Herbert Spencer and Social Theory

Also by John Offer

AN INTELLECTUAL HISTORY OF BRITISH SOCIAL POLICY: Idealism Versus Non-Idealism

HERBERT SPENCER: Critical Assessments (*editor*)

HERBERT SPENCER: Political Writings (*editor*)

SOCIAL WORKERS, THE COMMUNITY AND SOCIAL INTERACTION: Intervention and the Sociology of Welfare

INFORMAL WELFARE: A Sociological Study of Care in Northern Ireland (with Fred St Leger and Rosanne Cecil)

Herbert Spencer and Social Theory

John Offer
University of Ulster, UK

palgrave
macmillan

First published 2010 by
PALGRAVE MACMILLAN

Palgrave Macmillan in the UK is an imprint of Macmillan Publishers Limited,
registered in England, company number 785998, of Houndmills, Basingstoke,
Hampshire RG21 6XS.

Palgrave Macmillan in the US is a division of St Martin's Press LLC,
175 Fifth Avenue, New York, NY 10010.

Palgrave Macmillan is the global academic imprint of the above companies
and has companies and representatives throughout the world.

Palgrave® and Macmillan® are registered trademarks in the United States,
the United Kingdom, Europe and other countries.

ISBN-13: 978–0–230–20379–2 hardback

This book is printed on paper suitable for recycling and made from fully
managed and sustained forest sources. Logging, pulping and manufacturing
processes are expected to conform to the environmental regulations of the
country of origin.

A catalogue record for this book is available from the British Library.

A catalog record for this book is available from the Library of Congress.

10 9 8 7 6 5 4 3 2 1
19 18 17 16 15 14 13 12 11 10

Transferred to Digital Printing in 2012

Contents

Acknowledgements

My interest in Spencer goes back quite a long way. While I was 'directed' to Spencer by neither Ronnie Frankenberg nor Antony Flew, an interest in the singular marriage of the sociological imagination and evolutionary ethics that Spencer represents was something that their utterly different but inspiring teaching at Keele nurtured. Although since those days I have written on other topics as well, Spencer remained a key interest. I may add that I suspect I have not yet finished with him. As, perhaps, other authors experience, the things which at the start of the writing process I expected could all be dealt with adequately in one book have left me challenged by new complexities and my own ignorance that demand an unravelling and a rectification possible only in another.

In the preparation of this study specialist Library staff in the social sciences at the University of Ulster, Pam Compton, Janet Peden and Seamus Wray, have unfailingly provided prompt, cheerful and invaluable assistance in the face of my requests to track down esoteric Spenceriana. I also remain deeply impressed by the ready willingness of staff caring for special collections in a wide range of institutions to share their knowledge with a researcher who parachutes into their midst, most recently at Senate House, University of London (where Spencer's papers are housed), the British Library of Political and Economic Science at the London School of Economics, and at the West Sussex Record Office at Chichester. I wish to record my gratitude to all of them.

Conversations with Bob Pinker and Tim Gray, both of whom have written with insight on Spencer, have helped to sharpen my thoughts. I owe especial thanks to Tim for quite unexpectedly passing to me care of his extensive archive of published and unpublished material on Spencer. This archive is a collection particularly rich in the relatively early critical responses in America which Spencer's work attracted. In due course it is hoped to make its contents available to other researchers. All interested in Spencer's life and works are in Robert Perrin's debt for his *Herbert Spencer: A Primary and Secondary Biography* (1993). I am very grateful to the British Academy for awards which have been of the greatest assistance in allowing me to reassess Spencer's contribution to social thought in the late nineteenth and early twentieth centuries. My own colleagues have supported me with teaching relief through the Social and Policy Research Institute. Some have even joined with me in discussing Spencer: it is a pleasure to be able to thank Derek Birrell and Julian Leslie, friends as well as colleagues.

I must express particular thanks to Elizabeth McNeill who, in addition to cataloguing painstakingly the archive material from Tim Gray, has processed successive drafts of every chapter of this book, and insisted on keeping me to the Palgrave Macmillan guidelines. I am grateful too to Rosanne Cecil for her invaluable contribution to the preparation of the Index. In terms of style the outcome would have been much worse than it is but for Janet Mackle's sharp eye for ambiguity and incoherence, and also fudge. There is no doubt that carving out the time to write on Spencer has caused the neglect of other things, and I share her regrets over that.

University of Ulster, Coleraine

Introduction

How small, of all that human hearts endure,
That part which laws or kings can cause or cure.
Still to ourselves in every place consign'd,
Our own felicity we make or find

(Oliver Goldsmith, The Traveller)

Over a century after his death, Herbert Spencer still polarizes opinion. Incompatible estimations flow from a bewildering diversity of commentators. In 1994, he was singled out by one historian as 'an extremely unpleasant man and theorist' (McClelland, 1994: p. 394). W. H. Greenleaf, however, had come to evaluate his work as 'one of the ablest intellectual achievements in British thought and letters of the Victorian age' (1983: p. 32). Laland and Brown, concerned to distance Darwin from a political set of beliefs known often as 'social Darwinism' suggest that 'Social Spencerism would be a more appropriate term, since it derives far more from Spencer than from Darwin' (2002: p. 42). Michael Taylor, however, in the most recent study of the whole broad sweep of Spencer's ideas robustly resists the premise lurking behind this advice: 'To see his comprehensive world system through the lens of social Darwinism is thus to miss everything that enabled him to hold an entire generation in thrall' (2007: p. 149). While the anthropologist Tim Ingold found there to be 'good grounds for arguing that Spencer, and not Darwin, was the first sociobiologist' (1986: p. 225), the author of a recent biography, Mark Francis, characterized Spencer as first and foremost a psychologist, yet one who proved to be 'a corporate theorist who was also a utopian individualist' (2007: p. 311). Halsey's historical survey of sociology in Britain emphasizes that 'modern sociology was born out of political prejudice in the wake of Spencerian, individualistic interpretations of Darwinian evolution' (2004: p. 33). The contemporary American sociologist Jonathan H. Turner, explicitly concerned with Spencer's significance for sociology today rather than

1

historically, believes 'we should look at Spencer because we have not used his ideas to develop theory to the extent that we have employed the ideas of other historical figures. We have spent, indeed wasted, a great deal of time rediscovering Spencerian sociology; it would be more efficient to examine it firsthand' (1985: p. 153). Turner's conviction that there is neglected value in Spencer can be juxtaposed ironically with the American sociologist Robert Merton's own potted analysis of Spencer's attitude to antecedent literature: 'Herbert Spencer – of whom it can be said that never before had anyone written so much with so little knowledge of what others before him had written on the same wide range of subjects – elevated both his hostility toward authority and his illness (he was dizzied by reading) into a philosophy of investigation that gave little room to acquaintance with predecessors' (1968: p. 33). Another sociologist, however, Steve Fuller, has written more acidly of 'one of the false fathers of social science, Herbert Spencer, a man who fancied the term "sociology" but who always meant the natural history of social life' (2006: p. 35). On the other hand, Lee and Newby have observed that Spencer matters for sociologists, since 'there are very few ideas employed within the mainstream of evolutionary sociology which cannot be traced back to his writings' (1983: p. 73, see also Kerr, 2002: p. 355). In 1904, the neoclassical economist, Alfred Marshall, stepped back from his subject to comment: 'There is probably no one who gave as strong a stimulus to the thoughts of the younger Cambridge graduates thirty years or forty years ago as he (H. Spencer). He opened out a new world of promise, he set men on high enterprise in many different directions, and though he may have regulated English intellectual work less than Mill did, I believe he did much more towards increasing its vitality' (Marshall, 1925: p. 507. On Marshall and Spencer see Black, 1990). For Boyd Hilton, Spencer counted as 'a key figure in the mid-Victorian slide into unbelief' (1988: p. 311). In Hilton's perspective, 'Incarnational economists assumed a natural harmony of society and the probability of a future reign of natural justice'. Within this framework even Herbert Spencer, 'often thought of as a crude exponent of laissez-faire theory', slotted in well 'within this anti-Malthusian tradition' (1988: p. 322). Michael Freeden has judged the intellectual territory covered in the varied characterizations of Spencer as curiously wide: 'He has been wheeled out as a modern evolutionist, a laissez-faire liberal, an individualist, a functionalist, a synthesiser, a moral ethicist, to name but a few of his reincarnations' (2000: p. 1006). In the course of reviewing the historiography of political thought, elites and the state, Julia Stapleton emphasizes that while 'Spencer was of course renowned for his attack upon the state as an instrument of social reform' it needs to be added that 'however negative his attitude towards the state, the latter occupies a central position in his political thought' (1999: p. 262). Thomas Gondermann declares Spencer 'one of the most important contributors to the Victorian discourse on social evolution', but finds the fact overlooked 'that he did not just design an evolutionary theory of upward, yet branched development' but injected 'elements of retrogression into his theory' (2007: p. 21). Elliott (2004: p. 391), unstinting in his admiration for Spencer, identifies another, sometimes neglected, dimension: 'Herbert Spencer the evolutionary philosopher and educationist was, of course, one of the most famous intellectuals of the nineteenth century and his book on education became probably the most influential text on the subject in the late nineteenth and early twentieth centuries. However, he was educated by his father and many of the ideas in the book and his later evolutionary philosophy were developed with his advice.' For Carroll, Spencer was 'primarily a social philosopher . . . integrating Lamarckian progressivism, utilitarian ethical theory, and an extreme form of libertarian individualism associated with laissez-faire economics' (2003: p. 31). Carroll adds that his influence 'has now sunk into extinction' (2003: p. 34), with his many volumes 'like the skeletal remnants of an extinct people, kept in cabinets as objects of antiquarian curiosity, a little dusty and strange, icons of an evolutionary dead end, and thus melancholy mementos of an ultimate failure and futility' (2003: p. 35). According to Jose Harris in her contribution on Spencer to the *Oxford Dictionary of National Biography*, recent reassessments 'have been much less concerned with Spencer's reputation as one of the "founding fathers" of sociology, and much more interested in locating his role in nineteenth-century intellectual history, as a mirror of certain aspects of the Victorian age and as a contributor to specific debates on physiology, psychology, epistemology, political and social theory, ethics, and religious belief'. The conclusion drawn is that Spencer was 'not . . . the triumphal author of a holistic "total structure", but . . . an innovative and significant figure on a number of different fronts'.

Conscious of such discordant opinions, a shrewder writer might well have chosen a less contentious figure to interpret than Spencer, or at least elected to concentrate on a much narrower focus than Spencer's contribution to the study of social life. Yet the extraordinary breadth and depth of this current controversy around Spencer, after well over a preceding half century of at best benign neglect and at worst malign distortion, nicely seasons the many-layered and labyrinthine search for the real Spencer and contrives to make what *someone* has to undertake a fulfilling voyage of discovery. Nearly every opinion holds at least a grain of truth, although not one of the verdicts can be swallowed whole. And this sample of differing opinions is a very small fraction of those available and in need of appraisal as will become apparent as this reassessment progresses.

One regrettable difficulty with Spencer is that he has on many occasions been more a subject for caricature than fair-minded interpretation: a foil against which to headline the 'advantages' of some other way of thinking about social and political life, or indeed the merited achievements of Darwin in biology. Writing on Spencer would have been easier if he had been studiedly ignored. As it is, one can at this stage only urge readers to suspend, for now at least, any assumption that his social thought is fairly described, as conventional wisdom has it, as 'atomic individualism' and as an apologia for *laissez-faire*. Darwin's monumental and partly posthumous triumph in biology too can colour how we come to Spencer. For, in attempting a fresh approach to this particular eminent, independent-minded and not inconsiderably vain Victorian, we will disadvantage ourselves by compromising such efforts as may be made to lay bare his arguments, his impact on his contemporaries and his potential value in our own times unless, of course, we purge ourselves of yesterday's academic *parti pris*, or, in Darwin's case, the advantages of hindsight. On the other hand, one must suppose that merely undertaking an attempt to reappraise Spencer, on these lines, will no longer render the author liable to the accusation that thereby some championing of values associated with Spencer, rightly or wrongly, is the underlying motive. Intellectual history is not camouflaged political prescription, though it is compatible with a belief that Spencer merits more serious interest among historians of social science and within modern sociological endeavours.

In order to strip away the distorting patina of age which our picture of Spencer as a founding figure in sociology has acquired a great deal of ground must be covered. Partly this arises because of the nature of his basic orientation as a thinker. He was indeed a system-builder and synthesizer of knowledge, though he was also an observer of his times: he was not, however, a specialist researcher of any sort, unlike some of those with whom he rubbed shoulders. Partly it arises simply because of the very distinctive and perhaps idiosyncratic way in which he saw the subject matter of the new discipline. The journey involves excavating what Spencer meant by 'society' and by describing a society as a 'superorganism'. In several places, Spencer developed the idea that human societies could be envisaged as a kind of organism (from *Social Statics* of 1851, the essay 'The social organism' of 1860 through to the later *Principles of Sociology*). Spencer's version of what it has become routine to refer to as the 'organic analogy' (as will be discussed later, Spencer may have meant more than analogy) remains perhaps his most familiar contribution to sociological theory. Spencer's own late opinion on the 'social organism' was that the conception was little referred to in the *Principles of Sociology*, and that neither in *Social Statics* nor in 'The social organism' 'is there any assertion that this analogy between animal-structures and social structures is to be taken as the basis for sociological interpretations' (1896a: pp. 475–6). Spencer's 'social organism' idea, however, remains controversial. Wiltshire's *The Social and Political Thought of Herbert Spencer* furnishes but one instance of the perceived dilemma: 'Spencer took his ethical stand on the autonomy of the self-directed individual. This individualism is the antithesis of the organismic model of society, which presupposes the sacrifice of individual *autonomy* (not merely of self-interest) to the needs of society (1978: p. 235). Thus a new examination of the central question of whether the oft-declared incompatibility of Spencer's 'individualism' with his 'organicism' in understanding social life is a just view of his stance is indispensable.

Rediscovering Spencer's sociology also entails unravelling his ideas of 'social relations', including the fundamental contrasts he invoked between 'militant' and 'industrial' social relations, and between 'justice' and 'altruism' in the lives of individuals. It involves too examining his idea of evolution as orthogenesis and the derived idea of social evolution, and his two associated mechanisms of individual and social change. These were, firstly, the inheritance by offspring of characteristics acquired by their parents in their interaction with their surroundings and, secondly, but used alongside of the first, his own tailored interpretation of 'natural selection' (to which he preferred to refer as the 'survival of the fittest') after Darwin had advanced it in 1859. It involves investigating Spencer's conception of the relationship between biology, psychology and sociology as subjects, and in particular his understanding of psychological factors as the product of interaction between physical and psychical phenomena and the division of psychology as a subject between objective and subjective dimensions. Neglect of the close epistemological connection Spencer believed he established between psychology and sociology, neglect of his accompanying denial of freedom of the will and his rejection of ideas of social institutions as 'manufactured', and neglect of the implications he himself detected for sociological enquiry quite commonly afflict accounts of his sociology. Since his positions on these matters reflected his abstract analysis of the competing claims of 'idealist' and 'empiricist' approaches to the interpretation of reality and his attempt to provide a reconciliation, this dimension too demands reassessment. The journey also involves a study of the substantive matters which most systematically concerned Spencer, domestic, ceremonial, political, ecclesiastical, professional and industrial institutions, and other interests such as education, public finance, the governance of railway companies and the administration of prisons. It involves too examinations of his account of the 'evolution' of ethical and political principles, and the lesson he drew that the roles of the state were principally protection from external aggression and to enforce 'justice'. Nor can it exclude consideration of the stress Spencer placed on 'spontaneous associations' and 'private beneficence' in the conduct of social life, whereby altruism enhanced welfare, and the special but now rather neglected attention he devoted to the development of music in testing out his evolutionary perspective.

As might be expected, Spencer also attracted criticism, to which he himself often replied in print, or persuaded others (such as Eliza Lynn Linton) to do so on his behalf. His most perceptive contemporary and sociologically minded critics included John Stuart Mill (who prompted Spencer into a precise expression of the nature of his commitment to utilitarianism), John

Elliot Cairnes, Frederic William Maitland, Thomas Henry Huxley, Henry Sidgwick, St George Jackson Mivart (labouring to harmonize evolutionary thought with his Catholicism), Benjamin Kidd, Emile Durkheim, Ferdinand Tönnies, William James, John Dewey, W. H. Mallock, A. J. Balfour and Beatrice Webb, and also Thomas Hill Green, Bernard Bosanquet, David George Ritchie and James Seth, who represented idealist social thought towards the end of the nineteenth century, often pointedly pitting itself against what it regarded as Spencer's 'materialism'. For den Otter (1996: pp. 127–8), sociology, at least in the 1880s and 1890s, 'tended to refer to those theories which sought to apply biological evolutionary principles to the investigation of human societies. Attacks on the new discipline, therefore, were most often levelled at the kind of sociology advanced by Herbert Spencer... a figure who perhaps more than any other single contemporary shaped debate about the discipline of sociology'. Each of these critical engagements requires notice since they illuminate and parse both the actual difficulties and the perceptions of difficulties in Spencer's thought.

Nor can the voices of Spencer's comparatively unqualified admirers be neglected, who include the American-based Scottish businessman and philanthropist Andrew Carnegie, Edward Livingston Youmans, who tirelessly promoted Spencer's ideas and the publication of his books in the United States, Auberon Herbert, the English libertarian and voluntaryist, Thomas Mackay, prominent in the Charity Organisation Society and historian of the poor law, and John Morley, editor, author and Liberal statesman.

Spencer himself, notably in his posthumously published two-volume *An Autobiography* of 1904, always emphasized the independence and individuality of his own contribution to the world of ideas, both in respect of his general theory of evolution and his interpretation of social life in particular. He became sensitive to the point of neurosis on occasions when his originality was questioned and whenever allegations were made of intellectual debts which he himself had not acknowledged. There have been claims that he owed more to his father, or to Thomas Hodgskin, than he declared, but perhaps the best known example arose in relation to the work of Auguste Comte. Spencer repeatedly acknowledged very specific debts to Comte but went to great lengths to demonstrate his ideas owed nothing to the Frenchman's 'positivism' (Comte's *Cours de Philosophie Positive* appeared between 1830 and 1842, and was available in a shortened version in English, translated by Harriet Martineau, in 1853). However, for Michael Taylor (2007: p. 43), Comte's positivism 'was without doubt the primary model for the synthetic philosophy. While Spencer consistently denied Comte's influence and played up their various points of disagreement – some important, others quite trivial – he absorbed many of the French philosopher's ideas at an almost subliminal level'. The question of Spencer's indebtedness to Comte cannot be avoided in a reassessment, though here the nub of Merton's character sketch must be recalled, but it may be emphasized that the two men disagreed deeply over the practical consequences that publicizing the very idea of sociology as a science could produce within social life itself (for Spencer, in the short term, very few indeed).

Such questions can only be adequately answered alongside of a wider consideration of the intellectual environment and the form of ideas which surrounded Spencer as his own insights found expression. Spencer himself acknowledged that he grew up in a Christian household in which religious nonconformity and an informed and practical scientific gaze on the world went hand-in-hand. But an impressive body of recent research by historians has added immensely to our understanding of Spencer's kind of intellectual nursery through a focus on 'Christian political economics' (see Hilton, 1988; Mandler, 1990; Waterman, 1991). Christian political economics, in broad and brutally simple terms, covers much of what we would differentiate as theology and economics but which at the time were indissolubly entwined, and it left a mark on Spencer. At the end of the eighteenth century, ideological concerns may be discerned which reflect an enlightenment rationalism and anxiety over human destiny, coming to a head around the Christian idea of atonement. Thomas Robert Malthus's *An Essay on the Principle of Population* of 1798 quickly became influential as a bracing antidote to the unflagging but misplaced optimism, so it was argued, of William Paley's *The Principles of Moral and Political Philosophy* of 1785, with its Christian utilitarianism in which man seemed to have no need to display intelligence and nature offered no tests. Scarcity, starvation, war and the threat of atheism were what concerned Malthus, whose understanding of existing society was nevertheless of its essential stability, in accord with nature and its laws, with natural laws as God's laws. One of Malthus's objectives was to 'replace the doctrine that human life is a state of discipline and trial for eternity with the less familiar theory that it is, rather, "the mighty process of God ... for the creation and formation of mind"' (Waterman, 1991: p. 98). Inequality then is conceived of as a *perennial* requirement of and spur to human intellectual and spiritual development; it is an *indispensable* part of all social movement, including that of *civilized* society. God's power was in this manner revealed in nature. Richard Whately too, later to become Archbishop of Dublin, read Malthus in this manner, pointing out that it was not a case of God having ' "made Man too prolific, or the earth too barren". It was rather that having made man rational, God had placed him in just the sort of ecological trap to stimulate rational thought, and to direct him towards the long-term advantages of sexual abstention .... For though Malthus had shown that man has a *tendency* to overpeople the world, in order to do so he would have to behave like the savage he is not' (Hilton, 1988: p. 79, quoting from Whately's *Introductory Lectures*). Instead of producing a difficult case of the problem of evil, Malthus was showing God's wisdom.

The prose of Paley, Malthus and Whately, and others in a Christian political economics tradition would have been familiar to the Spencer household.

Indeed, Spencer went on to refer in particular to Whately in his own writings, a significant point of departure since he comparatively seldom referred directly to his sources. It will be suggested that, of all those who combined economics with theology, Whately, who was a widely read author in the second quarter of the nineteenth century, was a larger formative influence on Spencer than has hitherto been proposed. And this influence would scarcely have waned while Spencer's education was in the hands of his uncle, the Cambridge-educated Rev Thomas Spencer, Perpetual Curate of Hinton Charterhouse (in the countryside south of Bath): Thomas himself produced numerous pamphlets firmly in the Christian political economics style, with some of which his nephew gave a little assistance.

Spencer's intellectual odyssey, undertaken free of a university education, was at the outset pre-Darwinian in form and nourished by the traditions of evolutionary deism and, though this was perhaps approached more questioningly, natural theology, in which order in nature was evidence of God as Designer. 'Pre-Darwinian' is not here meant to refer to a simple and true chronological point, but to some of Spencer's major beliefs as being diametrically opposed to Darwin's thought. The extensive range of his mature articles and books, united by a concern with 'development' in some form, and expeditiously distributed by the railways he had in a small way helped to put in place, fanned out around the country, and beyond, ever augmenting the equipollent forces of attraction and repulsion among his followers and his critics in theology, philosophy, history, psychology and sociology and in a variety of emerging specialisms, such as music historiography. Moreover, his work permeated a very much wider, less academically minded popular audience, reflecting the fact that for most of his life he was perforce publishing his articles in the relatively 'generalist' Victorian periodical literature; only in the last few decades of his long life were specialist journals appearing, such as *Mind* and *Nature* (to which he contributed), associated with a professionalization of science which his intellectual sparring-partner Thomas Henry Huxley had devoted much of his unquenchable enthusiasm to bringing into being. One reason why Spencer still matters is that few Victorians of substance escaped noticing him, or being noticed by him: to list them all is impossible, but the remarkably diverse paths of scientists such as Darwin, Huxley, Joseph Dalton Hooker, John Tyndall, figures interested broadly in social life and science, such as Mill, Alexander Bain, E. B. Tylor, Henry Buckle, W. E. H. Lecky, W. S. Jevons, Marshall, Beatrice Webb, T. H. Green and Bernard Bosanquet, and those connected with the arts, politics and business, including Sir Hubert Parry, W. E. Gladstone, A. J. Balfour, John Morley, Auberon Herbert, W. S. Blunt, Grant Allen, George Eliot, David Masson, Lynn Linton, and Andrew Carnegie all crossed Spencer's path. Indeed, his reach was genuinely global, truly transcending anglophone boundaries. On his death the *New York Times* recorded that his works had been extensively translated; 'All are rendered into French, nearly all into German and Russian, many into Italian and Spanish, and his work on education has appeared also in Hungarian, Bohemian, Polish, Dutch, Danish, Swedish, Greek, Japanese, and Chinese'.

Spencer held no appointment in any academic institution, gave no lectures on his work, and travelled intent solely on relaxation. His visit to America from August to November in 1882 was in part an exception. It came about largely at Youmans's instigation. Youmans, as editor of the *Popular Science Monthly*, had whipped up interest in Spencer's theory of evolution, and now he had the chance to present his hero in person to American notables. However, Spencer, often fatigued or unwell, mostly kept himself secluded during his visit, speaking in public only at a farewell banquet for him attended by a large number of highly successful admirers in Delmonico's, New York, at which he rather unexpectedly developed the theme in his speech that life is not for work, but work for life. Accompanying him throughout his visit was Edward Lott, a friend from childhood days. William James Linton, writer and wood engraver, recalled in his *Memories* of 1895 that Spencer, 'after his visit to America, was my fellow-voyager to England. I had pleasant talks with him, rather from him, when he was well enough to be on deck. He appeared to me a very full man, full of knowledge and sure of it, and not anxious for more from me, even if I had had it at his command, but I had not even on wood-engraving. I was more attracted to his friend, Mr. Lott, a Derby stockbroker, who had special care of him, at whose house in the neighbourhood of Derby I afterwards spent a glad evening and a morning'.

One recent study of Spencer has opined that 'his reputation followed him to Highgate cemetery a century or more ago' (Taylor, 2007: p. xi). It is incontestable that by that time anyone who adhered to the Lamarckian inheritance of acquired characteristics as the chief mechanism of species change, as did Spencer, rather than to Darwinian natural selection, would be seen by informed opinion as flying in the face of the evidence. Even so, it should not be forgotten that Spencer still influences biology in at least one significant way, through the famous and readily available *On Growth and Form* by D'Arcy Wentworth Thompson, which relates the growth and structure of organismic forms according to mathematical principles and physical laws. Thompson paid homage to Spencer in this respect in his Herbert Spencer Lecture at Oxford, and noted more broadly that 'while Spencer lived his voice reached far and wide, even to the end of the earth. He was a philosopher not speaking to the philosophers, nor teaching in the schools; but he had a gift and a message, so in touch with the temper of his time, that it made him a speaker, *ex cathedra*, to the world' (1913: p. 3). Thompson added that Spencer had pointed out 'a way of emancipation, a path of deliverance from creeds outworn' (1913: p. 14).

In reality Spencer possessed a diverse plurality of reputations, ranging from that of the seer, who could reassuringly identify and account for underlying order amidst the apparent disorder of the experienced world, to that of the doyen among critics of socialism and 'big government'. In many of these areas a couple of decades had to pass before Taylor's assessment of his impact becomes plausible across the whole range of reputations.

His status as a scientific 'master of the universe' may have crumbled, and with reason, much as Taylor suggests. And certainly too, by 1901, the Fabian socialists Beatrice and Sidney Webb were exhibiting an effortless vainglory that Englishmen had had revealed to them a 'new world of relationships, of which they were before unconscious ... we have become aware, almost in a flash, that we are not merely individuals, but members of a community ... ' Gladstonian liberalism 'thinks in individuals', but 'the opening of the twentieth century finds us all, to the dismay of the old-fashioned individualist, "thinking in communities" ' (Webb, B., 1948: pp. 221–2). Writing in the same vein, shortly after Spencer's death, one prominent idealist philosopher again struck a triumphalist tone: 'the conception of man as essentially social, and of the state as the organ of the general will, has so firmly established itself that Spencer's pamphlets during the last twenty years sounded like a belated echo, and he had the air, even to himself, of one crying in the wilderness' (Pringle Pattison, 1904: p. 256). However, these were not Olympian judgements but the views of interested parties, and if there was an eclipse of Spencer it, was partial, not total. Not much earlier indeed, in 1890, W. E. H. Lecky, the Irish historian of ideas and acquaintance of Spencer (they enjoyed occasional games of billiards at their club, the *Atheneum*), expressed his view that 'I wish I could persuade those who form their estimate of the province of Government from Carlyle's "Past and Present" and "Latter-day Pamphlets" to study also the admirable little treatise of Herbert Spencer, called "The Man and the State," [*sic*] in which the opposite side is argued.' (1908: p. 109). Indeed, the *Manchester Guardian*'s obituary of Spencer in December, 1903, captured the likely afterlife of his political thought rather more accurately than Taylor: 'when socialism begins to produce reaction Spencer's political writings will be a mine of arguments for the critics of paternal government'. Sir Roland Wilson in his *The Province of the State* of 1911 continued the work of spreading this Spencerian message. In more recent times. Hiskes (1983) has stressed that, properly understood, Spencer's political individualism can generate a distinctive form of voluntary associationism and communitarianism, and Weinstein (1998) has argued that a liberal version of utilitarianism with potential applications for the present can be found in Spencer.

These comments conveniently permit a brief diversion to a few remarks on Spencer's *The Man versus The State* of 1884, these days his best-known book. For around it a new interpretative spat has been created, by Francis (2007), and to a lesser degree by Taylor (2007), who seek to characterize it as atypical. By contrast, in my judgement, *The Man versus the State* is a helpful point of entry to Spencer; it is contemporaneous with the System of Synthetic

Philosophy (*First Principles* and nine other 'Principles of' volumes on psychology, biology, sociology and ethics, which appeared between 1862 and 1896). Its message of small (but not no) government followed the logic of the System, contrary to Francis's reading of Spencer as a 'corporate theorist', to which his 'utopian' individualism played second fiddle (2007: p. 311). It has a quick-paced style ('dyspeptic' in Taylor's view), and merits canonical status as a passionate, if fretful, eye-witness account of a time abounding in new schemes for social legislation (Spencer targeted the Reverend W. L. Blackley's compulsory national insurance plan, but did not arraign it as representing as Francis claims, a 'selfish group'). In the face of such schemes governments on occasion capitulated, and grew commensurately. Spencer worried that thereby social evolution and adaptation to social life would be retarded or reversed, a theme of all his work. Francis though, on decidedly slender grounds, judges *The Man versus the State* to be aberrant Spencer. Certainly it was published outside the System, and it pursued sedulously the controversies of the day, but neither feature made it at all atypical. It has an anti-socialist message, but it does not posit an 'atomistic' view of individuals, rooting them rather in their relations with others. Spencer was no more 'senescent' than when he had completed the 'Political Institutions' part of the *Principles of Sociology* 18 months earlier. To sideline it as idiosyncratic is special pleading, by Francis in particular, on behalf of an interpretation of Spencer's social thought which, I shall be arguing, he fails to corroborate. Francis even ventures to offer the extraordinary advice not to interrogate *The Man versus the State* too closely. Francis fancies that 'the contradictions in the work...stem from Spencer's retrieval of his own family's involvement in welfare relief.... It was not the rational plans of socialists that had irritated him.... It was the prospect of a selfish group successfully demanding welfare relief. This struck Spencer as a coercive attack on the natural balance of politics, and superheated his response' (2007: p. 324). As it happens, for the sake of internal consistency at least, Francis's earlier and quite different interpretation of a previous objection raised by Spencer against poor relief as sapping the community rather than, as it is usually interpreted, the self (2007: p. 270) should have been revisited in this later context.

Returning now to the main path of these introductory comments on Spencer's social and political thought, it must be observed that to his mind there were three desirable and real 'social forces' observable in the modern capitalist societies of his time: self-interest (including 'unconscious cooperation'), sympathy, and governmental (negatively regulative) control (1871a: pp. 433–7). There was present as well 'positively regulative' control, also by government, which, although previously necessary, and no less tangible, now yielded social sclerosis, as social evolution manifested the ascendency of the other forces, which made for spontaneous social cohesion and personal fulfilment. But as Spencer sought to redirect praxis away from positive regulation, and a prospect of 'social regression', there arose a difficulty which

John Robertson noted (indebted, as he acknowledged, to D. G. Ritchie): 'In the same breath he protests that societies *cannot* be changed by purposive action, and that modern legislators are really making such changes' (1901: p. 83 Robertson, a writer and Shakespeare scholar, was also Liberal MP for Tyneside from 1906 to 1918). Why should one 'social force' count as less 'natural', and therefore less 'legitimate', than another? Spencer often uses the expression 'social forces', whose relationship to 'purposive action' will be questioned at some length. These forces were 'inosculated' with the forces of his essentially mechanistic law of evolution which was his paramount interest and, together with its elements, such as differentiation, specialization and integration, it determined and inscribed his signature inquisitorial stance towards human beings, physically and psychically, and towards the manifestations of sociality. As Letwin noted, 'Spencer was an engineer who had become convinced that "the astronomic, geologic, biologic, psychologic and sociologic groups of phenomena form a connected aggregate of phenomena", which nothing but the caprice of human convention had separated' (1965: p. 328). However, this distinctive science-minded focus, extended into the chronology and distribution of the yoked but interacting configurations of human psychology and social forms, tended to deprive the active agency of persons of any status. Many might suggest that charting neither the life of persons through society nor the life of society through persons gets us to the heart of the social life of persons, since the one recognizes exclusively only a stunted form of person agency and the other eliminates it (Ingold, 1986: p. 212). The question of whether Spencer's contribution to sociology is so disabled is one of the central ones that a study such as this has to confront.

For sure, defining 'social progress' in the technicist way he did seemed an unlikely overture to popular appeal: 'Social progress', Spencer remarked, 'is supposed to consist in the making of a greater quantity and variety of the articles required for satisfying men's wants; in the increasing security of person and property; in widening freedom of action; whereas, rightly understood, social progress consists in those changes of structure in the social organism which have entailed these consequences' (1857a: p. 9). Yet, in fact, the message of an underlying 'process of exuviation' (1854a: p. 50) as social life advanced, whereby the formal customs, rituals, fashions and expectations, blighting and cramping the desires of the young, the intelligent and the put-upon would be proved transient and consigned to oblivion, still stirred many imaginations. The irksome tyrannies of social conventions had feet of clay; they would be duly toppled and sent packing by a secular force in the order of things making for good. Here, then, is one source of Spencer's appeal to a much wider audience than might be expected for a 'philosopher', and it was fondly fleshed out by Arnold Bennett in his novel *Sacred and Profane Love*, when the young Carlotta, recoiling from life with her stuffy Aunt, discovers Spencer's *The Study of Sociology*. She read the book all night, amazed that 'anything so honest, and so courageous, and so simple, and so convincing had ever been written'. To forestall a domestic hiatus the book was secreted between the covers of a 'respectable' volume. Later reflection took nothing away from the encounter with Spencer: 'he taught me intellectual courage; he taught me that nothing is sacred that will not bear inspection; and I adore his memory'.

A related dimension to Spencer's impact is associated with the very fact of his unambiguous commitment to 'naturalistic' *social sciences*. That is to say, of his commitment to the comprehensive, diachronic, systematic and synthesized study by psychology, anthropology and sociology (but not, note, history) of psychic and social phenomena, embracing all human experience itself, not least social, political and moral change. This was notably undertaken in defiance of a faith in 'civilized' men as the outcome of divinely ordained interventions or creations, and in the absence of assurances that the wand of providence was discernible through 'evidences' of Design in the workings of the world. G. J. Holyoake, well-respected by Spencer and an advocate of cooperatives, mused that guided 'by the pole star of Evolution, Spencer sailed out alone on the ocean of Speculation and discovered a new empire of Law – founded without blood, or the suppression of liberty, or the waste of wealth – where any man may dwell without fear or shame. The fascination of Mr. Spencer's pages to the pulpit-wearied inquirer was that they took him straight to Nature. Mr. Spencer seemed to write with a magnifying pen which revealed objects unnoticed by other observers' (1905, ii, ch. 25).

For the naturalist and novelist, Grant Allen, it had always seemed, as he wrote to Spencer in 1882, that 'the value of your method and the importance of your results was at least quite as great in the department of human affairs as elsewhere: the dry light of scientific procedure is most wanted where the intellect is most often warped by social prejudices. But it is not astonishing that the Englishmen who hold India and would dragoon Ireland into submission think otherwise' (in Clodd, 1900: p. 119). Yet the science-mindedness could alienate as well. In 1880, Youmans had drawn to Spencer's notice a 'row' at Yale involving Professor William Graham Sumner's employment of *The Study of Sociology* as a textbook, with the President, Noah Porter, 'objecting to the use, in a college "intimately associated in its history and constitution with the Christian religion", of a book the tone of which was calculated to diminish respect for Christianity' (Duncan, 1911: p. 208). However, taking unexpectedly the opposite line, the Rev W. D. Ground contrived to 'astonish' Spencer, as he himself admitted in a letter to Beatrice Potter (Duncan, 1911: p. 251), by nominating him 'an instrument grasped by Christ's mighty hand, ... whose ideas "Christ intends to make structural in his Church"' (1883: p. 345). (Ground received no significant preferment within the Church of England, and featured in a chapter on 'eccentric and crazy persons' in the *Memoirs* of 1903 by the Cheltenham-born Chartist and newspaper editor, W. E. Adams.) This same scientific approach of Spencer to man proved by contrast a chief irritant to philosophical critics of an idealist conviction. In 1889, James Seth, Professor of Philosophy at the University of Edinburgh, not troubling to engage with much of the detail of Spencer's justifications for his position in his contributions to psychology, made what was thus a rather unreflective declaration: 'Self-conscious evolution is essentially different from unconscious evolution, and the former cannot be stated in terms of the latter. While all lower life evolves by strict unconscious necessity, man, as self-conscious, is free from its dominion; and has the power consciously to help on, or consciously to hinder, the evolution. Hence it is that we are at once conscious of the inadequacy of such categories as "adaptation to environment", "survival of the fittest", etc., as applied to moral life... they are only imperfect analogies drawn from a lower plane of existence' (Seth, 1889: pp. 350–1).

A further source of the frisson which Spencer generated was the whole cosmic evolutionary theory itself, sketched in an early version in the essay of 1857, 'Progress: its law and cause', and then refined and elaborated more influentially in *First Principles* of 1862. By the final and sixth edition the definition of 'evolution' had itself evolved to become (1900: p. 367): 'Evolution is an integration of matter and concomitant dissipation of motion; during which the matter passes from a relatively indefinite, incoherent homogeneity to a relatively definite, coherent heterogeneity; and during which the retained motion undergoes a parallel transformation'. Everything Spencer published after the 'Progress' essay related more or less directly to 'evolution'. The novelist Jack London exemplifies the stir flowing from *First Principles*, and although his semi-autobiographical novel *Martin Eden* of 1910 has been cited in this respect in other studies of Spencer, it makes the point too well to be ignored here. The eponymous hero found his encounter with Spencer's book and its idea of evolution teaching him what any amount of his sailing and wandering could not: 'He had merely skimmed over the surface of things, observing detached phenomena, accumulating fragments of facts, making superficial little generalizations – and all and everything quite unrelated in a capricious and disorderly world of whim and choice'. Martin awoke as if from sleep: 'here was the man Spencer, organizing all knowledge for him, reducing everything to unity, elaborating ultimate realities, and presenting to his startled gaze a universe so concrete of realization that it was like the model of a ship such as sailors make and put into glass bottles. There was no caprice, no chance. All was law.' Martin's epiphany left him 'drunken with comprehension': to abandon Spencer would be like 'a navigator throwing the compass and chronometer overboard'.

The earlier quotation from Alfred Marshall recorded this same shift in orientation as it impacted on intellectual life, and it was this change that led J. A. Hobson to rate Spencer's impact on his age over even Darwin's 'because the largest interpretation and application of the new scientific principles came from him' (1904; p. 12). Francis Galton praised the 'easy precision with which he dealt in generalizations; there was neither vagueness nor change in the sense in which he used them', attributing this feature of Spencer to the large number of observations habitually present to his mind (*The Times*, 9 December 1903). The newly married T. H. Huxley and his wife helped to check the proofs of the book: Huxley's view was that 'Someone had to publish the big evolutionary picture, and only Spencer had the cosmic gall' (Desmond, 1997: p. 286). In his own *Journals* Bennett hailed *First Principles* as one of the greatest books ever written. It had filled him up 'with the sense of causation everywhere', and, he alleged, could be seen 'in nearly every line I write' (1971: p. 335). It was also this unification of knowledge and demonstration of developmental order everywhere that bowled over the composer, music historian and principal of the Royal College of Music, Sir Hubert Parry. Parry had encountered Spencer in 1874 in Gloucester at the choir festival, becoming 'quite overwhelmed by the honour so that I could hardly speak without trembling' (Graves, 1926: Vol. 1, p. 146). Spencer's theory of evolution – and *First Principles* had also included discussions of the origin and development of music and music as a profession – in large measure structured Parry's *The Art of Music* of 1893, issued in a revised form 3 years later as *The Evolution of the Art of Music* in E. L. Youmans's influential *International Scientific Series*. Lady Courtney, who was Kate Potter, sister of Beatrice Potter (Spencer knew well their parents and the Potter children), recalled that 'even in the most unlikely quarters his name would be known as that of a distinguished man. I remember travelling from Aberdeen to Inverness in a third class carriage (not that this in Scotland was an unlikely quarter), and hearing some Scotch farmers, and a minister from a far away northern village, discussing his books, and finding myself unawares quite a centre of attraction when I remarked that I knew him in the flesh' (in Duncan, 1911: pp. 497–8).

Spencer's ideas on liberty and the role of government also stimulated wide interest. Although Spencer's libertarian message attracted a large range of individual followers, he cannot be said to have established a school. Moreover, in spite of contacts with senior political figures at a one-to-one level by the 1870s, and of much earlier participation in radical politics in the 1840s, he never cultivated access to the powerful organized political groupings of the day. His association with the Liberty and Property Defence League furnishes only a limited exception to this point, since he informed its secretary in February, 1890 that while he was 'quite willing to aid pecuniarily, I am desirous that my aid should not be publicly interpreted into membership of the League' (Duncan, 1911: p. 299).

Spencer was comfortable moving from generalizations about the conditions of social growth, unfailingly tethered to the underpinning larger principles of the theory of evolution, to judgements on the 'sins' of legislators, and the 'proper sphere' of governmental action. His normative authority was what he described as 'absolute political ethics': 'Its judgments on the relations between man and man are corollaries from its primary truth, that the activities of each in pursuing the objects of life may be rightly restricted only by the like activities of others: such others being like-natured (for the principle does not contemplate slave-societies or societies in which one race dominates over another); and its judgments on the relations between the man and the State are corollaries from the allied truth, that the activities of each citizen may be rightly limited by the incorporated body of citizens only as far as is needful for securing to him the remainder' (that is, of his activities, J. O., 1890: p. 227). Although perhaps in this form not immediately recognisable as such, Spencer is here detailing his 'equal freedom' or 'justice' principle, first articulated in *Social Statics* of 1851, and later given in *The Principles of Ethics* thus: 'Every man is free to do that which he wills provided he infringes not the equal freedom of any other man' (1910, ii: p. 46). This principle is founded on the dynamics of organic evolution at large, and is for Spencer an indispensable guide for present lives lived in present circumstances, both falling short of their wholly developed forms. In the late nineteenth century, there were some writers on political matters who were attracted by Spencer's libertarianism, but left comparatively unmoved, however, by the wider evolutionary philosophy notwithstanding the apparently considerable weight it lent to his judgements. Auberon Herbert belongs in this category, as do Mallock, Levy, Mackay and Carnegie, and John Morley. While comment on the others may be deferred for now, a few remarks on the two very different personalities, Morley and Carnegie, are appropriate here. Morley (1836–1923) was in fact on cordial terms with Spencer and in fundamental agreement with him as a free-thinker and over many matters of politics, including opposition to militarism, state intervention and ecclesiastical privileges. In 1908 (whilst in the Liberal cabinet as secretary of state at the India Office), he commented (1917, ii: p. 255), 'I'd rather have parliamentary rule with all its faults than Prussian bureaucracy' (with which in particular the idealist philosopher Bernard Bosanquet's ideas on the state were sometimes becoming associated). Morley combined journalism and scholarship with his parliamentary career, publishing studies of Voltaire and Gladstone, and editing the influential *Fortnightly Review* and *Pall Mall Gazette*. In the autumn of 1903, shortly in fact before Spencer died, Morley had accepted his invitation to give an address at his cremation. In the event Morley was, however, in Palermo and unavailable: the day of the funeral he marked by 'pondering... upon an indefatigable intellect, an iron love of truth, a pure and scrupulous conscience, a spirit of loyal and beneficent intention, a noble passion for knowledge and systematic thought' (1917, i: p. 116. It was Kate Potter's husband, the journalist and Liberal parliamentarian, Leonard Courtney, who substituted for Morley).

Carnegie encountered Spencer's ideas in the 1870s at a New York literary salon presided over by the poet Anna Botta. They first met later, travelling on the *Servia* to America in 1882. According to one biographer, Carnegie incorporated 'many of Spencer's ideas into his own life – especially the theory of the "survival of the fittest"... and the notion that "education has for a chief object the formation of character" ' (Lamont-Brown, 2005: p. 89, see also White, 1979). Most striking is that the thoughts of Spencer and Carnegie were in unison on the responsibilities that accompany wealth, and Carnegie's philanthropy certainly took the formation of character as a guide. In 'The morals of trade' of 1859 Spencer had looked forward to a 'new and better chivalry'. A more moral public opinion was showing itself, with the rich expected to devote some of their resources to matters of general welfare: 'Year by year is the improvement of the people occupying a larger share of the attention of the upper classes. Year by year are they voluntarily devoting more energy to furthering the material and mental progress of the masses' (1859: p. 151). Voluntary financial support of spontaneous organizations for specific ends which sprang from people themselves was a matter in general of approbation: a positive side to Spencer's arguments, based on the nature of the process of social evolution, which restricted action by the state to the enforcement of 'justice'. Later indeed, Spencer expressed serious reservations over the utility of interventions in social life undertaken by bodies he regarded as large, impersonal, bureaucratic and formalized voluntary organizations, such as the National Society for the Prevention of Cruelty to Children.

It should also be kept in mind that it is not only a reputation in one branch or another of 'public' life that counts. If an influence persists in the theories and judgements informing the conduct of everyday life, whether acknowledged there or not, this is of some importance too, not least of course to sociologists. Robert Pinker has captured this easily overlooked dimension to Spencer's warnings against dependence on governmental philanthropy as a source of legitimacy to enduring popular moral sentiments: 'There is, and always has been, a Spencerian underground in the public debate on social welfare. Spencer's language still has meaning to the marginally respectable who live in fear of imminent pauperization' (1971: p. 28). The editorial columns of the *Daily Express* may host ideas which still enjoy 'a vigorous continuity of existence at the level of everyday life' (1971: p. 29). Those famous four words 'survival of the fittest', in daily use in social life, were, after all, first joined together by Herbert Spencer.

A matter which several generations of scholars concerned with Spencer have been unable to sideline is his relationship to a later and retrospective 'ism' constructed to assist in interpreting the years around 1900, namely the unfortunate exspression 'social Darwinism' (see Hodgson, 2006, and also Halliday, 1971, and Rogers, 1972). I cannot recall from my own studies any source referring to Spencer as a 'social Darwinist' in his lifetime. Certainly, though, there was frequent confusion about what Spencer's theoretical position on evolution was as opposed to Darwin's in the minds of some interpreters, and this confusion was a source of frustration for Spencer.

On hearing about a lecture given by W. H. Hudson, a former secretary to Spencer, Spencer wrote to Hudson in 1892: 'I did not know ... that you had so thoroughly grasped the Synthetic Philosophy in its nature and bearings.... You have decidedly done me a service in putting forward so clearly the origin and development of the doctrine of evolution, and by correcting, as far as correction is possible, the erroneous views that are current respecting my relations to Darwin' (Duncan, 1911: p. 313). But to continue today what has become almost traditional, labelling Spencer a 'social Darwinist', is to partake of such a huge distortion of both the relationship between the two men and the relationship of their ideas that it should no longer be regarded as an available option. Fuller, for instance, first accuses Spencer of an 'insidious version' of 'premature naturalization' to be found in 'the proposition "*Laissez faire* is nature's way"', whereby one is always as one ought to be', adding too that the default 'is thus taken as *ipso facto* divine' (an interpretation explicitly denied by Spencer, as already suggested). Second, Fuller then piles anachronistic distortion on to misrepresentation by remarking that thereby 'Spencer's version of Social Darwinism' (2006: p. 61) gave wide public exposure to such economic naturalism. This unfortunate situation is in no way improved by rechristening, as Laland and Brown suggested, the 'ism' in question as 'social Spencerism', if only because 'Spencerism' has to be, *from the outset*, 'social'.

As will be explored, Spencer's scheme of evolution as orthogenesis was taken up and modified by many other writers, including W. H. Mallock, and, more interested in the scope for political intervention in the course of evolution, Benjamin Kidd, J. A. Hobson and L. T. Hobhouse. Often blended with this was an influence from Darwinian natural selection; indeed with both Darwin and Spencer in mind. Freeden has suggested that 'the incorporation within liberalism of notions concerning collectivism, community, and social reform can be attributed to biological and evolutionary currents rather than, as is common, to the elaboration of T. H. Green's political thought' (1976: p. 471). Francis Galton and others principally added on to Darwin's theory of species change through 'natural selection' 'applications' of it to human societies, seeking to augment the theory's workings. In this manner eugenics was born, the science and practice of altering the composition of populations to eliminate or favour particular inherited characteristics. Many aspects of early work associated with eugenics, relating to euthanasia and sterilization, and to the virtues of imperialism and ruthless colonialist policies, eventually fell foul of moral concerns, which the advocates had theorized as superseded through their naturalistic perspective on man as inseparable from animal life. (On the 'use' of 'Darwinism' in Germany in this area, and in psychiatry, ethnology, economics and sociology, covering the ideas of Ernst Haeckel, Ludwig Büchner, Alfred Ploetz, Albert Schäffle and Ludwig Gumplowicz, and others, see Weikart, 2004.) It is indeed questionable if either of these areas of development, in practice mostly separate if overlapping in theoretical content, is best understood by being placed without clear differentiation in the one category, 'social Darwinism'.

Moreover, and most importantly, 'social Darwinism', as designed to capture past thinking, has most commonly been deployed for subjective and negatively evaluative purposes, stemming in particular from the work of the American historian Richard Hofstadter (1944), initially on thought in America, to disparage supporters of *laissez-faire* and deterrent policies towards social 'failures', even though, as it happens, many of those so described owed little or nothing to Darwin, and even though, paradoxically, many who did draw on Darwinian biology were not described as 'social Darwinist', merely because they supported schemes of social and economic reform. (Spencer, who is a paradigm 'social Darwinist' for Hofstadter, did in some publications advocate deterrence, albeit in a circumscribed sense, and did find a place in his scheme for 'natural selection', which he reworked as 'indirect equilibration', but his orthogenesis marks the defining ideational difference.) Hofstadter's key innovation was calling *laissez-faire* 'social Darwinism', but whatever value as pure propaganda this may have had in ideological wars, it did no service to the understanding of Spencer. The serious conceptual shortcomings of Hofstadter's analysis and the quantitatively huge impact his work has had to this day in giving the expression wide currency is discussed in Tim Leonard (2009). Mike Hawkins, 1997, has tried *post hoc* to impose some rigour on the meaning of 'social Darwinism' but is undermined in various ways by the historical record of its use – as shown in the research of past usage by Hodgson and Leonard, by current usage remaining at odds with his strictures, by it being only with hindsight that *Darwin* appears as the driving force in the field in question, and by thereby producing the unfortunate consequence of rendering Spencer's own mostly distinctive voice in respect of sociality, justice and beneficence as marginal and muffled in an historically questionable manner. It follows therefore that this study of Spencer will not set out by viewing him through any lens supplied by the expression 'social Darwinist'.

Today, 'social Darwinism' is also increasingly used, and very appropriately, to refer specifically to a serious research effort which is thinking through how a suitably adjusted and applied Darwinian selectionist paradigm of explanation might prove worthwhile if applied by sociology itself to the understanding of novelty and oblivion in social phenomena (Laland and Brown, 2002). However, having now outlined how 'social Darwinism' will be approached in this study, further discussion of issues raised around an expression with a regrettably chequered history as applied to the interpretation of Spencer can indeed here be left on one side.

By the years which followed the First World War there is no obvious academic area, including sociology, in which Spencer's reputation can be regarded as other than at a low ebb. In 1919, A. D. Lindsay, a sociologically minded son of idealist social thought, declared the 'malignant theory' of 'scientific individualism' as swept into the dustbin of history (Harris, 1992: p. 135). In America Charles Horton Cooley was a seminal pioneer of sociology, his own research influencing the 'Chicago School'. In his 'Reflections upon the sociology of Herbert Spencer' of 1920 he paid Spencer a handsome tribute: 'I imagine that nearly all of us who took up sociology between 1870, say, and 1890 did so at the instigation of Spencer... he seemed to show us an open road into those countries which as yet we had only vaguely yearned to explore. His book, *The Study of Sociology*, perhaps the most readable of all his works, had a large sale and probably did more to arouse interest in the subject than any other publication before or since'. But, Cooley felt duty-bound to add in the very next line, 'nearly all of us fell away from him sooner or later and more or less completely' (1920: p. 7).

In 1933, Crane Brinton famously asked 'Who now reads Spencer?' He directly followed this question by noting it was 'difficult for us to realise how great a stir he made in the world. The *Synthetic Philosophy* penetrated to many a bookshelf which held nothing else quite so heavy. It lay beside the works of Buckle and Mill on the shelf of every Englishman of a radical turn of mind. It was read, discussed, fought over. And now it is a drug on the second-hand market, and hardly stirs the interest of the German or American aspirant to the doctorate in philosophy' (1962: p. 187). Indeed, second-hand booksellers in England, and in Dublin, still displayed a surfeit of Spencer (especially *First Principles*) well into the 1970s as the interest in Spencer of this author began. From American sociology, the answer to Brinton's question was, in due course, Neil Smelser and Talcott Parsons, a more positive answer than one imagines Brinton suspected possible, but sociology in Britain, after the time of the occupancy of its first sociology chair (at the London School of Economics) by Hobhouse, appeared to owe much less to Spencer than in America. Indeed, J. D. Y. Peel, who made one of the most influential contributions (Peel, 1971) to a later and continuing revival of interest in Spencer in social science circles which may be dated back to the late 1960s, has recently pinpointed when Spencer slid from view in British sociology for three decades: 'When the Herbert Spencer Trustees decided to wind up their posthumous publication programme of Spencer's *Descriptive Sociology* series, their last act was to commission Jay Rumney's *Herbert Spencer's Sociology* (1934) with a Preface written by Morris Ginsberg, Hobhouse's successor at LSE. For all its pious conclusions that sociology would do well to build on Spencerian foundations, the tone of Rumney's work was valedictory, and in fact it ushered in the 30-year trough in his reputation' (2003: p. 132). The years after the Second World War saw no quick revival. For the philosopher Frederick Copleston, he was now increasingly forgotten: 'I wonder how many people, even professional philosophers, could say that they had read the works of Herbert Spencer. Very few, I imagine' (1949: p. 105).

This, of course, is a far cry from the heady days when a bust of Spencer was emblematic of advanced thought: the stage directions of George Bernard Shaw's *Man and Superman* of 1903 call for 'two busts on pillars', one of John Bright, the other 'of Mr. Herbert Spencer', the two framing an engraved portrait of Richard Cobden and enlarged photographs of Martineau, Huxley and George Eliot. It also contrasts with signs of regard for Spencer at a high political level. At Gladstone's invitation he dined with him in April, 1877 (Spencer, 1904, ii: p. 297), and breakfasted with him in May, 1881 and June, 1882 (Duncan, 1911: pp. 215, 224). At Spencer's request John Morley brought A. J. Balfour (to become prime minister in 1902) to see him in 1896. Next day Balfour reflected (in a letter to Lady Elcho) that the request could not be taken as 'otherwise than a high compliment, so off we set together in a hansom to call on the old philosopher (he is 76 and has just finished the endless volumes of his so-called Synthetic Philosophy) in St John's Wood. He had put off his journey to Brighton for a day in order to see me, and we found him lying at nearly full length, with his feet on a chair, and, by his own account, in very poor health. Controversy, it appears, immediately brings on serious palpitations; we therefore avoided all subjects of difference and he talked interestingly of his early life as an engineer ... of the new edition of his Biology, and how he is employing five young men of science to bring it up to date, and so forth' (in Dugdale, 1939: pp. 150–1).

In traversing the territory to be surveyed, McClelland's pronouncement that Spencer was an 'extremely unpleasant theorist' should come to appear as injudicious, comprehensible only as a reflex action testifying to the baleful reach of the pernicious tag 'social Darwinist', used in the manner of Hofstadter. But was the man Spencer 'extremely unpleasant'? None of those who were well-acquainted with him volunteered traits worse than reserve, vanity, scorn of social conventions and authority derived from established status, and self-centredness. Beatrice Webb's sister, Kate, noted a nervous irritability, and recalled John Tyndall saying at her father's London house, with Spencer standing by, ' "He'd be a much nicer fellow if he had a good swear now and then" – and our hilarity at the very notion of Mr. Spencer swearing' (in Duncan, 1911: p. 510). Joseph Dalton Hooker, though, could find him 'a damper', with 'cribbed, cabined and confined' views (in Peel, 1971: p. 25). Most noted rectitude, loyalty, honesty, solicitude, kindness, clubbability, opposition to aggression and coercion, and a special rapport with children. Idiosyncrasies of habit and eccentricities of manner were legion, but as often as not associated with forms of nervous debility. Scarcely, then, the epitome of nastiness. Spencer was unarguably personally committed, because theoretically committed, to, as Robert Pinker expressed it, 'stringent limitations upon the scope of governmental administration, and especially so in the field of social welfare provision, irrespective of the short-run distress that might be caused' (1971: p. 26). Against this, however, needs to be set Spencer's novel and welfare-related emphasis on ready access, without cost, to the administration of justice, as interpreted with reference to his equal freedom principle. This certainly appeared to commit him to equal pay for equal work, and speedy redress when landlords, entrepreneurs and governments breached contracts, or polluters impaired health.

It will be helpful to give an indication of what each of the chapters of this book attempts to achieve. The first three chapters provide a fairly compact biographical study of Spencer and place the key questions that motivated his ideas regarding 'evolution' and other topics in an intellectual and historical context. I am aware that some readers with a 'presentist' take on dead sociologists may feel that a 'biography' is inessential. Nevertheless, Spencer's intellectual origins have on occasions been so brutally condensed as to eclipse the nuances which help to structure his wider work, and are essential in its interpretation. It makes sense then to try to retrieve the nature of his formative culture. Chapter 1 is concerned with Spencer's life and thought up until the late 1850s, when he was on the threshold of piecing together his general theory of evolution. It covers influences from his teachers, first his father George, himself an educationalist of significance, and then his uncle Thomas, Anglican cleric and Cambridge graduate. It deals with his early exposure to natural theology, evolutionary deism, geometry, science, and political economics. It also deals with his acquisition in the 1840s of a varied set of experiences associated with surveying and related work in railway promotion and construction, with writing short articles on political topics of the day and his first full-length book, *Social Statics*, and with his immersion in radical politics. His introductions to Lamarckian biology and Charles Lyell's geology, and, later, embryology, important events, are also considered. Chapter 2 covers a shorter period, up until the early 1870s, in which Spencer was principally tackling the foundational and biological dimensions of his distinctive perspective on the direction and mechanisms of evolution. It examines afresh what Spencer meant by 'survival of the fittest'. Chapter 3 chiefly deals with the extension of his evolutionary perspective into the interpretation of social life, including ethics, and thus the conclusion of his 'System of Synthetic Philosophy' in 1896. Each chapter considers as appropriate the significance for Spencer's intellectual growth of his wide circle of influential friends and personal contacts – including George Eliot, David Masson, Joseph Dalton Hooker, Thomas Henry Huxley, John Tyndall, Sir John Lubbock, W. E. H. Leaky, George Henry Lewes, Eliza Lynn Linton, Edward Livingston Youmans, Andrew Carnegie, Auberon Herbert, Beatrice Potter (later Webb), Charles Darwin, Alexander Bain, Charles Kingsley, John Morley, William Ewart Gladstone and Arthur James Balfour. The chapters discuss too the rise of his international reputation in his lifetime and provide an account of some of the general criticisms of his work and, where appropriate, his replies to them.

Chapters 4 and 5 provide an examination of Spencer's general theory of evolution, which he was developing from at least 1857 and to the exposition of which his 10-volume System of Synthetic Philosophy, published between 1862 and 1896, was entirely devoted. Chapter 5 in particular concentrates on Spencer's psychology in which associationism and evolution were integrated, and freedom of the will denied. It is no accident that Spencer regarded his *Principles of Psychology* of 1855 as central to his thought, nor was it an incidental dimension to the book that he explicitly rejected freedom of the will. Spencer's criticisms of socialism and positive attempts to achieve social reform through government initiative have bite precisely because he does not accept that a simple social determinism associated with ameliorative measures is an adequate theory of individual and social life. Now his own position here has problems, not least tending to 'biologize' accounts of individual and social change, but it does modify pretty radically 'traditional' interpretations of his social thought as straightforwardly 'functionalist'. The discussion thus brings back into the interpretation of Spencer the fact that he saw his psychology and sociology as intimately related. Spencer's own functional analysis itself will thus be given a 'critical and deconstructive' appraisal, and it will emerge that Spencer seems tolerably clear that a 'function' does not explain the origin of something, although he has been accused of this mistake. The psychology was highly influential, and an understanding of it is essential for a proper appreciation of his approach to sociology, studied in the following chapter. The structure of Spencer's theory of evolution is also contrasted with Darwin's theoretical position: there are key differences over the mechanisms of change and over the importance of direction in the change; for Spencer change takes the form of orthogenesis, that is to say it is holistic, linear and, in principle, reversible, whereas for Darwin change takes the form of phylogenesis, that is to say it is atomistic, branching, and irreversible. In the aftermath of the publication of Darwin's *On the Origin of Species by Means of Natural Selection* in 1859, Spencer, however, broadened his own understanding of mechanisms of organic change, and this development is examined. The Lamarckian mechanism was never abandoned by Spencer but now he, to varying degrees, emphasized in addition 'natural selection' (which he preferred to call 'the survival of the fittest' after 1864), characterizing its action as 'indirect adaptation', or 'indirect equilibration'.

Chapter 5 is also focussed on the *Principles of Sociology*. It discusses, as filtered through Spencer's evolutionary framework, his central substantive concerns relating to social structure and change in domestic, ceremonial, political, ecclesiastical, professional and industrial institutions. His discussions of the social phenomena associated with differentiation, specialization and integration, and also the possibilities of regression, are explored in detail. Spencer's distinctive treatment of culture, manners and fashion is also reviewed. However, his attempts to *explain* the detailed aspects of social life are rooted in his distinctive psychological perspective, evolutionary associationism, in which direct adaptation, physical and psychical to surrounding circumstances, rather than functions and teleology, seem central. For Spencer explaining social change involves seeing social circumstances as working as an adaptive pressure on individual psychologies (and individual psychologies as they adapt, psychically and physically, create new social features). In turn, adaptation is of course reconfigured in the face of major environmental disturbances, such as wars, aggressions and ruptures of all kinds. Part of the chapter offers a critical as well as contextual investigation of the specifically sociological responses to Spencer of Tönnies (who reviewed Spencer in several lengthy articles from the 1880s onwards) and Durkheim (taking into account in particular Ronald Perrin's defence of Spencer against Durkheim's interpretation of him).

Chapter 6 is focused on exactly what Spencer meant when he famously described a society as a 'social organism', which he did from at least 1851. It will discuss helpful distinctions made in Tim Gray's *The Political Philosophy of Herbert Spencer*, which indicate that Spencer's individualist/organicist conception of a society was, and remains, in principle coherent, contrary to the arguments from proponents of idealist social thought, and from within sociology as exemplified by Durkheim, that a society had to be seen as a moral or spiritual 'organic' whole.

The following chapter is concerned with another commonly noticed feature of Spencer's sociology, his contrast between 'industrial' and 'militant' forms of social relations. Societies are 'militant' when individuals are in all their main activities centrally and coercively controlled to resist real or supposed external aggression, but 'industrial', or peaceful, when the external threats are relatively dormant, thus enabled to display the ascendency of the law of equal freedom with its attendant spontaneous and unforced forms of cooperation and beneficence. Under 'militancy' the good of individuals is subordinated to the good of society as a whole, while under 'industrialism' the good of the component individuals is not sacrificed to the good of the whole. It will be argued that, contrary to some interpretations, for Spencer elements of both 'regimens' may be coeval in a society. Clarifying Spencer on these matters provides an opportunity to analyse his position on representative government, his conceptualization of the state and also his analysis of the causation and individual and social consequences of a range of social and international problems affecting the United Kingdom and United States as he saw it in the 1880s and 1890s. His three-volume *Principles of Sociology* is particularly important to this section.

Chapter 8 provides a particular assessment of Spencer on music and the evolution of professions related to music; these were topics on which he had written as early as the 1850s, before his theory of evolution and the *Synthetic Philosophy* had crystallized, and to which he often returned later. It serves as a case study of how he analysed a topic from his distinctive sociological and psychological perspectives. His apparently unique difficulty over settling on what he could regard as a satisfactory evolutionary account of the origin of harmony means that Spencer on music deserves much more attention in examinations of his ideas in general than it is normally accorded.

The next chapter turns the spotlight on to Spencer's extensive analysis of altruistic action in modern society, developed particularly in the *Principles of Ethics*. Spencer's approach is in the main naturalistic, a 'natural history' approach to moral sentiments which may be regarded as an exercise in the sociology of morals. The chapter covers Spencer's conception of individuals and social interaction, and explains the distinctive derivation, nature and importance of the law of equal freedom (or principle of 'justice') as the mechanism of change: for Spencer a process of adaptation to circumstances and the inheritance of acquired characteristics led to individual and social development which included cooperation and altruism as well as competition. Discussion of *Social Statics* and the *Principles of Ethics* form the core of this chapter. A topic of particular interest to Spencer is 'private beneficence', which takes positive and negative forms. The positive form is what we would call 'familial' or 'informal' care or welfare; the negative form involves waiving claims to redress in the face of 'injustice' if no serious harm results. But Spencer is also concerned with voluntary organizations, including professional associations and unions, and of course with distinguishing the state's legitimate role in enforcing 'justice', and thus policing violations of the equal freedom principle, such as breaches of contract, pollution, unequal pay for equal work and 'industrial slavery', from its positively regulating activities, coercive and comprehensive, characterizng 'militant' societies. Spencer's 'evolutionary ethics' attracted considerable critical attention, to which on occasion he replied, and the arguments of Henry Sidgwick and other moral philosophers, broadly urging that Spencer had missed the living heart of moral discourse in his natural history, are discussed – the points raise again of course the question of how adequately Spencer conceived of agency in individual and social life. It will also consider the response of idealist social analysis represented by Thomas Hill Green, Bernard Bosanquet, Henry Jones and David Ritchie, and of the 'new Liberals', J. A. Hobson and L. T. Hobhouse.

The Concluding Reflections argue that Spencer, as a sociologist with a liberal perspective, critical of state intervention beyond the maintenance of 'justice', directs some still relevant questions at holistic and normative assumptions about the concept of the 'good society', and at the legitimacy of the constraint and coercion of people deemed to have transgressed moral standards associated with, for example, 'responsible citizenship'. One essential step in making such an argument, though, is to bracket off or otherwise render anodyne Spencer's denial of free will (something he himself sometimes tended towards). This at least in principle yields a notion of agency in a purposive, conscious sense, inherent in social individuals. A further step is to build on the consideration that while Spencer's depersonalized concern with structures and functions at the specifically 'superorganic' level may be difficult to renovate within sociology, there is *already* in Spencer another kind of interpretation of social life, unshaped by that level of abstraction, and much more in tune with where sociology finds itself today (indeed various writers have found three or even four sociologies in Spencer). This is Spencer's own emphasis, once long out of sociological fashion, on competing and cooperating social individuals as forming a catallaxy, an unplanned and yet routinely reliable source of what is of benefit to other social individuals, themselves also similarly situated, and also a source of what would now be called 'social capital' (displayed, for example in his essay 'Specialized Administration' of 1871). With new priorities bringing that emphasis once more into the foreground, Spencer's classic contribution to it no longer deserves to be eclipsed from view. The Concluding Reflections also considers how Spencer might be assessed in connection with a successful application of the (Darwinian) 'selectionist paradigm' of explanation to sociology, now increasingly under consideration within sociology itself (as represented by Runciman's *A Treatise on Social Theory*). If there is no justification for re-introducing a neo-Spencerian version of social evolution as orthogenesis into accounts of social change, neither is it realistic to assume that aspects of social life survive merely because their 'designers' intend that outcome. It is suggested that the selectionist paradigm may, properly understood, provide not a threat to but an opportunity for developing sociological analysis. While in detail a viable selectionist paradigm in sociology would owe very little to Spencer, among the classical figures of sociology it is Spencer's absence of a 'silo' outlook in how to understand social life that would be most consonant with such a development.

1
Early Spencer: Influences and Ideas

The principle sources available on Spencer's life are the two volumes of his *An Autobiography*, published posthumously in 1904, the year following his death, and David Duncan's *The Life and Letters of Herbert Spencer* of 1908. The *Autobiography* gives the account of his life in some detail up to 1882, and is then thinner until as a chronological account it ceases altogether at the year 1889. Spencer relates that he systematically started collecting material in May, 1875, and then, 'for an hour on Saturday afternoon', dictated to a shorthand writer. Into the transcribed notes went letters and papers. The process continued for 'something like a year I think. Eventually the narrative was brought up to date and the process ceased' (*Autobiography*, 1904, i: p. 285). In 1886, he returned to the task while a sense of lassitude precluded more strenuous mental activity. Parts were composed out of chronological sequence. His objective was simple: 'It has seemed to me that a natural history of myself would be a useful accompaniment to the books which it has been the chief occupation of my life to write.... That I have fully succeeded is not to be supposed; but perhaps I have succeeded partially. At any rate, one significant truth has been made clear – that in the genesis of a system of thought the emotional nature is a large factor: perhaps as large a factor as the intellectual nature' (1904, i: p. vii). In essence, Spencer turned his own style of evolutionary analysis on to himself as a subject. 'Greatness and smallness surely never lived so closely in one skin together', thought William James, as he contemplated the 'admirably truth-telling' candour of the *Autobiography*: rarely had Nature performed an odder feat than when she 'designed, or accidentally stumbled into, the personality of Herbert Spencer' (1904: p. 19). Spencer's approach to autobiography has remained an interesting specimen for students of the genre, with Mark Francis, for instance, speculating that it 'was an act of expiation, and a warning to others to avoid his fate' (2007: p. 17).[1] Whatever there may be to be said in favour or against this interpretative orientation to the *Autobiography*, there are fortunately some recent historical studies which flesh out and revise Spencer's own account of early influences on him, for it is indeed the case that Spencer's own account of his intellectual development 'does not sufficiently acknowledge the debt that he owed to provincial scientific culture and its institutions' (Elliott, 2003: p. 28).

Duncan selected the material for and otherwise wrote the *Life and Letters* with Spencer's agreement and as requested in his will, and collected further mostly biographical evidence. The volume was progressed under the auspices of Spencer's trustees (H. Charlton Bastion, Auberon Herbert and Duncan himself). Duncan had become Spencer's first secretary in 1867, recommended by Spencer's friends David Masson and Alexander Bain. His main task at that time was to assist in the collection and tabulation of evidence from anthropologically orientated travellers' publications, preparatory to the writing of the *Principles of Sociology*. 'Very unfortunately for me, though perhaps fortunately for himself', wrote Spencer to Youmans on 9 March 1869, 'Mr. Duncan has been appointed Professor of Logic &c. at Madras; and leaves me for India some six weeks hence' (1904, ii: p. 215). In fact, Duncan coupled his new post with the provision of some continued assistance to Spencer. Duncan's book covers Spencer's whole life and is the only 'official' source after the 1880s with the exception of Spencer's own essay 'The Filiation of Ideas' of 1899 (included in Duncan), and his 'Reflections' of 1893 (included in the *Autobiography*).

Spencer was born on 27 April 1820 in Derby. His father, William George (usually referred to as George), was the strong personality in the household. George followed the example of his own father's commitment to teaching, himself building a career through carrying on school and private teaching, and by making contributions to educational thought, in both of which he achieved some importance. However, in 1824, he uprooted his family to Nottingham to try his luck in lace manufacture. Three years later, money lost and lessons learnt, he moved the family back to Derby, and returned to teaching. The boy's childhood was somewhat austere, mostly spent in the company of adult relatives: eight other children were born to his parents (Duncan, 1908: p. 7) but none survived infancy save one sister who died before he was four. In effect Spencer was an only child, and this he regretted. 'It was one of my misfortunes to have no brothers, and a still greater misfortune to have no sisters' (1904, i: p. 64). Spencer's mother, Harriet, apparently did not assert herself, living in the shadow of her slightly older husband. She retained throughout her life her adherence to Wesleyanism, displaying in her conduct and chapel-going a diligent fidelity to religious duty. Her husband originally shared this attachment to Methodism, but gravitated towards the Quaker meeting house during Spencer's early years. His busy life devoted to fostering enlightenment, enquiry and reason passed Spencer's mother by, and his periodic illness, depression and anxiety would trigger a frosty rudeness from him on occasion. Spencer judged him as 'not kind to my mother. Exacting and inconsiderate, he did not habitually display that sympathy which should characterize the marital relation' (1904, i: p. 54).

In addition to his teaching commitments, Spencer's father contributed to the wider life of Derby, particularly in the advancement of scientific culture. The town itself is to the north of Birmingham and Leicester, and west of Nottingham. In 1801, the first census recorded the town's population as just under 11,000. Forty years on, the population had grown to some 37,000. These years witnessed a process of change in Derby from a county market town into a strategic industrial centre. It already possessed an established wool industry, and in the middle of the eighteenth century a porcelain factory had opened, graced with a Royal Warrant in 1775 permitting the introduction of the famous name Crown Derby. Derby's enduring reputation as a major centre of engineering may be dated back to 1839 with the arrival of the railway. The town became a strategic railway junction, with workshops and locomotive building quickly developing once it had been selected as the headquarters in 1844 of the newly formed Midland Railway. At this time, Derby was no intellectual backwater, but 'a vibrant cultural and philosophical centre with a strong Dissenting community' (Elliott, 2003: p. 3). The town was especially noted for hosting the Derby Philosophical Society. The physician and poet, Erasmus Darwin, Charles Darwin's grandfather, who died in 1802, had been a founder member and its first president. Spencer's father held office as honorary secretary to the Society from 1814 and was a prominent figure in the Mechanics' Institute during Spencer's boyhood, arranging lecture courses. There was also, established in 1808, a Literary and Philosophical Society. George Spencer was probably 'one of the most industrious scientific activists in the region' (2004: p. 397) and among the 'great nineteenth-century educators..., a pioneer in the reception and development of pedagogical systems such as the Pestalozzian' (Elliott, 2004: pp. 391–2).

Dissent and science complemented each other in Derby. Erasmus Darwin's legacy may well have been decisive. His deistic evolutionary perspective 'included a model of biological evolution, a developmental associationist psychology, an evolutionary geology, and grand cosmological developmentalism' (Elliott, 2003: p. 28). His conception of the mutability of animate life, extending to include patterns of human life, rather than the belief that they reflected a given order of things was part of a scientific culture with practical and utilitarian ends, but it also possessed associations with radical reform, on political, religious and moral fronts. Unitarians were especially prominent in sustaining Derby's scientific and educational networks into which George Spencer was able to tap. The Unitarian textile-manufacturing Strutt family, Radical in politics and well-disposed towards the French Revolution, was wealthy and of exceptional influence, not least through a range of benefactions to the town – 'a library, an arboretum, a hospital, chapels and schools' (Peel, 1971: p. 35). There is a letter of 1819 from William Strutt to his son Edward which indicates that this Derby circle was not much impressed by the influential 'natural theology' of the time principally associated with

William Paley, in which the existence of a Creator was taken as demonstrated by evidence of 'design' or regularity observable in the world. Strutt drolly wrote, pleased on hearing that his son's tutor approved of the Rev. Thomas Robert Malthus's theory of population, 'I supposed his opponents, if the subject were in any way connected with what they call the benevolence of the Deity, would controvert the elements of Euclid' (quoted in Elliott, 2003: p. 16). Of George Spencer, Elliott suggests (2004: p. 398):

> It is likely that his early interest in science was stimulated by the activities of the Derby Literary and Philosophical Society (1808), created specifically to support... public lectures and raise funds for a laboratory to undertake original scientific research. The wealthy cotton magnate, William Strutt (1756–1830), the leading scientific activist in the area and second president of the Philosophical Society, had undertaken a series of electro-chemical experiments with Erasmus Darwin until 1801. This work received renewed stimulus when Sylvester moved to the town at Strutt's instigation in 1808. In addition to the Strutt brothers, William and Joseph and [the chemist Charles] Sylvester, leading members of this society included the physician Richard Forester, Higginson and the mayor and chemist, Richard Brown. After undertaking programmes of lectures on subjects such as chemistry and liberal education for about six years, the society was absorbed by the Philosophical Society, which appropriated its laboratory apparatus.

At home, as his father and uncles conversed, Spencer became accustomed to the discussion of moral, political, and religious matters, as well as scientific developments and educational methods. His father's scientific committee work, including serving on the Methodist library committee, meant that a range of books and journals on medical and scientific interests passed through the house, and Spencer read 'here and there on all kinds of topics, – mechanical, physical, medical, anatomical, and so forth' (1904, i: p. 88). Perhaps the greatest significance for Herbert of George Spencer's partiality for science was that it made him a participant in the demonstration of experiments: 'My father had an electrical machine and an air-pump; and from time to time classes of his pupils came to see electric and pneumatic phenomena. I had frequently to make preparations for the experiments and aid in performance of them. The result was that being on many occasions witness to the facts, and hearing the explanations given, I early gained some knowledge of physics' (1904, i: p. 86).

Beyond acting as a propagandist for science, George Spencer taught scores of private and institutional students, pioneering practical and experiential educative methods, particularly in mathematics and the sciences. He authored an instructional book, *Inventional Geometry: A Series of Questions, Problems and Explanations Intended to Familiarise the Pupil with Geometrical Conceptions, and to Exercise His Inventive Faculty.*[2] Elliott has also drawn attention to signs of professional recognition:

When superintending the first English translation of Pestalozzi's *How Gertrude Teaches Her Children* during the 1890s, the educationist Ebenezer Cooke argued that Spencer's *Inventional Geometry* 'stands alone' as 'our most Pestalozzian school-book' comparable in its practical approach to teaching to Huxley's *Biology*. He considered that it demonstrated that Spencer had 'perfected a method of teaching elementary geometry by a gradual transition from the concrete to the abstract, thus avoiding the obstacles that the realisation of mathematical conceptions presents to the ordinary student of Euclid'.

(2004: p. 415)

Among George Spencer's pupils who later distinguished themselves in life was Charles Fox, designer of the Great Exhibition building of 1851, the children of Henry Mozley, Thomas, Anne and James, all authors, and Thomas Rymer Jones, Professor of Zoology at King's College, London. Herbert's later renown would too have been a source of pride, though in this case it was the father's example rather than any formal teaching that left its mark. Spencer was taught by others, including his uncle William, George's brother, who had taken on their own father's school. Nevertheless, with his progressive philosophy and quizzical approach to political and social ideas, George Spencer played 'a decisive role in the development of his son's globally influential evolutionary system, surely his most lasting achievement' (Elliott, 2004: p. 417).

Herbert maintained that his father retained his religious faith, against claims to the contrary made by his former pupil Thomas Mozley[3] (Spencer, 1904, i: p. 46), though he conceded that he never referred 'to anything as explicable by supernatural agency. I presume from other evidence that he must at that time have still accepted the current belief in miracles; but I never perceived any trace of it in his conversation. Certainly, his remarks about the surrounding world gave no sign of any other thought than that of uniform natural law' (1904, i: p. 90). Spencer himself recalled his father coaching him towards the thoroughly practical utilitarian ambition 'to become "a useful member of society" ' (1904, i: p. 82), particularly in the aftermath of the son's challenges to authority and general disobedience, traits of his character to which he readily confessed. Yet while this ambition drove his father, beyond doubt he too showed no respect towards established social conventions or religious and intellectual 'authority', and he encouraged instead a sense of independence in his son in finding constructive answers as he faced up to the task of understanding the world about him, pressing him to identify the natural causes of puzzling events. Insects, and the countryside in general, were early enthusiasms of the boy, which his father helped him to turn into systematic entomological study. Rambles in the open air accompanied a thirst for novels (frowned upon by his mother) and a love of pursuing flights of his own imagination or, as he put it, 'castle-building'. He also discovered solace in fishing, which remained a passion into his adult life. His love of this sport nearly ended his young life; drowning in the River Derwent was once averted only by a youth, George Holme, plunging in to the rescue. Holme subsequently became a wealthy manufacturer and Mayor of Derby, and Spencer maintained contact with the family. In the *Autobiography* he offered a typically Spencerian character sketch of his saviour: 'As may be inferred from the fact that he was the one out of a considerable number of spectators who risked himself to save me, he was of superior nature morally; and he turned out in after life to be also a man of much faculty' (1904, i: p. 74). By the time he was 13, Spencer himself judged his education in Latin and Greek to have been thin, as mostly ignoring history, biography and matters of English grammar, and giving him merely 'the ordinary knowledge of arithmetic' (1904, i: pp. 88–9). By way of compensation he felt he had above-average knowledge of things and their properties, and places and their peoples: he was familiar too with aspects of physics and chemistry, and with some of the processes forming the subject matter of other sciences.

Now, however, an abrupt change was to hand. The small village of Hinton Charterhouse is situated on quite high and exposed land, south of the city of Bath, though the nearby Avon valley would count as picturesque. Here George's younger brother, Thomas, was the evangelically inclined Perpetual Curate, the village's first resident clergyman since Roman Catholic days. Thomas Spencer (1796–1853) had successfully graduated from St. John's College, Cambridge, where he achieved above average honours. Loans from his elder brother George had been instrumental in enabling him to pursue his university career. In June, 1833, shortly after Spencer's 13th birthday, he journeyed with his parents by coach, first, from Derby through Lichfield to Birmingham, then, the next day, onwards to Hinton, passing to the right the Malvern Hills ('the first objects in the nature of mountains I had ever seen' [1904, i: p. 91]), breaking for refreshment and the stretching of legs in Cheltenham, off again up by Leckhampton, the Cotswolds and the vale of Stroud, and only dropping down into Bath as the summer shadows lengthened. Nightfall beckoned as at the Hinton parsonage Thomas and his wife Anna welcomed the posse of Spencers from Derby.

Thomas had probably acquired his evangelicalism at Cambridge from Charles Simeon, evangelical preacher and Fellow of King's College. Though within the Church of England, Thomas was no liberal tory or 'noetic' but virtually a 'Nonconformist', as Hilton has described him, who 'combined evangelicalism with political radicalism' (1988: p. 311). His position possessed some affinity with the views of Thomas Chalmers, as expressed in his most systematic book, his first of 1808, *An Enquiry into the Nature and Stability of National Resources*. The 'master hand' of the divine will lies behind the following radical liberal paean from Chalmers: 'The greatest economic good is rendered to the community by each man being left to consult and to labour for his own particular good –...a more prosperous result is obtained by the spontaneous play and busy competition of many thousand wills, each bent on the prosecution of its own selfishness, than by the anxious superintendence of a government, vainly attempting to medicate the fancied imperfections of nature, or to improve on the arrangements of her previous and better mechanism' (in Waterman, 1991: p. 248). Boyd Hilton considers that, like economists, evangelicals believed in 'a "hidden hand"; unlike economists, they believed that the "hidden hand" held a rod' (Hilton, 1988: p. 114). Within the field loosely described as Christian Political Economics, with Thomas in the evangelical camp, there is, says Hilton, 'a symbiosis between the optimistic, *adaptational* approach of neo-Paleyans like Southwood Smith and Richard Whately, and the more fundamentalist, *conversionist* approach of the evangelicals, Sumner, Bicheno, and Chalmers. The two approaches had much in common, and both pointed towards freer trade and a *laissez-faire* social policy' (1988: p. 70). The contrast hinges on conflicting diagnoses of the nature of man's moral psychology. The differences are not always expressed in a clear-cut manner, and often emerge in matters of emphasis and nuance, derived from their differing spiritual contexts and respectively weak or strong anxieties about the imminence of disorder, and divine judgement. 'Thus', Hilton adds, 'when Southwood Smith writes of Malthusianism as a "moral discipline" ... his phraseology is typical of the Age of Atonement, but the sentiments are not in his case evangelical. More like Richard Whately, he saw the march of civilization, education, and generosity as a gradual process of tuition, fitting men for a future existence in heaven. Having no concept of natural depravity or of the urgent need for conversion, Southwood Smith was not only a post- rather than a pre-millenialist but a very relaxed millenialist altogether'. When James Ebenezer Bicheno observes that 'the human mind cannot be stationary', he too 'seems to share the evolutionary cosmic optimism of Southwood Smith', but his references to struggle and his use of a jungle metaphor help to establish the difference, 'as does his emphasis on fear more than on hope, on punishment and suffering more than on rewards and satisfaction . . . . The crucial difference is, of course, that for Chalmers and Sumner the world was merely an "area of moral trial", an "imperfect state" capable of but a limited amount of "welfare", whereas for Southwood Smith the world was cherished by God and designed for ultimate perfection' (1988: p. 80). This evangelical mode, shown by Chalmers, Bishop Sumner and Bicheno,[4] and also by Thomas Spencer, was perhaps more widespread than the general assuredness about economic and social progress which radiated from Southwood Smith and the Church of Ireland Archbishop of Dublin, Richard Whately (who had done much in his *Introductory Lectures on Political Economy* of 1831 to purge Malthus's theory of its appearance of enervating determinism and hence 'irregular' theological implications).[5]

Herbert had arrived at Hinton with joy and in innocence anticipating a holiday; lessons came as a disagreeable surprise. A month or so passed and then to his dismay it transpired that he was to remain at Hinton as his parents departed for Derby, to be taught by Thomas. Thomas sought to obtain obedience from him, and bring discipline and structure to his education for manhood. He also found it difficult to work alongside of a fellow-pupil. The upshot of these uncongenial experiences was that Spencer rose early one Thursday morning, about 10 days into the new regime, and set off to retrace his way to his Derby home, attaining his goal on the Saturday. Some free rides had hastened his path but he had still walked 115 miles in three days. Consternation met his unexpected arrival, but letters recording his contrition for his action, soothing hurt feelings at Hinton, saw him return about a fortnight later, none the worse for his escapade.

Spencer's life now became more austere and ascetic under his uncle's influence. His aunt and uncle had no children, and his only company of his own age were one or two other pupils of his uncle's towards whom Herbert was inclined to be dictatorial. Public 'amusements' represented temptation and vice: 'My uncle was never, I believe, within the walls of a theatre; and I never heard of his attending a concert' (1904, i: p. 28). When uncle and nephew together attended an evening party in Bath and the hostess was puzzled why the young man did not join other young people who were waltzing, it was Thomas who announced 'No Spencer ever dances' (1904, i: p. 28). Spencer found to his taste studies in Euclid, algebra and trigonometry, but made little progress in and showed no appetite for Latin, Greek and French. A year on, Thomas recorded in a letter to George that his son's talents were doubtless 'of a very superior order, and when he is under the restraining effect of an observing tutor and all trivial pursuits are banished from his thoughts, then a calm and grave diligence in study and cheerful quickness of intellect distinguish all he does'. But commendation of his achievement brought displays lacking modesty: 'The grand deficiency in Herbert's natural character is in the principle of *Fear*. And it is only so far as his residence with me has supplied that principle in a degree unusual to him, that after a few struggles he entirely surrendered himself to obey me with a promptness & alacrity that would have given you pleasure to witness, & the more obedient I have observed him the more I have refrained from exercising authority. By *Fear*, I mean both that "Fear of the Lord" which "is the beginning of wisdom", and that fear of Parents, Tutors &c' (in Spencer, 1904, i: p. 105). In quoting this letter Spencer himself acquiesced in his uncle's verdict.

Spencer spent the early part of the summer of 1834 with his parents, in or close to London. They visited Charles Fox, his father's former pupil, who was now a sub-engineer engaged on work for the new railway being constructed between London and Birmingham. Spencer's interest was aroused in going over the works, particularly by the Watford Tunnel, then being pierced. He visited also the Zoological Gardens through the offices of another of his father's former pupils, Thomas Rymer Jones, by then a fellow of the Zoological Society. Back at Hinton in the autumn his thin grasp of English grammar was a sore point, and Thomas, in a letter reporting on Spencer's progress, still singled out his general slackness when left to his own devices: 'with this exception of a *main spring* in this machine, all other things go on well' (in Spencer, 1904, i: p. 109). He continued to work on Euclid and mechanics, but he also read Martineau's *Tales of Political Economy*. This book had been dipped into before at home, but Spencer considered that then he 'read for the stories and skipped the political economy. However, from remarks in my letters written in the spring of 1835, it appears that I had gathered something of a solid kind' (1904, i: pp. 110–11).

Spencer's very first publication also appeared, a note on the formation of common salt crystals, in the newly launched *Bath and West of England Magazine*. This attempt at turning his hand to writing for publication, successful as it proved, was triggered by his uncle's example. Thomas Spencer was, as Lyon has noted, 'a prodigious writer of tracts and pamphlets' (23 in total), which were widely read and distributed.[6] His subjects included church reform, the corn laws, reform of poor law administration and practice, and teetotalism. Some of his 'causes' were highly controversial, locally, in his Church, and nationally. Herbert, with ample justification, noted Thomas's rare, unforced and unsettling instinct to denounce wrongdoing, expose political injustices and demand fair laws. He worked hard on behalf of the cause of the repeal of the corn laws:

> How conspicuously active he was, is shown by the fact that he said grace at the first Anti-Corn Law banquet, and that, continuing his relations with the league to the end, he said grace also at the last Anti-Corn-Law banquet. Among the state-appointed teachers of rectitude there was, I believe, one other avowed Free-trader, though not an active one; but with this qualified exception my uncle was, strange to say, the only clergyman out of fifteen thousand who contended that the people of England, mostly poor, should not be compelled to buy corn at artificially-enhanced prices to enrich English landlords. This was not his only endeavour to further political equity. He entered with energy into the movement for extending the franchise. He was a member of the first conference at Birmingham to initiate the Complete Suffrage movement, and was a delegate to the subsequent conference, also held there, to frame, if possible, a basis of agreement with the Chartists – a futile experiment.
>
> (1904, i: p. 30)[7]

A friend of Spencer's (E. A. B.) left him in no doubt that Thomas's politics unsettled the orthodox political outlook in the Church of England: 'My brother asked a fellow collegian of his (who comes from Bath) if he knew a clergyman of the name of Spencer there; his friend said: "Do you mean

Spencer of Hinton Charterhouse, for if you do, he is as mad as a March hare". What do you think of that! I see he has been figuring lately at some radical meeting for the repeal of the Corn Laws, where he proposed the first resolution. –Pretty well that for a clergyman!' (in Spencer, 1904, i: p. 30). Another topic dealt with by Thomas in his pamphlets, of especial significance for his nephew's intellectual development, was the reform of the poor laws. When first at Hinton, Thomas had not emulated some fellow clerics, such as Thomas Whately (Richard Whately's elder brother) at Cookham in Berkshire, who had sought from the 1820s to reform and reduce poor law expenditure and poor rates in a semi-experimental attempt to encourage industrial habits and virtue among their parishioners. According to his nephew, although he was known 'during the earlier part of his parochial life as a pauper's friend, he ultimately saw that it was a false humanity to encourage idleness at the expense of industry, and through much opposition succeeding in working out a reform for which his parishioners eventually thanked him' (1904, i: p. 37). The appointment of a Royal Commission to enquire into the poor law in 1832 and the publication of its Report 2 years later, specifically urging the curtailment of outdoor relief to the able-bodied, with relief instead available within a workhouse, provoked extensive national discussion. Legislation to implement these reforms and to group together parishes into 'unions' for the more effective administration of relief was proceeded with rapidly, and it was as the Bill was being debated in parliament that Thomas's eyes were opened. As soon as the Poor Law Amendment Act of 1834 was passed 'he began to apply its provisions to Hinton, before yet the Bath Union was formed' (1904, i: p. 104).

Thus in 1836, the poor law was a burning topic for discussion in the Hinton parsonage. Moreover, Thomas found a new and associated outlet for his unusual reserves of energy by becoming the first chairman of the Bath Union Board of Poor Law Guardians. One of Thomas's pamphlets on the poor law was *The Successful Application of the New Poor Law to the Parish of Hinton Charterhouse* of 1836. A combination of sound theology and political economics had delivered to the village an upswing in employment and a reduction in poor rates: political economy was 'inferior only to religion itself in importance' (Thomas Spencer, 1836: p. 5). Here Thomas's sentiments nicely underline Hilton's insistence in his *Age of Atonement* that evangelical ideology probably contributed 'more than "classical economics" or utilitarianism to the formation of that public morality (or doctrine) in the context of which the new economic policy emerged and by which it was sanctioned' (1988: p. viii). Spencer himself returned to his uncle's reforms in his *The Man versus The State* of 1884, adding to the narrative that 'out of a population of 800, only 15 had to be sent as incapable paupers to the Bath Union (when that was formed), in place of the 100 who received outdoor-relief a short time before' (1884: p. 83). By 1836, Spencer was checking the proofs of his uncle's current pamphlet, correcting typographical errors and punctuation. By now he himself could boast not one but two articles published in the new local magazine, the second of which was a short note defending poor law reform. A letter home to his father captured the boy's delight in his early success with this new enthusiasm:

> what with my uncle writing his pamphlet and articles in the newspapers, &c., &c., I began to think of trying my hand at writing something. Just at this juncture a new magazine was started.... After some consideration I sent *an article* on those little boats which we discovered when I was trying to crystallize salt. I did not tell this to my uncle and aunt for fear that *my article* would not appear in the magazine, but now it is published and after a little search.... I found *my article* looking very pretty. You can imagine my delight when I first saw it. I began shouting and capering about the room until my uncle and aunt did not know what was amiss; but they were very much surprised and pleased when I showed them *my* article.... And now that I have started I intend to go on writing things for this magazine now and then, and in the next number will be my second attempt. In this same number that mine was in there was a very ignorant and prejudiced article on the Poor Laws, which I intend to reply to. I suppose I shall be getting quite proud very soon; indeed upon reading the above over I find that it savours a good deal of it, but I must try to strive against it as well as I can.
>
> (In Duncan, 1911: pp. 19–20)

In June, 1836, Spencer returned to Derby, education at Hinton concluded. His own view was that he had profited intellectually and morally. He had acquired a 'fair amount' of mathematics, though he felt only a 'trifling success' had been realized in languages and other areas. He readily admitted that 'but for my life at Hinton I should have gone on idly, learning next to nothing' (1904, i: p. 115). If more sympathy and affection would have been welcome he acknowledged the value of being trained in self-discipline, adding that 'criticism is somewhat out of place' since he believed that had the roles been reversed he would have relinquished the task. He owed 'very much' to Thomas and Anna, and they had had to deal 'with intractable material – an individuality too stiff to be easily moulded' (1904, i: pp. 116–17).

Mark Francis has suggested that in these years Spencer 'had not held his own at all; he had been broken' (2007: p. 32). It is difficult to reconcile Spencer's own account with such a harsh verdict. After a dreamy and largely unstructured childhood the acquisition of the concept of a self as but a member of a wider world was essential for manhood to be attained. Nearer the truth may be the observation that he faced too few effective challenges to his early idea of himself from too few people. In Duncan's opinion, writing much nearer Spencer's own lifetime and with first-hand experience of him, there was an excess of confidence in his own judgment. Duncan added: 'Had he been sent to a large school, this feature would have been toned down; the application of a wider standard to his own achievements would have diminished his super-abundant self-confidence' (1911: p. 16). But whether this or some other experiences would have allowed him unself-conscious immersion in social and emotional life, not the air of detachment that characterized so much of his later existence, is probably not a matter for profitable speculation.

Back home in Derby, in his 17th year, the question duly arose of what was to happen next. In 1834, his aunt had suggested medicine (Duncan, 1911: p. 20), but in Derby it would be hard to avoid a commitment to teaching. There is no trace of any consideration of attending university. Perhaps funds were short, perhaps the curriculum he had followed had been too narrow to entertain the idea, perhaps his ability or his temperament was thought ill-suited to embarking on that course of action. After briefly undertaking some property surveying for his father Spencer did take up a temporary opening in teaching. But a friend proposed engineering to him. He suggested this as a way forward in a letter to his father, temporarily absent: 'I had not thought of it before, but since I have thought of it [I] think it would be a very eligible profession for me ... since it is just the kind of thing for which my past studies have fitted me' (in Duncan, 1911: p. 21). In November, 1837, his uncle William reported he had obtained a post for his nephew with Charles Fox, a permanent resident engineer on the nascent London and Birmingham Railway. Spencer's ready acceptance of this offer coincided with the inauguration of Victoria's reign; in the capital he witnessed the 'State-pageant' of the royal procession associated with her visit to the Lord Mayor on November 9 (1904, i: p. 129). Surveying out on the line and associated office-work were his chief activities, though he also made drawings by himself to develop his skills. By his own account, throughout a half-year in London he shunned places of amusement. Evenings not spent in drawing or calling on friends were 'devoted to rambles about London'. Oil lamps rather than 'modern' gas lighting in Grosvenor Square brought the insight that 'in this centre of fashionable life' it was 'curiously significant' that there should still survive the old system of illumination when it had elsewhere been replaced by a better' (1904, i: p. 132). With work based at Harrow and Wolverton, Spencer moved out to Wembly. Needing to return from Wolverton one evening, he arranged for a brakeless 'coach-truck' to be attached to a train, reasoning that if he uncoupled the truck from the moving train at a given point friction and gravity would see it coast to a stop at Harrow. Calculations and predictions badly awry, he sailed on down the gradient and through Harrow, alarmed an astonished workman, and rolled to a halt some 2 miles on. With the begrudging help of a gatekeeper's muscle the runaway truck was stowed out of harm's way; this incident, Spencer recorded drily, 'caused a good deal of laughter at my expense' (1904, i: p. 138). That in some quarters the story might be taken as a metaphor for the 'System of Synthetic Philosophy' was not recorded.

As the expiry of his employment approached, Fox brokered new employment for Spencer at Worcester, with an enhanced salary, on the Birmingham and Gloucester Railway under the chief engineer, Captain W. S. Moorsom. Of Spencer's character at this time, Duncan captured an independent observer's impression: 'Mr. Mosse, perhaps in 1904 the only survivor of those who served with him at Worcester, writes to me: "For some 18 months I worked with him at the *same table*... Spencer's office comrades found him an agreeable man, though we thought him a little bumptious"' (1911: p. 22). Spencer's own impression was that many of his colleagues 'belonged largely to the ruling classes' (1904, i: p. 141). However, Spencer became friends with one colleague, G. B. W. Jackson, the German-educated son of the foreign secretary of the Bible Society. Spencer judged himself against most of his colleagues as 'Alien in culture, ideas, sentiments, and aims' and as regarded by them as 'an oddity' (1904, i: p. 143). He and Jackson believed the dissolute habits of these companions spoke of wasted adult lives to come, about which, however, he later admitted, they turned out to be quite wrong. Spencer fretted over his own 'idleness' and whether it was expedient to force the mind against inclination: to his father he wrote early in 1839, 'I should like to hear what my uncle Thomas says upon this head. It seems to me to be rather important to be able to distinguish between idleness and mental debility' (in Spencer, 1904, i: p. 147). But later in the year George Spencer, while visiting his son, wrote with an unexpected complaint to his wife, craving respite: 'I must leave Worcester in my own defence for Herbert provides me with problems of so interesting a kind both to himself and to me that I find it difficult to relax entirely from mental pursuits and allow my mind to run wild' (in Spencer, 1904, i: p. 148). By 1840, he was sharing experiments in chemistry with Jackson and boasting to his father that his 'inventive faculties' were improving, with contrivances schemed to measure the velocity and the tractive force of engines. Still badgered by letters from his father, as he had been at Hinton, to reveal the state of his religious faith, he declined. Thin as he thought it was, it was growing thinner still; the idea of a breach 'in the course of creation had come to be, if not an impossible thought, yet a thought never entertained' (1904, i: p. 153).

Spencer was being entrusted with greater responsibilities at Worcester, including bridge and track layout design. He published several technical pieces in the *Civil Engineer and Architect's Journal* between 1839 and 1842, but writing on social and political matters had stalled. Moorsom thought him highly competent in railway work and administration, and well brought up, with gentlemanly habits – he wrote to Spencer's father to this effect (Duncan, 1911: p. 28) – enough so to offer him, in March, 1840, the temporary post of acting as his secretary. Spencer accepted, and lodged in the nearby village of Powick to be close to Moorsom's residence there. Work on correspondence was interspersed with frequent travels in the vicinity of the line, finessing engineering matters, assisting with experiments on locomotives and witnessing the trials of new American locomotives for the steep Lickey incline near Bromsgrove (he also travelled further afield with Moorsom, to Deepdene, near Dorking, on non-company business). On a different note, with the arrival of summer he was often alone in Moorsom's house with a young lady much his own age. She was a relative of Moorsom, and, unknown to Spencer, engaged. She struck Spencer as 'intelligent, unconventional, amiable, and in various ways attractive', and, excepting contact with a sister of one of the pupils at Hinton, this was his first informal contact with the opposite sex. He thought her company softened his '*brusquerie*', though it detracted from 'the fulfilment of duties'. After some time, the man in her life duly appeared, and with a vivid freshness of memory, spearing through the decades, Spencer shares with us that, out walking, she took the man's arm, and then 'looked over her shoulder smilingly, and rather mischievously, to see what effect was produced on me: there being an evident suspicion that I should not be pleased. The revelation was not agreeable to me; but still it did not give me a shock of a serious kind. Matters had not gone far enough for that' (1904, i: pp. 167–9). Subsequently, however, direct contact and then correspondence by letter continued.

A few months earlier, on 15 April 1840, his letter to his father had announced a new aspiration: 'I was thinking the other day that I should like to make public some of my ideas upon the state of the world and religion, together with a few remarks on education', though he concluded that he could employ his time better at present (1904, i: p. 158). Work with Moorsom was drawing to a close and he declined the offer of new employment as an assistant locomotive engineer. A degree of alienation from Moorsom had crept in, on the basis of little more than hearsay that Moorsom had stinted the payment of Jackson, away surveying a potential new line for their chief. In the *Autobiography* he acknowledged that his judgment was hasty, with 'some facts overlooked'. If 'the sentiment of justice' was strong it may on this occasion have been misapplied (1904, i: p. 184). Spencer had also made a very positive impression on Moorsom and his wife and children, and he fully recognized that much kindness had been shown to him. It is, however, stretching matters somewhat to gauge his regard for the Moorsoms as bestowing upon them the status of a 'substitute family' (Francis, 2007: p. 40). Jackson himself, away in Cornwall, wrote good-naturedly ribbing him about his 'philosophic theories' and 'everlasting grumbling' (in Spencer, 1904, i: pp. 178–9). On 26 April 1841, the eve of his 21st birthday he returned home to Derby, with a good deal of experience and discipline acquired over the 3½ years, a new blend of practical and theoretical knowledge under his belt, and perhaps some rough edges to his character smoothed by almost daily contact with men and women not part of his family.

A new interest was geology, prompted by the fossils which excavations for the railway revealed aplenty. Since 1840, he had possessed a copy of Charles Lyell's *Principles of Geology* (1830). By now, he recalled, he was already aware of the hypothesis that 'the human race has been developed from some lower race' (1904, i: p. 176). In Lyell, Spencer discovered a refutation of Jean-Baptiste Lamarck's views concerning the origin of species. Lyell's criticisms

> had the effect of giving me a decided leaning to them. Why Lyell's arguments produced the opposite effect to that intended, I cannot say. Probably it was that the discussion presented, more clearly than had been done previously, the conception of the natural genesis of organic forms. The question whether it was or was not true was more distinctly raised. My inclination to accept it as true, in spite of Lyell's adverse criticisms, was, doubtless, chiefly due to its harmony with that general idea of the order of Nature towards which I had, throughout life, been growing. Supernaturalism, in whatever form, had never commended itself. From boyhood there was in me a need to see, in a more or less distinct way, how phenomena, no matter of what kind, are to be naturally explained.
>
> (1904, i: p. 176)

Spencer thus responded by accepting Lamarck's idea that organic forms had arisen by 'progressive modifications, physically caused and inherited' (1904, i: p. 177).[8] He found the idea fitted his view of the natural causation of things, and his belief in it 'never afterwards wavered, much as I was, in after years, ridiculed for entertaining it' (1904, i: p. 177). The questions of by what mechanism 'inherited' modifications were actually transmitted, why were changes to be counted as 'progressive', and whether the Malthusian concern with scarcity and a struggle for resources was of significance do not appear at this time to have given Spencer cause for concern.

In Derby, the work he had planned with his father on developing an electromagnetic engine was dropped as impracticable. Instead he rowed on the Derwent, in the process cementing into a lifelong friendship his acquaintance with Edward Lott, and took to singing glees and madrigals. A letter he received in the September of 1841 proved to Spencer that his idea of a government's proper sphere of action was already roughly formed by him in his days at Powick, for his friend E. A. B. had written to him that he had called government 'a national institution for preventing one man from infringing upon the rights of another' (in Spencer, 1904, i: p. 197). He now gave phrenology some serious attention.[9] In the 1830s, he had attended Johann Spurzheim's lectures on phrenology in Derby, and his interest was rekindled by a visit to the town of J. Q. Rumball, who was examining heads for the personal characteristics they allegedly revealed. With Derby's town centre flooded in 1842, Spencer donned again his engineering hat and made a report to the Town Council on how a recurrence might be averted; it was not adopted.

Of more moment than schemes for flood prevention is Spencer's visit to Thomas at Hinton in the early summer of 1842. Within the Spencer family he noted there was 'a common tendency towards Individualism', or a resistance to unjust subordination by governments, at odds with 'loyal' support for a party either in office or wishing to be in office, which uncle and nephew now tested out in their conversations (1904, i: p. 208). Thomas suggested that he should write for the *Nonconformist*, a recently established radical newspaper, whose editor, Edward Miall, was known to Thomas. In due course 12 'letters' were published serially in the paper, with the omnibus title 'The Proper Sphere of Government'. Given Spencer's own explicit statement of his orientation towards government power, it needs to be recorded here that it is indeed difficult to see a justification for Francis's comment that in these 'letters' Spencer's view was that 'the people had submitted to their government and that, as a result, they must tolerate the exercise of coercive authority over them' (2007: p. 262).[10] On the contrary, Spencer insists the people should expect the legislature to behave as 'a body deputed by the nation to keep order, to protect person and property', for these are the 'original and all-important functions' of our governors. However, experience shows there occur grave sins of omission regarding this pre-eminent task of 'the administration of justice': the state fails to provide courts which are easy of access, speedy in their decisions and free of cost in which every man could obtain the protection of the law (1843: p. 50). Far from acquiescing in this state of affairs in which government is so remiss, Spencer asks with some urgency 'How long will men allow themselves to be cheated by an empty name?' (1843: p. 52).

On the origin and significance for his own work of the 'letters', and the part played by his visit to his uncle, Spencer commented:

Had it not been for this visit to Hinton – had it not been for these political conversations with my uncle – possibly had it not been for his letter of introduction to Mr. Miall, the first of these letters would not have seen the light, and the rest of them would never have been written. Had they never been written, *Social Statics*, which originated from them, would not even have been thought of. Had there been no *Social Statics*, those lines of enquiry which led to *The Principles of Psychology* would have remained unexplored. And without that study of life in general initiated by the writing of these works, leading, presently, to the study of the relations between its phenomena and those of the inorganic world, there would have been no *System of Synthetic Philosophy*.

(1904, i: p. 212)

The 'letters' cover a range of topics including poor laws, state education (a prime locus of dispute between state and Church), public health, and war, as well as offering an abstract analysis of government's proper sphere. 'Nature', Spencer insists, 'provides nothing in vain' (1843: p. 48). Back again in Derby having completed the 'letters' he was temporarily ambushed, being drawn into one of his father's areas of original enterprise, phonography, or shorthand. However, he now also 'became an active politician' (1904, i: p. 217). The Philosophical Radicals, and the allied Society for the Diffusion of Useful Knowledge – or the 'steam intellect society' in Thomas Love Peacock's sceptical gaze –[11] had failed to secure either a Benthamite refocusing within government on 'scientific' administration or popular support. Chartism tended to be too cavalier towards political economy to attract the likes of Spencer and Miall, and Spencer was never a utopian socialist. Miall had been a Congregational minister in Leicester in the 1830s but left his ministry to found the *Nonconformist*, to which as we have seen Spencer was an early contributor. Miall traced most social shortcomings to the existence of the Church of England as the established church, although his commitment to religion was strong and underpinned his political radicalism (Peel, 1971: pp. 64–5). Certainly Miall and Spencer shared a desire for disestablishment, the demise of a 'rich man's tyranny' (Spencer, 1843: p. 51) and political rights; and there was also common cause with Cobden and the Anti-Corn Law League. It was Miall's associate, Joseph Sturge, a prosperous Birmingham Quaker, committed to the abolition of slavery, who established the Complete Suffrage Union in 1842, and which quickly gained support in many important Midland towns, including Derby. Sturge breakfasted at the Spencer home when visiting Derby, and Spencer became the honorary secretary of the town's branch, reporting to the *Nonconformist* on its activities. At the first meeting in Birmingham, attended by Thomas Spencer, the aim was clear, to agree upon a morally acceptable home for essentially 'moderate radical' opinion between the Chartists and the Anti-Corn Law League whose support Cobden identified as 'we of the middle classes – the unprivileged men who live by our capital and labour' (in Peel, 1971: p. 89). Thomas's political leanings worried the High Church *Christian Remembrancer* which wondered how he could 'be allowed to propagate such pestilential opinions...without being made to feel the just punishment for his apostasy by being degraded and excommunicated' (in Vidler, 1961: p. 94). There was a subsequent meeting with the Chartists in December, which Spencer attended as a delegate, later remarking that they 'would listen to no compromise. Fanatics soon acquire passionate attachments to their shibboleths' (1904. i: p. 219). The Anti-Corn Law League, it may be added, despite the precise aim of its title, 'was part of a great wave of public opinion, possessed of "a moral and even a religious spirit", which had other cultural objects. The main moralizer of the movement was Bright, "Rochdale John", who with Cobden saw in the industrial cities of the north the germ of a new civilization. Their ideals were grounded ultimately in a Christian notion of natural rights, made historically feasible, it seemed to them, by the appropriate shaping of character by evangelicalism, or by a purely secular moral enlightenment' (Peel, 1971: pp. 75–6).[12] Indeed, this statement of ideals would not unfairly capture the essence of his 'letters' to the *Nonconformist*, 'The Proper Sphere of Government', except in one vital respect: Spencer did not share in the widespread heady optimism of the reformers and their assumption that individual 'character' and social life were readily or painlessly malleable into unaccustomed configurations. Spencer's tone was that of a post- rather than a nervy pre-millenialist, but his position may best be qualified in these years as a filleted and almost vicarious post-millenialism: a letter to Lott of October, 1843 discloses his stance as a bystander and reveals his maturing thought significantly enough to warrant its quotation at some length.

I think you have heard me say that whenever we believe a given line of conduct to be a right one, it is our duty to follow it without confusing our fallible minds respecting the probable result, of which we are rarely capable of judging. The fact that it is right should be sufficient guarantee that it is expedient; and believing this, I argue that if any proposed course of national conduct is just, it is our duty to adopt it, however imprudent it may appear. No doubt many will consider this a very silly doctrine, and perhaps yourself among the rest. When, however, you consider the changes that must take place before the *general reception* of such principles as those advocated in the 'Proper Sphere of Government', and the length of time that must elapse before they can be put into practice, I think that you will see that your objection respecting the unfitness of the nation will vanish. Such principles, it must be remembered, are to be carried out by moral agency.... Such being the case they can never be acted upon until the majority of the people are convinced of their truth; and when the people are convinced of their truth, then will the nation be fitted for them.... It is in this light also that I viewed the question of complete suffrage. I admit that were the people placed by some *external* power in possession of the franchise at the present moment, it would be deleterious. Not that I believe it would be followed by any of the national convulsions that are prophesied by some; but because it would put a stop to that development of the higher sentiments of humanity which are necessary to produce permanent stability in a democratic form of government. I look upon despotisms, aristocracies, priestcrafts, and all the other evils that afflict humanity, as the necessary agents for the training of the human mind, and I believe that every people must pass through the various phases between absolutism and democracy before they are fitted to become *permanently* free, and if a nation liberates itself by physical force, and attains the goal without passing through these moral ordeals, I do not think its freedom will be lasting.

(In Duncan, 1911: p. 41)

In the spring of 1843 Spencer moved to London in a 'campaign' to advance his prospects, still open to opportunities in both engineering and literature. An early step was to arrange for the publication of 'The Proper Sphere' as a pamphlet, which duly appeared in late August: in its first year it sold a hundred copies, and only 10 per cent of the printer's costs were met. Meanwhile articles were drafted, submitted and rejected, though he had some success with the *Nonconformist* and with a periodical with known sympathies towards phrenology, *The Zoist*. No money was earned. To the mixture of political economy, phrenological psychology and deistic optimism apparent in *The Proper Sphere* he was now adding the reading of Bentham's works, so he reported to Lott (1904, i: p. 226), and also Adam Smith's *Theory of Moral Sentiments* (1759). Money vanishing and clothes shabby, he resorted to borrowing from his father. He had to admit that having a 'name' mattered as editors made decisions on what to publish. His friend Jackson had already counselled in forthright terms for a resumption of engineering – 'You've never studied properly' (in Spencer, 1904, i: p. 222). The only appreciation he had been given was in an encouraging reply from Thomas Carlyle when he received his copy of *The Proper Sphere*. A little engineering work indeed came his way, but, success eluding him, he retreated to Derby for the New Year.

He was long enough in Derby to write further essays for *The Zoist*, though he failed at this stage to get his father to publish his shorthand. The Philosophical Society library was available to him and he read at least some parts of John Stuart Mill's *A System Of Logic*. Carlyle and Emerson he also read, with mixed reactions. Then in August he left for Birmingham, initially to stay with Sturge, where the post beckoned of assistant editor to James Wilson on a planned paper associated with the Complete Suffrage Union, *The Pilot*. From his contact with Wilson he came to read parts of Kant's *Critique of Pure Reason*, but summarily dismissed as incredible the doctrine that 'Time and Space are "nothing but" subjective forms – pertain exclusively to consciousness and have nothing beyond consciousness answering to them' (1904, i: pp. 252–3). Kant though, by Spencer's own admission, brought a latent interest in philosophical psychology to the surface, leading him to ponder on the authority of reason as 'one of the cardinal problems which the theory of human intelligence presents' (1904, i: p. 252). However, after a mere 3 months he was released from *The Pilot*, at first temporarily, then permanently to undertake some pressing railway surveying work for a nearby stretch of new line between Stourbridge and Wolverhampton. The *Autobiography* lists seven articles of his published by *The Pilot*. In one, 'Honesty is the best policy', he observed that the 'life and health of a society are the life and health of one creature. The same vitality exists throughout the whole mass. One part cannot suffer without the rest being ultimately injured' (1904, i: p. 255).[13]

Thus Spencer reverted for a while to engineering. He had, however, made new contacts through his political activity, including Lawrence Heyworth, who later became MP for Derby. Early in 1845, Heyworth hosted Spencer at his Liverpool home, and Spencer met both his daughter, Laurencina, who shared in their political endeavours, and her husband, Richard Potter. Spencer warmed to the couple (she was 'perfectly feminine' and 'unusually graceful', and he commanded his 'highest admiration' [1904, i: p. 260]). This encounter was the commencement of a long-lasting and deep association: 'The friendship thus initiated lasted until the deaths of both. It influenced to a considerable extent the current of my life; and through their children and grandchildren, influences it still' (1904, i: p. 261). His engineering work was now a combination of surveying, steering private bills sanctioning proposed railways through the examinations of the Committee on Standing Orders, and explaining the details of lines to potential backers. The second area of work entailed attendance at Westminster. In 1845, he recounts, 'the new Houses of Parliament were in course of erection. The part eventually provided for committee-rooms had not been built, and there ran along the Thames-side a temporary wooden structure, divided into the many compartments at that time required for those who dealt with the many railway-bills brought before Parliament. A long corridor, carpeted with cocoa-nut matting to diminish noise, flanked these chambers of inquisition; and, during the day up to 4 o'clock, this corridor served as a promenade for various of those who were concerned in the schemes...' (1904, i: p. 273). The third area of work struck him as less congenial. In meeting with promoters of the line from Weedon to Warwick he encountered an 'eager grasping at pecuniary advantage' which was 'very conspicuous', and he recalled one London barrister left him with an impression of greed such as we hear of in those around a Monte Carlo gambling table' (1904, i: p. 285).

The financial speculation associated with the 'railway mania' was in full swing, but his father followed his advice to sell his shares in October, before panic savaged their value.[14] Spencer also continued expanding his intellectual horizons, finding Strauss's *Life of Jesus* (1846)[15] an antidote to Paley (1904, i: p. 265), approving of Shelley's poetry, declaring opera construction in the shape of Mozart's *Don Giovanni* unappealing on account of 'a great departure from naturalness' (1904, i: p. 274), and noting to his father that *Vestiges of the Natural History of Creation* (later known to be by Robert Chambers) had appeared but had not yet been read by him (in Duncan, 1911: p. 53). He responded to Carlyle and Goethe by opposing their psychology of the will: 'The common idea, as well as the Goethe–Carlyle idea, is that the feelings constitute an assembly under the autocratic control of "the will"; whereas they constitute an assembly over which their reigns no established autocrat, but of which now one member and now another gets possession of the presidential chair (then temporarily acquiring the title of "the will") and rules the rest for a time....' Spencer adds a comment on this 'common idea' which reflects the course his evolutionary psychology later assumed: 'The entire mechanism of animate life, brute and human, would be dislocated if the desires which prompt actions were governable in this easy way' (1904, i: p. 279). Thomas, meanwhile, had been in America lecturing in favour of temperance and against slavery, returning from this considerable challenge, Spencer observed, with a 'lowered estimate of the Americans', perhaps partly due to the 'unfavourable reception' accorded to his lectures (1904, i: p. 294).

By early 1847, Spencer declared his career in railway engineering and associated work at an end (1904, i: p. 299), although an interest in working on inventions continued and he profited from the marketing of a binding pin he had devised (Duncan, 1911: p. 52). Of greater moment was his decision to write his first book, made early in 1846.[16] The background to the decision was dissatisfaction with the earlier 'letters': 'not so much with the conclusions set forth, as with the foundations on which they stood. The analytical tendency had begun to show itself. What was the common principle involved in these conclusions? Whence was derived their ultimate justification? Answers to these questions had become clear to me; and it was the desire to publish them which moved me to write' (1904, i: p. 305). Once he was at work on the book he secured access to the library of the British Museum, but he was not tied to the capital. In Derby, he slipped back into an old routine (he liked to be walking in the countryside while thinking), and in the Wye Valley he visited the Potters. In 1847, he took a holiday in Scotland and then in the autumn he was at Hinton, where Thomas had announced his resignation from his incumbency, planning to move into Bath. The process of writing was apparently slow in 1847; by April, the book, he told his father, was 'beginning to ferment violently' (1904, i: p. 314) but he was anxious to improve his style. By the next year, however, he had to address the still unresolved question, at the age of 28, of how he was to secure stability in his income.

Emigration to New Zealand was one option, though as an only child leaving behind parents in their declining years he considered cruel (1904, i: p. 371). Another was a joint educational venture with his father, tailored to meet the needs of individual children loosely along the Pestalozzian lines of a school they had both known of earlier through contact with Benjamin Heldenmeier, a member of the Derby Philosophical Society, who had established it in Nottinghamshire. It was thought there might be a demand in the Bath area, but a reconnaissance suggested otherwise. Thomas was losing money on some railway shares, and Spencer travelled to London to examine the plans and prospects for the line in question.[17] It was in fact a grateful and reciprocating Thomas who was instrumental in releasing Spencer from his impasse, penning in May, 1848, a letter of introduction for him to his fellow opponent of protectionist corn laws, James Wilson, the proprietor and editor of the *Economist*.[18] Wilson had steered the paper to influence in the mercantile world. Spencer met Wilson, giving him a copy of *The Proper Sphere*, and they explored the idea of a subeditorship on the paper for him. Months passed, and then, on November 15, Wilson wrote to offer him the post at 100 guineas per annum; regular attendance at the office was required, but free residence there was also available. An additional allowance would cover the contribution of leading articles. Wilson added: 'The vacancy has existed for some time (it has been temporarily filled), and as I have about seventy applications for it – to none of which I have replied – you will please say by return post if you feel inclined to take it, and if so I will appoint a time for you to meet me in town' (in Spencer, 1904, i: pp. 333–4). Spencer accepted forthwith.

At the end of April, Spencer could write to Lott that the post suited him well. He was in effect his own master, and the work was light: 'On Saturday, Monday and Tuesday, I have nothing to do but to read through the *Times* and *Daily News*..., extract what may be needful, and put it aside for subsequent use. On Wednesday and Thursday my work occupies me from ten until four. Friday is my only hard day, when I have to continue at it until 12½ or 1 at night. This, however, is a very small payment to make for having so much time at my own disposal' (1904, i: pp. 341–2). His own writing was done in the evenings, when he was not putting complimentary tickets to use in attending opera performances (at which he discovered a taste for Meyerbeer) or theatre performances. In the summer of 1849, Thomas and his wife Anna moved to Notting Hill: their migration to London was welcome to Spencer, for Thomas's character had softened, and Spencer himself now had independence (1904, i: p. 345). Spencer's employment also served as an *entrée* to new social and intellectual stimulation through a link with the current *enfant terrible* of publishing, John Chapman, whom he had first met in 1846. At gatherings at Chapman's combined shop, publishing house and *avant-garde* guest house, inhabited by Chapman's wife, regular mistress and, periodically, Marian Evans, and nearly opposite Spencer's office, he met, among others, the writer Eliza Lynn (later Lynn-Linton), John Froude, author of *Nemesis of Faith* (1849), Francis Newman, and George Henry Lewes. It was Chapman who had published Evans's translation from German of David Friedrich Strauss's *The Life of Jesus, Critically Examined* which profoundly affected orthodox interpretations of the foundation of Christian faith. On the domestic front, Spencer found he preferred to live away from the office and, in due course, after a stint in Westbourne Grove (and a short experiment as a vegetarian, which he abandoned finding his writing was losing vigour), he settled for a while at 20, Clifton Road, St John's Wood.

By the early spring of 1850, work on the book was well-enough advanced to address the question of how to get it published. Chapman agreed to publish it, with Spencer taking financial responsibility. Chapman also had, as Taylor has remarked, 'an extraordinary knack of gathering into his salon some of the finest emerging intellects in mid-Victorian Britain' (2007: p. 14). While it was Wilson who provided the means for Spencer's first book to see the light of day, it was Chapman and those around him who were largely instrumental in shaping the development of his thought over the next decade: 'For the largely self-taught Spencer, the Chapman salon was both a substitute university education and a surrogate senior common room' (2007: p. 15). The question of what title the book should carry proved a tougher challenge. His preference for 'A System of Social and Political Morality' was replaced by 'Demostatics', of which neither his colleague Thomas Hodgskin at the *Economist* nor Chapman approved. In the end he selected 'Social Statics', against his uncle's counsel, but supported by Hodgskin.[19] For him the choice of 'statics' was a means to indicating 'how an aggregate of citizens may stand without tendency to conflict and disruption – how men's relations may be kept in a balanced state: my belief being that the conforming of social relations to the law of equal freedom, or to the system of equity deducible from it, insured the maintenance of equilibrium' (1904, i: p. 359). Spencer was unaware that 'social statics' had been used by Comte, and regretted the choice since in his opinion it fuelled the idea of harmony, whereas their thoughts in reality were 'profoundly opposed' in respect of 'avowed or implied ideals of human life and human progress' (1904, i: p. 360).[20] *Social Statics* was dated 1851 (Spencer noted it was available late in 1850) and appeared with the subtitle *Or the Conditions Essential to Human Happiness Specified with the First of them Developed*. The book was reviewed quite widely, if sketchily, and for the most part well-received. Spencer in fact created his own review, including it in the *Autobiography* and in which he described *Social Statics* as 'a kind of Natural-History ethics' (1904, i: pp. 360–4).

The most apparent innovation compared with what Spencer had published up to this point was that he asserts a clear and absolute moral principle – the law of equal freedom – from which the right role of the state is to be derived: *Every man has freedom to do all that he wills; provided he infringes not the equal freedom of any other man* (1851: p. 103). This idea, however, although not formulated so precisely, nor characterized as a 'law of nature' is apparent in outline in *The Proper Sphere of Government* (see Letters 9 and 10), and was familiar to him as far back as 1841, according to the letter from his friend quoted earlier in the chapter. The observance of this principle permits the optimal exercise of men's 'faculties' (Spencer's use of the word 'faculties' reflects the continuing faculty-based phrenological nature of his psychological theory at this time) and thus their optimal adaptation to their surroundings. In this manner progress is assured, for the progressive modifications which mankind is undergoing and inheriting are the result of a wider principle at work, 'a law underlying the whole organic creation' (1851: p. 65). For Spencer, the law of equal freedom:

> broadly generalizing as it does, the prerequisites, both personal and social – being on the one hand the law under which each citizen may attain complete life, and on the other hand being, not figuratively, but literally, the vital law of the social organism – being the law under which perfect individuation, both of man and of society, is achieved – being, therefore, the law of that state towards which creation tends, the law of equal freedom may properly be considered as a law of nature.
>
> (1851: p. 462)

The 'doctrine of individuation' had appealed to him after reading Samuel Taylor Coleridge's essay of 1848, *Hints Towards the More Comprehensive Formulation of a Theory of Life* (not *Idea of Life* as Spencer gives the title) in 1849 or 1850 (1904, i: p. 351). Coleridge in turn leant on Friedrich Schelling who bracketed together human beings and nature. There were several themes here which Spencer was to incorporate over the next decade into his law of evolution. Taylor has identified in particular the ideas of 'a whole being formed from mutually dependent parts', of 'progressively more advanced forms of life' as exhibiting 'more advanced forms of organization', and of the outcome of this developmental process as combining 'highly individuated component parts into a whole in a way in which their individuality was nonetheless preserved' (2007: p. 62). The second and third of these ideas Spencer later described as the processes of integration and differentiation.

Social Statics will figure at several points in later chapters. In part this is because Spencer's normative focus on 'social' not only political morality, that is, a concern with how social beings *should* relate to each other in everyday life, is to be concerned with an area of social theory that is sociologically interesting, whether or not it is actually itself directly an area in which *sociologists* have special expertise (Spencer takes it to be such an area, since the normative and the natural are taken to be tethered). In the main, though, it is because the book confronts head on heartland sociological matters, even though Spencer as yet never describes himself as doing sociology: Spencer does discuss what 'social life' is and the place of 'sympathy' in the relationship between 'individual life' and 'social life', and he discusses also the nature of 'society', and the need, unless there is to be instability, for congruity between popular character and political organization (1851: p. 468).

A separate version of one chapter was republished separately as requested by the Congregational Board of Education, with the title 'State-Education Self Defeating'. A more significant development came with eight short articles written for the *Leader*, without his authorship being directly acknowledged, published between 1852 and 1854. His topics included 'Gracefulness', 'Use and Beauty', and 'The Valuation of Evidence' (on the difficulties of accurate perception when faced with the strange or 'miraculous'), but 'The Development Hypothesis' deserves special mention. This yields his first general discussion of the idea of special creations versus development and transmutation. If an acorn can become a tree, what is so outrageous about the idea of adaptations as leading to new species? On changes in dogs, for instance, as they adapt 'it is a matter of dispute whether some of these modified forms are varieties or separate species' (1852a: p. 3). Edited by Thornton Hunt, and contributed to by G. H. Lewes and J. A. Froude, the *Leader* was a short-lived paper in support of calls for democracy and the liberalizing of Christianity. Evangelical spiritualism was a special interest with much attention devoted to Francis Newman's *The Soul* (1849) and *Phases of Faith* (1850), and Leigh Hunt's *The Religion of the Heart* (1853). The *Leader* indeed offered its warm praise in print for Spencer's vision of human progress and its grounding in a psychology focused on belief and its 'unknowable' foundations. According to Spencer, it was Lewes, as the 'literary editor' of the *Leader*, who persuaded him to write for the paper (1904, i: pp. 376, 385–6). In 1851, the two men enjoyed walking tours in the Thames Valley and in Kent. Lewes was good company, well-informed and versatile, being an actor, dramatist, critic, novelist and writer on general literature. Most importantly, Spencer was prompted to read Lewes's *Biographical History of Philosophy*, probably his first systematic encounter with philosophical thought. Lewes had one day brought with him, Spencer recalled, 'a volume by (Henri) Milne-Edwards, and in it for the first time I met with the expression – "the physiological division of labour". Though the conception was not new to me, as is shown towards the end of *Social Statics*, yet the mode of formulating it was; and the phrase thereafter played a part in my course of thought' (1904, i: p. 377).[21]

Spencer's position with the *Economist* brought him free access to the Great Exhibition of 1851. Many hours 'were passed with pleasure and profit in studying the arts and industries of the various European peoples' at this unprecedented parade of modernity, and 'a good deal of time was spent in playing the guide to country relatives and friends' (1904, i: p. 373). A quashed attempt to keep the iron and glass structure *in situ* on the Exhibition's closure as a winter-garden for Londoners illustrated the truth, in Spencer's eyes, that 'a small body of men deeply interested and able easily to co-operate, is more than a match for a vast body of men less deeply interested and unfavourably circumstanced for co-operation' (1904, i: p. 374). More substantial, and more demanding than his writing for the *Leader*, was work requested of him by Chapman, who had in 1851 newly acquired the *Westminster Review* and drawn in Marian Evans, although unnamed, as an intellectual heavyweight on the editorial team to reassure readers and contributors, such as John Stuart Mill, that its high standards and reformist stance would not be compromised. Spencer at first hesitated, but his 'A theory of population, deduced from the general law of animal fertility' appeared in the *Review* for 1852 (1852b). Spencer candidly admitted in the *Autobiography* that this essay failed to recognize that the pressure of population and scarcity produced a competition with a tendency for 'the select of their generation to survive' among all living things, not mankind alone (1904, i: p. 390). He was persuaded that the inheritance of acquired characteristics was a sufficient explanation for most change, and he had 'slurred over' its difficulties. Nor was he familiar with 'the phenomena of variation', lacking, therefore, 'an indispensable idea' (1904, i: p. 390). In his own mind the gulf between himself in this essay and what Darwin would argue 7 years later was understood with brutal honesty: 'Even had I become distinctly conscious that the principle of the survival of the select must hold of all species, and tend continually to modify them; yet, not recognizing the universal tendency to vary in structure, I should have failed to recognize a chief reason why divergence and re-divergence must everywhere go on – why there must arise multitudinous differences of species otherwise inexplicable' (1904, i: pp. 390–1). Spencer's assessment is in tune with the essay's contents. Peel errs in asserting that 'in it Spencer coined the phrase "survival of the fittest"' (1971: p. 137). That precise expression was indeed coined by Spencer, but in 1864 in the *Principles of Biology*.[22]

The population essay was the start of quite a long association with the *Westminster*, and later in the same year his lighter 'The philosophy of style' also occupied its pages. In the 'style' essay, it should be noted, Spencer singles out Archbishop Richard Whately for comment, making two references to him in discussing literary style (1852b: pp. 349, 352).[23] Chapman provided a further service to Spencer by asking him to review for the *Westminster* a new edition of W. B. Carpenter's book of 1842, *Principles of Physiology, General and Comparative*. In Carpenter's book Spencer 'came across Von Baer's formula expressing the course of development through which every plant and animal passes – the change from homogeneity to heterogeneity'.[24] Spencer considered that *Social Statics* had contrasted 'high' and 'low' 'types' of 'society' along these lines. However, Von Baer's phrase expressing the law of individual development drew his attention 'to the fact that the law which holds of the ascending stages of each individual organism is also the law which holds of the ascending grades of organisms of all kinds'. For Spencer it possessed a further advantage 'in that it presented in brief form, a more graphic image of the transformation, and also facilitated further thought. Important consequences eventually ensued' (1904, i: pp. 384–5). As it happens, Spencer's meeting and subsequent friendship with the biologist Thomas Henry Huxley was at this point still a little in the future. However, to earn a crust Huxley was odd-jobbing, with one source of income being the translation from the German of items of general scientific interest, including Karl Ernst Von Baer on embryology. Huxley's biographer, Adrian Desmond, amplifies how Von Baer's formula appealed to Spencer and his friends, records Huxley's own caution, and introduces Marian Evans to the scene:

Huxley's translations were tuned to contemporary needs. Chapman's clique wanted to make man and morality as climate and cosmos. It wanted laws that stretched from stars to society. But to find them it was forced to plunder the microscopic realm, Huxley's.

The key turned up in the work of a brilliant Estonian embryologist, who had trained at Würtzburg and settled in St. Petersburg. Karl Ernst Von Baer had described how the foetuses of chicks, lizards and dogs all diverged and specialized away from a common homogeneous 'germ'. The notion of specialization and division of labour was elastic enough to satisfy everyone. It became the watchword; it explained embryos; it explained evolution; it explained the co-existence of creatures in a habitat, like so many trades in the same tenement; it explained an industrial society based on division of labour – for Spencer it explained everything. Growth from homogeneous to heterogeneous was 'the law of all progress'.

It was even the flirtatious babble of lovers, Marian Evans' come-hither call to Spencer. She would, she swore, presently 'be on equality, in point of sensibility, with the star-fish and sea-egg.... You see I am sinking fast towards 'homogeneity' and my brain will soon be a mere pulp unless you come to arrest the downward process'.

Huxley actually stuck to the letter of Von Baer's law, damning its extrapolation to heaven and earth.... Moreover he believed that Von Baer himself had pulled the rug from under the 'progressive development' nonsense. Von Baer's study of the great groups – the vertebrates, molluscs, starfish and insects – had shown each to be based on a unique archetypal plan. They could not be stacked into a chain, none was 'higher' than any other.

(Desmond, 1997: pp. 190–1)

Spencer's place in Chapman's circle had made it inevitable that he would meet Marian Evans (later better known as George Eliot). This happened in the summer of 1851. Both shared Midlands roots and cerebral pursuits, and they were soon seen together at cultural gatherings. Spencer's only difficulty in making an emotional commitment, in his view, was her deficiency in physical beauty. With an acute sense of drawbacks in her appearance, she had already experienced painful rejection. Her letters to him from Broadstairs at the time reveal a self-denying desire to please and an eagerness to commit, one which Spencer did not and, it seems, could not reciprocate. Some commentators have spent much effort in recent years in speculative theorizing to unravel why marriage did not happen.[25] I am reluctant to compete in this dubious pastime. However, something must be said on the matter to indicate the kind of person I take Spencer to have been at this point, and indeed later in his life. He had set himself to be an intellectual figure, though he was in this respect by temperament and background a teacher and journalistically inclined general essayist rather than a specialist research-grounded writer of monographs. This self-image fulfilled the paternal pressure to be a 'useful member of society' but it was a fragile matter and might shatter under criticisms pointing up his lack of formal education or his 'borrowings' from others, conscious or not. It was a precarious edifice, and one suspects he understood this about himself. His upbringing had not equipped him at all, probably the reverse, to commit himself easily and spontaneously to giving and receiving love: he had only encountered this vicariously, if at all. The giving of love, to his mind, possibly risked compromising or wrecking his main identity: the idea that it might have been in the process complemented had no precedent in his experience of the familial relationships with which he had grown up. To be given love risked a selfish response from the recipient, again something he had witnessed and deprecated. These considerations perhaps gain weight, since Spencer remained a bachelor. On the other hand, for many years yet he was far from 'established' and not in a social position likely to find a sympathetic partner. And his own protestation that physically Evans was not to his liking need not be seen as insufficient, or hollow. That in ensuing years he may have envied the settled life Evans and Lewes found with each other or reflected on his opportunity foregone or even been felt by a friend (Richard Potter) to 'lack instinct' (in Webb, 1926: p. 21), arguably merely makes him human rather than a milksop forced to 'recognize his own failure in masculinity' (Francis, 2007: p. 57).

The period of Evans's emotional involvement with Spencer appears to have terminated late in 1852, and a long friendship between the two in fact ensued. Kathryn Hughes's biography of Eliot probably strikes an appropriate note over the entanglement: 'In Spencer's support it should be pointed out that he could, if he had wished, made public the two Broadstairs letters, which proved conclusively that he was the jilter and not the jilted. Instead, he sealed them up, together with a few others, and instructed that they should not be opened until 1985. For a man so vain about his public image it was a generous gesture. In effect he was allowing George Eliot's reputation as a wise, self-contained sybil to continue at the cost of his own cherished sense of inviolability. It was the closest Herbert Spencer ever came to love' (1998: pp. 175–6).

However, this interlude did not slow the expansion of Spencer's circle of acquaintances and friends. Following the meeting of the British Association in 1852, Spencer sent Huxley a copy of the population essay. Huxley then called on Spencer at his Strand office, and there began 'an acquaintanceship, growing presently into a friendship, which became an important factor in my life' (1904, i: p. 402). In 1851, he had been introduced to Octavius Smith, who was the prosperous proprietor 'of the largest distillery in England'

(1904, i: p. 375) and shared the aversion of *Social Statics*, to the 'meddling policy'. Smith was destined to be Spencer's appreciative host over many years at his homes overlooking the island of Mull in western Scotland. Through Lewes, Spencer became personally acquainted with Thomas Carlyle, but after a few encounters was disillusioned by his outbursts, and with his antipathy to philosophy in general and utilitarianism in particular: 'one who scornfully called utilitarianism "pig-philosophy", and thereby identified the pursuit of material gratifications with the egoistic pursuit of material gratifications, spite of the proofs before him that it comprehends the pursuit of others' welfare and the exercise of the highest sentiments, displayed an inability to think discreditable to an ordinary cultivated intelligence, much more to one ranked as a thinker' (1904, i: p. 381). In contrast, as a result of his association with the prominent sanitary reformer, F. O. Ward, there came a congenial encounter with his contemporary, the author of *Yeast*, Christian Socialist, and Rector of Eversley in Hampshire, Charles Kingsley, later Regius Professor of Modern History at Cambridge.

> He is a capital fellow; I might with propriety say a *jolly* fellow. We met at a pic-nic. No one would suspect him of being a clergyman. We had a great deal of talk together.... He is evidently a man of immense energy.... He said amongst other things that he believed that man, as we know him, is by no means the highest creature that will be evolved. I took this as an admission of the development hypothesis; but I am not sure that he meant it as such.
>
> (1904, i: p. 408)

Other friendships cemented at this time were with Sara Hennell (later to write *Thoughts in Aid of Faith*, 1860), David Masson, a specialist in English literature and from 1852 Professor at University College London, and Cara and Charles Bray (Charles Bray was the author of *Philosophy of Necessity*).

Spencer himself suggests that by late 1851 he had decided to attempt a book on psychology, and was reading Mill's *A System of Logic* in preparation, although the writing of the book did not begin until 1854 (1904, i: pp. 391, 456). In the early 1850s, he was in addition heavily occupied with six further and substantial essays for the reviews, and in dealing with the death of his uncle Thomas. Thomas died in January, 1853, after spells of illness which his nephew attributed to years of overwork and a failure to rest. Spencer was left a bequest of £500 which transformed his financial position. In consequence he resigned in the summer from the *Economist* in order to devote more time to his own writing. The six essays outstanding were 'Over-Legislation' and 'The Universal Postulate', both published in 1853, and 'Manners and Fashion', 'The Art of Education', 'The Genesis of Science' and 'Railway Morals and Railway Policy', published in 1854. Spencer contended that these essays shared, in their different contexts, a search 'for an ultimate element which gives community of character to things superficially different' (1904, i: p. 417). Some brief comments on each here are in order.

'Over-Legislation' appeared in the *Westminster Review* for July, 1853. Spencer exposes the 'bungling' actions of the state and its employees in administration, justice, and defence: an inverted form of the parable of the talents appears to apply. People may have lost their theological beliefs but not their equivalent 'faith' in rulers. The state fails to protect subjects against aggression. It is not the role of the state to *prevent* 'justice' from prevailing, as has become common practice. Indeed, when the state acts to try to save individuals from the consequences of their nature, it is likely to be serving its own narrow political advantage as it sees it rather than acting out of pure, philanthropic love of neighbours. The agencies people *themselves* form to promote such ends are the only actions that can effectively be adopted. Spencer now appeals to a distinctive model of social life as he makes his main thrust: 'It is one thing to secure to each man the unhindered power to pursue his own good; it is a widely different thing to pursue the good for him' (1853: p. 235). To do this would require the 'superhuman power and intelligence' to come to know each man's needs better than he knows them himself. Examples of failure arising from state inefficiency (drawn from the areas of public sanitary interventions, housing, and railway accidents) show 'the folly of trusting a theorizing benevolence rather than an experienced self-interest' (1853: p. 238). Not only is harm done but good stopped. There has grown up a mutual dependence between the members of a society, and imposed change triggers unanticipated consequences. The state *cannot* be as efficient as spontaneous organizations – it has, after all, taken as long as 20 years for the legislature to get itself a new house. By the nature of their origins in coercive control government agencies are slow-moving, unsuited to adapting to changes in their surroundings. Spencer also considers the claim that there are wants which only the state can satisfy. This he denies. They will be otherwise met, and trying to meet them before they are so met 'naturally' will be wasteful and will detract from the strong and effective need-meeting activities which already exist. Persons themselves will meet the most urgent needs first, as their aggregated desires move them to take action. Spencer concludes with a reprise of the theme that the state is neglecting its true function: at present persons seeking 'justice' are neglected, and 'oppressed, cheated, robbed' (1853: p. 272), with government turning them over to solicitors, abandoning them to incur expenses innumerable. The state is producing 'negative evil' – harming the good – because its attention is all on a 'meddling policy' producing what is 'positive evil': 'The badness of our judicial system vitiates our whole social life: renders almost every family poorer than it would otherwise be; hampers almost every business transaction' (1853: p. 274). Indeed, it itself adds to the badness by neglecting to punish the breach of contract occurring, for instance, when trains are late, the remedying of which would also serve to prevent accidents. Invoking the name of

Monsieur Guizot, Spencer diagnoses a 'national enervation' (1853: p. 276) bred by a misplaced reliance upon the state. In England, men have been comparatively little helped by governments, and even less so in the United States. In these places progress is comparatively rapid, but it is less evident on the Continent: it is the enterprising and progressing English who bring water supplies to the cities of Berlin and Amsterdam (1853: p. 278). Men in general have not yet advanced enough from a superstitious respect for government, which will die hard, and not until the 'mental type' changes through a process of 'character' being modified (1853: p. 282).

'The Universal Postulate' was published in the *Westminster Review* for October, 1853. Its argument in essence was that the inconceivability of the negation of a belief was the ultimate criterion of its certainty. Spencer incorporated this essay into a part of his *Principles of Psychology*, and further discussion belongs at the point when the *Psychology* is examined later. Spencer's essay 'Manners and Fashion' was also published in the *Westminster Review*, for April, 1854. As we saw in the *Introduction*, Spencer discusses the evidence in favour of processes of 'exuviation' in social life, with practices cast off as men become more adjusted to social life. The control exercised by law, religion and manners and fashion in society was originally unified, but an 'increasing division of labour' marking 'the progress of society' has separated one structure into three structures (1854a: p. 11). Furthermore, he adds, 'In conformity with the law of evolution of all organized bodies, that general functions are gradually separated into the special functions constituting them, there have grown up in the social organism for the better performance of the governmental office, an apparatus of law-courts, judges, and barristers; a national church, with its bishops and priests; and a system of caste, titles, and ceremonies, administered by society at large.... Law and Religion control behaviour in its essentials; Manners control it in its details' (1854a: p. 23). As social life evolves certain instances of control become needless and lacking in support, or ridiculed: 'Knighthood has so far ceased to be an honour, that men honour themselves by declining it' (1854a: p. 28). The evolution involved is to a progressive outcome:

> The social discipline which has already wrought out great changes in men, must go on eventually to work out greater ones. That daily curbing of the lower nature and culture of the higher, which out of cannibals and devil-worshippers has evolved philanthropists, lovers of peace, and haters of superstition, may be expected to evolve out of these, men as much superior to them as they are to their progenitors.... As it is now needless to forbid man-eating, so will it ultimately become needless to forbid murder, theft, and the minor offences of our criminal code. Along with growth of human nature into harmony with the moral law, there will go decreasing need for judges and statute-books; when the right course has become the course spontaneously chosen, prospects of future reward or

punishment will not be wanted as incentives; and when due regard for others has become instinctive, there will need no code of ceremonies to say how behaviour shall be regulated.

(1854a: p. 30)

To a true reformer 'no institution is sacred, no belief above criticism' (1854a: p. 31); Spencer draws in both Emerson and Swift as examples of kindred thinkers. Perhaps, Spencer adds, 'the tyranny of Mrs Grundy is worse than any other tyranny' (1854a: p. 36). However, change can only succeed if existing practices are no longer fitted to 'the humanity to be controlled' (1854a: p. 50).[26]

The *North British Review*, edited by A. Campbell Fraser, was the quarterly that published 'The Art of Education' in May, 1854. It later became one of the components of his book, *Education*. Work began while he was staying in Suffolk at Earl Soham Lodge with Mrs Trevanion, an admirer of Thomas's preaching which she had heard at Halesworth. Education, Spencer thought, should aim at 'self-instruction' (1904, i: p. 438). Mind was interpreted as developing from the homogeneous to the heterogeneous, and as becoming more definite in form. A style of thought to appear prominently in the *Principles of Psychology* is the mainspring of the essay: 'Every lesson learnt, every fact picked up, every observation made, implies some molecular re-arrangement in certain nervous centres. So that not only that effect of exercise by which the faculties are fitted for their functions in life, but also the acquirement of knowledge serving for guidance, is, from the biological point of view, an adjustment of structure to function' (1904, i: p. 437).

'The Genesis of Science' appeared in the *British Quarterly Review* for July, 1854. Scientific knowledge, argues Spencer, does not differ *in nature* from ordinary, common knowledge. The sciences are best understood as 'severally evolved out of the chaos of primitive ideas' (1854b: p. 8), not the product of creation or revelation. If we neglect this growth of science, we misunderstand its nature and organization. Spencer was critical of Comte, whom he had read in Harriet Martineau's abridged translation, and explored through articles by Lewes in the *Leader*. He was also critical of German *Naturphilosophie*, in particular Lorenz Oken's, and Hegel's 'bastard *a priori* method' (1854b: p. 12) as a substitute for observation and induction (although Spencer of course acknowledges that there are legitimate *a priori* arguments). It is anthropomorphic to assume that nature itself, and the sciences, are serial, linear developments just because we think in terms of separate things and sequences. The real story is not one of simple movement from high generality to decreasing generality as science develops. Rather, likenesses and unlikenesses, and equality and number, are recognized from savage life on, shown in the evolution of language (Spencer suggests a kind of logical atomism and a naming view of the nature of language here). The sciences display no neat seriality; divisions and subdivisions reunite: 'They inosculate; they severally send off and receive connecting growths, and the intercommunion has been ever becoming more frequent, more intricate, more widely ramified. There has all along been higher specialization, that there might be a larger generalization; and a deeper analysis, that there might be a better synthesis. Each larger generalization has lifted sundry specializations still higher; and each better synthesis has prepared the way for still deeper analysis' (1854b: p. 29).

'Railway Morals and Railway Policy' appeared in the *Edinburgh Review* for October, 1854 (1854c). The *Edinburgh* was then edited by George Cornewall Lewis, who had been one of the permanent Poor Law Commissioners and was to become Palmerston's Chancellor of the Exchequer in 1855. Spencer reported 'pleasant recollections' of an interview with him, retaining 'a clear picture of his remarkable face' (1904, i: p. 450). Spencer adjudged the essay a 'terrific exposure' (1904, i: p. 445) of serious allegations of irregularity. Directors of railway companies pursued goals other than those original to their proprietorship, leading to falling income for shareholders as directors and their key officials themselves benefit by making further lines, buying land and 'dealing' with competitors. To protect shareholders, the limits of the enterprise as understood when first entered into need to be insisted upon, not modified – there needs to be proper legislative regulation, so that later supplementary plans for hotels, docks and other developments are not smuggled in. This is one of Spencer's essays which amply demonstrated that he was no friend to unqualified *laissez-faire*. Spencer also had the essay issued later by Longman in a series for travellers: this essay, Spencer reflected, 'attracted much attention – much more attention than anything else I ever wrote' (1904, i: p. 451).

Amidst this hard graft, Spencer met John Tyndall, introduced to him by Huxley in 1853, and to prove a firm friend until his death. Tyndall, 'a rising man of science' (1904, i: p. 418) had that year at the Royal Institution demonstrated the existence of dia-magnetic polarity, in front of Faraday who had denied its existence. Spencer also managed a stay at the Potters' new residence at Standish House near Stonehouse, on the flank of the Cotswold Hills, followed by a visit to Switzerland with Lott, and some strenuous walking, from which subsequently he felt his heart had suffered. When Thomas had been ill, he tried hydropathic therapy at Umberslade Hall near Birmingham. Now Spencer followed him, though did not find it beneficial.

The way was now clear for sustained work on the *Psychology*. He judged that 'Easy access to other books was not requisite; for its lines of thought had scarcely anything in common with lines of thought previously pursued; and of such material as was needed for illustration, my memory contained a sufficient stock' (1904, i: p. 453). Accordingly in August, 1854, he took himself across the English Channel to the small port and resort of Le Tréport, not far from Dieppe, which his father had once visited. Settled in the *Grande Rue*, elevated from the shoreline, writing began: 'The house had a garden

running up the slope towards the western cliffs, and at the top of this garden was a summer-house which made an agreeable writing-room for me
in fine weather' (1904, i: pp. 455–6). Some welcome occasional company
appeared fortuitously in the form of the culture and 'pleasant facetiousness'
of George Rolleston, later Linacre Professor at Oxford. A little later, Spencer
was in Paris, Jersey and Brighton (where he disputed with Louis Blanc), subsequently dividing his time between London (reporting in December to his
father that the book was 'going on very well', though not fast enough [1904,
i: p. 461]) and his parents' home in Derby up until the summer of 1855.
With only a few chapters to complete, Spencer went to Snowdonia for the
fishing, having the company of the artists A. O. Deacon and Alfred Hunt. At
Pen-y-Gwyrd, at the foot of Snowdon, Spencer later believed his nervous system 'finally gave way', as he recalled the onset of his unwelcome symptom
(1904, i: p. 466). He had begun work one morning, when 'there commenced
a sensation in my head – not pain, not fullness, nor tension, but simply
a sensation, bearable enough but abnormal. The seriousness of the symptom was at once manifest to me. I put away my manuscript and sallied out,
fishing-rod in hand, to a mountain tarn in the hills behind the hotel, in pursuance of a resolve to give myself a week's rest; thinking that would suffice'
(1904, i: p. 467).

The *Principles of Psychology* was published in August, 1855. To his father he
confided that he hoped 'it will ultimately stand beside Newton's *Principia*'
(in Duncan, 1911: p. 75). Lewes thought highly of it, but a small sale of
200 in the first year surely dampened expectations. Some reviewers noted
that it treated mind as part of nature, and thus judged it atheistic, doubtless
deterring wary potential purchasers. Taylor has given a succinct expression
of the book's core, as adopting a developmental perspective not merely in
terms of the individual (as in traditional psychology), but also in terms of
the species and the race. Through this paradigm, Spencer aimed to reconcile
the associationist psychology of Mill's *Logic*, the notion that human mind
was constructed from atomic sensations held together by the laws of the
association of ideas, with the apparently more 'scientific' theory of phrenology which located specific mental functions in specific parts of the brain.
Spencer argued that both these theories were partial accounts of the truth:
repeated associations of ideas were embodied in the formation of specific
strands of brain tissue, and these could be passed from one generation to
the next by means of the Lamarckian mechanism of use-inheritance (2007:
p. 19).

An acknowledgement of Spencer's distinctive psychology of man's constitution and capacities is essential in coming to a sound understanding of
his conception of social life and of the scope of sociology, and also of his
distinctive normative stance. Subsequent editions of the *Psychology* saw the
book recast pretty radically, but the core just outlined remained intact. To
the extent that the *Psychology* is ignored in appraisals of Spencer's sociology

and ethics the full content of his analytical perspective is unlikely to be appreciated.

With the *Psychology* published Spencer embarked on travels as a restorative, though not before attending a dinner in London at which leading figures in the public health movement were present, including Edwin Chadwick and Sir John Simon, with whom Spencer, as might be expected from the author of *Social Statics* and 'Over-Legislation', picked a lengthy but good-natured fight around their trust in 'positive' legislation and government agencies. Then he was away again to Le Tréport, this time with Lott. Locations in England too were tried, but no lasting improvement to his symptoms ensued and no nostrum worked for long, even after consultation with a physician, Dr. W. H. Ransom, who had helped his father. The disorder was probably psychosomatic; no organic trouble was ever detected. However, he was fit in the early summer of 1856 for a yachting trip to Cherbourg (meeting Victor Hugo), and then to visit Octavius Smith and his family at Achranich near Oban, where he found enjoyment: 'I think scarcely at all about myself or my ailments' he wrote to Derby (1904, i: p. 490). An autumn visit to Paris brought a meeting with Comte, but Spencer recalled no intellectual exchanges, only to have found his appearance unflattering (1904, i: p. 493). Back in Derby, faced with dwindling resources, persistent insomnia and an inability to concentrate on work for more than three hours at a stretch, he decided his best option was to return to essay writing in London for the quarterlies. There he met Mill for the first time, following his receipt of the new edition of Mill's *System of Logic* in which he had replied to Spencer's criticism of him: Spencer wrote to his mother in March, 1857, 'I called on John Mill a short time ago. We had a long chat. He was very friendly and asked me to call again' (1904, i: p. 504). Spencer was also introduced to Henry Buckle, whom in fact he had encountered in earlier days in London. It was Buckle's *History of Civilization in England* (whose first volume appeared that year) that Adrian Desmond gazetted as 'the first of the mythopoeic extravaganzas, a gigantic tome with its replacement naturalistic cosmogony. Spencer', Desmond added, 'would perfect the technique, leaving Darwin and Huxley to fill in the fine texture and Tyndall to capture the cosmic warp and weave. Credos were becoming the rage' (1997: p. 234).

2
Middle Spencer: Towards a Tapestry of the World

In due course four more essays were published in 1857. The first, 'Progress: Its Law and Cause', appeared in April in the *Westminster Review*, and the three others in October: 'The Ultimate Laws of Physiology' in the *National Review*; 'The Origin and Function of Music' in *Fraser's Magazine*; and 'Representative Government: What Is It Good For?' in the *Westminster Review*. In providing the first public signal of what was to emerge as the 'System of Synthetic Philosophy' the 'Progress' essay marks a turning point in Spencer's writing.

At the outset of the essay on progress Spencer rejects a human purpose-serving type of teleological approach to interpreting 'progress' as a concept: 'Leaving out of sight concomitants and beneficial consequences, let us ask what progress is in itself' (1857a: p. 9). For individual organisms the Germans have already furnished the answer: 'Wolff, Goethe, and Von Baer, have established the truth that the series of changes gone through during the development of a seed into a tree, or an ovum into an animal, constitute an advance from homogeneity of structure to heterogeneity of structure' (1857a: p. 9).

Goethe had made the point in 1807 in his *Zur Morphologie*, laying down as a law, as the biologist Wentworth D'Arcy Thompson recognized in his *Herbert Spencer Lecture* of 1913, that 'the more imperfect a being is, the more do its individual parts resemble each other, and the more do these parts resemble the whole. The more perfect the being is, the more dissimilar are its parts. In the former case the parts are more or less a repetition of the whole; in the latter case they are totally unlike the whole. The more the parts resemble each other, the less subordination is there of one to the other; and subordination of parts is the mark of high grade of organization'.[1] The inference may be drawn that it was the poet's insight 'quite as much as Von Baer's, that crystallised in Spencer's famous formula of evolution' (Thompson, 1913: p. 6). It should be noted, however, that Spencer also found in Goethe a flawed view of 'nature' as a kind of personified causal agent (1894, ii: p. 164). Spencer certainly believes that some kind of process moving towards heterogeneity is true also of the changes associated with the nebular hypothesis of the genesis of the solar system, and further believes that the process stands as 'the law of all progress', with the 'development of society' (1857a: p. 10) and 'the evolution of all products of human thought and action' (1857a: p. 23), including language and music, all explicitly included. There is a cause or principle which this law reflects: 'Every active force produces more than one change – every cause produces more than one effect' (1857a: p. 37). This principle is to be understood as compatible with the local occurrence of change of a 'degraded' type (1857a: p. 53). In societies, the increase in heterogeneity is exemplified through the multiplying differentiation and specialization of tasks which has occurred consequent upon the introduction of steam power, and Spencer provides instances from industrial activity to make the point. This principle has the property of a rational rather than an empirical generalization – but it is not to be considered as noumenal (1857a: p. 35). However, 'reality' still remains an ultimate mystery, what 'reality' is man cannot possibly understand. There remains the 'inexplicable', but an enquiry that specifies this in the process gives 'a firmer basis to all true Religion' (1857a: p. 60). Properly understood, 'the Materialist and Spiritualist controversy' is rendered 'a mere war of words' (1857: p. 61). Instead, one is brought 'face to face with the unknowable' (1857a: p. 62), which transcends experience. However, if Spencer intended theistic aporia, he could also be, and was, construed as nurturing a new locus for faith.

'Transcendental Physiology' was Spencer's own preferred title for the 'Ultimate Laws' essay, and he reverted to this title when it was republished in his collected *Essays*. He had already invoked the expression in *Social Statics*, where morality became grounded not only in phrenological psychology, but was characterized as 'a species of transcendental physiology' (1851: p. 436). In the new essay he proposed a balance between organ development and organ function, passed on cumulatively through the inheritance of acquired characteristics. With differentiation of organs comes integration, reflecting their 'community of function' in an organism (1857b: p. 71). In organs, structure grows, with a concomitant separation from other structures with other functions. These varying features are explained by the key idea, which Spencer projects as an improvement over the 'every cause produces more than one effect' formulation of the 'Progress' essay, that a condition of relative homogeneity is a condition of relatively unstable equilibrium: each specific organ in its context is thus subject to differing forces affecting its development. Spencer expressly addresses societies in this context, describing them as consisting of 'mutually-dependent parts' (1857b: p. 101).

On the precise processes concerned in the transmission of heredity Spencer admits ignorance: 'though the manner in which hereditary likeness, in all its complications, is conveyed, is a mystery passing comprehension, it is quite conceivable that it is conveyed in subordination to the law of adaptation.... Various facts show that acquired peculiarities resulting from the adaptation of constitution to conditions, are transmissible to offspring' (1857b: p. 91).[2] Adaptation with the characteristics acquired passed on through inheritance was the mechanism of 'progress' in life adopted in *Social Statics*.

'Transcendental Physiology' also confronted the contrast in the positions of Huxley and Richard Owen over the *a priori* determination of the existence of an inescapable kind of correlation between an organism's parts. In Spencer's understanding, Owen follows Georges Cuvier by adopting the *a priori* idea of distinct 'forms' underpinning families of species. Owen was by now a distinguished anatomist and an exceptionally powerful figure in the politics and patronage of mid-century science. In 1836, he became Hunterian Professor of Comparative Anatomy and Physiology at the Royal College of Surgeons and, 20 years later, moved to be superintendent of the natural history departments of the British Museum. From 1859, he lobbied for a new purpose-built museum in South Kensington, officially opened in 1881. Owen, though, damaged his standing with many younger scientists by maintaining that there was a physical locus for the unique status of man in the human brain, and by his inflexible adherence to the fixedness of species (indicative of design) over the transformationist perspective argued for by Darwin. Spencer's father knew Owen (1904, i: p. 194). Spencer himself attended Owen's lectures on comparative osteology in 1851; and in February, 1855, went, in company with Owen and his wife, as he recorded, 'to hear him give a lecture at the Royal Institution, on the relation between Man and the anthropoid apes. It was the same thing that I had heard before in his lectures [at the college of surgeons], and anything but logical...' (1904, i: p. 462). Spencer's own 'A Criticism of Professor Owen's Theory of the Vertebrate Skeleton' appeared in 1858 in the *British and Foreign Medico-Chirurgical Review* (reprinted in *Principles of Biology*, 1894, ii: pp. 517–35). Much later, in 'The Filiation of Ideas' of 1899 Spencer remarked: 'Of course, his theory, which was a modern application of the Platonic theory of Ideas, conflicted with the evolutionary view of the organic world. The purpose of the essay was two-fold – to show the inconsistencies of his reasoning, and to show how, by mechanical actions and reactions between organism and environment, the segmentation of the vertebral column might be produced' (in Duncan, 1911: p. 553).[3]

Huxley, who understood well that professionally Owen was feared, perhaps hated, lined up against Owen and with Geoffroy St. Hilaire and Henri de Blainville, doubting that nature adhered to such imposed fixed types. On the whole, Spencer appears to side with Huxley (see also 1904, ii: pp. 438–9). One upshot of this important debate is, for Spencer, that since as he argues particular *social* establishments can be observed arising which exhibit a 'direct metamorphosis of the organic units into the destined structure' (1857b: p. 107) – exemplified by *ab initio* rather than gradually 'developed' manufacturing establishments – the general proposition can be entertained that transitional steps 'usually' passed through as 'organs' are developed may be omitted. As a consequence, the contemplation of 'physiology' considered 'transcendentally' may be of unexpected assistance in biological physiology itself: 'study of organised bodies may be indirectly furthered by study of the body politic. Hints may be expected, if nothing more' (1857b: p. 107).[4] The essay establishes that for Spencer the understanding of neither 'life' nor 'mind' was advanced by a search for foundations in an extra-natural source. Nature itself could offer the transcendental organization which reason might conjecture. I know of no evidence suggesting Spencer was familiar with T. C. Morgan's *Sketches of the Philosophy of Life* of 1819, but Morgan like Spencer was adamant that a non-naturalistic account of the origin of life, mind and morals involved a kind of transcendental hypothesis that was flawed (see Jacyna, 1983).

Spencer's essay on the origin (as a growth out of the 'natural language' of emotional expression) and the function of music (1857c) is too often sidelined in discussions of Spencer's sociology. Music was one of the first topics to which Spencer related his law of all progress. When this 1857 essay is considered along with other analytical comments on music by Spencer, it becomes clear that in his early writing he asserts that 'harmony' evolved from melody, but later tends to deny that it can be considered as evolved, unless one stretches unduly the meaning of the word. There is no other 'thing' at which Spencer baulks in offering an evolutionary account and his reasons for withholding one are instructive. A focus on Spencer on music as a social product may thus serve as a valuable 'case study' in showing how Spencer practised sociology: the significance of music in interpreting Spencer is considered in detail in Chapter 8.

'Representative Government: What Is It Good For?' begins with a quotation from Shakespeare (a rarity for Spencer) as a promise to the reader that there is indeed a nugget of good in the eponymous institution. However, repeated experience shows elected representatives as tending to be selfish, ill-informed and nepotistic, and chosen by the unwise looking for short-term pecuniary or other gain (Spencer invokes Carlyle's support here). Those few who have a grasp of social science and understand societies are not chosen to stand, or not elected; military men, lawyers and peers are preferred. Their interests, though, are far from identical to the interests of those whom they represent, and they may regard the cherishing of cheap and prompt enforcement of law as a needless luxury: 'If the intelligence of the mass is thus not sufficient to choose out men who by position and occupation are fit representatives, still less is it sufficient to choose men who are the fittest in character and capacity' (1857d: p. 299). The work they do attempt goes beyond external defence and rectifying internal civil aggression: they 'seek to realize some undefined ideal community' (1857d: p. 302). Against this view Spencer argues: 'There is no growth, decay, evil, improvement, or change of any kind... but what has its cause in the actions of human beings. And there are no actions of human beings but what conform to the laws of Life in general' (1857d: p. 304). Actions may indeed be right or wrong, but are so regardless of the 'authority' of the law. Legislators, however, persevere in believing that Acts and their enforcement can achieve ends, with 'no question being put whether Laws of Nature permit' (1857d: pp. 306–7).

A monarchical system is not a better option. It may be more directly acting in its nature, but subordinating a nation to a man is not wholesome once a vicious humanity is 'outgrown' and sympathetic feelings woven into the interactions of daily life. No one person, *contra* Carlyle and his model hero, Cromwell, can rule the doings of a complex society. Its welfare and progress are independent of any one person. Representative government is best in origin, theory and results in respect of 'securing justice between man and man, or class and class'. It is representative government that best can ensure equitable social relations; its laws will 'prevent men from murdering and robbing... enforce the payment of debts,... prevent the strong from tyrannizing over the weak', and be 'the same for rich and poor'. The objections to representative government only apply, he declares, when circumstances have permitted its focus to wander elsewhere: representative government 'is good, especially good, good above all others, for doing the thing which a government should do. It is bad, especially bad, bad above all others, for doing the things which a government should not do' (1857d: p. 323).

While in Brighton in the autumn of 1857, Spencer prepared for publication, at the year's end, a collected edition of his articles entitled *Essays: Scientific, Political and Speculative*. With the essays in this form he created the bedrock of his reputation as a 'philosopher'. H. T. Buckle, whom Huxley and Spencer thought had himself amassed too much material to organize it effectively in his *History of Civilization in England*, published that year, wrote that very rarely had he read 'a volume containing so much thought', clear, but almost troubling in its 'wealth'. Buckle though considered that the essay on progress was in advance of the knowledge required to verify 'the whole generalisation it contains' (in Duncan, 1911: p. 88). Darwin found the 'general argument of the so-called Development Theory... admirable' (in Duncan, 1911: p. 87); Mill too was complimentary, telling Spencer he had read the essays 'he had not before seen and... re-read the others' (in Spencer, 1904, ii: p. 19). Spencer also passed on to his father that unexpected news about the impact of *Social Statics* in India had ensued from an encounter at Chapman's with Captain Pelly (later Sir Lewis Pelly). The book was apparently much read by officers on the northern frontier, who were circulating a dozen copies. Moreover, 'Colonel Jacob, the Chief Commissioner in Scinde, who is in fact the Governor of Scinde, swears by it, and acts completely on its principles. This Colonel Jacob has just written a book... in which he gives his political experiences illustrating these doctrines to which he has been converted. I little thought that Social Statics was already regulating the government of some millions of people' (in Duncan, 1911: p. 86).[5]

Spencer kept up the pressure on himself. Two more essays germinated, one on 'State Tampering with Money and Banks' featured in the *Westminster* for January, 1858, and the other on 'Moral Discipline of Children' for the *British Quarterly Review* was out in April. The sesquicentenary of the first was naturally celebrated by a few for its unanticipated poignancy. The state's role is as the enforcer of 'justice', so that bankers and traders, anxious therefore to avoid bankruptcy, will act with prudence and restraint in the use of paper bills. Honesty in society is indispensable for banking and currency to operate with success. When, as had been occurring in the wake of the Bank Act of 1844, a government or the Bank of England goes beyond 'justice' and imposes restrictions on the autonomy of provincial banks, it usurps honesty, and leads to the disruption of normal commerce. The state may cause and exacerbate commercial disasters, but cannot prevent them (1858a: p. 334). The words of wise opponents, such as James Wilson and John Stuart Mill, against 'currency-theorists' should be heeded. Such doctrines when implemented by the state are 'restrictionist from beginning to end', incompatible with free trade. Gold, as a commodity like any other, is best traded freely without interference. The second essay later reappeared in his book *Education*. In the *Autobiography* he interpreted it as evolutionary in tone. Allowing a child to 'discover' through experience is crucial: since 'inherited constitution' is the chief factor in determining character, 'it is absurd to suppose that any system of moral discipline can produce an ideal character, or anything more than some moderate advance towards it. "The guiding principle of moral education" especially insisted on, is that there shall habitually be experienced the natural reaction consequent on each action' (1904, ii: p. 18).

Underway too was the gestation of a hugely more ambitious enterprise. Spencer dated the 'inception of the general doctrine of evolution' back to January, 1855, (1904, i: p. 462) but now he was scheming how to give it substance. A draft plan was written on 6 January 1858. Although modified later, it is an unmistakeable outline of what became the 10-volume 'System of Synthetic Philosophy'. Eight divisions of a part on the 'laws of the unknowable' were summarized, destined to be the core of the first volume, *First Principles* (1904, ii: p. 15):

1. Though the Omnipresent Activity is unknowable, experience proves its laws to be uniform and ascertainable (illustrated by the law of all Progress).
2. The first law – Instability of the homogeneous.
3. The second law – All force follows the line of least resistance.
4. The third law – Every cause produces more than one effect.
5. The fourth law – The correlation of forces.
6. The fifth law – The conservation of forces (force indestructible).

7. The sixth law – The Equilibration of Forces (tendency to ultimate equilibrium).
8. These, being the laws of all force whatever, underlie all phenomena whatever.

Over the next 2 years a detailed programme for the 10 volumes was devised. Yet neither the time nor the financial resources to undertake the project was to hand. The money inherited from Thomas following his death was mostly spent, and the state of Spencer's health precluded the thought of accompanying writing with arduous remunerative employment. Initially he hoped to secure a public office as a kind of sinecure, and approached Mill, Dr. Joseph Dalton Hooker, Lord Stanley and George Cornewall Lewes, but all paired their sympathy with little hope of a post. However, he did harvest some supportive testimonials which underlined the considerable regard in which his publications were held, supplied by, among others, Mill, Hooker, George Grote, Professor Campbell Fraser, Sir Henry Holland, and Professors Huxley and Tyndall. To provide finance, Spencer decided to promote the venture by issuing parts serially to subscribers. Invitations to subscribe were circulated in the spring of 1860, accompanied by a list of names of those already committed: the support of Mill, Charles and Erasmus Darwin, Huxley, George Eliot, Lewes, Carpenter, Froude, Buckle, Masson, F. W. Newman, Lyell, Hooker, Tyndall, Sir John Herschel and the psychologist Alexander Bain was on display, as was that of Charles Babbage, Charles Kingsley and Octavius Smith. Kingsley's position in the Church of England had not deterred him from offering his approval: 'Anything from your pen will be important to me; and from your programme you are facing the whole matter from that side from which it *must* be faced, sooner or later' (in Duncan, 1911: p. 97. The list is in Spencer, 1904, ii: p. 484). Robert Chambers, who had authored *Vestiges of Creation*, was not included in the list, but wrote with encouragement; 'It is certainly a very grand design, such as few living men could have grappled with, or even conceived. If you execute it in a manner at all attractive you will obtain a great fame' (in Duncan, 1911: p. 97). The number of committed subscribers eventually reached around 600 (Spencer, 1904, ii: pp. 52–4), with well over 150 secured by two committed Americans, E. A. Silsbee and Edward Youmans. Youmans became a friend and tireless supporter. Spencer began *First Principles* on 7 May 1860, at 18 Torrington Square, in Bloomsbury.

However, up to this point the stream of essays had still been flowing. Those of direct sociological interest alone are noted here. 'The Morals of Trade' was an essay for the *Westminster*, for April, 1859. The main business is ostensibly an exposure of the deceits practised by manufacturers, merchants and wholesalers to boost their income. But there is novel sociological comment with the deployment of a concept of 'social self-consciousness':

As it is true of individual beings, that their height in the scale of creation may be measured by the degree of their self-consciousness; so, in a sense, it is true of societies. Advanced and highly-organised societies are distinguished from lower ones by the evolution of something that stands for a social self-consciousness. Among ourselves there has, happily, been of late years a remarkable growth of this *social self-consciousness*; and we believe that to this is chiefly ascribable the impression that commercial malpractices are increasing.

(1859: pp. 140–1)

Nevertheless, wealth, however indiscriminately accumulated, brings applause and power, because an indiscriminate public opinion in our 'present phase of progress' (1859: p. 149) is still an accomplice: 'Something, however, may even now be done by vigorous protest against adoration of mere success' (1859: p. 150). While many attempts at reform are fore-doomed because the character of the men forming a society is not ready, this 'intervention' is seen as potent because society is now prepared for 'stern criticism'. A more moral public opinion is showing itself, with the rich expected to devote themselves to general welfare. 'Year by year is the improvement of the people occupying a larger share of the attention of the upper classes. Year by year are they voluntarily devoting more energy to furthering the material and mental progress of the masses.' We are already witnessing a nascent 'new and better chivalry' (1859: p. 151).[6]

'The Social Organism' was included in the *Westminster Review* for January, 1860. It will be discussed more fully later in this study, but a summary of this signature but often misinterpreted essay will be helpful at this point. As the title suggested, societies were to be seen as growths and as natural, not as manufactures and as artificial. The article needs to be read in the context of the earlier essay on transcendental physiology. By considering physiology 'transcendentally' one can conceive of and identify a 'social' physiology; even though there is no single, direct precedent, one can build up through myriad suggested parallels with organisms of all sorts (which Spencer furnishes) a case to this effect. The shared general ground between the 'social' and other organisms includes gradual increases in mass and complexity, growing mutual dependency of parts (Spencer emphasizes the analogy between progressive economic and physiological 'divisions of labour'), and the continuation and development of the whole while generations of the parts perish. Spencer indeed criticizes the limitations of the conceptions of society based on an analogy with the human mind (Plato) and with the human body (Hobbes).

Societies have their origin neither in the heroic efforts of a 'great man', nor in supernatural intervention. The past of his whole society contributes to the making of a man. A government's enactments reflect the average desire and 'nature' of the men governed. For this reason, a ruler cannot by himself change the type of society he rules. 'It is well that the lives of all parts of an animal should be merged in the life of the whole', Spencer argues, 'because the whole has a corporate consciousness capable of happiness or misery. But it is not so with a society; since its individual units do not and cannot lose individual consciousness, and since the community as a whole has no corporate consciousness'. The difference of greatest consequence then is the fact of individual consciousnesses, which means that the welfare of individuals 'cannot rightly' (1860a: p. 276) be sacrificed to some supposed benefit of the state. Indeed, what Spencer desires for the idea of the 'social organism' is that it should encapsulate the 'physiology' presented by the 'spontaneously evolved' economic organization of a society, a conception which Spencer stresses as 'all-essential', with this spontaneous and dynamic evolution itself being achieved through the pursuit of 'individual welfare' involving the division of labour as a natural development (1860a: p. 267). As discussed in the previous chapter, Spencer is presenting a secularized version of a picture of 'society' with which he would have been familiar from Whately and Thomas Chalmers (especially his *Inquiry into the Extent and Stability of Natural Resources* of 1808) – the popular contributors to Christian Political Economy. Spencer also quotes from Guizot's *History of the Origin of Representative Government* to highlight processes whereby neighbouring aggregations of men become joined, with the politically strong tending to subjugate the weak, and he points to an organismic parallel with the class Hydrozoa. Spencer had made references to Guizot's work at least since *Social Statics*.[7]

'Parliamentary Reform: the Dangers and the Safeguards' was yet another contribution to the *Westminster Review*, for April, 1860. Spencer charges that legislators will favour their own class interests indirectly, if not directly. Bringing working men into parliament will increase pressure from their unions for their favoured, but unjust, limitation on individual and free contracts, for their idea of a wage irrespective of hours worked, and for measures to promote welfare in the 'socialistic' style of Chadwick and Shaftesbury, and as advanced by the 'absurdly self-entitled "National Association for the Promotion of Social Science" ' (1860b: p. 369), for all of which untaxed workmen make no contribution. One check on utopian parliamentary pursuits would be to broaden the base of taxation. Another check might come through education on the proper sphere of government, and he refers back to the conclusions on the failings of government when it acts beyond 'justice' as presented in the essay on representative government. Administering justice is in the interest of all, but once the state seeks to 'bring home positive benefits to citizens', or to interfere 'with any of the special relations between class and class', there enters an incentive to injustice. For in no such cases 'can the immediate interests of all classes be alike' (1860b: p. 380). Spencer's reservation here refers to the average constitution and character of men, and at a particular time: the 'working classes' or 'the masses' (1860b: pp. 375, 379) are as yet unready to participate in the 'new and better chivalry', although a 'superior few' of men of 'lower status' are already to be excepted from this stricture (1904, ii: p. 55).

'Prison Ethics' was written ahead of 'Parliamentary Reform' but appeared a little later, in the *British Quarterly Review* for July, 1860. Spencer distinguishes, as he did in *Social Statics*, and elsewhere, between 'a priori' and 'a posteriori' routes to the formulation of ethical propositions. Now, though, he asserts without qualification that both forms of reasoning have a capacity to yield truth in the field of moral thought:

> From the fundamental laws of life and the conditions of social existence, are deducible certain imperative limitations to individual action – limitations which are essential to a perfect life, individual and social; or, in other words, essential to the greatest happiness. And these limitations, following inevitably as they do from undeniable first principles, deep in the nature of life itself, constitute what we may distinguish as absolute morality. On the other hand it is contended, and in a sense rightly contended, that with men as they are and society as it is, the dictates of absolute morality are impracticable. Legal control, which involves infliction of pain, alike on those who are restrained and on those who pay the cost of restraining them, is proved by this fact not to be absolutely moral; seeing that absolute morality is the regulation of conduct in such way that pain shall not be inflicted. Wherefore, if it be admitted that legal control is at present indispensable, it must be admitted that these *a priori* rules cannot be immediately carried out. And hence it follows that we must adapt our laws and actions to the existing character of mankind – that we must estimate the good or evil resulting from this or that arrangement, and so reach, *a posteriori*, a code fitted for the time being. In short, we must fall back on expediency.
>
> (1860c: pp. 152–3)

With society and persons as they are, adjustments and compromises must occur, but the requirements of 'absolute' morality must become absorbed into the relative judgements made. Otherwise the changes made on grounds of 'expediency' may lead in a direction travelling away from meeting those requirements unless the 'existing character' of mankind halts it. The desirability of free trade could have been discerned more readily had a consciousness of absolute ethics been developed: 'Government which, in protecting citizens from murder, robbery, assault or other aggression, shows us that it has the all-essential function of securing to each this free exercise of faculties within the assigned limits, is called on, in the due discharge of its function, to maintain this freedom of exchange; and cannot abrogate it without reversing its function, and becoming aggressor instead of protector' (1860c: p. 155). Mill in *On Liberty* (1859), it should be noted, emphasized that the arguments for personal liberty needed to be considered as separate from arguments for a particular economic doctrine, such as free trade.

Spencer contends that the condemnation of robbery, for instance, is to demand that there be 'no breach of the natural sequence between labour and the rewards obtained by labour', which amounts to the demand 'that the laws of life shall be protected. What we call the right of property, is simply a corollary from certain necessary conditions to complete living' (1860c: p. 165). These conditions are matters of nature rather than mere dictates of human legislation. Breaches of the conditions indicate the need for restitution and prevention of recurrence, but not the infliction of pain or retribution. The convict's life after all continues. He must therefore be permitted to live 'as completely as consists with social safety. It is commonly said that the criminal loses all his rights. This may be so according to law, but it is not so according to justice . . . . Those exercises of faculty, and consequent benefits, which are possible under the necessary restraint, cannot be equitably denied' (1860c: p. 167). From 'justice' we may infer, observes Spencer, that the right of the prisoner to labour to provide for self-maintenance while 'living in durance' should be enforced (1860c: p. 168).

Moreover, that prisoners should labour to secure self-maintenance is a practicable ideal, demonstrated by the successful applications already initiated by Obermair in Kaiserslauten and Munich, by the 'Colonie Agricole' in Mettray, in Ireland's 'intermediate system', in Australia through the geographer and penal reformer Captain Alexander Maconochie's 'mark system', applied in the penal colony of Norfolk Island, and in the regime of Colonel Montesinos in Valencia prison.[8] Spencer also proposes that those who are convicted of certain crimes should be released after restitution if someone 'of good character and means' will employ them, bound by a sum should default occur within a specified period. Here indeed, Spencer adds, is a 'self-acting test' of a fit length of sentence (1860c: p. 185).

Work on *First Principles* was by now in hand. However, in the previous year evolutionary thought had seen a new idea presented – natural selection – which from the outset was considered likely to have profound consequences. Spencer recorded his response in the *Autobiography*:

> up to the time at which the papers by Mr. Darwin and Mr. Wallace, read before the Linnaean Society, had become known to me, I held that the sole cause of organic evolution is the inheritance of functionally-produced modifications. The *Origin of Species* made it clear to me that I was wrong; and that the larger part of the facts cannot be due to any such cause. Whether proof that what I had supposed to be the sole cause, could be but at best a part cause, gave me any annoyance I cannot remember . . . . But I doubt that any such feelings, if they arose, were overwhelmed in the gratification I felt at seeing the theory of organic evolution justified. To have the theory of organic evolution justified, was of course to get further support for that theory at large with which . . . all my conceptions were bound up.
>
> (1904, ii: p. 50)

On 2 February 1860, Darwin wrote to Spencer surprised by news that he had apparently not received a copy of the *Origin*. Darwin had asked Murray, the publisher, to send a copy to Spencer in November, among the first to be distributed. By February 10, Spencer could write to Lott: 'I am just reading Darwin's book (a copy of which has been searching for me since November and has only just come to hand)' (in Duncan, 1911: p. 98). To second and subsequent editions of the *Origin* Darwin added a succinct historical sketch of Spencer's salient contributions to the theory of the development of organic beings:

> Mr. Herbert Spencer, in an Essay (originally published in the 'Leader', March, 1852, and republished in his 'Essays' in 1858), has contrasted the theories of the Creation and the Development of organic beings with remarkable skill and force. He argues from the analogy of domestic productions, from the changes which the embryos of many species undergo, from the difficulty of distinguishing species and varieties, and from the principle of general gradation, that species have been modified; and he attributes the modification to the change of circumstances. The author (1855) has also treated Psychology on the principle of the necessary acquirement of each mental power and capacity by gradation.
>
> (1968: p. 60)

Given the accumulation of assaults on creationist theory to which Spencer was a notable contributor, it is puzzling that he makes no mention of the position of Baden Powell, Savilian Professor of Geometry at Oxford (and father of the founder of the Boy Scouts and Girl Guides). One imagines they had met, since in the 1850s Baden Powell was on visiting terms with Buckle, Mill, Francis Newman, Marian Evans, Charles Bray and Lewes, though Baden Powell himself makes no mention of Spencer in his Journal (Corsi, 1988a: p. 204). However, in July, 1858, the *Westminster Review* published Spencer's 'Recent Astronomy and the Nebular Hypothesis'. Some months after, Spencer recorded that it 'had been very favourably received everywhere. It was ascribed to Baden Powell' (in Duncan, 1911: p. 426). That something written by Spencer was so attributed was for him evidently a source of pride. By now Baden Powell's arguments against creationist thought were placing him in a vulnerable position in the Church of England, and Darwin had drawn attention to his supportive conclusions in his historical sketch: 'The "Philosophy of Creation" has been treated in a masterly manner by the Rev. Baden Powell, in his "Essays on the Unity of Worlds," 1855. Nothing can be more striking than the manner in which he shows that the introduction of new species is "a regular, not a casual phenomenon," or, as Sir John Herschel expresses it, "a natural in contradistinction to a miraculous process" ' (1968: p. 62). Baden Powell was also the contributor of 'Study of the Evidences of Christianity' to *Essays and Reviews* of 1860. Spencer certainly knew of this celebrated collection of essays related to theology because he wrote to Mrs. Potter: 'Have you seen the volume of Essays by Jowett and Co.? They appear to be creating a considerable sensation. As coming from some of the most influential men connected with the Church, they are extremely significant of the progress of opinion' (in Duncan, 1911: p. 102). In his contribution to *Essays and Reviews*, Baden Powell gave his own blessing to Darwin over those who doubted that the new emphasis on mutability and extinction could engender a shift in biological science which would explain the emergence of new species and apparently make redundant a transcendent, creationist account. This was brave and controversial: Baden Powell would have risked the charge of heresy had he not died prematurely. It is already acknowledged, he wrote, 'under the high sanction of the name of Owen' (in his British Association Address of 1858),

> that 'creation' is only another name for our ignorance of the mode of production ... while a work has now appeared by a naturalist of the most acknowledged authority, Mr. Darwin's masterly volume on *The Origin of Species* by the law of 'natural selection' – which now substantiates on undeniable grounds the very principle so long denounced by the first naturalists, – *the origination of new species by natural causes*: a work which must soon bring about an entire revolution of opinion in favour of the grand principle of the self-evolving powers of nature.
>
> (1860: p. 139)

Richard Whately and Baden Powell had shared theological concerns during Whately's Oxford days (Whately had held the Drummond Chair in Political Economy) which continued after his removal to Dublin as Archbishop in 1831. But Whately held that 'civilisation' seemed to imply revelation, and this Baden Powell now chided him over, also in *Essays and Reviews*. Whately gave a measured response to both Darwin and Baden Powell in 1861: 'Mr. Darwin', he wrote, 'has indeed been understood to teach that Man may possibly be a descendent of the Ape, and originally, of a Reptile or a Mollusc. But even supposing this possible, there would still remain an insuperable difficulty – which Mr. Darwin seems to have perceived – in the last step of all; the advance of the unaided savage to civilisation'. For Whately 'brutish, improvident, unthinking savages, such as the Papuans of Andaman, or the Fuegians' were in an 'unimproved and *stationary* condition' (Whately, 1861: p. 58). It is urged against this assertion that a long view of time must be taken, Whately notes, but this, he adds, is to overlook 'that Time is of itself no Agent' (1861: p. 59).

Spencer, however, was not diverted by the excitement surrounding 'variations', a 'struggle for existence' and 'natural selection'. While accepting natural selection he held too to the inheritance of acquired characteristics (as to a limited extent did Darwin), mindful of its apparent potential to bridge the gap Whately identified. He continued constructing the honeycomb of linked concepts populating *First Principles*. The book was composed by dictation given to an amanuensis, a method he had recently discovered to be less exhausting than direct writing. Even so, concern about his health led to absences from London 'to recruit' – within five months he visited Brighton, Standish (to join the Potters), Llandudno (in company with the Lotts), and Le Tréport (accompanying his parents, and where work resumed with some three hours dictation a day), followed by stays in Derby and Achranish (with the Smiths). When his uncle William died in November, Spencer was a beneficiary, lifting financial anxieties at a time when a number of subscribers were withdrawing. Work on the book in fact proceeded on singular lines, as his father learnt from a letter in June, 1861; 'I am much better this week and am doing some work. I am doing it in a very odd way – uniting dictating and rowing. I take my amanuensis on the Regent's Park water, row vigorously for five minutes and dictate for a quarter of an hour; then more rowing and more dictating alternately. It answers capitally' (1904, ii: p. 66). When the author of *Primitive Marriage*, J. F. McLellan, recommended racquets Spencer duly selected an open racquet-court at Pentonville and a nearby room. At the same time the friendship between Spencer and Huxley had developed into one in which Spencer could discuss his developing ideas on organic evolution: they lived nearby and met often. Huxley was encouraging, and Hooker too was helpful. Since Spencer had counted on their 'information, advice and criticism', he had exempted both from needing to pay subscriptions (Duncan, 1911: p. 101). Huxley's reaction to reading proofs of *First Principles* in previous weeks had buoyed Spencer. Huxley wrote to Spencer on September, 1860:

> To my mind nothing can be better than these contents whether in matter or in manner, and as my wife arrived independently, at the same opinion – I think my judgment is not one sided.

> There is something calm and dignified about the tone of the whole – which eminently befits a philosophical work which means to live – and nothing can be more clear or forcible than the argument.

> I rejoice that you have made a beginning and such a beginning – for the more I think about it the more important it seems to me – that somebody should think out with a connected system – the loose notions that are floating about more or less distinctly in all the best minds. It seems as if all the thoughts in what you have written were my own and yet I am conscious of the enormous difference your presentation of them makes in my intellectual state. One is thought in the state of hemp yarn and the other in the state of rope. Work away thou excellent rope maker and make us more rope to hold on against the devil and the parsons.

> (In Francis, 2007: pp. 146–7)

However an undated letter to his friend, the physicist John Tyndall, shows that a question had been raised which Spencer at this stage, in effect, evaded. Tyndall had demanded of Spencer 'But how does it all end?' (in Duncan, 1911: p. 555). Spencer had held that equilibrium would eventually be attained with the highest state of humanity being reached. Tyndall's answer to his own question was that equilibration was death, in line with the second law of thermodynamics which Clausius had formulated in 1854. Spencer admitted to Tyndall that he was 'staggered': 'Indeed, not seeing my way out of the conclusion, I remember being out of spirits for some days afterwards. I still feel unsettled about the matter...' (in Duncan, 1911: p. 104). More to his satisfaction, he had moved his publishing affairs away from Longmans (who had published the *Psychology* and the *Essays*) – 'my business transactions with the firm had been such as rendered me undesirous of continuing them, and still more undesirous of extending them' (1904, ii: p. 70). Certainly sales figures had been disappointing and he must have envied the success of, say, Lewes. Improved arrangements were entered into with Williams and Norgate. New friends too were being added to his large circle, George Busk and John Lubbock, and their wives.

First Principles was an attempt at a 'theory of everything' through a synthesis of the knowledge of the day. It is concerned primarily with shared patterns and trajectories in the *outputs* of processes of change. Problems about the *mechanism* of change itself, concern with which was central to Darwin's science, were in this book of lesser prominence for Spencer. Spencer was concerned with orthogenesis, with evolution as directional and indeed essentially progressive. This presumption of the benign in evolution rendered Spencer formally dependent on a deistic mode of thought. The Unknowable seemed after all to behave like a benevolent celestial being, with its manifest laws of nature uniquely well-disposed towards the interests of the best of civilized mankind. Closer examination of Spencer's theory of evolution, however, is deferred to Chapters 4 and 5. *First Principles* is not as wholly abstract as such a summary can make it sound. Spencer quite systematically introduces discussion of psychical and social life to bear out his general analysis, and it seems sensible to join the detailed discussion of the book with a special focus on the consideration of the psychological and sociological dimensions of his theory of evolution.

With all the component serial numbers issued, the complete volume was published in June, 1862. During work on *First Principles*, Spencer had also drawn some earlier essays together to compile his short book *Education*, which appeared in 1861.[9] So by now he had earned some respite. For the first time he met Youmans and his wife, in Glasgow. Youmans had championed his interests in America, and the meeting and further days spent touring together cemented the bond. Both fortunately favoured the North's cause in the Civil War in America. Nevertheless, by November, he had begun composition of the *Principles of Biology*. In book form there were two volumes, the first appeared in 1864, the second 2 years later. As Huxley had intimated, someone needed to think through the 'loose ends' swirling around, and an outsider's perspective on the disarray might yield dividends. Spencer candidly admitted 'it is manifest that I was inadequately equipped for the task' but he had committed himself: 'Whoever carries out such an undertaking must either have a knowledge of all the concrete sciences greater than any man has ever had, or he must deal with some sciences of which his knowledge is but partial, if not very imperfect. Either the thing must not be done at all or it must be thus done' (1904, ii: p. 103).

Darwin might have had his expectations of Spencer raised by a letter singing his praises from Alfred Wallace

> If you are able to bear reading will you allow me to take the liberty of recommending you a book? The fact is I have been so astonished & delighted with the perusal of Spencer's works that I think it a duty to Society to recommend them to all my friends who I think can appreciate them. The one I particularly refer to now is *Social Statics*, a book which is by no means *hard* to read; it is even amusing, & owing to the wonderful clearness of its style may be read & understood by any one. I *think* therefore as it is quite distinct from your special studies at present, you might consider it as 'light literature' and I am pretty sure it would interest you more than a great deal of what is now considered very good. I am utterly astonished that so few people seem to read *Spencer*, & the utter ignorance there seems to be among politicians & political economists of the grand views & logical stability of his works. He appears to me as far ahead of John Stuart Mill as J. S. M. is of the rest of the world, and I may add as Darwin is of Agassiz. The range of his knowledge is no less than its accuracy. His '*Nebular Hypothesis*' in the last vol. of his essays is the most masterly astronomical paper I have ever read, and in his forthcoming volume on *Biology* he is I understand going to shew that there is something else besides '*Nat. Selection*' at work in nature. So you must look out for a 'foeman worthy of your steel'. But perhaps all this time you have read his books – If so excuse me, & pray give me your opinion of him as I have hitherto only met with one man (Huxley) who has read & appreciated him.
>
> (letter from Wallace to Darwin, 2 January 1864)[10]

But if Darwin's hopes of the *Biology* were indeed raised he found as we shall see shortly 'nothing'.

Today the main interest of the *Biology* is in the first volume in which Darwin's theory of natural selection is ingested by Spencer's wider theory of evolution. For Spencer, the physical laws of change point to processes of equilibration in the redistribution of motion and matter always and everywhere going on. The Lamarckian inheritance of acquired characteristics, or use-inheritance, which Spencer had hitherto favoured, could be presented as a process of 'direct equilibration' (though what biological process of transmission was involved was not specified). Spencer never abandoned this mechanism in his theoretical scheme. The idea of a struggle for existence out of which 'variations' with some advantage in that environment survived to reproduce, with those lacking it perishing, the essence of Darwin's 'natural selection', was now, Spencer proposed, to be incorporated as a further mechanism of change, to be called 'indirect equilibration' – the equilibria of some individuals in a species are more easily overthrown than that of others and hence they fail to survive. 'This survival of the fittest', Spencer writes, 'which I have here sought to express in mechanical terms, is that which Mr. Darwin has called "natural selection, or the preservation of favoured races in the struggle for life". That there is going on a process of this kind throughout the organic world, Mr. Darwin's great work on the *Origin of Species* has shown to the satisfaction of nearly all naturalists' (1894, i: pp. 444–5). To Darwin, Spencer adds, 'we owe the discovery that natural selection is capable of producing fitness between organisms and their circumstances; and he, too, has the merit of appreciating the immensely-important consequences that follow from this' (1894, i: p. 446).

That particular job was done, but only after a fashion. 'Natural selection' was domesticated into the 'mythopoeic extravaganza' that was Spencer's 'System' but not in a straightforward and comprehensive way. While Darwin's central concern was *not* the *direction* of change (he very seldom even used the word 'evolution'[11]) but the identification of a *mechanism* of biological change accounting for the diversity of life, this important difference in prime focus was not at all the cause of the difficulty in question. The cause the difficulty instead is over what 'natural selection' means. Darwin's own core argument as presented in his Introduction to the *Origin* specified what *he* understood by 'natural selection' (1968: p. 68):

> In the next chapter the 'Struggle for existence' amongst all organic beings throughout the world, which inevitably follows from the high geometrical ratio of their increase will be treated of.... As many more individuals of each species are born than can possibly survive; and as, consequently, there is a frequently recurring struggle for existence, it follows that any being if it vary however slightly in any manner profitable to itself, under the complex and sometimes varying conditions of life, will have a better chance of surviving, and thus be *naturally selected*. This fundamental subject of 'Natural Selection' will be treated at some length...; and we shall then see how natural selection also inevitably causes much extinction of the less improved forms of life, and leads to what I have called divergence of character.

What Darwin showed was that, granted the premises, at least some natural selection must be a fact and so must some modification, by descent, of species. Other mechanisms of change were not ruled out, including sexual selection among animals and the Lamarckian use-inheritance. Whilst hereditary modification could be observed in domestic breeding, it was true that, as Darwin observed, '[o]ur ignorance of the laws of variation is profound' (1968: p. 202). Only later would empirical advances configure 'variations' in genetic terms, discrediting use-inheritance.

For Darwin, then, in what he means by 'natural selection', the 'struggle for existence' and 'variations' cannot be broken apart, the process called 'natural selection' is made up of both. However, Spencer, in a key note to the text of the second volume (1894, ii: pp. 500–1) details what *he* understands by 'natural selection', beginning with a reference back to his essay on population of 1852:

> Though the process of natural selection is recognized; and though to it is ascribed a share in the evolution of a higher type; yet the conception must not be confounded with that which Mr. Darwin has worked out with such wonderful skill, and supported with such vast stores of knowledge. In the first place, natural selection is here described only as furthering direct adaptation – only as aiding progress by the preservation of individuals in whom functionally-produced modifications have gone on most favourably. In the second place, there is no trace of the idea that natural selection may, by co-operation with the cause assigned, or with other causes, produce *divergences* of structure; and of course in the absence of this idea, there is no implication, even, that natural selection has anything to do with the origin of species. And in the third place, the all-important factor of variation – 'spontaneous', or incidental as we may otherwise call it – is wholly ignored. Though use and disuse are, I think, much more potent causes of organic modification than Mr. Darwin supposes – though, while pursuing the inquiry in detail, I have been led to believe that direct equilibration has played a more active part even than I had myself at one time thought; yet I hold Mr. Darwin to have shown beyond question, that a great part of the facts – perhaps the greater part – are explicable only as resulting from the survival of individuals which have deviated in some indirectly-caused way from the ancestral type.

In this passage Spencer presents *his* understanding of 'natural selection' in terms simply of the 'struggle for existence', hiving off 'variations' as a separate, and, optional ingredient. In itself this 'reconfiguration' is not illegitimate, but it is to sunder what Darwin had deliberately united, with consequences which are confusing unless the position is disentangled, and of significance once it is. When *Spencer* refers to 'natural selection', *he* means a struggle for existence combined with the Lamarckian inheritance of acquired characteristics – the effects of use and disuse – with a *contingent* contribution of 'variations' also admissible. Thus when Spencer refers to 'direct equilibration' it is a reference to the Lamarckian inheritance of acquired characteristics alone, but when he refers to 'indirect equilibration' it is a reference to the presence of struggle in that process, and only as a *possibility* to the presence of Darwinian 'variations'. There is, therefore, no simple equation for Spencer, unlike Darwin, of 'natural selection' with a struggle for existence and the presence of 'variations'. Spencer's introduction in the *Biology* of 'the survival of the fittest' is strictly as a synonym for his 'indirect equilibration', not for, in Darwin's sense, 'natural selection', even though a casual reading would give just that impression (the absence of isomorphism here is not identified in Paul's treatment of the 'selection' of the 'survival of the fittest' by Darwin as an alternative expression to 'natural selection', Paul, 1988). Whatever Spencer's motives, the upshot was that 'variations' were marginalized in this exercise in conceptual reconfiguration, perhaps enhancing the plausibility of Spencer's evolutionary schema as he saw it, in a way to be described shortly (it is not entirely clear that Spencer had even grasped what Darwin meant by 'variations' when he discussed the matter, since the examples he chose for discussion appear to be environmentally induced cases, such as the outcome of nutritional differences for certain plants between soils [1894, i: pp. 446–9]). For the sake of completing the picture it should be added that 'natural selection' and the 'survival of the fittest' can be used today to refer to the mechanisms contributing to the selection of individuals that reproduce regardless of whether or not the basis of the selection is in fact heritable. This use of 'natural selection' in the sense of 'phenotypic natural selection' is not what Spencer had in mind, since it is covering non-heritable factors in selection.

There was though a great deal more to the *Biology* than a concern with the origins of biological change: morphological and physiological development is exhaustively covered. Hooker at Kew was one botanist from whom Spencer often sought expert advice. Both Hooker and Darwin were receiving the *Biology* by instalment, and their correspondence referred to it, seldom to Spencer's advantage. On 24 January 1864, Hooker wrote to Darwin

> You ask about H. Spencers works, I cannot appreciate them so highly as Huxley, they are too purely speculative for me. I wonder at & worship the man's astonishing power of assimilation & incomparable fluidity of diction: he seems to have the whole English language in his inkstand; added to which, he is a sort of imaginative Carpenter – What I dislike most is the assumption of finality he claims, for all his speculations: or rather his treating all his speculative conclusions as realized facts. I cannot think him deep, but *very* ingenious, & very voluble. He sends me sundry chapters to revise & I have cut up some, – (The Botany in Number 10, this moment arrived, is all new to me however) – His chapters on variation interest me a good deal – I totally dispute his reasoning regarding *induced* modifications being transmitted, & think

them weak & inconclusive – without however denying the fact of such heredity. – The man is I think often out of his depth. I believe he is very poor & makes his bread by these books.

On October 26, Hooker unburdened himself to Darwin again:

I always admire his wonderful grasp & admirable illustrations, but his whole work is cumbrous to my mind, & reminds me of a huge mill-sluice of scientific diction & ideas: fluid, very noisy, the noise never discordant; the stream full & powerful, but never adding an inch to the depth of the river it pours into. Much of it seems to consist in clothing biological science in the language of physical science. He often comes to me for illumination, & I reel under him, like a drunk man: he is the toughest cross questioner I ever had to deal with.

Darwin's sense of relief that he was not isolated in his own reservations is palpable in his reply to Hooker of November 3: 'I am quite delighted with what you say about H. Spencer's book: when I finish each number I say to myself what an awfully clever fellow he is, but when I ask myself what I have learnt, it is just nothing'. In mid-summer, 1866, as the succession of instalments from Spencer came to a climax, Darwin alerted Hooker to the fact that Spencer was confused over his own special concern, natural selection: 'I have almost finished the last number of H. Spencer & am astonished at its prodigality of original thought. But the reflection constantly recurred to me that each suggestion, to be of real value to science, w^d require years of work. It is also very unsatisfactory the impossibility of conjecturing where direct action of external circumstances begins & ends, as he candidly owns in discussing the production of woody tissue in the trunks of trees on the one hand, & on the other in spines & the shells of nuts' (Darwin to Hooker, 30 June 1866). As Christmas approached Hooker reported back his own astonishment at the original thought in the *Biology*, but added, echoing Darwin's earlier doubt: 'how unfortunate it is that it seems scarcely ever possible to discriminate between the direct effect of external influences & "the survival of the fittest". It is all very easy for Spencer to wriggle without facts, & if he spent a fraction of his brain & time in observing & experimenting, he would not wriggle so lithely – he is all oil & no bone' (Hooker to Darwin, 14 December 1866). It was Spencer's ignoring or deliberate blurring of a distinction of utterly cardinal importance to Darwin between use-inheritance and 'variations' that understandably irritated Hooker and Darwin himself. Darwin was postulating and hunting for a biological mechanism that *produced* 'variations' in the first place, opening the door as it happens to subsequent discoveries in genetics. As discussed above, environmentally induced 'selection' (not production) of some but not all 'variations' was of course an integral part of 'natural selection' as he defined it, whereas environmentally produced 'adaptations' in populations of organisms, which Darwin did not in fact deny occurred, could not account for the biological diversity over time in the world. Spencer's blurring in his use of 'natural selection' of this distinction served to camouflage what Darwin's most innovative point was, and to permit Spencer to continue to emphasize, as he did, even as time passed, the centrality of environmentally acquired characteristics and their inheritance in accounting for changes in organisms, while adding in *as a widely operative and progressive* selective feature Malthus's point that scarcity and struggle was a check on the growth of (human) populations, which was what Spencer himself had specified *simply in terms of human populations* in his 1852 essay.

In these exchanges, then, come specific criticisms and serious suspicions that Spencer's 'System' overall might prove merely a lumbering and potentially tautological redescription of the world, explaining nothing. John Stuart Mill expressed his own reservation that Spencer's method of working was incautious to the psychologist Alexander Bain in a letter of 1863: 'He is a considerable thinker though anything but a safe one.... The conservation of force has hardly yet got to be believed, & already its negation is declared inconceivable. But this is Spencer all over; he throws himself with a certain deliberate impetuosity into the last new theory that chimes with his general way of thinking & treats it as proved as soon as he is able to found a connected exposition of phenomena upon it' (in Mineka and Lindley, 1972, Vol. 15: p. 901). Yet in the *Biology* Spencer was making sterling efforts to observe carefully: he recorded his indebtedness 'to Mr. Flower for the opportunity of examining the collection of skulls in the Museum of the College of Surgeons' in verifying the diminution in the size of teeth in the 'civilized' races as contrasted with 'savage' races (1894, i: p. 455).[12] Furthermore, George Busk communicated Spencer's *own* paper on the movement of sap, 'On Circulation and the Formation of Wood in Plants', to the Linnaean Society in 1866,[13] a paper which even the sceptical Hooker rated highly; 'I must confess that his sap & wood paper in the Linnaean is a confoundedly good piece of scientific work' (letter to Darwin, 14 December 1866).

In the *Biology*, and in his other work, Spencer combined his essentially secondary concern with *how* species changed, and with the significance of the phenomena of extinction or failure, with his primary focus on understanding the change *that* had occurred. He was concerned to affiliate the morphological and physiological 'differentiations' in plants and animals which reflected their changing structuration and functioning to the concepts and principles he had advanced to capture how evolution in general worked. This task was pursued unconstrained by the classification of organic forms into species, let alone 'higher' or 'lower' species. Indeed, no clear demarcation between 'organic' and 'inorganic' phenomena was insisted upon. Frances has suggested a 'cataclysmic shift' in Spencer's ideas concomitant with his breakdown while writing the *Principles of Psychology*, manifest in a loss of faith in 'progress' (2007: p. 192). But no instances of this shift are specified, and his essays from 1859, discussed above, certainly do not in general support the precise claim. However, the *Biology* is primarily about structural change or progress in the *non-moral sense* that the 'Progress' essay specified at its start, and, guided perhaps by Huxley in zoology and Hooker in botany, Spencer had not committed himself in analysing life-forms to a reliance on a simple linear trajectory: 'higher' organisms are so because of their degree, in terms of number and intricacy, of correspondence between internal and external relations (1894, ii: p. 87). Spencer did though suggest that there was a 'diminution of the jaws and teeth which characterizes the *civilized* races, as contrasted with the *savage* races' (1894, i: p. 455, italics added), which Spencer took to be explicable only in terms of the inheritance of disuse. This point also reinforces the observation already recorded that the Lamarckian mechanism of use-inheritance was not *abandoned* by Spencer for Darwinian natural selection or even his own version of it, to the contrary Spencer had retained use-inheritance and was to champion it further in later years at Darwinian natural selection's expense. Because Darwinian natural selection is intrinsically irreversible, its 'direction' cannot be predicted. The more Spencer can marginalize natural selection as understood by Darwin (in particular, the pivotal role of spontaneous 'variations') and emphasize 'direct equilibration' – use-inheritance – the more plausible in Spencer's evolutionary framework it is for him to claim it is not, as it were, going nowhere (Spencer's difficulty with what Darwin meant by 'variations' would have been how in detail to account for their origin in terms of 'equilibration'). And this is enough to prevent the orthogenesis which the whole evolutionary schema manifested being wrecked in terms of its overall direction – progress. Spencer had though now, in principle, already separated progress from the morally desirable. As a contingent matter of fact, nevertheless, mankind had been the beneficiary and 'good' things could reasonably go on being expected. The Divine Will had been replaced by a secular simulacrum of benign providence, and that was now in turn usurped by a set of laws that had so far produced a contingent – they could operate in no other way – and probably provisional good. As we shall see subsequently, Spencer could and did fall back from this position. At the end of the *Biology*, indeed, mankind is vouchsafed the prospect of an approaching equilibrium between his nature and his social and wider environment: 'in Man, all these equilibrations between constitution and conditions, between the structure of society and the nature of its members, between fertility and mortality, advance simultaneously towards a common climax' (1894, ii: p. 508).

Some other aspects of Spencer's work and life while he was engaged on the *Biology* cannot be passed over without comment, including his thoughts on utilitarianism, the classification of the sciences and Comte, and his part in the formation of the 'X Club'.

Mill had not mentioned Spencer or the equal freedom principle in *On Liberty* in 1859. However, in 1863, in *Utilitarianism*, Spencer was 'startled' to be classed by Mill as anti-utilitarian. Spencer's view was that direct appeals to expediency in identifying happiness were inferior to the guidance of laws of life that declared which *kinds* of action would 'necessarily' tend to produce happiness. Man's psychological constitution, the product of experiences of utility 'organized and consolidated through all past generations of the human race', themselves 'producing corresponding nervous modifications... by continued transmission and accumulation' (1904, ii: p. 89), was thus a potent source of 'guidance'. Mill cordially inserted a note recording Spencer's comments, though maintained in his opinion that differences remained between them.[14] Spencer's conception of himself as at least a 'transcendental' utilitarian (Duncan, 1911: p. 108) has gained fresh significance in the context of a revival of interest in Spencer as a 'liberal utilitarian' (Weinstein, 1998).

Spencer's essay 'The Classification of the Sciences' was first published as a brochure in 1864. It is a continuation of his critical engagement with Comte of 1854 on the genesis of science, and its subject matter was no doubt brought into focus as a consequence of his reappraisal more generally of schemes of classification in connection with his preparation of the *Biology*. No *serial* classification is tenable of the sciences, but they may be classified according to their concerns. Thus there are Abstract sciences, logic and mathematics, concerned with relations, Abstract–Concrete sciences, such as physics and chemistry, concerned with properties, and Concrete sciences, such as geology, biology, psychology and sociology, concerned with aggregates, 'inorganic, organic and super-organic (a society)' (1864: p. 102). Each tribe and nation to the sociologist is an aggregate 'presenting multitudinous phenomena, simultaneous and successive, that are held together as parts of one combination' (1864: p. 100). As the sciences grow they diverge and rediverge like the branches of a tree. Spencer suggests that 'objective' and 'subjective' psychology may be regarded as *two* subjects because of the difference in what they are concerned with – objective psychology is concrete, subjective is analytic. Subjective psychology 'stands entirely apart from all other sciences' (1864: p. 100). It is 'the correlative of all the sciences of objective existences; and is as absolutely marked off from them as subject is from object' (this significant elucidatory comment was made in connection with a response to Bain, in an added 'Postscript', 1864: p. 105). Spencer's subjective psychology in fact largely embraces philosophical and sociological concerns as Chapter 5 discusses.

In November, 1863, Spencer had written to the *New Englander* rejecting the growing idea that he was a follower of Comte:

> On all... points that are distinctive of his philosophy, I differ from him. I deny his hierarchy of the Sciences. I regard his division of intellectual progress into three phases, theological, metaphysical and positive, as superficial. I reject utterly his religion of humanity. And his ideal of society I hold in detestation. Some of his minor views I accept; some of

his incidental remarks seem to me profound; but from everything which distinguishes Comtism as a system, I dissent entirely.

(In Duncan, 1911: p. 113)

Shortly afterwards, Auguste Laugel, the French historical and philosophical writer with an interest in evolution, had described Spencer as a follower of Comte in his review of *First Principles* in the *Revue des Deux Mondes* in February, 1864. The time had arrived for this erroneous impression of his relationship to be given a more elaborate treatment. 'Reasons for Dissenting from the Philosophy of M. Comte' appeared as an Appendix to the 'Classification' essay. Spencer declares that he is no enemy of science but that nothing specifically Comtean is thereby involved. He rejects Comte's reorganization of scientific knowledge and method. He himself and Comte share the view that knowledge is phenomenal or relative, but again this is not an especially Comtean position. Philosophers such as William Hamilton had added to his own understanding, but not Comte. Spencer accepts that he adopts from Comte the word 'sociology' and the conception 'of a social *consensus*', adding that 'when the time comes for dealing with this conception, I shall state my indebtedness' (1864: p. 133). *Social Statics* uses the words of its title with reference to the keeping of relations in a balanced state, and thus the words are used in a *sense* different from that of Comte: 'So far from alleging, as M. Comte does, that society is to be re-organized by philosophy; it alleges that society is to be re-organized by the accumulated effects of habit on character. Its aim is not the increase of authoritative control over citizens, but the decrease of it. A more pronounced individualism, instead of a more pronounced nationalism, is its ideal' (1864: p. 136). Spencer refers to *Social Statics* and to the *Proper Sphere of Government* to emphasize his conception of laws of change operating through conditions and circumstances, rather than to a role for opinion. Spencer chastises Comte for his belief that species are immutable,[15] and for rejecting a subjective psychology.[16]

There was a further important essay generated in the mid-1860s while Spencer toiled on the *Biology*: 'Mill *versus* Hamilton – The Test of Truth', which appeared in July, 1865, in the new *Fortnightly Review*, edited by Lewes. Mill's *System of Logic* and his *Examination of Sir William Hamilton's Philosophy* had raised the issue of on what foundation knowledge is based. For Mill and for Spencer, Hamilton's appeal to 'belief' is unsatisfactory. For Spencer, Hamilton wrongly conflates 'belief' in the sense of states of consciousness the negation of which is inconceivable with 'belief' in a metaphysical sense where our consciousness is vague, and where truth cannot in fact be determined, in this way he is led astray from relativism. However, in respect of both Hamilton and Spencer, Mill rejects the anchorage in 'consciousness' as the test of truth as untenable. Spencer finds Mill's criticisms of him unfair. According to Spencer, he himself distinguishes between the negation of a

belief represented in a state of consciousness on grounds of it being unbe-
lievable (weak) from it being inconceivable. Inconceivability is a strong test,
but Mill, thinks Spencer, overlooks this point. By 'inconceivable beliefs' he
means such beliefs as are inherited from experience (not from outside it),
and thinks Mill should consider this seriously as an empiricist position.
One cannot on introspection negate 'Along with motion there is necessarily
something that moves' (1865: p. 207). Such a belief rules a man's thought
whether he wills it or not; it is necessary. Spencer suggests that similarly
we cannot negate the existence of an external world. An enquirer finds
'an indissoluble cohesion between each of those vivid and definite states of
consciousness which he calls a sensation, and an indefinable consciousness
which stands for a mode of being beyond sensation, and separate from himself' (1865: p. 211). Although not known, it cannot be counted a fiction: 'Any
conclusion into which he argues himself, that there is no objective existence
connected with these subjective states, proves to be a mere verbal conclusion
to which his thoughts will not respond. The relation survives every effort to
destroy it – is proved by experiment, repeated no matter how often, to be one
of which the negation is inconceivable; and therefore one having supreme
authority' (1865: p. 212). So reason takes us to a self and to an unknown
not-self, experience of relations in something beyond consciousness gives
rise to states of consciousness, and then to an ongoing adjustment of inner
to outer relations (including the consciousnesses of others) which moulds
a correspondence of thoughts and things 'going on through preceding generations', and 'inherited in the shape of modified organic structures' (1865:
p. 213). In this manner we arrive at what are known as 'forms of thought'
(1865: p. 213). Mill, it may be noted, remained unpersuaded by Spencer's
argument (see the exchange of letters in Duncan, 1911: pp. 119–22).

   In the autumn of 1864, the formation of what became known as the X
Club initiated an institution whose 'meetings' soon provided for Spencer
both an invaluable outlet for his high-minded conviviality and a flow of
intellectual stimulation from movers and shakers across an eclectic range of
scientific fields.[17] A brief indication of where other members stood in their
careers at about this time will be helpful. Huxley (1825–1895) held lecture-
ships at the School of Mines in natural history and palaeontology and was
hugely committed to the expansion of scientific instruction. John Tyndall
(1820–1893) was professor of natural philosophy at the Royal Institution,
prominent in physics education, and an enthusiastic mountaineer. Joseph
Dalton Hooker (1817–1911), a significant botanist, succeeded his father as
director of the Royal Botanic Gardens at Kew in 1865. John Lubbock (1834–
1913) was a banker, and later also a member of parliament, with strong
interests in natural history and archaeology – his *The Origin of Civilisation and the Primitive Condition of Man* appeared in 1870 (1882). Edward
Frankland (1825–1899) was professor of chemistry at the Royal Institution
and did pioneering work in the subject and its applications. George Busk

(1807–1886) had retired from a career as a naval surgeon, devoting himself to palaeontology and committee and editorial work in natural history in particular. Thomas Archer Hirst (1830–1892) was professor of mathematical physics at University College London. William Spottiswoode (1825–1883) was a publisher, mathematician and physicist, very active in scientific societies and administration. The nine members periodically invited 'interesting' outsiders to join their dinners: Spencer recalled the mathematician, Prof. William Clifford, Prof. David Masson, Professor of Rhetoric and English Literature at Edinburgh, Robert Lowe, Liberal Chancellor of the Exchequer from 1868 to 1874 (of whom, Spencer noted, he 'takes an intelligent interest in scientific matters [1904, ii: p. 235]), Auguste Laugel, , Prof Hermann Helmholtz, the German physicist, and Asa Gray, Professor of Natural History at Harvard, botanist and supporter of Darwin (1904, ii: p. 117). Huxley was the dominant originating force. This was an elite club for the London-based, and only illness or absence from town excused absence: for Peel it was the 'cynosure of scientific radicalism' (1971: p. 18).

Desmond as it happens errs in declaring none was Oxbridge educated (1997: p. 328), since Spottiswoode was a product of Balliol College. The rest for the most part were not silver-spooned, were at loggerheads with conservative Church-approved trimmers ruling the citadels of science, and had fire in their bellies. Sheer hard work, and resolve inured against failure through struggles won, meant this was not 'an outsider cadre trying to break in, but an insider caucus spreading out. For all its scientific exclusivity, the Club had direct access to the City, Parliament, medicine, industry and the liberal Church – to the cultural heart of the country. Huxley's irregulars had become a National Force' (Desmond, 1997: p. 328). Spencer's membership does not imply the others were 'Spencerians', and may itself seem strange since he was not a professional scientist, but it signifies that his project of a secular, evolutionary synthesis of the sciences of mind and nature, which would in turn yield guides to life, was seriously valued and encouraged, even if it were to end, as wise men understood it might, in a *cul-de-sac*. Many held important university Professorships in their subjects, and Hooker, Spottiswoode, and Huxley were in turn Presidents of the Royal Society between 1873 and 1885, and all, with the exception of Spencer, occupied powerful positions related to the administration and dissemination of science. In 1864, Spencer, along with fellow club members Huxley, Lubbock and Tyndall, and also Mill, a Christian Socialist the Rev. Llewellyn Davies, Thomas Hughes (the author of *Tom Brown's Schooldays*) and Octavius Smith, took on ownership of and recapitalized a weekly paper *The Reader*, to try to breathe new life into it and its commitment to liberal politics and science. But by the end of 1865, the venture was doomed, and the paper sold on into oblivion. An early triumph, however, was to secure the award of the Royal Society's Copley Medal to Darwin: 'the medal exhilarated Darwin, fortified the X, and incensed the evangelical Anglicans; no wonder Huxley told Darwin of the "satisfaction the award has given to your troop of friends" ' (Desmond and Moore, 1991: p. 526). Yet unanimity was sometimes elusive. The X mirrored wider polarization over the actions of Governor Eyre in Jamaica in 1866. In reprisals over the killing of magistrates, Eyre's troops had killed hundreds, leading to calls that he should be prosecuted issuing from the Jamaica committee, headed by Mill, on which served Huxley, Darwin and Spencer, but leading also to the Eyre Defence movement, which argued by contrast that a white blood-bath had been averted by his actions, a movement winning the support of Tyndall and Hooker (Charles Kingsley too sided with Eyre [Kingsley, 1877, ii: p. 235]). In general, though, the activities of the Club for Spencer were a focus of relaxation and friendship, both in London and in summer country picnics. The questions of how systematically and successfully the Club sought to advance its own interests in scientific life is a matter of debate within historical studies (Barton, 1990, 1998; Jensen, 1970; MacLeod, 1970).

Spencer had by now concluded that book reviewers could not be relied on to give fair-minded assessments, and their misleading criticisms deterred purchasers. No copies of the second volume of the *Biology* were sent out for review. More of moment was his realization in 1866 while working on the instalments of this volume that his income was draining away. This was a result partly of the withdrawal of some subscribers and partly because he was giving increased financial support to his parents, for his father was now 75 and less energetic, and his mother a 'confirmed invalid' and confused (1904, ii: p. 133). The cessation of publication was announced once the *Biology* was completed. The two responses which Spencer met with were a surprise and heart-warming. First, Mill offered to guarantee sums to the publisher as needed to ensure continuation, and second, unnamed individuals, 'under the guidance' of a posse of X Club members, together with Mill, would take 250 additional copies to distribute. Spencer found Mill's offer one involving such selfless sacrifice that it must be declined, yet ever afterwards admitting to 'pleasurable remembrance of it as a manifestation of feeling between authors that has rarely been paralleled' 1904, ii: p. 136). The 'group' proposal he accepted, if embarrassed at being so valued. In the event the arrangement was cancelled; at the end of April he was called back to Derby, where his father was ill, dying, recalled Spencer, 'in a morphia-dream, the subject of which was the high-handed action of Governor Eyre in Jamaica' (1904, ii: p. 139). The shock unnerved him greatly: to Youmans he wrote 'I found my system running down so rapidly, and such serious symptoms showing themselves, that I have been obliged to come up to town for a few days change of scene, lest I should fall into some nervous condition out of which it would take me a long time to recover' (1904, ii: p. 138). His mother's memory and mental debility was now such that she was spared the news since it would have scarcely registered. Although her care was to fall to a sister-in-law and a nurse, Spencer recognized the need to reorganize his life and work in order to be in Derby often as well as resident in London.

In July, Youmans arrived in London with unexpected news. He had organized a fund (amounting to 7000 dollars) from Americans desiring to support the continuation of Spencer's work, which had been invested in public securities in his name. The process had been overseen by Robert B. Minturn from whom Youmans brought a letter to Spencer. Spencer's acceptance was perhaps assisted by the impassioned argument of an accompanying letter from the Congregationalist preacher, abolitionist and friend of evolution, Henry Ward Beecher:

> The peculiar condition of American society has made your writings far more fruitful and quickening here than in Europe. We are conscious of great obligations to you, and perplexed because we cannot acknowledge them as we could were we your fellow citizens.

> But we cannot consent to lie under such obligations without some testimonial of our feelings respecting your eminent service to us, and to the cause of the emancipation and enlightenment of the human mind, so dear to us all.

> And we are sure that you will not allow any scruples of personal delicacy to make you unjust to us, or to compel us to forbear the only action which is possible to us at this distance, and in our circumstances.
>
> (In Duncan, 1911: p. 129)

Spencer and Youmans then met up with Huxley and Hooker at the British Association, conveniently held in Nottingham that year, with Huxley lobbying to get science teaching ensconced in public schools at the expense of Latin (Desmond, 1997: p. 350).

From the September of 1866, Spencer found lodgings in London that lasted him for 21 years, at 37 (later 37 and 38) Queen's Gardens, Lancaster Gate, where he had the company of a retired government officer, two naval officers (including an admiral), an army captain and a spinster, as well as others whose stay was less permanent. Content with this domestic regime, he also took space at 2 Leinster Place nearby to sequester himself in a study: 'Here I collected and arranged all my books, papers, and other things needful for work; and here I spent my mornings. I thus protected myself against all interruptions: the servants at Queen's Gardens being forbidden to give any further reply to visitors than that I was not at home' (1904, ii: p. 146).

In 1867, he rejected overtures that he should put himself forward for chairs in philosophy at University College, London and at Edinburgh (this from Masson). It is likely that his preoccupation with the continuing decline in his mother's health put such potential disturbances to the pattern of his life beyond serious reflection. He spent time designing and overseeing the construction of an invalid bed, which his mother used, apparently with benefit. An improved version for production was made, but, since Spencer did not want to patent it to keep the cost down, no manufacturer took up the invention. In the summer his mother died. Sorrow and self-criticism left him bereft, to observe and regret 'how small were the sacrifices which I made for her in comparison with the great sacrifices which, as a mother, she made for me in my early days. In human life as we at present know it, one of the saddest traits is the dull sense of filial obligations which exists at the time when it is possible to discharge them with something like fullness, in contrast with the keen sense of them which arises when such discharge is no longer possible' (1904, ii: p. 149). His pondering on 'filial obligations' as his mother's presence left his life shaped his social and ethical analysis in years to come, for in both the *Principles of Sociology* and the *Principles of Ethics*, while their rarity and thinness was bemoaned, social evolution would ensure their ubiquity and generosity in the future.

Derby from now on ceased to have any claim on him. Back in London,[18] the revision continued of *First Principles* for a new edition, principally to reflect his view that in evolution integration was the primary process and differentiation a secondary process (1904, ii: pp. 168–9). To Mill he had to report a modification of his view on women's suffrage since *Social Statics*. Short-term benefits and respect for authority appeal to women to the extent that the extension of suffrage to them is at present undesirable. The minds of men and women are unlike, 'quantitatively and qualitatively', and this difference results 'from a physiological necessity', which 'no amount of culture can obliterate'. This 'relative deficiency of the female mind' arises in exactly those 'most complex faculties, intellectual and moral, which have political action for their sphere' (Letter to Mill, 9 August 1867, in Duncan, 1911: pp. 138–9). Were the sphere of government already confined to being guided by the equal freedom principle, the extension might not be objectionable. In present circumstances, though,

> you must bear in mind that to me the limitation of the functions of the State is the question of questions. In comparison with which all other political questions are trivial; and that to me electoral changes and other changes in forms of government are of interest mainly as they promise to make men freer, partly by the removal of direst injustices, and partly by the removal of those indirect injustices which all undue legislative action involves.
>
> (In Duncan, 1911: p. 139)

In the *Biology* Spencer had relied on his own endeavours for such facts as were required for setting forth general conceptions; and for the subjective aspects of the *Psychology* (also now being revised) he had drawn on introspection. However, with work on the *Principles of Sociology* in prospect, he realized both the need for an enormous accumulation of classified facts 'arranged as to facilitate generalization' (1904, ii: p. 171). Some form of research assistance had become indispensible. On Masson's recommendation Spencer took on the young Scot, David Duncan. However, concentrated study was inducing head symptoms, and insomnia, to mitigate which he resorted to morphia. But with no sustained improvement obtained he arranged a solo tour of Italy for the early part of 1868. Before he embarked, however, he was elected to the Athenaeum Club (along with Masson and his colleague from *Economist* days, William Rathbone Greg), around which his daily life soon largely became organized. The Italian expedition took in the eruption of Vesuvius, the cities of Naples, Florence, Rome and Genoa, and the remains at Pompeii (which impressed him the most). In the *Autobiography* he joined his recollection to a comment on sociology and history: 'I take but little interest in what are called histories, but am interested only in Sociology, which stands related to these so-called histories much as a vast building stands related to the heaps of stones and bricks around it. Here, however, the life of two thousand years ago was so vividly expressed in the objects on all sides, and in the marks of their daily use visible on them, that they aroused sentiments such as no written record had ever done' (1904, ii: p. 185).

On his return to London by mid-April, and revising the *Psychology*, he treated Duncan to his patent regimen of dictation interspersed with racquets or, in warm weather, rowing on the Serpentine. Living only a stroll from Spencer at 'The Priory', Marian Evans and Lewes had asked him to lunch with them 'whenever I found it convenient' (1904, ii: p. 202). On one of these convivial occasions he had explained his 'method' of fishing only to get the retort: ' "Yes", she said, "you have such a passion for generalizing, you even fish with a generalization" ' (1904, ii: p. 203). Visiting Oxford in the spring of 1869, accompanied by George Rolleston, Linacre Professor of Anatomy and Physiology in the University, whom he had met in Le Tréport in 1854, he found *First Principles* and the *Biology* in use as textbooks; yet at the 'godless' University College, London the Council had apparently resisted their purchase, despite student requests, until at least late 1871. Indeed, in 1869, he was pleased to receive a work on longevity from E. Ray Lankester, 'one of the rising young biologists' The study was consonant with the perspective of the *Biology*, and one to which Oxford had awarded a prize: 'Fancy', he wrote to Youmans, 'the Oxford authorities giving a public endorsement to the doctrine of Evolution!' (1904, ii: p. 216). Lubbock, and J. T. Knowles, an architect and shortly to become editor of the *Contemporary Review*, and eventually his neighbour in Brighton at 3 Percival Terrace (Spencer would occupy number 5), urged him to join the eclectic mix of intellectuals at the Metaphysical Society, but he desisted, fearing too much 'nervous expenditure' would ensue (1904, ii: p. 209). In March, 1870, he learnt he must part with Duncan, who had been appointed to a Chair at Madras. While Duncan undertook to finish his tasks associated with the *Sociology*, the loss of his experience upset Spencer's plans (James Collier took Duncan's place). In 1870, his holiday period included time with the Lotts at Llanfairfechan, during which he teamed up with Sir William Gull and Sir James Paget, distinguished London medical men, to visit the slate quarries at Penrhyn. Over three decades later, Lott's son Frank recalled this visit (though giving 1871 as the year) 'at which Mr. Spencer pointed out the glacial scratches on some of the rounded rocks in the Pass of Llanberis; and his clear and vigorous description of the old glacier coming down from Snowdon, impressed me even more than when, a few years later at the School of Mines, Sir Andrew Ramsey explained the same phenomena in his usual interesting manner' (in Duncan, 1911: p. 497).[19] In 1870 in Liverpool and again the following year in Edinburgh, he attended the British Association meetings. At the 1871 meeting, the idea of an 'International Scientific Series' began to firm up. This was a venture driven by Youmans in connection with Spencer's American publisher, Appleton, to promote the work of British (and French) scientific writers.[20] Not long afterwards Huxley's pointedly critical article 'Administrative Nihilism' appeared in the *Fortnightly Review*, to which Spencer replied in December with a not ineffectual rejoinder, 'Specialized Administration'.

'Specialized Administration' is a useful early statement of what the 'mature' Spencer, understood as the pattern of thought established by the theoretical synthesis of the idea of evolution as represented by *First Principles*, considered of greatest moment in explaining the nature and value of sociology. Spencer demonstrates that the consequences of actions in social life may be quite unexpected; the coming of railways, for instance, brought more horses on to the roads than before. 'Social forces' have, indeed, wrought out a 'seemingly-impossible set of results'. Language may appear a miraculous gift, but it has no supernatural origin: men today 'are carrying on the process by which Language has been evolved' (1871a: p. 403). This process has been natural, spontaneous, unconscious and unplanned; the product of individuals unaware they were doing any more than communicating personal interests. These observations frame Spencer's direct response to Huxley's critique of his 'Social Organism' essay. Spencer insists that the state has a role in his account – the provision of justice, in the sense of negative not positive regulation (1871a: pp. 418, 423). While positive regulation is required in organizing defence from aggressors outside of a society, it is counter-productive applied to a society internally. The normal performance of 'internal social functions' will operate provided 'justice' is in place. He is at pains to make his meaning clear: 'So long as order is maintained, and the fulfilment of contracts is everywhere enforced – so long as there is secured to each citizen, and each combination of citizens, the full return agreed upon for work done or commodities produced; and so long as each may enjoy what he obtains by labour, without trenching on his neighbour's like ability to enjoy; these functions will go on healthfully – more healthfully, indeed, than when regulated in any other way' (1871a: p. 423). Here Spencer again appeals to the authority of Richard Whately (Lecture 4 of his *Introductory Lectures on Political-Economy*) on how great results may be achieved which are not planned or even thought of by those contributing, such as supplying a city efficiently with its manifold requirements. Spencer reminds us that men 'in addition to their selfish interests... have sympathetic interests, which, acting individually and cooperatively, work out results scarcely less remarkable than those which the selfish interests work out' (1871a: p. 433). He gives examples such as friendly societies, charities, and health and education establishments. Feelings both egoistic and 'altruistic' (that this is Comte's word Spencer acknowledges) are powers which suffice to maintain a 'healthy national life' (1871a: p. 437), provided a negatively regulative central power is in place and operative. Evils arise because government neglects this job (he points to the history of relations between government and banks). So his own position, Spencer concludes, contrary to Huxley's representation of it, is not 'administrative nihilism'. For Spencer at this stage, we should note, there are three 'social forces': selfish, sympathetic, and governmental; with language, for instance, evolved through 'unconscious cooperation' (1871a: p. 436).[21]

By late 1871, after much hesitation, Spencer had settled on a generic description of the series of linked volumes on the theory of evolution and its manifestations commencing with *First Principles*, now naming it the 'System of Synthetic Philosophy'. The Christmas week of 1871 was spent in the company of Busk and George James Allman, who had recently retired from his post as Regius Professor of Natural History at Edinburgh and been elected to the Athenaeum, 'walking and driving' round the south coast of the Isle of Wight (1904, ii: p. 235. He was later joined by Huxley, Tyndall and Hooker [1904, ii: p. 244]). At much the same time he rejected a proposal from St Andrews University to award him the degree of LL.D. On this occasion, and subsequently, such awards were declined for the reason that they should be directed to younger men of merit needing assistance in making their way. The award of honours to older men of 'known achievements' adds further to a bias hindering the advance of young writers (1904, ii: pp. 233–4). In March, having read parts of *The Descent of Man* he informed Darwin he had 'no idea that such multitudinous proofs of the action of sexual selection were forthcoming' (in Duncan, 1911: p. 148), though Spencer seems not to have adopted the concept. Translations of three of his books into French were underway, and sales at home had increased. The French translation of *First Principles* by Dr. Émile Cazelles was initially delayed by the need for Spencer to provide an account of his thought and its distinctiveness compared with that of Comte. The Franco-Prussian War of 1870–1871 and then the Paris Commune and its suppression in 1871 had further delayed its appearance.[22] But it saw the light that summer. Spencer was delighted with the lucidity of the 'Introduction' the translator had supplied, and arranged for it to be translated into English. He had, however, a pessimistic analysis of the prospects for France, as he explained to Cazelles in May:

> It has seemed to me for these many years past that from some cause difficult to trace (race, or the particular mixture of races, being perhaps at the root) there has arisen an obstacle to further development. The nature of the social units seems to have become different from that required for a higher type of social structure, and, in fact, there seems to be no type that is suitable. In the *average* French nature there appears to be an intolerance of despotism along with an unfitness for freedom – or, at least, if these characters do not co-exist in the same individual, they co-exist in the individuals of the same society, and prevent that society from organizing itself into a type under which the units can co-operate harmoniously.
>
> (In Duncan, 1911: p. 155)

Two months later, while he welcomed the promise of tranquillity in France, he feared that military preparations, exhausting economic resources, might still 'entail a further retardation, if not arrest, of social growth' (in Duncan, 1911: p. 155). Translations into German were in prospect as well through the German evolutionist Ernst Haeckel's encouragement. On 2 February 1872,[23] he recorded that 'Haeckel's assistant, of whom he speaks highly, a Dr. Vetter, has undertaken to translate *First Principles*, and proposes afterwards to translate the *Biology* and the *Psychology*. It seems that Brockhaus hesitates about undertaking the publication; but Haeckel speaks as though there will be no difficulty in finding another publisher, if Brockhaus should not shortly agree' (1904, ii: p. 235). The first volume of the new version of the *Principles of Psychology*, issued first in instalments, appeared in December, 1870 (the second volume was completed in October, 1872). One motive for his extensive and, as it happens, protracted recasting of the *Psychology* had been that the impact of Darwin's *Origin* was now giving a glow to subsequent contributions in psychology but eclipsing his own earlier and evolutionary perspective on the subject:

> Especially was this so with the work of Dr. Maudsley on the *Physiology and Pathology of the Mind*, which, proceeding throughout on the evolution view of mind, and adopting the cardinal conception of the *Principles of Psychology*, without at all indicating whence that conception was derived, was reviewed with applause and had a great success. In now returning to the *Psychology*, therefore, for the purpose of further developing it, I had the consciousness that something would be done towards rectifying the arrangement in which I had got all the kicks and others the halfpence.
>
> (In Duncan, 1911: p. 140)

A significant innovation in this version of the *Psychology*, in the second volume, is the part called 'Corollaries'. This section prepared the ground for developing sociology: 'Psychology underlies Sociology; and there had to be specified a number of those more special truths in Psychology which have to be handed on to Sociology as part of its data. The deduction of these special truths from the general truths set forth in the preceding parts of the work, was an interesting task' (1904, ii: p. 241).

3
Later Spencer: Crafting the *Principles of Sociology*, and Losing Hold

The path was now clear for more sustained labour to explain why a science of sociology was needed and to specify the method of study appropriate to the science. Spencer anticipated the task with naive optimism. To Youmans on 12 October 1872 he confided that he expected a quickening in the rate of progress towards the completion of the remaining volumes projected for the 'System'. The 12 years spent to date had included 2 years taken up with a number of interruptions:

> partly due to occasional relapses of health, partly to the second edition of *First Principles*, partly to various incidental essays and articles, and partly to the arrangement and superintendence of the *Descriptive Sociology*, which, during the early stages, occupied much time. Indeed, now that I put them down, these interruptions account, I think, for more than two years' loss of time. As I am much better now than I was when I commenced, and as I do not see the likelihood of much incidental writing hereafter, I am inclined to hope that, after completing the *Study* [*of Sociology*], ten years will suffice to carry me through.
>
> (In Duncan, 1911: p. 147)

The Study of Sociology came about almost accidentally. Unlike the *Principles of Sociology*, it was not part of his 'System', nor was it planned for any length of time. It fulfilled, though, the urgent need for a book which demonstrated that a science of social life was possible, explained why the science mattered, and which introduced readers to the difficulties involved if the science were to be done well. Crucially, Youmans wanted such a book for the *International Scientific Series*, and Spencer found it impossible to refuse his friend and champion. It was arranged that the successive chapters should be published first serially in Britain and the United States: Knowles was to take them in his *Contemporary Review*, and in America Youmans neatly launched *The Popular Science Monthly* in time to publish the chapters simultaneously there. Spencer attributed increased sales of his books to the *Contemporary Review* publication of the chapters, and estimated his income from the *Study* and its serializations as '£1500 or more', commenting that 'For a five-shilling book on a grave subject, such a result was hardly to be expected' (1904, ii: p. 255).[1] The success of the book was merited, its style is approachable and punchy, it parades, as Arnold Bennett detected, 'intellectual courage', and the message is direct: sociology, not theology, is the key to a true understanding of the underlying fluidity of social life and its liberal and secularizing tendencies. The economist John Elliot Cairnes had reservations (discussed later) but paid handsome tribute: 'Never before has the conception of a social science been put forth with equal distinctness and clearness; and never has its claim to take rank as a recognized branch of scientific investigation been placed upon surer grounds, or asserted with more just emphasis. The wealth of illustration lavished on the various topics discussed is almost marvellous; and, when one considers that Mr. Spencer has already on hand a great work on the same subject, augurs a rare profusion of resources' (1875a: p. 125). In more neutral language Spencer himself later made similar points about the book in his essay 'The Filiation of Ideas':

> Rather fortunately, it was written before the *Principles of Sociology* was commenced; and, while serving to prepare the public, was also a good discipline for me. The cultured classes and their leaders – Carlyle, Froude, Kingsley, etc. – were in utter darkness about the matter. They alleged the impossibility of a 'science of history', and were without any conception that there had been going on the evolution of social structures, not made or dreamed of by kings and statesmen, or recognized by historians. Two chapters 'Is there a Social Science?' and 'The Nature of the Social Science', explained that there is a distinction between history and the science of sociology like that between a man's biography and the structure of his body.
>
> (In Duncan, 1911: p. 567)

Spencer's unflattering perception of historical studies as superficial had long been a counterpoint to his advocacy of engaging the evolution idea in making sense of social change. And his own contact with evidence of the past had a detached quality, not lastingly altered apparently by his very personal response to the intimate detail on view in the Pompeii ruins. It was the poetry of a location, not its history, that he relished: 'To me the attractiveness of ancient buildings is almost exclusively that resulting from the general impression of age which they yield, and from the picturesqueness of decay. When I go to see a ruined abbey or the remains of a castle, I do not care to learn when it was built, who lived or died there, or what catastrophes it witnessed' (1904, ii: p. 187). Twenty years earlier, just after the publication of *Social Statics*, he had declared to Lott (on 23 April 1852):

> My position, stated briefly, is that until you have got a true theory of humanity, you cannot interpret history; and when you have got a true theory of humanity you do not want history. You can draw no inference from the facts and alleged facts of history without your conceptions of human nature entering into that inference: and unless your conceptions of human nature are true your inference will be vicious. But if your conceptions of human nature be true you need none of the inferences drawn from history for your guidance. If you ask how is one to get a true theory of humanity, I reply – study it in the facts you see around you and in the general laws of life. For myself, looking as I do at humanity as the highest result yet of the evolution of life on the earth, I prefer to take in the whole series of phenomena from the beginning as far as they are ascertainable. I, too, am a lover of history; but it is the history of the Cosmos as a whole. I believe that you might as reasonably expect to understand the nature of an adult man by watching him for an hour (being in ignorance of all his antecedents), as to suppose you can fathom humanity by studying the last few thousand years of its evolution.
>
> (In Duncan, 1911: p. 62)

The death of Mill in Avignon on 9 May 1873 brought Spencer a 'severe deprivation' (1904, ii: p. 247),[2] and entailed a short pause in the progress of the *Study* while he prepared an obituary notice for the *Examiner*. He extolled Mill's exceptional generosity of spirit as a feature of his character, which Spencer had witnessed first hand both in Mill's offer of assistance as his losses accumulated and in the cordiality sustained even when differences of opinion were aired in print: 'I had, both directly and by implication, combated that form of the experiential theory of human knowledge which characterizes Mr. Mill's philosophy; in upholding Realism, I had opposed in decided ways, those metaphysical systems to which his own Idealism was closely allied; and we had long carried on a controversy respecting the test of truth, in which I had similarly attacked Mr. Mill's positions in an outspoken manner' (in 1904, ii: pp. 507–8). Mill possessed an 'unusual predominance of the higher sentiments', from which he was perhaps led to regard learning and working as too exclusively the ends of his own life, neglecting his physical well-being and thus preparing the way for a premature death. But the life was a noble one: 'Extreme desire to further human welfare was that to which he sacrificed himself' (1904, ii: p. 508). With Mill, Spencer had found an intimacy in disputation.

A little time was also spent in late 1873 and early 1874 once the *Study* was issued in correspondence with W. E. Gladstone, the Prime Minister, shortly before the Liberals lost the 1874 general election. Gladstone demurred at

Spencer's casting him as 'a type of the anti-scientific public'. The matter was settled amicably, and 'established between us social relations of a pleasant kind' (1904, ii: p. 255).

Alongside of commitments to the *Study of Sociology* and the collection of sociological data by Duncan and Collier for utilization in the upcoming *Principles of Sociology*,[3] Spencer also undertook some further significant articles. 'Morals and Moral Sentiments' appeared in 1871 in the *Fortnightly Review*. It is a critical response to an article of 1869 by Richard Holt Hutton (a Unitarian) in *Macmillan's Magazine* under the title 'A Questionable Parentage for Morals' (first read at the Metaphysical Society). Spencer felt he needed to reverse the growing currency of Hutton's misleading criticisms (Duncan, 1911: p. 148). According to Spencer, Hutton found no basis furnished by his work for morals independent of utility narrowly understood (as in Mill). Spencer replied by pointing to the evolution of sympathy and the altruistic sentiment of justice under gregariousness, a subject which he had already promised to develop further. His project, he argues, is more concerned with the parentage of 'moral sentiments' rather than 'morals'. While Adam Smith's remarks on sympathy in his *Theory of Moral Sentiments* 'made a large step' by recognizing that sympathy gives rise to our superior 'controlling emotions', his account needs supplementing in two ways: 'The natural process by which sympathy becomes developed into a more and more important element of human nature has to be explained; and there has also to be explained the process by which sympathy produces the highest and most complex of the altruistic sentiments – that of justice' (1871b: pp. 346–7). Sympathy and gregariousness reinforce each other through reciprocal aid. Spencer points to the *Psychology* and *Social Statics* as offering accounts of how sympathy produced 'justice' as an abstract emotion and the highest altruistic sentiment (1871b: p. 347).[4]

'Mr Martineau on Evolution' appeared in the *Contemporary Review* for June, 1872. 'The Place of Mind in Nature, and Intuition of Man' by James Martineau, also a Unitarian, had been carried in the April issue. Spencer replies to some of Martineau's criticisms relatively easily. The idea of 'elementary substances' is not a difficulty for Spencer's theory of evolution from homogeneity, since few chemists would assert there are in fact undecomposable substances, with compounding (from hydrogen) suggested by, for instance, Sir John Herschel. Nor is it strong criticism to point either to a line of demarcation between plants and animals or to there being no transition from simple organisms to the existence of 'mind'. There is indeed evidence that such barriers and gaps do not exist (1872: pp. 376–8). In passages of significance Spencer also asserts against Martineau that he uses the word 'evolution' quite explicitly in a sense free of the idea of a settled future towards which events unfold prospectively – orthogenesis.[5] Spencer declares too that the law is the law of the survival of the *fittest*: 'the law is not the survival of the "better" or the "stronger", if we were to give to these words anything like their ordinary meanings. It is the survival of those which are constitutionally fittest to thrive under the conditions in which they are placed; and very often that which, humanly speaking, is inferiority, causes the survival' (1872: p. 379). Problems raised in this area by Martineau may be attributed to his own confusion about what Spencer has claimed. Spencer also denies coherence to the idea of an 'originating mind', preferring to theology's false humility the view that 'humility is better shown by a confession of incompetence to grasp in thought the Cause of all things' (1872: p. 388). His commitment to this conception is, he feels, a sufficient rebuttal of the claim that his thought represents 'materialism'.

Spencer's Martineau essay is of especial importance because of his comments on the meaning of 'fittest' in his own work. It must be recalled from the discussion of 'natural selection' and 'survival of the fittest' in the context of the *Biology* that, contrary to the impression perhaps given by Spencer and often subsequently assumed, there is no isomorphic relationship between how Darwin uses 'natural selection' and how Spencer uses 'survival of the fittest'. In his comments on Martineau, he introduces no reference to either the inheritance of acquired characteristics or Darwin's 'variations'. Had Spencer brought into the discussion his continuing willingness to invoke the Lamarckian process, as contributing to change through 'survival of the fittest' as *he* uses the expression, it would have been very much more difficult for him to maintain that he himself consistently observed the distinction between 'best' and 'fittest'. Though not as it happens impossible; for there is nothing directional in an evaluative sense in the mechanism of the inheritance of acquired characteristics operating by itself. This mechanism does, however, appear to suggest the occurrence of cumulative change, if the hand of providence is on your shoulder. We shall see in later chapters that Spencer can be accused of not holding consistently to the interpretations, which he has here adumbrated, of either 'evolution' or the 'fittest'. Darwin, it is interesting, liked the essay, for Spencer wrote to him on June 12: 'I cannot consent to let your letter pass without saying how much gratified I am by your approval. I should very well have liked, had time permitted, to deal somewhat more fully with the metaphysical part of Mr. Martineau's argument' (in Duncan, 1911: p. 60). Perhaps Spencer's 'economy' of expression eluded Darwin.

In 1873, Spencer published collected replies in the *Fortnightly Review* to some of his other critics, dealing in particular with criticisms of *First Principles*. In 'Replies to Criticism', Spencer addressed first Edward Caird's sermon delivered at the Edinburgh meeting of the British Association, in 1871. The sermon suggested that to reason that there is a limit to knowledge implies that in doing so you have crossed that 'limit', in other words a self-contradiction is involved. In reply, Spencer says that 'the product of thought is in all cases a relation, identified as such or such; that the process of thought is the identification and classing of relations; that therefore Being in itself, out of relation, is unthinkable, as not admitting of being brought within the forms of thought. That is to say, deduction explains that failure of Reason established as an induction from many experiments' (1873a: p. 221). In short, it seems that deductive reasoning can show without self-contradiction that we know we don't know something (for more on Caird's views of Spencer as a philosopher see Tylor, 2006).

The philosopher and theologian, Henry Mansel, had criticized Spencer in his *The Philosophy of the Conditioned* of 1866. Spencer repeats his own view that, contrary to Hamilton and Mansel, belief in a personal God cannot be held to be *unprovable* and thus a matter of faith, since this belief is not in fact a belief underlying all proof; after all, 'In works on Natural Theology, the existence of a personal God is *inferred* from these moral and religious feelings, to show that it is not contained in these feelings themselves, or joined with them as an inseparable intuition' (1873a: p. 223). Moreover, Spencer argues that Mansel has misunderstood his account of religious belief: the basis for religious belief, properly interpreted, is not negative, but positively manifested to us through our consciousness of phenomena, 'which supplies an indestructible basis for the religious sentiment' (1873a: p. 224).

Shadworth Hollway Hodgson had become a prominent figure in philosophy as President of the Aristotelian Society. In November, 1872, his Kantian critique of Spencer 'The Future of Metaphysic' appeared in the *Contemporary Review*. For Spencer, Kant held that Space was a form of intuition derived from all phenomena, a position which he continues to reject, against Hodgson's arguments. First Spencer argues that odours and sounds, for instance, are phenomena that do not require us to intuit Space. Then he declares that 'Space *by itself* cannot be conceived of as an existence' (1873a: p. 228). In his assessment, if Space, and Time, are, as Kant says intuitions themselves, these intuitions can be the *matter* but not the *form* of Space and Time: to get to the form would involve regress. So they can never be *forms* of thought, if they are thought about. Spencer regards Space as an abstract of all co-existent positions, generated out of the legacy of inherited experiences 'during the evolution of intelligence' (1870: p. 164). This relative reality of Space relates as effect to cause to some Absolute reality, the Unknown Cause (1870: p. 167). Spencer thus maintains his position that, since the Unknowable is *Power* manifested to us, 'what we call Space and Time answer to the unknowable nexus of its manifestations' (1873a: p. 234).

Spencer argues that philosophical systems, like theological ones, following the law of evolution in general, 'severally become in course of time more rigid, while becoming more complex and more definite; and they similarly become less alterable – resist all compromise, and have to be replaced by the more plastic systems that descend from them' (1873a: p. 234, 'plastic' was by now a word which implied acceptance of mutability among public intellectuals). This lack of adaptability applies to pure Empiricism and Transcendentalism as they stand. Spencer thus bridles at Max Müller seeing him as a Kantian (in *Fraser's Magazine* for May, 1873). Spencer by contrast suggests he is closer to Locke's experientialism than to Kant (1873a: p. 237). For Spencer, Kant's Space is 'supernaturally given', not derived over time from outward experience. Kant had not the benefit of the evolutionary form of thought: 'I contend that these subjective forms of intuition are moulded into correspondence with, and therefore derived from, some objective form or *nexus*, and therefore dependent upon it; while the Kantian hypothesis is that these subjective forms are not derived from the object, but pre-exist in the subject – are imposed by the *ego* on the *non-ego*.... In the absence of the hypothesis that intelligence has been evolved, it was not possible for him to regard these subjective forms as having been derived from objective forms' (1873a: p. 237). Indeed, Brian Magee's interpretation of Schopenhauer in his *Confessions of a Philosopher* (1997) as finding noumena as cause, in contrast to Kant, could serve as an avenue of comparison with Spencer's thought.[6]

Spencer next turns to Henry Sidgwick's comments on the *Psychology*: Spencer argues he is *not* suggesting a *point* at which consciousness arises in what we take to be intelligent animals but emphasizing the *process* of the 'changes constituting psychical life, arising as the nervous system develops' while physical life itself changes (1873a: p. 240). Against Sidgwick's probing, Spencer maintains that his 'transfigured realism' as an elucidation of 'objective reality' remains an improvement on both 'crude realism' and 'idealism'. But Spencer admits a need for greater precision in how he expresses himself on objective experience to avoid appearing to lapse into 'crude realism' (1873a: p. 246). Spencer also considers Martineau's 'Science, Nescience and Faith' in his *Essays, Philosophical and Theological*. Martineau objected to Spencer's assigned Absolute role for the Unknown; it is in a relation with the known. Spencer though explicitly objects to 'Absolute' because of its Hegelian associations as encompassing both object and subject. Spencer's position is that one may contrast the Relative with a consciousness, not a *conception*, of the 'Non-relative' (1873a: p. 252). However, if, as Martineau wishes, you try to attribute some shape or content to the Unknown, you will be forced into an Unknown behind that as Cause.

An anonymous writer in the *Quarterly Review* for October, 1873, suggested that Spencer's philosophy involved the denial of all truth, and opposed all sound principles of morals. In response, Spencer says he indeed holds to a doctrine of the relativity of knowledge, as do Mill, Lewes, Bain, Huxley, Mansel, Hamilton and Kant, but that his version improves on earlier versions with their self-refuting general claim that all knowledge is relative, and does not assert that no absolute truth is possible: 'I diverge from other relativists in asserting that the existence of a non-relative is not only a positive deliverance of consciousness, but a deliverance transcending in certainty all others whatever; and is one without which the doctrine of relativity cannot be framed in thought' (1873a: p. 260). The co-existence of subject and object is a deliverance of consciousness which precedes all reasoning. On the moral issue, Spencer refers to what was said in *Social Statics*: 'the principles of justice are primarily deducible from the laws of life as carried on under social conditions. I argued throughout that these principles so derived have a supreme authority, to which considerations of immediate expediency must yield' (1873a: pp. 262–3). Unmoved by Mill's comments in relation to 'inductive utility', Spencer still insists that 'good and bad results cannot be accidental, but must be necessary consequences of the constitution of things'. Moral science deduces 'from the laws of life and the conditions of existence, what kinds of action necessarily tend to produce happiness, and what kinds to produce unhappiness'. These deductions count as 'laws of conduct; and are to be conformed to irrespective of a direct estimation of happiness or misery' (1873a: p. 263).

In the *British Quarterly Review* for October, 1873, and again in January, 1874, another anonymous critic[7] criticized Spencer on physics and his 'a priori' approach, invoking the authority of the Scottish physicist Professor Peter Guthrie Tait. Spencer first defends his preference for the expression 'Persistence of Force' over 'Conservation of Energy' because force is more generic than energy and matter. Then, on the status of the *a priori*, Spencer insists that *a priori* truths and axiomatic truths are intuitions latent in the inherited brain, arising over time from 'thought' being moulded into correspondence with 'things' (1873a, 'Postscript' of 1874: p. 288); they are not arbitrary and indeed they properly feature in the reasoning of physical science. Spencer invokes W. S. Jevons in his *Principles of Science* as an ally on this matter. Jevons argued that 'there is no such thing as a distinct method of induction as contrasted with deduction... induction is simply an inverse employment of deduction' (*Principles of Science*, 1874: p. viii). In this matter Jevons aligned himself with the Cambridge polymath William Whewell against Mill in supporting what is sometimes known as the hypothetico-deductive method in science. But, as was the case for Hume, no inductive inference could be certain; only probabilities could be assigned to particular hypotheses. Harman has drawn attention to a letter at this time from James Clerk Maxwell to George Crystal, who had attended his Cambridge lectures in 1873: 'I am at present busy with the laws of motion and other mechanical matters and I am sore afraid that if I must choose between Mr. Herbert Spencer and his opponents as to the nature of the evidence I must side with Mr. Spencer... [for] the only proofs which are more than mere illustrations of the laws of motion are as à priori as Euclids proof that lines which make alternate angles equal will not meet' (in Harman, 2001: p. 188).[8]

Spencer probably relished these interludes of polemics. Certainly they bring into focus for us some significant but easily overlooked aspects of his thought, and demonstrate that by now he was a public intellectual too important to ignore. His main concerns, however, had now become the

Descriptive Sociology and the *Principles of Sociology*, although he squeezed in the time to plot with Miall, and also John Morley, Frederic Harrison, and Joseph Chamberlain, the disestablishment of the Church of England. Apart though from a draft Bill having been prepared, Spencer could not remember any further consequences (1904, ii: pp. 258–60). Work on the *Descriptive Sociology* involved the separate treatment of 'uncivilized races', 'extinct and decayed civilized races', and 'existing civilized races'. The first part was entrusted to Duncan, the second to Dr. Richard Scheppig, and the third to Collier. Each division was planned to occupy several volumes. Youman's enthusiasm over the value of the material animated Spencer to accelerate publication, stretching himself financially in the process. The series was, in the event, only completed after his death. Each volume contained tables of facts, abstracted and classified, together with quotations and abridged abstracts out of which the tables had been constructed. According to Spencer, his friend, like himself, had grasped

> that exhibiting sociological phenomena in such wise that comparisons of them in their coexistences and sequences, as occurring among various peoples in different stages, were made easy, would immensely facilitate the discovery of sociological truths. To have before us, in manageable form, evidence proving the correlations which everywhere exist between great militant activity and the degradation of women, between a despotic form of government and elaborate ceremonial in social intercourse, between relatively peaceful social activities and the relaxation of coercive institutions, promises furtherance of human welfare in a much greater degree than does learning whether the story of Alfred and the cakes is a fact or a myth...historical gossip which cannot in the least affect men's conceptions of the ways in which social phenomena hang together, or aid them in shaping their public conduct.
>
> (1904, ii: pp. 264–5)

The immediate purpose of the *Descriptive Sociology*, however, was to provide data for the three volumes of the *Principles of Sociology*. Moving from the 'raw material' of one to the textual composition of the other was a practically bothersome chore, but by 5 March 1874, two chapters were ready for the printers. Relaxation came in the form of the customary New Year's Day dinner with the Huxleys, and visits to the Higford Burrs at Aldermaston Court in Berkshire, near to the Roman remains of Silchester which imparted a vivid impression of the strength of Roman civilization in England, and to Spottiswoode at his home near Sevenoaks. His general policy now was to shun public dinners and large social gatherings. He was elected a member of the committee of the Athenaeum Club, learning slowly that tact and diplomacy assist greatly in achieving ends, but not, it seems, curbing his urge to meddle in day-to-day matters. He also served on the committee of the London Library. In August 1874, he was in Belfast, with Lott, for the meeting of the British Association and the unionist Tyndall's presidential address, memorable for Spencer because Tyndall referred to his evolutionary account of mind in the *Principles of Psychology*. The address became a focus of controversy in some religious circles since Tyndall joined scientific explanations of events in nature to the successful pursuit of humanistic aspirations, championing faith in science at the expense of faith in religion. To Youmans, Spencer vouchsafed a laconic comment: 'it called forth many sermons' (in Duncan, 1911: p. 172). There was also a variety of other calls on his time. Henry Sidgwick's *Methods of Ethics* of 1874 raised questions about the guidance provided by the equal freedom principle, and Harald Höffding, a Copenhagen philosopher and psychologist translating a selection of Spencer's essays into Danish, needed clarification from Spencer in late 1876 on exactly how he understood 'consciousness' in relation to parallel physical and psychical changes (see Duncan, 1911: pp. 176, 178–80, and Chapter 5). The music of Richard Wagner also gained his attention. Spencer adopted an unfashionably critical stance towards Wagner's music, which he heard at the Albert Hall. It struck him as melodically weak, but with 'progress' displayed in the form of increased heterogeneity on account of Wagner's innovations in orchestration.[9] On the *Sociology* front, the completion of the first volume was predictably taking much longer than anticipated: he had belatedly recognized the need to consider, ahead of ceremonial and other forms of governance, family life, or 'domestic institutions'.

The complete version of the first volume of the *Principles of Sociology* eventually appeared in June, 1877,[10] though accompanied by a debate in *Mind* with E. B. Tylor over the originality and interpretation of his ghost theory and the origins of religion. With its completion the distribution of serial versions to subscribers ceased. Individual chapters of future volumes, though, would appear in the form of magazine articles. In July he organized a celebratory picnic for his friends at St George's Hill, Weybridge. Rheumatism drove him to hunt a cure in Buxton, where he encountered Goldwin Smith, back from Canada on a visit. Smith, born in Reading, Berkshire, was a journalist, historian and radical liberal with an established base in Toronto, whose criticism of his work Spencer regarded as perversely combining sympathy with misrepresentation (1904, ii: pp. 304–5). Some 3 years earlier, Hooker had indicated his willingness to propose Spencer as a Fellow of the Royal Society, but Spencer declined, in terms similar to the 'feeler' from St Andrews. His usual practice was to refuse such honours. However, in 1876, he accepted election to foreign membership of the Roman Academy. Indeed, on 2 July 1878, he noted a further enhancement to his position from the Academy: 'Italian Ambassador called to say that the Roman Academy had elected me a member' (in Duncan, 1911: p. 194). These events, though, were incidental when compared with his decision to postpone work on the *Sociology* and concentrate his efforts on the *Principles of Ethics*. Early in 1878 he had felt sufficiently ill to change his whole plan of work:

> I begin to feel that it is quite a possible thing that I may never get through both the other volumes of the *Principles of Sociology*, and that, if I go on writing them, and not doing anything towards the *Principles of Morality* till they are done, it may result in this last subject remaining untreated altogether; and since the whole system was at the outset, and has ever continued to be, a basis for a right rule of life, individual and social, it would be a great misfortune if this, which is the outcome of it all, should remain undone.
>
> (1904, ii: p. 314)

After time in Brighton, though, he had recovered. Before he could concentrate on the *Ethics*, chapters forming the part on 'ceremonial institutions' were due to Morley for the *Fortnightly Review*. Then in May he was in Paris with Lott for the International Exhibition. Summer arrived before he could commit to the *Ethics*, leaving the *Sociology* in abeyance.

At about the same time Potter's daughter Beatrice was tackling *First Principles*, having already been captivated by the general law proclaimed in *Social Statics* that 'Always towards perfection is the mighty movement' (Webb, 1926: p. 79). She confided to her diary on December 15 the 'very great influence' of *First Principles* upon her

> It has made me feel so happy and contented....I do admire that still, reverent consciousness of the great mystery; that fearless conviction that no advance in science can take away the beautiful and elevating consciousness of something greater than humanity. One has always feared that when the orthodox religion vanished, no beauty, no mystery would be left, but nothing but what could and would be explained and become commonplace – but instead of that each new discovery of science will increase our wonder at the Great Unknown and our appreciation of the Great Truth.
>
> (1926: p. 83)

In 1878, in December, Spencer lost one of his intellectual guides, Lewes. He attended the funeral contrary to his customary practice of eschewing religious services. Spencer reflected that Lewes and George Eliot 'exceeded any married pair I have known in the constancy of their companionship; and his studious care of her was manifest', while in wider life Lewes was 'fair in his criticisms', and 'exceptionally open-minded' (1904, ii: p. 319). Then, as planned earlier, he decamped, with Youmans as company, to the anticipated therapeutic warmth of the French Riviera. Spencer had promised

Youmans in September that if he resolved 'to do a little idling in pleasant places' his health and life would benefit: he must abandon the 'absurd fanaticism' of believing 'the one thing impossible is to let business go' (in Duncan, 1911: p. 196). There was an amicable difference of opinion over what counted as time to 'recruit'. Youmans's letters to his sister reveal the frenetic pace Spencer adopted: 'working like ten horses in quest of what he came for – relaxation!'. Christmas Eve in Hyères was, perversely, bitterly cold. But warmer weather three days later ambushed any respite for Youmans:

> The morning is pleasanter; it has stopped raining; and now we shall have to start through the mud in quest of the 'rest' we are after. Spencer is the same and not the same; his qualities abide, but they grow; while not relaxing a jot of his theoretic *laissez faire*, he is still more irritably denunciatory of people doing as they can and may. He meddles with me, and interferes with me, and criticises me, and takes care of me, all for my good, of course, in the most assiduous manner. I am beginning to count on momentary escape from his vigilance to do a little writing or reading. – At this point he came for a walk, 'a slight ramble for half an hour'. It was very wet and muddy, but we rambled through the lanes and alleys, up and around the side of the mountain behind us, climbing for an hour, steady pull. Then he struck off into an obscure path that promised more direct descent. We lost the path, and lost our way, and had to plunge down a steep, broken, rocky, muddy side of the great hill full of gorges and deep channels. It was an old *olive orchard*, old and half dead; the trees are about the size of apple trees, and their tops look as if covered with sage leaves. We got back after a two hours' tramp, and I was quite used up. Then we had 'breakfast' at twelve o' clock. Then another tramp of twenty minutes, at the end of which I back out. He has gone on, but will be back for me for another pull before dinner.... He professes great benefit already, boasting of eight hours' sleep the three previous nights each, and he falls asleep almost every time he sits down. He slept nearly all the time in the cars, and is evidently making up for his past losses. If nothing happens, it will undoubtedly do him great good.
>
> (In Fiske, 1894: pp. 352–3)

Spencer had continued working on the text and proofs of his study of ethics while in France, and then at Wilton House as the guest of Lord and Lady Pembroke. Fruits appeared in June, 1879, as *The Data of Ethics*, the first of three Parts that eventually made up the first volume of the *Principles of Ethics*. On June 30, Spencer was on hand when the artist Jack Collier married Huxley's daughter Marian. Collier's sister-in-law Mary Collier, later Lady Monkswell, noted: 'very much pleased and amused by sitting in the little garden, talking & looking at Herbert Spencer, [Lawrence]Alma[-]Tadema, Sir Joseph Hooker, & Mrs. [Laura Theresa] Alma[-]Tadema' (in E. C. F. Collier,

1944: p. 36). The Alma-Tademas were noted London painters of the time.[11] Reviews of the *Ethics* encouraged Spencer; Bain's in *Mind* was 'extremely satisfactory', especially so since Spencer was aware that on many occasions he had been 'rather unsparing in my criticisms of him' (in Duncan, 1911: p. 201). Instead of proceeding further with the *Ethics* Spencer reverted to the *Sociology* to issue separately the Part 'Ceremonial Institutions' as a book with the same title, ahead of its planned inclusion in the second volume.

Spencer's renewed attention to sociological matters triggered in him fresh ideas about social evolution and contemporary political concerns. On 10 October 1879, he wrote to Youmans:

> While away in the country this time, I have been so frequently thinking of the question of Militancy v. Industrialism, and the profound antagonism between the two which comes out more and more at every step in my Sociological inquiries, and I have been so strongly impressed with the re-barbarization that is going on in consequence of the return to militant activities, that I have come to the conclusion that it is worth while to try and do something towards organizing an antagonistic agitation. We have, lying diffused throughout English society, various bodies and classes very decidedly opposed to it, which I think merely want bringing together to produce a powerful agency, which may do eventually a good deal in a civilizing direction. The Nonconformist body as a whole, through its ministers, has been manifesting anti-war feelings very strongly; the leading working-men, as was shown at the late Sheffield Congress, are quite alive to the mischief; the Secularists as a body will go in the same direction; so will the Comtists; so will a considerable number of rationalists; so will a considerable sprinkling of Liberal politicians; and so will even a certain proportion of the advanced Churchmen, such as Hughes, and of the clerical body. I have talked to several about the matter – Rathbone, member for Liverpool, Harrison, Morley and others – and I am about to take further steps. There is a decided sympathy felt by all I have named; and I think that it is important to move.
>
> (1904, ii: pp. 329–30)

This letter helps to furnish the background to three of Spencer's social and political concerns which feature in the 1880s. First, it displays the contrast between militant and industrial social types that became a central aspect of his account of social evolution. Second, its concern with 're-barbarization' resonates strongly in the four new polemical essays which became *The Man versus The State*, a book separate from his 'System'. Third, it provides the rationale for a period of active political engagement by Spencer in the Anti-Aggression League. An eventful excursion 'up the Nile' intervened first, however.

Once *Ceremonial Institutions* appeared in November, Spencer left immediately afterwards to cross Europe heading for Cairo with Margaret Potter, one of Beatrice's sisters. The trip up the Nile occupied December, 1879 (not September as given by Wiltshire, 1978: p. 79) and January, 1880. His main companions as well as Margaret were another Potter daughter, Kate (the visit seems to have originated with her), and Canon Samuel Barnett and his wife, Henrietta. Spencer, already dyspeptic, unexpectedly punctuated his trip by returning to Cairo. Having received reassurance about his health – 'fancies, afterwards seen to be morbid, took possession of me' (1904, ii: p. 340) – he rejoined the party. Spencer recorded no impression of the Barnetts, though their commitment to practical socialism and social reform[12] would have been uncongenial. They apparently had not read his work, and found him a prickly individual: 'unloved and unloving' (Barnett, 1921: pp. 230–1). He visited the Pyramids, tombs and temples, and went to dancing dervishes. He finally parted with the others at Philae, returning to Cairo. Spencer discerned a melancholy in Egypt, a triumph of decay and death. His own reflections dwelt on desert landforms, the indigenous aquatic life and weather patterns almost as much as on the relics of past human lives (1904, ii: pp. 335–43, Duncan, 1911: pp. 204–6). Journeying home, at least Milan's cathedral was admired, meriting two visits. In Paris, he met with Gustave Baillière, who published French translations of Spencer, and Théodule Ribot, who had translated the *Psychology* (on Spencer's psychological analysis and its value to the 'Solidarisme' of Léon Bourgeois see Beck, 2004). On February 12, he was in London: 'Heartily glad – more pleasure than in anything that occurred during my tour' (in Duncan, 1911: p. 206).

Returning to work he had to decide whether to continue at once with the *Sociology* or add to the *Psychology* a new Part on 'Congruities' to explicate how the 'Unknowable', or 'Transfigured Realism', reconciled the physical and psychical (or 'subjective') aspects of the subject which he now felt was needed. The 'Political Institutions' Part of the *Sociology* in the end won precedence, though completion took until March, 1882 (the addition to the *Psychology* was written later in 1880). The final stretch of 'Political Institutions' was covered by dictation to his secretary, Bridge, initially in or near to Brighton (by now a favourite place of Spencer's) and finally back in London. His diary entry of 24 March reads: 'Ended chapter on Political Retrospect and Prospect. Finished vol. ii. of the *Sociology*, SO ENDING HARDEST BIT OF WORK. Dined at Huxley's' (in Duncan, 1911: p. 222). Alongside of this work he was also 'guiding' an article by the poet and eventual anarchist Louisa Sarah Bevington ('The Moral Colour of Rationalism' for the *Fortnightly Review*) as a response to an essay by Goldwin Smith which had alleged a link between scientific doctrine and personal and political selfishness; with Spencer himself also replying to Goldwin Smith in the *Contemporary Review* for March, 1882. Bevington was interested in evolutionism – 'Nothing hinders, all enables/Nature's vast awakening' – and 'became a friend of Herbert Spencer. Both her philosophical essays and her poems, which question religion and its moral authority, betray the influence of his ideas' (McGowran,

2004).[13] In 1881, he fitted in a visit to Thomas's widow, his aunt Anna, now an invalid, at Weston-super-Mare. In October of the same year he finally issued a notice ceasing further publication of the *Descriptive Sociology*, principally for financial reasons: the series had cost £4426 and he was out of pocket by £3250 (1904, ii: p. 351). It was becoming clear that books and articles in one way or another critical of aspects of his thought were appearing at a faster rate than it was possible to reply to them all. Yet Spencer responded to some in an Appendix to a new edition of *First Principles*, and in a Postscript added to the *Study of Sociology*.

In December, 1880, George Eliot died. Spencer had talked with her shortly before her unexpected death. Lewes and Eliot had lived together since 1854 without being married, although after his death she had married John Cross. Spencer disparaged any claim that his ideas had greatly influenced her fiction, and recorded that 'A movement was commenced to obtain for George Eliot a place in Westminster Abbey; but, before any overt steps were taken, it was concluded that undesirable comments would probably be made, and the movement was abandoned. She was buried in the Highgate Cemetery; and though the day was continuously rainy, the funeral was attended by a very large concourse, including many distinguished men' (1904, ii: p. 365). Spencer also attended Darwin's funeral in the Abbey on 26 April 1882. In its listing of those present *The Times* made him a Fellow of the Royal Society in error. The two men had not met often, and for all that the public joined their names, then and still, the central question each sought to answer was distinct, one a problem in biology while the other a cosmic conundrum. But Spencer well knew Darwin had had no hand in diminishing his standing. Huxley had assumed, with good reason, that Spencer might not even be lured into the Abbey, let alone be a pall-bearer (Desmond, 1997: p. 520). Some misunderstanding must have arisen since he wrote in reply to George Darwin on May 4: 'I fancy some remark of Huxley's (made probably to Galton and then to you) to the effect that my very pronounced non-conformity in the matter of ecclesiastical ceremonies (which he knew had prevented me from being present at Tyndall's marriage) might perhaps be an obstacle to my attendance. But I felt the occasion of your father's funeral to be so exceptional that I could not let this feeling prevent me from manifesting my great respect' (in Duncan, 1911: p. 223).

In the interests of his health he had for long restrained himself from the stress of public involvement in controversial causes. Work on 'Political Institutions' had, however, further sensitized him to 'militancy' and sympathy with attempts to curb it. In 1881, Frederic Harrison tempted him into consultations with like-minded individuals, including John Morley and the Rev. Llewellyn Davies, which led him into drawing up an address that described their aims, involving not the non-resistance of the Peace Society but non-aggression, which in turn led him into making a speech at a public meeting in February, 1882, at the Westminster Palace Hotel. Spencer had tried, but failed, to elicit a contribution from Swinburne, and deemed Tennyson's poetry unsympathetic to the cause. Later, in June, Spencer breakfasted with Gladstone and talked with him about the League. Spencer reported to John Bright on the 24th: 'He expressed his entire sympathy with its aims. He felt the need for it, saying, to use his own words, that the Peace Society had "botched the matter" by its impracticable principle; and he recognized the fact that our aims were in harmony with the progress of Liberalism at large' (in Duncan, 1911: p. 224). Spencer forwarded to him material on the League, to which Gladstone replied, repeating his sympathy though not offering actual concurrence. On reflection, Spencer judged that the Anti-Aggression League was indeed doomed to achieve little in the primarily militant climate of the time, and regarded his expenditure of energy on it as a 'grievous mistake', doing him great evil: 'There was produced a mischief which, in a gradually increasing degree, undermined life and arrested work' (1904, ii: p. 378). Nevertheless, his anxiety was not of a magnitude to prevent the contemplation of a visit to America. Richard Potter wrote to Cunard on his behalf to secure a 'desirable room in the "Servia", sailing on the 12 of August' (1904, ii: p. 383).

Constituent sections of 'Political Institutions' had been appearing in various periodicals, including the *Fortnightly Review* (not as well received as he had hoped), and the completion of the Part, and thus of the second volume of the *Sociology* in March, 1882, was the occasion for a retrospective review in the *Autobiography*:

> If I did look for some acceptance of the leading ideas set forth in this volume, it was from the men of science that I looked for it. These general facts, – that in the course of animal evolution there arises a strong contrast between the method of co-operation among those organs which carry on the vital actions, and the method of co-operation among those organs which carry on dealings with the environment; and that there arises in the course of social evolution a kindred contrast between the mode of co-operation among the industrial structures which sustain social life, and the structures which perform actions of offence and defence against other societies (which form the social environment), – might, I thought, be recognized by the scientifically cultured, and their significance perceived. That there results the industrial type or the militant type according as one or other set of organs and mode of co-operation predominates; and that the phenomena of activity, structure, government, with the corresponding beliefs and sentiments, are determined by the relative predominance; proved to be conceptions no more appreciated by those who are in the habit of studying natural causation, than by those to whom natural causation is an unfamiliar thought.

> Beliefs, like creatures, must have fit environments before they can live and grow; and the environment furnished by the ideas and sentiments

now current, is an entirely unfit environment for the beliefs which the volume sets forth.

(1904, ii: p. 374)

Spencer was probably aware that Beatrice Potter, having already studied Lewes's *History of Philosophy*, was now setting off on her own voyage of 'a systematic study, lasting for over a year, of the Synthetic Philosophy', though possibly as yet had no inkling that 'in spite of the guidance of its author' she was to become 'a "doubting Thomas", though a miserably feeble one, about the validity of the Spencerian generalisations' (Webb, 1926: p. 119). For all his solicitation over her well-being, and although attending Darwin's funeral and taking breakfast with Gladstone would have been major events, Spencer's mind must mostly have been on his own approaching embarkation for America. Lott had generously agreed to accompany him. Spencer had ruled that he was giving no lectures; the overriding aim was relaxation. Before sailing, Spencer stayed in Liverpool with Robert Holt and his wife (his friend Potter's eldest daughter). Crossing the Atlantic was uneventful, though Spencer slept badly and became 'dilapidated' (1904, ii: p. 388); Youmans met them in New York. Later they journeyed to Saratoga and into Canada, and Montreal, Lake Ontario, Toronto and Niagara. After a week or so, in response to an invitation pressed on Spencer by Andrew Carnegie, they travelled on to Cleveland and Pittsburg, taking in a visit to the ironworks. Next it was Washington, and then Baltimore, to the Johns Hopkins University, where his chaperone was a supporter, the mathematician Professor J. J. Sylvester. In Baltimore Spencer stayed with J. W. Garrett, President of the Baltimore and Ohio Railway, whom he had met previously in England. Lott and Spencer then returned to New York, but with a glimpse of the New England states still in store. Stopping at New Haven, he visited Yale and Professor Othniel C. Marsh's collection of fossil mammals (the ones displaying the pedigree of the horse had galvanized Huxley on his visit in 1876 [Desmond, 1997: pp. 471–4]), and then arrived at Boston. He dined with the Saturday Club, made up of the great and the good from Boston and Concord, presided over by Oliver Wendell Holmes, whom Spencer enjoyed encountering as 'one whose writings had given me so much pleasure' (1904, ii: p. 404). He was also reunited with his admirer John Fiske, and Professor Asa Gray. Lott and Spencer visited Emerson's house at Concord, meeting family members, and appreciating the beauty of 'Sleepy Hollow' where Emerson had recently been buried. A chase to catch a train now weakened him which a few days quiet only partly overcame. And an ordeal was imminent. He was to deliver a speech to a large audience at Delmonico's in New York on November 9. His theme was 'that life is not for learning nor is life for working, but learning and working are for life'. Spencer prophesized, moreover, that the future 'has in store a new ideal, differing as much from the present ideal of industrialism as that ideal differs from [the] past ideal of militancy' (1904, ii: pp. 406–7; see also Werth, 2009). Shapin's modern assessment of the banquet was that it was 'the great event of the New York cultural season of 1882':

> Nowhere did Spencer have a larger or more enthusiastic following than in the United States, where such works as 'Social Statics' and 'The Data of Ethics' were celebrated as powerful justifications for laissez-faire capitalism. Competition was preordained; its result was progress; and any institution that stood in the way of individual liberties was violating the natural order. 'Survival of the fittest' – a phrase that Charles Darwin took from Spencer – made free competition a social as well as a natural law. Andrew Carnegie admired Spencer enormously and attributed to him the decisive metaphysical epiphany of his life: 'I remember that light came as in a flood and all was clear.... I had found the truth of evolution. "All is well since all grows better" became my motto, my true source of comfort.' Thanks to Spencer, Victorian capitalists knew that nature was on their side.
>
> (Shapin, 2007)

With their patience no doubt sorely tested, and with intensive cosseting, Lott and Youmans saw Spencer through. To avoid reporters, Spencer and Youmans conspired in an 'interview' for publication in the press. Presents from well-wishers, fair weather and good food on board the *Germanic* had Spencer in better form, undone by delay and overnight noise before docking at Liverpool. Instead of dining with the Holts, he took a fast train for the peace of home in London. Come the *Autobiography* the expedition represented an incubus: 'Setting out with the ill-founded hope that the journey and change of scene would improve my health, I came back in a worse state than I went; having made another step downwards towards invalid life' (1904, ii: p. 409).

On Spencer's return to England there was gratifying news from the physician and neurologist Dr Hughlings Jackson, working in London, which Spencer communicated to Youmans: 'The initiative he made years ago by applying the doctrine of dissolution to interpretation of nervous disorders...seems likely to lead to other results. The paper is very clearly and conclusively argued; and is to me just as much a revelation as that which Hughlings Jackson made of the doctrine' (in Duncan, 1911: p. 227). He also received from Youmans the pamphlet including his 'interview' with Youmans and the speeches delivered at or at least prepared for the Delmonico's dinner, *Herbert Spencer on the Americans and the Americans on Herbert Spencer* (see Spencer, 1883).

Spencer's own narrative of his life in the *Autobiography* was not extended in any detail beyond his return from America. The backbone of any consideration of the last 21 years of his life must be Duncan's *Life and Letters*.

Now into his 60s, more frequently concerned with variations in his health than hitherto, there was no discernible decline in the amount or intellectual quality of his work. The third volume of the *Principles of Sociology* remained to be written, with Parts on 'Ecclesiastical', 'Professional' and 'Industrial' institutions, and only one of the six Parts of the *Principles of Ethics* had been completed. In addition, he wished to revise 'Ceremonial Institutions' in the second volume of the *Sociology*. In due course, all such outstanding tasks were fulfilled. Nevertheless, he now also contemplated a new literary project, which, with its roots back in his Anti-Aggression League involvement of 1881–1882, itself reflected the signs of a recrudescence of belligerence abroad, as witnessed by the Triple Alliance of Germany, Austria–Hungary and Italy against Russia and France in 1882, and in calls at home for more intervention by the state as in Canon W. L. Blackley's proposed scheme of 'national insurance' of 1878. To Youmans he wrote on 13 November 1883:

> I shall probably commit myself to a series of four political articles. For some time past I have been getting more and more exasperated at the way in which things are drifting towards Communism with increasing velocity; and though I fear little is to be done I am prompted to make a vehement protest, and am intending to say some very strong things. Oddly enough, yesterday while exciting myself over it, as I have been doing lately, the editor of the *Contemporary Review* called on me, wanting me to take up the question, which has just been raised in a very startling way by an article of Lord Salisbury's on the dwellings of the industrial classes. Though I have not yet committed myself I shall probably do so. Of course I do not like to suspend other work, but the matter is pressing and important, and, in a sense, permanent; for, these four articles I contemplate, dealing with the questions not after a temporary, but after a permanent manner, will have their future value.
>
> (In Duncan, 1911, p. 238)

There were, though, even further diversions pressing on his time. One matter perceived as deserving immediate attention was the 'Kantian revival' within philosophy in Britain. Here he detected a threat to the whole approach adopted in his work, as he remarked to Richard Hodgson in January 1883: 'The Kantians think they have gone behind other philosophies. The thing to be done is to go behind them, and to show [that] the true "form of thought", is a relation between states of consciousness, and the true process of thought a survival of the more coherent relations in the struggle for existence' (in Duncan, 1911: p. 229. See also Spencer, 1888). Psychology, then, rather than 'logic' should be the focus. Preparation for a new and better referenced edition of the first volume of the *Sociology* commenced, and he started work on a revised edition of his *Essays*.

In the spring of 1883, the Council of the Birmingham Natural History and Microscopical Society had agreed upon a new Sociological Section for the study of Spencer's 'Synthetic Philosophy' (Spencer was an Honorary Vice-President).[14] The young Constance Naden, a scientist and poet (four poems formed a group called 'Evolutional Erotics') was a regular member until she left Birmingham: 'Of the many diligent and enthusiastic students of the doctrine of evolution who have assisted at our meetings in discussions and by readings, criticisms and expositions, from learned professors and local scientists down to tyros who were just beginning to understand and appreciate Herbert Spencer, not one was so highly valued as Miss Naden' (Hughes, 1890: p. 21). Taking her cue from the 'Synthetic Philosophy' that the laws of evolution are common to organic and super-organic phenomena, 'she rightly viewed society as an organism – a vast organism – as regards its genesis and many-phased development' (Hughes, 1890: p. 24).

Early in 1884 Spencer was approached to ascertain his willingness to accept nomination as a Liberal representative in Parliament (for Leicester). He declined on health grounds, and because the 'actual work of legislation is more the work of those who modify the ideas of electors than of those who give effect to their ideas.... I conceive that I should not gain influence, but rather lose influence, by ceasing to be a writer that I might become a representative'. A further reason was that his view of the chief business of legislation was not (yet) widely shared by political parties; the concern of legislation should be 'an administration of justice such as shall secure to each person, with certainty and without cost, the maintenance of his equitable claims' (in Duncan, 1911: p. 240). When these opinions were published, *The Times* commented that costless administration of legislation would increase litigation: Spencer's denial pointed to a reduction of civil aggression, and thus litigation, precisely because easier access to litigation and hence the enforcement of penalties would deter potential aggressors. To the Earl of Wemyss on March 1, he declined an invitation to join the Liberty and Property Defence League, fearing a formal association with a body perceived as Tory would devalue the attempt to change Liberal thinking in the essays, now being published despite the distractions (Duncan, 1911: p. 242).[15]

Indeed, 'The New Toryism', 'The Coming Slavery', 'The Sins of Legislators' and 'The Great Political Superstition' – the 'four political articles' of which he had provided prior notice to Youmans – appeared in the *Contemporary Review* between February and July during 1884. They were subsequently revised, furnished with a Postscript and published in book form as *The Man versus The State*. The first essay argued that Liberals had come to confuse the rectification of evils, reducing the range of governmental authority over persons, with the positive achievement of 'good'; the Liberal policies were thus tending towards a coercive or 'militant' type of society. This essay led into an exploration of why this trend must undermine social advance, and the ways in which legislators are ignoring the lessons of social evolution. The concluding essay criticized the idea that majorities have rights over minorities, except within definable limits. Spencer explicitly saw these essays as a summation of a process of gradual development in his thought on politics rather than as in any sense a rupture with previous statements he had published. On May 13, he wrote to Youmans:

> Beginning in 1842 and returning from time to time to the topic in the interval, with further developments, I now in 1884 reach what seems to me a sufficiently completed view – the politico-ethical doctrine set forth...being a presentation in a finished form of the theory gradually developed during these forty-two years. It will, I think, eventually form a new departure in politics. The definite conclusions reached, alike concerning the legitimate powers of Governments and majorities, and the reason why, beyond a certain range, their powers cannot be legitimately exercised, and along with them the definite conception presented of the nature of true Liberalism for the future, may, I think, serve presently to give a positive creed for an advanced party in politics.
>
> (In Duncan, 1911: p. 243)

Among responses to *The Man versus The State* there was an influential one from the Belgian economist Emile de Laveleye in the *Contemporary Review*, to which Spencer replied robustly in 'M. de Laveleye's Error'. The nature of Spencer's core arguments, and arguments against them, including de Laveleye's, are addressed in detail later in this study.

Spencer had also made inroads on 'Ecclesiastical Institutions' during 1883 and, with some chapters still outstanding, he ensured that the concluding chapter, 'Religious Retrospect and Prospect', was published in the *Nineteenth Century*. Frederic Harrison, in sympathy with Comte's positivism in the form of the religion of humanity, wrote a reply which as Spencer thought misrepresented his understanding of the foundations for agnosticism. According to J. H. Brooke, Spencer now posited a power behind evolution, an Unknowable Power that nevertheless made for righteousness, a power that 'stands towards our general conception of things, in substantially the same relation as does the creative power asserted by Theology' (Spencer, quoted in Brooke, 1991: p. 305).[16] In America, Youmans felt under pressure to ensure that the exchanges should be published in a more permanent form, and Spencer acquiesced on January 14 and 15, 1885 (in Duncan, 1911: pp. 259–60). The Appleton company published the volume as *The Nature and Reality of Religion* in May. Harrison raised objections and Spencer immediately realized that the whole question of Harrison's copyright had been overlooked. He acted to ensure the publisher suppressed the book. In the surrounding correspondence it is clear that Spencer felt wounded by some comments Harrison had made about the *Descriptive Sociology*, but it was Spencer who had erred primarily, and the quarrel subsided.[17] The drama had not prevented the completion of the entire 'Ecclesiastical Institutions', which came out in the autumn of 1885.

Still Spencer evaded devoting all his energies to the outstanding Parts of the 'Synthetic Philosophy'. For some time he had wanted to revisit the question of the 'factors of organic evolution', largely left aside since the *Biology*. He planned two articles and he neatly expressed his aims to his German translator, Vetter:

> They will be in the main a criticism upon the current conception of Mr. Darwin's views; showing that this conception is erroneous in ignoring altogether one of the beliefs set forth by Dr. Erasmus Darwin and by Lamarck – the belief that the inheritance of organic modifications produced by use and disuse, has been a cause of evolution. The thesis of the first paper will be that this cause has been all along a co-operative cause, and that in its absence, all the higher stages of organic evolution would have been impossible.

> The second paper will have for its object to point out that besides the factor of 'natural selection', now exclusively recognized, and besides the factor previously alleged, which has of late been improperly ignored, there is yet a third factor, preceding the other two in order of time, and universally co-operative with them from the beginning, which has to be taken into account before all the phenomena of organization can be understood – a factor which has to be recognized before organic evolution is rightly conceived as forming a part of evolution at large.
>
> (In Duncan, 1911: pp. 269–70)

'The Factors of Organic Evolution' appeared in the *Nineteenth Century* for May and June, 1886. Spencer regards the ideas of Cuvier, as a catastrophist, as dominant in geology until the 1850s over Lyell's uniformitarianism. While *Vestiges of the Natural History of Creation* was evolutionary in conception, it provided no plausible mechanism of change. Spencer places himself in the tradition of Erasmus Darwin and Lamarck in accepting the adaptation of parts to circumstances. It was indeed 'tenable' that they were inheritable; but much change, he admits with hindsight, was not thereby accounted for. The emphasis on natural selection in Darwin's *On the Origin of Species* produced a new picture. Spencer, however, notes at some length Darwin's acceptance of the effects of use and disuse in accounting for change in addition to natural selection. For Spencer, natural selection 'is the overthrowing of many individuals by agencies which one successfully resists, and hence continues to live and multiply' (1886: p. 429). Spencer insists that in the interpretation of his phrase 'survival of the fittest' an 'anthropomorphic' perspective on the meaning of fittest is to be avoided (1886: pp. 429–30).

Spencer provides a sketch of the relative chronological importance of mechanisms of change in the world. First, he emphasizes forces in the environment or medium of an organism as primordial factors of modification of structure (from homogeneity to heterogeneity). In this connection Spencer relates the detail of his argument to *A Treatise on Comparative Embryology*, by the late Francis Balfour. Variations in Darwin's sense then enter as a co-operating factor in change by natural selection. However, with 'higher grade' animals, observes Spencer, 'there came more and more into play as a factor, the inheritance of those modifications of structure caused by modifications of function.... in the case of the highest of creatures, civilized men, among whom the kinds of variation [it is tolerably clear contextually that Spencer does not intend to mean 'variation' in Darwin's sense here] which affect survival are too multitudinous to permit easy selection of any one, and among whom survival of the fittest is greatly interfered with [but Spencer does not say by what or whom, or in what way], it has become the chief factor: such aid as survival of the fittest gives, being usually limited to the preservation of those in whom the totality of the faculties has been most favourably moulded by functional changes' (1886: p. 462).

If the mechanism of the inheritance of acquired characteristics is discarded, psychological and social change, dependent on variations and natural selection alone, may be inferred to be much slower and less comprehensive than its acceptance implies:

> If functionally-produced modifications are inheritable, then the mental associations habitually produced in individuals by experiences of the relations between actions and their consequences, pleasurable or painful, may, in the succession of individuals, generate innate tendencies to like or dislike such actions. But if not, the genesis of such tendencies is, as we shall see, not satisfactorily explicable.

> That our sociological beliefs must also be profoundly affected by the conclusions we draw on this point is obvious. If a nation is modified *en masse* by transmission of the effects produced on the natures of its members by those modes of daily activity which its institutions and circumstances involve; then we must infer that such institutions and circumstances mould its members far more rapidly and comprehensively than they can do if the sole cause of adaptation to them is the more frequent survival of individuals who happen to have varied in favourable ways.
>
> (1886: pp. 464–5)

In advance of publication Spencer had asked Huxley and Flower for comments. Flower made no objections, but Huxley still found the transmission of inherited characteristics 'as far off sufficiently trustworthy evidence now as ever it was' (in Duncan, 1911: p. 270).

With his health and low spirits already causing anxiety, Spencer now had to face two painful losses: in the summer of 1886, Lott died, and then, early in 1887, Youmans died. Youmans had taken enormous trouble to advise Spencer sympathetically and constructively, and to advance Spencer's ideas, reputation and financial success in America, and more widely. Of course,

Youmans himself had also gained. Rather desperately, Spencer thought 'yachting would be the thing – yachting about the coasts with the ability to go into port every night so as to get quiet rest'. He felt Tyndall would be game, and tried the idea on Huxley: 'We all three of us want a lounging life in the open air, with just enough variety to keep us alive, and the exhilarating effects of a little pleasant company.... What do you say to our chartering a yacht for a couple months...and going hither and thither about the coasts of the English Channel, including Jersey, Guernsey, the Scilly Islands, &c' (in Duncan, 1911: p. 273). The prospect appalled Hooker: ' "Just fancy" being cooped up "with H.S. in a yacht", exclaimed Hooker: "I should go before the mast, & stay there" ' (in Desmond, 1997: p. 551). The X Club members were now consumed with aches and pains, and decrepit: 'for each of them, Death had a stalking-horse' (Desmond, 1997: p. 551). No yacht was ever chartered, of course, and nor did Spencer pursue the idea of staying in Folkestone and 'going backwards and forwards to France every day for the benefit of the sea air, motion and liveliness' (Duncan, 1911: p. 275). Instead he adjourned to Brighton, though not without offering friendly guidance to Beatrice Potter for an article she was preparing on understanding pathological social states: 'the course of treatment is not the readjustment of the principles of political economy, but the establishment as far as possible of free competition and free contract' (in Duncan, 1911: p. 276).

For the next winter he stayed with the Potters in Bournemouth. Potter's own health was failing, and Spencer, observed Beatrice, 'sits in his chair not daring to move body or mind...waiting with despondent patience for returning strength, pursued by his desire to finish his System of Philosophy. I sit in his room writing or reading, now and again saying some kind word...Yesterday as I sat there I heard a sudden moan as if he was in pain. "Are you suffering?" "No", groaned the poor old man, "a momentary fit of impatience. Why suffer more to-days?" a question I could not answer' (Webb, 1926: p. 27).

Yet a good degree of resilience returned for 1888, though Beatrice Potter failed to get his agreement for his portrait to be painted by Millais (Duncan, 1911: p. 383). After further rest in Dorking at Grant Allen's home, the next year he effectively saw off an inference that, because he had written articles on 'sociology' for the *Pilot* in 1844, he was a Comtean: Harrison searched on his behalf, finding no such articles (Duncan, 1911: p. 287). He also provided a Preface for an independent *vade mecum* by Howard Collins, *An Epitome of the Synthetic Philosophy*. The *Pall Mall Gazette* of 7 March 1889 carried a note referring to the Sociological Section of the Birmingham Natural History Society and urged the foundation of a Spencer Society in London. Next day, from the Athenaeum, came a letter in the *Gazette* from a key figure in technical education, Sir Philip Magnus:

Your suggestion about a 'Spencer Society' is too valuable to remain unnoticed. As a very humble student of philosophy and science, I know how much these two great branches of learning owe, in their mutual relation and dependence to the great thinker of the present century; but to Herbert Spencer more than to any other writer are undoubtedly due the recent advance of practical education and such improvements as have been introduced into our methods of instruction. His influence is now being felt in all our boys' and girls' schools. His advocacy of science-teaching has partially succeeded in revolutionizing our system of education from the elementary school to the University. What remains to be done can best be done by giving effect to the views expressed in his four articles, which appeared in the Westminster Review in the years 1854–9. If our scientists, philosophers, and educationists unite, a Spencer Society may be formed, which may do honour to the author of 'First Principles', and may perpetuate his influence. I believe there are many who, like myself, would be glad to assist in the formation of such a Society.

(In Hughes, 1890: p. 45)

Constance Naden was hooked on the idea and, with the co-operation of Magnus, sought to establish such a society in London.[18] Shortly before her death in 1889 intervened, she gave an address to the Sociological Section in Birmingham which advocated 'the new science of Sociology', defined the nature and scope of its aims and objects, gave some account of 'the various complicated factors which regulate its inter-dependence and progress, together with comparative illustrations from primitive and other races', and which concluded: 'A society like ours ought to find its ideal in that possible future social type which, in Mr. Spencer's words, will use the products of industry neither for maintaining a militant organization, nor exclusively for material aggrandisement, but will devote them to the carrying on of higher activities, – a type which, instead of believing that "life is for work", will hold the inverse belief that "work is for life" ' (Hughes, 1890: pp. 53–4).[19] Spirits lifted and strength renewed, Spencer abandoned boarding-house life and, following his summer break in the Wiltshire countryside near Pewsey, occupied a permanent residence of his own in London. To Tyndall he reported: 'I have taken a house in St. John's Wood, and am going to have three maiden ladies to take care of me!' (in Duncan, 1911: p. 289).

It was not the Spencer of the philosophy of evolution but of his essays on politics written in the 1850s and 60s and then *The Man versus The State* that appealed deeply to the former Liberal MP, Auberon Herbert, who in 1890 founded and edited a new libertarian paper *Free Life* which survived until 1901 and to which Spencer subscribed. Auberon Edward William Molyneaux Herbert, third son of the third Earl of Carnarvon, spent most of his early childhood at the family estate at Highclere. He went to St. John's College, Oxford in 1855. Here his 'social qualities' and delight in sports outstripped, according to Mansel, his devotion to studies. Later he became a Lecturer in History at his college. He resigned his Fellowship in December, 1869, giving as a reason his distaste for the restricted competition under which he himself had been appointed – college funds should be available to support wider access to university education. He developed a career in politics, and in November 1868, with Goldwin Smith's support (at Oxford, Smith had influenced him towards liberal thought), he stood unsuccessfully as a Liberal for Berkshire. A by-election at Nottingham in February, 1870, where he was supported by the radical, A. J. Mundella, saw him elected to parliament. However, by the end of 1872, he was disillusioned with party politics, with the Liberals divided over the merits of legislation designed directly to promote social advance. He left parliament on the dissolution in 1874. In the same year, he met Herbert Spencer at the Athenaeum: the conversation led to a profound and permanent distrust of the 'great law-making machine'. Later he recreated this epiphany:

> I have often laughed and said that, as far as I myself was concerned he spoilt my political life. I went into the House of Commons, as a young man, believing that we might do much for the people by a bolder and more unsparing use of the powers that belonged to the great law-making machine; and, great as it then seemed to me, were those still unexhausted resources of united national action on behalf of the common welfare. It was at that moment that I had the privilege of meeting Mr. Spencer, and the talk which we had – a talk that will always remain very memorable to me – set me busily to work to study his writings. As I read and thought over what he taught, a new window was opened in my mind. I lost my faith in the great machine; I saw that thinking and acting for others had always hindered not helped the real progress; that all forms of compulsion deadened the living forces in a nation; that every evil violently stamped out still persisted, almost always in a worse form, when driven out of sight, and festered under the surface. I began to see that we were only playing with an imaginary magician's wand; that the ambitious work we were trying to do lay far out of the reach of our hands, far, far above the small measure of our strength. It was a work that could only be done in one way – not by gifts and doles of public money, not by making that most corrupting and demoralizing of all things, a common purse; not by restraints and compulsions of each other; not by seeking to move in a mass, obedient to the strongest forces of the moment, but by acting through the living energies of the free individuals left free to combine in their own way, in their own groups, finding their own experience, setting before themselves their own hopes and desires, aiming only at such ends as they truly shared in common, and ever as the foundation of it all, respecting deeply and religiously alike their own freedom, and the freedom of all others.
>
> (Herbert, 1908: pp. 5–7)

In 1882, Herbert commenced the essays which became *A Politician in Trouble About His Soul*, praised by Spencer (Hutchinson Harris, 1943, p. 250). He established a Party of Individual Liberty to galvanize popular support for voluntary co-operation and 'justice' as interpreted by Spencer, and wrote articles for the *Newcastle Weekly Chronicle*, which formed his *The Right and Wrong of Compulsion by the State* of 1885.[20] Both Herbert and Spencer contributed to *A Plea for Liberty* of 1891 (edited by Thomas Mackay), a publication associated with the Liberty and Property Defence League (Spencer contributed the Introduction entitled 'From Freedom to Bondage'[21]). Early in 1890 Spencer reminded the League that while he was 'quite willing' to give financial aid he did not wish that aid to be 'publicly interpreted into membership of the League' (in Duncan, 1911: p. 299).

While Herbert acknowledged Mill's *On Liberty* as setting out a moral case for freedom, he believed that Spencer had provided a more comprehensive, compelling and robust justification for it as the *sine qua non* for the advance of social, political and moral life. In his *A Politician in Trouble About His Soul* (1884) 'Markham' is mostly a mouthpiece for Spencer's ideas. Government should defend individuals from rather than subject them to force and coercion. Variety and competition are the conditions of advance and necessitate liberty. Infringements tend towards uniformity and hinder advance. Majorities possess no rights over individuals. However, Herbert also advocated voluntary taxation, recognized as a step too far by Spencer, and they disagreed too over common ownership of the land. John Morley also shied away from aspects of Herbert's Individualist attack on state paternalism: 'I would not touch (in the way of repeal) a bit of the factory legislation' (in Hutchinson Harris, 1943: p. 223).

Herbert characterized his Individualist position as 'voluntaryist': in a free world there could be 'voluntary socialism', entered into freely as representing the interests of those concerned. 'Force socialism' was entirely different: it trampled individual freedom. The life of a nation could not be engineered or manufactured by parliament; it could only be moved by action arising from 'the living energies of free individuals', uniting as *they* chose, aiming at the ends that they *themselves* shared, and respecting the freedom of all others. This indeed was the central message of his Herbert Spencer Lecture in 1906 and *The Voluntaryist Creed*, which contained the Lecture, posthumously published in 1908.

The launch of the paper *Free Life*, founded to propagate radical and conservative ideas in the true sense, provided an occasion for Herbert to identify the substantive positions associated with voluntaryism. It was opposed to hereditary privilege, religious establishments, artificial regulations tending to monopoly in land, attacks on property, bureaucracy, and a centralized system of compulsory education. It deprecated enslaving education to examinations, making them master, not servant, and jeopardizing the independence of student and teacher. It also criticized growing taxation and sought to popularize instead the idea of voluntary national subscriptions. It praised efforts by labourers to improve their condition by voluntary methods alongside of opposition to state socialism and its imitations. In a nutshell, the aim was to make the country 'the freest, the most tolerant, the most enterprising, and, economically, the cheapest country a man can live in' (in Hutchinson Harris, 1943: p. 302). The delusions of governments too were to be exposed: in 1893, the *Nineteenth Century* published his 'A Cabinet Minister's *Vade-mecum*', a lampoon on the dynamics of parliamentary party politics. Herbert's voluntaryism was sometimes construed as anarchism, to which he demurred. The following year the *Contemporary Review* published his 'The Ethics of Dynamite', critical of anarchist violence, to clear the air.

In 1890, Spencer made clear to Herbert that he dissented from Home Rule for Ireland: 'To dissolve unions because they were inequitably formed I hold, now that they have been formed, to be a mistake – a retrograde step. Were it possible to go back upon the past and undo all the bad things that have been done, society would forthwith dissolve'. He was also more pessimistic about the possibility of achieving change in the short term in a libertarian direction, stressing the 'organic badness of existing human nature' and the resulting badness of any society organized out of it, and again discouraged Herbert from expressing his views on voluntary taxation, which would be regarded as impracticable and discredit the wider position (in Duncan, 1911: p. 301). In Spencer's own 'From Freedom to Bondage' one feature to be noted, familiar from later relative deprivation theory, is that, even as actual circumstances improve, the remaining difficulties may increase in the intensity by which they are felt: 'the more things improve the louder become the exclamations about their badness' (1891a: p. 445). For Spencer the growth of socialism is a major concern; from the perspective of social evolution ('force'), socialism does not bring the benefits its advocates anticipate.

In the autumn of 1889 through into 1890, there was a controversy initially in *The Times* and then the *Daily Telegraph* which had originated in the belief that Spencer still advocated land nationalization as he had in *Social Statics* in 1851. Both Huxley and Spencer were drawn in. Huxley's scorn towards Spencer's present position that considerations of 'absolute political ethics' could not be acted upon in circumstances that were short of ideal, and other criticisms, struck Spencer as instances of misrepresentation, and betrayal by a friend. Spencer withdrew from the X Club, sensing his friends, Tyndall excepted, perhaps did not appreciate how ill-used he believed he had been by Huxley. The rift was only healed in 1893.

In 1891, Spencer became concerned over the Society for the Prevention of Cruelty to Children, whose actions he feared would undermine rather than enforce parental responsibilities (or 'saddle these responsibilities on the community' [in Duncan, 1911: p. 304]). Discussion of the issues involved occupied both the *Pall Mall Gazette* and the Charity Organisation Society's *Charity Organisation Review*. For Spencer, the overarching point to be kept in mind by reformers is the danger of degradation when 'people are led to abrogate the order of Nature and to substitute an order of their own devising'. However, provided these dangers are kept in mind, then, although the children of 'bad parents' might well themselves be 'bad', and although by intervention 'there is some interference with the survival of the fittest, yet it is a defensible conclusion that in the social state, philanthropic feelings may, to this extent mitigate the rigour of natural law' (1891b: p. 3). Later in the same year,[22] in August, Spencer thought that the formation of 'The London Ratepayers' Defence League' would enhance the prospects for 'justice' among individuals.[23] For Spencer, though, the significant event of 1891 was the appearance of 'Justice', the fourth Part of the *Principles of Ethics* (the second and third Parts were still to be written). Spencer regarded 'Justice' as a revised and mature exposition of the systematic parts of *Social Statics*; a new edition of that book would now render it in a sense 'residual', containing ideas he still held and which were not more appropriately placed in 'Justice'.

In 1892, Spencer's concerns oscillated between the fine textured and the grand sweep. He rejected an overture to support a charter for the Royal British Nurses Association from Thomas Buzzard, neurologist and associate of Hughlings Jackson. Spencer feared the outcome would be regulation which prevented nursing practice without a certificate, an interference with liberty and a step which while it might ensure 'a due amount of technical knowledge... cannot secure sympathy and cannot secure unwearying attention' (in Duncan, 1911: p. 315). But the summer saw the first volume of the *Ethics* issued, with 'The Inductions of Ethics' and 'The Ethics of Individual Life' now completed and united with 'The Data of Ethics'. The 'abridged and revised' version of *Social Statics*, coupled to *The Man versus The State*, also appeared in 1892. As the description of the new edition implies, the two editions of *Social Statics* always need to be differentiated in assessments of the development of Spencer's ideas. In 1890, as already noted, he had argued to Herbert that to approve of Home Rule in Ireland would be to sanction the dismemberment of all societies since at some point they had all been formed inequitably. Now, however, he changed his tack. In a letter to the Earl of Dysart, a supporter of Home Rule, he produced a less abstract and more sociological argument against it: the goodness of governmental systems and institutions 'is purely relative to the natures of the men living under them' (in Duncan, 1911: p. 315), the implication being that Ireland was not yet ready for self-government. The libertarian Wordsworth Donisthorpe had published his *Individualism: a System of Politics* in 1889, broadly in tune with Spencer's conception of social life developing in line with the laws of evolution. A projected home-grown scheme involving Spencer and Donisthorpe to catalogue past legislation, its aims, effects and reasons for repeal, designed to underline the futility of the 'law-making machine', was not completed, though Spencer still regarded it as important in 1894 (Duncan, 1911: pp. 316, 360).[24]

Since 1890, Spencer had been in contact with Count Ito (who served four periods as Japan's Prime Minister between 1885 and 1901) and Kentaro Kaneko who had studied Spencer while engaged in revising the Japanese constitution. Spencer's own advice on the constitution when asked was conservative, anxious in case a hasty imposition of liberal and democratic structures on to a people conditioned to living under despotism would fail. Continuity could be preserved by working with existing structures to modify them, and by following the maxim *'keep other races at arm's length as much as possible'* (in Duncan, 1911: p. 323).[25] Spencer's idea of adaptation and social progress (in *Social Statics* in particular) could be drawn on by both sides of the popular rights movement (as it could by liberals and conservatives in Britain and America), since it championed 'justice', but frowned on other governmental action, and his organismic conception of 'society' permitted Japanese thinkers to 'produce new interpretations of Japan's past, present and future', and thus new ideas of political agency and development (Howland, 2000: p. 68).

In terms of Spencer's intellectual output, the main event of 1893 was the publication of the second volume of the *Principles of Ethics*. In addition to 'Justice' there were now Parts on 'Negative Beneficence' and 'Positive Beneficence', the first dealing with the exercise of voluntary and altruistic restraint on insisting on one's rights and the second with exceeding voluntarily and altruistically what 'justice' might indicate is required in conduct. However, other matters still swirled around Spencer and he dutifully tried to respond to them. On reading Horace Seal's *The Nature of State Interference*, Spencer emphasized to the author that the 'tacit assumption that Individualism means the solitary life of the individual is an entire misapprehension. It may and does go along with an elaborate form of mutual dependence' (in Duncan, 1911: p. 354). Youmans's death had compromised Spencer's ability to keep track of his impact on America. He had come to lean on James Skilton, Secretary of the Brooklyn Ethical Association, as someone who could protect his standing there, along with surviving members of the Youmans family. Skilton had published *The Evolution of Society* in 1889. One important intellectual challenge at home was posed by Huxley's 1893 Romanes Lecture on 'Evolution and Ethics'. In this Lecture, Huxley had again stirred the pot, and further irritated his huffy and disaffected friend. On June 29, he wrote to Skilton:

I am glad to hear that you think of taking up Huxley's 'Evolution and Ethics', ... Practically his view is a surrender of the general doctrine of evolution in so far as its higher applications are concerned, and is pervaded by the ridiculous assumption that, in its application to the organic world, it is limited to the struggle for existence among individuals under its ferocious aspects, and has nothing to do with the development of social organization, or the modifications of the human mind that take place in the course of that organization.... The position he takes, that we have to struggle against or correct the cosmic process, involves the assumption that there exists something in us which is not a product of the cosmic process and is practically a going back to the old theological notions, which put Man and Nature in antithesis. Any rational, comprehensive view of evolution involves that, in the course of social evolution, the human mind is disciplined into that form which itself puts a check upon that part of the cosmic process which consists in the unqualified struggle for existence.

(In Duncan, 1911: p. 336)

The difficulties raised by this response will be examined at a later stage. Eventually though, perhaps against the odds, their estrangement came to an end in the autumn of 1893. Yet the topic of land nationalization, one of the issues originally causing the rupture, was already taking on a new life. In his *A Perplexed Philosopher* Henry George took Spencer's change in his position since *Social Statics* as a betrayal reflecting venal interests, by which Spencer was affronted. As to the logic of the position, he maintained that the right of the community to the land remained his position, but that the cost of compensation to the value given to it by the labour of previous occupiers (and compensation in the face of nationalization was demanded by equity) would, he now calculated, leave the community at a loss. Guided by Spencer, Skilton and W. J. Youmans largely fielded the issues on his behalf in America.

Another important controversy, running from 1890 until 1895, and to a lesser degree beyond, involved the challenge to the mechanism of the inheritance of acquired characteristics, almost a presupposition for Spencer, posed by the work of August Weismann on 'germ plasm' and heredity. Spencer participated in an exchange of views in *Nature* in 1890, and then, having written to Norman Lockyer at *Nature* concerned that his position encountered a negative editorial bias, moved the exchange to the pages of the *Contemporary Review*, contributing himself between 1893 and 1895. To Sir Edward Fry, who had communicated to Spencer that his own work on mosses and the various ways in which they are reproduced yielded a strong argument against Weismann, Spencer wrote in June, 1893: 'The hypothesis of a "germ-plasm", as distinguished from the general protoplasm, seems to me a pure fiction, utterly superfluous, and utterly discountenanced by the facts; and the phenomena presented by the mosses are among those showing in the clearest way that there is but one plasm...' (in Duncan, 1911: p. 348). Fry was a judge who had taken an early interest in zoology, winning the London matriculation prize in zoology ahead of Flower in 1849. As well as Fry, Marcus Hartog, (Professor of Natural History at Queen's College, Cork), Burden Sanderson (a pathologist and physiologist, earlier consulted by Darwin on evidence of electrical currents in plants, and now Regius Professor of Medicine at Oxford) and David Sharp (a leading entomologist who knew Spencer from when Spencer had stayed in his father's house in the late 1850s) expressed sympathy with Spencer's arguments. His contributions were brave, but rather against the drift of biological opinion. In Peel's view his defence of the inheritance of acquired characteristics was, 'a serious piece of biology', adding though that it was 'as much required by his conception of sociology as it was a contribution to a debate in biology' (1971: p. 146).

In December, 1893, the death of Tyndall was followed 18 months later by the death of Huxley. In many respects the three had for 40 years worked on complementary pursuits; for Spencer their loss was a serious wrench. Still he was grinding on towards the completion of the *Sociology*. Before that business was concluded, instances of irreverence towards the 'Synthetic Philosophy' from others still merited the time for a rebuke. Henry Drummond's *The Ascent of Man* of 1894 was a case in point. Drummond was claiming for himself the accolade of revealing the importance of altruism in social life, which Spencer had indeed long insisted upon, yet transforming it into something akin to unbounded Love. Drummond, Spencer wrote on June 6, had set out 'with the airs of a discoverer and with a tone of supreme authority', to instruct Spencer himself, and other evolutionists, 'respecting the factor of social evolution which we have ignored – altruism' (in Duncan, 1911: p. 363). Spencer felt it unwise to respond to this travesty himself, and alighted on Eliza Lynn Linton as a proxy: 'With your vigorous style and picturesque way of presenting things, you would do it in an interesting and effective way, at the same time that you would be able to illustrate and enforce the doctrine itself' (in Duncan, 1911: p. 363). The writer obliged, with a coruscating 'Professor Drummond's discovery' in the *Fortnightly Review*. Its finale took no prisoners: 'He strips science of her divinity and sends her out as a cottage-maid, or rather as a young priest, of whom no one need be afraid. But he lets slip truth in this endeavour to extract milk for babes out of the meat for men; and his rendering of synthetic philosophy is both inadequate and shallow. Whatever is true is borrowed; whatever is false, strained and inconclusive, is his own. His sin is the sin of plagiarism, with the additional offence of distortion in the lifting' (1894: p. 457). Spencer had reminded Donisthorpe that in his own writing he could refer to Spencer's doctrine enunciated long ago of the State's responsibility to administer 'justice' gratuitously, and exhorted him to 'deal with Mr. Sidney Webb' on the 'beneficial achievements' of the London County Council (in Duncan, 1911: pp. 360–1).[26] Spencer himself upbraided Lester Ward over the claim that, in Ward's essay on the place of sociology in the sciences, Spencer had followed *Comte's* scheme of classification in his arrangement of the sciences in the 'Synthetic Philosophy' (in Duncan, 1911: pp. 376–7).[27]

Perhaps even to Spencer's own surprize the final hurdle of the third volume of the *Principles of Sociology* was at last cleared, and the 10 volumes of the 'System of Synthetic Philosophy', inaugurated by *First Principles* 34 years earlier, thereby concluded. Walter Troughton, Spencer's Secretary, recorded the red-letter day with due decorum:

> Mr. Spencer was seventy-six years of age when he dictated to me the last words of 'Industrial Institutions', with the completion of which the Synthetic Philosophy was finished – to be precise it was on the 13 August, 1896. Rising slowly from his seat in the study at 64, Avenue Road, his face beaming with joy, he extended his hand across the table, and we shook hands on the auspicious event. 'I have finished the task I have lived for' was all he said, and then resumed his seat. The elation was only momentary and his features quickly resumed their customary composure.
>
> (In Duncan, 1911, p. 380)

Given that sociology was becoming established in France and Germany, it is perhaps a little surprizing that in this final volume Spencer showed no sign of awareness of the work of Durkheim or Tönnies. Tönnies, half Spencer's age, and with *Gemeinschaft und Gesellschaft* just recently completed, had sent copies of some of his work to Spencer, but if Spencer was aware of its content no use was made of it. Of three surviving private communications from Spencer to Tönnies which survive the least peremptory was written by his secretary: 'He regrets that his ignorance of German prevents him from profiting by a perusal of your article, which, even did he understand German, he would be disabled from doing by his state of health'.[28]

With the 'System' known to be complete, Hooker communicated a letter of congratulation to Spencer on December 16. There were 82 signatories, drawn almost exclusively from within England and Scotland, with an additional appended approval from Gladstone. The letter registered that 'we are all at one in our estimate of the great intellectual powers it exhibits and of the immense effect it has produced in the history of thought; nor are we less impressed by the high moral qualities which have enabled you to concentrate those powers for so many years upon a purpose worthy of them...' Then the wish was expressed to Spencer that the signatories should employ an artist to provide a portrait, to be deposited in a national collection (in Duncan, 1911: pp. 383–5).[29] The distinguished names came mostly from the fields of politics, philosophy, psychology, the sciences, and medicine. There was Hubert Parry too, as Principal of the Royal College of Music, and Beatrice Webb. The letter of congratulation to Spencer openly acknowledged that not all who signed agreed 'in equal measure' with the conclusions of the 'System'. Some idea of the flexibility this phraseology permitted comes with the case of the Idealist philosopher Bernard Bosanquet. Bosanquet signed the letter, yet only a year earlier he had written of Spencer that 'a Dante of philosophers ought to grant him the distinction of the lowest circle in the inferno' (1895: p. 57). Less combatively, Bosanquet's review of Thomas

Mackay's *The English Poor* (Mackay was the editor of *A Plea for Liberty* to which Spencer had contributed and was a Spencerian Individualist) had noted that 'the inheritance of acquired instincts on which the author rests a good deal of his case was always exaggerated by Mr. Spencer, and seems likely now to topple over altogether' (Bosanquet 1889: p. 465).

The portrait was painted by Hubert von Herkomer and completed early in 1898. It was prepared from photographs without a sitting; the artist and Spencer apparently failed to find mutually convenient times for sittings. Spencer's approval was qualified; he expressed reservations to Herkomer over the appearance of his nose and a 'bulkiness of body' (in Duncan, 1911: p. 302).[30] While the completion of the 'System' did not signal retirement, Spencer did decide that he no longer benefitted from his London base in Avenue Road and his spinster household. Two of the women involved subsequently wrote up with some affection, and probably some invention, their impressions of the experience as 'Two'.[31]

Brighton suited him, and early in 1898 he moved into 5, Percival Terrace in the town. His secretary, Walter Troughton, noted among his visitors the novelist William Black and his wife, familiar as was Spencer with the Sound of Mull and who now lived nearby in Brighton (Black died at the end of 1898),[32] Anne Ritchie, Thackery's elder surviving daughter and a writer herself, and, perhaps motoring down from London in his Daimler, the distinguished urologist, and epicurean, Sir Henry Thompson, also instrumental in founding the crematorium at Golders Green opened in 1902 (1938: p. 200). The completion of the 'System' did not presage a hiatus in intellectual activity. Before the *Sociology* was finished, he had already initiated the preparation of revisions to the *Biology* (finished in 1899), with further revisions then being made to *First Principles*. On completing the German version Victor Carus wrote that it had been 'a great very treat' to undertake this, against which Spencer noted that this was 'the highest compliment I ever received, considering Professor Carus's age and position' (in Duncan, 1911: pp. 420–1).[33] Two Postscripts related to Idealism were added to the *Psychology*. Two new collections of essays were also issued, entitled *Various Fragments* (1897, later enlarged), and *Facts and Comments* (1902). The 16, mostly short, essays of *Various Fragments* are typically rejoinders to critics, such as Cairnes and Huxley, not brought together in his collected *Essays*; the essays of *Facts and Comments* were in general more discursive and valedictory in nature. Several of the essays will be discussed further at later points as the particular aspects of Spencer's sociological thought are explored more closely. As a counterpoint to Spencer's work in revision and the collation of occasional pieces, his correspondence covers his reactions to contemporary events. It displays despair at signs of growing militancy, in the war between Spain and America in 1898, and then the Boer War, and an increasing and general pessimism over the prospects for social progress in the world. Everywhere there was evidence of 'barbarism', 'war fever' and 're-barbarization'. These sentiments are hammered home in a letter to Moncure D. Conway of 17 July 1898:

> Now that the white savages of Europe are overrunning the dark savages everywhere – now that the European nations are vying with one another in political burglaries – now that we have entered upon an era of social cannibalism in which the strong nations are devouring the weaker – now that national interests, national prestige, pluck, and so forth are alone thought of, and equity has utterly dropped out of thought, while rectitude is scorned as 'unctuous', it is useless to resist the wave of barbarism. There is a bad time coming, and civilized mankind will (morally) be uncivilized before civilization can again advance.
>
> (In Duncan, 1911: p. 410)

In 1897, the trustees of the newly established British Library of Political Science, connected with the London School of Economics, requested a gift of copies of his publications. In Spencer this triggered a response questioning 'free' provision in general and the political outlook underpinning the School's origins (associated with the Fabian socialism of Sidney and Beatrice Webb). Spencer could no more approve of Free Libraries than of 'Free Bakeries'; he was 'profoundly averse to socialism in every form' and schemes for public instruction were socialistic. From the prospectus he inferred that the institution 'will be used by those who have in view the extension of State agencies. Alike from what I know of its inception and from what I now see of it, I am convinced that it will be an appliance not for the diffusion of political *science* but for the diffusion of political *quackery*' (in Duncan, 1911: p. 403). Spencer also responded to W. H. Mallock's *Aristocracy and Evolution* of 1898. Spencer insisted that his view of the members of a society was that they were not 'equal' in talents, contrary to the manner in which Mallock was representing his position (Duncan, 1911: pp. 407–8).

As the end of the century neared, Spencer was striking up a late friendship with the traveller, poet and libertarian, Wilfrid Scawen Blunt. Spencer suggested a poem exploring Satan's horror at the scale of the hypocrisy in the pagan lives lived by professed Christians: Blunt's response was 'Satan Absolved'. The two men lived in Sussex and subsequently corresponded in a codgerly manner. Spencer detested the conduct of the Boer War: on 5 September 1901, he exclaimed 'When is this dreadful state of things to end? I hope there may come a severe financial crisis, for nothing but the endangering of their personal interests will open the eyes of the war party'. A month later, Spencer imagines Blunt will share his satisfaction that affairs look black for government: 'A little pressure on the money market, a bank failure or two, and a consequent panic may open people's eyes and make them repent. However heavy the penalty they may have to bear, it cannot be too heavy to please me'. And, despite his quarrel with Frederic Harrison over the *Religion* volume, Spencer was at pains to sing his praises to Blunt in

October, 1899, as 'a cultured and acute critic'.[34] The guard of the branch-line train rolling through the South Downs from Southwater was so frequently entrusted with pheasant and partridge, the bounty of Blunt's land, that Spencer could scarcely match each gift with an original turn of phrase in thanking his benefactor. They had acquaintances in common, and Blunt visited Spencer at least twice, in March, 1899 and again in August, 1903, recording his impressions in his diaries. In 1899, he found Spencer 'lying on a sofa in a dressing gown, with slippers on of an ornamental feminine kind. He began by talking for ten minutes about his health ... then he got round to the subject of my visit, the militarisms and brutalities of the day, the idealization of Napoleon and other war-making scoundrels who had long been condemned as such, with the rewriting of history to suit the aggressive ideas now in fashion' (Blunt, 1932: p. 317). As the day's visit wore on Blunt came to reflect:

> On the whole I am rather disappointed with Spencer. He is so very dry, and so much wrapped up in himself, his ailments, his work and his ideas, to the exclusion, it seems to me, of individual sympathies. His mind is clear and logical, he expresses himself well, but without eloquence or such power as compels attention; not once was I able to feel myself in the presence of a great man, only of a well-informed one, a pedagogue and able reasoner. There was nothing in him of the softening character which old age so often gives, and which is so touching. Still I am glad to have spent this day with him, for his is one of the great names of our time, and his work has been great.
>
> (1932: p. 318)

Although living in Brighton, Spencer still spent the summer months in other places, between 1900 and 1902 he found country retreats not very far away elsewhere in Sussex (near Midhurst) or in Surrey. The preparation of the new essays for *Facts and Comments* was ticking over at a mere 'ten lines a day', so he told Bain in April (in Duncan, 1911: p. 457). The new and final book contained critiques of public health bureaucracy, state education schemes, and routinized gymnastics. Re-barbarization is seldom far away as a concern, and is even detected in the foundation of the Salvation *Army*. Less expected, perhaps are diverse musings on the value of euthanasia, on how the composition of music may evolve, and the disappearance of hedges and roadside flowers in Sussex. Spencer was also again exercised by what he perceived as a resurgence of idealism in philosophy. The specialist journal, *Mind*, he judged to have become an organ for this philosophical approach; he therefore ceased to subscribe. To his old friend Professor David Masson he wrote: 'I suppose Hegelianism is rife in Edinburgh as it is in Oxford and Cambridge. This is one of those inevitable rhythms which pervade opinion, philosophical and other, in common with things at large. But our Hegelianism, or German

Idealism in England, is really the last refuge of the so-called orthodox. As I have somewhere said, what could be a better defence for incredible dogmas than behind unthinkable propositions' (in Duncan, 1911: pp. 457–8). By the summer of 1902, however, Troughton, his secretary, saw unmistakeable signs that he was 'breaking up, physically, certainly, and also mentally; but the decay of mental faculty was less marked than the bodily decrepitude, which seemed now to be advancing with rapid strides' (in Duncan, 1911: p. 465). He was housebound for most of the winter, although watchfully monitoring his nurses and doctor, and still able to make his position about individual equality unambiguous in a letter to W. H. Hudson of 7 January 1903. Hudson had written a book on Rousseau which he proposed to dedicate to Spencer. However, Spencer wanted no confusion by association between his and Rousseau's different conceptions of what it meant to be equally free. Perhaps his experience with Mallock was still in his mind. In *Social Statics* (and elsewhere), wrote Spencer, the equality alleged 'is not among men themselves, but among their claims to equally-limited spheres for the exercise of their faculties: an utterly different proposition. Huxley confused the two and spread the confusion, and I am anxious that it should not be further spread' (in Duncan, 1911: p. 466). In May, 1903, though, aphasia accompanied by hallucinations became apparent (Duncan, 1911: p. 469). Charlton Bastian was called in, as a neurologist specializing in forms of speech loss and their relationship to cerebral disease, although he was also a friend of Spencer and an evolutionist in his mould.

Blunt's visit in August found Spencer very much weaker than on his first visit as he made a limited recovery. Differences between religious faiths were mulled over. The person who probably gained most from the visit was Mohammed Abdu, by whom Blunt was accompanied, since he had an ambition to meet Spencer and had translated his *Education* into Arabic. A more frequent visitor now was Beatrice Webb. On July 3, she noted:

> Melancholy letter from H. S. Ran down to see him. Again repeated that he and we agreed in essentials, differed only in form. Was extremely sensitive as to his reputation and influence, felt that he had dropped out and was no longer of much consideration. 'What you have thought and taught has become part of our mental atmosphere, Mr. Spencer', I said soothingly. 'And like the atmosphere we are not aware of it. When you cease to be our atmosphere, then we shall again become aware of you as a personality'. 'That is a pleasant way of putting it', and he smiled. I tried to suggest that he should give up the struggle against ill fate and accept the rest of his existence. 'Why should I be resigned?' he retorted almost angrily. 'I have nothing to hope for in return for resignation. I look forward merely to extinction – that is a mere negative. No', he added with intense depression, 'I have simply to vegetate between this and death, to suffer as little as I need, and, for that reason, I must not talk to you any

more: it prevents me sleeping and upsets my digestion. Good-bye – come and see me again'.

It is tragic to look at the whole of man's life as a bargain in which man gets perpetually the worst of it. But the notion of contract – a *quid pro quo* – is so ingrained in the poor old man that even illness and death seem a nasty fraud perpetuated by nature.

An arrangement preceding her marriage to Sidney Webb that Beatrice would act as Spencer's literary executor had already, by mutual agreement, been allowed to lapse, although she would, as Spencer wished, give her assistance to David Duncan in preparing a biography.

During November, Spencer's decline accelerated. On 7 December, he was at best semi-conscious until the evening, when he became unconscious and remained so until he died at 4.40 on the morning of Tuesday 8 December. Spencer had left thorough instructions for the disposal of the body. Thus on the morning of 14 December his remains were removed from his home, accompanied by the Mayor of the town, to Brighton station to be conveyed by the 8.45 train to Victoria. From there a plain closed hearse bore the body through London on to Golders Green Crematorium.[35] John Morley was out of the country and so unable to speak as he had agreed: Leonard Courtney, the prominent Liberal married to Kate Potter, took Morley's place. In accord with an announcement made at the cremation, Mr. Shyamaji Krishnavarma presented £1000 to found a Herbert Spencer Lectureship at the University of Oxford.[36] Later in the day the ashes were conveyed to Highgate Cemetery and placed in the sarcophagus prepared some time earlier.

Spencer's death was an occasion for reflection on his significance in science and social, political and moral thought around the world. On 9 December, *The Times* noted the depth of the impact of his death felt in New York and Paris, and similar reports were carried the next day from Budapest and Montevideo. It pondered whether the scale of his contribution to thought made him a nobler figure than Spinoza or Descartes, and indeed took the theme of comparisons further: 'By those who realized the vastness of his conceptions, he has been compared to Aristotle, sometimes also to Hegel, sometimes to Comte; and certainly there is more than a superficial likeness between him and the first of these thinkers in the range and amplitude of their investigation, in the greatness of the unities which they detected in Nature'. Nevertheless, the paper had reservations about how he would be estimated in the future, though it did single out as an enduring strength his 'application of scientific conceptions to the study of the conditions of social welfare'.[37] In the *New York Times*, *Social Statics* was singled out as still enjoying 'a wide popularity', especially in America, and although in some respects the author's views had further matured, it could nevertheless be regarded 'as the best text book of sound democratic political philosophy that has ever been published'.[38] *Mind*, by now the philosophers' trade journal, promised a full obituary though in the event does not appear to have printed one.

In 1904, a discreet campaign for a memorial in Westminster Abbey gathered momentum (see Gay, 1989). A letter to the Dean of 30 May accompanied by 59 appropriate signatures referred to 'the important and stimulating effect of Mr. Spencer's writings in the domains of Philosophy, Science and Education' (in Duncan, 1911: pp. 483–6). The decision to decline was made in 17 days. The Dean, Joseph Armitage Robinson, stated the reasons to Professor Meldola (in Duncan, 1911: p. 487):

> I observe that the memorialists do not claim that Mr. Spencer has or will have a high place as a philosophical thinker. When I ask with what important achievement in philosophy or natural science, or with what permanent contribution to thought his name is destined to be connected, I meet with no satisfactory reply. His philosophical system has called forth the severest criticism, and his views in various branches of knowledge, physical as well as metaphysical, are severely challenged by experts. Eminent he was in his own generation, and stimulating in a high degree. But these characteristics, apart from the enduring quality of work, do not constitute the highest claim to a national homage which is now necessarily restricted to a very few; and I have failed to find evidence that the results which Mr. Spencer has achieved are such as are certain to command recognition in the future.

Gay's examination of the surviving correspondence between Meldola and those who might at least in principle have been expected to support the request is interesting. Some refused, such as Morley, who had been after all well-placed to intuit Spencer's wishes. Others were not included, such as Carnegie, even though he had given his approval. Alfred Wallace appears not to have been approached at all. Often the correspondents, whether in the end supportive or not of the proposal, seemed, Gay concluded, unfamiliar with his work, although accepting that he had been an important figure. By living until he was 83 years old, and thus into the new century, he had outlived the majority of those who had known him well, and his time of greatest fame. In addition, as Gay stresses, the social organization of intellectual life had changed rapidly: 'professionalization within the sciences had left figures like Spencer in its wake'. By 1904, while it remained recognized that Spencer 'had exerted a great influence' in his pomp, 'only a few thought that Spencer's reputation would outlive him' (Gay, 1998: p. 53).

As a general comment on the view from university science and philosophy this is a fair conclusion to draw. At a broader cultural level though there is evidence that it is just too neat to marry his physical demise with that of his reputation. We need, for instance, a 'biography' of the posthumous career of his expression 'the survival of the fittest'. In its absence a couple of examples will have here to substitute. For the Fabian socialist, H. G. Wells, it was of his reputation outliving his demise that with a (partisan) reference to a decade later he wrote 'We but do emerge now from a period of deliberate happy-go-lucky and the influence of Herbert Spencer who came near raising public shiftlessness to the dignity of a national philosophy. Everything would adjust itself, if only it was left alone' (1914: p. 69). That acute student of social life, Arnold Bennett, spent a year working through *First Principles* before his 40th birthday, and, 40 years after the book's appearance, finished it on Good Friday, 1907, with no sense of anti-climax:

> I suppose I can never again have the same thrills of admiration as this book has given me. If any book could be called the greatest book in the world, I suppose this can. I have never read anything a tenth part so comprehensive. And it makes its effects by sheer honest argumentative force.... Faults there, of course, are in it but it is surely the greatest achievement of any human mind. This I do think. And Spencer has not yet come into his own, in England. As a *philosopher*, in the real sense – not as a discoverer, or a man of science – but as a philosopher, he is supreme in the history of intelligence. I say this, not because I have read all the other great ones, but because I cannot imagine the possibility of anyone having produced anything else as great as *First Principles*.
>
> (1971: p. 192)

Spencer's reputation as a contributor to social theory persists to this day, though there is little substantive consensus over the context of that reputation. Often, indeed, Spencer is demostrably misunderstood. I presume that few would disagree that biographical and contextual material on Spencer is essential to a faithful presentation of what he was trying to say about sociology and why. There is perhaps more here than might have been expected. Partly this is because many biographical essays attached to discussions of Spencer's sociology are so 'potted' as to be unreliably abbreviated or else in style unduly speculative. Mostly, though, it is because the way in which Spencer conceptualized sociology as related to psychology and biology, and to 'evolutionary' science in general, perforce propels a study of the Spencerian ambience into deeper waters than might be demanded by other figures in sociology's past. And then deeper still. For to understand Spencer on evolution the anchorage in deism and the turn away from Paley's natural theology with its presumption in favour of evidence for design has also to be considered. One must, therefore, go beyond the picture, as here, that Spencer painted of himself in his *Autobiography*. However, since that picture often provides plausible cautions against the interpretative *clichés* or wilder speculations which Spencer still seems to attract, it invites trouble to accord it only marginal status.

Nevertheless, we are still a long way short of the 'definitive intellectual biography we so badly need', as Peel, himself the author of an earlier important study of Spencer, has observed (2004: p. 145). Perhaps, by endeavouring to draw into this analysis some of the fruits of recent salient historical studies, of which there are gratifyingly many, it can at least be hoped that the cause has been helped, not hindered. However, the suggestion that our reading of Spencer should now be 'predominantly in the historicist mode' (Peel, 2004: p. 145), interpreted in the sense that Spencer has little of relevance with which to embellish contemporary sociology, seems regrettably myopic. Were there, however, to be ideas in Spencer of enduring value, or just value for us, it is improbable that they would be convincingly uncovered through an interpretative approach which had stripped away the meanings carried by them, derived from the wider structure and rationale of his thought.

4
Evolution and Mind

Spencer's general theory of evolution as set forth in *First Principles* is at the heart of his contribution to social thought, so that pushing it to the periphery distorts its whole morphology. One must therefore ignore Crane Brinton's often-quoted droll yet superficial aside that a full analysis of Spencer's system 'would be an intolerable infliction upon the reader' (1962: p. 188). Spencer provided a summary of his theory to accompany the publication of Collins's *Epitome of the Synthetic Philosophy* in 1889, and this summary provides a useful point of entry. I have further abridged the set of points which Spencer took to encapsulate the theory.

In the entire universe, in detail and generally, matter and motion are unceasingly redistributed. The redistribution constitutes evolution when there is a predominant integration of matter and dissipation of motion, and dissolution when the opposite occurs. Evolution is *simple* when integration, or the forming of a coherent aggregate, arises if the parts are in identical circumstances. Evolution is *compound* when other, secondary, changes ensue from the different circumstances of different parts of the aggregate. What was relatively homogeneous thus becomes relatively heterogeneous, a transformation found in the whole and in its inorganic and organic details (meaning each organism and the aggregate of organisms in geological time, and also mind, society and 'all products of social activity' (in Collins, 1889: p. ix)). Integration is combined with differentiation, and produces a heterogeneity which possesses an increasing relative definiteness. Redistribution of the matter making up an evolving aggregate is accompanied by a redistribution of its retained motion, itself becoming more definitely heterogeneous. The change that is evolution is inevitable, for Spencer argues that an original homogeneity is always relative, not absolute; any part on which a force falls subdivides and differentiates that force, creating a 'multiplication of effects', in which any one change leads to effects in a manner akin to the domino theory. Unlike units become separated and like units brought together, segregation thus arises. Equilibration is the final result for an evolving aggregate when the forces opposed to an aggregate are balanced by the forces it opposes to them. In inorganic bodies this is a state of rest; in organic bodies it is death. After rest is reached, or there is death, dissolution will set in, which is the counter-charge of unbalanced forces. Thus there is a 'rhythm of evolution and dissolution, completing itself during short periods in small aggregates and in the vast aggregates distributed through space completing itself in periods which are immeasurable by human thought' (in Collins, 1889: pp. x–xi). All of these phenomena result from 'the persistence of force' in its forms as matter and motion. Ultimately 'force' persists, is unchanging in quantity, but ever-changing in form, and 'transcends human knowledge and conception – is an unknown and unknowable power, which we are obliged to recognize as without limit in space and without beginning or end in time' (in Collins, 1889: p. xi).

Such, then, is Spencer's 'theory of evolution', which he condensed further into the famous definition given in *First Principles*. Although that definition has already been quoted, it will be convenient to give it again, in the form it took in the final edition of 1900: 'Evolution is an integration of matter and concomitant dissipation of motion; during which the matter passes from a relatively indefinite, incoherent homogeneity to a relatively definite, coherent heterogeneity; and during which the retained motion undergoes a parallel transformation' (1900: p. 367). As just implied, this definition of evolution must not be read as precluding the reverse antagonistic process of dissolution, for, as Spencer makes clear from the first edition of *First Principles* onwards: 'Just in the same way that a city, already multiform in its variously arranged structures of various architecture, may be made more multiform by an earthquake, which leaves part of it standing and overthrows other parts in different ways and degrees, and yet is at the same time reduced from definite arrangement to indefinite arrangement; so may organised bodies be made for a time more multiform by changes which are nevertheless disorganizing changes. And in the one case as in the other, it is the absence of definiteness which distinguishes the multiformity of regression from the multiformity of progression' (1862: pp. 178–9). In fact, Spencer exemplifies the implications of dissolution for social life in an explicit manner: When social ties, whether 'governmental or industrial', are destroyed, 'the combined actions of citizens lapse into uncombined actions. Those general forces which restrained individual doings, having disappeared, the only remaining restraints are those separately exercised by individuals on each other. There are no longer any of the joint operations by which men satisfy their wants; and, in so far as they can, they satisfy their wants by separate operations. That is to say, the movement of parts replaces the movement of wholes' (1862: p. 352).

The theory of evolution, embracing dissolution, thus specifies in formal terms the direction of change, and the physical forms to which all change conforms. The theory covers all phenomena, organic and inorganic, from the solar system to our cognitions. It is important to understand that Spencer is not advancing a simple linear idea of progressive change, followed by the change represented by dissolution: there is the rhythm of motion to consider in addition. For Spencer, 'rhythm is a necessary characteristic of all motion. Given the coexistence everywhere of antagonist forces... and rhythm is an inevitable corollary from the persistence of force'. It follows, then, that 'throughout that re-arrangement of parts which constitutes Evolution, we must nowhere expect to see the change from one position of things to another, effected by continuous movement in the same direction. Be it in that kind of Evolution which the inorganic creation presents, or in that presented by the organic creation, we shall everywhere find a periodicity of action and reaction – a backward and forward motion, of which progress is a differential result' (1862: p. 334).

The rhythm of motion is not a part of Spencer's theory to which much consideration is usually given. However, my view is that its neglect over the years has been reflected in overly simplified accounts of his theoretical approach to social life, so that Spencer's original message in this respect has become a palimpsest. Some sustained exposition of what he has in mind is probably the best remedial measure to adopt:

> A place at which some necessary of life is scarce, becomes a place to which currents of it are set up from other places where it is relatively abundant; and these currents from all sides lead to a wave of accumulation where they meet – a glut: whence follows a recoil – a partial return of the currents. But the undulatory character of these actions is perhaps best seen in the rises and falls of prices. These, given in numerical measures which may be tabulated and reduced to diagrams, show us in the clearest manner how commercial movements are compounded of oscillations of various magnitudes. The price of consols or the price of wheat, as thus represented, is seen to undergo vast ascents and descents whose highest and lowest points are reached only in the course of years. These largest waves of variation are broken by others extending over periods of perhaps many months. On these again come others having a week or two's duration. And were the changes marked in greater detail, we should have the smaller undulations that take place each day, and the still smaller ones which brokers telegraph from hour to hour. The whole outline would show a complication like that of a vast ocean-swell, on whose surface there rise large billows, which themselves bear waves of moderate size, covered by wavelets, that are roughened by a minute ripple. Similar diagrammatic representations of births, marriages, and deaths, of disease, of crime, of pauperism, exhibit involved conflicts of rhythmical motions throughout society under these several aspects.
>
> (1862: p. 331)

Spencer supplemented this outline of his fundamental perspective with a consideration of broader trends in societies within the perspective of undulating motion which encompassed religious observances, the valuation of rational thought, political ideologies, and national life in general:

> There are like characteristics in social changes of a more complex kind. Both in England and among continental nations, the action and reaction of political progress have come to be generally recognized. Religion, besides its occasional revivals of smaller magnitude, has its long periods of exaltation and depression – generations of belief and self-mortification, following generations of indifference and laxity. There are poetical epochs, and epochs in which the sense of the beautiful seems almost dormant. Philosophy, after having been awhile predominant, lapses for a long season into neglect; and then again slowly revives. Each science has its eras of deductive reasoning, and its eras when attention is chiefly directed to collecting and colligating facts. And how in such minor but more obtrusive phenomena as those of fashion, there are ever going on oscillations from one extreme to the other, is a trite observation.

The adjustments represented by social rhythms which result from the combination of several or many causes render the historical record non-recurrent. To the extent that

> the variations are those of one simple element in national life, as the supply of a particular commodity, we do indeed witness a return, after many involved movements, to a previous condition – the price may become what it was before: implying a like relative abundance. But where the action is one into which many factors enter, there is never a recurrence of exactly the same state. A political reaction never brings round just the old form of things. The rationalism of the present day differs widely from the rationalism of the last century. And though fashion from time to time revives extinct types of dress, these always re-appear with decided modifications.
>
> (1862: pp. 331–2)

A further sign of 'rhythm' is the changing predominance of at one time 'militant' and another 'industrial' social relations in a society, with which a later chapter deals in some detail. Here, however Spencer's emphasis on the rhythm of motion in evolution helps us to see how he has made room for 'backward' and 'forward' motion going on simultaneously in a single society, and between different societies and races. Indeed it makes room for the relatively permanent regression and degeneration, and the cessation within some societies to progress beyond a certain state of sociality, that can all, he believes, be shown to have arisen. In his discussion of 'rhythm' Spencer usually (but not always, as will be seen in the discussion of T. E. Cliffe Leslie later in this chapter) stops short of declaring that it shows the hallmarks of 'dissolution', which is, presumably, a larger process (the criteria for distinguishing between 'dissolution' and the perturbations associated with the rhythm of motion are not stated with adequate precision by Spencer). William Henry Hudson, who was Spencer's secretary from 1885 to 1888, later published a study of Spencer which allocated to the 'rhythm of motion' the kind of significance intended by Spencer: 'It is a common error to suppose that evolution is continuous and uninterrupted – that its course may be symbolised in a straight line. A wavy line would, roughly speaking, be a more correct expression... [T]hroughout the whole universe motion is rhythmical or undulatory. This is true of all phenomena, from the minutest cognizable by science to the latest transformation of societies studied by the economist and the historian' (Hudson, 1897, quoted in Taylor, 1992: p. 80).

Spencer's theory of evolution thus specifies the fundamental dynamics operating at all levels of reality, while distinctive mechanisms of change relating to organic life, and in conformity with the dynamic principles, are thus, in a logical sense, secondary matters. The theory of evolution for Spencer is not *primarily* about the mechanisms of how specific changes originate in biological or social life. The contrast with Darwin here cannot be emphasized too strongly. However qualified, a sense of direction to change is inseparable from Spencer's idea of evolution. Cornered one day into responding to Spencerian 'evolution', Spencer's great personal friend, Richard Potter, a perceptive, and an eminently successful man in the world of business, fought back swiftly. Beatrice Potter recalled that her father

> had a genuine if somewhat pitying affection for the philosopher on the hearth... but argue with him or read his books he would not... Herbert Spencer's 'synthetic philosophy', whether it concerned the knowable or the unknowable, bored him past endurance; he saw no sense in it. When I tried to interest him in the 'law of increasing heterogeneity and definiteness of structure and function' at work – so the philosopher demonstrated – throughout the universe, my father answered in this wise: 'Words, my dear, mere words. Experience tells me that some businesses grow diverse and complicated, others get simpler and more uniform, others again go into the Bankruptcy Court. In the long run and over the whole field there is no more reason for expecting one process rather than the other. Spencer's intellect is like a machine racing along without raw material: it is wearing out his body. Poor Spencer, he lacks instinct, my dear, he lacks instinct'.
>
> (Webb, 1926: pp. 20–1)

Nevertheless it was *First Principles* that cemented Spencer's reputation as a serious thinker. It did so in a paradoxical manner. In providing an underpinning for and synthesis of scientific work it appealed to opponents of orthodox theological views. In its acceptance of an inscrutable 'unknowable' order beyond our knowledge, however, it appealed to searchers after a revelation of grounds for faith in, as they thought, the implication of a new sort of providence. Spencer clearly hoped for the first kind of response; the second may have been unexpected. What is not in doubt is that *First Principles* is the theoretical foundation of the primarily illustrative ensuing volumes making up the 'System', *Principles of Biology, Principles of Psychology* (second edition), *Principles of Sociology*, and *Principles of Ethics*. Spencer's publications before 1862, including *Social Statics*, are thus not 'evolutionary' in this strong sense, though there is an omnipresent commitment to progressive development as assured. Our earlier discussion of his essays in the 1850s, especially perhaps 'The Development Hypothesis', and 'Manners and Fashion', will have shown how with hindsight Spencer was collecting the elements for his massive synthetic science of evolution.[1]

In an important and highly regarded paper Derek Freeman rightly emphasized that a 'lumping together of the evolutionary theories of Spencer and Darwin is, in the light of the evidence, unwarranted, for the theories of Darwin and Spencer were unrelated in their origins, markedly disparate in their logical structures, and differed decisively in the degree to which they depended on the supposed mechanism of Lamarckian inheritance and recognized "progress" as "inevitable"' (1974: p. 9). To which it must be added that, in the *Autobiography*, Spencer made the unfounded claim that Darwin's demonstration of 'natural selection' had justified his own theory of organic evolution (1904, ii: p. 50). Darwin's idea of natural selection as a mechanism of species change was itself agnostic in relation to pivotal Spencerian hypotheses about such matters as heterogeneity and integration. Nevertheless the temporal conjunction of the work of the two men, leaving aside the important differences between the sets of ideas, both helped the reputation of each and also whipped up a huge swell against creationist accounts of order, and of change. John Dewey grasped this clearly in 1904, perceiving the paradoxical significance of their independence:

> Because Spencer's thought descended from the social and political philosophy of the eighteenth century, . . . and employed the conceptions thus derived to assimilate and organize the generalized conceptions of geology and biology, it needed no particular aid from the specialized order of scientific methods and considerations which control the work of Darwin. But it was a tremendous piece of luck for both the Darwinian and Spencerian theories that they happened so nearly to coincide in the time of their promulgation. Each got the benefit not merely of the disturbance and agitation aroused by the other, but of psychological and logical reinforcement, as each blended into and fused with the other in the minds of readers and students.
>
> (1904: p. 39)

As was explained earlier in this study, Spencer retrospectively identified some key stages in his progress to his theory of evolution. The first was his reading of Lyell's *Principles of Geology* in 1840, and his acceptance, contrary to Lyell, of Lamarck's mechanism of organic change which he described as 'progressive modifications, physically caused and inherited' (1904, i: p. 177). The second was the 'doctrine of individuation' as a feature of progress which had struck him while working on *Social Statics* and reading Coleridge's essay *Hints Towards The More Comprehensive Foundation of a Theory of Life*. The third came in 1851 with the expression 'the physiological division of labour', which he encountered in Milne-Edwards' *Outlines of Anatomy and Physiology*. The fourth arose in the same year from his reading of Carpenter's, *Principles of Physiology*, where he met with the embryologist Von Baer's description of individual development as a change from the homogeneous to the heterogeneous, an idea which Spencer saw no reason not to apply to change in general and elevate as the law of all progress. Also important to Spencer by 1857 was that the scientific world 'was becoming everywhere possessed by the general doctrine of the "Conservation of Force", as it was then called' – he cites in this connection the earlier publication of Sir William Grove's *The Correlation of Physical Forces* (1904, ii: p. 13). His essays of the 1850s explicitly worked this range of ideas through in diverse contexts, and the first edition of the *Principles of Psychology* did so comprehensively in relation to mental organization. Spencer himself noted that by 1857 the word 'evolution' was replacing 'progress' in what he was writing (1904, i: p. 503). Indeed it is strongly present in the abstract discussions of the original 'Manners and Fashion' of 1854.[2]

A glance at other sources likely to have been familiar to Spencer fleshes out this rather skeletal and perhaps insular later account of the genesis of his 'big idea' which he proffered. Chambers in the *Vestiges*, although retaining the 'divine mind', unlike Spencer, had already claimed change and progress, as evident throughout creation, from the bodies of space through geology and the vegetable and animal kingdoms to man.

> The system of nature assures us that benevolence is a leading principle in the divine mind. But that system is at the same time deficient in a means of making this benevolence of invariable operation. To reconcile this to the recognised character of the Deity, it is necessary to suppose that the present system is but a part of a whole, a stage in a Great Progress, and that the Redress is in reserve. Another argument here occurs – the economy of nature, beautifully arranged and vast in its extent as it is, does not satisfy even man's idea of what might be; he feels that, if this multiplicity of theatres for the exemplification of such phenomena as we see on earth were to go on for ever unchanged, it would not be worthy of the Being capable of creating it. An endless monotony of human generations, with their humble thinkings and doings, seems an object beneath that august

Being. But the mundane economy might be very well as a portion of some greater phenomenon, the rest of which has yet to be evolved.

(1844: p. 385)[3]

George Combe, in his *Moral Philosophy; or The Duties of Man Considered in his Individual, Domestic and Social Capacities* of 1840, took the study of brain and character by phrenological science as a basis for the correctly informed guidance of human conduct. Spencer's first adult literary efforts were in the field of phrenology, and he is likely to have had familiarity with this book's leading ideas. Indeed Combe,[4] like Spencer, had had close contact with Chapman, and Combe's earlier *The Constitution of Man and its Relations to External Objects* of 1828 had circulated widely, establishing him as a significant intellectual figure (Taylor, 2007: p. 33).[5] According to Combe, in *Moral Philosophy*,

man is obviously progressive in the evolution of his mental powers. The moral and intellectual faculties bear a far higher sway in the social life of Europe in the present day, than they did five hundred years ago; and the development of the brain also appears to improve with time, exercise, and the amelioration of social institutions. Wherever skulls several centuries old have been disinterred, they have presented moral and intellectual organs less in size in proportion to those of the propensities, than are found in the average skulls of the modern inhabitants of the same countries. It is certain also, that, in civilized nations in general, the moral and intellectual organs are larger, in proportion to the organs of the animal propensities, than they are in savages.

(1846: p. 57)

Moreover, Combe was confident about a forthcoming era of enlightenment, optimistic that to the degree man 'shall evolve a correct knowledge of the elements of external nature, and of his own constitution ... will his means of acting wisely, and advantageously for his own happiness, be augmented' (1846: p. 58). While Chambers and Combe complemented Spencer's emphasis on liberty, progress and the exercise of faculties in *Social Statics*, they also envisaged quite clearly the larger treatment of the laws of all nature, including social life, which Spencer attempted to deliver in detail in *First Principles*.

New thinking on the foundations of Christian faith and the nature of knowledge more generally also touched Spencer in the 1850s, helping to shape the content of *First Principles*. Yet amid the 'evolutions' in Spencer's own thought he never departed from either a commitment to science as the key to unlocking the workings of the world, or the belief that this commitment did not justify describing his position on psychic and social evolution as 'materialist'. That a better future for mankind could be the product of evolution was a view never abandoned, though it was placed under pressure late in his life. The prominent place at the beginning of the book accorded to the 'unknowable', to which in his analysis the questing intellect was ultimately driven back, rather than to Hume's scepticism, gave some sort of scope for post-Christian spiritual reflection. Nevertheless, that *First Principles* was read by many as a contribution to religious thought apparently took him by surprise. In the *Autobiography* he explained that the opening chapters were to avoid the charge that he held a 'purely materialistic interpretation of things'. He expected that his subsequent explanation, the doctrine of evolution, of the order of the phenomena as manifested to us in the universe would lead readers to understand that the Ultimate Mystery must be left unsolved: to Spencer it seemed 'that the essential part of the book... may be held without affirming any metaphysical or theological beliefs; and though, to avoid the ascription of certain beliefs of these classes which I do not hold, I thought it prudent to exclude them, I presumed that others, after noting the exclusion of them by the first division of the work, would turn their thoughts chiefly to the second division. Nothing of the kind happened. Such attention as was given was in nearly all cases given to the agnostic view which I set forth as a preliminary' (1904, ii: pp. 75–6). In a later reflection on the order adopted in the book he declared: 'An absurd misconception resulted. While this was simply an introduction intended to exclude misinterpretations, it was, by the few who paid any attention to the book, regarded as its substance. Having inspected the portico, they turned their backs on the building' (1899: p. 554).

While Spencer quite clearly did not teach that the search for the 'meaning of life' was illegitimate as a human concern, his work gave no discernible support to any of the conventional answers available. In the 1850s, in London, his imagination was stimulated by the latest sources in philosophical and spiritual reflection, as well as by his scientific friendships with Huxley and Tyndall. Tyndall in particular also shared Spencer's belief that behind what evolution and science generally could reveal was mystery and, perhaps, purpose. But Spencer's explicitly acknowledged sources in discussing the 'unknowable', also characterized as the 'Inscrutable Power', 'Unseen Reality' and 'Unknown Cause' (1862: pp. 108, 117, 123), were the intuitionalist philosophers Sir William Hamilton and Henry Mansel. Mansel at the time had delivered the Bampton Lectures at Oxford in 1858, his controversial *Limits of Religious Thought*. Mansel in particular claimed to have found a place for a personal God, beyond the limits of knowledge (which Spencer could not accept). Spencer absorbed from both the twin ideas of essentially psychological limits to our understanding and intuition in some form of the absolute beyond.[6] Spencer concluded from his labours on metaphysics that the existence of the external world was not to be doubted, and nor was the existence of the 'unknowable': 'At the same time that by the laws of thought we are rigorously prevented from forming a conception of

absolute existence; we are by the laws of thought equally prevented from ridding ourselves of the consciousness of absolute existence: this consciousness
being ... the obverse of our self-consciousness' (1862: p. 96). We cannot see
the 'unknowable' as merely the negation of knowledge; it is part of our consciousness. Spencer thus concludes that 'Religion and Science are therefore
necessary correlatives'. They represent 'two antithetical modes of consciousness which cannot exist asunder. A known cannot be thought of apart from
an unknown; nor can an unknown be thought of apart from a known. And
by consequence neither can become more distinct without giving greater
distinctness to the other. To carry further a metaphor before used, – they
are the positive and negative poles of thought; of which neither can gain in
intensity without increasing the intensity of the other' (1862: pp. 107–8).

Spencer made no bones about the relativity of knowledge that accompanied his idea of our consciousness of the unknowable when contrasted
with the knowable: the transformation called evolution and its interpretation possessed a 'relativity which ... characterises all our knowledge' (1900:
p. 514). Spencer believed that the doctrine of the relativity of knowledge
had also been held by many others (Mill, Lewes, Bain, Huxley, Mansel,
Hamilton and Kant) but that his version improved on earlier versions and
their self-refuting nature when this belief is asserted, and did not assert that
no absolute truth is possible: 'I diverge from other relativists in asserting
that the existence of a non-relative is not only a positive deliverance of consciousness, but a deliverance transcending in certainty all others whatever;
and is one without which the doctrine of relativity cannot be framed in
thought' (1873a: p. 260). The 'co-existence of subject and object', he adds, is
'a deliverance of consciousness which precedes all reasoning' (1873a, p. 261).

This basic kind of contrast made by Spencer in relation to the nature of
knowledge, and by prior and subsequent philosophers, not least by his near
German contemporary Schopenhauer with his division between 'will' and
'idea', have long been topics of dispute within philosophical studies. Here it
is only needful to observe that in Spencer's postulate of the 'Unseen Reality'
may be detected a thin causeway by which his fundamental philosophical
outlook, in a restricted sense and the significance of which is not to be
exaggerated, came to partake of the company of phenomenologists, such
as Husserl, for whom ' "reality in itself", the "objective world out-there", is
without significance, unsignified, meaningless apart from man's conscious
attention to it' (Roche, 1973: p. 13).[7]

The posthumous publication of Spencer's *Autobiography* in 1904 was the
occasion for a no-blushes-spared round of critical reappraisal of his work,
with *First Principles* recurrently paraded as his Achilles' heel. The American
idealist philosopher, Josiah Royce explored the idea that the theory of evolution was by virtue of its conceptual breadth incapable of disproof, not
a merit in an explanatory programme. While a true process of evolution
will unite opposed tendencies, one wants to know *what principle*, in any

given case, gives the opposing tendencies that unity. 'This is', Royce notes, 'what Spencer's account does not tell us.... In sum what one learns seems to be that, in general, the evolution of the plastic bodies involves increasing differentiation, except where differentiation is diminished, and increased segregation, except where the incident forces mix things. Now, all this is unquestionably true; but does it tell us how to distinguish the true evolutionary combination of these opposed tendencies from that combination which leads towards dissolution? The vagueness of the Spencerian description of evolution', Royce adds, 'renders it possible, of course, to conceive the formula so interpreted as to fit any special case that may arise. But what one misses is any guide, in the formula, for the precise definition of types of cases *in advance of such special adjustments*. Any permanently and positively useful generalization, in a field like this, must be such as to define for us, not merely something abstract enough to be true whatever happens, but a more or less complete and exact *series of ideal cases* to which the formula can be deductively applied, in such wise as to show how the predicates used in stating the generalization are to be specified to suit each of these ideal cases. The law of gravitation, the theory of energy – these are not formulas such as:... "Everything changes" ' (1904: pp. 113–14). These laws, continues Royce, are by contrast

> formulas that can be applied, deductively, to predict in detail the characters of any one of an infinite series of ideal cases (such as planets moving about suns, masses of gas cooling, etc.). Now, nobody expects, as yet, any mathematical formula for evolution. But just because every case of evolution is obviously a case where mutually opposing tendencies somehow balance one another, and combine into higher unities, the requirement for the situation is, not that the philosopher should tell us (truly enough) that evolution involves both shrinkings and swellings, both mixings and sortings, both variety and order, – but that he should show us *how* these various tendencies are, in the various types of evolutionary process, kept in that peculiar balance and unity which, each time, constitutes an evolution.
>
> (1904: pp. 114–15)

It is the insufficient attention to the specification of unambiguously applicable criteria relating to the actual description of the world which renders Spencer's theory of evolution as it stands open to the charge that it is a cumbrous redescription of the world, incapable of *explaining* anything, because it was unfalsifiable in principle. Back in 1852, Huxley had said, half-jokingly: 'Oh! You know, Spencer's idea of a tragedy is a deduction killed by a fact' (1904, i: p. 403). Royce's overall verdict was that Spencer 'appears as a philosopher of a beautiful logical naivete. Generalization was an absolutely simple affair for him. If you found a bag big enough to hold all the facts, that was an unification of science. If, meanwhile, you were ready to present a beautifully ordered series of illustrations of your theory, this showed that your facts themselves were conceived with a due respect to their own orderly theoretical unification'. To which verdict Royce added perceptively that

> orderly exposition ... is not necessarily the same as the perfection of one's theory. The business of a theory of phenomena is the arrangement of systems of facts in ideal serial orders, according to concepts which themselves determine both the ordering of each series and the precise relations of its members to one another. Spencer's theory of evolution does not determine the relations of the essential processes of evolution to one another, does not define their inner unity, and does not enable us to conceive a series of types of evolutionary processes in orderly relations to one another.
>
> (1904: pp. 115–16)

Others had already adumbrated similar reservations over the grip on reality actually possessed by Spencer's conceptual schema and the associated morphological generalizations.[8] In the present context the anxieties expressed in 1879 by the Irish economist T. E. Cliffe Leslie (on whom see Black, 2002) merit discussion for two reasons. First, they were particularly directed at Spencer's working out of his theory of evolution in relation to social life, and, second, Spencer himself responded in print to Leslie. Spencer's 'corrections' may be read as tending to reinforce rather than to defuse the criticisms.

According to Leslie, Spencer's theorem 'that "a movement from the homogeneous to the heterogeneous characterises all evolution", in both the physical and the social world, is true in a number of instances; and he has connected it with *verae causae*, with ascertained natural forces and conditions, indubitably creating diversity where there had been similarity, and evolving new kinds and species of phenomena. Yet it is not', Leslie added, 'a universal law, or an invariable truth from which inferences respecting the course of social development can with certainty be drawn'

> In the civilized world the unification of language is rapidly proceeding; probably no Celtic tongue will be spoken in any part of Europe, Brittany or Wales not excepted, in a few generations. The diversities of English speech were so great four hundred years ago, that Caxton found them a great obstacle to printing; four hundred years hence the same English will be spoken over half the globe, and will have few competitors, there is reason to believe, over the other half. The movement of political organization is similar; already Europe has nearly consolidated itself into a Heptarchy, the number of States into which England itself was once divided; and the result of the American war exemplifies the prevalence of the forces tending to homogeneity over those tending to heterogeneity. Two systems of civil law, again the French and the English

now extend over a great part of the civilized world; and Sir Henry Maine has established many grounds for the proposition that 'all laws, however dissimilar in their infancy, tend to resemble each other in their maturity'. In customs and fashion civilized society is likewise advancing towards uniformity. Once every rank, profession, and district had a distinctive garb; now all such distinctions, save with the priest and the soldier, have almost disappeared among men; and among women the degree of outlay and waste is becoming almost the only distinction in dress throughout the West. In the industrial world a generation ago a constant movement towards a differentiation of employments and functions appeared; now some marked tendencies to their amalgamation have begun to disclose themselves. Joint-stock companies have almost effaced all real division of labour in the wide region of trade within their operation. Improvements in communication are fast eliminating intermediate trades between pro-ducers and consumers in international commerce; and the accumulation and combination of capital, and new methods of business, are working the same result in wholesale and retail dealing at home. Many of the things for sale in a village huckster's shop were formerly the subjects of distinct branches of business in a large town; thus also eliminating the wholesale dealer.

(1879: pp. 407–8)

For Leslie then, a wide range of examples suggest that a move to homogene-ity rather than heterogeneity can also be observed alongside of Spencer's overwhelming, even definitive, focus on the reverse direction. Spencer had also observed, remarked Leslie, that in the early stages of social progress a 'differentiation' takes place between political and industrial functions, which fall to distinct classes. But now, however, 'a man is a merchant in the morning and a legislator at night; in mercantile business one year, and the next perhaps head of the navy, like Mr. Goschen or Mr. W. H. Smith'. And while improvements 'in both manufactures and the art of war seemed to Adam Smith, with good reason, to necessitate a separation between the military and industrial occupations: now every able-bodied man is a soldier – on the Continent'. Finally comes the *coup de grâce*:

Were a tendency to division of labour and differentiation of functions still to display itself on all sides, it would not give us a fundamental law deter-mining the directions of human energies and their actual occupations. To take the case of another planet inhabited by human beings, astronomers might conceivably discover marks of a diversity of employments, and yet get no clue to the nature or course of the division of labour. We should need to know, for example, whether war and religion had any influence on their occupations.

(1879: pp. 408–9)

Spencer's reply to Leslie was mildly upbraiding, and appeared in the sixth and final edition of *First Principles* of 1900. The reply took the form of a set of comments included in an appendix (Appendix B) which dealt with other matters as well. A better apprehension of the formula of evolution, and of the meaning of individual words associated with it will, Spencer believes, meet Leslie's criticisms. In fact Spencer responds to most of Leslie's examples by suggesting that integration, or 'amalgamation', is occurring, not an increase in homogeneity, and that the change represented by the integration in question will lead on to differentiation and heterogeneity. Thus in answer to the potential disappearance of Celtic tongues, Spencer insists that the supplanting of a language, or languages, by another is not itself evidence of 'any tendency towards homogeneity in the proper sense' (1900: p. 526) – the surviving language(s) would after all continue the theoretically predicted tendency to heterogeneity. While Spencer may display internal consistency here in his own 'technical' use of 'heterogeneity', and with his suggestion that the Celtic languages would thus be undergoing 'dissolution' (but in both cases cross-cutting, though, a 'lay' application of the word 'heterogeneity'), the question occurs in the process whether this conceptual apparatus is at all, except in a self-serving sense, a clear or fruitful way of interpreting events.

Spencer's response to Leslie's allegation of an evident falling-off of differentiation between industrial and political functions is handled in a different way. Spencer reminds us that the process of evolution is not necessary but dependent upon conditions. If conditions change, adaptation proceeds differently. We should thus be prepared to find that 'the progress of a social organism towards more heterogeneous and more definite structures of a certain type, continues only as long as the actions which produce these effects continue in play' (1900: p. 528). If these actions alter

> We shall infer that the particular structures which have been formed by the activities carried on, will not grow more heterogeneous and more definite; and that if other orders of activities, implying other sets of forces, commence, answering structures of another kind will begin to make their appearance, to grow more heterogeneous and definite, and to replace the first. And it will be manifest that while the transition is going on – while the first structures are dissolving and the second evolving – there must be a mixture of structures causing apparent confusion of traits.... during the metamorphoses undergone by a society in which the militant activities and structures are dwindling while the industrial are growing, the old and new arrangements must be mingled in a perplexing way.
>
> (1900: p. 529)

Leslie's concern that differentiation was diminishing is thus, in Spencer's eyes, misplaced; rather there is a shift towards 'militant' social relations and even (a phase of) 'dissolution'. Here especially the difficulty is that the necessary, publicly available criteria for making and replicating such distinctions are not supplied by Spencer; we are confronted by the essentially protean and arbitrary definition and application of theoretical distinctions, itself driven only by, 'in a perplexing way', authorial fiat.

Spencer also brings into play a 'general' kind of reply to Leslie's probing of the language of evolution. Spencer notes that Leslie is concerned with 'detached groups of social phenomena'. Spencer's own preferred focus is a whole society, or even the entire aggregate of societies:

> the real question is, not whether we find advance to a more definite coherent heterogeneity in these taken separately, but whether we find this advance in the structures and actions of the entire society. Even were it true that the law does not hold in certain orders of social processes and products, it would not follow that it does not hold of social processes and products in their totality. The law is a law of the transformation of aggregates; and must be tested by the entire assemblages of phenomena which the aggregates present.
>
> (1900: p. 531)

On examination, though, Spencer's 'general' point here neatly contradicts what he commits himself to elsewhere. For in his Preface to Collins's *Epitome of the Synthetic Philosophy*, he asserted that in evolution the processes of integration and differentiation, leading to change towards not just heterogeneity but definiteness in heterogeneity, 'is exhibited in the totality of things and in all its divisions and sub-divisions down to the minutest' (1889: p. ix. See also 1900, pp. 501–2). Spencer's own practice too included applying the formula of evolution to 'detached groups of social phenomena', whether in the case of music and harmony, discussed later in this study, or to the development of printing and the division of labour to the extent that automatic printing and the 'Walter-Press' could be produced (1873b: pp. 126–32).

Once this apparently opportunistic avoidance of a difficulty for the theory by means of a resort to the radical redefinition of its scope is recognized, Spencer's earlier responses to Leslie must indeed themselves appear more as either an ill-advised, because inconsistent, evasion of the difficulties raised by Leslie or as a self-defeating resort to conceptual 'malleability' or plasticity in a desperate attempt to save the theory from collapse, than as a genuine demonstration of misunderstandings on Leslie's part. For a theory that is compatible with the occurrence of anything and everything can of course explain nothing. William James knew this when he declared *First Principles* 'almost a museum of blundering reason', with terms of 'vagueness and ambiguity incarnate' (1911: pp. 26, 27). Hobson too thought the book the 'least convincing of his works and the most open to the onslaughts of destructive logic' (1904: p. 13). In the case of Spencer we are no further helped than by the 'law', as Royce noted, of 'everything changes'.

Spencer and Peter Tait had already been at loggerheads over the role of the *a priori* in scientific theory. One presumes that Tait in 1879[9] relished quoting the lampoon of Spencer's definition of 'evolution' conjured up by the mathematician Thomas Penyngton Kirkman in his *Philosophy Without Assumptions*, where it is rendered as 'a change from a nohowish untalkaboutable all-likeness, to a somehowish and in-general-talkaboutable not-all-likeness, by continuous somethingelse-ifications and sticktogetherations' (Kirkman, 1876: p. 292). In his response Spencer ignored the thrust that his grand formula might be somewhat vacuous when it came to capturing how and why changes in nature and events in history were actually generated, which clearly also worried Royce and Leslie. His faith in his unified synthesis of processes was unshaken (that he wanted to record change in *this kind* of way is of some telling significance as will be discussed later when considering an interpretation of Spencer's theory advanced by Valerie Haines). Spencer is instead at first affronted that an up-to-date version of his definition has not been used as the target (1900: p. 519); and then disdainful, and deadpan:

> a formula expressing all orders of changes in their general course – astronomic, geologic, biologic, psychologic, sociologic – could not possibly be framed in any other than words of the highest abstractness. Perhaps there may come the rejoinder that they (Spencer's critics, J. O.) do not believe any such universal formula is possible. Perhaps they will say that the on-going of things as shown in our planetary system, has nothing in common with the on-going of things which has brought the Earth's crust to its present state, and that this has nothing in common with the on-going of things which the growth and actions of living bodies show us; although, considering that the laws of molar motion and the laws of molecular action are proved to hold true of them all, it requires considerable courage to assert that these modes of cooperation of the physical forces in the several regions of phenomena, present no traits in common'.
>
> (1900: pp. 520–1)

Indeed, the interpretation of the 'persistence of force' in *First Principles*, in relation to social life in particular, constituted one of the reasons William James refused to be swept along. In part this was because James detected it had an eclectic and discordant miscellany of unanalysed functions in Spencer's text. Out of this general vagueness for James was spawned the special vagueness of 'social force' – 'what on earth is "social force"? Sometimes he identifies it with "social activity" (showing the latter to be proportionate to the amount of food eaten), sometimes with the work done by human beings and their steam-engines, and shows it to be due ultimately to the sun's heat'. On both what one might indeed consider as a 'social force' and on an alleged force's 'magnitude', acting as a stimulus to change, Spencer is silent. James asks if a leader, a discovery, a book, a new idea, and a national insult would count as 'social forces', and emphasizes 'that the greatest of "forces" of this kind need embody no more "physical force" than the smallest. The measure of greatness here', James declares, 'is the effect produced on the environment, not a quantity antecedently absorbed from physical nature. Mr. Spencer himself is a great social force; but he ate no more than an average man, and his body, if cremated, would disengage no more energy. The effects he exerts are of the nature of *releases*, – his words pull triggers in certain kinds of brain' (1911: p. 29).

As discussed earlier, Tyndall had raised with Spencer in about 1857 the implication of Clausius's Second Law of Thermodynamics that the perfect equilibrium of forces in the universe would be death. Spencer's eventual response was to draw out the process of equilibration, particularly in respect of society, into the far distant future. Indeed, Spencer's interpretation of the physics of 'force', the lynchpin of his theory of evolution, was itself radically unstable.[10] The First Law of Thermodynamics did not assure 'growth' in any ordinary meaning of the word, and the Second Law 'was not...particularly helpful for Spencer's theory' (Taylor, 2007: p. 66). In 1923, Bertrand Russell, celebrated by that time for his achievements in the philosophy of mathematics and logic, advised Beatrice Webb, then in the process of clarifying her own reflections on Spencer, that if Spencer had indeed realized the implications of the Second Law 'he might well be upset. The law says that everything tends to uniformity and a dead level, diminishing (not increasing) heterogeneity. Energy is only useful when unevenly concentrated, and the law says that it tends to become evenly diffused. This law used to worry optimists about the time when Spencer was old. On the other hand, his optimism was always groundless, so his pessimism may have been equally so' (in Webb, 1926: p. 78).

In 1905, the Comtean positivist Frederic Harrison, who had collaborated over the years with Spencer in lobbying for the disestablishment of the Church of England, and non-aggression, and sparred with him in print over religion and positivist humanism, gave the newly founded annual 'Herbert Spencer Lecture' at Oxford. Harrison first quoted from Leonard Courtney's generous eulogy spoken over Spencer's coffin at Golders Green,[11] then gently but firmly demurred:

'All history, all science, all the varying forms of thought and belief, all the institutions of all the stages of man's progress were brought together; and out of this innumerable multitude of data emerged one coherent, luminous, and vitalised conception of the evolution of the world'. It is a noble ideal towards which Spencer toiled with heroic constancy for forty years. It is an ideal which no English philosopher has ever essayed to reach, an ideal towards which Spencer contributed germs of imperishable truth. Would that I could join in the confidence that this mighty Ideal had been achieved! When I reflect on the enormous gaps in the Synthetic System, the absence of any continuous theory of general history, the absence of any systematic treatment, or even of any sketch, of all the Inorganic Sciences – Mechanics, Astronomy, Physics, Chemistry – I reluctantly am forced to regard the claim, that out of all history, all science, Spencer has evolved 'one coherent conception' as being far beyond the truth. And when I reflect on the claim, that the one supreme conception of Evolution, with its monotonous, rigid, mechanical dogmas, sufficed to illustrate and even to co-ordinate all phenomena, both cosmical and human, I even begin to doubt if the very basis of the Evolution system were on sound philosophical lines.

(1905: pp. 28–30)

It is true that Harrison had had serious differences with Spencer while he was alive. Yet these punishing verdicts owe little to the settling of old scores. Harrison was pinpointing genuine and profound deficiencies.

Spencer's *First Principles* may justly be regarded as a watershed in the structure of his thought, though it is of some importance to keep in mind that the 'Progress' essay of 1857 was an early sea trial of his new way of ideas. Prior to this point he simply had no cosmic theory of evolution. Instead there were 'laws of life', formulated for social life in the equal freedom principle, and for all organic life in terms of the process of adaptation by organisms to their circumstances, with characteristics thereby acquired inherited by offspring. On view most familiarly in *Social Statics*, these 'laws', it is widely agreed among writers on Spencer, were teleological. That is, there is a specific end towards which the operation of the laws leads. Providence ensured they operated throughout nature in a direction that was progressive; however, man could and did so act as to 'pervert' these laws of life thereby engendering 'evil', stagnation, and regression (the problematic conflation of descriptive and normative senses of laws of life in which such reasoning apparently indulges can for now be left aside). The point of real controversy relevant here, in relation to the question of teleology, comes with the Spencer of *First Principles* and the 40 or so subsequent years of productive effort: is the 'mature' theory of evolution teleological?

Towards the end of the first edition of *First Principles* progress seemed at least tolerably assured:

from the persistence of force follow, not only the various direct and indirect equilibrations going on around, together with that cosmical equilibration which brings Evolution under all its forms to a close; but also those less manifest equilibrations shown in the re-adjustments of moving equilibria that have been disturbed. By this ultimate principle is provable the tendency of every organism, disordered by some unusual influence, to return to a balanced state. To it also may be traced the capacity, possessed in a slight degree by individuals, and in a greater degree by species, of becoming adapted to new circumstances. And not less does it afford a basis for the inference, that there is a gradual advance towards harmony between man's mental nature and the conditions of his existence. After finding that from it are deducible the various characteristics of Evolution, we finally draw from it a warrant for the belief, that Evolution can end only in the establishment of the greatest perfection and the most complete happiness.

(1862: p. 486)

This passage remains unaltered in the 1870 edition, with the persistence of force thus promising at least a 'warrant for the belief' that evolution ends in the 'greatest perfection' (1870, p. 517). However, by the final, 1900, edition the whole concluding sentence of the passage, and with it any mention of greatest perfection and complete happiness, has been struck out (1900, pp. 472–3).

Moreover, as Spencer concluded the final volume of the *Principles of Sociology*, and thus the entire 'System of Synthetic Philosophy', he cautioned against heady optimism about the future: 'Evolution does not imply a latent tendency to improve, everywhere in operation. There is no uniform ascent from lower to higher, but only an occasional production of a form, which in virtue of greater fitness for more complex conditions, becomes capable of a longer life of a more varied kind' (1896b: p. 599). Earlier in the same volume he had declared that 'social progress is not linear but divergent and re-divergent. Each divergent product gives origin to a new set of differentiated products' (1896b: p. 325). Regression, or dissolution, accompanies evolution, for the 'cosmic process' is responsible for 'retrogression as well as progression, where the conditions favour it' (1896b: p. 599). The mood is different in the 1850s, as *Social Statics* signifies, for while already 'civilization no longer appears to be a regular unfolding after a specific plan', it is 'a development of man's latent capabilities under the action of favourable circumstances; *which favourable circumstances, mark, were certain some time or other to occur*' (1851: p. 415, italics added).

The publication of *First Principles* thus saw an explanatory framework that was quite different to that of *Social Statics*. Now physical properties, not deism, not metaphysical properties, but properties which include the 'persistence of force', the 'instability of the homogeneous', the 'multiplication of effects', the 'rhythm of motion', and 'equilibration', ultimately unify and determine, it is argued, the processes of inorganic and organic evolution, such as integration and differentiation, with dissolution as a complementary reverse process. The framework is no longer teleological, but nor is it agnostic over direction, whether concerned with parts or wholes. Evolution may now go 'backward' as well as 'forward' (though it does not 'jump' from one 'stage' to another), but it possesses direction in morphological terms, given surrounding conditions. The theory is intended to be foundational science, as liberated from the sediment deposited by natural theology. Moreover, social evolution, excluding now 'dissolution', is, according to the evidence in Spencer's view, a process likely to deliver human happiness, at least in the long run. In his essay of 1883 'The Americans' Spencer assured his readers that 'Either unknowingly or in spite of themselves, Nature leads men by purely personal motives to fulfil her ends: Nature being one of our expressions for the Ultimate Cause of things, and the end, remote when not proximate, being the highest form of human life' (1883: p. 491). For Spencer, therefore, according to David Wiltshire, 'Evolution ... is good. The idea of a determined, unimpeded upward growth was discarded by 1851 in favour of the more arduous process of alternating progress and regression, and of human effort rising above distressful circumstances. Evolution, however, is always invested with an aura of beneficence ... and its imperatives superceded (*sic*) the Deity in Spencer's eyes as supreme moral arbiter. The definition of "right" conduct as "conduct tending to increase life" (in other words conduct tending to facilitate evolution) entails the assumption that the evolutionary consummation is devoutly to be wished' (Wiltshire, 1978: p. 193).

However, the basic kind of interpretation which I have just sketched of the structure of Spencer's theory of evolution needs to be protected from the potential challenge that it is 'immanentist' in character, a variant of teleology. It requires some elaboration to show that it respects the distinction between the causes and the processes of change. Valerie Haines (1988) has suggested that in Spencer's theory the specific theory of *organic* evolution is the logical core: the wider theory must be regarded as 'a generalization and respecification, in ultimate terms, of his theory of organic evolution. As the core of his system of synthetic philosophy, the theory of organic evolution determines the explanatory form of Spencer's theory of social evolution' (1988: p. 474). In particular it was Von Baer's idea of epigenesis, of a developmental process moving from homogeneity to heterogeneity, coupled with, as the causal mechanism producing particular changes, adaptation passed on through the Lamarckian inheritance of acquired characteristics which, for Haines, formed Spencer's core argument. Haines has as a particular target some interpreters of Spencer (Nisbet, 1969; Peel, 1971; Freeman, 1974; Hirst, 1976) who find his theory of evolution 'immanentist' in the sense that it is guilty of confusing a *process* of change with a *cause* of change.[12] Haines is convincing on two central points: that Spencer had a theory of the *cause* of change in organic, human and social life before *First Principles*, and that this Lamarckian theory was Spencer's effective mechanism of change, with a place accorded to some version of Darwin's natural selection as well, in and after *First Principles*. However, it must be noted that the large-scale 'envelope' in which these causes of change operate is provided for, according to Spencer, by the more abstract processes detailed in *First Principles*, involving 'force' and its manifestations. Lamarckian adaptation in the language of *First Principles* becomes 'direct equilibration' and natural selection 'indirect equilibration' (as discussed in Chapter 2). Spencer explicitly argues in the *Principles of Biology* that the changes in an organism which arise from a new equilibrium becoming established between it and its surroundings 'must also be transmitted, however obscurely, from one generation to another', adding that this 'appears to be a deduction from first principles – or if not a specific deduction, still, a general implication. For if an organism A, has, by any peculiar habit or condition of life, been modified into the form A^1, it follows inevitably, that all the functions of A^1, reproductive function included, must be in some degree different from the functions of A.... It involves a denial of the persistence of force to say that A may be changed into A^1, and may yet beget offspring exactly like those it would have begotten had it not been so changed' (1894: pp. 255–6). The 'persistence of force' here is *not* serving as the *cause* of change but as a reference to the framework of principles of change in which that cause occurs. There is no direct 'immanentism' at work.

Haines's own statement, however, of what Spencer understands by organic and social evolution in and after *First Principles* is unfortunate. This is because the more fundamental foundations, in Spencer's own estimation, which he had put in place in *First Principles* are described by Haines, reductively and deprecatingly, as generalizations from and as a 'respecification, in ultimate terms' of his pre-*First Principles* ideas of *organic* evolution. In fact, though, these foundations *materially supplemented* his Von Baerian understanding of organic change with elements which Haines, perhaps understandably, downplays, including the persistence of force (as just demonstrated), integration (as emerges for instance in Spencer's reply to Leslie) and the rhythm of motion (see the later discussion of Spencer on a regression to militancy). Haines thus dismisses Spencer's own claim to have 'deduced' from (or found as 'a general implication' of) his general law of evolution his biological mechanism(s) to explain actual changes. The reality is, however, otherwise, as Taylor has noticed:

The theory of evolution propounded by Spencer was not a generalization of a biological theory, but an independent account of the process which resulted in the growing complexity of the cosmos. The theories of biological evolution put forward by both Lamarck and Darwin did not inspire this overarching vision but were incorporated as parts of it, since the purpose of the Synthetic Philosophy was to demonstrate the mutually reinforcing nature of these apparently incompatible theories. These biological theories were simply special cases of the cosmic process Spencer set out to describe, and hence his doctrine of evolution was neither Lamarckian nor Darwinian.

(1992: pp. 84–5)

Spencer then, at least, believed he had deduced the mechanisms from, or found them a 'general implication' of, the general law of evolution. But this does not mean, it seems to me, that for Spencer the mechanisms of change therefore operate necessarily in a manner that would have to represent a strong immanentist 'conspiracy' in terms of the actual content of outcomes, which Haines appears to presume.[13] Spencer does after all often emphasize that evolutionary change in phenomena depends upon 'conditions' (including the 're-adjustments' of moving equilibria that have been disturbed). While this feature makes a non-nuanced immanentist interpretation of *First Principles* difficult to sustain, the problem of deep conceptual ambiguities remains unresolved in his attempts to characterize and interpret through the general theory of evolution the morphological processes involved in actual change. As has been suggested, for Spencer the *whole* environment of a biological organism or an individual human being, an environment of course itself subject to the 'persistence of force' and 'rhythm of motion' as ultimately shaping its own changing nature, is also regarded as an active or 'direct' agent engendering change in an organism, rather than as an unfreighted and self-acting 'test' of the viability of changes produced otherwise in the organism, as in Darwin's case.[14] The mechanisms of change themselves, as renamed as 'direct' and even as 'indirect' 'equilibration', thus convey baggage derived from the natural history of first principles working in the relevant environments (Taylor thus oversimplifies matters when he claims 'no necessary connection' between the Lamarckian mechanism and the Malthusian competitive pressures on an organism in respect of selection outcomes represented by Spencer's indirect equilibration, 1992: p. 83). I doubt, though, that this deserves to be considered as more than a weak variant of immanentism. In this precise kind of selectionist context Spencer seems, in the main at least, to reject the hallmark of immanentism as Haines expresses it, 'the unfolding of preexisting potentials inherent in an individual organism at the time it begins life' (1988: p. 472). Contributing to the interpretative difficulties, however, is that Spencer did not always carefully 'distinguish between processes like the development of the embryo, where the outcome is genetically programmed at the outset, and ones like the evolution of a species or the socialization of infants, where the form of the outcome is in no sense innately determined right from the beginning' (Peel, 1971: p. 135). Even so, Spencer was aware of the essential distinction between the two kinds of enquiry, even in respect of social phenomena: the arrival of harmony in music could be described, to his own satisfaction at least, in an unfolding narrative of music's 'development' in quasi-embryological Von Baerian terms, where the story was bestowed with, so to speak, its own momentum. However, in causal terms, music for Spencer arose out of the 'natural language of emotion' or excited feeling, and such music was originally single-part. The sudden arrival and success of harmony could not be causally explained, *as he felt it needed to be*, except by the successful identification of an equivalent change in the human physiology of feelings and emotion, which on his theory should accompany the shift from melody to simultaneous differing tones. He demanded such a causal explanation of himself, yet he had to admit failure (see Chapter 8).

A rather different kind of argument against Spencer, but likely too to allege his theory was not what it seems, should be noticed. If valid, this argument would lead not as in Haines's case to a sophisticated, though, I suggest, flawed re-reading of Spencer's theory, but to a blanket dismissal of it as a theory deserving serious attention. According to Wiltshire, Spencer 'has hitherto been regarded as an evolutionist whose contribution to political thought was a by-product of his scientific theory', to which interpretation Wiltshire takes exception, contending instead that 'a close survey of his writings reveals a "primacy of politics". Spencer was an individual liberal first and an evolutionist second; individualism is, both genetically and structurally, the core of his thinking' (1978: p. 1). As a simple chronological claim this is contentious: both *The Proper Sphere of Government* and *Social Statics* commingle ideas of progress, laws of life and radical liberalism. As a potentially much more significant claim about the structure of, say, *First Principles*, it can only coherently be read as referring speculatively to an underlying desire on Spencer's part ultimately to rationalize his political preferences. However, even if such an interpretation were plausible, it would be a mistake to derive directly from the fact of such a motivation the conclusion that his work was thereby 'unscientific', and thus not in principle deserving of serious rational examination. For whatever their historical or psychological 'causes', scientific arguments could still be valid and scientific statements could still in fact be true. Quite clearly it is possible to criticize Spencer's contribution to evolutionary thought comprehensively, then proper to suggest reasons for his style of reasoning to be as it is. Wiltshire's point, either when read as a chronological observation or as an observation on Spencer's motives, provides no sound alibi for refusing at the outset to consider Spencer's theory of evolution seriously. Wiltshire's claim to have found a new interpretation of Spencer is a *cul-de-sac*. Note though that to resist an interpretation which concludes on weak grounds that Spencer could not have been attempting to do science does not entail a commitment, as Gondermann has hastily inferred, to the general propositions either that motives are of no consequence at all in this kind of context, or that Spencer did actually do good science (2007: p. 35).

That *First Principles* is seriously flawed remains a judgement widely, though not universally, shared. Spencer's law of evolution is also in the main regarded as deeply defective, seen as having, for instance, the emptiness of a 'rather fruitless cosmic cliché' (Young, 1967: p. 379); though Robert Carneiro is one sociologically minded writer who has gamely found it to have merits, with Spencer nominated as the person 'who gave the world the first precise, rigorous, and systematic concept of evolution' (1972: p. 427), and who in the process gave recognition to 'a profound and universal transformation, proceeding at many levels toward greater complexity and increased integration' (1981: p. 613). It is not, however, part of this book's remit to climb Everest and rehabilitate *First Principles* and its protean theory, though a carefully critical understanding of what Spencer undertook to deliver is, I believe, a necessary foundation for an adequately sympathetic reading of how he conceives of sociology and its subject matter and central questions. I must, therefore, part company with Jonathan Turner when he declares that *First Principles* is not to be counted 'a crucial work *in Spencer's sociology*' (1985: p. 43, italics added).[15]

5
Mind and Society

In the process of elucidating Spencer's *First Principles* and the cosmic theory of evolution, it has proved helpful already to touch on his treatment of social life in that general context. It is essential now, however, to address the theory as manifested in respect of 'psychical' and 'social' evolution, themselves intimately linked in his discussions.

In these matters modern critical commentary on Spencer is confronted by great difficulties. Academic specialization has comprehensively usurped work across 'disciplines' in scholarship, and this means that normally Spencer's work is 'naturally' compartmentalized by discipline. Yet Spencer, an incomparable generalist in his approach, is especially vulnerable to misinterpretation under what has become the ordinary division of academic labour. Normal intellectual comfort zones have to be transcended to achieve an adequate understanding of Spencer on any topic; the unique breadth of his odyssey demands nothing less. Sociologists will not unnaturally home in on his *Study of Sociology*, the *Principles of Sociology*, and essays such as 'The Social Organism' while moral philosophers will focus on the early *Social Statics* and the *Principles of Ethics*. In practice it is a struggle for both groups, who tend nowadays to be most interested in Spencer, to acquire the grasp of his *Principles of Psychology* which his sociology and moral argument presuppose. Historians too face similar problems of their own specializations in coming to Spencer. The very nature of Spencer's encyclopaedic endeavour entailed that there would be intimate logical linkages from the beginning to the end of his 'System'. Of course one *may* for specific purposes explore one part in particular but if Spencer's distinctive voice is to be heard it is usually counter-productive to bracket off other parts for long: the cuts tend to bleed. As Weinstein discovered, interpreting Spencer is 'an exegetical labyrinth even for the initiated' (1998: p. 9). In the present discussion of the nature of Spencer's thought on social life and the underlying difficulties involved, paying, though, the attention due to his overall scheme of things, I have tried to avoid one tempting but unprofitable line of approach. That approach is to argue that because Spencer said so-and-so in one place or another he cannot 'really' hold its converse at some other point. Inconsistency of course ought not to occur, but it can: apparent contradictions can be real. On some matters it would simply be dogmatic to insist on one 'correct' reading.

A good place to commence is with Spencer's unusually minimalist attitude to the matter of the relevance and impact of his writings on everyday life. In the *Principles of Sociology* he remarked:

> A general congruity has to be maintained between the social state at any time necessitated by circumstances, and the accepted theories of conduct, political and individual. Such acceptance as there may be of doctrines at variance with the temporary needs, can never be more than nominal in degree, or limited in range, or both. The acceptance which guides conduct will always be of such theories, no matter how logically indefensible, as are consistent with the average modes of action, public and private. All that can be done by diffusing a doctrine much in advance of the time, is to facilitate the action of forces tending to cause advance. The forces themselves can be but in small degrees increased; but something may be done by preventing misdirection of them.
>
> (1891c: p. 666)

In a more avuncular tone, *The Study of Sociology* concluded that the man of 'higher type' should understand that social reform requires that 'philanthropic energy' must be united with 'philosophic calm', since before there can arise in human nature and human institutions changes which possess 'that permanence which makes them an acquired inheritance for the human race, there muse go immeasurable recurrences of the thoughts, and feelings, and actions, conducive to such changes. The process cannot be abridged; and must be gone through with due patience' (1873b: pp. 402–3). A letter dated 1895 to J. A. Skilton, the American author of *The Evolution of Society* of 1889, expressed the point more bluntly: 'No adequate change of character can be produced in a year, or in a generation, or in a century. All which teaching can do – all which may, perhaps, be done by a wider diffusion of the principles of sociology, is the checking of retrograde action...' (in Duncan, 1911: p. 367). Neither governments nor individuals can achieve change unless the time is right in terms of prevailing human character, though their actions can delay it.

These passages are entirely characteristic and encapsulate Spencer's signature but problematic conceptualization of human beings at large in social life, and of 'society' as a unit. In social life, according to Spencer, human beings are bound into a process by which 'character' or 'human nature' is gradually transformed, adapting or adjusting to the acknowledged existence of others and of social institutions. As a consequence of the inheritance of acquired characteristics achieved by adaptation, the passing of generations ensures human beings become more fitted to social life, and, *simultaneously and as a direct consequence*, social life and its institutions also undergo social evolution: 'The truth is that a society and its members act and react in such wise that while, on the one hand, the nature of the society is determined by the natures of its members; on the other hand, the activities of its members (and presently their natures) are re-determined by the needs of the society, as these alter: change in either entails change in the other. It is an obvious implication that, to a great extent the life of a society so sways the wills of its members as to turn them to its ends' (1883: p. 490). This mechanism of social change is in essence based on the method of change for individual members of species developed in the *Psychology*, as discussed shortly.

In both his own time and more recently Spencer has often been interpreted as viewing a person's capacity to believe or feel certain things as determined by their levels of psychological and social adaptation (as examples see Mivart, 1873; Cairnes, 1875a; Wiltshire, 1978), an interpretation which intuitively meshes in well with the circumscribed scope for 'teachings' which Spencer has conceded, given his proviso that the contents of books and lectures and so forth can possess only an unconscious, part-of-the-environment variety of impact on the process of adaptation. Of course, in this scenario, the further question at once raises itself – how can a new thought to be taught arise in the first place, except of course as a result of the author having superior psychic and social adaptation? In this framework conscious human agency can at best seldom be what it seems.

A different interpretation in principle, however, can be advanced. Spencer does from time-to-time refer to 'average modes of action, public and private' (1891c: p. 666) and 'average human nature' (1873b: p. 395). It seems likely that Spencer is attempting to identify 'structural', 'underlying', or 'relatively permanent' impersonal levels of personal and social reality in contrast to 'surface' levels of relatively unimportant and transitory ideas, feelings and happenings. Sociologists today would now mostly disparage this kind of putative explanatory focus, on 'social forces' for instance, considering it to exclude from view much of the purposive activity that is of central importance in the 'social work' of producing and reproducing social and individual life, and thus for sociological study itself. But contrary to such reticence, Spencer pursued a headlong dash for causes and order, in an echo of a Calvinist's pressing desire to discern the providential Will of God. In this connection Peel has discerned that in Spencer

> A dangerous distinction is set up between events, the particular doings of men, on the one hand, and the stuff of social change, on the other, to which they are epiphenomenal. The evolution of structures and functions thus becomes 'reified'.... The distinction is untenable, however, because events are the primary evidence for establishing what institutions and social structure are. Where it is believed that a uniform evolutionary law

runs through history, and has been determined, detailed data of all kinds are dispensable; for either they fit the law, in which case they are super-fluous, or they do not, in which case they are incidental. Either way, as Spencer put it, *'you do not want history'*: sociology is no sooner begun than it is completed.

(1971: pp. 162–3)

Nevertheless, such an interpretation would yield up in principle the log-ical space in which Spencer might accommodate a non-reductionist idea of conscious agency. With some people capable of actions above 'average' human nature, here would be scope for the conscious production of new ideas and for teaching to have some familiar point of substance, a con-scious reaction on the part of some individuals. That Spencer on occasion maybe interpreted as suggesting the contrast pinpointed by Peel is indis-putable. In practice, though there would be a negligible effect on social life precisely because such individuals are in advance of average modes of action and average human nature. That the world was not yet able to listen to what Spencer had to say was a view he comforted himself with in later life. We are in essence brought back to the first interpretation, and thus (most) people are again very differently conceptualized than they are ordinarily understood to be.

Spencer considered several cases of historically significant and relatively rapid political transformations in a range of societies. It might be expected that a close examination of his analyses of social reconfiguration would further illuminate the question of Spencer's attitude towards the idea of conscious human agency. However, again, his discussions of major political and social transformations in France, America and Britain make reference to the changes as produced by 'accident', with the course of events displaying the consequences of a lack of 'duly adapted character' in the countries con-cerned, and only obliquely at best refer to aspects of the changes which in principle might indicate a role for innovative human agency. His outlook remains that a country's political institutions cannot be effectually modi-fied faster than the characters of its citizens are modified. It follows, Spencer declares:

> that if greater modifications are by any accident produced, the excess of change is sure to be undone by some counter-change. When, as in France, people undisciplined in freedom are suddenly made politically free, they show by some *plebiscite* that they willingly deliver over their power to an autocrat, or they work their parliamentary system in such way as to make a popular statesman into a dictator. When, as in the United States, repub-lican institutions, instead of being slowly evolved, are all at once created, there grows up within them an agency of wire-pulling politicians, exer-cising a real rule which overrides the nominal rule of the people at large.

When, as at home, the extended franchise, very soon re-extended, vastly augments the mass of those who, having before been controlled are made controllers, they presently fall under the rule of an organised body that chooses their candidates and arranges for them a political programme, which they must either accept or be powerless. So that in the absence of a duly adapted character, liberty given in one direction is lost in another.

(1891c: pp. 661–2)

Confronted by this position four preliminary observations seem appropriate. First, that it is highly doubtful that Spencer subscribed to what might be assumed to be common sense ideas of conscious human agency. Second, that to any possible extent that Spencer did so subscribe, conscious human agency was nevertheless thickly shrouded and muffled by a preoccupation with causal factors, both psychical and social. Third, the power of such human agency, deliberate or otherwise, to change social life, whether of parochial or international proportions, was much more severely limited than would ordinarily be supposed. And, fourth, the possibilities need to be considered whether Spencer is vulnerable to the charge of internal inconsistency over his conception of human agency, and whether his position can be more decisively determined by a wider consideration of other aspects of his theory of evolution, particularly his evolutionary psychology.

In connection with examining more closely these four points of orientation it is of assistance to begin by noting how Spencer himself saw sociology in relation to biology and psychology. In his 1896 essay 'Biology, Psychology, and Sociology', Spencer criticized the sociological contributions of Ward and Giddings for underplaying the importance that he placed on the relationship between sociology and psychology. Spencer considers that *Social Statics* makes clear his emphasis upon a strong role for mental science in sociology. In an earlier essay, 'The Comparative Psychology of Man' of 1876, originally presented as a paper read to the Anthropological Institute on what its section on psychology might undertake, Spencer billed comparative psychology as excellent therapy for the vagueness of thought which accompanies 'the wandering about in a region without known bounds or landmarks. Attention devoted to some portion of a subject in ignorance of its connexion with the rest, leads to untrue conceptions. The whole cannot rightly be conceived without some knowledge of the parts; and no part can be rightly conceived out of relation to the whole' (1876a: p. 351). In considering human types and races he drew attention to their mental evolution and 'the accompanying social states, which it largely determines – the forms and actions of governments; the characters of laws; the relations of classes' (1876a: p. 369). The comparative study of the emergence of the altruistic sentiments, categorized as pity, generosity, and justice, resulting from a learned capacity for sympathy, was of especial significance. The paper concluded by connecting the need to understand the human mind to the study by psychology of mental evolution:

> A true theory of the human mind vitally concerns us; and systematic com-
> parisons of human minds, differing in their kinds and grades, will help us
> in forming a true theory. Knowledge of the reciprocal relations between
> the characters of men and the characters of the societies they form, must
> influence profoundly our ideas of political arrangements. When the inter-
> dependence of individual natures and social structures is understood, our
> conception of the changes now taking place, and hereafter to take place,
> will be rectified. A comprehension of mental development as a process
> of adaptation to social conditions, which are continually remoulding the
> mind and are again remoulded by it, will conduce to a salutary conscious-
> ness of the remoter effects produced by institutions upon character; and
> will check the grave mischiefs which ignorant legislation now causes.
> Lastly, a right theory of mental evolution as exhibited by humanity at
> large, giving a key, as it does, to the evolution of the human mind, must
> help to rationalise our perverse methods of education; and so to raise
> intellectual power and moral nature.
>
> (1876a: pp. 369–70)

Spencer's *Principles of Psychology* is now one of Spencer's least read titles. By common consent it is dense in style and organization. It is, though, one of his most original and important legacies and in many respects holds the key to understanding the Spencerian trope in respect of human beings and their social life. The *Psychology* was first published in 1855, an attempt to find a more secure foundation in science for his understanding of the nature of mind and its development. An extensively revised and reorganized second edition in two volumes came out in 1870 (volume 1) and 1872 (volume 2), incorporated as constituent volumes of the 'System of Synthetic Philosophy', with a third edition following in 1880. Common to all editions is a promi-nent denial of freedom of the will, which would now appear to be seldom discussed. Thus in the 1880 edition, Spencer affirms that whilst everyone is at liberty to do what he or she desires to do (supposing there are no external hindrances) no one is at liberty 'to desire or not to desire'. The underpin-ning reasoning is that 'all actions whatever must be determined by those psychical connexions which experience has generated – either in the life of the individual, or in that general antecedent life of which the accumu-lated results are organised in his constitution' (1881b, i: p. 500). For Spencer, the very plausibility of the idea of a general theory of evolution specifically requires the denial of free-will, and this particular point is made expressly in the 1855 and 1870 editions (though not in the 1880 edition) in an arresting staccato:

To reduce the general question to its simplest form:- Psychical changes either conform to law or they do not. If they do not conform to law, this work, in common with all works on the subject, is sheer nonsense: no science of Psychology is possible. If they do conform to law, there cannot be any such thing as free-will.

Respecting this matter I will only further say, that free-will, did it exist, would be entirely at variance with that beneficent necessity displayed in the progressive evolution of the correspondence between the organism and its environment.

(1855: pp. 207–8)

The denial of free-will was never retracted. Spencer, though, very largely left the point to be tacitly understood in the *Principles of Sociology*, assuming that readers would have some familiarity with the *Psychology* on which the *Sociology* in many respects clearly leant. Spencer was not alone in adopting a secular, scientific determinism. David Hartley, Joseph Priestley, James Mill, Harriet Martineau, Henry Buckle, and John Stuart Mill had taken the same path; and in its sacred and not unconnected form of God's transcendent Will in Calvinism it was familiar territory (Peel, 1971: pp. 102–11). For Spencer, still relatively young and experimenting with ideas, ineluctable determinism did not yet appear as an 'enervating fatalism', which potential consequence troubled George Eliot (Cross, 1885: p. 538). The book's treatment of the will in particular drew criticism that its 'materialism' undermined morality and religious belief, but it was also perceived as audaciously repositioning psychology as a science by G. H. Lewes and George Eliot, with its advance over phrenolological faculty psychology, and also associationism, then being refined by Alexander Bain in *The Senses and the Intellect* (1855).

By the time of the second edition, St. George Jackson Mivart was one who homed in on the denial of free-will. Mivart, son of a famous London hotelier, was 7 years younger than Spencer, and converted to Roman Catholicism in 1844. He pursued a distinguished career as a zoologist.[1] Stiffened with Owen's and Huxley's backing, he attained the position of lecturer in comparative anatomy at St. Mary's Hospital, Paddington in 1862. Darwin took Mivart seriously as a critic, but what was presumed to be personal criticism of himself and his family led to Mivart's exclusion from a circle of evolution-minded scientists with which he was previously on good terms. Commencing in 1873, Mivart published 10 articles (one in the *Quarterly Review* and an epic series of nine in the *Dublin Review*) painstakingly dissecting the *Psychology* though the examination was accompanied by a desire to divert encroachments on Cartesian dualism and Christian beliefs about the place of man in the world. Mivart considered Spencer to be denying 'any more power of choice' to human will 'than a fragment of paper thrown into a furnace has a choice concerning its ignition' (1873: p. 220). In Mivart's view, the *Psychology* undermined a sense of choice and moral responsibility, and possessed a form of expression which 'would lend itself to confusion between the sorting faculty of the apertures of a sieve and the sorting faculty of the man who employed it for sorting' (1873: p. 222). In the *Psychology* we have, he says:

> the most ingenious and interesting construction of sensible perceptions of increasing degrees of complexity wrought out with an abundance of illustration and a facility of research truly admirable. But what is the outcome? We feel indeed we have an insight into the power of mere sensation and the consequent faculties of brutes, such as we never had before, as also into the *materials* of our own thoughts; but we have no increased knowledge of our own *intelligence* itself. Our cat's mind is indeed made clear to us, but not our own.
>
> (1873: p. 221)

As it happens, once reaction set in among the Catholic hierarchy, this invective was not enough to assuage his church's perception of Mivart as apostate, and he was excommunicated in 1900. Another of Spencer's early critics, John Elliot Cairnes, exploited a link between Spencer's denial of free-will and the apparent shortcomings presented by one of the main thrusts of *The Study of Sociology*.[2] In his 'Mr. Spencer on Social Evolution', written shortly before Cairnes died, he noted Spencer's commitment to causal antecedents operating everywhere, but then added that Spencer:

> refuses to admit that an individual has the power, by an effort of will, to make his character other than it must inevitably be. He thus, no doubt, escapes a difficulty; but only, as it seems to me, to encounter another still more formidable. For, on the supposition that self-improvement is impossible, and that consequently the whole course of human affairs is predetermined, to what purpose devote ourselves to the study of sociology? To what purpose warn mankind against the dangers of over-legislation? Or to preach the duty of letting social evolution go on unhindered? Is Mr. Spencer prepared to accept the conclusion that these too – his own words and actions – are but links in the chain of destiny, and that he himself is but a 'conscious automaton'?
>
> (1875a: p. 143)[3]

Spencer had a response of sorts to concerns of this nature, although it had been fashioned in anticipation of the need to deflect a rather naively developed criticism of his naturalistic view of persons: it was of course absurd to think of social evolution going on apart from the activities of the component individuals of a society. Thus towards the close of *The Study of Sociology* Spencer commented (1873b: 400–1):

If, as seems likely, some should propose to draw the seemingly awkward corollary, that it matters not what we believe, or what we teach, since the process of social evolution will take its own course in spite of us; I reply that, while this corollary is in one sense true, it is in another sense untrue. Doubtless, from all that has been said, it follows that, supposing surrounding conditions continue the same, the evolution of a society cannot be in any essential way diverted from its general course; though it also follows (and here the corollary is at fault) that the thoughts and actions of individuals, being natural factors that arise in the course of the evolution itself and aid in further advancing it, cannot be dispensed with, but must be severally valued as increments of the aggregate force producing change.

Later, Spencer returned to this kind of criticism of the logic of his conception of social individuals in an essay 'Social Evolution and Social Duty', written in 1893 and published 4 years later in *Various Fragments*. But now the emphasis had shifted to account for the 'misconception' of his views held by his critics, deriving from the false idea that a society was a kind of thing in itself. It is supposed that societies 'passively evolve apart from any conscious agency; and the inference is that, according to the evolutionary doctrine, it is needless for individuals to have any care about progress, since progress will take care of itself. Hence, the assertion that "evolution erected into the paramount law of man's moral and social life becomes a paralyzing and immoral fatalism" '. Spencer declares, however, that it is absurd to expect that social evolution 'will go on apart from the normal activities, bodily and mental, of the component individuals'. The error which at the root of the misconception of his position is diagnosed as the failure to grasp 'that the citizen has to regard himself at once subjectively and objectively – subjectively as possessing sympathetic sentiments (which are themselves the products of evolution); objectively as one among many social units having like sentiments, by the combined operation of which certain social effects are produced. He has to look on himself individually as being moved by emotions which promote philanthropic actions, while, as a member of society, he has to look on himself as an agent through which these emotions work out improvements in social life' (1897: 120–1).

Now, while this 'clarification' of his own position touches helpfully on how Spencer divided sociology from psychology, he has still not escaped from the dilemma posed by Cairnes. Spencer's comments merely repeat the problematic conception of persons as pawns from which Cairnes had started his criticism: there is no room for indeterminacy, or for authentic voluntary or co-operative action, and no escape from the imputation of a fatalism which Cairnes pinpointed so graphically. Spencer has not retracted his denial of free-will for individuals nor met Cairnes's 'conscious automaton' challenge. Spencer made a further comment on the topic of human agency, on this occasion as an explicit reply to Cairnes (first published in 1875 as a rejoinder appended to Cairnes, 1875b), declaring that: 'the difficulty lies in recognizing human actions as, under one aspect, voluntary, and under another pre-determined. I have said elsewhere all I have to say on this point. Here I wish only to point out that the conclusion he draws from my premises is utterly different from the conclusion I draw' (1897: 17–18). As an answer this is gnomic, and opaque. When Huxley in his Romanes Lecture of 1893, *Evolution and Ethics*, raised concerns about the place of man in an evolutionary context and the need to struggle against or correct the cosmic process, no better response was forthcoming from Spencer. In his comments on the lecture to Skilton, discussed earlier, Spencer merely regarded Huxley as recycling 'old theological notions, which put Man and Nature in antithesis'. A sound conception of evolution, for Spencer, considers that, through social evolution, the human mind is 'disciplined into that form which itself puts a check upon that part of the cosmic process which consists in the unqualified struggle for existence'. Unexceptionable in itself, the view of evolution Spencer gives here cuts right across the apparent contrast between the principles of Nature and the effects of government legislation and action to which he himself had appealed, early on in the *Proper Sphere* and *Social Statics*, and later in *The Man versus The State* and elsewhere, discussed in detail later. Again the implications of his denial of free-will are not even confronted let alone resolved.

To understand why Spencer denied freedom of the will, it is necessary to delve more deeply into the *Principles of Psychology*. A key part of Spencer's project was to go beyond the sensationalist and associationist psychology of the time, and also the static faculty structure of the phrenologists, which possessed no evolutionary or developmental dimension beyond that of the individual. The project would also locate psychology as a subject much more within the general developmental theoretical framework of biology than in philosophy. If mind was part of nature, as he believed, then it must evolve; there must be mental, or psychic, evolution. Through the Lamarckian mechanism of an organism's adaptation to its circumstances and the inheritance of mental characteristics acquired in the process, animal organisms, including man, responded to experience and in the process cumulatively acquired a mental structure through the generations. This approach served to reconcile the current polarized emphases on experience (Mill) and *a priori* mental equipment (Whewell):

> Mill was correct in claiming that all laws governing mental operations ultimately derived from experience, but wrong in supposing that each individual had to acquire such modes of activity anew. According to Spencer's novel theory, the laws of mind resulted from the adaptational experiences of the race. Hence Whewell was also correct: the structures of thought and perception in each individual were a priori and necessary,

but as the evolved consequences of the inheritance of acquired mental habits.

(Richards, 1987: p. 286)

From a longer perspective Spencer was seeking a route between Locke's rejection of innate ideas and the Kantian alternative, while scotching Hume's scepticism. That this endeavour ushered in a new way of ideas of epochal significance to psychological thought the psychologist Douglas Spalding, whose own experimental work on young chicks' unlearned behaviour chimed in with Spencer's innovation,[4] was evidently in no doubt as, jubilant at Spencer's refulgence, he reviewed the second edition of the *Psychology* for *Nature*. For Spalding, Spencer's imposing achievement came with 'the doctrine that the brain and nervous system is an organised register of the experiences of past generations, that consequently the character and intelligence of individuals and races depend much more on this, on the experiences of their ancestors, than on their individual experiences'. And then Spalding continued, praising the *Psychology* lavishly

The flood of light thrown by this conception on so many things previously dark and unfathomable, its power of bringing about harmony where before there was nothing but confusion and unsatisfactory wrangling, ought to have been sufficient to have secured it a universally favourable reception. This, however, has not been the case, and partly, perhaps, because of the very merits that recommend it. It may be that veterans who have won their laurels on, say, the battle-field of innate ideas, love the old controversy, and are not anxious to learn that both sides were right and wrong. Moreover, it is the misfortune of this important addition to psychology, that it shows that previous workers in this field of enquiry have at times been labouring in the dark to solve problems like in kind with the famous difficulty of accounting for the supposed fact, that the weight of a vessel of water is not increased by the addition of a live fish. For instance, should Mr. Spencer be right, the celebrated theory of the Will, elaborated by Prof. Bain, the able representative of the individual-experience psychology, becomes a highly ingenious account of what does not happen. Thus, the new doctrine can be accepted only at the expense of giving up much of what has hitherto passed for mental science.

(1873: p. 299)

In essence, the *Psychology* developed a dualist 'inner–outer' psychoneural theory of mind (see Smith, 1982). The evolutionary process of compounding and recompounding of sensations and feelings was paralleled by a process whereby the central nervous system, in response to external stimuli, grew in complexity, definiteness and heterogeneity. The human brain had emerged in this manner. What is 'subjectively' (that is, for a person) a new association

of ideas has as its 'objective' structure a new nerve fibre, and repeated associations arising from the environment on an organism build up strands of
nervous fibre, which in turn permit more complicated adjustments to the
environment, ultimately to be passed on to the next generation. Spencer
was shifting the approach required in understanding mind to an emphasis
on the continuity of psychological phenomena and to the relation between
a being and its environment. Mind and life could not be divorced: 'no one
in the associationist tradition had gone so far in substituting a biological
approach for the traditional epistemological one' (Young, 1970: p. 169). The
neurologist, Hughlings Jackson, repeatedly and warmly acknowledged a debt
to Spencer's work on psychology, continuity and evolution.[5]
    According to Spencer, for each occurrence of a sensation,

> there was a corresponding disturbance of the nervous system,
> and ... these were to be regarded as the mental and physical instanti-
> ations of the same event. This was not a materialist theory of mind,
> a charge Spencer repeatedly denied, but was a species of what modern
> philosophers would describe as 'psychophysical parallelism', the theory
> that for every mental phenomenon there must be a neural counterpart.
> Spencer argued that what was subjectively a mental event was objectively
> a molecular motion.
>
> (Taylor, 1992: p. 109)

To the extent that Spencer is committed to 'psychosocial parallelism' he need
claim no more than that what are, conventionally, examples of the exercise
of free-will, or, I think we might add, original thought, always have some
parallel neural story. There is not much discussion by Spencer which yields
clear answers to such questions as what disturbances in my central neural
system parallel my efforts to master and criticize the *Principles of Psychology*, or my choice to visit someone today or tomorrow. But I assume the
parallels are to be in some way so intimately textured as to apply to all of
the 'subjective' mental life of individuals, as indeed suggested by Spencer's
discussion of 'original' ideas in thought in this context: 'Gaining greater
freedom as it reaches the advanced stages of complexity and multiformity,
thought acquires an excursiveness such that with the aid of slight suggestions – slight impulses from accidental circumstances – its highly-composite
states enter into combinations never before formed; and so there result conceptions which we call *original*' (1881b, ii: p. 534). In which case no negative
indication in relation to ideas of or acts of free-will might seem called for,
the matter might seem untouched. However, once it is noted that these co-
evolving parallel tracks are the 'inner' and 'outer' manifestations of a unified
evolutionary process – neural activity on the one hand, consciousness on
the other, both evolving together – it becomes clear that the evolutionary
process of the adaptation of an individual to the environment (including

of course and especially the social environment), in union with the inheritance of acquired mental characteristics (physical and psychic), is indeed determining and locking together the form and content of both consciousness and the parallel neural structures and associated nervous discharges. Spencer's psychological understanding is driven by a biological determinism which eliminates much of what for us, in a conventional sense, would be considered as 'the social aspects of human mental development' (Rylance, 2000: p. 223).

Spencer's psychology, then, precludes free-will, and in turn explains his insistence that expecting results from trying to alter the course of people's lives directly through reason, as opposed to doing so by impacting on their environment, is mostly futile, or worse. Habit and value become identical. There was indeed a contradiction between his determinism and his efforts, for instance, to stem aggression by lobbying the political establishment. R. H. Hutton in his 'A Questionable Parentage for Morals' of 1869 pressed on Spencer the need to explain precisely how moral conceptions can be passed from parent to child biologically, but, as Rylance has observed, 'he cannot specify a means, or even a mode of existence, for such a process, let alone a formal description of an infant's moral inheritance' (2000: p. 230). Mivart's pungent objections to Spencer's elimination of free-will have already been noted. Cairnes's charge that Spencer construes individuals as 'conscious automata' needs revision only to the extent that their 'programmes' are slowly updated during their lives. But Spencer's analysis did not change. The human beings whose activities are so indispensable for social evolution to go on are shackled, and only have the appearance of exercising free-will; they may believe in the voluntary nature of actions, but the belief is unfounded. And thus, contrary to the Cartesian tradition of dualism and immensely to the chagrin of his religious and idealist contemporaries, Spencer accords human consciousness no special status.

Thus fortified by the *Psychology* and the general evolutionary theory, proscribing all but the gradual psychical and social change which reflects the pace of 'equilibration' and actual change in an individual and the individual's social environment through their adaptation to each other, Spencer accented the pointlessness and the likely damaging consequences for evolution in 'advanced' societies of political campaigns for rapid legal, policy and social reforms to remodel individuals. The *Psychology* also explained, in the section entitled 'Corollaries' (Spencer's nascent social psychology, and preparation for the treatment of social evolution), the relative lack of 'higher' social and psychical sentiments among primitive men, a consequence of limited opportunities to develop the power of representation and the cognizance of general truths (1881b, ii: pp. 521–38). Elsewhere in the *Psychology* Spencer offered physical and psychical explanations of individuals with 'undeveloped' intelligence, of the 'impulsiveness' of 'lower' races, and of the generally more 'emotional' nature of women (1881b, i: pp. 582–3). Two further examples of Spencer's style of analysis, one on intellectual life and the other on moral conduct, will illustrate how he applied his evolutionary associationism to contemporary man. On the development of 'imagination' Spencer observes that at the 'highest' level: 'we pass in the most civilized to constructive imagination – *or rather, in a scattered few of the most civilized* (italics added). This, which is the highest intellectual faculty, underlies every high order of intellectual achievement.... Instead of constructive imagination being, as commonly supposed, an endowment peculiar to the poet and the writer of fiction, it is questionable whether the man of science, truly so called, does not possess even more of it' (1881b, ii: pp. 534–5). In relation to conduct, he argues that in considering the distance of the 'average mind' from complete fitness for the social state,

> we see how far men at present are from that highest moral state, in which the supreme and most powerful sentiments are those called forth by contemplation of conduct itself, and not by contemplation of other persons' opinions of conduct. In the average mind the pain constituted by consciousness of having done something intrinsically wrong, bears but a small ratio to the pain constituted by the consciousness of others' reprobation: even though this reprobation is excited by something not intrinsically wrong. Consider how difficult it would be to get a lady to wheel a costermonger's barrow down Regent-street, and how easily she may be led to say a malicious thing about some lady she is jealous of – contrast the intense repugnance to the one act, which is not in itself reprehensible; and then infer how great is the evolution of the moral sentiments yet required to bring human nature into complete fitness for the social state.
>
> (1881b, II: pp. 605–6)

Spencer's social beings, certainly the most intellectually developed, are in many ways indistinguishable from people as we would ordinarily understand them. They have consciousness and moral sentiments. However, they do not *choose* what to say or do, even if it appears so; instead what is said or done is the result of complex and subtle causes which determine how incoming 'sensations' are received and structured in consciousness, and which are paralleled by slowly evolving complex neural structures and processes, all of which are modifying and being modified by surroundings, including social circumstances, and in due course yielding up more advanced minds through use-inheritance over time. In an appendix in the second volume of the *Principles of Ethics*, Spencer later offered a reply to the Rev. J. Llewelyn Davies, prominent Christian socialist and friend of the Huxleys, in which he declared that 'the consciousness of "ought" as existing among men of superior types is simply the voice of certain governing sentiments developed by the higher forms of social life, which are in each individual endorsed by transmitted beliefs and current opinion' (1910, ii: pp. 449–50). This represents consolidation of the position which Spencer had advanced in the *Psychology*, not recantation. The image is reminiscent of a locomotive rather than its driver being described as in charge of the train. Spencer, as we have seen, goes to great lengths to emphasize how little a practical impact a theoretical argument or moral exhortation can have. Encounters with theory and moral 'oughts' may be understood by men of 'higher intelligence', but they can impact more widely only as 'average' character adapts to them initially as environmental factors, in which form they may remove 'friction' impeding possible progress through adaptation and the inheritance of acquired characteristics over the generations. Ideas 'far ahead' of the competence of component individuals and their level of adaptation to the social state are doomed either to wither, at least temporarily, or to have negative consequences for the social fabric (there remain difficulties for Spencer in explaining how these ideas might come about at all).

At this stage it will be apparent that the transition has been reached in Spencer from his conception of thinking in psychological to sociological terms. In his treatment of the transition Spencer considers sociality and sympathy among other animals as well as human beings, since in his evolutionary perspective there can be no sudden break. Sociality, which reflects the mental states produced by the presence of others and sympathy, which reflects the mental states produced by the actions of others, emerge around the fact of the proximity of others, permitting simple gregariousness, permanent sexual relations, and double parental relations, and embody in their form the stage of evolution of the psychological characteristics of intellectual and emotional development, feebler or stronger as may be.

> Sociality can begin only where ... there is less tendency than usual for the individuals to disperse widely. The offspring of the same parents, naturally kept together during their early days, may have their proneness to stay together maintained for a longer time – they may tend to part only at a somewhat later age. If the family profits by this slight modification, dispersion will in subsequent generations be more and more postponed, until it ceases entirely ....

> Sociality having thus commenced, and survival of the fittest, tending ever to maintain and increase it, it will be further strengthened by the inherited effects of habit.
>
> (1881b, ii: pp. 560–1)

Continued co-operation in a social state means that the amounts and proportions of the original mental powers 'may be modified, and some modified form of co-operation may result; which again reacting on the nature is itself again reacted upon' (1881b, ii: p. 508). Spencer identifies and discusses in three chapters three 'sentiments': 'egoistic'(self-gratification), 'ego-altruistic' (where the gratification of others gratifies the ego), and 'altruistic' (the gratification of others). Altruistic sentiments are likely to flourish in industrial rather than in predatory social conditions in which a desire for the 'ill-being' of others dominates. Since, under the conditions of an industrial society 'the inter-dependence of its parts increases, and the well-being of each is more bound up with the well-being of all, it results that the growth of feelings which find satisfaction in the well-being of all, is the growth of feelings adjusted to a fundamental unchanging condition to social welfare' (1881b, ii: p. 609). The most complex altruistic sentiment and idea to evolve is 'justice': in Spencer's assessment, justice 'primarily serving to maintain intact the sphere required by the individual for the due exercise of his powers and fulfilment of his desires, secondarily serves, when sympathetically excited, to cause respect for the like spheres of other individuals – serves also, by its sympathetic excitement, to prompt defence of others when their spheres of action are invaded' (1881b, ii: p. 617). A sense of justice to self accompanies a sense of justice to others. Spencer also points to the emergence of what he terms 'aesthetic' sentiments. When there is energy to spare from meeting the conditions of life, actions related to play, or art, can be undertaken because they are pleasurable in themselves.

In the *Principles of Sociology* 'social phenomena' – the coordinated actions of co-operating individuals – display as a primary truth that they 'depend in part on the natures of the individuals and in part on the forces the individuals are subject to' (1893: p. 14). These 'forces' include the presence of other individuals who become a factor in adaptation and the inheritance of acquired characteristics, itself modifying the original 'nature' which then goes on to be a cause of and subject to new circumstances, leading to further cycles of adaptation and influence. In this context, Spencer's 'primer', the *Study of Sociology* of 1873 discussed the need for sociology, the difficulties involved in its study, and the subject's essential focus: by the characters of individuals 'are necessitated certain limits within which the characters of the aggregate must fall. The circumstances attending aggregation greatly modify the results; but the truth here to be recognized is, that these circumstances ... can never give to the aggregate, characters that do not consist with the characters of the units' (1873b: p. 50). An accurate preparation in the science of psychology is, therefore, indispensable according to Spencer for the study of sociology:

Nothing comes out of a society but what originates in the motive of an individual, or in the united similar motives of many individuals, or in the conflict of the united similar motives of some having certain interests, with the diverse motives of others whose interests are different. Always the power which initiates a change is feeling, separate or aggregated, guided to its end by intellect; and not even an approach to an explanation of social phenomena can be made, without the thoughts and sentiments of citizens being recognized as factors.

(1873b: p. 382)

Spencer acknowledges that the student of society is studying facts which are exhibited 'by an aggregate of which he is a part'. While the sociologist can *strive* to avoid bias, he is nevertheless as a citizen 'helped to live by the life of his society, imbedded in its structures, sharing in its activities, breathing its atmosphere of thought and sentiment' (1873b: p. 386), and hence will find sustained detachment from its orthodoxies a difficult objective to realize. The lesson an understanding of evolutionary sociology can impart is one of deep caution over trying to achieve rapid social change. There are contradictions in current opinions, arising out of re-adjustments: a process of perpetual compromise between the ideas of the past and of the future is the counterpart of natural development in the present (1873b: p. 396). A true theory of social phenomena shows that there can be no more good done 'than that of letting social progress go on unhindered', with great mischief being a consequence of 'policies carried out in pursuance of erroneous conceptions' (1873b: p. 401). One associated deduction from this perspective is that 'misconduct among those in power is the correlative of misconduct among those over whom they exercise power' (1873b: p. 398). Misconduct by rulers would lead otherwise to their eviction unless the misconduct in fact reflects the disposition and character of the ruled.

In Spencer's discussion of the relationship of individuals and society there is a remarkable continuity between *Social Statics* and the *Study of Sociology*, although the earlier upbeat optimism over the future has waned, and all trace of a 'creative purpose' has been obliterated. The idea of progressive individuation, which Spencer attributes to Coleridge, informs *Social Statics*, and man is the highest manifestation of this tendency – he is complex in structure, long-lived, and self-conscious. As individuation becomes perfect, so must the moral law, the law of equal freedom, become shared and embedded in humanity, for the highest individuation requires the greatest mutual dependence (1851: p. 441):

Paradoxical though the assertion looks, the progress is at once towards complete separateness and complete union. But the separateness is of a kind consistent with the most complex combinations for fulfilling social wants; and the union is of a kind that does not hinder entire development of each personality. Civilization is evolving a state of things and a kind of character, in which two apparently conflicting requirements are reconciled. To achieve the creative purpose – the greatest sum of happiness, there must on the one hand exist an amount of population maintainable only by the best possible system of production; that

is, by the most elaborate subdivision of labour; that is, by the extrem-
ist mutual dependence: whilst on the other hand, each individual must
have the opportunity to do whatever his desires prompt. Clearly these
two conditions can be harmonised only by that adaptation humanity is
undergoing – that process during which all desires inconsistent with the
most perfect social organization are dying out, and other desires corresponding to such an organization are being developed.... Just that kind
of individuality will be acquired which finds in the most highly-organised
community the fittest sphere for its manifestation – which finds in each
social arrangement a condition answering to some faculty in itself –
which could not, in fact, expand at all, if otherwise circumstanced. The
ultimate man will be one whose private requirements coincide with public ones. He will be that manner of man, who, in spontaneously fulfilling
his own nature, incidentally performs the function of a social unit; and
yet is only enable only so to fulfil his own nature, by all others doing the
like.

(1851: pp. 441–2)

In social life, then, the welfare of each individual is bound up with the
welfare of all; failures to act in accord with the equal freedom principle
by individuals will entail 'disastrous consequences somehow or other coming back upon them' (1851: p. 446). Spencer's concern with individuality
here is quite at odds with an expression of self-centred 'individualism'.
Most of Spencer's writings had been translated into French, and were of
considerable influence on French intellectual life. Yet in 1898, the French
sociologist Emile Durkheim (1858–1917) pigeonholed Spencer as the author
of a 'narrow utilitarianism and utilitarian egoism'. In a passage brought to
prominence by Steven Lukes, Durkheim declared that it was not hard

to denounce as an ideal without grandeur that narrow commercialism
which reduces society to nothing more than a vast apparatus of production and exchange; and it is only too clear that all social life would be
impossible if there did not exist interests superior to the interests of individuals. Nothing is more just than that such doctrines should be treated
as anarchical, and with this attitude we are in full agreement. But what
is inadmissible is that this individualism should be presented as the only
one that there is or even that there could be. Quite the contrary; it is
becoming more and more rare and exceptional. The practical philosophy of Spencer is of such moral poverty that it now has scarcely any
supporters.

(In Lukes, 1990 [1969]: p. 172)

Durkheim's understanding of Spencer, particularly in his *De la division du
travail social* of 1893, has attracted substantial commentary, often concerned

not with how accurately or sympathetically Durkheim represented Spencer, but with the historical reconstruction of Durkheim's own 'awareness' or perception of Spencer (see Jones, 1974: p. 270; 1975) while he was amplifying and refining his own moral and sociological analysis of modern social life as the life of a collectivity which possessed a *conscience collective*. However, when, as here, Spencer himself rather than Durkheim is the centre of attention, the main concern must become the question of Durkheim's reliability and probity as a reporter on and critic of Spencer. This focus gains in pertinence inasmuch as Perrin is correct in depicting off-the-shelf verdicts on Durkheim's study of the division of labour as presuming it 'to have superseded Spencer's theory' and 'routed' Spencer's larger theory of 'man and society' (1995: pp. 339, 340).[6] The key matters at stake are whether or not, unlike Durkheim, Spencer believed co-operation comes before solidarity in social life, and, if he did, is this belief in the event misguided.

Giddens has plausibly argued in this connection that Durkheim was mostly aware of and concerned to elaborate 'a difference between two types of "individualist" philosophy';

> Whereas utilitarian individualism must be rejected as a methodology – sociology cannot be based upon a theory which treats the individual as the *starting-point* of analysis – ethical or 'moral individualism' refers to a social process which is of the greatest significance in modern society. The latter form, which Durkheim also frequently refers to as the 'cult of the individual', is created *by society*; it is this very fact which demonstrates the inadequacy of utilitarianism as a social theory, because what it takes as its premise is actually the outcome of a long-term process of social development.
>
> (1971: p. 301)[7]

My view on these matters is that Spencer shares with Durkheim what Giddens calls here 'a conception of moral individualism', although it has roots in both social life and psychology for Spencer. If one takes, purely for present purposes, Spencer's idea of 'militant' social life as, roughly, equivalent to Durkheim's conception of 'mechanical' solidarity, then the difference appears to be only that whereas for Durkheim moral individualism will not be present where there is the mechanical form of solidarity, it may be present alongside of Spencer's militant form of social life, and thus in 'early' societies. However, in both Spencer's 'industrial' form of social life and in Durkheim's (modern) organic form of solidarity it is an essential feature, sanctioned, enabled and regulated in social life for Durkheim by the *conscience collective* (Giddens, 1971: p. 302; Allcock, 1982: p. 224).[8] Indeed, though not noticed by Durkheim in his branding of Spencer as a simple 'utilitarian individualist', Spencer himself had introduced the concept of a 'social self-consciousness' which men might possess (as presented in his essay 'The

Morals of Trade' of 1859), in addition to concepts of justice, sympathy and altruism by which he himself distanced his thought from being committed to *laissez-faire*. But what, then, of so-called 'utilitarian individualism' and Spencer? Was there really an argument in Spencer, one which Durkheim certainly believed existed and which he was attempting to counter, which held that 'the social order could be derived from egoistic cooperation (from the calculus of mutual self-interest)' (Corning, 1982: p. 318)?

It should first be noted that the basic form of Durkheim's reservations about 'utilitarian individualism' also extended into reservations about socialism, with both systems of thought for Durkheim excluding the 'social' in their understanding of the 'economic' (Steeman, 1963: p. 60): 'over against both Socialism and Economic Liberalism which exalted egoism and were in the last analysis materialistic, Durkheim holds his banner of human brotherhood based on spiritual values' (Steeman, 1963: p. 74).[9] For Durkheim, in the absence of a *conscience collective*, there can be no norms governing contract, and thus basic egoism cannot produce what is social: 'a set of rules cannot function properly if it is not accepted by the individuals and... this acceptance is incompatible with a basic egoism' (Steeman, 1963: p. 65). Social life entails solidarity, which entails altruism. Altruism is the basis of social life, not an ornament to it. Thus, for Durkheim, 'no real social order would be possible if the individual were really the kind of egoist Spencer makes him to be. The very fact of an existent social order proves that the individual is not purely egoistic, and, for this reason, the individualizing trend in social evolution cannot lead to the type of society Spencer had in mind: a harmony of egoisms' (Steeman, 1963: p. 65).

Corning, however, questioned Durkheim's theoretical premise that 'a moral order – a normative infrastructure – is a necessary pre-requisite to a division of labor.... All that is required', Corning added, 'is a common or complementary set of goals among various parties, appropriate motivation, a means of communication, and the ability to coordinate efforts (a cybernetic infrastructure in other words)' (1982: p. 315). A formula on these lines stops far short of spiritual values and human brotherhood, components of the 'solidarity' which Steeman reasonably interprets as being required in Durkheim's perspective before a division of labour in social life is possible. Whether or not such solidarity is morally desirable is not here in question. The point is that, contrary to Durkheim, some much weaker sense of sociality among individuals may be sufficient to permit the emergence of a division of labour and interdependence. And it is certainly the case that Spencer worked with such a formula, and that he did so is not recognized at all by Durkheim. For Spencer, 'As soon as a combination of men acquires permanence, there begin actions and reactions between the community and each member of it, such that either affects the other in nature' (1893: p. 11).[10] Primitive man's gregariousness became sociality, which was stimulated by a love of approbation, which in turn fostered 'ego-altruistic' sentiments. As Zafirovski has noted, since Spencer 'considers that in the absence of "common ends", no cooperation and society would be possible, this implies a latent normative solution to the problem of social order' (2000: p. 556). Spencer marked off the realm of the superorganic (the social) from that of individual organisms as including all those processes and products which imply 'the co-ordinated actions of many individuals' (1893: p. 4), and noted that there are distinctively super-organic products, 'the potency of which can scarcely be over-estimated', such as culture, tools, language and knowledge, ranging from caves with rude markings to galleries of pictures, gestures to involved conceptions, numeration on the fingers to far-reaching mathematics, and roughly chipped flints to steam engines (1893: pp. 12–13).[11] All of these factors interact with, and modify, each other, for 'they are ever modifying individuals and society, while being modified by both' (1893: p. 14). This reciprocal influence of the society and its units in the course of evolution is of cardinal importance to Spencer. As we have already seen from the *Principles of Psychology*, continued co-operation in a social state brings, for Spencer, the consequence that the original mental powers may undergo modification, possibly with some modified form of co-operation resulting, which 'again reacting on the nature is itself again reacted upon' (1881b, ii: p. 508). Indeed, as already noted, Spencer identifies three 'sentiments': 'egoistic'; 'ego-altruistic'; and 'altruistic'. Altruistic sentiments are not necessarily 'late' evolutionary outcomes, but they are most likely to flourish in uncoercive societies based on spontaneous co-operation. The evolution of the advanced altruistic sentiment and idea of justice serves both to maintain intact the necessary sphere for an individual's exercise of his powers and fulfilment of his desires, and, when sympathetically excited, to cause respect for the like spheres of other individuals, extending to defence of others when their liberty is under threat (see Spencer, 1881b, ii: p. 617).

Durkheim's treatment of Spencer on the psychical constitution of individuals and of 'individualism' is sketchy, immoderately opportunistic and unreliable. It eliminates *without comment* Spencer's own version of 'moral individualism', and elevates instead the contrast, misleadingly articulated insofar as Spencer is in question, between society as a 'solidary moral community' and as a utilitarian 'network of self-interested "exchangists" ' (Perrin, 1995: p. 352). From Durkheim's point of view, Ingold has remarked, 'Spencer was proposing a programme for the *elimination* of society. Yet for Spencer, the sphere of social relations would have been entirely encompassed in the residue' (1986: p. 230). However, absent from such a summary is the recognition that Spencer did not confuse unplanned spontaneous order with amoral chaos: individuals were moral and capable of altruism, and, as social life developed, the role of government was to protect where necessary the equal liberty of all. This idea of a society as catallaxy, which Spencer encountered in reading Whately, is central to understanding

Spencer, although it is seldom discussed, with George Smith being a noteworthy exception:

> Herbert Spencer, in my judgment, is a major theorist in the spontaneous order school of social theory. The similarities, for example, between Spencer and F. A. Hayek are remarkable, yet Hayek pays little attention to Spencer's contributions. And it should be noted that Spencer did more than simply repeat the principles of spontaneous order defended by Adam Ferguson, Adam Smith, and others. In a sense, Spencer's entire social theory may be seen as an elaboration of the spontaneous order model. Spencer explicated this model in far more detail than his predecessors.
>
> (1981: p. 424)

Of no less significance, then, than Durkheim's arguably exaggerated specification of the conditions for sociality is his defective recording of how Spencer understands the origins of sociality in terms of ego-altruism associated with relatively permanent proximity, and, therefore, of his accounts of how the division of labour arises, and how it contributes further to the growth of the altruistic sentiments, including the sentiment of justice. It is not needful here to try to resolve the differences between the positions of Spencer and Durkheim, but it has been important to show that Durkheim's account of Spencer is a seriously compromised one, and that, for this reason, Spencer was not 'routed' by Durkheim.

Durkheim was profoundly committed to the institutionalization of sociology as a subject in French education; he taught the first course in the subject in a French university at Bordeaux in 1887 (Alpert, 1937: p. 15), and his influence was strong on the compilation of the noted yearly reviews of significant sociological publications from 1898 of *L'Année sociologique* (Clark, 1968). Durkheim adopted a signature focus on solidarity, and the 'abnormal' consequences in behaviour which flowed from its weakness in daily social life: he was critical of, for example, divorce by mutual consent and its socially dysfunctional nature (Bynder, 1969: p. 302). This intellectual orientation appeared, for a time at least, to give the subject a secure and distinctive identity, a concern with the social, serving to distinguish it clearly from, for example, psychology. Such a sharp division simply could not appeal to Spencer, given his all-embracing theory of evolution. In England, Spencer had no access to such platforms from which to manipulate the development of sociology – he lacked his friend Huxley's gene for organized action – and by the 1890s, he fretted that, with Beatrice Potter's embracing of Sidney Webb, the study of socialism would in any case subvert or squeeze out the serious study of society along the lines advanced by his general evolutionary science. Spencer's own desire to contribute to sociology as a science was simpler in scope and motivation, being 'the direct consequence of his affirmation that the laws of nature operated without exception and thus there must be laws of mind and society that were equivalent to the physical and organic worlds' (Taylor, 2007: p. 93).

Taylor, however, proceeds to argue that rather than 'forming the centrepiece of his system, as some commentators have claimed, his sociology was, in reality, just another aspect of his overall project of bringing to completion the programme that had been sketched out by Combe and Chambers' (Taylor, 2007: p. 93). Given the logical structure of Spencer's System, this view is understandable. Indeed, if there was a centrepiece to it in Spencer's mind, it was surely the *Principles of Ethics*. However, provided one accepts that the *Proper Sphere of Government* and *Social Statics* were in large measure devoted to discussions concerning the laws of social life and of life in general, as were many of his essays, it becomes undeniable that, when to these writings are coupled the *Study of Sociology* and the especially large scale of the *Principles of Sociology* (one may add too that substantial sections of the *Principles of Ethics* are sociological in nature), then sociology bulks uniquely dominant in Spencer's output. If in theory sociology was not special to Spencer, in practice it was of course outstandingly special, no less so than for Durkheim.

How, then, did Spencer himself understand societies and their evolution? Further consideration of Spencer's *conception* of 'society' itself and its regulative, productive and distributive aspects involves a close investigation of his idea of the 'social organism', the special topic of the next chapter. At this point our concern is with how Spencer depicted in synthetic form the 'general order of co-existence and sequence' (1893: p. 585) of social phenomena through the lens of his developmental interpretation of evolution, a task he attempted in the three-volume *Principles of Sociology*, published between 1876 and 1896.

By way of an introduction, part of what he called the 'data of sociology', Spencer attempted, through comparative evolutionary anthropology, to construct a picture of early man's social life by reading 'backwards' from the extant 'uncivilized' races apparently closest to that state, and to identify also more recent 'primitive' intellectual and emotional traits. Man in the early state was hardier than in the civilized: 'Survival of the fittest must ever have tended to produce and maintain a constitution capable of enduring the pains, hardships, injuries, necessarily accompanying a life at the mercy of surrounding actions' (1893: p. 49).[12] Primitive man is interpreted as impulsive and improvident, but sociality, stimulated by a love of approbation, fostered ego-altruistic sentiments. Evidence suggests women were treated as inferiors, and that distrust and general emotional conservatism were common (hence little altruism) and with the bonds of social units relatively feeble (1893: p. 71). Primitive man imitates rather than reflects and innovates, and is weak on abstract ideas, amassing instead a mass of 'facts'. The absence of a fit environment serves to explain the primitive man's intellectual state: no social growth means a low level of stimulation to progress, in contrast with the case of 'ourselves' (1893: p. 90).

Early social organization as best it can be reconstructed suggests the presence of regression as well as advance; the ability to flourish must depend heavily on habitat and upon the dispositions of other surrounding 'societies'. With early social organization there comes the growth of a system of ideas themselves formed out of earlier life, and further acting on social life. Spencer insists that these ideas should be accorded the status of rational and natural thoughts, thoughts different in their content from our thoughts, but not those of a different human nature. These ideas include perception of a difference between the capacities of inanimate and animate objects in early man. Without the conception of a mind in the body, dreams produce sensations interpreted as part of ordinary experience and thus, by our standards, a strange conception of reality. Death is not readily distinguished from forms of sleep, hence ideas of reanimation arise. Ideas of an afterlife and of another world take shape out of the experience of migration. There arise too ideas of the spirits of the dead as agents in environmental changes and in bodily changes, such as illness. The dead can be friendly as well as hostile, and thus their sprits may 'inspire' and take over the living. Spirits may be invoked by men through witchcraft and sorcery, and pacified through propitiation and worship. Sacred places, temples and altars are demarcated. Spencer is at pains to draw parallels with Roman Catholic practices; primitive altars are related to burial places, while Catholic altars contain the relics of saints. The dead become friends in the other world, needing nourishment from the living. Fasting heightens the senses to the departed spirits, surviving today as acts of self-ennoblement. Ancestor worship emerges, still to be found in Catholicism in Europe. Spencer advances a methodological precept: 'Whatever is common to men's minds in all stages, must be deeper down in thought than whatever is peculiar to men's minds in higher stages; and if the later product admits of being reached, by modification and expansion of the earlier product, the implication is that it has been so reached' (1893: p. 281).Thus idolatry and fetichism became derived from ancestor worship once the notion of dead spirits took hold. Animals that haunt the house or are found with the dead may become objects of worship. Ancestral spirits can inhere in animals, and indeed a name in early language may not distinguish between a man and an animal. Nature worship too will arise, where spirits inhere in the dawn, the sun and the moon, and mountains. In these phenomena, observes Spencer, we have the genesis of deities. The remarkable man or superior stranger is exalted, and is deified. Over time, the emergence of unambiguous proper names permits maintenance of human individuality rather than a merging into nature (1893: p. 385).

Spencer's review of anthropological material has thus demonstrated that when we cease to look back upon early life 'from our advanced stand-point', and instead 'look forward upon it from the stand-point of the primitive man' (1893: p. 412), we can see sense and order in early social life. Spencer ties in his evolutionary psychology to this point: generalizations and abstractions familiar to us are not familiar to early men, just as they are not to our children. The development of supernatural beliefs which he has outlined conforms with what the theory of evolution leads us to expect in its interpretations and in its perceptions of the objects interpreted – increasing heterogeneity, integration and differentiation are in evidence. Fear of the dead leads to religion and differentiated religious practices, and fear of the living leads to politics and government as specific activities.

Setting out, then, with social units thus conditioned and constituted Spencer turns to a systematic survey over time of the phenomena of growth, structure and function resulting from the combined actions of these social units. First he deals with the means of production of successive generations, family life, and then successively moves the focus on to ceremonial, political, ecclesiastical, professional and industrial institutions. Consideration of the coordinating arrangements as well as the phenomena coordinated, in terms of their structures and sustaining, distributing and regulating functions, is at the heart of each of the discussions presented under these six grand organizational categories. In each case the focus is placed initially on inductions, only later does Spencer advance deductive interpretations, drawing on the law of evolution as adumbrated in *First Principles*.

Spencer commences his discussion of 'Domestic Institutions' by noting that the fundamental welfare of a species is its survival, and that survival entails expenditure of energy and resources by parents, whether animals or humans. A trade-off occurs between the welfare of individuals and species in biological terms, and reproduction and survival rates vary enormously. Spencer proposes a test of 'higher' life: 'In proportion as organisms become higher they are individually less sacrificed to the maintenance of the species; and the implication is that in the highest type of man this sacrifice falls to a minimum' (1893: p. 598). Analysis in terms of evolution suggests that 'in relation to its component individuals, each social aggregate stands for the species. Mankind survives not through arrangements which refer to it as a whole, but by survival of its separate societies; each of which struggles to maintain its existence in the presence of other societies. And survival of the race, achieved through survival of its constituent societies, being the primary requirement, the domestic arrangements being most conducive to survival in each society, must be regarded as relatively appropriate' (1893: p. 598). The primitive customs of which we have evidence 'must have been those which most favoured social survival; not because this was seen, but because the societies that had customs less fit, disappeared' (1893: p. 610). It is notable that here again the structure of explanation is essentially Darwinian, rather than cast in terms of Lamarckian adaptations or their inheritance. Spencer suggests that the ideal of the family in the organic world in general appears as that suggested by higher stages of human progress.[13]

Turning to the topic of promiscuity, Spencer makes no claim as to an aboriginal order: 'the initial social state must have been one in which there were no social laws. Social laws presuppose continued social existence' (1893: p. 632).[14] If children from relatively permanent unions were more vigorous, they would tend to be favoured over others: 'Where they favoured race-maintenance, survival of the fittest would further the establishment of them' (1893: p. 639). Again a selectionist rather than a Lamarckian approach provides the framework for explaining change. While changes in family life show a general increase of coherence and definiteness, in accord with the general law of evolution, the changes associated with the move to monogamy are attributed to the rise of industrial society, not changes in religious belief (1893: p. 680). Spencer also expresses appreciation and some criticism of the work of Sir Henry Maine, in his *Ancient Law, Village Communities in the East and West*, and *Early History of Institutions*. Spencer is critical in particular of his view that patriarchy is fundamental: evidence suggests, believes Spencer, that the data indicate that the required female obedience is not the rule. Maine has been tempted into constructing a vision of the past based on modern assumptions.

Maine and Spencer agree, however, that the individual rather than the family is now becoming the basic unit of social composition. Laws, including the poor law, are occupied in substituting for the established roles of families' direct provision for the welfare of individual children by government. The family as a responsible unit is in decline. The relations of domestic life have been partially dissolved, and substituting for them are 'the relations of social life' (1893: p. 712). In evolutionary terms the rhythm of change has taken us from one extreme (the compound family as unit) to another. Spencer raises too the topic of elderly parents as neglected by their adult offspring (explored further in the second volume of the *Principles of Ethics*). Historically, sons in their afterlife would have been expected to have cherished their parents in old age (1893: p. 736). Apart though from appealing to reciprocal altruism, Spencer does not explain why children should care for ageing parents – rather surprisingly he does not, for instance, explore the value of their wisdom being absorbed and passed on by the inheritance of acquired characteristics. However, although the Lamarckian mechanism is less visible in the *Principles of Sociology* than in earlier works it is not entirely eclipsed: 'the superior domestic relations have become possible only as the adaptation of man to the social state has progressed' (1893: p. 748). In principle, therefore, Spencer remains committed to equity in political power for women, but in practice, for Lamarckian reasons, he advises caution. Women favour the encroachment of need-meeting family ethics into social life in general, where it would cut against adaptation to circumstances and hence delay progress (1893: p. 758). Only as industrial society becomes fully developed and the proper sphere of action by the state is generally accepted will such risks evaporate. In the future too filial responsibility will develop, Spencer judges, once the state ceases to interfere and general education and the culture of parents improve.

The next division of the *Sociology* concerns the evolution of 'Ceremonial Institutions', the primordial institutions of governance, established in practice before political and ecclesiastical institutions became differentiated. Ceremonial control involves 'manners' from very early on, in groups 'scarcely to be called social' (1891c: p. 4), since most ceremonies may be traced back 'to certain spontaneous acts which manifestly precede legislation, civil and ecclesiastical. Instead of arising by dictation or by agreement, which would imply the pre-established organization required for making and enforcing rules, they arise by modifications of acts performed for personal ends; and so prove themselves to grow out of individual conduct before social arrangements exist to control it' (1891c: pp. 34–5). Indeed, ceremony 'precedes not only social evolution but human evolution' (1891c: p. 113). (As noted earlier, Spencer was aware that 'agreements' as such assumed some pre-established sense of 'rule', although not in the thickly social form upon which Durkheim insisted.)

Spencer's location of the origin of 'ceremony' in pre-human and not just pre-social evolution points to 'the ceremonial' both as ubiquitous and as growing from 'basic' conduct modified in some way to be 'mannered'. Ceremony was venerable, intimate, and everywhere. Building on this basis, Spencer argues:

> If, disregarding conduct that is entirely private, we consider only that species of conduct which involves direct relations with other persons; and if under the name government we include all control of such conduct, however arising; then we must say that the earliest kind of government, the most general kind of government, and the government which is ever spontaneously recommencing, is the government of ceremonial observance. More may be said. This kind of government, besides preceding other kinds, and besides having in all places and times approached nearer to universality of influence, has ever had, and continues to have, the largest share in regulating men's lives.
>
> (1891c: p. 4)[15]

The theme of ceremony as regulation is pursued in a discussion of the gathering up and exhibition of trophies as proof of significant deeds. Spencer also comments on the development of mutilations, which characterize societies in which warfare is a preoccupation.[16] In discussing the propitiatory nature of 'presents', oblations and obeisance, he finds it declines in significance as we move away from societies which predominantly exhibit militant social relations. Forms of address and titles, badges and costumes, location of residence and sumptuary regulations show a kindred decline. 'Fashion' though receives a more complex and suggestive treatment from Spencer: 'Throughout the several forms of social control thus far treated, we have found certain pervading characters traceable to common origins;

and the conclusions reached have hence been definite. But those miscellaneous and ever-changing regulations of conduct which the name Fashion covers, are not similarly interpretable; nor does any single interpretation suffice for them all' (1891c: p. 205). Fashion as imitation can as much debunk as flatter.[17]

Spencer concludes that the phenomena associated with ceremonial institutions conform to the deductions of the laws of evolution at large – displaying advances in integration, heterogeneity, differentiation and coherence. Three orders of the ceremonial have in fact emerged, the political, the religious and the social. With the advance of social evolution we may observe, Spencer adds, that 'as law differentiates from personal commands, and as morality differentiates from religious injunctions, so politeness differentiates from ceremonial observance. To which I may add, so does rational usage differentiate from fashion' (1891c: p. 224).

Spencer's discussion of 'Political Institutions' also contains key ideas relating to his contrast between 'militant' and 'industrial' forms of political and social life. Consideration of these particular comments is thus deferred to Chapter 7. However, other important matters are raised which must be mentioned here.[18] In Spencer's judgement, the 'survival of the fittest' has produced the evolution of higher creatures, and higher social organisms (1891c: p. 240). This discipline of Nature has achieved progress such that new purposes for inherited mental structures are now possible, and that the brutality, ceasing to be necessary, may disappear, if not the struggle itself. The benefits of the earlier 'predatory-period' will, Spencer insists, remain a permanent part of our inheritance – showing itself in our intelligence and social co-operation. Social co-operation, indeed, 'is initiated by joint defence and offence; and from the cooperation thus initiated all kinds of cooperations have arisen' (1891c: p. 241). A mere gathering of individuals into a group does not make them into a society: a society, 'in the sociological sense, is formed only when, besides juxtaposition there is cooperation.... Cooperation, then, is at once that which cannot exist without a society, and that for which a society exists' (1891c: p. 244). In whatever way a society originates, mutual dependence replaces independence. This co-operation comes in two 'architecturally' contrasted forms, with both featuring divisions of labour, which arise from the experience of facilitating life. 'There is a spontaneous cooperation which grows up without thought during the pursuit of private ends; and there is a cooperation which, consciously devised, implies distinct recognition of public ends' (1891c: p. 245). Co-operation, though, implies organization. In the two kinds of co-operation, the organization of production and distribution, and of regulation, are contrastingly established and observed. Each type of co-operation and organization mingles, and each ramifies through the other, according to the respective degree of predominance. Out of the second type of co-operation and organization, conscious co-operation and organization, comes agencies both forcing individuals to labour for public ends (an aspect that declines as militancy declines), and restraining 'individual actions in such wise that social safety shall not be endangered by the disorder consequent on unchecked pursuit of individual ends' (1891c: pp. 246–7). Both kinds of co-operation and organization are instrumental to social welfare, but in converse ways. Thus we have 'combined action which directly seeks and subserves the welfares of individuals, and indirectly subserves the welfare of society as a whole by preserving individuals... (and) combined action which directly seeks and subserves the welfare of the society as a whole, and indirectly subserves the welfares of individuals by protecting the society' (1891c: p. 247). It is the sphere of *conscious* co-operation which forms the focus of 'political institutions'. Political organization can, though, come to negate some of the benefits of co-operation in general. It may encourage a fixity if it involves a system whereby tasks are inherited, whereas plasticity results from a system of succession according to a record of efficiency. Thus distinctions of the parts in the form of rank and class evolve – exemplifying integration and differentiation, but when a predominant militancy yields to industrialism there is a political dissolution out of which arises non-militant integrations and differentiations on the basis of aptitude for function.

The power of government, or of a single ruler, is constrained by the public opinion of the living, which also embodies the public opinion of the dead, and by the aggregate will of the community, or of that part of it able to manifest its opinion as the source of political power. Spencer discusses rulership in terms of kings, oligarchies ('compound political heads'), and consultative bodies. The nature of headship is determined by conditions and average 'character', not by intentions. Spencer's treatment of political institutions also examines the emergence of representative bodies, ministers, local government agencies, and the military, and judicial and executive systems. As circumstances come to favour manufacturing and commerce, so grow up representative bodies to deal with rulers, who can themselves less and less compel but need instead people's assent. A separation thus arises of representative from consulting bodies. Spencer's dismissive attitude to new political 'manufactures' as atypical in evolutionary terms lies behind his decision that 'an account of representative bodies which have been in modern days all at once created... is not here called for' (1891c: p. 439). This decision carries the consequence that Spencer excludes from his narrative colonial legislatures and imitative representative bodies established after revolutions as reactions to despotisms: 'we are concerned only with the gradual evolution of such bodies' (1891c: p. 440). Sacred law and secular law were not originally distinguished in political institutions. Later a split became discernible, and also between laws which were in favour of the interests of rulers, and of 'those which have the aggregate of private interests as their predominant sanction' (1891c: p. 531). In social evolution the aggregate of private interests more and more come to dominate over the interests of rulers. The consensus of individual interests becomes the fount of law, not religion and not the formulated 'will' of a majority. Spencer notes support for the idea of natural law in France: a warrant for law comes from claims 'anteceding political authority and its enactments' (1891c: p. 533).

Spencer's discussion of 'Ecclesiastical Institutions' begins with the idea that the propitiation of ghosts is the natural origin of religion – anthropological evidence tells against the idea that a religious sense is innate. Medicine men arise to deal with evil ghosts, but their power dwindles as a priestly concern with benign ghosts gains influence, with the chief as a priestly figure, a public intercessor. A process of differentiation leads to the emergence of a priesthood, with hierarchical structures, with forms of political dominance in a society fuelling a move from polytheism to monotheism. A distinction emerges between the concerns of this world and the other. For Spencer, 'along with that development of civil government which accompanies social integration, there usually goes a development of ecclesiastical government' (1891c: p. 751). Ecclesiastical institutions have doubly conservative influences: 'In several ways they maintain and strengthen social bonds, and so conserve the social aggregate; and they do this in large measure by conserving beliefs, sentiments and usages, which, evolved during earlier stages of the society, are shown by its survival to have had an approximate fitness to the requirements, and are likely still to have it in great measure' (1891c: pp. 770–1). Ecclesiasticism, indeed, stands for social continuity: 'Above all other agencies it is that which conduces to cohesion; not only between the coexisting parts of a nation, but also between its present generation and its past generations. In both ways it helps to maintain the individuality of the society' (1891c: p. 773). It has value in its function of conserving accumulated experience as a resource in adapting to new experiences. Militancy and priestly functions are closely linked, with the attitude of mind fostered by industrialism – 'insisting on self-claims while respecting the claims of others' (1891c: p. 801) – not favouring unqualified submission. In religion, nonconfomity accompanies the nations in which the industrial type of society dominates. In militant contexts, maintaining subordination to the deified progenitor is the 'fundamental function' of religion (1891c: p. 810).

Over time, dissolution operates for Spencer as a Darwinian 'selective' force on religion:

> the antagonist Dissolution eventually gains predominance. The spreading recognition of natural causation conflicts with this mythological evolution; and insensibly weakens those of its beliefs which are most at variance with advancing knowledge. Demons and the secondary divinities presiding over divisions of Nature, become less thought of as the phenomena ascribed to them are more commonly observed to follow a constant order; and hence these minor components of the mythology slowly dissolve away. At the same time, with growing supremacy of

the great god heading the hierarchy, there goes increasing ascription to him of actions which were before distributed among numerous supernatural beings: there is integration of power. While in proportion as there arises the consequent conception of an omnipotent and omnipresent deity, there is a gradual fading of his alleged human attributes: dissolution begins to affect the supreme personality in respect of ascribed form and nature'.

(1891c: p. 833)

In the future, ecclesiastical institutions will come to have the conduct of life in general as their principal object, rather than propitiations. Indeed, Spencer was himself witnessing a move towards Incarnation rather than Atonement as the primary focus in Victorian theology (1891c: p. 831), though he is concerned that the threat of increased control by the state of production and distribution may reverse such trends. Trends in protestant cathedral music had already made it, he suggested, the most impersonal and expressive of life as transitional in comparison to the Power behind it (1891c: p. 825). The future functions of religious reflection would be on the Infinite and Eternal Energy, on the Inscrutable Existence and the Unknown (1891c: p. 843).

In turning next to 'Professional Institutions', Spencer discusses the evolution and secularization of professions in general, and in particular in relation to the arts, to law, and to education. Since a detailed review comes in Chapter 8 of this book of how Spencer treats one profession, musician, the coverage of this section of the *Principles of Sociology* is comparatively brief. Spencer emphasizes that the professions emerge by being differentiated over time from the general regulation of social life sustained and managed by the politico-ecclesiastical agency. For Spencer, 'No group of institutions illustrates with greater clearness the process of social evolution; and none shows more undeniably how social evolution conforms to the law of evolution at large. The germs out of which the professional agencies arise, forming at first a part of the regulative agency, differentiate from it at the same time that they differentiate from one another; and, while severally being rendered more multiform by the rise of subdivisions, severally become more coherent within themselves and more definitely marked off' (1896b: p. 311). This part of Spencer's understanding of professions continues to attract interest in sociology (see Dingwall and King, 1995). Spencer's conception of the functions of professional institutions accords with his conception of the relationship between a society and its members: 'The lives of a society and of its members are in one way or another subserved by all of them: maintenance of the life of a society, which is an insentient organism, being a proper proximate end only as a means to the ultimate end – maintenance of the lives of its members, which are sentient organisms' (1896b: p. 179). With the growth of professions at a general level in mind, Spencer takes the opportunity to underline that 'society is a growth and not a manufacture, and has its laws of evolution' (1896b: p. 315): social arrangements 'have come about by small accumulated changes not contemplated by rulers', an open secret 'which only of late has been recognized by a few and is still unperceived by the many – educated as well as uneducated' (1896b: p. 315). These 'natural forces' are ignored in politics; everyday social life and economic activity are originated 'naturally and not artificially' (1896b: p. 316). It is, however, transparent that the transformation 'by which, in thousands of years, men's occupations have been so specialised that each, aiding to satisfy some small division of his fellow citizen's needs, has his own needs satisfied by the work of hundreds of others, has taken place without design and unobserved' (1896b: p. 316). Spencer maintains that 'immense injuries have been done by laws – injuries afterwards healed by social forces which have thereupon set up afresh the normal course of growth' (1896b: p. 316). Governments are blind to this reality of social life as 'catallaxy' (though this is not an expression of which Spencer makes explicit use), unaware of what he calls 'the unprompted workings of this organized humanity' (1896b: p. 317).

In terms of the date of its composition, the final Part of the *Principles of Sociology*, 'Industrial Institutions' brings to a conclusion the whole of the 'System of Synthetic Philosophy'. On the movement observable in social evolution Spencer is now unequivocal: 'social progress is not linear but divergent and re-divergent. Each differentiated product gives origin to a new set of differentiated products' (1896b: p. 325). Spencer indicates that the idea of 'specialization' of function is taken to refer to his large-scale systems divisions, production, distribution and regulation (discussed in the next chapter), with the 'division of labour', with which he is here mostly concerned, referring to actual work functions.[19]

The social foundation of industrial activities derives from 'the very idea of exchange, without which there cannot begin commercial intercourse and industrial organization'. In turn, this idea has been a growth 'out of certain ceremonial actions originated by the desire to propitiate' (1896b: p. 381). Once established, industrial differentiation is accompanied by integration – a co-operation between processes. Labour is by this process already organized. In respect of the multitudes of men favouring the 'organization' of labour, he hence remarks: 'A fly seated on the surface of the body has about as good a conception of its internal structure, as one of those schemers has of the social organization in which he is imbedded' (1896b: p. 403). Over time, the paternalistic and patriarchal regulation of industry has yielded to communal-based regulation in the form of gilds, and serfdom. Gild regulation was not a 'social invention', but arose undesigned. Custom and conservation, not inventiveness, is the overwhelming power for savages and the partially civilized: we may therefore presume that the origins of institutions 'have arisen not by design but by incidental growth. Familiar as we are with the formation of societies, associations, unions, and combinations of all types, we are led to think that the savage, similarly prompted, proceeds in analogous ways; but we are wrong in thus interpreting his doings' (1896b: p. 441).[20] Proof, Spencer adds, is furnished by the truth 'that the initial step in social evolution is made in an unintended way. Men never entered into any social contract, as Hobbes and Rousseau supposed'. Rather, subordination began 'when some warrior of superior prowess' (1896b: p. 441), conspicuous in battle, gathered the less capable men as followers and led as a matter of course. In the same manner, gilds are thus in origin, according to Spencer, a form of coercive government growing from an occupation associated with a particular family.

Slavery too was once normal and common, and not uniformly repressive. It declined with the decline of militancy, rather than because of Christianity, for slaves and serfs were more deficient in their motivation to work than those less coerced. In such circumstances, voluntary co-operation emerged. Spencer draws the contrast with an explicit nod in Maine's direction:

> to state the fact in the language of Sir Henry Maine, the members of a society may be united under relations of *status*, prescribing and enforcing their graduated positions and duties, or, in the absence of these relations of *status*, they must fall into relations of contract – relations determined by their agreements to perform services for specified payments.
>
> Hence, if social life is to go on at all, it is necessary that as fast as the one system of cooperation decreases the other system must increase.
>
> (1896b: p. 484)

Factory work is compound labour, many hands performing the same task. Spencer recognizes that poor physical conditions exist and that the choices a free labourer faces involve making contracts at will only in a nominal sense. Industrial development during the nineteenth century has, with its repetitive tasks and demands on posture, mentally and physically 'proved extremely detrimental to the operative' (1896b: p. 515). In the course of social progress, therefore, parts of each society have been 'sacrificed for the benefit of the society as a whole'. Trade unions, according to Spencer, were not formed out of gilds but independently, though with, in fact, a similar function for wage earners: 'it occasionally happens that social institutions of a kind like some which previously existed, arise *de novo* under similar conditions; and the trade-union forms one illustration' (1896b: p. 527). The 'redivergence' here pinpointed is consistent with his adoption of a non-linear interpretation of evolution, though it is unusual in Spencer in that it is tacitly supported by an appeal to a quasi-Darwinian kind of social 'variation' ('it occasionally happens') as the cause of the innovation in question, not the Lamarckian mechanism of the inheritance of acquired characteristics. The emergence of this rather casually introduced nuance is of significance in Spencer's work, and it complements the more common occurrence of references in the later Parts of the *Sociology* to evolutionary success as a result of indirect equilibration or the 'survival of the fittest'. For Spencer himself this may have amounted to no more than an opportunistic finessing of aspects of his theory, when evidence had to be accommodated which told against the expected evolutionary continuity. On the other hand, it is arguable that Spencer was undergoing a late bout of real doubt over the viability of his lifelong commitment to the Lamarckian mechanism of change. The potential criticism that there might be potentially trivializing and tautological consequences for the applicability of his theory *in toto* to the world was not addressed. The problem would of course have become especially acute if Spencer really was embracing wholeheartedly the idea of chance, and also perhaps freedom of will, so castigated in the *Principles of Psychology*.

According to Spencer, the formation of trade unions depends on a separation of payers of income and earners, and upon there being a mass of earners. Given a community of interest, unions will arise out of festive social gatherings of a ceremonial sort, such as friendly society meetings: 'Germs usually differ in character and purpose from the things evolved out of them' (1896b: p. 529). Spencer here explicitly draws on the *History of Trade Unionism* by Sidney and Beatrice Webb (formerly, of course, Beatrice Potter), describing it as 'comprehensive and elaborate' (1896b: p. 528). Wiltshire has portrayed Spencer as possessing a near-hysterical distaste for and 'inveterate opposition' to trade unions (1978: pp. 141, 161). Spencer certainly had reservations about their understanding of economics and policies over wages, and expressed these without inhibition. Nevertheless, Wiltshire's view is a very selective one. In the *Sociology* the unions are regarded as 'natural to the passing phases of social evolution, and may have beneficial functions under existing conditions. Everywhere aggression begets resistance and counter-aggression; and in our present transitional state, semi-militant and semi-industrial, trespasses have to be kept in check by the fear of retaliatory trespasses' (1896b: p. 542). Employers are prevented by them from doing unjust things that would otherwise be done in terms of the wages paid, and may be disposed to grant members respect, and better moral and physical treatment, so softening divisions of status. And trade unions serve to prepare their active members with the discipline of living and working together with others for fitness to serve in higher forms of organization.

Paying tribute to the research in G. J. Holyoake's *The History of Co-operation in England*, and especially in Beatrice Potter's *The Cooperative Movement in Great Britain*, published in 1891, Spencer regards the signs of success of examples of formalized co-operative endeavours as suggesting that 'character' has for some men reached that of the higher type. We may, therefore, be witnessing the 'germs of a spreading organization' (1896: p. 564). Perhaps, then, a 'transcendence' of his two fundamental types of co-operation may emerge, with an absence of coercive rule becoming combined with reward allocated according to work done. Yet socialism as a political theory, however, remains without merit in the future as Spencer foresees it. Socialism will prove to be against the nature of things and self-defeating; the organization and bureaucracy it requires flies against the 'fructifying causation' characteristic of social life. While an 'average of benefit' will be secured by the mitigation of the miseries arising from inferiority which are prompted by 'the spontaneous sympathies of individuals for one another' (who will not permit the rearing of their own children to suffer in the process), the socialist does not ask what must happen if, generation after generation, the material well-being of the inferior is raised at the cost of lowering that of the superior: 'people who, in their corporate capacity, abolish the natural relation between merits and benefits, will presently be abolished themselves. Either they will have to go through the miseries of a slow decay, consequent on the increase of those unfit for the business of life, or they will be overrun by some people who have not pursued the foolish policy of fostering the worst at the expense of the best' (1896b: p. 574). Coupled to the biological difficulties of socialism are psychological difficulties. The whole relation between effort and benefit would be suspended in favour of an 'absurd' and 'impossible' mental structure: the character of all is to be 'so noble that it causes continuous sacrifice of self to others, and so ignoble that it continuously lets others sacrifice to self' (1896b: p. 572). Love of one's own offspring at the expense of love of the offspring of those beyond the family group becomes outlawed under the equalization of means prescribed by 'communistic arrangements' (1896b: p. 573). A civil regimentation parallel in nature to military regimentation would result, establishing 'an industrial subordination parallel to the military subordination' (1896b: p. 578).

Spencer's conclusions about the prospects for industrial institutions are bound up closely with his discussion of militancy and industrialism. So too are the prospects for social evolution as a whole as he brings the *Principles of Sociology* to its conclusion. Consideration of these matters thus properly belongs in the chapter specifically dealing with Spencer's contrast between militant and industrial social forms. Here it may be worthwhile to end with Spencer's own concluding words to the *Sociology*, with which he closed a circle by deliberately quoting some of his own words from *Social Statics*. They administer, after all, a corrective to the misconception of Spencer's sociology as a naive apologia for selfish individualism: 'The ultimate man will be one whose private requirements coincide with public ones. He will be that manner of man who, in spontaneously fulfilling his own nature, incidentally performs the functions of a social unit; and yet is only enabled so to fulfil his own nature by all others doing the like' (1896b: p. 601).

6
The Social Organism

Spencer's conceptualization of a society as an organism remains one of the contributions to sociological thought with which his name is still routinely associated. It is fair to say it is commonly held that Spencer's organicism is incompatible with his emphasis on the proper sphere of government as the protection of individual liberty in accord with the principle of 'justice' or equal freedom, thus discrediting at a stroke his value to sociology and his reputation as a thinker in general. Taylor's summary remains substantially true: 'Many of Spencer's critics have regarded the attempt to marry organicism with Individualism as fundamentally misconceived, and he has been accused of having failed to recognize that his sociology made use of two irreconcilable ways of conceptualizing society' (1992: p. 132). There are, however, compelling grounds on which to call this deeply entrenched conviction into question. The first step to make in this connection is to establish afresh what Spencer himself claimed as his position, and the structure of the reasoning he deployed to underpin its adoption. This chapter then reappraises responses to Spencer's idea of the social organism and its implications for sociological study developed by some of his contemporaries, and in more recent interpretations.

Conceptualizing a society as a kind of organism served Spencer in a variety of ways. It appeared to bolster criticism of the habits and the legislation which he identified as hindering natural progress and of the demands of 'socialist' reformers which ran the risk of throwing such progress into reverse. In fact, according to context, the idea of the social organism in Spencer's hands could make life difficult for both liberals and conservatives. It also allowed him to argue that a science of society could be built without a hiatus on the foundations of natural science (Freeden, 1978: p. 95).

In *The Proper Sphere of Government* Spencer had committed himself to the view that everything in nature has its laws, including man socially as well as individually: 'Society as certainly has its governing principles as man has' (1843: p. 5). These principles ensure that 'there is in society, as in every other part of creation, that beautiful self-adjusting principle, which will keep all its elements in equilibrium; and, moreover, that as the interference of man in external nature often destroys the just balance, and produces greater evils than those to be remedied, so the attempt to regulate all the actions of a community by legislation, will entail little else but misery and confusion' (1843: p. 6). Indeed, in a review of the alleged 'benefits' of war the expression 'social organism' is introduced, though it is not subjected to analysis. 'Many entertain the opinion', writes Spencer, 'that war is essentially beneficial to the community – that it invigorates the social organism; and they refer to the commercial energy, exhibited during the late continental campaigns, in proof of their assertion'. Spencer, though, judges such benefits as 'accidental', and accompanied by much suffering among the 'lower orders'. And even if war does yield some temporary good, 'it infallibly inflicts a more than equivalent injury. It acts upon a nation as wine does upon a man. It creates the same unnatural activity – the same appearance of increased strength' (1843: p. 23). To such harbingers of 'mature' versions of the social organism idea was joined, as we saw earlier, his observation in a *Pilot* article for 1844 that the life and vitality of a society and a creature are the same, and if one part suffers the whole suffers.

By the time of *Social Statics* Spencer perceived the need for a more explicit formulation of what constituted a society. One approach he adopts is to use an analogy drawn from construction and the forces acting on materials: 'Let us never forget that institutions are *made* of men; that men are the struts, ties, and bolts, out of which they are framed; and that, dovetail and brace them together as we may, it is their nature which must finally determine whether the institutions can stand. Always there will be some *line of least resistance*, along which, if the humanity they are wrought out of be not strong enough they will give way; and having given way, will sink down into a less trying attitude' (1851: pp. 261–2). An analogy drawn from mechanical engineering, Spencer admits, does not capture the living connection between a society and those who form it. The idea of the 'social organism' thus makes its appearance: 'Men cannot break that vital law of the social organism – the law of equal freedom, without penalties in some way or other coming round to them. Being themselves members of the community, they are affected by whatever affects it' (1851: p. 443). There is an 'essentially *vital*' relation between each person and the society of which he is a unit: 'we commonly enough compare a nation to a living organism. We speak of "the body politic", of the functions of its several parts, of its growth, and its diseases, as though it were a creature. But we usually employ these expressions as metaphors, little expecting how close is the analogy, and how far it will bear carrying out. So completely, however, is a society organised upon the same system as an individual being, that we may almost say there is something more than analogy between them' (1851: p. 448). What the expression 'more than analogy' points to is duly amplified. We find, says Spencer, not only that the analogy between a society and a living creature is borne out to a degree quite unsuspected by those who commonly draw it, but also, that the same definition of life applies to both. This union of many men into one community – this increasing mutual dependence of units which were originally independent – this gradual segregation of citizens into separate bodies, with reciprocally subservient functions – this formation of a whole, consisting of numerous essential parts – this growth of an organism, of which one person cannot be injured without the rest feeling it – may all be generalized under the law of individuation. The development of society, as well as the development of man and the development of life generally, may be described as a tendency to individuate – to become a thing. And rightly interpreted, the manifold forms of progress going on around us, are uniformly significant of this tendency.

(1851: p. 455)

The process to which Spencer here refers as 'individuation' would, come *First Principles*, be described in terms of 'integration' and 'differentiation'. This development of life in individuals and society is the outcome of the natural and beneficent operation of the equal freedom principle: 'broadly generalizing, as it does, the prerequisites of existence, both personal and social – being on the one hand the law under which each citizen may attain complete life, and on the other hand being, not figuratively, but literally, the vital law of the social organism – being the law under which perfect individuation, both of man and of society, is achieved – being, therefore, the law of that state towards which creation tends – the law of equal freedom may properly be considered as a law of nature' (1851: p. 462).

As already noted, in 'Manners and Fashion' of 1854 Spencer again referred to the 'social organism'. Here the expression was invoked in the course of exemplifying how generalized forms of control become more specific, and reflect a 'division of labour', as development occurred. Particular functions become differentiated and associated with particular structures, also differentiated. So we see, 'in the social organism' (1854a: p. 23) at the appropriate point of development, a legal apparatus, a national church, and rituals and ceremonies, each with their own officers, called on to maintain and administer society at large. However, three questions are as yet unanswered by Spencer. The first is what makes a society, or 'social organism', possible. The second is what morphological features may be taken to characterize as distinctive this 'organism'. And the third is how is the relationship between the whole and the parts to be interpreted, though, importantly, the law of equal freedom for all individuals had already been identified in *Social Statics* as 'vital' to the social organism. These are questions centrally, if not definitively, addressed in the 1860 essay 'The social organism'.

Once the idea that societies are 'arranged' by 'direct interposition of Providence', or 'the wills of individual men' is questioned, the idea they are natural 'growths' appeared a truth to Spencer of such obvious authority that 'it seems wonderful that men should ever have overlooked it' (1860a: p. 266). The course of the division of labour on reflection demonstrates that, by 'steps so small, that year after year the industrial arrangements have seemed just what they were before – by changes as insensible as those through which a seed passes into a tree, society has become the complex body of mutually-dependent workers which we now see' (1860a: p. 267). Economic activity, the most vital part of our social structure has thus 'spontaneously evolved', and we may regard other parts of the structure as having arisen similarly. When a parliament or a ruler orders some thing to be done, no exception to this conception is required. The true sources of change lie deeper than within these acts by themselves, the acts indeed only survive if they 'fit' with circumstances. Under representative government the 'national will' determines the ultimate fate of enactments, which is to say that their fate results 'from the average of individual desires; or, in other words – from the average of individual natures' (1860a: p. 267). The law then 'grows out' of 'character', and it will do this too in a divided society where one class monopolizes power and another acquiesces. The 'character' of a people is the original source of political form, and a form which has departed far from that character as at the time it is will not endure. The 'great man' is a product of his society, and if he to some extent re-moulds his society, he was 'before and after birth' moulded by it, he is the result of the influences which bred the ancestral character which gave him the 'creed, morals, knowledge, aspirations' that he possesses (1860a: p. 269).

A perception that there is some analogy between a social body and a living individual body has been asserted from time to time, but it is only with the growth of physiological science, 'especially of those comprehensive generalizations which it has but lately reached', that the 'real parallelisms' become clear (1860a: p. 269). Plato saw a society as made up of castes of men which mirrored the 'faculties' of Reason, Will and Passion inherent in each man in some balance or other, whereas Hobbes compared a society to the human *body*, not the mind.[1] As well as seeing a society as something 'made' rather than as a growth, both made the cardinal mistake of looking to the human being for their model, for which there is no warrant. Science can take us further towards an apt analogy.

Societies 'agree' with individual organisms in four ways. First, they begin as small aggregations but grow in mass, sometimes very greatly. Second, while they begin with little if any discernible structure, during growth an increasing complexity of structure arises. Third, in their early forms there is little mutual dependence of parts, but mutual dependence becomes marked in advanced forms. Fourth, the lives of an individual organism and a society both outlive and are independent of the 'lives' of its component units, and they go on to increase in mass, structure and functional activity. No such agreement is to be found with inorganic objects. However, there are apparent differences between individual organisms and societies. First, societies have no specific external form. This though can also be said of some vegetal and lower animal life. Second, there is no continuous mass of living tissue in a society. However, some organisms have bodies of differentiated parts 'dispersed through an undifferentiated jelly' (1860a: p. 274). The 'jelly' ministers to its life. The idea of a social organism needs to incorporate this model: 'the members of the body-politic are not to be regarded as separated by intervals of dead space, but as diffused through a space occupied by life of a lower order. In our conception of a social organism, we must include all that lower organic existence on which human existence, and therefore social existence, depend. And when we do this, we see that the citizens who make up a community may be considered as highly vitalised units surrounded by substances of lower vitality, from which they draw their nutriment' (1860a: p. 275). This observation might be taken to suggest that all mankind might be viewed as one social organism, though Spencer does not here make this claim. The third difference is that the living (human) elements of the social organism are capable of movement from place to place, the living elements of an individual organism are mostly fixed in their relative positions. Yet this disagreement is much qualified. For Spencer, 'while citizens are locomotive in their private capacities, they are fixed in their public capacities'. Where there is absence, deputies will be appointed. And just as in a living body cells perform for a time and then make way for others, so 'in each part of a society the organ remains, though the persons who compose it change' (1860a: p. 275). Spencer thus does not regard locomotion as vitiating the analogy. The fourth disagreement is the most important, and one always insisted upon by Spencer subsequently: 'while in the body of an animal only a special tissue is endowed with feeling, in a society all the members are endowed with feeling' (1860a: p. 276).[2] The contrast highlighted is 'tolerably decided' and must be kept constantly in mind: 'while, in individual bodies, the welfare of all other parts is rightly subservient to the welfare of the nervous system, whose pleasurable or painful activities make up the good or ill of life; in bodies-politic the same thing does not hold, or holds to but a very slight extent'. Corporate life in bodies-politic must therefore serve the lives of the parts (1860a: pp. 276–7), a central point in the development of his conception of a society as a 'social organism'.

Spencer next explores physiological variety as a resource for building up a picture of the variety of 'social organisms'. Just as protozoa may unite into monadic aggregates with no organic mutual dependence, so with the human 'societies' of the 'lowest races' we find exhibited no division of labour but 'an undifferentiated group of individuals, forming the germ of a society'. As with the *Hydra*, where the creature's parts have many functions, so with most aboriginal societies, where there is some structure of governance but much indefiniteness of function. While with the oceanic *Hydrozoa* and the *Physophoridae* a variety of organs appear, so that 'a *Physalia* is, morphologically considered, a group of *Hydrae* of which the individuals have been variously transformed to fit them for various functions', so with civilized society this 'differentiation upon differentiation is just what takes place during... evolution'. Alongside of the economic division of labour there is also a 'physiological division of labour itself', already familiar to 'scientific naturalists' (1860a: p. 283).

Spencer now introduces to his exposition a major division observable within organisms, the contrast between the ectoderm, which develops an apparatus for dealing with the outside and the endoderm, which develops an apparatus for processing food into nutriment for the organism itself. We have as an analogue in a society a warrior class to deal with threats from the outside, and an inferior class devoted to alimentation. As vascular systems grow to take nutriment to the nervo-muscular system, developing out of the ectoderm, so as 'social progress' develops a distributive system arises, a middle class of tradesmen and brokers (1860a: p. 286). In both individual organisms and a society, when structures or 'faculties' are exercised, growth occurs, provided that nutriment for support is supplied, and specialization among organs fulfilling the supply of nutriment arises, improving its quality and quantity. Spencer observes that 'what in commercial affairs we call *profit*, answers to the excess of nutrition over waste in a living body' (1860a: p. 290). Similarly the 'capital' which has been consumed by one activity may have been diverted from another, which perhaps permanently declines as a consequence.[3]

Moreover, in the same manner as more elaborate arrangements for circulating the blood evolve in higher animals, we see in advanced societies the evolution of better channels of distribution in terms of roads and two-way double-track railway lines. Nerves for communication have their parallel in telegraph wires running in parallel with them (1860a: pp. 295, 306). Just as the brain resolves conflicting demands 'reported' to it, by averaging the interests of life, physical, intellectual and moral, so does a parliament average the demands brought to it by 'representatives' according to the interests of the classes in the community.[4]

A key objective in reappraising 'The Social Organism' must be to convey a sense of the wide-ranging *physiological* grounding in organic variety which Spencer marshals to persuade us that societies should be viewed as organisms.[5] That grounding partly matters because, as Elwick (2003) has argued, while Spencer was at this time pondering the nature of 'societies' he was also involved with practically based but ultimately conceptual problems in biology over the puzzling 'compound individuality' then predicated of certain organisms.[6] Mainly though it matters because the essay needs to be understood as a successor to his 'Transcendental Physiology' essay, which speculated about possible or hypothetical physiological structures beyond the specimens available in the anatomy laboratory of the day. As we know Spencer was not likening a society to any one known individual organism or set of organisms. The focus was on organisms and their physiologies as forms, and the modification of these forms by the forces associated with the exercise of functions. The first paragraph of 'Transcendental Physiology' adumbrates the perspective:

> The title Transcendental Anatomy is used to distinguish that division of biological science which treats, not of the structures of individual organisms considered separately, but of the general principles of structure common to vast and varied groups of organisms, – the unity of plan discernible throughout multitudinous species, genera, and orders, which differ widely in appearance. And here, under the head of Transcendental Physiology, we purpose putting together sundry laws of development and function which hold not of particular kinds or classes of organisms, but of all organisms: laws, some of which have not, we believe, been hitherto enunciated.
>
> (1857b: p. 63)

'Transcendental Physiology' indeed had considered the phenomenon of 'direct' metamorphosis in the 'body politic',[7] and it more generally sought to compare physiological phenomena with social phenomena. Spencer ventured to declare that 'the general principles of development and structure displayed in organised bodies are displayed in societies also'. Both display a mutual dependence of parts, which involves 'a community of various characteristics'. Specialists acquainted with 'the broad facts of both physiology and sociology, are beginning to recognize this correspondence not as a plausible fancy, but as a scientific truth' (1857b: pp. 101–2). The 'new' physiology contemplated by Spencer is stated boldly. Sociology and physiology will 'more or less interpret each other'. Relations of cause and effect in 'the social organism' may lead 'to the search for analogous ones in the individual organism; and may so elucidate what might else be inexplicable'. Moreover, the laws of growth and function 'disclosed by the pure physiologist, may occasionally give us the clue to certain social modifications otherwise difficult to understand. If they can do no more', Spencer maintains, 'the two sciences can at least exchange suggestions and confirmations; and this will be no small aid' (1857b: p. 102). As it happens Spencer's conception of a 'transcendental physiology' also figured briefly in his *Social Statics*, 7 years earlier. In the concluding part, which dealt not with 'statics', the equilibrium of a perfect society, but with 'dynamics', the forces by which a society is advanced towards perfection, he reflected that 'we may discern how what is termed in our artificial classifications of truth, *morality*, is essentially one with physical truth – is, in fact, a species of transcendental physiology. That condition of things dictated by the law of equal freedom – that condition in which the individuality of each may be unfolded without limit, save the like individualities of others – that condition towards which … mankind are progressing, is a condition towards which the whole creation tends' (1851: p. 436).

By 1860, therefore, Spencer's idea of the 'social organism' had a considerably more deeply rooted, complex and sophisticated underpinning in his theoretical outlook than is by convention acknowledged. A society was stipulated to be essentially a unique organism, and objections to Spencer's conclusions which relied on suggesting that, 'properly' presented, the implication of the organic analogy 'must' be that the government in a 'social organism' should have controlling powers equivalent to the brain certainly short-changed the logic of his position. Moreover, Spencer's general theory of evolution embraced both individualism and organicism, not self-evidently in a form which involved contradiction. It postulated a movement over time from relative homogeneity to relative heterogeneity, with an accompanying process of integration, dependent on community of function, and this of course applied to social organisms, which duly would become more integrated while their parts ('units') became more individuated. As Taylor has observed: 'Greater individuation did not preclude the possibility of, or need for, strong central control, but it defined the form that such control could take. An extensive sphere of state action was ruled out as incompatible with the greater individuation of the social organism's component parts; but it also followed that within its proper sphere of protecting liberty government should be capable of enforcing its will' (2007: p. 101). Spencer could thus consider that on these two counts Huxley was offering unfair criticisms of him in his 'Administrative Nihilism' of 1871, in which Spencer was a target. In this essay Huxley had insisted

> if the resemblances between the body physiological and the body politic, are any indication, not only of what the latter is, and how it has become what it is, but of what it ought to be, and what it is tending to become, I cannot but think that the real force of the analogy is totally opposed to the negative view of State function.

> Suppose that, in accordance with this view, each muscle were to maintain that the nervous system had no right to interfere with its contraction, except to prevent it from hindering the contraction of another muscle; or each gland, that it had a right to secrete, so long as its secretion interfered with no other; suppose every separate cell left free to follow its own 'interests', and *laissez faire*, Lord of all, what would become of the body physiological?

> (1871: p. 65)

Huxley was by 1871 in militant, proselytizing mode, eager to swing the power of the state behind technical and scientific education, in the economic and social interests as he saw it of all in Britain. But Spencer's position was not so easily routed. His reply, 'Specialized Administration', has, in general terms, been reviewed earlier, but his specific defence of the 'social organism' idea must now be introduced. He reminds Huxley of both the sheer range of organic forms (as outlined in 'The Social Organism') in which, in his view, parts have the autonomy of 'individuals'. The visceral nervous system can involve processes, such as peristalsis, which are relatively self-acting, particularly in respect of the cerebro-spinal nervous system (1871a: p. 443). He iterates his unyielding adherence to the point that governments have 'external' protective responsibilities, but, on internal matters, where peaceful 'industrial' social relations have evolved and pertain, insists on the distinction between legitimate 'negative' and illegitimate 'positive' regulation (1871a: pp. 419–20), adding significantly, on negative regulation, that 'were the restraining action of the State prompt, effective, and costless to those aggrieved, the pleas put in for positive regulation would nearly all disappear' (1871a: p. 437).[8] Spencer's description of the creation of unplanned but real social satisfactions out of individual actions is augmented by an emphasis on a 'spontaneous cooperation', which he finds 'habitually ignored in sociological discussions' and omitted by Huxley, but which satisfies certain needs – men, he insists, have 'sympathetic interests' (1871a: pp. 432–3).[9] Huxley had charged Spencer with 'astynomocracy', support for *laissez-faire*, to which Spencer objects with vigour: 'Far from contending for a *laissez faire* policy in the sense which the phrase commonly suggests, I have contended for a more active control of the kind distinguishable as negatively regulative. One of the reasons I have urged for excluding State-action from other spheres, is, that it may become more efficient within its proper sphere. And I have argued that the wretched performance of its duties within its proper sphere continues, because its time is chiefly spent over imaginary duties' (1871a: p. 438).

Two years later, in *The Study of Sociology*, Spencer overtly denied that the 'social organism' was a metaphorical construction: 'That there is a real analogy between an individual organism and a social organism, becomes undeniable when certain necessities determining structure are seen to govern them in common' (1873b: p. 330). However, with the exception of this point, the concept was generally treated thinly in the new book, which is more concerned with the attitude of mind required for sociological investigation, and the value of its enquiries, than with sociology's actual concepts and theories, discussion of which is deferred to the *Principles of Sociology*. As in 'Transcendental Physiology' and 'The Social Organism', Spencer emphasizes in *The Study of Sociology* the idea of the division of labour, taken by Milne-Edwards into biology and now brought back to sociology to cover divisions in social practices above and beyond divisions in purely industrial and working practices. Once man himself is rightfully regarded as an object of biology, we are made familiar with the slowness of adaptation and the inheritance of characteristics, and thus of change in social life, rather than encouraged to think in the superficial terms of opportunistic 'mechanical' change. A more directly political message is borne by the deployment of the 'social organism' idea in *The Man versus The State*. The legislation which embodies positive regulation in the circumstances of 'industrial' society has its root in 'the error that society is a manufacture; whereas it is a growth'. The 'machinery' associated with legislation lacks a scientifically based conception of society. Each society possesses 'a natural structure in which all its institutions, governmental, religious, industrial, commercial, &c., &c., are interdependently bound – a structure which is in a sense organic... incorporated humanity is very often thought of as though it were like so much dough which the cook can mould as she pleases into piecrust, or puff, or tartlet. The communist shows us unmistakably that he thinks of the body politic as admitting of being shaped thus or thus at will; and the tacit implication of many Acts of Parliament is that aggregated men, twisted into this or that arrangement, will remain as intended' (1884: pp. 136–7).

By contrast, the discussion of the 'social organism' in the *Principles of Sociology* is more directly sociological, and breaks relatively new ground by setting it in the novel context of 'super-organic' evolution. The concept of the 'super-organic' goes back to Spencer's 'Classification of the Sciences' essay of 1864 in which sociology is classed as a 'concrete' science, one that deals with an aggregate (a society) and pluralities of aggregates (societies). Each social aggregate presents 'multitudinous phenomena, simultaneous and successive, that are held together as parts of one combination' (1864: p. 100), and such an aggregate is 'super-organic' as distinct from 'organic' (1864: p. 102). The concept can be found too in passing in second (and subsequent) editions of *First Principles*. In the second edition of 1867 Spencer remarks that although 'social aggregates differ so much from aggregates of other kinds, formed as they are of units held together loosely and indirectly in such variable ways and by such complex forces', they do in appropriate conditions display features established as associated with aggregates of other sorts, including 'dissolution'. Then, at this point, as the analysis of 'dissolution' is explored *beyond* its application to societies, Spencer quietly describes the shift in the subject matter under consideration as being one of a departure 'from these super-organic aggregates' to what is a separate concern with 'organic aggregates' (1867: p. 522). Although super-organic evolution has come about out of organic evolution, Spencer marks it off from the organic in the first volume of the *Principles of Sociology* of 1876 'as including all those processes and products which imply the co-ordinated actions of many individuals' (1893: p. 4). Insects and other organisms may exhibit super-organic features, but such manifestations are quintessentially transcended in human societies (the primary focus for the application of the concept), and are on display in their growths, functions, structures, and products.

The factors of this 'super-organic' evolution are the units themselves and their conditions – intrinsic (physical and psychical), and external (climate, for instance). There are also derived factors which social evolution introduces: a society transforms its environment, and it is likely to do this more the more it grows in mass. There are also actions and reactions between the community and its members, again according to mass. There is too the existence of other societies forming a social environment with which a society comes into contact. Lastly, there are distinctively super-organic products as already noted in Chapter 5, such as culture, tools, language and knowledge. All of these factors interact with, and modify, each other. This reciprocal influence of the society and its units in the course of evolution is emphasized by Spencer: once a combination of men acquires permanence, actions and reactions begin between the community and each member of it 'such that either affects the other in nature. The control exercised by the aggregate over its units, tends ever to mould their activities and sentiments and ideas into congruity with social requirements; and these activities, sentiments, and ideas, in so far as they are changed by changing circumstances, tend to re-mould the society into congruity with themselves' (1893: p. 11).

One important question for Spencer to answer is whether society is an entity, and if so of what sort (1893: p. 435). It is an entity, because its arrangements, coordinated rather than accidental, are relatively permanent (unlike a lecturer's audience which disappears at the end of the lecture). According to Spencer, 'we consistently regard a society as an entity, because, though formed of discrete units, a certain concreteness in the aggregate of them is implied by the general persistence of the arrangements among them throughout the area occupied. And it is this trait which yields our idea of a society. For, withholding the name from an ever-changing cluster such as primitive men form, we apply it only where some constancy in the distribution of parts has resulted from settled life' (1893: p. 436). By 1882, in the 'Political Institutions' division of the *Sociology*, Spencer emphasized co-operation rather than co-ordination (co-operation now subsuming 'co-ordination') as a key criterion of what can be called a 'society': 'The mere gathering of individuals into a group does not constitute them a society. A society, in the sociological sense, is formed only when, besides juxtaposition there is cooperation.... Cooperation, then, is at once that which cannot exist without a society, and that for which a society exists. It may be a joining of many strengths to effect something which the strength of no single man can effect; or it may be an apportioning of different activities to different persons, who severally participate in the benefits of one another's activities' (1891c: p. 244). A society grows, as do living things, and there are structures which develop. Moreover, 'the changes in the parts are mutually determined, and the changed actions of the parts are mutually dependent' (1893: p. 439). As we saw in the previous chapter, Spencer seems to leave no effective scope for *genuinely deliberative* agency innovation on the part of the 'units'; whatever appearances may suggest, any change is itself caused by what went before or results from surrounding conditions. Neither 'co-ordination' nor 'co-operation' implies purposive action; the phenomena involved instead reflect the working out of highly specific psychological 'forces'.

According to Spencer, in a society exchange develops and permits specialization: 'This division of labour, first dwelt on by political economists as a social phenomenon, and thereupon recognized by biologists as a phenomenon of living bodies... is that which in the society... makes it a living whole' (1893: p. 440). There is though the 'extreme unlikeness' upon which Spencer insists between the social and (most) other organisms – the living units composing a society are in Spencer's special sense at liberty, dispersed and often not in physical contact. There cannot be the directly physical co-operation as in a biological organism. Language, emotional and intellectual, takes its place, however. Given the factor of distance, each and every 'unit' has had to continue to possess a brain, and thus 'consciousness is diffused throughout the aggregate: all the units possess the capacities for happiness and misery' (1893: p. 449). This feature of the 'social' organism is a 'contrast of great significance – a contrast fundamentally affecting our idea of the ends to be achieved by social life' (1893: p. 448). It permits a 'catallaxy'[10] of interactions and transactions, made viable by a government ensuring agreements are kept and that reward is proportionate to merit (both elements of the equal freedom principle). According to Spencer, 'the welfare of the aggregate, considered apart from that of the units, is not an end to be sought. The society exists for the benefit of its members; not its members for the benefit of the society. It has ever to be remembered that great as may be the efforts made for the prosperity of the body politic, yet the claims of the body politic are nothing in themselves, and become something only in so far as they embody the claims of its component individuals' (1893: pp. 449–50).[11] While in the 1860 essay Spencer may have left the door open in respect of the idea of the whole of mankind as one social organism, it is not pursued further here. At the time of writing, Spencer saw little prospect of a unified 'mankind': 'in relation to its component individuals, each social aggregate stands for the species. Mankind survives not through arrangements which refer to it as a whole, but by survival of its separate societies; each of which struggles to maintain its existence in presence of other societies' (1893: p. 598).[12]

Spencer next examines the 'inductions' of sociology pertaining to social growth, and its associated structures and functions. Growth of the social 'germ' occurs through the compounding and recompounding of societies by conquest, and by an indigenous increase of population. Such accumulation of heterogeneity, the unlikeness of parts, is accompanied by the appearance of co-ordinating structures, which foster both the integration of the parts and establish a sharper differentiation between them (1893: p. 459). Each 'organ' of a society, be it a university, a port or a specialist manufacturing area, has, as in an individual organism, its own regulation and supply mechanisms (1893: p. 466). Once evolved, the process of reproducing the particular development is abridged (the 'direct metamorphosis' outlined in 'Transcendental Physiology'). Universities are now built with all features in place from the start; and factories appear without a stage of domestic production preceding them. 'Changes of structures', Spencer declares, 'cannot appear without changes of functions' (1893: p. 473). Often it is a change in function that indicates a change in structure. Specialist functions are especially dependent on other relatively more generic functions being executed; cut off from them they wither quickly, because the maintenance of this diversification becomes difficult.

Spencer also introduces the conception of 'systems of organs' as a feature of the social organism: a primary differentiation is the contrast between 'organs' according to their focus on outer or inner relations. Hence, we find early divisions (already noted in connection with the 1860 essay) between 'warriors' and 'slaves'. Between these arises a third system, of co-operation. So, sustaining, distributing and regulating systems become established. Industry develops with division of labour and geographical specialization, and with local level control to deal with 'outer' relations. With a spatial spread come communications in the form of roads and railways: this distributing system communicates between the inner and outer original systems, and their sub-divisions. The regulative system, concerned with the 'outer' world, develops compound regulation, with local regulating organs under central control. The sustaining system also becomes regulated through markets and self-regulation (as with reports on trading); and both the political and sustaining regulating processes are added to by banking and credit systems, which speed the processes of adjustment in times of rapid change.

One important question which arises is the connection in Spencer between societies regarded as such super-organic holistic systems and social life regarded as evolving toward the model of spontaneous co-operation across his 6 'institutions', and this is one which as far as I can tell Spencer does not directly address. The basic potential problem was recognized by Peel, as noted earlier on: 'A dangerous distinction is set up between events, the particular doings of men, on the one hand, and the stuff of social change, on the other, to which they are epiphenomenal. The evolution of structures and functions thus becomes "reified" ' (1971: p. 162). Yet while Spencer's conception of change in social life including change in spontaneous co-operation is idiosyncratically sclerotic, for reasons already discussed, the doings of men are not in this context 'epiphenomenal', and the structures and functions are not 'reified' as in principle external to men's doings. The structures and functions arise out of the co-operative doings, and then shape the doings further, and these newly modified doings modify afresh the structures and functions. Spencer denied repeatedly there was a one-way street in this connection, though on occasion he suggested that the doings of men might be of comparatively more significance than the impact of surrounding societal structures and functions on them. Change to structures and functions is the outcome of a 'natural' process of adaptation between men and circumstances, in which both men themselves and their circumstances may alter. Spencer's objections to 'artificial' change made by legislatures remain in force. The underlying dynamics of social change may be incommensurate, but Spencer could have declared with no less authority than Marx in *The Eighteenth Brumaire of Louis Bonaparte* that 'men make their own history, but they do not make it just as they please; they do not make it under circumstances chosen by themselves, but under circumstances directly encountered, given and transmitted from the past' (1934: p. 10).[13] There is then no contradiction involved here in Spencer adhering to his altruistic 'spontaneous co-operation' or catallaxy 'model' of interaction and to social structures and functions *conceived as mutable*, and clearly he does so conceive of them. Where Werner Stark (1961) believed *three* sociologies could be detected in Spencer – that is of a social 'system', of voluntary co-operation, and of evolving altruism – there is in reality only one, which possesses closely interrelated facets. There was in fact no inconsistency such as Stark asserts.

We need to note, however, a further point in respect of the social organism idea in particular, for an unheralded change to Spencer's argument is sprung upon us. In a chapter preparing the reader for the application of the general theory of evolution, as informed by the 'inductions' generated through the idea of societies as 'social organisms', Spencer declares that the idea of the social organism itself can now be dropped. First he reminds us that there are 'no analogies between the body politic and a living body, save those necessitated by that mutual dependence of parts which they display in common', and adds that the social organism 'is not comparable to any particular type of individual organism, animal or vegetal' (1893: p. 580). But then, here's the thing. Without warning, Spencer announces: 'now let us drop this alleged parallelism between individual organizations and social organizations. I have used the analogies elaborated, but as a scaffolding to help in building up a coherent body of sociological inductions. Let us take away the scaffolding: the inductions will stand by themselves' (1893: pp. 580–1). In another place Spencer denied outright that he considered the 'social organism' idea as basic to *sociology* at all. In 1896, in an essay 'The Relations of Biology, Psychology, and Sociology', a reply to American critics, he quite clearly declared in relation to the 'social organism' that neither in *Social Statics* nor in 'The Social Organism' 'is there any assertion that this analogy between animal-structures and social structures is to be taken as the basis for sociological interpretations' (1896a: pp. 475–6). He points out that with the idea of the division of labour there have been two way influences between biology and social science around the application of the idea (originating from social science). The same he holds is true of 'organism'. And Spencer adds that 'any one who reads through *The Principles of Sociology*, or even reads the titles of its chapters, will see that this analogy plays but a relatively inconspicuous part' (1896a: p. 474).

I take these declarations to amount to the view that societies *are* organisms, and hence 'natural', but essentially *sui generis* in their structures and functions (they are 'super-organisms', as he terms them). 'Parallels' with other organisms have simply ceased to matter to Spencer. Such a position accords entirely with the 'thought experiment' over possible organic structures which 'Transcendental Physiology' represented. It establishes what mattered to Spencer in his project of founding a thoroughly scientific sociology, that societies were not the product of divine interventions, or indeed of Acts of Parliaments: 'nations acquire their vital structures by natural processes and not by artificial devices' (1896b: p. 315).[14] Of course Spencer's natural versus artificial division is precarious, as Mill most comprehensively if indirectly argued.[15] But he had to make out the case that a *science* of social life was a serious proposition in an often unsympathetic historical context, and it is hard to see how better was this job of persuasion to be done than by appeal to a 'community in the fundamental principles of organization' in both the actual and the 'transcendental' physiology of organisms, as Durkheim, with an eye on functions and structures, and who thus made the same journey on different pathways, also recognized.[16]

Certainly Spencer did not desist from invoking the social organism idea. In the later, third volume of the *Sociology*, he concluded his chapter on the evolution of professions in 'Professional Institutions' by reminding us once more of prevalent but 'unscientific' ideas of society as something 'made', and the nightmare threat they represent to spontaneous co-operation and its outcomes through their associated support for 'positive regulation'. Such ideas have in the past injured a wide range of enterprises, 'injuries afterwards healed by social forces which have thereupon set up afresh the normal courses of growth'. The incubus still indwells:

> So unconscious are men of the life of the social organism that though the spontaneous action of its units, each seeking livelihood, generate streams of food which touch at their doors every hour – though the water for the morning bath, the lights for their rooms, the fires in their grates, the bus or tram which takes them to the City, the business they carry on (made possible by the distributing system they share in), the evening 'Special' they glance at, the theatre or concert to which they presently go, and the cab home, all result from the unprompted workings of this organized humanity, they remain blind. Though by its vital activities capital is drafted to places where it is most wanted, supplies of commodities balanced in every locality and prices universally adjusted – all without official supervision; yet, being oblivious of the truth that these processes

are socially originated without design of any one, they cannot believe that society will be bettered by natural agencies.

(1896b: pp. 316–17)

It should also be recorded that in his 'Reflections' of 1893 Spencer had a further try at characterizing aspects of the 'social organism', explicitly distancing himself now from what he saw as Comte's holism in the form he characterized as incorporated humanity, and the supreme being (in 1904, ii: p. 465). Men are less products of this body than the reverse: 'the society is created by its units, and...the nature of its organization is determined by the natures of its units. The two act and re-act; but the original factor is the character of the individuals, and the derived factor is the character of the society. The conception of the social organism necessarily implies this'. Advanced human societies are still quite new, and they seem to a degree fluid compared with the earlier animal forms of society. Still, any such society 'inheres in so considerable a degree that complete change from one social type to another is impracticable; and a suddenly-made change is inevitably followed by a reversion, if not to the previous type in its old form, yet to the previous type in a superficially different form' (in 1904, ii: p. 466). If institutions can re-make men only gradually, essentially the same constraint furnished by 'human nature' applies, less only in degree, to men's re-making of institutions. It takes some *deus ex machina*, classically aggression from outside, to engender a comparatively rapid change in social type (as discussed in the next chapter).

In the *Principles of Sociology*, the changes which Spencer's 'social organism' may undergo in accord with his theory of evolution have been allocated a special division of evolution, *super-organic* evolution. Any substantive novel content to evolution intended by Spencer through this new description is unclear. Spencer himself does not appear to have elaborated on it elsewhere, being content to refer simply to 'social evolution' rather than 'super-organic evolution. It is Ingold's opinion that the word 'super' for Spencer 'denotes not a transcendence of the organic by an emergent domain of reality but an extension of organization beyond the boundaries of the individual. Spencer's society was a resultant, not an emergent, containing nothing that was not already prefigured in the properties of its original constituents'. For Spencer, Ingold continues, 'the essence of sociality lies in the association, interaction and co-operation of numerous, discrete individuals, each equipped with a set of purposes in advance of their entry into mutual relations, purposes that must therefore be a property of their constitution as organic things (and in that sense, of their "nature"). Whether our concern is with insects, birds or human beings, the rationale for social co-operation is to be found in the net advantages it brings to each and every one of the contracting individuals' (1986: p. 224). This is a somewhat questionable view of Spencer that we shall need to consider further (especially in the Concluding Reflections), though to the extent that it merely implies no more than that Spencer did not believe that membership of a 'social organism' presaged a qualitative shift whereby 'social' concepts such as the 'general will' acquired ultimate moral supervenience in the lives of citizens, it seems to accord with Spencer's position.

We need to row back a little for now and try to capture the kind of conception of sociology it is that Spencer believes his social organism idea serves. For Spencer, the nature of the units pre-determine the aggregate (though those units will have acquired characteristics from earlier social or pre-social circumstances), but it must be noted that he specifies 'the *nature,* meaning, of course, the essential traits, and not including the incidental' (1873b: p. 50). Sociology must contemplate the modifying of the units and society which goes on in respect of 'essential traits': 'it has for its subject-matter the growth, development, structure, and functions of the social aggregate, *as brought about by the mutual actions of individuals* whose natures are partly like those of all men, partly like those of kindred races, partly distinctive' (1873b: p. 53, emphasis added). Sociology thus conceived, Spencer declares, yields generalities of prevision, not specialities. Unlike our concerns in everyday life, sociology is concerned with the comparative constancy, not the fleeting ephemera, of interaction. Thus 'in the nation there are structures and functions which make possible the doings its historian tells of;...it is with these structures and functions, in their origin, development, and decline that science is concerned' (1873b: p. 58). Both the anthropological detail of interactions of ordinary social life and, to a limited extent, the narratives of historians are treated by Spencer as repositories of particular illustrations appropriate to the morphological configurations he identifies, in conformity with evolutionary truths. His primary focus may be placed elsewhere than the humdrum of everyday interaction, but that does not entail that he must be read as ascribing to it the logical status of being 'epiphenomenal'.[17] It is merely that *one* aspect of an evolutionary approach to the sociology of societies is to be understood as forming a part of the much wider study of morphology and physiology in general. Indeed, 'social organisms' will be found classifiable in terms of classes and sub-classes (1873b: p. 59). The subject matter of this 'structural' sociology complements but does not undermine his familiar focus on social and economic life as catallaxy. For Spencer, sociology after all is concerned with the forces shaping the general 'doings' of 'incorporated human nature' (1873b: p. 60) not simply with the 'physiology' involved in its production of 'things' called 'societies'.

Undertaking sociology, Spencer admits, is no easy task. We must be mindful of the elusiveness of the 'objective', of the risk of being 'led away by superficial, trivial facts, from the deep-seated and really-important facts they indicate'. The 'significant', or 'real relations' must be identified: 'Always the details of social life, the interesting events, the curious things which serve for gossip, will, if we allow them, hide from us the vital connexions and the vital actions underneath' (1873b: p. 96). The sociological gaze for Spencer must thus regard human nature as indefinitely modifiable, yet appreciate that it 'can be modified but very slowly' (1873b: p. 120). It is impossible to achieve change to a society's structure through political revolution, since the underlying human nature will not be ready to cope with suddenly encountered new arrangements: the political instability of France is highlighted as a salutary lesson. Good sociology requires an informed awareness of complex relations and a plasticity of mind. People tend to be unconscious of the natural complexities of the 'social organism' (1873b: p. 132). Imaginative growth is needed in the conduct of sociology to transcend the confusion of partial perspectives, deriving from the particular circumstances of one's upbringing, in order to envisage the appropriate broader picture:

> The child of Puritanic parents, brought up in the belief that Sabbath-breaking brings after it all kinds of transgressions, and having had pointed out, in the village or small town that formed his world, various instances of this connexion, is somewhat perplexed in after years, when acquaintance with more of his countrymen has shown him exemplary lives joined with non-observance of the Sunday. When during continental travel he finds that the best people of foreign societies neglect injunctions which he once thought essential to right conduct, he still further widens his originally small and stiff conception.
>
> (1873b: pp. 132–3)

Spencer also recognizes that while the 'sociological conclusions of its units' about the society to which they belong are partisan and constrained that fact itself is of great sociological significance. Certainly, the individual citizen, 'imbedded in the social organism as one of its units, moulded by its influences, and aiding reciprocally to re-mould it, furthering its life while enabled by it to live, cannot so emancipate himself as to see things around him in their real relations' (1873b: p. 175). Considered more deeply, though, sociological 'emancipation' on any large scale among citizens as they are presently constituted *must* be impossible, since unless the mass of citizens 'have sentiments and beliefs in something like harmony with the social organization in which they are incorporated, this organization cannot continue. The sentiments proper to each type of society inevitably sway the sociological conclusions of its units' (1873b: p. 175). The sociologist must avoid recapitulating an exaggerated sense of the importance of political power and government held by the units of a society to get to true sociology. In English society, an 'awe of embodied power', rather than of the law itself, still displays itself among the people (or 'units').[18]

Over time, each person in a society will come to develop both a rounded individual self-consciousness and a rounded sense of their society: 'A well-balanced social self-consciousness, like a well-balanced individual self-consciousness, is the accompaniment of a high evolution' (1873b: p. 291).

Our consciousness of others was seen by Spencer as an essential constituent of social relations in the social organism. His position was summarized in his 'Mill *versus* Hamilton' of 1865. Reason has taken us to a knowledge of a 'self' and an unknowable 'not-self' as a dictum of consciousness, and our experience of relations in something beyond our consciousness has given us states of consciousness, interpretable as an ongoing adjustment of inner to outer relations (including the consciousnesses of others), one which has moulded a correspondence of thoughts and things 'going on through preceding generations', and which has been inherited by us 'in the shape of modified organic structures' (1865: p. 213). In the social organism, Spencer adds, life requires some balance to be struck by each 'unit' between egoism and altruism: 'Were A to be careless of himself, and to care only for the welfare of B, C, and D, while each of these, paying no attention to his own needs, busied himself in supplying the needs of the others; this roundabout process, besides being troublesome, would very ill meet the requirements of each, unless each could have his neighbour's consciousness' (1873b: p. 183).

Huxley, as we have already seen, believed that Spencer had built his organic analogy in a way that was unpersuasive. How did Spencer's other contemporaries respond to the idea of society as a (quasi-)organic 'growth'? One of his first and most penetrative sociologically minded critics was the Irish economist, John Elliot Cairnes (1875a,b), intellectually aligned with John Stuart Mill (see Boylan and Foley, 1983, 1992). Cairnes believed Spencer neglected that societies of men become conscious of a corporate existence, and as a consequence neglected that 'the improvement of the conditions of this existence becomes for them an object of conscious and deliberate effort'. To Cairnes, the improvement of conditions '*is a new social force*, wholly different in character from any which had hitherto helped to shape human destiny – wholly different, also, from those influences which have guided the unfolding either of the individual animal or of the species' (1875a: p. 133). The formation of political institutions and private altruism are two ways in which efforts to this end may be made. To describe, as Spencer does, political institutions as having 'grown' or as having 'spontaneously developed', when the case is that the institutions 'have been deliberately created or adopted by intelligent beings for the precise purpose which they serve' is objectionable: the use of a word such as 'grown' is 'unwarrantable, and ... a cover for fallacious inference' (1875a: p. 134). Indeed it was with a Millian attention to the meaning of words that Cairnes elaborated his line of criticism:

> Political institutions ... do not 'grow' in the sense in which plants and animals grow: they are not the 'products' of a community in the sense in which the fauna and flora of a country are its products; but are due to causes and to processes of an entirely different kind. Under these circumstances, to describe them as examples of spontaneous development,

and to class them with the ordinary phenomena of organic life, is to use language, and to adopt a classification, fitted to obscure and to confound, rather than to elucidate, the problems of social existence.

(1875a: p. 135)

Similarly, Cairnes continued, voluntary associations are founded by conscious, not 'spontaneous', effort, with deliberate aims and purposes in mind. Spencer's concern with society as an 'organism', with 'growth', and with the evolution of 'structure', 'integration' and 'differentiation' has led him astray into the neglect of acts of creation 'by the human will in the deliberate pursuit of public well-being' (1875a: p. 138). The complexity of the historical record of effort and variation is thereby not explained, but rather explained away, by the evasive generalities of what Spencer proclaims as 'the workings-out of sociological processes' (1875a: p. 139), in which a man's status, it is to be observed, whether pauper or parliamentarian, or even a philosopher of evolution, is but as a 'conscious automaton' (1875a: p. 143). Spencer might well have replied to Cairnes that his conception of individuals as possessing a 'social self-consciousness' encompassed consciousness of a corporate existence. To neutralize the remainder of the critique, though, Spencer would have been forced to compromise his psychology and grand evolutionary narrative in sociology.

In contrast, the response of J. A. Hobson, was to adopt Huxley's line that the idea of the social organism in Spencer's hands was simply incorrectly drawn. For Hobson, Spencer was 'the first English thinker clearly to apply the organic conception of growth to the structure of Society. This he combined with a strangely perverse refusal to apply this same principle as a formative progressive force in the perfection of the organic nature of Society in politics and industry. He finds Society a low-grade organism, without a sensorium, and thinks it must remain so' (1904: p. 15). In a similar manner, Benjamin Kidd sought to undermine Spencer's version of the social organism idea to promote a holistically spiritual idea of social evolution. Thus, having outlined Spencer's position in his 1860 essay, Kidd considers the state of contemporary thought in 1908, in which a 'more organic' conception of society is coming to the fore, changing how evolution may be seen in relation to society:

It will be apparent, on reflection, that Spencer's conception of a corporate life subordinate to the interests of the units comprising it, is in the nature of things invalid. It is the correlative of that conception of the individual struggle for existence which was first presented by Darwin. It is evident that it is impossible to conceive society in any scientific sense as a mere mob of units of this kind whose individual interests could be paramount over the corporate interests.

(1908: p. 24)

The American sociologist, Harry Elmer Barnes, took an unusual position, finding inconsistency in Spencer's idea of the social organism, yet doubting the wisdom of reinterpreting it in the manner of Hobson or Huxley. He acknowledged that (by 1921) Spencer's idea had been 'roundly criticized by many writers', noting the contribution of the idealist philosopher David Ritchie in particular, and admitted that between the social organism and the inference that the regulating structure of government (except for its negatively regulative functions) would 'disintegrate' with the evolution of society there was a 'discrepancy' which Spencer's 'ingenuity was never quite able to explain away'. However, the contrasting belief that the logical fulfilment of the idea of society as an organism implied that 'the function of government must become more and more all-inclusive' was, for Barnes, 'hardly more satisfactory'. Barnes noted that, while Comte and Lester Ward had been adamant that, in contrast to Spencer, man's intellect could guide social development by devising advantageous legislation, and thus hastening progress through 'an extension of state activity', there were serious difficulties: 'in view of the present level of general intelligence and moral character of the usual run of the governmental officers in modern political systems, many modern thinkers would rather trust to the efficacy of voluntary organization. It seems', added Barnes, 'that this was essentially the view of Spencer' (1921: p. 40).

   In Kiel, the liberal sociologist Ferdinand Tönnies was writing quite extensively on Spencer (his *Gemeinschaft und Gesellschaft* of 1887 contains several references to Spencer), and in 1904 he pronounced his idea of the social organism unimpressive: 'wanting in clear conception, and unworkable' (1974: p. 109). His chief objection was that the conception fails to distinguish between accidental unity and social unity – a social whole has to be conceived as such by its members. In fact it is far from established here that Spencer, with his emphasis on 'permanence' and the presence of 'cooperation' and 'co-ordinated actions', is in breach of such a stipulation, though his commitment to his evolutionary perspective would rebel against the existence in practice of a sharp line of demarcation of the kind Tönnies invokes. Spencer, as already noted, emphasizes that cultural products, including tools, language, knowledge, customs and art-objects, are social or super-organic phenomena (1893: pp. 12–13). Moreover, as already discussed, Spencer insists that men have altruistic feelings, and give voice to 'sympathetic interests, which, acting individually and cooperatively, work out results scarcely less remarkable than those which the selfish interests work out' (1871a: p. 433). Tönnies (1892) also calls into question the idea that mankind as a whole could count as a single social organism (to which idea Spencer was not committed). And in so doing he also called into question Spencer's use of the 'division of labour' as evidence of the actual organic unity of a particular 'social organism'[19]:

If we illustrate his international division of labor by the commerce between Britain and China, as a typical example, it may be seen at once that the separateness of the partners is not preceded by their unity; as though there had been at first a combined if less efficient activity of tea-growing and cotton goods manufacture, to be followed by concentrating all tea-growing energies in China, and all cotton goods manufacturing energies in Britain. Nothing of the sort. Even on the most favourable assumption, that is, of the whole nation being the agent of the commercial exchange each nation is independent and entirely without any organic relation to the other. If they engage in exchange transactions with one another, they do so with a view to the benefit to be derived to themselves. As the contracts continue, they become a more important relation. This latter can even be considered as a unit. But the unity of the thing resides not in the different nations as such, but it arises from each of their social actions which are as building blocks being put together to a single structure. All such actions and hence the whole action system, can be considered a unit in the sense that it is the result of naturally opposite aims. There just is no unit to begin with; it is constructed by the deliberate actions of its independent subjects, acting the way they do in their own interests....

(In Jacoby, 1974: pp. 109–10)

Tönnies had idealist sympathies. Other idealist thinkers were notably vocal critics of Spencer's idea of the social organism. Bernard Bosanquet's criticisms of Spencer on the social organism covered materially similar ground to Cairnes, though Cairnes did not share the idealists' analysis of 'society' as a moral entity. For Bosanquet, little has been gained 'by applying inadequate conceptions, drawn from the life of plants and of lower animals, to the life of man .... For this evil we have largely to thank Mr. Herbert Spencer ... in spite of his great abilities and untiring industry, or rather because of them and their abuse' (1895: pp. 56–7).[20] According to Ritchie, Spencer thought of the individual as if 'he had a meaning and significance apart from his surroundings and apart from his relations to the community of which he is a member' (1885: p. 106). Like T. H. Green, Ritchie and Bosanquet, Henry Jones was also an idealist philosopher. He was a close contemporary of Bosanquet's, but, like most prominent idealists, was less hostile to positive action by the state (as opposed to voluntary action) than Bosanquet.[21] Jones considered that a society 'must exist for the benefit of its component parts, and the component parts must also exist for the benefit of society. Nay, more, if society is an organism, then it is impossible to separate the welfare of the whole from the welfare of the members, or the welfare of the members from the welfare of the whole. To separate the one from the other is to give independent existence to unreal abstractions and to empty the notion of organic unity of its distinctive content' (1883: p. 7). In Jones's assessment, the real meaning of the doctrine that society is an organism is that 'an individual has no life except that which is social, and that he cannot realise his own purposes except in realising the larger purposes of society.... Whatever the difficulties may be in finding the unity of the social organism, if we hold to the doctrine and make it more than metaphor, we must recognise that society and individuals actually form such a whole, and that apart from each other they are nothing but names; and we must cease to speak of individuals as if they ever could exist apart from society, or could attain their purposes except by becoming its organs and carrying out its purposes. It seems to me that the first and last duty of man is to know and to do those things which the social community of which he is a member calls upon him to do'. A life a man 'perverts' to selfish ends 'is not merely his own but that of the moral organism which lives in him' (1883: p. 9).[22] In idealist hands the idea of society as an organism was rapidly mutating into a metaphor for the moral or 'organic' community with a capacity for *moral* growth and in which there was a communion of souls, with neither individuals nor the state construed as the *means* to the other. Natural processes as such of growth in terms of structure and function, moreover, were simply ceasing for idealists to be appropriate ways of understanding social phenomena, it was the *meaning* in human and moral terms of such phenomena to which students of social life should direct their attention, because, through their consciousness and reflexive use of language, the members of a community as a *collectivity* gave meaning and moral significance to social phenomena, constructing the *sense* of social phenomena rather than 'observing' them as mere brute objects for study in the world. Compared with Tönnies, and T. H. Green and the other idealist philosophers, owing debts to Hegel, and Rousseau's 'general will', Spencer was in an enemy camp, well brought out by Jose Harris:

> Green, like Herbert Spencer, viewed society as an 'organism', and like Spencer he believed that the true arena of social progress lay in voluntaristic cooperation among human beings rather than in direction by the state. Unlike Spencer, though, he saw the 'organic character of society' as rational and purposive rather than natural and predetermined, and the true sphere of rights and laws as being not nature but human consciousness and will. A fully organic 'society' was a group of interdependent rational beings with a common moral purpose, embodied in a 'general will'. Only in 'society' could human beings find true freedom or 'moral liberation'; and morality did not consist merely in private acts of virtue, but in the bringing of the individual will into conformity with the rules and well-being of the wider organic whole.
>
> (1993: p. 228)

Idealists were concerned, first, to criticize Spencer's 'individualism' as embodying a social ontology, which they rather hastily assumed was discredited, and, second, to recreate the social organism idea to serve their own ends, advancing the idea of society as a holistic collectivity and a moral unity. Little time was thus devoted to sedulous dissection and scrupulous argument that *in its own terms* Spencer's idea of the social organism lacked legitimacy. There is indeed a distinction to be made between the social organism regarded as a collectivity, and Spencer's own position, that the social organism 'was an aggregate possessing definite relations which remained comparatively constant while the individuals occupying them changed' (Taylor, 1992: p. 165).[23] Once the logic of Spencer's position is properly recognized, there is no contradiction between his organicism and his opposition to collectivist ideas. Spencer saw his sociology as furnishing robust arguments against Comtean and indeed Idealist schemes of collectivist interference with the social organism in the interests of 'social engineering', meaning to say programmes of legislation by which a government would engage in positive regulation and direct provision in such areas as the education of children, health services and the public subsidy of housing costs. It did, though, support the growth of both a more accessible and efficient administration of justice as a safeguard for well-being against infringements of liberty and the blossoming in each individual of a 'social self-consciousness'. It was not therefore opposed to all types of social reform as Taylor tends to imply (1992: pp. 131–2). The message married a comparatively distant prospect of gradual, but 'natural' and not chimerical change, an element of 'real' progress, with a trenchant critique of the counter-productiveness of mechanistic legislative interference in the social and economic relations of the status quo. Should the State do more than protect freedom and administer 'justice' it would inflict harm upon the working of the whole social organism.

It may be that, historically, most conceptions of societies as organisms have accompanied and perhaps been designed to encourage essentially authoritarian or Burkean conservative social and political arrangements, with significant responsibilities for government beyond the 'negatively regulative'. There is, though no necessary or 'natural' connection here: the analogy could be legitimately formulated to point in the opposite direction. And this Spencer does, taking pains to argue unambiguously that since social individuals have consciousness there is in society no social sensorium. The coherence of Spencer's position has been expounded with magisterial elegance by Tim Gray (1996: p. 233)

> Spencer enunciated a conception of individualism which was opposed to collectivism, not to social organicism; and he enunciated a conception of social organicism which was opposed to mechanism, not to individualism. The general consistency of Spencer's position is made clear by the additional facts that his 'true' model of individualism was opposed to mechanism, and his 'true' model of organicism was

opposed to collectivism. At the root of the critics' misinterpretation of Spencer's theory was their mistaken assumptions that the 'opposite' of individualism was organicism, and that the 'opposite' of 'organicism' was individualism. The truth is, however, that if there *is* an 'opposite' of individualism it is collectivism, not organicism, and if there *is* an 'opposite' of organicism, it is mechanism not individualism. Spencer consistently developed an individualistic/organicist theory, and consistently opposed it to a collectivist/mechanistic theory.

David Wiltshire, in a widely quoted study of Spencer's social and political thought, recognizes that, for Spencer, a society apart from its units has no feeling, or perception. However, Wiltshire then adds that this point, 'substantially contradicts the organic analogy, but is a vital concession to the nominalist theory of society, which Spencer denied. If society can "feel" only through the perception of its units, then only through the perception of its units has it any existence'. Nevertheless, for Spencer, as Wiltshire acknowledges, society *was* real, 'existing independently of the perception of its constituent members. Only if thus conceived', Wiltshire continues, 'can its development be considered subject to the immutable laws of nature'. But this 'vital concession' allegedly made by Spencer to nominalism is in reality a damp squib. The perceptions of a society's government and other institutions are indeed for Spencer decomposable into those of the society's relevant individuals, or 'units', themselves of course key parts of the social organism in question. And this view is not at all a departure from or invalidation of Spencer's own idea of the social organism. In fact Wiltshire's 'problem' is of his own making: the reality of a social organism for Spencer quite simply, and legitimately, does not inhere *in it itself possessing* perceptions independent of its members but in the consciousness of all members of the society of each other as members. According to Wiltshire: 'The absence, in society, of a collective consciousness thus neatly incorporates three related problems; first, it sets up an insuperable barrier to literal acceptance of the social organism; second, it confounds Spencer's realist view of society, and third, it raises the questionable status of the individual in evolutionary philosophy' (1978: pp. 234–5). In logic, however, once Spencer's version of the social organism is given a fair hearing, the absence of a 'collective consciousness' within it does not appear to do any of these things.

Wiltshire proceeds to argue that Spencer's response to Huxley 'virtually jettisoned the literal interpretation of the social organism' (1978: p. 240). For in 'Specialized Administration' Spencer himself suggests that in a 'physically incoherent aggregate of individuals distributed over a wide of area' there cannot be 'analogies of a visible or sensible kind; but can only be analogies between the systems, or methods, of organization. Such analogies as exist result from the one unquestionable community between the two organizations: *there is in both a mutual dependence of parts.* This is the origin of all organization; and determines what similarities there are between an individual organism and a social organism' (1871a: p. 411).[24] Wiltshire's overall judgement is that ' "Administrative Specialization" marks the grave of Spencer's organic analogy.[25] Society cannot be regarded as literally "organic" in the sense that it is a natural outgrowth of pre-social evolution, and to describe it as organic in any other way is to dissipate the force of the analogy' (1978: p. 241). Wiltshire thus insists that, with the drawing of the physiological parallel with organic life in fact unavailable because, in his assessment, of the lack of a 'continuous physical structure' (1978: p. 241), to point to the presence of what Wiltshire considers to be simple mechanical functionalist relations in a society is a much weaker observation to have made. Yet this is surely to miss the point and significance of Spencer's attempt to stretch ideas of organisms and their morphologies in 'Transcendental Physiology'! With the idea of the social organism, Spencer was striving to achieve a coherent, subtle and sophisticated approach to answering the challenge of how to think about society and social relations, and this merits sympathetic analysis rather than a misplaced condescension, as if he were hooked on an elementary mistake in the construction of the analogy. Indeed, the implied 'conventional' and 'correct' form of the 'social organism' clearly diminishes to vanishing point individual autonomy, which would hardly itself represent a fair encapsulation of social reality. The deeper issue at stake is, I submit, the question of what Spencer thought counted as doing sociology. His model was, on the one hand, a natural history approach to social evolution, in which 'history' and agency are ironed out to give a kind of 'objective' narrative, but one readily open to disproof unless the grounds for criticism from historical studies are removed as well, of which step Spencer is, perhaps unawares, not entirely innocent. On the other hand, it was of sociology as engaged and normative, focused on social transactions and their outcomes, and concerned with contemporary matters in a society. In the first, we have a natural history of forms of society as resulting from successive and successively 'higher' manifestations of the law of equal freedom as an evolutionary law of life, in the second, derived from the same law, a sociology focused on a conception of lived social life as a spontaneous co-operation between socially self-conscious persons, on the conditions under which this conception can have stability in its existence, and on its outcomes, planned and unplanned.

The 'social organism' scaffolding enabled Spencer to get to this point, and it was buttressed by a train of reasoning of much greater insight and sophistication than admitted when caricaturing him as an abuser of an in fact arbitrarily selected template of the 'true' analogy. These, in principle, complementary, not contradictory, components of what Spencer perceived as the appropriate gaze for sociology remain in vogue in sociology, even if acknowledging Spencer's earlier effort does not. For, on the one hand, there is Runciman's *A Treatise on Social Theory* (especially the third volume of 1997), concerned with evolution of social forms in respect of the changing distribution of economic, ideological and political power, and, on the other, James Coleman's *Foundations of Social Theory* (1990), with a focus on rational choice, and outcomes. These issues are revisited later in 'Concluding Reflections'.

7
Militant and Industrial Social Types

> If men had always been secured in person and property, and left at full liberty to employ both as they saw fit; and had merely been precluded from unjust interference with each other – had the most perfect freedom of intercourse between all mankind been always allowed – had there never been any wars – nor (which in that case would have easily been avoided) any taxation – then, though every exchange that took place would have been one of the phenomena of which Political-Economy takes cognizance, all would have proceeded so smoothly, that probably no attention would ever have been called to the subject. The transactions of society would have been like the play of the lungs, the contractions of the muscles, and the circulation of the blood, in a healthy person; who scarcely knows that these functions exist.

This elegantly expressed speculation came not from Spencer but from Richard Whately, in the third of his *Introductory Lectures on Political Economy* published in 1832. Spencer was by no means a lone voice in the first half of the early nineteenth century in identifying war and militancy as a source of distinctive and disturbing forms of social life. Whately perceived, no less keenly than Spencer was later to do, an antinomy between the waging of wars and social progress, with progress understood in terms of enhanced personal liberty, augmented wealth and increased moral sensibility. Like Spencer too, Whately faulted the conventional historical analysis of his day for failing to grasp the fundamentals of social organization and the most salient factors involved in interpreting economic and social life. In his ninth and last Lecture he remarked.

> For not only are many of the transactions which are, in the historian's view, the most important, such as are the least important to the Political-Economist, but also a great proportion of them consists of what are in

reality the greatest *impediments* to the progress of a society in wealth: viz. wars, revolutions, and disturbances of every kind. It is not in consequence of these, but in spite of them, that society has made the progress which in fact it has made. So that in taking such a survey as history furnishes of the course of events, e.g. for the last 800 years, ... not only do we find little mention of the causes which have so greatly increased national wealth during that period, but what we chiefly do read of is, the *counteracting* causes; especially the wars which have been raging from time to time, to the destruction of capital, and the hindrance of improvement. Now if a ship had performed a voyage of 800 leagues, and the register of it contained an account chiefly of the contrary winds and currents, and made little mention of favourable gales, we might well be at a loss to understand how she reached her destination; and might even be led into the mistake of supposing that the contrary winds had forwarded her in her course. Yet such is History!

Spencer's own analysis of social relations in terms of two contrasted types, 'militant' and 'industrial', was a major constituent of his sociology, and remains an often cited point of orientation in contemporary sociological thought, in name if not in substance. It is indeed no exaggeration to find 'the importance of the distinction between militant and industrial societies to Spencer's sociology ... hard to overestimate' (Bell and Sylvest, 2006: p. 225). For Spencer the contrast facilitated the comparative analysis of a variety of societies, and gave some assurance that in the future civilized societies might resolve differences and contribute to a stable international political order. The germ of the contrast may be discerned as far back as 1842 in the Letters which formed *The Proper Sphere of Government*:

> War has been the nurse of the feudal spirit so long the curse of all nations; and from that spirit has flowed much of the selfish and tyrannical legislation under which we have so long groaned. If, for the last four or five centuries, the civilised world, instead of having been engaged in invasions and conquests, had directed its attention to the real sources of wealth – industry and commerce, science and the arts – long since would our nobility have found that they were mere drones in the hive, and long since would they have ceased to glory in their shame.
>
> When to the commercial and political evils of war, we add the moral ones, when we remember that it is inconsistent with the spirit of Christianity – that it unduly encourages the animal passions – that it exalts brute courage into the greatest of human virtues – that it tends greatly to retard the civilisation of the world – that it is the grand bar to the extension of that feeling of universal brotherhood with all nations, so essential to the real prosperity of mankind: when, in addition to these collateral

evils, we call to mind the immediate ones – the horrors of battle, and the lamentations of kindred – we shall rather feel that, a principle which of necessity excludes these things, should, on that account alone, earnestly commend itself to our notice.

We are told that the time shall come, when nations 'shall beat their swords into ploughshares, and their spears into pruning hooks'. That time may be yet afar off, but we are advancing towards it – we shall eventually arrive at it, and that too, we may assure ourselves, not by any sudden revolution, but by a continued moral and intellectual progression. We must not wait for a direct interposition of the Almighty to bring about this change; we must use proper means; we must put our shoulders to the wheel, and then look for the fulfilment of the promise as the result of our obedience to the commands. But what are the means? One of them we have before us. Confine the duty of our rulers to their only duty, the administration of justice; and ... the prophecy is fulfilled.

(1843: pp. 23–4)

The concern was retained in *Social Statics*, though now framed within the pre-Darwinian evolutionary framework of direct adaptation to conditions, at the expense of faith in a simple 'shoulders to the wheel' mode of exhortation and the expectation of a direct and immediate consequential impact on social life (see 1851: p. 247). Once sociality was established, human character changed only slowly in history because it has been subject to two sets of conditions which conflict with each other:

On the one hand the discipline of the social state has been developing it into the sympathetic form; whilst on the other hand, the necessity for self-defence partly of man against brute, partly of man against man, and partly of societies against each other, has been maintaining the old unsympathetic form. And only where the influence of the first set of conditions has exceeded that of the last, and then only in proportion to the excess, has modification taken place. Amongst tribes who have kept each other's anti-social characteristics in full activity by constant conflict, no advance has been possible. But where warfare against man and beast has ceased to be continuous, or where it has become the employment of but a portion of the people, the effects of living in the associated state have become greater than the effects of barbarizing antagonisms, and progress has resulted.

Regarded thus, civilization no longer appears to be a regular unfolding after a specific plan; but seems rather a development of man's latent capabilities under the action of favourable circumstances.

(1851: p. 415)

However, the contrast in terms of a systematically constructed sociological division between 'militancy' and 'industrialism' as distinct types of social structure (not, note, 'societies') was first given public shape in the first edition of *First Principles* of 1862. It was introduced as Spencer sought to rebut the possible criticism to his theory of evolution, as applied to social life, that in fact there was *not* an unwaveringly uniform process of an increase in definiteness, or integration. To this potential objection, Spencer pointed in response to a further aspect evident in social evolution that must be incorporated into the theory: 'Should it be objected that among civilized nations there are examples of decreasing definiteness, (instance the breaking down of limits between ranks,) the reply is, that such apparent exceptions are the accompaniment of a social metamorphosis – a change from the military or predatory type of social structure, to the industrial or mercantile type, during which the old lines of organization are disappearing and the new ones becoming more marked' (1862: p. 190; also 1870: p. 374). The same passage is present in the sixth and final edition of 1900, save that 'or predatory' and 'or mercantile' have been omitted. In the second and subsequent editions, but not as far as I can trace in the first edition (except for the final sentence), he also says,

> A civilized society is made unlike a barbarous one by the establishment of regulative classes – governmental, administrative, military, ecclesiastical, legal, &c., which, while they have their special bonds of union, constituting them sub-classes, are also held together as a general class by a certain community of privileges, of blood, of education, of intercourse. In some societies, fully developed after their particular types, this consolidation into castes, and this union among the upper castes by separation from the lower, eventually grow very decided: to be afterwards rendered less decided, only in cases of social metamorphosis caused by the industrial regime. The integrations that accompany the operative or industrial organization, later in origin, are not merely of this indirect kind, but they are also direct – they show us physical approach. We have integrations consequent on the simple growth of adjacent parts performing like functions; as, for instance, the junction of Manchester with its calico-weaving suburbs.
>
> (1867: pp. 317–18)

The whole passage is interesting and difficult to interpret with certainty. It could be read in the sense that the *integrations* accompanying industrial organization are later in origin than all of those associated with militarism. Or it may be read as asserting in general that *industrial organization* is a later evolutionary product than militant organization. However, neither of these meanings, if intended at all, was adhered to as the typology was developed in the *Principles of Sociology*, as we shall shortly see. There Spencer made specific references to 'early' societies displaying 'industrial' or peaceful social life. A third reading is possible, and I think the most plausible one, in which the passage is simply concerned with militancy and certain forms of industrial integration in 'advanced' societies. This reading preserves consistency, with other forms of industrial integration not ruled out in 'early' industrial societies.

By the *Principles of Sociology*, Spencer had adopted the terminology of 'militant' and 'industrial' 'types *of society*'.[1] In discussing types of society, Spencer declares that, unlike in the case of individual organisms, classification is difficult, because 'higher social aggregates propagate their respective types in much less decided ways' (1893: p. 537). However, societies may be grouped, in a 'natural manner', in two ways – 'primarily' by their composition, how complex the process of compounding they have undergone (political amalgamation and unification), and secondarily, 'though in a less specific way', they may be divided 'into the predominantly militant and the predominantly industrial – those in which the organization for offence and defence is most largely developed, and those in which the sustaining organization is most largely developed' (1893: p. 538). This second grouping refers to the kinds of social activities which have preponderance in a particular society at a particular time, and the resulting contrasts in the organization the society possesses. Compulsion or coercion into co-operation contrasts with voluntary co-operation. In this context Spencer's meaning would have been clearer had he referred to 'types of social relations' rather than to 'types of society'. It is important to note too that Spencer now points explicitly to instances of 'early' societies that are 'industrial', giving as examples the Arafuras, the Todas, the 'amiable Bodo and Dhimáls', and the Mishmis (1893: pp. 552–3).

In considering advanced societies of his own time, Spencer stresses that 'multitudinous objects' are already being achieved 'by spontaneously-evolved combinations of citizens governed representatively' (1893: p. 556). In other words, we have in our midst aspects of social organization which represents 'industrial' society. Of particular concern to Spencer is a contemporary metamorphosis in Britain away from the industrial type and towards the militant type, associated first with perceived external threats to security, but which has also manifested itself in internal matters, at the expense of individual freedom and local autonomy.[2]

Whatever are Spencer's own normative preferences about the nature of social relations (they are not difficult to discern), he attempts to present a neutral evolutionary perspective on the types: 'Social organization is to be considered high in proportion as it subserves individual welfare, because in a society the units are sentient and the aggregate insentient; and the industrial type is the higher because, in that state of permanent peace to which civilization is tending, it subserves individual welfare better than the militant type' (1893: pp. 587–8).[3] However, Spencer also briefly introduces the possibility of a *third* social type in the future, as different to the two types as they are to each other. This third social type would be one

> which, having a sustaining system more fully developed than any we know at present, will use the products of industry neither for maintaining a militant organization nor exclusively for material aggrandizement; but will devote them to the carrying on of higher activities. As the contrast between the militant and the industrial types, is indicated by inversion of the belief that individuals exist for the benefit of the State into the belief that the State exists for the benefit of individuals, so the contrast between the industrial type and the type likely to be evolved from it, is indicated by inversion of the belief that life is for work into the belief that work is for life. But we are here concerned with inductions derived from societies that have been and are, and cannot enter upon speculations respecting societies that may be. Merely naming as a sign, the multiplication of institutions and appliances for intellectual and aesthetic culture, and for kindred activities not of a directly life-sustaining kind but of a kind having gratification for their immediate purpose, I can here say no more.
>
> (1893: p. 563)[4]

We may now turn to the detailed analytical exposition of the militant and industrial types which Spencer provided in 'Political Institutions', a later Part of the second volume of the *Sociology*, written in 1882.

In the chapter devoted to the militant type of society, Spencer adopts the approach of identifying 'the several traits which of necessity militancy tends to produce', and then observing 'how far these traits are conjointly shown in past and present nations distinguished by militancy'. In this way, having contemplated the society 'ideally organized for war, we shall be prepared to recognize in real societies the characters which war has brought about' (1891c: p. 569). Corporate action is required if corporate life is threatened; in a 'struggle for existence' the victorious society may have produced warriors not inferior to its opponents but be better supported by the non-combatants organized in their support. The militant type of society, 'produced by survival of the fittest, will be one in which the fighting part includes all who can bear arms and be trusted with arms, while the remaining part serves simply as a permanent commissariat' (1891c: p. 570). Such corporate control requires that individuality is lost; the individual is at the disposal of his society, owned by the state which curtails his liberty. In the process the social organization at large becomes characterized by centralization, with the members assigned ranks, and status, exhibiting degrees of hierarchical subordination and regimentation. The militant form of government is regulative both negatively and positively: it restrains and also enforces, so that voluntary co-operation becomes controlled and coerced. Status becomes fixed, and consequently inheritance of rank and position by descendants grows, bringing both stability and inflexibility to the social structure. In general the militant society is associated with resistance to change. Self-sufficiency rather than exchange in the society becomes normal as commercial intercourse is hindered or prevented: economic autonomy accompanies political autonomy. Ancient Peru, Sparta, the Roman Empire and Russia are among examples Spencer discusses to indicate the social range and geographical spread of typical militant social organization. The German Empire too is taken as one contemporary exemplar of such features, with Spencer's choice of illustrations including railway ownership by the state, and Bismarck's 'scheme of State-insurance, by the help of which the artisan would, in a considerable degree, have his hands tied' (1891c: p. 590). The largely reactive 'revival of military activity' in 'our own society' is having, suggests Spencer, a creeping and extensive impact, restraining or usurping private action by central control: 'There is the "endowment of research", which, already partially carried out by a government fund, many wish to carry further; there is the proposed act for establishing a registration of authorized teachers; there is the bill which provides central inspection for local public libraries; there is the scheme for compulsory insurance – a scheme showing us in an instructive manner the way in which the regulating policy extends itself: compulsory charity [that is, the poor law] having generated improvidence, there comes compulsory insurance as a remedy for the improvidence' (1891c: pp. 591–2). In the organization of even the Liberal party, the party traditionally not disposed to militancy, 'we see that militant discipline is spreading; for the caucus system, established for the better organization of liberalism, is one which necessarily, in a greater or less degree, centralizes authority and controls individual action' (1891c: p. 592).

The characters of the men themselves who are members of a militant society both shape and reflect their social condition. They have revenge as a sacred, religiously sanctioned duty. Individual initiative is repressed in favour of a passive acceptance and expectancy of being commanded. Where the militant type of society is fully developed, men accept that 'everything must be done by public agencies; not only for the reason that these occupy all spheres, but for the further reason that did they not occupy them, there would arise no other agencies: the prompting ideas and sentiments having been obliterated' (1891c: p. 599). With the idea of omnipresent rulers entrenched, there comes the sequel that the idea of impersonal causation is not understood: 'the course of social evolution is unperceived. The natural genesis of social structures and functions is an utterly alien conception, and appears absurd when alleged. The notion of a self-regulating social process is unintelligible. So that militancy moulds the citizen into a form not only morally adapted but intellectually adapted – a form which cannot think away from the entailed system' (1891c: p. 600).

In his summary of the industrial type of society (or type of social relations), Spencer observes at the outset that since societies nearly always have to defend themselves against aggression from outside as well as internally to ensure 'sustentation', they 'habitually present us with mixtures of the structures adapted to these diverse ends. Disentanglement is not easy' (1891c: p. 603). Depending on which type of structure predominates it closely affects the other: where militant structures prevail the worker is no freer than the soldier, and where industrialism prevails the soldier, 'volunteering on specific terms', acquires the position of a free worker. In the first type of structure the system of status prevails even in the workplace, in the second the system of contract affects military organization. Where, as in many societies, the militant type of social relations is so far displayed as to be readily apparent, the industrial type 'has its traits so hidden by those of the still-dominant militant type, that its nature is nowhere more than very partially exemplified' (1891c: p. 603). Spencer now emphasizes strongly that industrialism is not to be confused with industriousness: 'the social relations which characterize the industrial type may coexist with but very moderate productive activities' (1891c: p. 604). It is, rather, *the form that co-operation takes* that is the key consideration in identifying the industrial type of social relations. For Spencer, this criterion indicates that socialism and communism as forms of control replicate the characteristics of the predominantly militant form of society: the industrial type of society must therefore be distinguished sharply from a type

> very likely to be confounded with it – the type, namely, in which the component individuals, while exclusively occupied in production and distribution, are under a regulation such as that advocated by socialists and communists. For this, too, involves in another form the principle of compulsory cooperation. Directly or indirectly, individuals are to be prevented from severally and independently occupying themselves as they please; are to be prevented from competing with one another in supplying goods for money; are to be prevented from hiring themselves out on such terms as they think fit. There can be no artificial system for regulating labour which does not interfere with the natural system. To such extent as men are debarred from making whatever engagements they like, they are to that extent working under dictation. No matter in what way the controlling agency is constituted, it stands towards those controlled in the same relation as does the controlling agency of a militant society.
>
> (1891c: p. 605)

In industrial societies it is voluntary contract rather than status that is the predominant form of social relations, with individual liberty limited only by the like liberty of others, reinforced by 'a representative agency' (government) mediating on disputed matters. It is an essential requirement of 'industrial' social relations that 'the individuality of each man shall have the fullest play compatible with the like play of other men's individualities' (1891c: p. 608). Without an external threat with which to contend, the role of government becomes solely to maintain conditions for 'the highest individual life' (1891c: p. 609), life which encompasses spontaneous voluntary aid. A society in which life, liberty and property are secure 'must prosper more than one in which they are not' (1891c: p. 608). The equal freedom principle rules: 'Living and working within the restraints imposed by one another's presence, justice requires that individuals shall severally take the consequences of their conduct, neither increased nor decreased' (1891c: p. 610). Public action abstracting from this is vetoed as handicapping those whose lives are adjusting to the demands of the industrial type of society. While the industrial type has come into being by the operation of the 'survival of the fittest' when the decline of external aggression which suits the emergence of industrial society is present, there persists an 'industrial struggle for existence' between societies of the industrial type (1891c: pp. 608, 610). An overall relative plasticity of form and flexibility in the interests of accommodating adaptation to new circumstances and the exercise of liberty must characterize the organization of this social type. The processes involved usher in a diminution of economic isolation: 'the great nations themselves, at present forced in large measure to maintain their economic autonomies, will become less forced to do this as war decreases, and will gradually become necessary to one another. While, on the one hand, the facilities possessed by each society or nation for certain kinds of production will render exchange mutually advantageous, on the other hand, the citizens of each will, under the industrial *régime*, tolerate no such restraints on their individualities as are implied by interdicts on exchanges or impediments to exchange' (1891c: pp. 614–15).

As noted earlier, there are for Spencer some 'early' tribes already indeed endowed with at least a sprinkling of the qualities associated with industrial society. Spencer notes that 'while the status of women is habitually very low in tribes given to war and in more advanced military societies, it is habitually very high in these primitive societies' (1891c: p. 631). It is not made entirely clear if Spencer believes these societies must have all possessed a militant earlier history. Records simply indicate that 'no civilized or semi-civilized nation has fallen into circumstances making needless all social structures for resisting aggression' (1891c: p. 615). Some may have fled before invaders, finding localities 'in which they are able to carry on their peaceful occupations unmolested' (1891c: p. 616). Certainly, though, the discussion is clear that forms of industrial social relations are not confined to 'civilized societies'. Spencer does, however, offer us a broad-brush view of European societies as embracing in varying degrees industrial forms of social life in 'modern' times, contrasting their appearance now with their prior conditions:

First, with the formation of nations covering large areas, the perpetual wars within each area have ceased; and though the wars between nations which from time to time occur are on larger scales, they are less frequent, and they are no longer the business of all freemen. Second, there has grown up in each country a relatively large population which carries on production and distribution for its own maintenance; so that whereas of old, the working part existed for the benefit of the fighting part, now the fighting part exists mainly for the benefit of the working part – exists ostensibly to protect it in the quiet pursuit of its ends. Third, the system of status, having under some of its forms disappeared and others become greatly mitigated, has been almost universally replaced by the system of contract. Only among those who, by choice or by conscription, are incorporated in the military organization, does the system of status in its primitive rigour still hold so long as they remain in this organization. Fourth, with this decrease of compulsory cooperation and increase of voluntary cooperation, there have diminished or ceased many minor restraints over individual actions. Men are less tied to their localities than they were; they are not obliged to profess certain religious opinions; they are less debarred from expressing their political views; they no longer have their dresses and modes of living dictated to them; they are comparatively little restrained from forming private combinations and holding meetings for one or other purpose – political, religious, social. Fifth, while the individualities of citizens are less aggressed upon by public agency, they are more protected by public agency against aggression. Instead of a *régime* under which individuals rectified their private wrongs by force as well as they could, or else bribed the ruler, general or local, to use his power in their behalf, there has come a *régime* under which, while much less self-protection is required, a chief function of the ruling power and its agents is to administer justice. In all ways, then, we are shown that with this relative decrease of militancy and relative increase of industrialism, there has been a change from a social order in which individuals exist for the benefit of the State, to a social order in which the State exists for the benefit of individuals.

(1891c: pp. 619–20)

Spencer's summary here should not be taken as signalling a Gnostic and panoptic complacency on his part. Repeatedly he deprecates the deep-seated militant personal traits in our own 'civilized society': 'In independence, in honesty, in truthfulness, in humanity, its citizens are not likely to be the equals of the uncultured but peaceful peoples above described' (1891c: p. 632). In practice, however, England appears to be closer to the industrial type than France, and Spencer provides a condensed comparative history to underpin this conclusion, citing Buckle's *History of Civilization* in support. France, for instance, exhibits a continuing preoccupation with external aggression, and a concomitant concern with the control of internal social relations, a consequence of that external preoccupation. In England, there is a trait of independence in men's character, linked to industrialism, which is more marked and joined with less worship of the state than in the country's European neighbours. The controlling agency possessed by countries approaching advanced industrialism applies itself in the main to the administration of justice, that is to say, it is concerned primarily with negatively regulative functions. Such regulation, and sympathetic self-regulation, should ensure that 'each citizen gains neither more nor less of benefit than his activities normally bring' and refrains from all public action 'involving any artificial distribution of benefits' (1891c: p. 638).

In assessing the two types of society more generally Spencer concludes that there is as he would expect an evolution in the various political institutions towards integration, an overall movement from homogeneity to heterogeneity. But each society can evolve and has evolved internally in different ways according to external circumstances: 'the phenomena become complicated by a simultaneous evolution of one part of the social organization and dissolution of another part – a mingling of changes well illustrated in our own society' (1891c: p. 646).[5] Spencer's disenchantment with England in the 1880s prompts him to celebrate the peaceful tribes that he has described as lacking the moral and religious hypocrisy found in England, the emblem of militant sentiments:

> The truth disclosed by the facts is that, so far as men's moral states are concerned, theory is almost nothing and practice is almost everything. No matter how high their nominal creed, nations given to political burglaries to get 'scientific frontiers', and the like, will have among their members many who 'annex' others' goods for their own convenience; and with the organized crime of aggressive war, will go criminality in the behaviour of one citizen to another. Conversely, as these uncultivated tribes prove, no matter how devoid they are of religious beliefs, those who, generation after generation remaining unmolested, inflict no injuries upon others, have their altruistic sentiments fostered by the sympathetic intercourse of a peaceful daily life, and display the resulting virtues. We need teaching that it is impossible to join injustice and brutality abroad with justice and humanity at home. What a pity these Heathens cannot be induced to send missionaries among the Christians!
>
> (1891c: p. 642)[6]

Spencer infers from past developments that at some future time the industrial type will become permanently established. And in the exemplars of this type there will be a devolution of administration concerning affairs that are purely local matters. The state, moreover, will undertake the administration of justice free of cost to the citizen (1891c: p. 660).

Spencer reiterates his analytical imperative that ultimately the characters of the units will determine the aggregate. The aggregate cannot be advanced 'all at once', since character needs to adapt, and slowly, to conditions.

Moreover, the conditions in principle suited to 'advanced' industrialism had not been encountered before. There was thus no reservoir of experience as there was to assist adaptation to conditions of militancy redivivus. As revolutionary France shows, if liberty is won in a sudden burst, character will show itself as not ready for it. In ultimate terms, the permanent ending of war is the key to the future; war has given all that it can give to social evolution – the building of nations and the discipline of continuous application in work. All that teaching can achieve, however, is to deter 'here and there one from doing mischief by imprudent zeal' (1891c: p. 667), thus serving in small measure to prevent the misdirection of 'forces' in support of militancy (1891c: p. 666).

What has been discussed so far respecting Spencer's presentation of the militant and industrial types of society in the *Principles of Sociology* is drawn from sections which are specifically planned to elucidate systematically the types as aids to sociological analysis. However, other chapters of that same large division ('Political Institutions') of the *Sociology*, and indeed other divisions, furnish many supplementary references to the types. The types are deployed as aids to analysis throughout the volumes. A glance at the chief instances of these applications completes the picture of the insights into social relations which Spencer believed the binary contrast that the types represent was equipped to unlock.

In the division devoted to 'Domestic Institutions' Spencer concludes that women acquire an enhanced position in social life when social organization is industrial in type. The associated peacefulness encourages the development of altruistic sentiments, more favourable consideration of children, and respect for liberty. It is the rise of industrial social relations, with their less predatory and coercive characteristics, that has permitted the growth of monogamy as the family unit, not other factors such as the influence of religious beliefs (1893: p. 680). However, as discussed in Chapter 5, he expresses ready agreement with the historian, Sir Henry Maine, that there is a trend towards the individual usurping the family as the basic unit of social composition (1893: pp. 704, 712). The trend has arisen from traits within both the militant *and* industrial types of society. Forced co-operation weakens voluntary co-operation, but in industrial social relations it is an individual distinct from their family and kin who is regarded as infringing liberty or as having their liberty infringed, and who is thus separated out from family and kin (1893: pp. 704–5). Laws, including the poor law, have replaced the roles of families as a source of financial assistance and in providing directly for the welfare of individual children: 'Legislation has of late further relaxed family-bonds by relieving parents from the care of their children's minds, and replacing education under parental direction by education under governmental direction'. The family as a responsible unit is thus in the present in decline: 'This recognition of the individual, rather than the family, as the social unit, has indeed now gone so far that by many the paternal duty of the State is assumed as self-evident; and criminals are called "our failures"' (1893: p. 705). Spencer's fundamental explanation, provided by a derivation from his basic evolutionary tenet of the persistence of force, is that the 'rhythm of change', once in motion, has in this case taken us from one extreme (the compound family as unit) to another, and 'we may expect a recoil towards that medium state in which there... is a renovation of the family group proper, composed of parents and offspring' (1893: p. 707).

A contrast between the regime appropriate to the family and the regime appropriate in particular to the state must be observed. If the two are confused in practice then either society weakens or children suffer. In order to survive, Spencer argues, 'every species of creature must fulfil two con-flicting requirements. During a certain period each member must receive benefits according to its incapacity. After that period it must receive benefits in proportion to its capacity' (1893: p. 708). In human life it is the fam-ily that cares for the young, or the sick: 'Import into the family the law of the society, and let children from infancy upwards have life-sustaining sup-plies proportioned to their life-sustaining labours, and the society disappears forthwith by death of all its young. Import into the society the law of the family, and let the life-sustaining supplies be great in proportion as the life-sustaining labours are small, and the society decays from increase of its least worthy members and decrease of its most worthy members. It fails to hold its own in the struggle with other societies, which allow play to the natural law that prosperity shall vary as efficiency'. To this exposi-tion, Spencer adds that the cardinal distinction between family ethics and state ethics must be publicly maintained to avoid the fatal results conse-quent upon its erosion: 'Unqualified generosity must remain the principle of the family while offspring are passing through their early stages; and generosity increasingly qualified by justice, must remain its principle as offspring are approaching maturity. Conversely, the principle of the society, guiding the acts of citizens to one another, must ever be, justice, qualified by such generosity as their several natures prompt; joined with unqual-ified justice in the corporate acts of the society to its members' (1893: p. 709).

The contrast, it must be said, is a somewhat infelicitous one, since the drawing of a distinction between *family* relations and *social* relations (by which, in fact, Spencer appears to mean all other relations, all associated chiefly with the predominant regime of the state at the time in question) may well appear a problematic process. Moreover, while the idea of mili-tant family relations as different to industrial family relations is not itself a difficulty, the potentially cross-cutting complication of a non-isomorphic relation between militant and industrial *family* relations and militant and industrial *social* relations, introduced with the reference to the rhythm of change, ought to be noted. Part of the explanation may be that Spencer himself had not anticipated including a treatment of 'domestic relations' until already preparing the first volume of the *Sociology*, making it a very late modification to the structure of the volumes.[7] Nevertheless, the basic point is clear enough. Biologically driven requirements related to the meeting of needs of offspring, mediated differently if under conditions of militancy rather than industrialism, demonstrate to Spencer that family life and not the State must fulfil these requirements.[8] In fact, as already noted, Spencer believes that the excess in family disintegration which is evident will be followed by a 'recoil' and 'partial re-integration' (1893: p. 712).

In another Part of the *Sociology*, 'Ceremonial Institutions', dating from 1879, Spencer finds 'Catholic societies...relatively more militant in type of organization' than Britain (1891c: p. 104). Obeisance, one form of social control, may be considered in general as reflecting the inability to resist; it declines as a feature as we move away from militant societies. Imitations of a ceremonial kind aimed at pleasing a superior indeed account for some of what Spencer categorizes as 'fashion', but in themselves would not produce the evident and widespread kind of social effect: 'There is a co-operating cause which takes advantage of the openings thus made. Competitive imitation, ever going as far as authority allows, turns to its own advantage every opportunity which reverential imitation makes' (1891c: p. 207). Spencer proposes that imitation in 'fashion' can be both a sign of reverence and an assertion of equality. Between these two forms of fashion, prompted by unlike 'motives', no clear line can be drawn. There results a possible transition 'from those reverential imitations going along with much subordination, to those competitive imitations characterizing a state of comparative independence' (1891c: p. 206). Evidence suggests that the two motives emerge at the same time, and develop in a range of forms in early societies, especially in industrial forms of society where rank and wealth do not always coincide. Although entangled and confused as 'ceremonial' and 'fashion' are, they represent respectively, as behaviour required by subordination to the great and as behaviour resulting from imitation of the great, the two different militant and industrial types. Both ceremonial and fashion are today 'enforced' by 'unembodied opinion', but the opinion of 'class-rule' and 'social opinion' can neverthelesss be differentiated (1891c: p. 209). As government is a form of political regulation, fashion is a form of 'social regulation'. Just as there has been a transition to voluntary co-operation which involves 'a growth of the representative agency serving to express the average volition', so too there has come growth of an 'indefinite aggregate of wealthy and cultured people, whose consensus of habits rules the private life of society at large' (1891c: p. 210). The changing balance between restraint and freedom has moved towards a balance between equalization and freedom.[9]

The general analysis of political matters contained in 'Political Institutions' also presented Spencer with the opportunity to put to use the militant/industrial typology beyond the specific sections that explained the typology itself. Of particular significance is his consideration of the ownership of land, which later embroiled Spencer in controversy, involving in particular Henry George (see Chapter 9). Communal proprietorship of land is, Spencer remarks, apparent in early social life, but militarism with its predatory and coercive characteristics seriously limits this pattern, producing a graduated ownership of land according to the status of the owner. However, although the individualization of land ownership at present accompanies industrial society, this pattern may nevertheless decline as a feature, since its roots are in militarism. For in general labour cannot create land: thus as the individual partially or wholly loses ownership of himself during the militant regime, but gradually resumes it as the industrial regime develops, 'so, possibly, the communal proprietorship of land, partially or wholly merged in the ownership of dominant men during evolution of the militant type, will be resumed as the industrial type becomes fully evolved' (1891c: p. 556). Thus a form of ownership with the community as landowner and the individual as tenant may emerge, with due compensation allowed for the value hitherto gained by the previous owner. An analogy with the decline of slavery is offered. We might once have inferred ownership of man by man was becoming permanently established, yet a later stage of civilization has destroyed ownership of man by man. In the same way, it seems possible that the primitive communal ownership 'which, with the development of coercive institutions, lapsed in large measure or wholly into private ownership, will be revived as industrialism further develops' (1891c: pp. 553–4).

Other aspects of the future of life and work within the industrial type of society are explored in the final and eighth Part of the *Sociology*, 'Industrial Institutions'. While militant activity will foster certain industries, associated with the manufacture of arms, for instance, 'in most respects the destroying activities have been antagonistic to the productive activities' (1896b: p. 360). Militant social life fractures industrial organization – and also distribution mechanisms – makes production reliant on women, which restricts and stagnates it, and generally lowers its status in social life. Once more, Spencer returns to the fundamental contrast that he wishes to make between militant and industrial co-operation, here describing the first as 'conscious' action and the second as 'unconscious':

> The commander, officers, and common soldiers forming an army, consciously act together to achieve a certain end. The men engaged in businesses of all kinds, severally pursuing private ends, act together to achieve a public end *unthought of* by them. Considered in the aggregate, their actions subserve the wants of the whole society; but they are not dictated by an authority, and they are carried on by each with a view to his own welfare, and not with a view to the welfare of all.
>
> (1896b: p. 544, italics added)

The first form is adjudged coercive and illiberal. The second, of course, accords with the idea of 'catallaxy' as described by Whately, and is voluntary and liberal. Spencer recognizes that the choices a contemporary labourer faces often amount to 'little more than the ability to exchange one slavery for another' (1896b: p. 516), a state of affairs arising from the low regard for justice adopted in commercial struggle and competition: 'men are used up for the benefit of posterity; and so long as they go on multiplying in excess of the means of subsistence, there appears no remedy' (1896b: p. 516). Current orthodox co-operation for industrial purposes, saving that apparently possible in self-styled 'cooperative' ventures (to which Spencer gives approval), means that, for the wage-earner, and, 'using Sir Henry Maine's terms', 'the marks of status do not wholly disappear'. During his work, a wage-earner does not act purely voluntarily: 'he is coerced by the consciousness that discharge will follow if he idles, and is sometimes more manifestly coerced by an overlooker'. But agreed contracts between men concerning who 'will perform certain work for a certain sum' transcend the coercion of temporary slavery represented in the status employee, a man's activity 'becomes entirely voluntary'. Thus, under 'present arrangements', the transition from 'the compulsory cooperation of militancy to the voluntary cooperation of industrialiam' is, in fact, 'incomplete' (1896b: p. 563).

Spencer also approaches current political theory through the lens of his binary divide: 'the socialist theory and practice are normal in the militant type of society, and cease to be normal as fast as the society becomes predominantly industrial in its type' (1896b, p. 567). A socialist perspective 'fits' with militancy, but not with industrialism, because of the overarching need in a militant form of society for joint action in the face of aggression. While much coercion of working people has disappeared, that which remains is fuelling a socialist cause:

> There is to be a re-institution of *status*, not under individual masters but under the community as master. No longer possessing themselves and making the best of their powers, individuals are to be possessed by the State; which, while it supports them, is to direct their labours. Necessarily there is implied a vast and elaborate administrative body – regulators of small groups, subject to higher regulators, and so on... to a central authority, which coordinates the multitudinous activities of the society in their kind and amounts.... A complete parallelism exists between such a social structure and the structure of an army.
>
> (1896b: p. 577)

Looking to the future, Germany and France are militant and bureaucratic already in social type, and fertile ground in which socialism can root itself (as spread by Marx, Lassalle, St. Simon, Fourier, Proudhon and Louis Blanc, whom Spencer all names [1896b: pp. 585, 588]). This kind of concern with the nature of French social relations was one of Spencer's specialities, and it had figured also in the *Principles of Ethics*. In France, the idea of equality 'has always subordinated the idea of liberty', and, under 'the guise of a free form of government, citizens have all along submitted without protest to a bureaucracy which has been as despotic under the republican form of government as the monarchical'. According to Spencer, reversions to 'the completely militant type of structure have more than once occurred; and have more than once almost occurred'. Compared with the case of England, 'the industrial freedom of the individual, in common with other freedoms, has never been established so fully as here; where *la gloire* has not been so prominent an aim and militant organization has never been so pronounced' (1910, ii: p. 135).

England too has been again becoming increasingly militant in type, with an increase in government controls of civil organization and socialist agitation. Yet, in the middle of the century, and consequent upon centuries of the slow diminution of coercive rule, 'a degree of individual freedom greater than ever before existed since nations began to be formed' (1896b: pp. 596–7). However, 'the movement which in so large a measure broke down the despotic regulations of the past, rushed on to a limit from which there has commenced a return movement' (1896b: p. 597). But this 'return movement',[10] if handed over to socialism, will take a new form: 'Instead of the rule of powerful political classes, men are elaborating for themselves a rule of official classes, which will become equally powerful or probably more powerful – classes eventually differing from those which socialist theories contemplate, as much as the rich and proud ecclesiastical hierarchy of the middle ages differed from the groups of poor and humble missionaries out of which it grew' (1896b: p. 597). Spencer indeed closes the whole analysis of the *Principles of Sociology* with a view of the future constructed partly through the prism of the militant–industrial typology. Spencer emphasizes that there are no guarantees of progress in evolution, though an understanding of it offers 'guidance' to achieving progress.[11] Evolution 'does not imply a latent tendency' to improve; there is no uniform ascent from lower to higher (1896b: p. 599). It may be the fate of a 'minor nation' to be left to its niche if it becomes less fit than others for complex conditions. While a Darwinian element of chance in survival is thus once more introduced, the distinctively Spencerian theory of evolution is not abandoned. The entire assemblage of societies

> fulfils the law of evolution by increase of heterogeneity, – while within each of them contrasts of structure, caused by differences of environments and entailed occupations, cause unlikenesses implying further heterogeneity; we may infer that the primary process of evolution – integration – which up to the present time has been displayed in the

formation of larger and larger nations, will eventually reach a still higher
stage and bring yet greater benefits.

(1896b: p. 600)

Indeed, Spencer proceeds to imagine that the future may involve the integration of the highest developed nations into a federation committed to
advanced industrialism, and hence to individual liberty. Such a federation
'may, by forbidding wars between any of its constituent nations, put an end
to the re-barbarization which is continually undoing civilization' (1896b:
p. 600).

Calmness and resignation are the words best capturing Spencer's mood
in this final section of the *Sociology*. But 12 years before he wrote as a
nervy Jeremiah, foretelling and fearing catastrophe. As its title may suggest,
The Man versus The State of 1884 deployed the contrast between militant
and industrial types of society as a leading idea. Here it served a clearly
polemical purpose, buttressing a passionately argued critique of British government intervention and socialist thought. Uninhibited by the constraints
of his putatively scientific 'System of Synthetic Philosophy', he could recon-
nect with his roots in the 1840s as a political journalist. Many Liberals, he
contended, had become Tories of a new type, in favour of paternalistic legislation and regulation. They had come to confuse the good achieved by
freeing people from shackles with the good outcomes achieved by people
under freedom, seeking to provide such outcomes and 'freedom' directly. In
the beginning, believes Spencer

> the two political parties at first stood respectively for two opposed types
> of social organization, broadly distinguishable as the militant and the
> industrial – types which are characterized, the one by the *régime* of sta-
> tus, almost universal in ancient days, and the other by the *régime* of
> contract, which has become general in modern days, chiefly among the
> Western nations, and especially among ourselves and the Americans. If,
> instead of using the word 'cooperation' in a limited sense, we use it in its
> widest sense, as signifying the combined activities of citizens under what-
> ever system of regulation; then these two are definable as the system of
> compulsory cooperation and the system of voluntary cooperation.
>
> (1884: p. 63)

For Spencer the message to the Liberals accused of a flirtation with compulsory co-operation was essentially straightforward: 'The function of Liberalism in the past was that of putting a limit to the powers of kings. The
function of true Liberalism in the future will be that of putting a limit to
the powers of Parliaments' (1884: p. 169). At present, however, advanced
societies are of a 'semi-militant semi-industrial type' (1884: p. 170). The
theory of social evolution shows that 'only little by little can voluntary

co-operation replace compulsory co-operation, and rightly bring about a correlative decrease of faith in governmental ability and authority' (1884: p. 172). At every stage of social evolution 'there must exist substantial agreement between practices and beliefs – real beliefs I mean, not nominal ones' (1884: p. 170). In other words, the way to the fully developed industrial type *had to involve* experience of 'the militant type; which, by discipline generates in long ages the power of continuous application' and also 'the willingness to act under direction (now no longer coercive but agreed to under contract)' (1884: p. 172).[12] That England's own militancy and need of a degree of coercive government is not outgrown is undeniable: 'While among ourselves the administration of colonial affairs is such that native tribes who retaliate on Englishmen by whom they have been injured, are punished, not on their own savage principle of life for life, but on the improved civilized principle of wholesale massacre in return for single murder, there is little chance that a political doctrine consistent only with unaggressive conduct will gain currency' (1884: p. 173). Nevertheless, to promulgate new forms of socialistic, coercive co-operation is to expand militant characteristics in government and society, and in this retrogressive sin of legislators the Liberals are now indulging. Thus Spencer complains that in these days 'of active philanthropy, hosts of people eager to achieve benefits for their less fortunate fellows by what seem the shortest methods, are busily occupied in developing administrative arrangements of a kind proper to a lower type of society—are bringing about retrogression while aiming at progression. The normal difficulties in the way of advance are sufficiently great, and it is lamentable that they should be made greater. Hence', Spencer adds, restating the rationale for his analysis, 'something well worth doing may be done, if philanthropists can be shown that they are in many cases insuring the future ill-being of men while eagerly pursuing their present well-being' (1884: p. 174).

Spencer's distinction between militant and industrial social formations also shaped the discussion in his *Principles of Ethics* of the evolution of 'sympathy', and the conduct called 'moral'. The component Parts of the *Ethics* were published between 1879 and 1893. Conduct which gives full expression of sympathy to the existence of others surrounding us is not possible under the antagonisms accompanying a militant regime: 'conduct gains ethical sanction in proportion as the activities, becoming less and less militant and more and more industrial, are such as do not necessitate mutual injury or hindrance, but consist with, and are furthered by, co-operation and mutual aid' (1910, i: p. 20). Spencer paints a comprehensive picture of the contrast in the social and moral relations in the two forms of social life. Where militancy prevails and social co-operations hinge around fighting

> there grows up a pride in aggression and robbery, revenge becomes an
> imperative duty, skilful lying is creditable, and...obedience to despotic

leaders and rulers is the greatest virtue; at the same time there is a con-
tempt for industry, and only such small regard for justice as is required
to maintain its existence. On the other hand, where the predominant
social co-operations have internal sustentation for their end, while co-
operations against external enemies have either greatly diminished or
disappeared, unprovoked aggression brings but partial applause or none
at all; robbery, even of enemies, ceases to be creditable; revenge is no
longer thought a necessity; lying is universally reprobated; justice in the
transactions of citizens with one another is insisted upon; political obedience is so far qualified that submission to a despot is held contemptible;
and industry, instead of being considered disgraceful, is considered as, in
some form or other, imperative on every one.

(1910, i: pp. 467–8)

These contrasted relations, Spencer adds, are complicated and qualified in
their appearance by the 'varieties of nature inherited by different kinds of
men from the past', and by customs, creeds and circumstances, but in their
broad outlines 'they are sufficiently clear – as clear as we can expect them
to be' (1910, i: p. 468). Militarism is antagonistic towards both the egoistic
sentiment of justice (an individual's sense of freedom to exercise one's faculties, while reaping the consequences) and the altruistic sentiment of justice
(respect for the liberty of others). 'Predominant militancy' in a society tram-
ples on the egoistic sentiment of justice and cuts across or 'sears' the altruistic
sentiment. However, as fast as voluntary co-operation, the *sine qua non*
of industrial society, becomes more general than compulsory co-operation
which characterizes the militant type of society, 'individual activities become
less restrained, and the sentiment which rejoices in the scope for them is
encouraged; while, simultaneously, the occasions for repressing the sympathies become less frequent. Hence, during warlike phases of social life the
sentiment of justice retrogrades, while it advances during peaceful phases,
and can reach its full development only in a permanently peaceful state'
(1910, ii: pp. 33–4).

By his final collection of essays, *Facts and Comments*, a movement towards
militancy in England was to Spencer beyond doubt: 'the retrograde movement now going on towards the militant social type' is inevitably accompanied by enforcement of authority (1902: p. 103). A passion for imperialist
mastery of other peoples complements a ready merging of 'personal liberties
in the power of the State' (1902: p. 121). The culture of aggression, coercion
and rank is resurgent, set again to colonize ordinary life. Spencer singles out
in ecclesiastical life the rise of 'General' William Booth's Salvation Army,
the Church Army, and the Church Lad's Brigade, with its uniform, arms
and drill (1902: pp. 126–7), and more generally bemoans the cultivation of
skilled physical force in the shape of 'athleticism' rather than 'sports'. Thus
in the public schools and universities, while 'bodily superiority is coming

to the front, mental superiority is retreating into the background' (1902: p. 130). Signs of the re-barbarization in process were also offered by the visual arts, with forms associated with coercion regaining popularity, such as in William Morris's typography, and the return to vogue of medieval architectural styles (1902: pp. 187–8). To Spencer, the current pulse of 'popular feeling' was indicated by the 'immense popularity' of Rudyard Kipling, 'in whose writings one-tenth of nominal Christianity is joined with nine-tenths of real paganism; who idealizes the soldier and glories in the triumph of brute force; and who, in depicting school-life, brings to the front the barbarizing activities and feelings and shows little respect for a civilizing culture' (1902: p. 131).

Fears of this type for the present and the immediate future of society both at home and abroad form a leitmotif of Spencer's writing on political matters from the time of *The Man versus the State*. While pessimism about social matters had taken hold, and while Spencer felt the Liberal party as a whole was abandoning its core values, one should be cautious about leaping to an interpretation of Spencer as 'drifting to conservatism' (see Wiltshire, 1978 and, for reservations, Miller, 1982). His principal concern was the momentum driving militancy in all aspects of social life, made worse by the conviction that reason was pretty much powerless to combat it. This all spilled out in the letters between Spencer and Blunt in the late 1890s. Blunt grumbled to Spencer on 5 October 1898 that religious leaders' groups (including Quakers) and men of science 'have convinced themselves that wars of extermination are in accordance with Evolution .... More than words, I expect, is required to bring about a change of opinion – nothing short of a disastrous war against an invader here in the Southern counties'. Spencer answered the next day:

My beliefs are pretty much as pessimistic as those you express – in respect at least of the approaching condition of mankind; but holding though I do that we are commencing a long course of re-barbarization from which the reaction may take very long in coming, I nevertheless hold that a reaction will come, and look forward with hope to a remote future of a desirable kind, to be reached after numerous movements of progress and retrogression. Did I think that men were likely to remain in the far future anything like what they now are, I should contemplate with equanimity the sweeping away of the whole race.

By 14 December 1899, the press and the journalists who might be expected to voice tolerance and caution were counted by Spencer among the vehicles and spokesmen of militant fashion and culture 'Our critical journals are mainly officered by those who have passed through the public-school regime – who have the militant spirit and passion for mastery cultivated there'. And on 5 October 1900, Spencer bemoans more 'political burglaries', of a kind to leave him 'ashamed of my country'.[13]

The exact function of Spencer's contrast between militant and industrial types of society in his wider evolutionary scheme has caused a good deal of trouble to his interpreters. According to Wiltshire, Spencer's scheme of social evolution possessed definite stages, with progress 'from the "militant" to the "industrial" type of society'. The distinction made is so sharp, Wiltshire continues, as to render questionable 'the principle of continuity which links them. Each is a perfect theoretical model (almost a Weberian "ideal-type"), its characteristics deriving from the exigencies of the stage of civilization which it represents. Spencer rejected the suggestion that a society might exhibit characteristics of both types simultaneously, because the "industrial" type is the "perfect" state, and anything falling short of it is stigmatized as being semi-evolved' (1978: p. 247).

Let me begin to assess Wiltshire's comments by starting from his last point. It was made clear above that in the *Principles of Sociology* Spencer envisaged a future form of society that transcended both militancy and industrialism, so for Spencer the industrial type of society was *not* the perfect form. It is thus deeply misleading to suggest *for this reason* that he would have 'stigmatized' as 'semi-evolved' some combination of the two types in one society.[14] Spencer did *not* reject the idea that a society could embrace both types; indeed England and 'advanced societies' were explicitly and often described by him as part-militant and part-industrial. One of the characteristics even of Max Weber's ideal types is that, when applied to the analysis of actual world circumstances, they are not going to be, and were not intended as, perfect matches of that *part of reality* to which it is proposed that they relate. Ideal types are simply not themselves historical generalizations, but aids towards them.[15] It is difficult to see why Wiltshire finds the distinction between Spencer's two 'types' as so sharp as to suggest discontinuity. Spencer indeed often talks about types of *society* when in fact types of social *relations* would have been a clearer expression, but I would have thought the context usually makes this sense fairly obvious. It is clear that Spencer recognizes not only that societies may well possess features of both types at the same time, but that societies evolve in ways that alter the balance between the relative presence of the types.[16]

Much the same misconception comes into play in Jose Harris's contribution on Spencer to the *Oxford Dictionary of National Biography*, with the statement that 'his social theories were rooted in the assumption that industrialization and militarism were mutually exclusive (although the most cursory glance at the history of nineteenth-century Europe and America might have suggested otherwise)'. What Spencer calls 'militant' societies can contain 'industrial' activities, and for that matter, as remarked earlier, in what he calls 'industrial' societies there may be 'but very moderate productive activities' (1891c: p. 604). Indeed, for Spencer, all societies of which we have knowledge have both militant and industrial dimensions. This is because all societies have to deal with external threats, and have to sustain themselves; all have to some extent a division, as explored in his arguments for the social organism idea, between 'outer' and 'inner' activities. Spencer's nomenclature did not really help his cause; his meaning is perhaps better expressed in the way that he himself frequently presented it, by contrasting social relations exhibiting 'compulsory cooperation' with those exhibiting 'voluntary cooperation'. Once this is grasped, it becomes clear that 'militant' organization is compatible with a considerable degree of 'industrialization' and indeed may be present in industrial organizations, though they would be less efficient, being coercively organized, than if they were the product of the division of labour and exchange associated with the 'spontaneous organization' of the catallaxy.

Harris also comments that in the *Principles of Sociology* Spencer identified 'a universal law of socio-political development, from regimes based on military organization through to regimes based on industrial production (analogous to, and tacitly borrowed from, Sir Henry Maine's account of the transition from status to contract)'. In fact, as recorded above, Spencer explicitly acknowledged Maine's signature distinction. Harris is not to be faulted in detecting in Spencer *some form* of the idea of development from militant regimes, though it is misleading to suggest the path is towards regimes based on 'industrial production' rather than being 'industrial' in character in the sense Spencer specified. But the change involved is over the 'long run': the advanced societies Spencer commented on in 'Political Institutions' and *The Man versus The State* were analysed unequivocally as part-industrial and part-militant, with in fact a tendency to become more militant from the 1870s.

We must note too that Weinstein also subscribes to an interpretation of Spencer's types in terms of sequential 'development', although specified in greater detail. Weinstein's view is that after *Social Statics* Spencer came to hold the view that societies passed through four phases in terms of political history: '(1) primitive societies characterized by informal political co-operation, (2) "militant" societies dominated by regimented, centralized political authority, (3) "industrial" societies distinguished by the relaxation of centralized political authority and the emergence of liberal values and, finally, (4) liberal utopias where government withers away' (1998: p. 16). It is not made clear by Weinstein what is meant by 'informal political co-operation' in early societies. For Spencer, in fact, once formed such societies are most likely to be, but certainly not always, preoccupied with warding off predators, human and other. Next, Weinstein offers a restatement of the 'either-or' view of a society in respect of how Spencer's typology is to be applied to its interpretation. Finally, Weinstein notes Spencer's 'third' and future 'type'. On the detail of this 'type' Spencer is somewhat reticent. In the first volume of the *Principles of Sociology*, as already noted, it takes the form of what we might call 'relaxed industrialism': men of the future will work to live rather than live to work – the gist of the challenge that he believed American society would encounter hammered out as the thrust of his speech in Delmonico's in 1882.[17] This form has similarities with, but is not identical to, comments in the first volume of the *Principles of Ethics*, in a Part which first appeared in 1879. These comments appear to have passed unnoticed in most discussions of Spencer on social 'types' but they do enable us to understand his emphasis not only on justice but also on beneficence as a feature of developed social life. Spencer cautions that there is 'a theoretically-possible form of society, purely industrial in its activities, which, though approaching nearer to the moral idea in its code of conduct than any society not purely industrial, does not fully reach it' (1910, i: p. 146). Industrial life requires that citizens refrain from aggressions on each other, but does not require of each citizen that his life 'be such that it shall directly further the lives of other citizens'. It is not, therefore, a necessary implication of industrialism, 'as thus far defined, that each, beyond the benefits given and received by exchange of services, shall give and receive other benefits'. However, Spencer reasons from experience that the 'gratuitous rendering of services' avoids the serious losses and damages which would be incurred if each person had to face the contingencies of life single-handedly. Moreover, public interests would suffer 'if no one did for his fellows anything more than was required by strict performance of contract', and private interests would suffer from 'the absence of attention to public interests. The limit of evolution of conduct is consequentially not reached, until, beyond avoidance of direct and indirect injuries to others, there are spontaneous efforts to further the welfare of others'. The addition of beneficence to justice is thus a concomitant of full adaptation to the social state.[18] Spencer, though, does not conclude that these particular features of social life characterize a 'third type' of society. To do so would suggest a more substantial contrast than is appropriate. He merely observes instead that, 'since sympathy is the root of both justice and beneficence', it is needless to 'qualify greatly that conception of the industrial state above set forth;' (1910, i: p. 149).

However, in a further contrast, by the close of the third volume of the *Sociology* in 1896 the social type of the future has itself 'evolved' into a rather different conception than it was given in the first volume, featuring new and essential steps towards the 'final stage of human evolution' (1896b: p. 600). Now the new type appears principally to depend upon multi-lateral agreements to foreswear aggression and war. It has become, in other words, an entirely post-militant form of society with work-place relations free from coercion. Both variants may indeed, though, be taken as 'liberal utopias', since men will have become well-adapted to the social state, and, since war is outlawed in both, governments will be needed neither for defence nor the maintenance of justice to protect liberty (for the imperatives associated with acting justly will have become internalized through adaptation to the social state as 'natural' conduct).

It is perhaps unnecessary to dwell for longer on Spencer's third type. The key concern now must be that, if the evolutionary sequence interpretation of Spencer's objective in making the contrast between militant and industrial social forms is accurate, it perforce becomes an embarrassment that most (probably all) advanced societies are for Spencer a mixture of the two. On this interpretation the contrast seems to offer such a vacillating and fuzzy 'path' of 'development' in political history as to be virtually without value. If Weinstein is capturing faithfully Spencer's position, then Wiltshire and Harris too would be vindicated in finding Spencer lacking in coherence.[19] There is, however, more to be said. In contrast, Turner has declared that Spencer's militant–industrial distinction is not 'an evolutionary classification, as some authors have argued. Rather, it is a way to fine-tune the description of a society, whatever its stage of evolutionary development' (1985: p. 93). In Turner's interpretation, Spencer recognized that militancy or political centralization 'is a fact of social life in all types of systems, from very simple to complex ones'. Moreover, he grasps that ' "Industrial" does not denote a mode of production, but rather, the degree to which operative and distributive processes are free from extensive political regulation. "Militant" does denote military organization to pursue conflict, but it also describes the regulation of operative and distributive processes by political authority' (1985: p. 79). Turner, though, over-simplifies the point, for, as we have already noticed, in the *Principles of Sociology,* Spencer makes beyond doubt a relevant directional claim, referring to 'that state of permanent peace to which civilization is tending' (1893: p. 588).

There is a way forward. The contrasts in social reality which Spencer describes in terms of militancy and industrialism are in a sense 'frozen', diachronic contrasts of change across the spectrum of social relations in each society. Within the ever-changing synchronic processes producing the evolution of each society and its component individuals, the contrasting phenomena which the militant/industrial dichotomy depicts as embedded in the factual nature of actual social relations, can at best be interpreted as only conditioning the production of further psychical and social evolution, and not by themselves producing it. That is to say, while they form some of the (relatively impermanent) social circumstances or environment under which both the psychical adaptation of the component individuals and super-organic adaptation occur (just as their outer – and inner – structures and environments condition the adaptation of individual organisms), it is the underlying laws of the persistence of force and rhythm of motion which frame the evolutionary tendency to integration, differentiation and equilibrium, which make possible adaptation (and natural selection, or 'indirect equilibration') in the first place, *and to which, whatever it is these mechanisms of change produce, they conform.* And individuals, with their varying but accumulated psychical inheritances, both write on and are written on by their environment. When, for instance, Jose Harris refers to Spencer as asserting a 'universal law of socio-political development' from militancy to industrialism, she ascribes to 'the militant type of society' or 'militant social forms' a socially deterministic causal force which Spencer does not give to them. For Spencer, the super-organic was not in this connection considered as supra-individual (Ingold, 1986: p. 227). 'Militant' and 'industrial' stand for Spencer as ideal-typical descriptions of 'temporary' and evolving reality, not as explanations of it in the terms of an intrinsically evolutionary scheme of classification. So when Spencer asserts that civilization is tending towards permanent peace this is not *because* 'militarism' or 'industrialism' precede it, although they do, but because of the deeper evolutionary processes at work, established to his own satisfaction in *First Principles,* through the mechanism of adaptation, and also Darwinian 'natural selection'. In short, evolutionary explanations for Spencer are separate from the sociologically descriptive work on the products of individual and social or super-organic evolution that the militant and industrial contrast is designed to capture. Indeed the (evolving) phenomena, brought into appropriate analytical syntheses by the militant and industrial models of contrasting social relations as applied to social contexts past and present, are themselves what *the laws of* evolution, including the 'rhythm of motion', have to explain; they are not of themselves explained by being described thus. If for Spencer the way to the fully developed industrial type indeed had to be 'through the militant type; which, by discipline generates in long ages the power of continuous application' and also 'the willingness to act under direction (now no longer coercive but agreed to under contract)' (1884: p. 172), the 'type' itself stood for no explanatory 'force', as indeed logically it could not, and the actually evolving phenomena concerned themselves were, firstly, the evolutionary product of the pre-existing psychical adaptation of social individuals and of their specific environment of social relations, and, secondly, one factor among others, including the extant psychical inheritances of individuals, of the evolution to occur subsequently. Indeed, in proximate terms, the phenomena referred to as 'militant' and 'industrial' arise through adaptation and survival: 'Whether the organization for offense and defense or the sustaining organization is more "largely developed" depends on the nature of the interactions that occur between a society and its neighboring societies in the struggle for existence. If these interactions are hostile, then militancy evolves; if peaceful, then industrialism is adaptive' (Haines, 1988: p. 482). The complex but I think accurate analysis now advanced should spare Spencer the fate of being misread in the Wiltshire, Harris, Weinstein tradition,[20] and corrects the overly 'static' interpretation of the 'types' as advanced by Turner.

One of Spencer's main contributions to the nascent subject of sociology was thus an attempt to map, in the manner of a Victorian territorial explorer, what he saw as the fundamental differences between forms of social life, particularly between the nature of routinized and regimented social life, in which the state displays a coercive and compulsory 'militant' type of activity, and private, personalized and yet unselfish life – a classic illustration of which was, for Spencer, the spontaneous efforts to further the welfare of others through positive, and negative, private beneficence (on which see Chapter 9). The help given, or debts waived, are not matters of justice, of the essentials for co-operation to endure, but are matters of voluntary altruistic sociality. Such beneficence is the hallmark of an advanced peaceful society and its citizens. Control exercised by the state over matters relating to welfare epitomized for Spencer what he nominated as the 'militant' type of society, whereas autonomy in these matters characterized the 'industrial' type. Private beneficence was a sign of evolutionary progress because of the developed sense of altruism and sociality which it displayed; it was also a sign of normative progress for Spencer because 'industrial' social life was itself an advance on 'militant' life – the Fabian socialist surveillance by the state of personal welfare as a means to collective ends desired by Beatrice and Sidney Webb represented a personal nightmare of militancy. Yet an ill-judged excess of unforced beneficence could 'spoil' children and foster dependency. In this context a passage in the *Ethics*, dealing chiefly with pecuniary inequality and the risks of passing on great riches through parental beneficence, is of significance. It ties in a hypothesized growing parental enlightenment on the matter to the militant and industrial types, themselves freshly blended into an ad hoc sub-type. Spencer suggests that, just as our existing but transitional social regime is witnessing a decrease in the political inequalities which characterized former times, so future times 'will most likely see a decrease in those great pecuniary inequalities which now prevail. Having emerged from the militant social type, we appear to be passing through a social type which may be distinguished as militant industrialism – an industrialism which, though carried on under the system of contract, instead of under the system of *status*, is in considerable measure carried on in the old militant spirit; as, indeed, it could not fail to be, seeing that men's characters and sentiments can be changed only in the course of long ages'.[21] Pausing only to muse that 'socialisms and communisms' may have temporary triumphs, Spencer infers that in the future, while there will be pecuniary inequalities, 'under higher social forms and a better type of humanity, they will be nothing like so marked as now. There will be neither the possibilities nor the desires for accumulating large fortunes: decrease in the desires being, in part, caused by the recognition of the truth that parental beneficence, instead of enforcing them, interdicts them' (1910, ii: pp. 348–9).

In Spencer's view, the compulsory co-operation 'characterizing the militant *régime* necessarily represses sympathy – exists only on condition of an unsympathetic treatment of some by others' (1910, i: p. 245). The late nineteenth-century 'revival' of belligerent militancy was thus the fly in the ointment, and to this militancy Spencer attributed a *volte face* from the State's mid-century commitment to personal freedom, and a consequent and ruinous diminution in the protection of rights to liberty (a recidivism by stealth, which smiled upon a broader recrudescence of a form of social relations that Spencer characterized disparagingly as *laissez-faire*). In contrast, state-sponsored 'generosity' now eclipsed citizen-growth and its practical expression in terms of spontaneous beneficence and community participation. Established in Germany, this general trend was insinuating itself into England. According to Spencer, the recent re-development of militancy was manifested in actual reductions of freedom in everyday life, accompanying 'multiplied restrictions and exactions':

> The spirit of regimentation proper to the militant type, has been spreading throughout the administration of civil life. An army of workers with appointed tasks and apportioned shares of products, which socialism, knowingly or unknowingly, aims at, shows in civil life the same characters as an army of soldiers with prescribed duties and fixed rations shows in military life; and every act of parliament which takes money from the individual for public purposes and gives him public benefits, tends to assimilate the two. Germany best shows this kinship. There, where militancy is most pronounced, and where the regulation of citizens is most elaborate, socialism is most highly developed; and from the head of the German military system has now come the proposal of regimental regulations for the working classes throughout Europe.

> Sympathy which, a generation ago, was taking the shape of justice, is relapsing into the shape of generosity; and the generosity is exercised by inflicting injustice. Daily legislation betrays little anxiety that each shall have that which belongs to him, but great anxiety that he shall have that which belongs to somebody else. For while no energy is expended in so reforming our judicial administration that everyone may obtain and enjoy all he has earned, great energy is shown in providing for him and others benefits which they have not earned. Along with that miserable *laissez-faire* which calmly looks on while men ruin themselves in trying to enforce by law their equitable claims, there goes activity in supplying them, at other men's cost, with *gratis* novel-reading!

> (1910, ii: p. 44)

The actual prosecution of a war was not logically necessary for Spencer to count a society as militant, nor did it have to be industrious to count as industrial. Rather, the description and analysis of fundamentally contrasting social relations, whether domestic, ceremonial, religious, moral, or regarding political structures and functions, were his central focus. This contrast he identified as driven by the laws of evolution as made manifest in the dominant concerns of the 'average character' of the time; by the 1890s in England, for Spencer, these had become imperialism and 'positive regulation' at home, rather than peaceful production, self-development, and spontaneous co-operation. Yet the functions he chose to highlight through this choice of terms in presenting the 'types' – militant and industrial – have I think served to divert attention from his deeper descriptive purpose. For the 'militant' or 'predatory' social type might with advantage be re-described, although cumbrously, as capturing social life as characterized by a tightly controlled and closed form of collective life, in fact as politically centralized, and the 'industrial' or 'mercantile' type might be re-described, again cumbrously, as capturing social life as characterized by light-touch regulation and open and innovative forms of economic and social co-operation, in fact as decentralized. Indeed, in his *Dynamic Sociology*, Lester Ward, later to become the first President of the American Sociological Association, pinpointed Spencer's selection of labels, in particular 'militant', as misleading: 'If he merely means that certain tribes and nations are far more warlike than others, it is true enough; but he seems to convey the idea of societies in which war is the chief and permanent occupation. The impossibility of such a state, considered as at all permanent, is manifest. And when warlike nations plunder industrial ones they are soon compelled in some way to restore in some way the industrial state. In fact, all "militant societies" must rest upon an industrial class, while the military operations, however incessant, depend chiefly upon simultaneous industrial operations' (1897, i: p. 527). In terms of substance, however, as has been discussed already, there was no real disagreement here at all between Ward and Spencer.

Spencer's younger contemporary, Tönnies, who as noted in the previous chapter explicitly criticized and engaged with Spencer's writings, worked up the well-known binary contrast between informal and 'natural' *Gemeinschaft*, or community, life, and formal, impersonal *Gesellschaft*, or societal, life. To Tönnies, Spencer's categories suggested that his own preferences had dimmed his judgement. One might say that, Tönnies remarked, 'because he did not keep himself free from patriotic bias, he succumbed to free-trade bias' (in Cahnman, 1973: p. 209), adding subsequently, in 1904, that Spencer's conceptualization was 'infused by the predominant outlook at the peak time of Victorian Britain' (Tönnies, 1974: p. 111). In an article which dissected Spencer's theoretical sociology into a collection of uncoordinated fragments, Werner Stark considered that had Spencer believed that 'a militant society, fighting, as a whole, against other societies, is more like a unity than a multiplicity, whereas an industrial society, which subserves individual welfare, is more like a multiplicity than like a unity ... he would have anticipated, in its essentials, the deep insights which Ferdinand Tönnies was soon to present to the world. But it is a fact that he does not take this line' (1961: p. 120). Stark's basic premise echoed Huxley's argument against Spencer that the idea of the social organism implied that a society was itself a moral collectivity, which, with reason, as we have already seen, Spencer could deny. For Spencer a militant society was no more or less 'organic' than an industrial society. Now it is not to be decided here whether Stark's unity versus multiplicity distinction does justice to the *Gemeinschaft* versus *Gesellschaft* distinction made by Tönnies. However, once freed of misinterpretation, it does seem at least plausible that Spencer's distinction between militancy and industrialism, whether applied as a characterization of complete societies, basic structural features of complete societies, or to the contrasted forms of the types of social relations to be found *within* a complete society, is not necessarily to be regarded as a poor relation to the distinction made by Tönnies. Through their dichotomous models both sociologists – Spencer anchored in the sciences, Tönnies less so – were striving to say something fundamental about the anatomy of social relations, and about changes in their texture over time, and also, and more generally, to identify the overall nature, the most appropriate questions and methods, and the value to social life itself of sociology. Each viewed the subject through a different lens, though Tönnies certainly adopted Spencer's basic proposition that 'all life consists of development from the general to the particular' (Tönnies, 2001: p. 9; see also pp. 211, 213). For all Spencer's hand-wringing over the revival of militancy to which he considered he was a witness, his outlook remained optimistic in the sense that his normative preferences and his expectation of the eventual triumph of forms of industrialism were aligned. This seems not to have been so for Tönnies and the flow he observed towards *Gesellschaft*. However, Tönnies emphasized that 'opposing relationships of individual man to mankind in general are the very heart of the matter' (2001: p. 13) in explaining his contrast between *Gemeinschaft* and *Gesellschaft*; Spencer was attempting to capture an indisputably similar kind of contrast with his militant and industrial 'types'. Perhaps the language he chose with which to make the contrast reflected too narrowly of its time, but he seems to have left behind no suspicion that he romanticized either militancy or industrialism.

8
Understanding Music

Across *First Principles*, the *Principles of Sociology*, and several essays Spencer developed interpretations of music as a social phenomenon, particularly its origin, function and growth, and the social organization associated with the performance of music. This interest in music may serve as a case study of the nature of Spencerian sociology as applied to a particular substantive area. Moreover, this relatively rare instance of a key sociologist taking pains over music certainly deserves wider recognition than it is usually accorded, particularly so since what Spencer said has had a history of influence on music and associated matters. Neither his efforts to make sociological sense of music within the framework of his evolutionary theory nor his substantial impact on the writing of the history of music has received much discussion in recent years. The present chapter tackles both concerns.

As always with Spencer, it must be emphasized that his sociological analysis cannot be divorced from its distinctive anchorage in his work as philosopher, biologist, psychologist and even physicist. His sociological interpretation of music as a social phenomenon is no more open to the charge that it is not 'sociological' than is the remainder of his sociology; psychological and biological dimensions of analysis always force themselves into play in Spencer's process of constructing sociological analysis. Sociology sometimes appears to be uniquely prone to schisms, nevertheless any temptation to rebuff the claim that Spencer was doing sociology (whether of music in particular or social life in general) can be met by pointing to the broad activity that in reality it remains, with even the most cherished and burnished of sectarian and divisive assumptions about 'real sociology' being contested by some other practitioners of a different disposition. While Spencer was certainly not only a sociologist, his heart does seem most to have been in social science, in particular in forging a sociology with a scientific approach to the study of social phenomena in a broad sense, embracing ethics and politics. Although it hardly proves the point, it seems too that his contribution to social science in this broad sense is what has remained of greatest interest to those who write on Spencer today. His ambition in connection with sociology was of course enormous: the description and classification as well as the explanation of all social phenomena. And in Spencer's view music clearly counted as a significant constituent of social life. It provided both a significant source of 'inductions' about super-organic activities and a 'test-bed' for his all-embracing deductive framework.

Undoubtedly, Spencer's major sociological interests in music were its origin (the first to manifest itself, before the System of Synthetic Philosophy had been thought of), and its evolution since its origin. Both were to prove to be influential. Spencer's 1857 essay on the origin of music also initiated a debate that is not unimportant in the history of aesthetics, for its claims were, as we shall see, keenly countered by, amongst others, Darwin, Edmund Gurney, Ernest Newman and Richard Wallaschek.[1] There is also a matter of especial interest in trying to understand Spencer: he is torn over whether or not harmony can be described as 'evolved', and the important question is why there is this internal disunity.

Quite why Spencer troubled himself over music as a phenomenon is obscure, possibly it seemed simply an obvious area of concern to which to apply some of the ideas recently advanced on 'feelings' (covering 'emotions' and 'sensations') in his *Principles of Psychology*. There is no evidence that his parents or his uncle Thomas were particularly interested in music. Significant encounters with music or musicians seem absent from his early life, and his first career as a civil engineer with various railway companies brought no changes in this respect. He used his free hours to deepen his knowledge of the sciences and to apply it in mechanical inventions. It was not until the late 1840s, when he was resident and employed in London, with access to complementary tickets, that he began to attend opera performances and concerts at all regularly. This belated blooming of an interest in music is emblematic of the capital's stimulation of intellectual growth in Spencer. Surrounded by new and inspiriting friends and culture, he made the decision to commit himself to a life as an author. The new taste for music did not lead him to any formal musical education beyond learning to sing from Hullah's highly popular 'manual' of 1841 (see Leinster-Mackay, 1981), and it engendered only a modest practical involvement. He was, to meddle with a phrase of Beatrice Webb's, a 'performer of the hearth'. For a time George Eliot was a close friend and it is with a reference to her that he reveals his chief experience of making music. Recording that he and some friends had amused themselves by singing glees, he notes that she 'never joined us: why I do not know for her voice would greatly have improved the harmony' (1904, ii: p. 73).[2] From Spencer's fireside experience of singing, his secretary in the 1870s, James Collier, rather casually inferred that 'his striking essay on "*The Origin and Function of Music*" was no accident', though he correctly perceived that Spencer's essay was not the work, as Emerson ungenerously and untruly said of all his writings, 'of a "stock writer who could write equally well on all subjects" ' (1904: p. 194). Spencer was unable to play any instrument himself, as his last secretary, Walter Troughton, recorded (1938: p. 199), but enjoyed hearing the piano played for him; from 1891 the instrument was a Bechstein, the gift of Andrew Carnegie. Spencer was thus not by his background in any way a 'natural' to go on to write with authority on the origin and growth of music, nor on any other aspect of it. There appears, then, to be no explanation available beyond a general desire to 'validate' the *Psychology* except, perphaps, an inquisitive desire to make sense of all the areas of social life hitherto, to Spencer's mind at least, not adequately understood.

This chapter discusses first Spencer's theories of the origin of music and the origin of harmony. It then turns to how Spencer interpreted the function and growth of music itself, and music as an organized and co-operative activity, which over time became more integrated and more differentiated from other activities, in accord with the general evolutionary movement towards increasing heterogeneity. Within this framework his own comments on particular musical styles and individual composers are introduced and examined briefly. I have also endeavoured to indicate some of the difficulties that are raised by Spencer's ideas, and to indicate also, where the point applies, how these difficulties derive from his more general and distinctive style of evolutionary analysis. The body of thought which constitutes his main contributions to the sociology of music was by no means flawless, but an identification of the flaws, as I have argued in the final section, should itself be of positive value. Although many of the critical concerns that are introduced had, in some form or another, been advanced by the 1890s and thus during Spencer's lifetime, this critical climate did not prevent music historiography, itself then in the process of emerging, from taking up his ideas on the origin of music and its evolutionary development. Thus this chapter also offers a sketch of the dimensions of this influence. This will, I hope, contribute both towards the goal of assessing the full impact of evolutionary theory on social and cultural thought in general and towards an understanding of the intellectual history of music historiography in particular, especially in Britain.

Spencer's first comments on the origin and growth of music come as selected illustrations in support of the general statements advanced in his wide-ranging essay, 'Progress: Its Law and Cause', which appeared in the *Westminster Review* for April, 1857 (1857a). For Spencer, rhythms in words, sounds and motions 'were in the beginning parts of the same thing, and have only in process of time become separate things. Among existing barbarous tribes we find them still united' (1857a: p. 30). Dancing, poetry, and music thus had an original unity from which there has been a 'gradual differentiation', displaying an 'advance from the homogeneous to the heterogeneous' (1857a: p. 31). Having thus already selected music for some attention, a more thorough examination of how it in particular might exemplify his law of progress in the contexts of psychological and social development would probably have struck Spencer as a pressing necessity. Accordingly, later in the same year his theory of how music originated received a much more detailed presentation in 'The Origin and

Function of Music', published in *Fraser's Magazine* for October. Subsequently, he returned to music in *First Principles* (also drawing in material from the 'Progress' essay) and the *Principles of Sociology*. He also issued replies to critics, and in his final book *Facts and Comments* (1902) as an octogenarian he gamely presented some autumnal reflections.

'The Origin and Function' essay (1857c) is thus relatively early, but, even so, it still comes after *Social Statics* and the *Principles of Psychology* in its first form, volumes which included many elements of the evolutionary theory later developed more systematically. It is also an essay that contains some troublesome traps for the interpreter. According to Spencer's *Autobiography*, the essay was written, at least in part, in agreeable surroundings in southwest Scotland.[3] Spencer assumes in this essay that music is originally vocal, and then seeks an explanation for its existence by looking at vocal phenomena in general. Vocal sounds, he declares, 'are produced by the agency of certain muscles. These muscles, in common with those of the body at large, are excited to contraction by pleasurable and painful feelings. And therefore it is that feelings demonstrate themselves in sounds as well as in movement' (1857c: p. 403).

In Spencer's view, variations of voice are one of 'the physiological results of variations of feeling'. It follows, therefore, as considered in the *Principles of Psychology*, 'that the explanation of all kinds of vocal expression must be sought in this general relation between mental and muscular excitements' (1857c: p. 404). As a consequence, he embarks on tracing back to 'feelings' the various peculiarities of all vocal phenomena. He classifies these under the heads of loudness, quality or timbre, pitch, intervals, and rate of variation. From this discussion Spencer concludes that he has adequate data to support a theory of the origin of music. Those vocal peculiarities 'which indicate excited feeling *are those which especially distinguish song from ordinary speech. Every one of the alterations of voice which we have found to be a physiological result of pain or pleasure is carried to an extreme in vocal music*' (1857c: p. 410). Spencer emphasizes this consequence of extreme feelings as the basis of music a little later in the essay: 'in respect alike of *loudness, timbre, pitch, intervals, and rate of variation*, song employs and exaggerates the natural language of the emotions; – it arises from a systematic combination of those vocal peculiarities which are physiological effects of acute pleasure and pain' (1857c: p. 411).

In a subsequent reference to the essay Spencer insisted that he had meant that music evolved from excited speech: 'the whole argument of the essay is to show that it is from this emotional element of speech that music is evolved.' (1891c: p. 536). However, the actual words he used in the key passages introduced above are compatible with the view that emotional speech and music have evolved independently from feeling rather than sequentially – Ernest Newman (1905: pp. 191–3) noted this ambiguity but also that other passages do confirm Spencer's own reading, as when Spencer writes 'we may infer that vocal music originally diverged from emotional speech in a gradual, unobtrusive manner' (1857c: p. 414). One further passage shows that Spencer's drafting of the essay was indeed ambiguous on this matter: 'music takes its rise from the modulations of the *human voice* under emotion' (1857c: p. 419, italics added).

We need briefly to note some further points with relevance to the origin of music from Spencer's 'Origin' essay. At one stage he might be interpreted as making, rather clumsily, the point that music is a specifically human phenomenon: 'That music is a product of civilization is manifest: for though some of the lowest savages have their dance-chants, these are of a kind scarcely to be signified by the title musical: at most they supply but the vaguest rudiment of music properly so called' (1857c: p. 420). However, Spencer makes it clear that, even if we do not *call* the sounds 'music', there are phenomena to which music is to be affiliated – the vocal productions of sounds by animals. There are relevant references to dogs, cats, and lions.[4] The implication of this idea, to which we shall return, is that there is at best only some apparently arbitrary difference of degree in a continuum of sounds marked off by the term 'music'.

In his later remarks on the origin of music Spencer enlarged upon his original comments, most extensively in an essay which was a rejoinder to points made by Charles Darwin, and by Edmund Gurney, a psychical researcher and psychologist, deeply interested in music. It appeared as a 'postscript' to his earlier survey in a collected edition of his essays, and in *Mind* for 1890. Two matters with which it is concerned may be mentioned briefly. The first matter arose as a consequence of the formulation of his mature ideas on evolution in the 1860s, namely the provision of an explicit linkage of his account of the origin of music to his general evolutionary law of a progressive movement to increasing heterogeneity:

> The genesis which I have described conforms to this fundamental law. It posits the antecedent fact that feeling in general produces muscular contraction in general; and the less general fact that feeling in general produces, among other muscular contractions, those which move the respiratory and vocal apparatus. With these it joins the still less general fact that sounds indicative of feelings vary in sundry respects according to the intensity of the feelings, and then enumerates the still less general facts which show us the kinship between the vocal manifestations of feeling and the characters of vocal music – the implication being that there has gone on a progressive specialization.
>
> (1857c, postscript of 1890: pp. 437–8)

It should be noted that in this passage Spencer once more fails to specify that vocal music arose out of emotional *speech*, rather than 'feeling'. The second matter to mention is the restatement of what he had already argued elsewhere, and indeed alluded to in 1857, that there is progress running through the history of music. Both particular compositions and the body of music as a whole display an 'immense progress in heterogeneity', which is witnessed 'on putting side by side the monotonous chants of savages with the musical compositions familiar to us: each of which is relatively heterogeneous within itself, and the assemblage of which forms an immeasurably heterogeneous aggregate' (1857c, postscript: p. 449). This idea of progress in the history of music turned out to have a substantial impact, explored later in this chapter.

In considering Spencer on the origin of music a more significant feature of this postscript to his 1857 essay is that it contains new clues as to what Spencer means by 'music'. Darwin in his *Descent of Man* had proposed a competing theory of the origin of music which claimed a central role for amatory feeling rather than feeling in general. In his response, Spencer by implication seems to commit himself to what in logic he came close to saying in 1857, that 'music' names some of both the human and the animal sounds manifesting strong feeling. Spencer criticizes Darwin on the ground that 'certainly the animals around us yield but few facts countenancing his view'. However, there is also a passage which may appear to be a contradiction of this point about the meaning of 'music' for Spencer:

> Even did the evidence support the popular view adopted by Mr. Darwin, that the singing of birds is a kind of courtship – even were there good proof, instead of much disproof, that a bird's song is a developed form of sexual sounds made by the male to charm the female – the conclusion would, I think, do little towards justifying the belief that human music has had a kindred origin.

However, on reflection Spencer's reference here to 'human music' may be taken as corroboration of the point rather then contradiction. For the introduction of the expression 'human music' would seem to imply that for Spencer there are indeed other sorts of music. A consequence of this state of affairs is that it would be eccentric, to say the least, to insist that *all* sorts of music are evolved from *speech*. Note too that Spencer significantly advances no special criteria as a basis for distinguishing 'human music' from bird 'song' or 'animal' music.

A degree of imprecision in Spencer's thoughts on music's origin has been established in the course of this examination and it is now appropriate to take stock. In the 1857 essay we saw Spencer vacillating somewhat over the place of speech in the evolutionary sequence leading to (human) music. To this the later postscript adds further evidence which suggests that Spencer entertained the concept of 'animal music', which, in the absence of statements to the contrary, appears for Spencer to be assimilable to 'human music', although presumably it is not to be seen as a sequel to excited speech. Some justification for each of the following diagrammatic interpretations of the exact nature of Spencer's theory on the origin of music can be found in what he published:

1. Excited Feeling → Emotional (Human) Speech → Human Music
2. Excited Feeling → (Human) Music
3. Excited Feeling → Human and Animal Music
4. Excited Feeling → Emotional (Human) Speech → Human Music *and*
   Excited Feeling → Animal Music

The first and the fourth interpretations fit most comfortably with the general drift of Spencer's comments. The first interpretation was the one intended by Spencer according to his responses to critics, and, indeed, the one to which critics mostly directed their observations. Gurney's opinion, for instance, of the 1857 piece was that 'Mr. Herbert Spencer...has written an ingenious essay in which he derives the sense of music from the cadences of emotional speech' (1876: p. 107). Later, in the *Principles of Ethics*, Spencer referred back to this argument in the 1857 essay to emphasize the evolution of 'feeling' and its results: 'cadences are the comments of the emotions on the propositions of the intellect' (1910, i: p. 248). And although Spencer did not care for the theory being called by Gurney the 'speech theory', he had in essence no serious quarrel with the label. He believed that all of his work on music had uniformly shown that it had been produced, by evolution, by having originated naturally (i.e. unconsciously) in the extension of emotional speech. Whatever ambiguities Spencer's formulation of his theory contained, it was mostly interpreted by others in the kind of way it appears he had intended. Nevertheless, it is the fourth interpretation, accommodating non-human 'music' which captures best the overall logic of his comments, in which no difference in kind between (human) music and non-human sound is indicated, nor, indeed any criteria by which such a distinction might be drawn.

Those of Spencer's contemporaries who responded to his theory did so with elegance and penetration. Each to some degree demurs at Spencer's treatment of the facts; both at the interpretations put upon the ones he marshals and at the disregard of many which, it is submitted, would have proved instructively less amenable to his thesis. Gurney in particular worked on these lines, offering many examples to show that music had characteristics at odds with Spencer's claim that it took to extremes elements already to be found in speech. He concluded that a great many of his key propositions were not true.[5] Gurney's comments were largely echoed by the German phenomenologist, psychologist and musicologist, Carl Friedrich Stumpf – taught by Brentano, and supervisor of Husserl's habilitation thesis – in his review of English 'Musikpsychologie' (1885).

Richard Wallaschek, a comparative musicologist and Gestalt music psychologist, published an article in *Mind* in 1891 widely critical of the structure of extant origin theories and which propounded his own alternative (see also his *Primitive Music* of 1893). We have already seen that Spencer apparently equivocated over the then quite popular idea of 'animal music'. Particular concerns of Wallaschek were to discourage the idea of even tacitly suggesting that animals produce music, and instead to exhort us to seek the *social* origins of music: he does both on the grounds that the concept of music is so constructed, socially, as to make the alternatives quite inappropriate. Wallaschek thus observes that we are 'accustomed to speak of "music" in the animal kingdom, and especially among birds, but in so doing we do not use the word in its proper meaning. The emission of sounds such as we hear in nature is by no means real music' (1891: p. 378).[6] By 'music', he continues, 'we always understand a musical composition, or at least its reproduction, that is to say, a consciously designed and constructed work of art' (1891: p. 379). Wallaschek is thus deeply at odds with both Spencer and Darwin on how the origin of music might be detected:

> Of course, in following the utterances of the animal kingdom down to a very primitive stage, we must go back as far as the bird's song, but we are not more or less justified in discerning in it the origin of music, than we should be in saying that all animals equipped with sound apparatus speak English, the English language being just as peculiar an order of utterance – of which the peculiar origin is still *sub judice* – as is human music. The origin of music is not to be sought in the fact that birds call 'cuckoo', cluck; 'go-back' or imitate our speech, but in our connecting certain things and ideas with certain sounds.
>
> (1891: p. 380)

Ernest Newman too, emerging as a leading writer on music in the 1890s, mounted similar campaign against the logic of Spencer's theory:

> We are prepared to admit ... that in moments of emotional excitement the ordinary speech of men becomes more rhythmical, acquires a more pronounced *timbre*, and generally varies in the ways Spencer has enumerated. What we are *not* prepared to admit is that this is either a lower form of music, or the stuff out of which music has grown. Our contention is that while the difference between speech and excited speech is one of degree only, *the difference between speech and music is one not merely of degree, but of kind* – we are dealing with similar physiological but widely separated psychological phenomena.
>
> (1905: p. 193)[7]

Such was the texture of the critical replies which were delivered whilst Spencer's own essays were still relatively fresh, although, as we shall see below, this did not prevent his theory having a considerable vogue. Within the ranks of more recent critics there has been little sign of a readiness to resuscitate Spencer's theory. The music educator and critic Percy Scholes talked of Spencer as 'guessing' (1954, i: p. 5),[8] and also observed a general downwards drift in his reputation: 'Philosophy and psychology are over-turned. It seems but a few years since Herbert Spencer's was a great name, and now nobody mentions him' (1954, iii: p. 132). More recently, Marius Schneider has claimed that the theories of Darwin and Spencer are no longer tenable, and preached agnosticism as far as the origin of music is concerned: 'It is very difficult to say anything definite about the origin of music, because the phenomenon is quite outside the range of our observation. Even in those primitive civilizations that still exist there is no race so primitive that it can be considered a relic of the very beginning of human culture' (1957: p. 5).

There seems to be no reason to dissent from any of the above comments critical of Spencer's theory on the origin of music. We may say that Spencer's account is vitiated by the assumption that social phenomena could be reduced to, and explained in, biological or in quasi-biological psychological terms. If we were to try to locate the origin of music, we should instead need to look to the realm of purposive action in the field of expression in cultural forms by social individuals. Nor is it only with 'music' that Spencer takes unconscionable conceptual liberties, for 'feeling', on which the whole theory is constructed, is also reduced to some putatively biological states. 'Feelings' and allied terms are ordinarily used to refer not to private, ghostly, inner events but to a wide variety of publicly identifiable occurrences.[9] To say the least, a great deal of highly sophisticated argument would be necessary to show that 'feelings' can legitimately be reduced to events in the neurophysiological make-up of individuals. No such arguments are adduced by Spencer to support his reductionism. Instead, Spencer simply declares that the 'feelings' relevant to the origin of music may be understood as the overflow of (biological) energy coming from 'an excess of those absorbed materials needful for self maintenance' (1857c, postscript: p. 431). Spencer's kind of approach is deeply unsatisfactory. Couple this with the general doubts expressed by Schneider, and the prospects for a sociological account of the *origin* of music seem dim indeed.

Yet to say what has just been said is not, however, to speak against the more limited set of enterprises of exploring how novel kinds of music are established as such, how children acquire a category 'music', and so forth. Valuable things can be said on such matters, though not through a Spencerian approach. As D. F. Wright has indicated, the style of research that is required is one that seeks 'to explicate the taken-for-granted assumptions, the trustworthy recipes by which meaning is given to a group of sounds', and one that can thus discover 'the rules by which sounds are constituted as music' (1975: p. 432).[10] These assumptions, recipes and rules are contested and eventually in some way reinterpreted in their application when unfamiliar kinds of sound move from being seen in such terms to being counted as music, or as a new kind of music. The accomplishment of such activity must be a key topic for the sociology of music to study. And as new kinds of music have become established as such, the hitherto settled procedures adopted in areas of activity not necessarily involved in any direct way with that process may in turn be challenged and modified. This can, I think, be observed in the field of the formal analysis of compositions, where one analyst, Wilfrid Mellers, deliberately set out to make the point that the relevant language could be as illuminating in the understanding of widely acclaimed 'popular' music as in the 'art' music to which it had been tacitly assumed it must be restricted.[11]

Spencer's speculation on the origin of music also tipped over into a discussion of the origins of harmony. This is perhaps another matter on which even when the approach adopted appears to be in order it is difficult to come to solid conclusions. Spencer handled the matter of the origin of harmony in one way in his general statement and illustration of his theory of evolution, *First Principles*. There, in discussing the forms of differentiation shown in music as the 'advance' to the heterogeneous is displayed, he notes that while differentiation was occurring in music towards the close of Greek civilization 'there existed nothing but melody: harmony was unknown'. Only with some development in Christian church-music was music in parts evolved:

> then it came into existence through a very unobtrusive differentiation. Difficult as it may be to conceive, *à priori*, how the advance from melody to harmony could take place without a sudden leap, it is none the less true that it did so. The circumstance which prepared the way for it, was the employment of two choirs singing alternately the same air. Afterwards it became the practice (very possibly first suggested by a mistake) for the second choir to commence before the first had ceased; thus producing a fugue. With the simple airs then in use, a partially harmonious fugue might not improbably thus result; and a very partially harmonious fugue satisfied the ears of that age, as we know from still preserved examples. The idea having once been given, the composing of airs productive of fugal harmony would naturally grow up; as in some way it *did* grow up out of this alternate choir-singing. And from the fugue to concerted music of two, three, four, and more parts, the transition was easy.
>
> (1862: p. 172)[12]

Together with the phenomena of the harmonic arising 'differentiated' from the phenomena of the antiphonal melodic came the 'integration' or consolidation of the two into new musical forms. In music, 'progressive integration' is displayed in numerous ways:

The simple cadence embracing but a few notes, which in the chants of savages is monotonously repeated, becomes, among civilized races, a long series of different musical phrases combined into one whole; and so complete is the integration, that the melody cannot be broken off in the middle, nor shorn of its final note, without giving us a painful sense of incompleteness. When to the air, a bass, a tenor, and an alto are added; and when to the harmony of different voice-parts there is added an accompaniment; we see integrations exemplified of another order, which grow gradually more elaborate. And the process is carried a stage higher when these complex solos, concerted pieces, choruses and orchestral effects, are combined into the vast ensemble of a musical drama; of which, be it remembered, the artistic perfection largely consists in the subordination of the particular effects to the total effect.

(1862: p. 210)[13]

In this manner, then, what was relatively diffuse becomes relatively concentrated, and what was relatively incoherent homogeneity becomes relatively coherent heterogeneity. In terms of Spencer's theory of evolution, what is here depicted in connection specifically with music are processes observable in the cosmos, reflecting the instability of an original homogeneity, given the persistence of force, and a consequent redistribution of matter and dissipation of motion.

Spencer's remarks on harmony in these passages, designed to illustrate the general processes associated with his theory of evolution, are, however, of singularly compelling interest because, when he turns to write in the specific context of discussions in which music itself is the central focus, he does not produce this sort of analysis. In his 1890 postscript he clearly declared that that 'relatively modern element in musical effect', harmony, 'cannot be affiliated on the natural language of emotion, since in such language, limited to successive tones, there cannot originate the effects wrought by simultaneous tones' (1857c postscript: p. 448). He claims instead that harmony is *not* a product of evolution. The American psychologist, James McKeen Cattell, helpfully tried to plug the gap in a rejoinder (1891) by suggesting that harmony had evolved through a natural extension of the overtones associated with each note of a melodic line. Yet Spencer, in reply to Cattell (1891), stressed he did indeed find unacceptable that harmony had evolved from melody:

To establish the evolution of the one from the other, there must be found some identifiable *transitions* between the combinations of tones constituting timbre, which do not constitute harmony to our perception and those combinations of tones which do constitute harmony to our perception; and I know of no such transitions. So far as I know (and I speak from memory, for I write far away from books), harmony commenced with the fugal repetition of a melody in ecclesiastical chants. Though the melody was the same, and the effect was produced by one choir commencing a bar or two after the other, yet the new kind of effect suddenly achieved cannot be considered as *evolved*, without stretching somewhat unduly the meaning of the word.

(1891c: p. 537)

All this is extraordinary. No other topic makes Spencer hesitate so when he is attempting to engineer evolutionary explanations. While the process of 'differentiation' which he sketched *may* describe the public arrival of harmony, it does not provide a cause. But this being so, I cannot quite see *Spencer's* difficulty, in his own terms, in finding the origin of harmony in what he calls the natural language of the emotions. Persons forming a society are likely to share emotions, and the voices of men and women, will, after all, have expressed emotion at different pitches, on occasion, doubtless, at the same time. A unique and deep sort of qualm appears to have struck him, which, unparalleled in the coverage of the numberless other subjects over which his writings ranged, made him intuit in the sole case of 'harmony' that it 'cannot be considered as *evolved*, without stretching somewhat unduly the meaning of the word'. What seems to have happened is that Spencer sensed it was problematic to equate accidental simultaneous soundings of two or more notes with hearing this as 'harmony'. In effect he was realizing that the publicly ascribed and negotiated meaningful, rule-governed nature of harmony could not be ignored (see also Offer, 1983). Alas, when writing on other and, of course, equally rule-governed aspects of social life, not least the origin of 'music', he did not have the same kind of doubt or sociological sensitivity. Hence such work is particularly vulnerable to criticisms of its methods. And this is of course a familiar concern in sociology in approaching its subject matter. A different kind of illustration may help. In an important sense people have always networked, for example, but only with the adoption relatively recently of a concept of 'networking' has the activity as such become recognized, in the process acquiring criteria and rules by showing competent compliance with which one may be counted as 'networking'.

A concern with the origins of music and harmony were only two of Spencer's set of interests related to music. The other constituents were the function of music, music's evolution through the centuries together with its associated institutions and equipment for sound production, and his critical discourse in respect of a variety of compositions and composers.

First we need to consider Spencer on the function of music. Francis has argued that in the 1850s Spencer held an anti-functional approach to art, believing that the arts and beauty uniquely excited our feelings, directly and naturally. Certainly Spencer wrote that the love of music seems to exist for its own sake, and that 'the delights of melody and harmony do not obviously minister to the welfare either of the individual or of society' (2007:

p. 82. Francis is here directly quoting from Spencer, 1857c: p. 421). However, in promoting a Procrustean 'reinterpretation' of Spencer's life and work, in terms of a public, self-denying intellectualism and repressed private passion, Francis oversimplifies Spencer's actual analysis of music and its functionality. While he muses that Spencer 'never recovered from unconsummated love' (2007: p. 52), and speculates over the 'bondage of his love' for Marian Evans (2007: p. 62), he omits any mention of the reality that Spencer's following sentence is 'May we not suspect, however, that this exception is apparent only?' (1857c: p. 423). For Spencer, music, having evolved from emotional speech, reacts on and advances emotional dimensions of our language. It indeed has a function: developing emotional expression, nurturing in hearers the capacity to empathize with others beyond an intellectual level. Music promotes 'sympathy' on which 'our general welfare and our immediate pleasures' depend (1857c: p. 424). It is one of the 'chief media of *sympathy*', and whatever makes sympathy greater is of large importance to civilization (1857c: pp. 424–5). An agency which communicates and enhances fellow-feeling 'can scarcely be overrated in value' (1857c: p. 425). Music, Spencer asserts, in almost Schopenhauerian style, 'must take rank as the highest of the fine arts – as the one which, more than any other, ministers to human welfare' (1857c: p. 426).[14] An allusion to such a convergence of styles of thought is not mere ornament. Spencer alighted on music towards the climax of the 'Ecclesiastical Institutions' Part of the *Principles of Sociology* in discussing the future functions of these institutions, and remarked that, from the evident decline of dogmatic theism and the growth of agnosticism,

> it does not follow that there will lapse all observations tending to keep alive a consciousness of the relation in which we stand to the Unknown Cause, and tending to give expression to the sentiment accompanying that consciousness. There will remain a need for qualifying that too prosaic and material form of life which tends to result from absorption in daily work, and there will ever be a sphere for those who are able to impress their hearers with a due sense of the Mystery in which the origin and meaning of the Universe are shrouded. It may be anticipated, too, that musical expression to the sentiment accompanying this sense will not only survive but undergo further development. Already protestant cathedral music, more impersonal than any other, serves not unfitly to express feelings suggested by the thought of a transitory life, alike of the individual and of the race – a life which is but an infinitesimal product of a Power without any bounds we can find or imagine; and hereafter such music may still express these feelings.
>
> (1896b: p. 157)[15]

Spencer adds, indeed, that it is in the most developed musical intelligence of the day that we may catch a glimpse of the demanding holistic and synthesizing intelligence required in the future 'for symbolizing in thought the totality of things' (1896b: p. 174): 'We may say that just as an undeveloped musical faculty, able only to appreciate a simple melody, cannot grasp the variously-entangled passages and harmonies of a symphony, which in the minds of composer and conductor are unified into the involved musical effects awakening far greater feeling than is possible to the musically uncultured; so, by future more evolved intelligences, the course of things now apprehensible only in parts may be apprehensible all together, with an accompanying feeling as much beyond that of the present cultured man, as his feeling is beyond that of the savage' (1896b: p. 175). Yet Spencer was adamant that the function of music was not to be interpreted as the didactic transmission of a normative instruction to the intellect, and he criticized Wagner and Newman for holding to the view that the purpose of music was to teach. It was precisely in this specific context that in a late short essay, 'The Purpose of Art', he argued: 'the primary purpose of music is neither instruction nor culture but pleasure; and this is an all-sufficient purpose' (1902: p. 34).

Secondly, we should acknowledge Spencer's identification of trends in music history since its origin through the lens of his theory of evolution, a topic which, indeed, was touched upon in the section discussing harmony in connection with differentiation and integration in music. Spencer's key claim is that we may find in music over time 'a simultaneous advance in heterogeneity, in integration, and in definiteness' (1902: p. 53). Perhaps in recognition of Hubert Parry's sympathies with his theory of evolution, Spencer makes several references to his *The Art of Music*, which had appeared in the 'International Scientific Series' of volumes originated by Youmans and in which Spencer had a hand.[16] These references are particularly in connection with very early music, which for Spencer, drawing on Parry, displays 'vocal utterances little above the howls and groans in which inarticulate feeling expresses itself. There is but an imperfect differentiation of the tones into notes properly so called. So that we see well exemplified that indefiniteness which characterises incipient evolution in general' (1902: p. 50).[17] Spencer's own illustrations of differentiation, beyond that made early on between dance and music, tend to point to the multiple differentiations of compositional from which music has come to display. Thus in *First Principles* he enumerates the 'many different genera and species' of musical types exemplifying an undoubted increase in heterogeneity accumulating over time. He notes, for example, divisions between vocal, instrumental and mixed forms of music, and 'their subdivisions into music for different voices and different instruments'. In sacred music there is 'the simple hymn, the chant, the canon, motet, anthem &c. up to the oratorio' And in secular music, there are still more numerous forms 'from the ballad up to the serenata, from the instrumental solo up to the symphony' (1862: p. 173). In the *Principles of Sociology* he offers illustrations of differentiation becoming established between, for instance, professional musical performers and teachers of music, and also between 'the multitudinous local musical societies; the local musical festivals with their governing organizations; and the several incorporated colleges, with their students, professorial staffs, and directors' (1896b: p. 214). Spencer also illustrates integration in the form of the unifying consequences of the growth of a periodical literature, made up of 'sundry music journals devoted to reports and criticism of concerts, operas, oratorios, and serving to aid musical culture while they maintain the interest of the teachers and performers' (1896b: p. 214).

The third of the trio of Spencer's interests in music with which this section is concerned is his music criticism. William Henry Hudson was Spencer's secretary in the late 1880s, and recalled that for Spencer 'music was a never-failing source of satisfaction'. He was a critical and responsive listener, especially enjoying having played to him Handel and Bach, and Beethoven and Gluck. Most modern composers he thought 'clever technicians merely', and he was 'wholly indifferent to any music, no matter how brilliant, which seemed to him to want the note of genius – which, in a favourite phrase of his, struck him as simply "manufactured" ' (1904: p. 10). Most of Spencer's critical comments on music appeared in his *Facts and Comments* of 1902, though the roots of his perspective are clearly discernible in the 'Origin and Function' essay. There, having reminded readers that 'the tones, intervals and cadences of strong emotion were the elements out of which song was elaborated', he adds that 'we may expect to find that still stronger emotion produced the elaboration'. Spencer duly finds composers of music to be 'men of acute sensibilities', and he identifies Mozart, Beethoven, Mendelssohn and Chopin as characterized by an 'unusually emotional nature', which is 'just the agency required for the development of recitative and song' (1857c: p. 417).[18] One of Spencer's prime interests is to defend the reputation of Meyerbeer as an opera composer, often at the expense of Mozart or Wagner. To counter the charge that Meyerbeer makes excessive use of arpeggios and scale-passages, sometimes regarded as mere combinations of notes, substituting for musical thought, Spencer dragooned his lady-pianist to undertake a meticulous comparative count of such devices in three operas by Meyerbeer and three by Mozart. Mozart, it was discovered, had significantly more of them (full details are in 'Meyerbeer' in Spencer, 1902: pp. 80–2). Spencer's idiosyncratically flat-footed and, for its time, typically cross-grained defence of Meyerbeer has not stood the test of years. As Grew observed, insofar as there is an implication that his figures suggest Meyerbeer is underestimated as a composer, Spencer loses sight of the fact that 'it is the way the construction is used that makes it good or otherwise' (1928: p. 136. See also Hill, 1928).

Spencer's taste for reductionism emerges again when he adopts a questionable position on the nature of opera as an artistic form. He disputes the claim that Meyerbeer's operas are 'theatrical' in the pejorative sense of that term. A piano arrangement of Meyerbeer's operatic music shows, he says, that the 'effects' are not the product of empty display and noise. However, it would be widely judged as unwise to imply that if the *music* is not theatrical the conclusion follows that the *opera* is not. That is to assume that operas should be evaluated in terms of the calibre of their constituent artistic elements, with one (music) being predominant, rather than in total, in line with the conception held by Wagner of opera as *Gesamtkunstwerk*, under which operas are *sui generis* works of art (a conception not precluding a focus on operatic *music* as such).[19]

Another topic from the field of Spencer's music criticism merits some mention. For Spencer, 'orchestras are very defective'. They lack 'adequate impressiveness'. The volume and quality of tones from a pipe organ produce a 'massive emotion' unparalleled by orchestras. Orchestras rely too much on the strings, particularly violins, which are lacking in 'dignity' and, since their presence is continuous, contribute small rather than massive contrasts in sound. Indeed, they serve to make orchestral sound top heavy. Spencer attributes these 'defects' to an as yet imperfect evolution of instrumental specialization in the make-up of the conventional orchestra:

> Achieved by arrangements of contrast, great and small, art of every kind forbids that monotony caused by the directing of constant attention to one element. Orchestral effects need much greater specialization. Sounds of kindred qualities should at one moment be used for one purpose and then sounds of other kindred qualities should be used for another purpose: thus differentiating the *masses* of sound more than at present. In fact, there requires a larger step in evolution – a more marked advance from the indefinitely homogeneous to the definitely heterogeneous.

> Further contemplation of the contrast between the emotion produced by an organ and that produced by an orchestra, shows that a large part of this contrast is due to the far greater predominance which the bass has in the organ than in the orchestra. It is from the volume of an organ's deep tones that there comes that profound impressiveness which an orchestra lacks. As a masculine trait, deep tones are associated with power, and their effect is therefore relatively imposing. To show that this is so, it needs but to recall a part of an organ performance in which the upper tones only are used, to see that but little of the dignity and grandeur remain. Necessarily, therefore, in an orchestra, while the sounds of the violins are predominant, the trait of dignity is absent.

(1902: pp. 178–9)

Spencer's critical comments on music do quite frequently display a jejune 'simplification' of complex products of the social world; a consequence, it seems, of his 'scientific' intellectual priorities and theoretical procedures in applying the idea of evolution to social life as if each person is a conscious automaton and as if the work of mankind through history is but a series of sedimentary deposits. Events may happen over time but the whys and hows of innovation often seem left untouched. However, from the points of view of both the sociology of knowledge and Spencer studies his music criticism is of real significance. It parades in an important but unusual setting the theories and methods of his own brand of scientistic sociological rationalism, conventionally assumed to be confined to the analysis of more 'mainstream' social, economic and political concerns. In taking music so seriously Spencer impressed Tönnies that he was no 'zealot of a shallow utilitarian outlook' (1974: p. 116). However, William James's comment encapsulated the difficulty: 'In all his dealings with the art products of mankind he manifests the same curious dryness and mechanical literality of judgment' (in Elton, 1954: p. 136).

There were three ways in which nineteenth century evolutionary thought became linked with music, in the political and social awareness of certain composers, in occasional uses of evolutionary themes for the purpose of 'program' music and in the interpretation of the historical development of music (Oldroyd, 1980: p. 333). It is especially with the third of these largely neglected levels which this section deals, with particular reference to Britain. It is, I think, fair to claim that on this topic and in that country Spencer's idea of evolution made a real difference. This is not to say either that some sense of progress in music had been absent in previous British histories or that other countries manifested no such Spencerian influences. Both of these dimensions are discussed by Allen in his *Philosophies of Music History* of 1939 (1962). However, in Britain the influence of Spencer's contributions to thought on the origin and subsequent evolution of music was but little diluted by, for example, the concerns pursued in the writings of Wagner on the future of music. The tangible result was a major change of direction and style in the native music historiography in which Spencer was a prime mover.

The reputation of Spencer's general evolutionary theory reached its zenith in the 1870s and 1880s. The theory was taken up eagerly by many and it was expounded especially but not only in science-minded studies which were largely aimed at a broad readership. It is easy nowadays not to appreciate this abundant enthusiasm excited by Spencer's evolutionism. The central idea of the ubiquity of change was in essence simple and opened up new horizons, the 'explanations' it could yield were apparently endless and attractively unorthodox, and the associated panoply of terminology seemed to ooze the magisterial authority of science. It fascinated and it converted. The young Hubert Parry was not slow to respond.

Charles Hubert Hastings Parry, who lived from 1848 to 1918, was to earn high esteem as composer, teacher and music historian. His compositions figure prominently in what is often called the 'Renaissance of English music' (see Dibble, 1992). He was appointed as a professor at the Royal College of Music in 1883 and became the Director in 1895. He was also appointed Professor of Music at Oxford in 1889, the year following his knighthood. The very breadth of his interests was somewhat Spencerian as indeed was those of his predecessor as Director of the RCM, Sir George Grove, most famous for his *Dictionary of Music and Musicians*: Grove's biographer in fact draws the parallel with Spencer but gives no evidence of any influence from the latter (Young, 1980: p. 271). It is, however, specifically with Parry's music historiography that we are concerned, in particular his *The Evolution of the Art of Music* (first published as *The Art of Music* in 1893 after nearly a decade of gestation).[20]

Parry had been reading and discussing Spencer's *First Principles* and *Principles of Psychology* with enthusiasm in the mid-1870s. It was noted in the Introduction to this study that an apparently flustered Parry met Spencer in 1874 at the Choir Festival at Gloucester, and the claim has been advanced that this meeting constituted the birth of ethnomusicology (Wachsmann, 1973: p. 6). Parry's interest in Spencer and evolution does not appear to have diminished during the 1890s and he and Spencer, both members of the Athenaeum Club, met occasionally, and corresponded on early music in 1890. Indeed, in 1899, Spencer sought Parry's advice on the applications he had received for a 'domestic musician' whom he wished to secure (Graves, 1926: p. 12). When Parry's book on the history of music appeared, it contained many novel features reflecting his interest in Spencer's ideas. Kennedy, a leading historian of the musical life of the period, tells the story concisely: 'Parry, in fact, was truly Victorian in the best sense of the term. He tried to relate music to life, philosophy, and science. He admired the ideas of Herbert Spencer and this led to his book *The Evolution of the Art of Music* in which he traced music back to its primitive folk origins' (1964: p. 5).

Parry's book reflects Spencer's preoccupations both in its discussion of the origin of music and, much more significantly, in the way in which it organizes the material according to the conceptions associated with his law of evolution. Parry in fact was at the forefront of the reaction against the prevalent Romantic music historiography with its emphasis on a divine origin and great names, 'those of the leaders in musical thought upon whom the gods or the muse had smiled at birth' (Allen, 1962: p. 87). In Parry's view, music history should be the study not of a few great names but of the gradual organic development of music, with the movement from homogeneity to heterogeneity given pride of place. Parry was already an 'ardent student' of and 'full of' Spencer (in Graves, 1926, i: p. 152). He was someone who had caught the message that, as Allen commented, 'Spencerian laws of progress and evolution' offered to music historians 'a new solution to their problems. Music history need not be a mere chronicle of men and events; to be scientific one need only envisage music as an evolving organism' (1962: p. 110; see also Oldroyd, 1980).

When Parry discussed the origin of music, he shrewdly refrained from actually claiming that music evolved from excited speech, whilst sharing Spencer's language: 'The raw material of music is found in the expressive noises and cries which human beings as well as animals give vent to under excitement of any kind.... Such cries pass within the range of art when they take any definite form' (1931: pp. 12–13). But on other matters Parry is generally faithful to Spencer, presenting the material to show a gradual progressive evolution at work, and ultimately treating all music as if it were itself a single evolving organism. Repeatedly he introduces Spencer's own terms, especially 'homogeneity' and 'heterogeneity'. One may take as an illustration his discussion of the music of the early baroque, where he declares:

> The progress of this somewhat immature period shows the inevitable tendency of all things from homogeneity towards diversity and definiteness. In its widest aspects art is seen to branch out into a variety of different forms. The difference in style and matter between choral movements and instrumental works begins to be more definite and decisive. The types of opera, oratorio, cantata, and of the various kinds of church music become more distinct, and are even subdivided into different subordinate types, as was the case with Italian and French opera.
>
> (1931: p. 155. See also, for example, pp. 121–4)

Such passages are characteristic of the framework of analysis which Parry embraces. Nonetheless, within the Spencerian parameters, Parry often assesses the merits of individual composers quite openly, with little or no attempt to clothe them in evolutionary jargon. And his own common sense protects him from 'ranking' 'great' composers in line with their evolutionary position. Whatever the evolutionary state of the musical vocabulary and instrumental resources that were to hand, if composers possess consummate mastery of their potentialities, if their compositions are in this sense 'mature', then for Parry this gives a special status to these composers: the limits of evaluation by evolution have been reached.[21]

Parry, then, normally follows Spencer's lead in presenting changes in the nature of music as travelling in an onwards and upwards direction, but he explicitly retains the capacity to make judgements independent of the point reached on that path. Allen summarizes well what Parry had abstracted from Spencer and was adapting to his own purposes

(1) that music 'created itself', like other organisms.
(2) that the various divisions of music were at first united.
(3) that this unity was that of undifferentiated homogeneity.
(4) that progressive evolution took place to the definite, clear-cut forms of modern art.

(1962: p. 115)

Similar themes were recapitulated in other British music histories of the time, most notably in *A History of Music* by Sir Charles Villiers Stanford and Cecil Forsyth (1916).[22] This book presents a version of Spencer's origin theory (1916: Ch. 10). It is punctuated by references to a process of progressive evolution. Thus, for example, the compositions of Josquin and his contemporaries, whilst their historical importance is readily acknowledged, are deemed to be artistically immature; they are but stations on a line leading to the glories of Palestrina (1916: pp. 153–7).

The themes also infiltrated a less academic and more discursive literature on the development of the history of music. The English composer Ralph Vaughan Williams professed a distinctly Spencerian view of the origin of music to which possibly he was introduced by Parry in his student days at the RCM. In 1902, he was delivering a series of lectures on the history of folk song in which he declared it to be 'the natural development of excited speech' (in Kennedy, 1964: p. 31). And elsewhere Vaughan Williams observed that song is 'nothing less than speech charged with emotion' (1963: p. 17). He also showered praise on Parry's book, which, so Vaughan Williams claimed, had 'shown how music like everything else in the world is subject to the laws of evolution, that there is no difference in kind but only in degree between Beethoven and the humblest singer of a folk-song' (1963: p. 5).

The omnipresence of evolutionary theories, of the origin of music especially, whether attributed to Darwin or Spencer, made some comment on them advisable by the musicologist, Percy Carter Buck, in his *The Scope of Music*, first issued in 1924:

> When I was a young student there were two theories that held the field sponsored by names of such eminence that musicians accepted them as the only possible alternatives, and for the most part (if interested in the matter) became partisans of one or the other. Darwin told us that the origin of our art was sex, instancing the male birds who, in the mating season, sung in competition before the female. Spencer, on the other hand, said the art arose from the deliberate (sic) attempt to reproduce the inflexions of speech.
>
> (1969: p. 27)

Yet Buck coupled this recollection with a perceptive expression of caution which gave voice to the spreading critical detachment from the vogue for 'evolution' which had ensnared earlier historians of music: 'The mere musician may say, without impertinence, that we have come to look to the anthropologist, who studies mankind as a whole rather than man as an organism, for enlightenment as to the earliest practical efforts. From him we can learn what is actually being done today by primitive peoples, and finding certain lines of action normal and others exceptional can feel some assurance in piecing together the artistic history of the human race' (1969: pp. 27–8).

The years between the First and Second World Wars also evince a dwindling of the grand, all-embracing Spencer and Parry mode of undertaking historical research into music. Of course there were, and perhaps still are, 'survivals'. However, the painstaking preparation of scholarly editions of early music from manuscript sources and of books on specialized historical topics, seldom embellished with the language of evolution, became much more the rule. Spencer and Parry, in drawing attention to early music, folk-song and also 'differentiation' through their evolutionary scenarios, may well have contributed a spark to ignite such interests, but their condescending attitudes towards musical ancestors were seldom found either constructive or congenial. Allen's pioneering and invaluable study also points to the waning of the influence of Spencer's theory of evolution in that, whilst the first edition of the *Oxford History of Music*, which began to appear in 1901, manifested Spencerian principles, the second edition of 1929 onwards, under the editorship of Buck, tended markedly to distance itself from a crudely progressive framework (1962: pp. 128–9, and pp. 136–7). And Allen himself, forcefully urging rejection of the 'belief that peoples and arts of different times and places are ipso facto inferior', was a part of the process, for his book, it must be remembered, was first issued in 1939 (1962: p. 342).

Critical commentary on the mechanical perpetuation of Spencerian ideas in the presentation of music history persisted into the 1950s. Austin in particular argued that, although the application of evolutionary perspectives to music history usefully reminded us of its continuities and complexities, music could not be said to evolve in any but a metaphorical sense: rather than 'evolving' from one composition to another or one style to another, separate pieces of music are made by men and women. A phrase such as 'evolution of 20th-century music' refers only to 'relations among certain events in the minds of men' (Austin, 1953; see also Lissa, 1967). A little later, Sir Jack Westrup, in his *An Introduction to Musical History*, distanced himself from the adoption of Spencerian evolutionary perspectives in the history of music, pointing a finger in the process at one specimen of the genre, to which reference has already been made: 'evolutionary theory has induced authors to regard a period as a time of steady progress from small, or even insignificant beginnings to heights of supreme mastery. The method is seen in its most grotesque form in the *History of Music* by Sir Charles Stanford and Cecil Forsyth' (1955: p. 54).[23]

This chapter has indicated that Spencer's ideas were a significant force in structuring the style and content of music historiography in Britain for a period of at least, speaking approximately, the four decades around the beginning of the twentieth century. This verdict applies to both his specific evolutionary theory of the origin of music and the general evolutionary theory of change in all things from homogeneity to heterogeneity, including of course musical style, genres, and education, as elaborated in the 'System of Synthetic Philosophy'. The impact came in spite of the criticisms by Gurney, Newman and others of Spencer's origin theory in particular, noted already. Spencer's evolutionism thus penetrated far further into the business of making sense of human activity than is usually recognized in accounts of the impact of evolutionary thought. The chapter has not only established that Spencer's ideas on music were historically significant, but also in the process underlined how broad was the 'take-up' of 'evolutionary' ideas. This of course makes his distinctive ideas of real significance in intellectual history and the sociology of knowledge, especially as the impact of nineteenth-century evolutionary modes of thought in general is of indisputable significance.

However, it seems to me that much of the ground covered has additional significance. In the first place, it has emerged that music was elevated to a position of unusual prominence by Spencer in his discussions of substantive sociological matters. A recognition of this fact demands a modification to what at present seems to be the prevalent opinion, that Spencer was, in his sociology, almost exclusively concerned with relationships between the state and the individual. Secondly, it is apparent that, in connection with the origin of harmony, Spencer advances statements and arguments which ought to force some revision to the widespread belief that Spencer considered he had provided explanations of *all* phenomena by his law of evolution. Thirdly, Spencer's theory of the origin of music imperfectly distinguishes between the levels of explanatory account offered by biology as such and sociology of the origins of social phenomena. The criticisms which have been discussed show that a clear distinction is desirable between studying the biological/physiological development of sound production and the sociology of music.[24] As Allen observed of Spencer's theory, it confused unorganized sound with music: 'Music is, in one sense, a language, an art which communicates tonal ideas in organised form. The study of sound, *per se*, whether vocal or otherwise, is a branch of physiology or physics that may have nothing whatever to do with art' (1962: p. 139). In turning next to Spencer's treatment of moral conduct we shall see that in conceptual terms the idea of the 'the moral' received more refined consideration than did 'music'.

9
Sociology, Ethics and Well-Being

This chapter is concerned with Spencer's evolutionary and liberal vision of the future for the well-being of individuals. It thus deals with his morphological and developmental interpretation of moral values as grounded in and expressive of social and individual life, and also with the political structures and functions to which he regarded it as closely connected. Spencer's ideas relating to well-being are mostly to be found in his *Principles of Ethics*, the two volumes of which were in terms of their place in its logical sequence the conclusion of his 10-volume 'System of Synthetic Philosophy'. However, these volumes were both composed and first published in finished form (in 1892 and 1893) before the 'System' was actually completed with the third and final volume of the *Sociology* in 1896. The *Ethics* itself is in many important respects a development of his earlier *Social Statics* of 1851, which had preceded his *Principles of Psychology,* and the theory of evolution as systematically expounded in *First Principles*. A chief task of the *Ethics* was therefore to expand upon and connect structurally to his evolutionary theory the ideas which Spencer remained satisfied were the correct positions which had been adumbrated in the earlier book. However, Spencer also issued a much abridged and revised version of *Social Statics* in 1892, essentially containing discussions not directly superseded by the *Ethics*.

It seems fair to say that sociologists have tended to regard the *Ethics* as falling into the territory of philosophers. This is a matter for regret, since his analysis of ethics is approached through the lens of his distinctive theory of social evolution. For Spencer, our understanding of how men ought to live must begin from the position that actual and possible moral conduct is tethered to the natures of men as formed by psychical and social evolution over generations through the mechanism of the inheritance of acquired characteristics. The *Ethics* draws on animal behaviour, anthropological studies and sociological conjecture to construct a speculative kind of sociological natural history of the origin, current practice and potential development of ethics. Spencer indeed traces elements of the sentiment of 'justice' back to a nascent 'animal ethics' (his expression); from which origin the development of man's ethical ideas and sentiments may be charted, being the product of adaptation which has yielded the unfinished odyssey of his evolution as a psychical and social being. Social arrangements at any one time have formed an important part of the 'circumstances' of man to which adaptation has taken place. Spencer's adoption of this form of narrative, although coupled with an approach indebted to his own psychological thought, resulted in the production of a *sociology* of morals. As well as Spencer's analytical style in approaching ethics being recognizably sociological in spirit, he provides for its time a uniquely sympathetic perspective on everyday moral beliefs and practices, which he describes in some detail, notably so in his consideration of 'positive beneficence'. He also relates patterns of moral thought and action in social life, as in the case of contrasted weightings attached to the value placed on 'justice', to more abstract elements of his sociology, especially his contrast between militancy and industrialism. With this sociology of morals perspective, moreover, Spencer deliberately attempted to transcend the more usual concerns, theological or philosophical, about how the authority of moral obligations might be justified. Spencer also utilized his own sociological generalizations, themselves closely tied in with his general evolutionary thought, to argue that particular normative contents be adopted within moral thought and conduct.

In places the detailed structure of the *Principles of Ethics*, particularly in the first volume, is not always easily discerned, and Spencer appears to retrace his steps at certain points in a rather confusing manner. This chapter nevertheless tries to provide a fairly comprehensive exposition of Spencer's understanding of ethics as part of social life. Doing so should serve to emphasize his distance from the conventional wisdom that in his ethical analysis he was an apologist for selfishness (to which the claim that he was a 'social Darwinist' usually seems to refer) and a naked, nuance-free *laissez-faire*, whether in economics, politics, social life or international relations. It also should compensate for the fragmented and incomplete picture of his contribution to understanding ethical thought and conduct which is often displayed by, and on occasion weakens, specialist philosophical studies of his ethics, which have tended to focus on specific problems such as the precise nature of his utilitarianism, and whether or not Spencer committed the 'naturalistic fallacy' in his reasoning. This is not, of course, to deny that there are philosophical problems, often it seems to me deep-seated, in respect of these and kindred concerns.

Spencer was confident that his principles of evolution, once they had been demonstrated to be as true of ethics as of everything else, would provide an explanation of the manifest ethical diversity within and between societies over time and place; they would yield also, he believed, the principles of 'absolute ethics', which depicted the state of moral life for men and societies as ultimately evolved, thus serving as a guide by which the imperfect present (our world, in which for Spencer forms of 'relative ethics' obtain) might gradually be improved upon over the generations 'without resort to the supposed supernatural sanctions of right conduct' (1910, i: p. vii).[1] Spencer interpreted his objective as necessitating an account of conduct in general as well as of that part of it of ethical significance, and the part of ethical significance was conceived of as larger than he thought usual, embracing facets of individual conduct not normally considered to be matters of ethical concern. Spencer also sought to combat the popular identification of ethics with repression and enforcement: 'just as the rampant egoism of a brutal militancy' cannot be suppressed by subjection, neither can 'the misconduct of ordinary humanity as now existing' be remedied through 'upholding a standard of abnegation beyond human achievement'. Trying to achieve the impossible demoralizes those persons who *are* attempting to achieve 'higher life', for by association 'with rules that cannot be obeyed, rules that can be obeyed lose their authority' (1910, i: p. xv). These concerns entice Spencer into a sustained contemplation of the ethically impregnated interactions in which 'ordinary humanity' routinely engages, an important dimension of Spencer as a sociologist often obscured in studies of his sociology that omit the *Ethics*, and which thereby perpetuate an approach that short-changes Spencer and compromises the just assessment of the breadth of his conception of and contribution to sociological enquiry.[2]

The *Ethics* begins with the Part entitled 'The Data of Ethics' first issued, it will be recalled, in 1879. For Spencer, conduct in general is action that is adjusted to ends, and conduct to be judged as good is well adjusted to ends, it 'conduces to life in each and all' (1910, i: p. 45). It is important to set out clearly the connection Spencer sees between evolution and 'good'. The conduct which is 'highly-evolved conduct, is that which ... we find to be what is called good conduct', and is thus also well-adjusted to ends. Spencer adds that the 'ideal goal to the natural evolution of conduct ... is the ideal standard of conduct ethically considered' (1910, i: p. 44). Thus conduct which exhibits militancy in otherwise 'advanced' societies is not 'highly-evolved' because it involves mutual injury and hindrance. What we call 'good' conduct is itself the outcome of our inheritance of characteristics acquired through adaptation to surrounding conditions over generations. The fundamental connections here specified are much contested in philosophical appraisals of Spencer's conception of 'good', and will be returned to later in the chapter.

The conduct with which morality has no concern passes into conduct which is immoral or moral 'by small degrees and countless ways' (1910, i: p. 6). We have, therefore, to frame a conception of the evolution of conduct 'as correlated' with the evolution of structures and functions throughout the ascending types of animals (1910, i: p. 8). In terms of the subject matter of the *Ethics* the objective aspect of moral conduct considered in terms of the 'Evolution-Hypothesis', corresponds with the same conduct considered subjectively or individually (1910, i: p. 20). Spencer is clear that all of this conduct is made up of external motions for which, 'if we could trace the cerebral processes which accompany these, we should find an inner physiological co-ordination corresponding with the outer co-ordination of actions' (1910, i: p. 10). However, the exploration of these cerebral physiological co-ordinations is explicitly excluded by Spencer from the *Ethics*.

In mankind, 'the adjustments of acts to ends are both more numerous and better than among lower mammals'. The same contrast characterizes 'the doings of higher races of men' compared with 'those of lower races'. If we take any one of the major ends achieved, such as nutrition, shelter, or political discussion and agitation, 'we see greater achievement by civilized than by savage' (1910, i: p. 13). Life is both prolonged and increased in amount: species life as well as individual life is advanced. Yet as long as antagonisms between and within groups remain the evolution must be incomplete. A greater completeness of the adjustment of acts to ends can be achieved (not only by mankind) when there is peace, not aggression, that is, when the adjustment of the acts of each may be undertaken without hindering the like adjustments of the acts of others (the core of the equal freedom principle). A further advance, though, remains to be achieved:

> beyond so behaving that each achieves his ends without preventing others from achieving their ends, the members of a society may give mutual help in the achievement of ends. And if, either indirectly by industrial co-operation, or directly by volunteered aid, fellow citizens can make easier for one another the adjustments of acts to ends, then their conduct assumes a still higher phase of evolution; since whatever facilitates the making of adjustments by each, increases the totality of the adjustments made, and serves to render the lives of all more complete.
>
> (1910, i: p. 19)

The idea of good is thus understood as the progressive adjustment of acts to ends. Pleasure and happiness are thereby enhanced: 'the good is universally the pleasurable' (1910, i: p. 30). Right principles of conduct, however, need to be affiliated on our knowledge of causation, that is, to the laws of life as stated in general by the theory of evolution and in particular within the special sciences, including psychology and sociology. While utilitarianism best captures the central place in moral reasoning of happiness, the unscientific utilitarianism of John Stuart Mill, 'which recognizes only the principles of conduct reached by induction, is but preparatory to the utilitarianism which deduces these principles from the processes of life as carried on under established conditions of existence' (1910, i: p. 51). The provision of such deductions is one of the principal tasks of the *Ethics*.

The appropriate evidence on causation furnished by the sciences must thus inform the process of placing our understanding of moral conduct on a sound basis. The physical sciences show us that the conduct of the habitually moral man is more definite and coherent in its nature, and thus more advanced, than that of the habitually immoral man. Biology shows us that the ideally moral man 'is one in whom the functions of all kinds are duly fulfilled' (1910, i: p. 75). Psychology explains why moral feelings and the associated restraints have arisen 'later than the feelings and restraints that originate from political, religious and social authorities' (1910, i: p. 121) and have not yet entirely disentangled themselves:

> only by these lower feelings and restraints could be maintained the conditions under which the higher feelings and restraints evolve. It is thus alike with the self-regarding feelings and with the other-regarding feelings. The pains which improvidence will bring, and the pleasures to be gained by storing up things for future use and by labouring to get such things, can be habitually contrasted in thought, only as fast as settled social arrangements make accumulation possible; and that there may arise such settled arrangements, fear of the seen ruler, the unseen ruler, and of public opinion, must come into play. Only after political, religious, and social restraints have produced a stable community, can there be sufficient experience of the pains, positive and negative, sensational and emotional, which crimes of aggression cause, as to generate that moral aversion to them constituted by consciousness of their intrinsically evil results. And more manifest still is it that such a moral sentiment as that of abstract equity, which is offended not only by material injuries done to men but also by political arrangements that place them at a disadvantage, can evolve only after the social stage reached gives familiar experience both of the pains flowing directly from injustices and also of those flowing indirectly from the class-privileges which make injustices easy.
>
> (1910, i: pp. 121–2)

However, the conception of duty as self-compulsion, as intrinsic rather than imposed from outside, is itself in evolutionary terms ultimately transitional, for the complete adjustment of acts to ends entails that 'the sense of obligation ... will be awakened only on those extraordinary occasions that prompt breach of the laws otherwise spontaneously conformed to' (1910, i: p. 131). Meanwhile, social life requires that a true ethical principle must specify the manner in which it may be carried on to ensure to best effect that 'the complete living of each consists with, and conduces to, the complete living of all (1910, i: p. 148). The 'highest degree' of man's life in the social state is characterized by the emergence of a formula 'which specially recognizes the relations of each individual to others, in presence of whom, and in co-operation with whom, he has to live' (1910, i: p. 133). However, evolution has also presented men in society with contingent circumstances in which the life of the social organism must 'as an end, rank above the lives of its units' (1910: i: p. 133): the presence of antagonistic societies, and the

interests of all in a particular threatened society that it should survive, has
served to subordinate 'personal to social welfare' (1910, i: p. 133). When,
though, in due course, danger to the society has receded, the 'final object
of pursuit, the welfare of the units' (1910, i: p. 133) becomes the immediate rather than merely the ultimate object of pursuit. Once war ceases
to be endemic, 'growing industrialism habituates men' to the principle of
'maintaining their own claims while respecting the claims of others', and in
respect of private actions the authority of the ruler becomes open to challenge: 'the political independence of the citizen comes to be regarded as
a claim which it is virtuous to maintain and vicious to yield up' (1910, i:
p. 135). Since the processes of adjusting acts to ends, which conduce to
the continuance of life, simply render acts of aggression incompatible with
conduct attaining its highest level, the limit to the evolution of conduct
is arrived at by the members of each society 'only when, being arrived at
by members of other societies also, the causes of international antagonism
end simultaneously with the causes of antagonism between individuals'
(1910, i: p. 137). At present, the 'civilized man' may be approaching such
a state, yet the moral code of 'enmity' remains in existence alongside of
the code of 'amity'. There is an inconsistent and relatively precarious but
nevertheless transiently authoritative compromise between the codes, an
unavoidable consequence of the persisting residual forms of aggression. It
is a fact, Spencer observes, that the individual man while living with due
regard paid to the lives of others in the same society, experiences it on
occasion commanded that he act 'regardless of the lives of those belonging to other societies. The same mental constitution having to fulfil both
these requirements, is necessarily incongruous; and the correlative conduct,
adjusted first to the one need and then to the other, cannot be brought
within any consistent ethical system' (1910, i: p. 135).

Co-operation, whether it takes the form of a physiological or a sociological division of labour, requires that the benefits received are proportionate
to the services rendered. Just as an organ needs due nutriment to perform
well, in like manner each bargain must be kept between persons. Harmonious co-operation in social life when the division of labour is established
can only be carried on with voluntary agreements: individuals must have
so adapted not only to eschew direct aggression at the expense of another's
liberty, but also so as to eschew indirect aggression through the breaking
of agreements. As noted already, Spencer supplements his emphasis on the
avoidance of direct and indirect aggressions by highlighting beneficence
as a form of altruism which adaptation to the social state produces and
by which each citizen 'shall directly further the lives of other citizens'
(1910, i: p. 147).

Spencer regards Bentham's analysis of utility as inferior to his own: the
complexity and individual and social relativity of 'happiness' demand *not*
its direct but its *indirect* pursuit. Spencer declares that while the greatest

happiness may vary widely in societies which, though ideally constituted, 'are subject to unlike physical circumstances', there are certain fundamental conditions to the achievement of this greatest happiness' which are common to all such societies (1910, i: p. 169). A true conception of 'justice', maintaining harmonious co-operation between men by proscribing direct and indirect aggression, expresses the requirement: it provides the unvarying condition for the greatest happiness in all societies, 'however much the greatest happiness attainable in each may differ in nature, or amount, or both' (1910, i: p. 170). Living up to this condition facilitates to the maximum extent the adaptation of individuals to social existence, and therefore enables social evolution to take place and good conduct to flourish. To the extent that what is at present unpleasurable is consistent with the maintenance of life in social conditions, it will become pleasurable over time, and to the extent that what is at present pleasurable is inconsistent with the maintenance of life in social conditions, it will become unpleasurable over time: 'pleasure will eventually accompany every mode of action demanded by social conditions' (1910, i: p. 186). To work satisfactorily, the indirect pursuit of happiness in social life thus demands conformity with the principle that each creature 'shall take the benefits and the evils of its own nature, be they those derived from ancestry or those due to self-produced modifications' (1910, i: pp. 188–9. Militancy of course renders imperfect this relationship between natures, benefits and evils as compared to the higher individual development which industrial social relations permit). Egoism is thus an ultimate principle of conduct. Without due attention to self-preservation there is death, and others left without care, and if all neglect self-preservation there will be none to be cared for. Where self-preservation is attended to the individual tends to radiate happiness and also has the powers for altruistic activities. Altruism, though, is 'no less essential than egoism' (1910, i: p. 201).[3] Altruism embraces social as well as family life. If justice involves neither directly nor indirectly aggressing on others, altruism leads to the making of sacrifices for social welfare which enhance personal welfare, exemplified by the benefits coming to all through the responsible participation by individuals out of altruism in public affairs. Spencer underlines the importance of altruism by adding:

> The well-being of each is involved with the well-being of all in sundry other ways. Whatever conduces to their vigour concerns him; for it diminishes the cost of everything he buys. Whatever conduces to their freedom from disease concerns him; for it diminishes his own liability to disease. Whatever raises their intelligence concerns them; for inconveniences are daily entailed on him by others' ignorance or folly. Whatever raises their moral characters concerns him; for at every turn he suffers from the average unconscientiousness.
>
> (1910, i: p. 216)

In short, altruism works; it yields beneficial results. Nevertheless, egoism and altruism *appear* to come into conflict under the form of the 'greatest happiness principle' and its assertion that the general happiness ought to be the object of pursuit. Spencer considers this principle as a potential guide for both governmental action and individual action. He argues that happiness is not the kind of thing that can 'be cut up and distributed equally' (1910, i: p. 223). There appears no viable basis on which purchasing power, for instance, can be apportioned to individuals, except according to the 'efforts' made by each, subject to the like liberty of all. Other principles are self-defeating. Spencer concludes that reason thus forces us back to an idea of justice: the principle of general happiness is meaningless 'save as indirectly asserting that the claims of each should be duly regarded by all. The utilitarian altruism becomes a duly qualified egoism' (1910, i: p. 226). Egoism therefore cannot be abandoned.

Given, therefore, the problematic and indeed evolutionary nature of happiness, both corporate happiness and individual happiness 'must be pursued not directly but indirectly' (1910, i: p. 238). Once this point is accepted, it is possible to argue that the action of social evolution will effect a 'conciliation' between egoism and altruism. The demand for actions prompted by altruism comes from social conditions. Spencer again stresses that these actions if not already pleasurable (thus conflicting with egoism) will become so with adaptation to the social state duly advancing:

> They are actions which maintenance and further development of social organization tend ever to increase; and therefore actions with which there will be joined an increasing pleasure. From the laws of life it must be concluded that unceasing social discipline will so mould human nature, that eventually sympathetic pleasures will be spontaneously pursued to the fullest extent advantageous to each and all. The scope for altruistic activities will not exceed the desire for altruistic satisfactions.

> In natures thus constituted, though the altruistic gratifications must remain in a transfigured sense egoistic, yet they will not be egoistically pursued – will not be pursued from egoistic motives. Though pleasure will be gained by giving pleasure, yet the thought of the sympathetic pleasure to be gained will not occupy consciousness, but only the thought of the pleasure given. To a great extent this is so now.
>
> (1910, i: p. 250)

At the same time, receiving help from others will become less pleasurable, since it will arrest what has become a more pleasurable activity. Competition between self-regarding and other-regarding actions will no longer be felt since all are pleasurable. The scope that remains for 'altruism' that consciously involves sacrifice will be limited to cases such as aid when accidents occur and the giving of advice; all will want to share in these activities, leaving no individual overtaxed.

'The Data of Ethics' had mapped out in some detail, with particular reference to Spencer's own contributions to evolutionary thought in biology, psychology and sociology, how the field of ethics was to be conceptualized, and how he intended to advance the understanding of the field. The next Part, 'The Inductions of Ethics', though, is concerned chiefly with 'the actual ideas and feelings concerning conduct which men entertain' (1910, i: p. 324). However, in the first two chapters there is more of what might be considered 'framework analysis'. Ethics originate in religion; in the propitiation of the spirits of deceased ancestors and chieftains in the hope of gaining benefits and avoiding evils in the present. While arrangements for defence against other societies or their conquest have been requirements of life, the ethics of enmity have largely held sway, with appropriate sanctions for the deeds entailed in terms of their 'rightness' and 'wrongness'. Nevertheless, the combined action of tribesmen that this has implied

> must be impossible in the absence of some mutual trust, consequent on experience of friendliness and trust. And since a behaviour which favours harmonious co-operation with the tribe conduces to its prosperity and growth, and therefore to the conquest of other tribes, survival of the fittest among tribes causes the establishment of such behaviour as a general trait.
>
> The authority of ruling men gives the ethic of amity collateral support. Dissension being recognized by chiefs as a source of tribal weakness, acts leading to it are reprobated by them....
>
> (1910, i: p. 314)[4]

Without some such codes of amity and a degree of conformity to them, 'there must result social dissolution' (1910, i: p. 316). The two sets of ethics, enmity and amity, correspond to external and internal conditions within a society, and may be counted as the ethical counterparts of militancy and industrialism. While as already noted the differing sentiments and ideas are inconsistent, contradictory and impossible to harmonize, yet individuals live with and act upon this confusion of ethical thought.

Spencer now adds to his account that observation of the *consequences* which followed particular actions has encouraged the differentiation of utilitarian ethics from theological ethics.[5] In particular, living under *social* conditions itself encourages opinions which chime in with whatever is perceived as promoting 'human welfare' (1910, i: p. 320). Manifestly, 'such a moulding of human nature has been furthered by survival of the fittest; since groups of men having feelings least adapted to social requirements must, other things equal, have tended to disappear before groups of men having feelings most adapted to them' (1910, i: p. 320). Nor does Spencer omit to note the emergence of the conception of a 'moral sense' in man, though he emphasizes that its 'intuitions' are not divinely implanted but the secular and natural product of the inherited experience of generations: they thus have 'a co-ordinate authority with the inductions of utility' (1910, i: p. 322).[6] Spencer subsequently reports that while in his earlier book, *Social Statics,* he espoused the moral sense doctrine associated with the intuitionists, it had now become clear that 'the qualifications required practically obliterate the doctrine as enunciated by them' (1910, i: p. 470).

There is then, across history, the playing out of a kind of competition between ethical codes, and the sources of authority behind them. In addition, however, there is not even a clear consensus across societies about the ideas and sentiments which are in principle to be considered as ethical:

> the conceptions of *right, obligation, duty,* and the sentiments associated with those conceptions, have a far wider range than the conduct ordinarily conceived as the subject-matter of moral science. In different places and under different circumstances, substantially the same ideas and feelings are joined with classes of actions of totally opposite kinds, and also with classes of actions of which moral science, as ordinarily conceived, takes no cognizance.
>
> (1910, i: p. 335)

It has, though, often been merely the *weight* of authority and coercion that has in practice largely generated what come to be the particular feelings of obligation and conceptions of what is 'right'. For Spencer, this field of conduct for the purposes of the *Ethics* has to be seen as part of ethical conduct, though he wishes to mark it off as 'pro-ethical'; 'for the mass of mankind' it stands 'in place of the ethical properly so called' (1910, i: p. 337). The authentic conceptions of moral consciousness and moral ideas which are to be associated with the properly ethical are not derived from external authority and constraints.

> The true moral consciousness which we name conscience, does not refer to those extrinsic results of conduct which take the shape of praise or blame, reward or punishment, externally awarded; but it refers to the intrinsic results of conduct which, in part and by some intellectually perceived, are mainly and by most, intuitively felt. The moral consciousness proper does not contemplate obligations as artificially imposed by an external power; nor is it chiefly occupied with estimates of the amounts of pleasure and pain which given action may produce, though these may be dimly or clearly perceived; but it is chiefly occupied with recognition

of, and regard for, those conditions by fulfilment of which happiness is achieved or misery avoided.

(1910, i: pp. 337–8)

Spencer's survey of this field of 'pro-ethical' ideas and feelings derives from the conduct recorded in anthropological studies and the recollections of other travellers to distant cultures. He interprets his comparative evidence to show that aggression, robbery and revenge within a society tend to diminish as external militancy diminishes. Moreover, the 'peaceful uncivilized tribes' (1910, i: p. 359) are notably honest and honourable in commercial dealings (Spencer cites the Wood-Veddah, Esquimaux and Fuegians). Where militant despotism prevails in societies, its coercive practices prevent a distinction from emerging between 'generosity' and 'justice'. Generosity itself is a simpler sentiment than justice, and appears earlier:

The one results from mental representations of the pleasures or pains of another or others – is shown in acts instigated by the feelings which these mental representations arouse. But the other implies representations, not simply of pains or pleasures, but also, and chiefly, representations of the *conditions* which are required for, or are conducive to, the avoidance of pains or procuring of pleasures. Hence it includes a set of mental actions superposed on the mental actions constituting generosity.

Recognition of this truth makes comprehensible the order of their succession in the course of civilization. And this order will be rendered still more comprehensible if we remember that generosity, among people of low intelligence, often results from inability to represent to themselves distinctly the consequences of the sacrifices they make – they are improvident.

(1910, i: p. 379)

Mendacity rather than veracity prevails where the chronic coerciveness usually associated with external enmity has developed. However, the evidence suggests that the *reprobation* of lying characterizes societies where a 'non-coercive social structure' (1910, i: p. 409) develops, which is usually a reflection of peaceful social relations. Where compulsory co-operation declines, so too does obedience, whether worshipful or merely robotic in nature. Obedience to political control too gradually yields to an obedience to conscience: 'in an advanced state, the sphere of political obedience will have comparatively narrow limits; ... beyond those limits the submission of citizen to government will no more be regarded as meritorious than is now the cringing of a slave to a master' (1910, i: p. 421). The valuing of industry and labour can only develop as militancy wanes, and becomes associated with a properly ethical sense that labour is associated with the 'duty of self-sustentation' (1910, i: p. 433), of not robbing the common stock.[7]

Thus, in broad terms, there is a contrast between the pro-ethics associated with societies primarily concerned with external enmities and the pro-ethics associated with societies primarily concerned with internal voluntary co-operation. However, Spencer is judiciously cautious about the sources of the evidence on which his conclusions are based: 'Not all travellers are to be trusted. Some are bad observers, some are biased by creed or custom, some by personal likings or dislikings; and all have but imperfect opportunities for getting at the truth. Similarly with historians. Very little of what they narrate is from immediate observation...Testimonies concerning moral traits are hence liable to perversion' (1910, i: p. 464). Spencer, however, singles out as significant in his review the evidence concerning 'those various uncivilized peoples who, inferior to us in various respects, are morally superior to us' (1910, i: p. 471). They are free from inter-tribal enmities and militancy. Peace therefore appears as the key to moral development.[8]

Spencer's analysis now proceeds to uniting an evolutionary understanding of ethics proper with present circumstances and future prospects. Integration leads us to expect that the totality of conceptions forming ethics will enlarge, while increasing heterogeneity, definiteness and coherence will characterize the component ethical conceptions. As well as encompassing new dimensions of social conduct, ethics must be seen as taking into its sphere what is essentially private conduct, for injury and benefit to self must form a division of ethics. Ethics should be seen as a strand in 'the great mass of acts constituting normal life' (1910, i: p. 479). Disregard of self compromises the health and rearing of children, and risks the individual becoming a burden on others, disappointment to fellow-men whose lives are bound up with his own in business, and an inability to contribute to the benefit of society as a citizen. Thus the third Part of the *Ethics* is devoted to 'The Ethics of Individual Life'. It treats the responsibility to sustain oneself through useful activity, and the often unacknowledged but vital contribution made by each individual to social life by their observance of periods of rest, by new experiences gained through recreation and travel, by wise nutrition, and by the stimulation of the sympathy which arises from acquiring tastes in intellectual and aesthetic culture.[9] While given his evolutionary perspective Spencer's desire to highlight as a neglected field 'individual' ethics is understandable, the Part mostly signifies simply as a prelude to the discussion in the next Part of the ethics of social life, and of 'justice' in particular.

Spencer begins this Part with what he calls 'animal-ethics'. Species that survive conform to a natural principle: 'among adults there must be conformity to the law that benefits received shall be directly proportionate to merits possessed: merits being measured by power of self-sustentation'. Otherwise, Spencer adds, 'the species must suffer in two ways. It must suffer immediately by sacrifice of superior to inferior, which entails a general diminution of welfare; and it must suffer remotely by further increase of the inferior which, by implication, hinders increase of the superior, and causes a general deterioration, ending in extinction if it is continued' (1910, ii: pp. 6–7).[10] Regarded biologically, this law implies survival of the fittest; regarded ethically each individual must be subject to the effects of its own nature and consequent conduct. In non-gregarious 'sub-human' life there exists 'no agency by which, among adults, the relations between conduct and consequence can be interfered with' (1910, ii: p. 8), a point which applies to individual organisms and to the relations between the parts of each organism. With gregariousness, however, appears passive and active co-operation, and this feature introduces the new condition that an individual 'shall not seriously impede the like pursuits of others' (1910, ii: p. 12). Without this condition, an *a priori* condition for harmonious co-operation, the association would be unprofitable; 'survival of the fittest' will 'exterminate that variety of the species in which association begins' (1910, ii: p. 12). The condition is thus 'an imperative law for creatures to which gregariousness is a benefit' (1910, ii: p. 15). 'Human' justice is simply a development of this sub-human form. The part of 'justice' which is embodied in the relation between conduct and consequences is an egoistic sentiment whose development is easily explained within the theory of evolution. However, the essentially altruistic element involving equitable relations between individuals is, Spencer acknowledges, more difficult to conceive in an evolutionary framework in a manner that avoids circularity: 'On the one hand, the implication is that the altruistic sentiment of justice can come into existence only in the course of adaptation to social life. On the other hand the implication is that social life is made possible only by maintenance of those equitable relations which imply the altruistic sentiment of justice'. Spencer submits that 'a pro-altruistic sentiment of justice' (1910, ii: p. 29) temporarily supplies the place of the altruistic sentiment of justice proper. This emerges, for instance, around a fear of the pain of retaliation and is seen in animals. Function, in other words, precedes structure (1910, ii: p. 29). To such feelings, 'which come into play before there is any social organization, have to be added those which arise after political authority establishes itself' (1910, ii: p. 30). Once the associated state has been maintained courtesy of the 'pro-altruistic sentiment of justice', the conditions are in place 'in which the altruistic sentiment of justice itself can develop' (1910, ii: p. 31). Sentiments of justice and, later, ideas of 'justice' develop slowly and in accord with the nature of social surroundings, militant or peaceful. Even in 'civilized' societies, a tension may be detected between ideas of justice related to the conduct of war and to internal co-operation. Where there are militant social relations, characterized by coercion, there is not a natural achievement of greater rewards by greater merit but an 'artificial apportionment of greater rewards to greater merit' (1910, ii: p. 40. The altruistic element is little in evidence. By now, in the 1890s, Spencer was certain that socialism was seeking to cement this principle into the social relations associated with the industrial form of society).[11]

Only at this point does Spencer move towards the definitive presentation of the 'formula' of 'justice'. Following a discussion of the past in which Spencer points to the intellectual dominance of at one time a conception of justice understood in terms of inequality (as displayed in the philosophies of Plato and Aristotle) and at a later time a conception of justice understood in terms of equality (as indicated by Bentham and Prince 'Krapotkin'), he declares (1910, ii: pp. 42–3):

> if each of these opposite conceptions of justice is accepted as true in part, and then supplemented by the other, there results that conception of justice which arises on contemplating the laws of life as carried on in the social state. The equality concerns the mutually-limited spheres of action which must be maintained if associated men are to co-operate harmoniously. The inequality concerns the results which each may achieve by carrying on his actions within the implied limits. No incongruity exists when the ideas of equality and inequality are applied the one to the bounds and the other to the benefits. Contrariwise, the two may be, and must be simultaneously asserted.

Spencer then substitutes for the reference to 'inequality' the idea of a 'positive' element in 'justice', and substitutes for the reference to 'equality' the idea of a 'negative element'. Thus, for Spencer, a satisfactory, evolution-based 'law of life' formulation of 'justice' must unite 'positive' and 'negative' elements in respect of each and every person: 'It must be positive in so far as it asserts for each that, since he is to receive and suffer the good and evil results of his actions, he must be allowed to act. And it must be negative, in so far as, by asserting this of everyone, it implies that each can be allowed to act only under the restraint imposed by the presence of others having like claims to act' (1910, ii: p. 45).[12]

Spencer's statement of how justice is to be defined in the *Ethics* is not significantly changed from its form in *Social Statics*. It is 'every man is free to do that which he wills, provided he infringes not the equal freedom of any other man' (1910, ii: p. 46). This grounded and specific sense of 'justice' is of cardinal importance to Spencer. He makes it clear that he means his definition to be interpreted 'obviously' as covering both 'positive' and 'negative' elements: 'by asserting that in each individual the inter-actions of conduct and consequence must be restricted in the specified way; it tacitly re-asserts that these inter-actions must be maintained in other individuals, that is in all individuals' (1910, ii: p. 15). This view of 'justice' is bedrock Spencer, consistently held and argued for onwards from *Social Statics*. The idea of 'justice' so understood has its origin 'in the experiences of the race', and we are, Spencer reflects, 'entitled to affiliate it on the experiences of living creatures at large, and to perceive that it is but a conscious response to certain necessary relations in the order of nature. No higher warrant can be imagined' (1910, ii: p. 61). 'Justice' then may be reasonably defined as a 'natural right', though to avoid confusion with other applications of that expression Taylor's preference for 'naturalistic right' may be commended (2007: pp. 117–18). Its appearance as the cardinal principle of ethics is of course not its only incarnation; for Spencer the formula in its essence encapsulates the core of the process of living as manifested throughout the biological, psychical and social worlds.

Spencer next turns to 'deductions' from his equal freedom principle or principle of 'justice'. Here what is said is mostly of more interest to political philosophers than social scientists, though the general ground covered needs to be noted, since Spencer argues that behaviour in congruity with its 'corollaries' is arising 'naturally' in social life across societies rather than as the result of legal injunctions. Thus what Spencer calls 'the right to physical integrity' (essentially a right to life) has been, 'in the course of social evolution and the accompanying evolution of Man's mental nature, gradually establishing itself. Prolonged converse with the conditions under which alone social life can be harmoniously carried on, has slowly moulded sentiments, ideas, and laws, into conformity with this primary ethical truth deducible from those conditions' (1910, ii: p. 70).[13]

On land-ownership, however, some discussion is here required. In *Social Statics* Spencer's position was that private property in land contravened the necessary 'co-heirship' of men to the soil, and that ownership of land should be returned to the community, with compensation paid as appropriate. Later, in 1879, the American social critic, journalist and political economist, Henry George, published a widely read book, *Progress and Poverty*. This book contained a chapter 'How Equal Rights to the Land May Be Asserted and Secured', in which *Social Statics* was quoted approvingly. During the 1880s, in published Letters and *The Man versus The State*, Spencer argued that his position had altered and that he now no longer supported the idea as a present practicable policy. This position Spencer now re-stated in the *Ethics*. George responded to what he took as betrayal in his *A Perplexed Philosopher* of 1892, accusing him and his works of bad faith: 'No one can boldly utter a great truth, and then, when the times have become ripe for it, and his utterance voices what is burning in hearts and consciences, whisper it away' (1892: p. 72). The episode was painful for Spencer, and George fought dirty. In a relatively recent review of the issues at stake Jeffrey Paul concluded that Spencer's theoretical opposition to private property in land

> was as unequivocally supported in 'Justice' and other late writings as it had been in the earlier *Social Statics*. What changed was the application that he was willing to make of his theory. The younger Spencer

believed that moral philosophy erected a standard with which mankind, however morally inept, must strive to comply. The evolutionism which suffused the thought of the later Spencer convinced him that such moral demands were metaphysically impossible to meet and, therefore, ought to be supplanted by ones that were congruent with the present limited potentialities of mankind.

(1982: p. 197)[14]

Spencer next turns to the principle of 'justice' as underpinning rights to property in things and ideas, of making gifts and bequests, to free exchange, free contract, free worship, and also to free speech and publication.[15] Spencer also considers the rights of children, and women. In respect of their life and liberty, the rightful claims of children against their parents are increasingly acknowledged in practice. In discussing the rights of women in *Social Statics* he had contended with radical passion that their rights 'must stand or fall with those of men' (1851: p. 171). In the *Ethics*, 40 years later, his comments are much cooler in tone and infused again with a consciousness of the 'present limited potentialities of mankind'. While no restraints are justified on the careers women may adopt – in this respect they must have like freedom with men (1910, ii: p. 160) – Spencer now argues that a difference in the political rights of women should be observed for so long as, unlike men, they are not called on to defend the country by furnishing contingents to the army and navy, thus suffering no corresponding loss of their liberty, or risk of injury or death (1910, ii: p. 184). In the present transitional state of even the most advanced societies, with the idea of 'justice' but shallowly rooted, and a revival of militancy and coercion a prospect, extending the franchise to women would risk further breaches of rights. The risk arises because 'it is especially in the nature of women, as a concomitant of their maternal functions, to yield benefits not in proportion to deserts but in proportion to the absence of deserts – to give most where capacity is least' (1910, ii: pp. 195–6). They prefer generosity over 'justice'.

Spencer's discussion of 'rights' culminates in a critique of the idea of *political* rights. Individuals have rights prior to the emergence of government, not as a consequence of it. The idea of a political right to vote is based on endowing government with a spurious legitimacy: governments have duties, a right if you will, *to maintain rights*, but otherwise its legislation subtracts from rather than augments the right to liberty

> rights, truly so called, originate from the laws of life as carried on in the associated state. The social arrangements may be such as fully recognize them, or such as ignore them in greater or smaller degrees. The social arrangements cannot create them, but can simply conform to them or not conform to them. Such parts of the social arrangements as make up what we call government, are instrumental to the maintenance of rights, here

in great measure and there in small measure; but in whatever measure, they are simply instrumental, and whatever they have in them which may be called right, must be so called only in virtue of their efficiency in maintaining rights.

(1910, ii: p. 176)

Voting is but one means for creating an appliance to protect rights. This it may indeed achieve, but a 'right to vote' may not check corruption and a majority vote may usher in tyranny, and trespasses upon freedoms.[16]

From the consideration of rights Spencer turns more directly to consider the role of the state. As threats from other societies recede, and as within a society peace and uncoerced co-operative life come to prevail, the nature of the role of the state changes too. Transgressions of liberty will in these circumstances tend to be scattered and continuous, and a diffused administration of 'justice' will be appropriate. The duties of the state for Spencer are straightforward. First there is defence against external aggressors, and second the administration of 'justice', 'without cost, in civil as well as criminal cases' (1910, ii: p. 211).[17] Spencer adds that the state, as trustee of its land for the nation, has the duty of protecting the rights of present citizens and the interests of future generations in respect of proposed undertakings to use land in such manner as to make it useless for other purposes, by the building of a road, a railway or a dock. Also to the state, on behalf of the community, falls the responsibility of protecting all members of the community from uncontrolled breaking up of roads, and regulating the use of rivers and the adjacent sea. For Spencer, arguments that the state should have further duties fail to succeed. The master point is that taxes and public expenditures[18] raised for other purposes are at variance with the basic principle of an equitable social order; they diminish freedom, and are thereby unjust:

A man's liberties are none the less aggressed upon because those who coerce him do so in the belief that he will be benefited. In thus imposing by force their wills upon his will, they are breaking the law of equal freedom in his person; and what the motive may be matters not. Aggression which is flagitious when committed by one is not sanctified when committed by a host.

(1910, ii: p. 224)

In addition, Spencer argues that the state administers its existing responsibilities inefficiently. Progress is displayed when the state relinquishes functions beyond its proper sphere to more specialist agents, more adapted to performing the functions required. He reiterates that progress in social life comes not through state direction but through the 'natural method' of the 'spontaneous adaptation of citizens to social life', free from 'artificial' attempts to mould character (1910, ii: pp. 257–8). Severance of the tie between conduct and consequence would entail the 'extreme absurdity' of 'proposing to improve social life by breaking the fundamental law of social life' (1910, ii: p. 260).

The *Principles of Ethics* culminates in two Parts devoted to the discussion of 'beneficence', divided into 'negative' and 'positive', occupying fully 170 pages thereby underlining that Spencer attached uncommon importance to the topic. In a less fastidious age 'benevolence' might have been the word chosen.[19] In Spencer's evolutionary narrative of social life, the idea of 'justice', together with governments and other institutions to protect it, become necessary for social equilibrium. Justice is a matter of public concern. There is, however, another form of altruism, that of beneficence (sometimes described by Spencer as a 'secondary' form of altruism, 1910, ii: p. 275). Equitable social relations need to be supplemented by 'the promptings of kindness'. Beneficence, the rendering of services beyond what merely accords with 'justice', is a required capability 'before life, individual and social, can reach their highest forms' (1910, ii: p. 270). However, beneficence is of *private* not public concern; it is not needful for social equilibrium. If beneficence was exercised by society in its corporate capacity violations of the principle of justice would be ineluctable, with the anti-progressive consequence of the relatively unadapted being rewarded and the relatively adapted punished, and, with social equilibrium thereby disrupted, agitation and unrest would ensue from both those persons 'unjustly' penalized and those who have come to expect even more in terms of unearned benefits. Private beneficence, however, responsibly and knowledgeably endowed, increases social coherence and stability through its reciprocal benefits to benefactors and beneficiaries, outweighing any risk of such consequences. Spencer is careful to insist that irresponsible private beneficence, beneficence which ignores conduct and character in the beneficiary, shares in the difficulties associated with corporate beneficence. It too could discourage industriousness and promote dependency.

Negative beneficence concerns restraint and passivity when egoistic advantage might otherwise be won, perhaps to be compensated for by sympathetic pleasure. Seeing that a monopoly might ensue, and the public suffer, a competitor might hold his fire when faced with an opportunity to eliminate another (1910, ii: p. 282), and, if circumstances have unexpectedly changed, insistence on the agreed detail of a contract may be waived. In some circumstances restraints on both blame and praise may be appropriate: 'If it is a function of beneficence to mitigate, so far as consists with other ends, the injustices of Nature, then the lowly-endowed should not have those injustices of nature from which they suffer, made harder to bear by the needlessly harsh treatment of men. Negative beneficence requires that such blame as their failures call for, shall be sparing in amount and gentle in kind' (1910, ii: p. 317). The need for restraint on praise where it has become a matter of convention is similar.[20]

By addressing 'positive beneficence', Spencer was touching on issues of serious concern to the late Victorians, the need for and difficulties associated with charitable activity, and the responsibilities of family members towards each other.[21] The consideration of Spencer's detailed comments on positive beneficence is best undertaken by first turning to his comments on the redistribution of income, or cash transfers, since in this connection he divided contemporary welfare activities in a simple but original way, itself of considerable significance yet almost universally omitted in studies of the development of policy analysis. 'We have,' writes Spencer:

> the law-established relief for the poor by distribution of money compulsorily exacted; with which may fitly be joined the alms derived from endowments. We have relief of the poor carried on by spontaneously organised societies, to which funds are voluntarily contributed. And then, lastly, we have the help privately given – now to those who stand in some relation of dependence, now to those concerning whose claims partial knowledge has been obtained, and now hap-hazard to beggars.
>
> (1910, ii: p. 376)

Spencer is of course here distinguishing between the state, the voluntary sector and 'private beneficence' (the area today loosely referred to in discussions of social policy as informal care) as sources of cash aid. Spencer iterates his critical stance towards beneficence for the poor when provided by the state. State beneficence makes dependent the recipient and hinders the natural process of that person's adaptation to surrounding circumstances. It penalizes those persons who have adapted and are therefore able, through the payment of rates, to fund relief. It is also, of course, contrary to his conception of justice. In addition, beneficence provided by government is extravagant in the sense that much of the total fund raised out of rates goes to maintain the machinery involved – to pay the salaries of poor law officers and other staff – staff who may indeed, moreover, have the sentiment of their own self-interest most at heart, since their connection to those who pay their salaries and wages is remote and impersonal, rather than framed by personal encounters and knowledge. Hannah Gay has noted that if, according to Spencer, human beings are 'forced to cope with difficult situations, the results would be beneficial all round. Not the least of these beneficial results would be that coping strategies, and related behaviours, would have positive results in inheritance. If there was state assistance for the poor, the evolution of these good qualities would not occur' (1999: p. 58). This is true. But Gay paints a slightly unbalanced picture, since she omits that Spencer contemplates arrangements that might ensure 'the degraded were to leave no progeny' (1910, ii: p. 393), though finds them likely to be wanting in effectiveness. He despairs at the 'mass of effete humanity' (1910, ii: p. 393), mostly the product of lax poor law administration. There are 'large numbers unadapted to the requirements of social life, and ... consequently sources of misery to themselves and others', but this body of 'relatively worthless people' cannot be diminished 'without inflicting much pain' (1910, ii: p. 394). The transition from a reliance on the poor law to 'a healthy condition of self-help and private beneficence' is akin to 'the transition from an opium-eating life to a normal life – painful but remedial' (1910, ii: p. 394).[22]

Charities and other forms of formally arranged voluntary organization also present difficulties for Spencer. In the last quarter of the nineteenth century, particularly in London, the Charity Organisation Society emerged as a well-connected charity seeking to improve 'character' and a sense of the responsibilities of 'citizenship' by the casework method of relief which it adopted and publicized (Harris, 1989; Lewis, 1995). In fact, the givers of charity as well as the recipients were expected to 'grow' in moral terms through the interactions. Although Spencer has been nominated as a source of the Society's ideas (Heraud, 1970: p. 4), the main influential figures in fact were independent of and mostly intellectually detached from Spencerian thought. As Harris observes: 'Within the Charity Organisation Society – a body often typecast as the last bastion of laissez-faire individualism – there was in fact a striking contrast between the atomistic philosophy of older members like Thomas Mackay and a younger generation who supported the organic "social collectivism" preached by Bernard and Helen Bosanquet and Thomas Hancock Nunn' (1993: p. 231). The poor law historian and Individualist Mackay, 'a permanent fixture on the council of the Charity Organisation Society' (Taylor, 1992: p. 24), appears to be the only significant Society figure for whom Spencer was a mentor.[23] Had Spencer believed that the Society's *modus operandi* was in harmony with his precepts he would have exempted it by name, it may be presumed, from his criticisms of voluntary relief (he does though, as noted earlier, substantiate his criticisms by reference to the Society's own accounts of lax practice by charities). Evils akin to those found in state beneficence abound: 'They force on us the truth that, be it compulsory or non-compulsory, social *machinery* wastes power, and works other effects than those intended. In proportion as beneficence operates indirectly instead of directly, it fails in its end' (1910, ii: p. 386). These reservations, uttered with some force by Spencer, appear to have been overlooked in Robert Pinker's account of Spencer's 'positive' disposition towards charity (1971). Spencer does, though, give an indication of what he *could* approve as 'non-compulsory social machinery'. It comes with reference to the 'provident beneficence' secured through the acquisition of surgical and medical knowledge, permitting ordinary people to provide help to sufferers before the arrival of professional help: 'Unqualified applause, then, must be given to those Ambulance Societies and kindred bodies, which seek to diffuse the requisite information and give by discipline the requisite skill' (1910, ii: p. 361).

Spencer's incubus, the threat of social regression, is at least much diminished when beneficiary and benefactor are known to each other. Beneficence is then appropriate and desirable. 'Within the intricate plexus of social relations surrounding each citizen,' Spencer says, 'there is a special plexus more familiar to him than any other and which has established greater claims on him than any other' (1910, ii: p. 390). Spencer surmises that the substitution of the system of contract for the system of status has meant that the principle of so much service for so much money has weakened the impulse to acts of kindness. Yet the impulse could and should be strengthened; it would be so strengthened 'by the gradual disappearance of artificial agencies for distributing aid', in particular the poor law (1910, ii: p. 391).

However, Spencer clearly interprets private beneficence as encompassing more than straightforward pecuniary assistance. The relevant discussion mostly adopts the family as its point of contextual reference, with a review first of beneficence in general within marriage and from children towards parents. On both of these themes his position can be indicated briefly. If, as Spencer says, marital beneficence must be reciprocal he nonetheless begins by underlining discrepancies: 'In the history of humanity as written, the saddest part concerns the treatment of women' (1910, ii: p. 336). On filial beneficence towards elderly parents the reciprocity required is of a kind to avoid mental starvation in addition to physical starvation, which he considers is in fact usually forthcoming. When Spencer turns his attention to aid to the ill and injured, the topics are still addressed from a familial perspective. Illness or accident requires, according to circumstance, marital beneficence, paternal beneficence and filial beneficence from within the family, in the form of 'solicitous care': 'In the natural order of things the house becomes at need a hospital and its inmates nurses' (1910, ii: p. 355). Some comments follow which help to guard Spencer against accusations of bias in terms of gender, and underline that beneficence should be neither expected nor provided unconditionally: 'Husbands in the decline of life who have married young wives, and presently make them little else than nurses – objecting even to have other nurses share the burden with them – require awakening to a due sense not of others' duties to them but of their own duties to others. A man is not absolved from the obligations of beneficence because he is ill; and if he rightly feels these obligations he will insist that others shall not injure themselves for his benefit' (1910, ii: p. 357). Spencer's points are essentially about the 'costs' and 'burdens' of caring, topics which he is here raising in a picaresque but effective manner. Beneficence does not demand the loss of the lives of the healthy:

> A wise and duly proportioned beneficence does not countenance loss of the relatively worthy for preservation of the relatively worthless, Every-one can name persons wrecked in body and mind by cherishing invalid

relatives – relatives who often thanklessly receive the sacrifices made for them. Here is a wife whose sole occupation for a decennium has been that of nursing a gouty husband; and who, as a result, dies of a worn-out physique before he does. Here is a daughter who, after many years' attendance on an invalid mother, is shortly after required to give similar attendance to an invalid aunt; and who, now that she has lived through these long periods of daily abnegations and wearisome duties, is becoming mentally unhinged. And here is a husband whose latter days are made miserable by the task of safeguarding, in his own house, an insane wife.

(1910, ii: pp. 356–7)

If Spencer was lacking a solution to the dilemma of self-sacrifice versus self-preservation in the face of such demands on beneficence – and he was – he nonetheless ought to be acknowledged as confronting the difficulties early and forcefully within the contexts of the social science and practical moral thought of the 1890s.

Spencer's treatment of 'positive' and 'negative' 'beneficence' and the location of 'private beneficence' within it thus emerges as analytically perceptive; its prominence in the *Ethics* underlines that he accorded it considerable significance in his general theoretical perspective on social life.[24] There is sociological shrewdness about who gives care and to whom, and the morally charged negotiations in social life connected with the provision of care. Indeed, he advances a descriptive hierarchy of caring responsibilities.

If, as all will admit, the care of one who is sick devolves primarily on members of the family-group, and devolves secondarily on kindred, it devolves only in smaller measure on unrelated persons. These may rightly limit themselves to indirect aid, where this is needed and deserved, Only in cases where there are no relatives, or none capable of undertaking relatives' duties, does it seem that beneficence demands from unrelated persons the requisite attention.

(1910, ii: p. 358)

In Spencer's eyes, private beneficence, whether it takes the form of cash or care, must reflect the moral conduct and character of the beneficiary, the more direct the contact, the less the risk of a demoralizing effect upon the beneficiary, with practical ethics suggesting that there are legitimate limits to what it is reasonable to supply or to demand as to beneficence, according to the circumstances of the beneficiary and benefactor. Most importantly, the existence and further expansion of positive private beneficence is pivotal for Spencer in its ability to contribute to social and moral development; it combines the merits of advancing altruistic sentiments in the benefactor and enhancing the welfare of beneficiaries. Private beneficence, negative as well as positive, benefits both benefactor and beneficiary, is needful for individual and social life to reach their highest forms, and increases social coherence and stability. Already, in 'a few finely-constituted natures', this fellow-feeling shows itself 'to have become with them organic'; as beacons, as 'natural centres of happiness', they radiate well-being to all around (1910, ii: p. 423). It is the conduct associated with private beneficence that 'affects others from hour to hour' (1910, ii: p. 422). In short, according to Spencer, it permits social evolution to progress, unlike beneficence, as distinct from justice, provided by the state. As time goes on, 'there will be more and more of those whose unselfish end will be the further evolution of Humanity. While contemplating from the heights of thought, that far-off life of the race never to be enjoyed by them, but only by a remote posterity, they will feel a calm pleasure in the consciousness of having aided the advance towards it' (1910, ii: p. 433).[25]

In the *Principles of Ethics*, then, the sole essential function of the state is any necessary maintenance and accessible administration of 'justice'; if this function is neglected or poorly executed in a modern state, psychical and social evolution will regress. In the process, coercive arrangements characterizing militancy may arise again to displace the spontaneity, enterprise, self-realization and social growth associated with industrialism. In advanced societies, individuals act in a 'thick' social manner, displaying altruism and a social self-consciousness (although, it must be recalled, they remain 'handcuffed' by their inheritance and environment), with the state enforcing 'justice' as required. This picture represents a species of political individualism.[26] The proper task of government, then, is to enforce justice, no more and no less. Spencer himself is in no doubt that, the acme of altruism is life lived 'organically' according to 'justice', but complemented by beneficence.

Much of the contemporary critical reaction to the *Ethics* concerned Spencer's conception of 'justice'. Lester Frank Ward was a distinguished American scientist and sociologist, perhaps most noted for his *Descriptive Sociology*. In his 'Political Ethics of Herbert Spencer' of 1894, Ward charges Spencer with being 'utterly blind' to 'the most conspicuous fact in society, that under an unregulated or "competitive" *régime* there is very little relation between "benefits" and "merits" or "fitness". It is partially to enforce such a correspondence that the state exists, and the essence of the idea of "justice", in the human sense, is the proportioning of benefits to merits, which "Nature's methods" do not secure' (1894: p. 87). On the same topic, but from a different viewpoint, and with the vexed matter of the right to the use of the land uppermost in his mind, the Cambridge philosopher, Henry Sidgwick, alighted on

> the inadequacy of the single formula of justice offered by Mr. Spencer. When we are inquiring into what compensation is justly due to persons whose rights have admittedly been encroached upon, supposing

the encroachments have been sanctioned by law and custom and complicated by subsequent exchange, it is evident that the Law of Equal Freedom cannot help us; we want some quite different principle of Distributive or Reparative justice.

(1892: p. 379)

Sidgwick's comment seems to identify a lacuna in Spencer's thought. Ward, though, neglects the element in Spencer's conception of justice relating conduct to consequences. In the context of human social life, this principle seems to be violated, *according to Spencer himself*, in the wage levels and conditions of some mills, which represent a form of slavery (1896b: pp. 515–6), and Spencer also credits trade unions with preventing employers from 'doing unfair things' with wages (1896b: p. 542). Indeed the principle appears to suggest too that equal work should bring equal rewards. And the equal freedom element itself indicates that where contracts are entered into with honesty and without coercion they may be enforced to repair breaches, though kindness, through beneficence, negative and positive, allows flexibility, even by employers towards their economic competitors, according to circumstances. Nor do Ward's comments propose an alternative to some version of an open-ended organization or catallaxy that might be compatible with a liberal outlook (a topic considered in John Gray, 1995: pp. 67–8). Ward thus seems unduly selective in the way he presents Spencer's position for criticism. Spencer's liberalism is not blind to the need for limits to men's behaviour in markets. It should be added that a recent point of dispute in political philosophy concerning Spencer has been over the importance in principle which he attached to considerations of desert, as opposed to entitlement, once the 'positive' element of 'justice' applies, as of course it does for Spencer in social and economic life.[27]

Another important strand of criticism questioned the general value of a sociological interpretation of ethics and especially the value of Spencer's particular approach derived from his theory of evolution. The American Unitarian, James Bixby, responded to 'The Data of Ethics' in 1882 by criticizing Spencer's account of the origin of moral sentiments and ideas as utterly inconsistent 'with the received principles of Ethics'. To Bixby, Spencer's account appeared to be 'in blank contradiction to our moral consciousness. The idea of duty is granted only an "illusive independence". In Spencer's analysis our moral ideas are not what we individually see to be right, but what preceding generations thought most useful' (1882: p. 305). Bixby pressed home his concerns in a memorable passage:

By the subtle operations of heredity these ideas of our ancestors as to what was conducive to their happiness have not only smuggled themselves into our brains, but have assumed a sacred authority. As the suggestion of a companion may take possession of the brain of a delirious person, and the thought and will of a hypnotizer seize control of the mind of his patient, and make him do what his own reason and will would never order, so do the experiences of past generations as to the pleasurable and the painful, obsess our brains with their illusory convictions of self-evident right and solemn duty. Not only is our general idea of duty an illusion, but our special ethical ideas are hallucinations....

(1882: p. 305)[28]

This type of reservation was also echoed and developed within the idealist thought at home, associated especially with T. H. Green, Bernard Bosanquet, and David George Ritchie. However, as Spencer already well knew, there was an unbridgeable chasm between his philosophical position and that of Green and Bosanquet. Bosanquet was the Charity Organisation Society's leading intellectual luminary (Lewis, 1995; Gaus, 2001). He may indeed have signed the letter of congratulation to Spencer in 1896 to mark the completion of his 'System'; only a year before, however, he had dipped his pen in vitriol (Bosanquet, 1895, see also MacBriar, 1987: p. 126). As Vincent remarks, 'Bosanquet contrasted what he called the ethical individual against the Spencerian atomic individual' (1984: p. 353). Bosanquet, his teacher Green, and the many other idealist philosophers, with debts to Hegel, and Rousseau's 'general will', were in a different camp altogether in respect of their 'philosophical sociology'. Idealist versions of the social organism insisted that it was in their membership of a society that individuals became meaningful: society was the genesis of the moral self, or as Green put it 'without society, no persons' (1883: Sect. 288). Alienated most perhaps by Spencer's *Psychology*, idealists considered a society itself as a moral unit: 'Society was a "moral organism", for it was the only sphere in which individuals could realize themselves' (den Otter, 1996: p. 157). Moral action demanded a sense of a permanent, higher good, only realizable in a society. Spencer's commitment to the 'individual', the idealists considered, was a commitment to an unintelligible abstraction: Spencer's model of 'the autonomous, unencumbered individual was false, they argued, for it denied that all our aspirations and actions are embedded within a social whole' (den Otter, 1996: p. 151). Sidney and Beatrice Webb, sharing ground with idealist social thought (Harris, 1992) sought to realize 'social health' (Webb S. and Webb B., 1910: p. 319), and believed that the opening of the twentieth century 'finds us all, to the dismay of the old-fashioned individualist, "thinking in communities" ' (in Webb, B., 1948: pp. 221–2). For the idealist F. H. Bradley the idea of the individual was accompanied 'in every fibre' by 'relations of community' (1876: p. 155).

In *Mind* in 1889, James Seth, professor of philosophy at the University of Edinburgh, called into question whether morals could be a subject for natural science at all. Seth adopted the view that while the character and conduct of man is not separate from or independent of the evolving phenomena of the universe, 'moral life', in contrast, 'refuses to be identified with the life of nature, or to be interpreted in its terms'. Seth regarded 'freedom', or 'will-power', as fundamental in ethical life, and as something natural science cannot recognize. It implies 'a different attitude in man to the universal course of things' and makes necessary 'a different interpretation of Evolution as applied to human character and conduct'. Self-conscious evolution 'is essentially different from unconscious evolution, and the former cannot be stated in terms of the latter. While all lower life evolves by strict unconscious necessity, man, as self-conscious, is free from its dominion, and has the power consciously to help on, or consciously to hinder, the evolution' (1889: p. 350).

On the basis of similar considerations, Henry Calderwood, another idealist professor of philosophy at Edinburgh, insisted on the special and privileged status of men as moral beings, laying siege in 1892 to Spencer's conception of man as moral merely in terms of an extension to a continuum joining human ethics with 'animal ethics'[29]:

> there is not any indication of reference to law, or purpose, or obligation, or merit, on the part even of the higher vertebrates; and in absence of this we can speak only of natural laws, not of ethical principles, nor even of 'ethical aspects' of these principles, unless we rise to deal with the moral government of the world as determined by the moral governor himself. Animal necessities we can see clearly; animal benefits we can reckon up accurately; but animal ethics we cannot find even in faintest outline. The weakest life dies off; the completest survives, and contributes to the advance of the species; but the laws applicable are physical, not ethical.
>
> (1892: p. 358)

Although with substantial differences of emphasis, most idealist thinkers concerned with social life added to their general standpoint a greater openness towards positive action by the state in the field of welfare than Spencer would have countenanced (on the definition and nature in general of idealist social thought see Harris, 1992). Early in the new century, L. T. Hobhouse, sympathetic to idealism and the social reform associated with 'New Liberalism', espoused a decidedly post-Spencerian version of social evolution in his *Social Evolution and Political Theory*. Having praised the recent innovation represented by state-funded pensions for older people (in 1908) – an earlier version of which idea advanced by W. L. Blackley (1878) had disturbed Spencer in *The Man versus The State* – Hobhouse commented

> The turning-point in the evolution of thought...is reached when the conception of the development of humanity enters into explicit consciousness as the directing principle of human endeavour, and, in proportion as the phrase is adequately understood, is seen to include within

it the sum of human purpose in all its manifold variety. In particular, it can be seen to be the conception necessary to give consistency and unity of aim to the vastly increased power of controlling the conditions, external and internal, of life, which the advance of knowledge is constantly yielding to mankind.

(1911: pp. 155–6)

Although the philosophical respectability of idealist thought ebbed substantially early in the twentieth century, it continued to have a strong influence on social theory and ideas relating to the reforming objectives of social policy, clearly detectable in the writings of Richard Titmuss (Titmuss, 1970; Harris, 1992; Offer, 1999a, 2006a). Certainly in 1939 the 'late' idealist philosopher, J. H. Muirhead could claim, ironically in the Herbert Spencer Lecture of that year, entitled 'The Man Versus The State as a Present Issue', that the conception adhered to by Spencer

both of the Individual, and the State, was inherited from a philosophy and from circumstances which by the time of his book with the above title was published in 1884 may be said to have no longer existed except as a survival. The freedom of the individual was no longer conceived of as merely freedom from State-control. State-action was no longer conceived of as 'interference with natural liberty', but as itself a natural attempt to limit the excesses of such liberty in the interest of the physical and moral welfare, and so of a truer kind of freedom, in the mass of the people.

(1939: p. 5)

Muirhead here omits to refer to the meaning and importance of 'justice' in Spencer's sociological and ethical understanding of individuals and society: few idealists, as it happens, seem to have schooled themselves deeply enough in Spencer to acquire a comprehensive familiarity with his thought ahead of trying to land punches.

Spencer had not 'overlooked' the position insisted upon by these adversaries. He was deliberately aiming to seize and destroy their citadel. It was not defensible to insist on the 'special' status of man. It was not plausible to exempt moral, political and religious ideas from natural causation. Society was not a machine to be tinkered with by governments outside of their proper and natural sphere, but a growth, changing in line with laws of life which applied to all organisms, though taking the particular form of the law of equal freedom in social life. With a psychology predicated upon the inheritance of acquired characteristics cumulatively acquired in a process of adaptation to circumstances (including surrounding society), Spencer was arguing that sociality could indeed be understood, and that the very foundations of the ideas of 'conscience', 'duty' and 'virtue' to which idealists appealed had been pulled from under them. Cherished assumptions about the authority and efficacy of moral thought and action were misconceived: they were grounded, Spencer declared, in the survival of faith in the super- natural. In this respect, Spencer's evolutionary analysis renders questions of moral justification 'otiose', and yields a 'sort of moral pragmatism in which moral principles are themselves regarded as the perishable products of social evolution' (John Gray, 1982: pp. 237, 247). Consistent with this unapologet- ically deterministic position were Spencer's minimalist expectations of the practical effects of his own ideas; they would not, and could not, change minds directly, at best they could change minds gradually by becoming part of the environment to which individuals were adapting. Perhaps, indeed, the idealist had a beam in his own eye. We will return to this clash of 'paradigms' in the Concluding Reflections and deal directly there with the wider and essentially epistemological point which we earlier and briefly saw raised by Bosanquet that Spencer was committed to an objectionable 'atomic individualism' in his analysis of social life.

Early in the *Ethics*, we found Spencer to declare that the conduct which is 'highly-evolved conduct, is that which ... we find to be what is called good conduct'. A few philosophically minded commentators have attempted recently to develop from Spencer a moral theory sometimes described as 'liberal utilitarianism', in which non-defeasible rights to liberty are upheld in conjunction with consequentialism. If Spencer can be mined without collat- eral damage as a means to such an end well-and-good, but there is a real risk that in the process his actual position becomes distorted in favour of what it suits the miners to attribute to him. John Gray rightly admitted that, 'once purified of its various inadvertences, the moral and political theory that emerges will seem to have little in common with Spencer's' (1982: p. 248). One major 'purification' to result, displayed by both Gray in the same arti- cle and Weinstein (1998) is the failure to acknowledge, let alone examine the implications of, Spencer's unambiguous and prominent denial of free- dom of the will, never withdrawn, in his *Principles of Psychology* – Weinstein as it happens nonchalantly refers to Spencer's human beings as 'choosing' happiness, without inserting the inverted commas Spencer's actual analysis demands (1998: p. 155). However, the main issue of concern to be noticed here is the presence of a newly minted and dubious representation in these accounts of what Spencer meant by 'good', for, compared with what his words quoted above would indicate, the contrary interpretation has been substituted. Much weight in this connection (Weinstein, 1998: pp. 143– 4, 151–4) is accorded to occasions when Spencer claims, as already noted in Chapter 2, that the 'survival of the fittest' 'is not the survival of the "better" or the "stronger", if we give to those words any thing like their ordinary meanings' (1872: p. 379, see also 1897: p. 114). But it was argued there that in so elucidating the meaning of 'survival of the fittest' Spencer was referring only to *Darwin's* process of natural selection (which Spencer had so renamed), *not* the inheritance of acquired characteristics. He is thus only referring to one relatively subordinate ingredient of his own theory of evolution. Indeed, when it comes to the social evolution 'of the highest of creatures, civilized men' it is, by contrast, this other mechanism of change, the inheritance of acquired characteristics, *never* discarded by Spencer, which had for him, as he emphasizes, 'become the chief factor' (1886: p. 462). And this mechanism in Spencer's view is precisely the mechanism that produces 'highly-evolved conduct', the conduct which 'is called good conduct'. It is in the interest of the modern liberal utilitarian cause to minimize connections in Spencer between 'more evolved' and 'good', since that might vitiate Spencer's value to the cause by rendering him open to the allegation of committing some form of the 'naturalistic fallacy' (as Moore, 1901, indeed controversially claimed). It is of course essentially a technical philosophical question, inappropriate to pursue in this sociological study, whether or not Spencer does commit some form of the naturalistic fallacy (on which see Flew, 1967; Richards, 1987, Appendix 2). It does seem hard to imagine, though, a successful escape from a quasi-theological commitment on Spencer's part to 'the concept of the normativity of nature as being at the heart of his evolutionary analysis' (Taylor, 2007: p. 126).

To Spencer, in matters pertaining to ethics, well-being and conduct in general, progressive evolution shows itself through modifications to outcomes as individuals adapt to their circumstances and in particular in the products of specialization associated with an increasing social division of labour. And in its *proper sphere of action* government has a crucial role to play. If government does not perform its duties in this sphere any social advance will be thrown into reverse. Government action *outside* of its 'proper sphere' will protect people artificially from the consequences of non-adaptation. 'Artificial' protection is doubly counter to evolutionary advance in Spencer's sense because it both retards the ability of individuals to adapt and punishes and discourages those who have adapted, through the raising of taxes and so forth to finance the intervention of government. The fundamental character of individuals cannot be changed 'artificially', it must adapt naturally to circumstances, which includes surrounding society: as the aggregate of adapting individual characters duly makes up the social relations, the social relations themselves thereby change. As Taylor has noted, the objective of Spencerian social theory, unlike the theory of Comte or Mill (or Durkheim), 'was not to serve as a basis for social engineering, but rather to show that all such engineering was an impossibility' (1992: p. 132). Much less often recalled, though, is another side to Spencer's evolutionary theory as it relates to ethics and well-being: his emphasis, first, on the growth of prompt, accessible and free-of-cost administration of 'justice', and, second, on the near open-ended amelioration which can issue from acts of beneficence driven by fellow-feeling (though see Hiskes, 1983).

The traditional portrayal of Spencer as placed intellectually on the defensive by the 1890s contains some truth. Yet it would be misleading to go on to conclude that the concerns of the *Ethics*, for instance, failed to resonate with wider shifts in Victorian thought. If his earlier political and moral thought appeared to have slipped its moorings in evangelicalism, a benevolent direction to the course of life, provided of course militancy remained in abeyance, rested there complacently unquestioned, though it was acknowledged as contingent upon individuals participating diligently and capably in his Whately-inspired vision of economy and society as catallaxy, and in particular in acting in accord with the discipline demanded by adaptation to circumstances. Never far away, moreover, was the Malthusian prospect of demise, which was reworked by Spencer into a consequence of non-adaptation, itself the product of a failure or a deficiency in faculty-exercise, and thus in 'character'. In its key features, here was social philosophy that still chimed in well with Hilton's portrayal of the evangelical theology of atonement, the conquest of sin through redemption, as probably the characteristic style of social thought, conceived in broad terms, in the first half or so of the nineteenth century. Spencer's optimism was of the form that out of the struggle of hard grind would arrive the sunny uplands of prosperity, virtue and harmony; it probably reached its peak for Spencer in the 1870s. To Huxley's critique of his normative outlook as administrative nihilism he retorted in 'Specialized Administration' of 1871, as we have seen, that the power of man's egoistic and altruistic 'spontaneous cooperation', and 'the effects of fellow-feeling... supplementing the effects of self-regarding feelings' (1871a: p. 433), considered together, 'amply suffice to originate and carry on all the activities which constitute healthy national life' (1871a: p. 437), provided men are under the negatively regulative control of government in the manner indicated by his liberty-guaranteeing principle of justice. It was evident to Spencer that social life as catallaxy, in embodying wider natural principles, and thus linking conduct to consequences, was enlarging to mutual benefit the worlds of producers and consumers, and set fair to conquer not only scarcity, disease and ignorance, but also sin.

In the *Ethics* the focus on beneficence, negative and positive, is a focus on the promise of persons, of course, rather than faith in an expansion of powers for 'positive' governance and the enlarged conceptualization of the state favoured by many idealists (Meadowcroft, 1995). Voluntary restraints on competition, and reasonable flexibility over the fulfilment of contracts and the making of due payments, are the hallmarks of the highly evolved behaviour of sympathetic, advanced social individuals no less than the spontaneous provision of advice, support and care as appropriate. These individuals eagerly acquire knowledge, culture and discrimination. They travel, they think of mankind, they engage in public affairs, adding to their own fulfilment and the fulfilment of others at the same time. They are 'natural centres of happiness'. Given what Spencer himself has said, as we have seen, it has proved easy to dwell on his great fear that these attainments might be swept away in a tidal wave of militancy, war and re-barbarization.

This scenario was real enough to Spencer. But the pessimism, it seems to me, was significantly offset for Spencer by an appreciation of the nobility and chivalry expressed in the degree of adherence to the maxims of justice and beneficence reached by the sympathetic members of mankind. Here was the judicious consumer, the wisely caring parent, the attentive son and daughter, the responsible citizen. In Spencer in this mode we catch a scent of the later nineteenth century theology of the Incarnation, in which the goodness of man was granted ascendancy over his propensity for sin, inspiring from at least the 1850s Charles Kingsley's yoking of his nature science pastimes to lofty new ambitions for Anglican pastoral and social commitments (as expressed for instance in Kingsley, 1877, i: pp. 378–80, 392, 468). For the historian Peter Mandler, 'a little bit of Jesus was found in every individual' (2002: p. 659). Of course Spencer would not consciously have seen his analysis of late-century individuals in these precise terms. Nor am I implying that there is some discernible change in the fundamentals of Spencer's thought. There are clear signs, though, of new nuances of expression, catching a subtle difference of emphasis. Spencer was perhaps not as remote and immune from the currents of his time as he probably thought he was, and certainly not as remote and immune as most modern historiography choreographs his appearance. Hilton's properly well-regarded study does more than most to bring Spencer in from the cold, but he deserves yet more reappraisal. Those fecund labels applied with facility and a whiff of effortless superiority by critics, such as 'apologist for laissez-faire', have to be stubbornly resisted if he and his work are to be judiciously reassessed, and if his wider significance as a public intellectual in nineteenth century life and as a witness to that life are to be sympathetically evaluated. As the translations of his writings into numerous other languages would suggest, there are few countries for which histories of their biological and social sciences, educational institutions, and political and cultural experiences can be counted as having trawled deeply enough unless Spencer and the remarkable scope of his ideas have exercised the indexers.

Concluding Reflections

One might have expected that Spencer's former employer, the *Economist*, would have insisted on accuracy when it commented on him over a century after his death, but this was not to be so. In one short paragraph in an anonymous leading article for 20 December 2005 there came the false claim that Spencer minted the phrase 'survival of the fittest' *before* Darwin's *On the Origin of Species* was published in 1859, followed by the further false claim that he took what he 'thought were the lessons of Darwin's book' and applied them to human society. In the same paragraph is the umpteenth repetition of the misleading judgement that he became 'one of the band of philosophers known as social Darwinists', coupled with the enigmatic thought that for Spencer 'the criterion of desert was genetic'. That this can still happen, in the face of sustained and substantial scholarly endeavour by many hands, is extraordinary, and if this book helps to stop it happening again it will have had at least one worthwhile outcome. Words written by Mary Midgley a quarter of a century ago remain pertinent: 'Spencer's bold, colourful and flattering picture of evolution has constantly prevailed over Darwin's more sober, difficult one, not only in the public mind, but also surprisingly often in the minds of scientists who have reason to know its limitations' (1985: 158). Certainly, though, there are some quite large deficiencies in Spencer, and it will be well to summarize these at the outset. It would be irresponsible and foolhardy to try to breathe new life into the 'inheritance of acquired characteristics'. That Spencer was indissolubly tied to it is a fact and he proved to be utterly mistaken in so committing himself. As a plausible mechanism of biological and psychological change it is as discredited as it is possible to imagine, and was so before the very end of Spencer's life. In 1891, as Lord Rector of the University of Glasgow, the philosophically minded politician, A. J. Balfour, pinpointed the threat to Spencer's philosophy:

> there is one systematic philosopher of our own day who has applied
> this principle so persistently in every department of his theory of Man,

that were it to be upset, it is scarcely too much to say that his Ethics, his Psychology, and his Anthropology would all tumble to the ground without it. Yet this doctrine has for many years been questioned by a great English authority, and, as many of you are aware, it has been directly controverted by one of the most eminent living German biologists... Weisman's (sic) conclusions are largely based on the extreme difficulty of conceiving any possible theory of heredity by which the transmission of acquired qualities could be accounted for; on the relative simplicity and plausibility of his own theory of heredity, according to which the transmission would be impossible; and on the absence of any conclusive proof that the transmission has ever taken place.

(1892: pp. 46–7. On Balfour see Jacyna, 1980)

In making this concession it may be noted that Benjamin Kidd quickly stepped in to exploit the situation at Spencer's expense. Kidd was a policeman's son from County Cork. He gained his education outside of the universities and became a civil servant in England. His *Social Evolution* of 1894 was widely read and much translated; and *The Principles of Western Civilization* (1902) and *The Science of Power* (1918) followed (on Kidd see Crook, 1984). Kidd readily accepted Weismann's rejection of the inheritance of acquired characteristics and in effect imported genetic variations into sociology as a basis for his understanding of various social outcomes. For Kidd this meant that individuals and social life were in perpetual conflict, rather than moving to a Spencerian harmony. However, religion for Kidd became a key force making for a new order in which a socialist equality of opportunity would become a state duty, allowing all persons to compete efficiently and fairly in social life.

To this concession that Spencer's commitment to the Lamarckian inheritance of acquired characteristics proved untenable two further concessions should be added. To the extent that Spencer interpreted 'the moral' (in the sense of what *should* be done rather than in the factual sense of what it is *believed* should be done) as tethered to 'the natural' the grounding of his normative propositions must fail to convince. And it should also be added that the whole process of change associated with Spencer's all-embracing theory of evolution, amended as it was over the years, must appear to us as casuistry, just as it did to Beatrice Webb (1926: p. 23), and to many others of his informed contemporary critics. The theory appears so structured that once Spencer perceived a potential empirical threat to one component proposition it became confirmation of another, the public criteria are lacking to discriminate clearly between, for instance, 'dissolution' and 'differentiation'. The theory is, in effect, defined as true. My own view is that it is very unlikely indeed that re-workings of Spencer's theory could lead to anything substantial being resurrected. Even if this view were to emerge as incorrect, Spencer's faith in the ultimately benign direction of the change to which his theory referred seems now simply an unwarranted and arbitrary assumption, a simulacrum of design in natural theology. In a spectacularly comprehensive manner, John Stuart Mill exposed the fractured logic of Spencer's appeals to 'laws of nature' as sources of 'authority' for normative declarations. By 1854, Mill had completed his essay 'Nature', though it was not published until 1874. It was an argument against the proposition that God reveals himself through Nature, and in particular directed at a process of reasoning he found commonplace in natural theology. Yet he might as well as have had Spencer in mind. By virtue of its elegance and economy Mill's summary deserves to be given in full. He writes:

> The word Nature has two principal meanings: it either denotes the entire system of things, with the aggregate of all their properties, or it denotes things as they would be, apart from human intervention.
>
> In the first of these senses, the doctrine that man ought to follow nature is unmeaning, since man has no power to do anything else than follow nature; all his actions are done through and in obedience to some one or many of nature's physical or mental laws.
>
> In the other sense of the term, the doctrine that men ought to follow nature, or, in other words, ought to make the spontaneous course of things the model of his voluntary actions is equally irrational and immoral:
>
> Irrational, because all human action whatever consists in altering, and all useful action in improving, the spontaneous course of nature:
>
> Immoral, because the course of natural phenomena being replete with everything which when committed by human beings is most worthy of abhorrence, anyone who endeavoured in his actions to imitate the natural course of things would be universally seen and be acknowledged to be the wickedest of men.
>
> (1961: pp. 400–1)

Spencer reacted to Huxley's criticisms in 1893 (see Ch. 3, p. 79) by declaring, in effect, that Huxley's points misfired because he was defining 'nature' in the second of the senses Mill had distinguished, in which it was plausible to contrast man's doings with nature's doings, whereas man's doings had to be seen as *part of* nature's doings: Spencer in his response was calling into play the first sense of 'nature' as identified by Mill. In doing so, however, Spencer escaped from one trap into another. Now any criticism of some idea or innovation as against 'nature' in this first sense as specified by Mill (as opposed simply to being 'undesirable') became in logic inadmissible; it was 'unmeaning'. Yet Spencer did want to claim, as in *The Man versus The State*, that 'every proposal to interfere with citizens' activities further than by enforcing their mutual limitations, is a proposal to improve life by breaking through the fundamental conditions to life' (1884: p. 167). Spencer could not seem to shake Nature and Providence apart. One indeed senses that Huxley 'understood what was at risk in forsaking monotheism in a way Spencer did not' (Fuller, 2006: p. 141).

Once these concessions to critics are made, it is possible to move towards a more generous attitude. With Spencer a touch of irony at this point enters the picture for, with the abandonment of the inheritance of acquired characteristics, the reality of course becomes that we have actively to learn about the past, rather than inherit it as filtered and sedimented in our mental apparatus, and it follows that the accounts we produce of dead theorists shoulder a heavy responsibility in their task of transmitting those theorists' endeavours into the consciousness of the present. But is it the case that any redemption is possible for Spencer? Of course, as is so often stated, there are shifting priorities over time in the questions of concern to sociology and to other subjects, and in the perceived relevance of particular academic outlooks; just as in social life itself, manners and fashions wax and wane. Yet the glib sound bites, as exemplified by the article in the *Economist,* represent more than transitory prejudices. They seem so entrenched in the repertoire of public intellectuals that it is hard to imagine any shift in the questions and fashions dominating social enquiry which would permit Spencer to be brought back into play as a source of useful ideas. Hard, certainly, but not, I will suggest, impossible. Spencer might, of course, have been so fundamentally misguided and muddled that untruths and half-truths about his ideas hardly matter, but a summary dismissal of him in this manner can, I believe, be shown to be a mistake. While the sound bites beyond doubt distort, the distortion rides on the back of dated and careless, or worse, misrepresentations of Spencer by older critics. It is not too late to challenge these deeper dispositions towards Spencer with the aid of text and reason. Moreover, it must be kept in mind that we ourselves create priorities and fashions no less than they create us: it is in this spirit, therefore, that we should respond to John Gray's shrewd observation that 'Among the causes of Spencer's decline as a formative influence on thought...the prejudiced and ignorant treatment given his writings by moral philosophers of the late nineteenth and early twentieth centuries cannot be the least important' (1982: p. 234).

There are, as it happens, many significant interpretational issues arising over Spencer. It became clear to me, before writing this study, that if they can be resolved at all, not simply brought into sharper focus (itself always a constructive step), they required new assessments of what Spencer was arguing. In each case this would mean peeling back layers of accumulated assumptions and trying to establish connections across a rather large number of his long list of publications. By drawing on recent work in a range of disciplines, and on the detailed texture of Spencer's own work, the present study has offered extensive reassessments of how best to inter-pret his own understanding of the contrast between militant and industrial social relations, and, in the light of his essay 'Transcendental Physiology', his own conception of a society as a 'social organism'. It has also excavated the interdependence of psychology and sociology which Spencer regarded as essential in making sense of social life, and his detailed analysis of the structure of relations between the individual and the social. It has empha-sized the often overlooked social nature and social production of ethical sentiments and ideas argued for in the *Principles of Ethics*. It has also recon-sidered the nature of the causes of 'social evolution' for Spencer, finding in particular that there is reason to believe that the relationship between the phrases 'natural selection', as used by Darwin, and 'survival of the fittest', as used by Spencer, may not be quite the one of isomorphism Spencer him-self often suggested, which interpretation has subsequently gained general acceptance (that Spencer also retained his adherence to the mechanism of the inheritance of acquired characteristics is not in question). In a sense such efforts might be counted as exercises in, to invoke Spencer's lexicon, 'nega-tive beneficence'. That is to say, the aim involved took the form of trying to remove interpretative obstacles that have arisen which have served to hinder the appreciation of his true positions.

Has something more 'positive' become available by combing through and re-thinking Spencer? Before tackling this question directly we need at this point to confront with some care the primarily idealist challenge to Spencer, potentially very damaging, that he was committed to a flawed 'atomic indi-vidualism' as Bernard Bosanquet alleged and as Vincent (1984) and den Otter (1997: p. 69) have in modern times repeated. In a sense the con-flict between Spencer and Durkheim within sociology over how society was possible, reviewed in Chapter 5, was a microcosm of this wider debate.

In the last two decades of Spencer's life and further on into the new cen-tury the idealists and the partly associated rise in the political arena of 'New Liberalism'[1] helped to reconceptualize the role of the state, and, it has been argued, 'transformed liberalism by ridding it of its self-centred, narrow indi-vidualism ... Green brought together Kant, Aristotle and Hegel, Hobhouse relied on biology and sociology, while Ritchie sought to reconcile Darwin and Hegel' (Simhony and Weinstein, 2001: p. 8). Simhony and Weinstein suggest that any political theory possesses an ontology, or philosophical anthropology, and advocacy, or prescriptivity. In terms of ontology, 'atom-ism and holism are principal rivals', and in terms of advocacy 'individualism and collectivism oppose each other fundamentally' (2001: p. 14). Spencer it may be assumed – he is fact not mentioned by Simhony and Weinstein, in spite of the fact that his thought was the point of departure for many ideal-ist and new liberal writers – belongs to the 'untransformed' liberalism, and would thus be categorized as wedded to atomic or ontological individualism, where 'only individual wants, interests and preferences exist' (Vincent, 1995:

p. 128). Ritchie, an idealist who also recognized the importance of Darwin, certainly 'reacted violently to Spencer' (den Otter, 1996: p. 96), though tellingly he paid tribute to Spencer in his *Principles of State Interference* of 1891 by nominating him as, perhaps, 'the most formidable intellectual foe with whom the New Radicalism has to reckon' (1902: p. 3. On Ritchie and evolution, see also Neill, 2003). The simple distinction between ontology and advocacy, although further refined by Simhony and Weinstein for other purposes, is very helpful in permitting some steps towards freeing Spencer from conventional (mis)representations. It can be argued that Spencer is not wedded to 'atomism', or, as Ritchie insisted in *Darwinism and Politics*, 'old fashioned individualism' (1895: p. 12), in any especially objectionable ontological sense.

We need to get beneath these abstract expressions. The rejection of 'atomism' entailed rejection of the idea of social life 'as little more than an aggregative gathering of duelling self-interest', and the re-conception of individuality in terms of mutual self-development through co-operation in 'social life's sociability' (Simhony and Weinstein, 2001: p. 17). The new thought in liberalism in particular, and idealist social thought more generally, rejected atomism by embracing 'the interdependence of the self-development of individuals, the interdependence of individuals and society, and the mutual recognition of each as a personality' (2001: p. 19). This rejection means that mutual dependence and common enjoyment are emphasized over competitive independence and private enjoyment. However, the role of institutions aimed *directly* at advancing towards this moral goal, as opposed to allowing it to happen voluntarily or spontaneously, was a matter of dispute. Although an important idealist, Bernard Bosanquet wished to limit the role of government in social reform because it was unable to respond, he held, to the uniqueness of each individual's circumstances, unlike the more personal approach intended as the hallmark of the Charity Organisation Society's approach to 'social work' (Gaus, 2001: pp. 143–4). Helen Bosanquet and Charles Loch, members of the exhaustive and ideologically freighted Edwardian Royal Commission on the Poor Laws established in 1905, were able to bring this brand of idealist social thought to the fore in the Majority Reports issued in 1909.[2]

While the naturalistic approach of Spencer and the idealist approach of Bernard Bosanquet to society and its members possessed few apparent points of convergence, it is interesting that both men wholeheartedly supported versions of economic individualism and energetically opposed social reform as an objective to be undertaken by the state. While Bosanquet was the least far apart of the idealists from Spencer *in a political sense*, the alleged differences in philosophical anthropology between them should still stand out in stark relief. However, as we have seen repeatedly, Spencer saw men as gregarious and as social from very early on in social evolution. His own version of the social organism explicitly modelled individuals as thoroughly inter-dependent parts, belonging to a whole. We have also seen that in the *Principles of Sociology* Spencer insisted that once 'a combination of men acquires permanence, there begin actions and reactions between the community and each member of it, such that either affects the other in nature' (1893: p. 11), to which in the *Ethics* he added, first, that the limit of the evolution of conduct is not reached until, beyond the avoidance of direct and indirect injuries to others, 'there are spontaneous efforts to further the welfare of others' (1910, i: p. 147), second, that 'unceasing social discipline will so mould human nature, that eventually sympathetic pleasures will be spontaneously pursued to the fullest extent advantageous to each and all' (1910, i: p. 250), and, third, that the well-being of each 'is involved with the well-being of all' (1910, i: p. 216). Each person was capable of possessing, as Spencer elsewhere expressed it, a 'chivalry' and a 'social self-consciousness' (in 'The Morals of Trade' of 1859, discussed in Chapter 2). This type of concern with sociality from Spencer is not open to rejection as unrepresentative of his thought in general. Its palpable reality points therefore to Bernard Bosanquet and other idealist thinkers in presenting Spencer as an 'atomic individualist' as noted earlier in this study, as culpable (den Otter is kinder, suggesting idealists tended to represent atomic individualism in a 'rather overly stylised manner', 1997: p. 69). For Spencer voluntary co-operative associations which serve to express and foster altruism form the heartland of naturally advancing social evolution.

The Spencerian idea of community which this picture embodies is both an everyday necessity for the successful pursuit of personal growth and part of the process leading to the near-utopia of complete adaptation to the social state, in which voluntarism renders entirely residual the coercive functions and powers of the state:

> What makes liberal individualism appear 'brutal' is the neglect of the cooperative elements which must accompany the pursuit of self-interest in a social environment. Herbert Spencer is innocent of such negligence. Too often those who consider themselves critics of the liberal tradition ignore the fact that Spencer's 'altruistic interests' are crucial aspects of his ethical and political position and form the basis of community in the liberal state.
>
> (Hiskes, 1983: p. 53)

Spencer's limitations on government action (which themselves were predicated on the general welfare-enhancing proclivities of its non-negotiable role in the enforcement of the 'justice' or equal liberty principle) were tightly coupled to an analysis of the growth and centrality of 'community'. As Hiskes indicates, it has been the neglect of this second element, in the widespread misconstrual of older liberal individualism, that has rendered 'brutal' Robert Nozick's (1974) advocacy of liberal individualism (Hiskes,

1983: p. 53). Sociologists too still overlook Spencer's stress on altruism and the social self-consciousness of persons. Steve Fuller has compounded weakness on these fronts by offering a rash and unhistorical account of Spencer's reaction to Darwin's *On the Origin of Species* and the suggestion that he was committed to 'genetics'. Thus he claims incautiously that Spencer read Darwin's *Origin* as a 'naturalized version of Adam Smith's "invisible hand" argument for the conversion of private vices into public virtue... Spencer simply extended Smith's conception of self-interest to an interest in reproducing one's genetic material' (2006: p. 171).

However, in a more penetrating and fruitful critical approach to Spencer, Ingold has contended, very plausibly, that a sound conceptualization of sociality must enable us 'to comprehend social life as a creative process whereby human beings relate to one another as the authors as well as the players of their parts' (1986: p. 244). 'Action', Ingold adds, 'is *carried on* by persons in mutual relationships; behaviour is emitted by interacting individuals' (1986: p. 338). Does Spencer rise to these particular demands in conceptualizing sociality? The answer I believe must be that he does not. His denial of freedom of the will, held at least from the first edition of the *Principles of Psychology*, and given momentum through his insistence on psychical change as resulting from the inheritance of characteristics acquired through adaptation to circumstances (included in which are social surroundings), means that Spencer can understand 'behaviour' but not 'action' as distinguished by Ingold, partly at least because Spencer makes no consistent distinction between the innate and the acquired. As with Goffman's stripped-down sociology of encounters between the 'discredited' and the 'normal' (see below, and Goffman, 1968; Offer, 1999b), so with Spencer's sociology overall: fulfilling a 'role' is not the same as 'revealing a plan lodged in the mind of the enculturated individual' (Ingold, 1986: p. 337). For as Ingold adds, the effect of 'the dramatic metaphor... is to take the intentionality out of action, leaving only prior intentions and execution, status and role, norms and behaviour' (Ingold, 1986: p. 331). We will need to return to intentionality and Spencer's denial of freedom of the will shortly. First, though, the significance for Spencer's sociology of his idea of 'spontaneous cooperation' must be clarified in this context.

Spencer's social whole was quite consistently not accorded an internal moral authority over citizens *beyond* the sphere of the maintenance and administration of 'justice', as he had always and unambiguously defined it, except in times of 'militant' social relations when aggression from without had necessitated central control to ensure the survival of the whole. In Chapter 5, George Smith was noted as classing Spencer as 'a major theorist in the spontaneous order school of social theory. The similarities, for example, between Spencer and F. A. Hayek are remarkable...' (1981: p. 424). Spencer had indeed aligned himself with Richard Whately, discussed earlier in the present study, in regarding economic market transactions, and also to a degree social transactions, as forming a catallaxy, though of course with the government responsible for maintaining equal liberty where individuals failed to do this themselves (it was with this role for government in economic and social life, 'specialized administration', that Spencer met Huxley's charge that he was endorsing 'administrative nihilism'). The outcomes in terms of production and distribution of a spontaneous order or catallaxy would be, Spencer judged, superior to coercive efforts in the same direction, not least because the information that would be necessary on the needs and capabilities of individuals could not be known adequately by governments to marry policy to outcomes. Perrin too noted Spencer's emphasis on networks of 'exchangists', and its more recent manifestations (as in Coleman, 1990; Randall Collins, 1994) 'under the aegis of contemporary exchange and rational-choice theory' (1995: pp. 352–3). Spencer's part in highlighting the importance of economic and social outcomes as the product of a spontaneous order in transactions, congruent with his idea of social evolution, and given, of course, the psychical predispositions of the transactors, may pass largely unacknowledged and unexploited. Nevertheless, Perrin notes, he remains 'an intellectual ally of exchange and rational choice theory' (1995: p. 353). Spencer's extended discussion of private beneficence, dealing with the relatively ordinary exchanges of assistance and information in everyday life, pointed similarly to the networks of relatives, friends and contacts which people typically establish around themselves in which 'caring' as a form of beneficence was a significant feature. Since the 1980s, research has contributed substantial empirical information on this area of social life (for example Parker, 1990; Finch and Mason, 1993). Yet Spencer's comments in the *Ethics* also drew attention to the 'theories' relating to responsibilities towards others held by ordinary people in this context, about which our knowledge remains regrettably sketchy. Robert Pinker called for a 'sociology of morals' in this connection over 30 years ago, unconsciously perhaps echoing Spencer, but the call merits a more sustained response than it has yet received:

> One of the tasks of a sociology of morals would be to clarify the nature and consistency of individual and public attitudes towards the varieties of mutual aid practised ... within families. We need to know far more about the preferred and actual forms of reciprocity and obligation which occur between strangers sharing a common citizenship and members of the same kin. A second task would be to re-examine the extent which the values and assumptions which are implicit in social legislation support, weaken or modify the moral beliefs and practices of ordinary people.
>
> (1974: pp. 8–9)

Spencer's participants in a catallaxy are of course almost certain to be in a society in which 'industrial' not 'militant' social relations predominate, imbued with a social self-consciousness and altruism, and predisposed to go beyond 'justice' in their relations with others and to offer to them and receive from them positive and negative beneficence. All of which, it must be observed, is compatible with his analysis of each society as possessing in common a *sui generis* kind of organic quality, and as exhibiting evolving structures or institutions, and functions, shaping and in turn shaped by the psychical make-up of the individuals forming it. It is compatible too with the inheritance of acquired characteristics, operating without hindrance, holding the promise of a more virtuous future, though perhaps with spasms of militant recrudescence intervening, courtesy ultimately, as in other matters, of the rhythm of motion reflecting as yet imperfect adjustments or equilibrations in this instance in individual and social life. And all of these points are compatible with individuals and societies as still inhabiting a world that in its changes is without guarantees, since they are elements in a Darwinian struggle for existence, out of which some may dwindle or even perish as others find themselves best suited to, or 'fittest' for, the circumstance they are in (the process Spencer renamed 'indirect equilibration'). There is indeed an integrated structure to Spencer's evolutionary analysis of social life. Although Stark (1961) found 'three sociologies' in Spencer, and Perrin (1976) 'four theories of social evolution', there is in fact one overarching Spencerian sociology integrated into one overarching Spencerian theory of social evolution, but with, as one would surely reasonably expect, a range of interlocking and theoretically unified components.

Ingold, I think, would contend that in the catallaxy Spencer still omits intentionality from action. Neither a purely interactive nor a purely regulative or coercive sense of sociality 'enables us to comprehend social life as a creative process whereby human beings relate to one another as the authors as well as the players of their parts' (1986: p. 244). Ingold argues that Spencer's society was 'a resultant, not an emergent, containing nothing that was not already prefigured in the properties of its original constituents' (1986: p. 224). Thus for Spencer

> the essence of sociality lies in the association, interaction and co-operation of numerous, discrete individuals, each equipped with a set of purposes in advance of their entry into mutual relations, purposes that must therefore be a property of their constitution as organic things (and in that sense, of their 'nature'). Whether our concern is with insects, birds or human beings, the rationale for social co-operation is to be found in the net advantages it brings to each and every one of the contracting individuals...this Spencerian conception underwrites much of the most recent ethological and sociobiological discussion of social behaviour in animals and man. Indeed there are good grounds for arguing that Spencer, and not Darwin, was the first sociobiologist. Conversely the roots of the contemporary anthropological critique of socio-biology are to

be found in the anti-Spencerian superorganicism of Durkheim, Boas and Kroeber.

(1986: pp. 224–5)

Although one sees Ingold's point, his account seems to me rather unsympathetic in respect of what Spencer actually claimed. Apart from the unintended and novel results engendered by spontaneous co-operation, it is clear that for Spencer 'advanced' 'social individuals' are much more sophisticated, socially self-conscious and adept at culturally freighted 'creative' interaction than Ingold's snapshot of them captures. The real difficulty again derives from Spencer's negative attitude to the 'liberty to desire or not to desire' (Spencer, 1881b, i: p. 500). It is this underlying orientation rather than the reference to reified 'sets of purposes' that gives force to the 'first sociobiologist' charge.

Persons, then, need to be conceptualized as constituting and reconstituting each other through a continuous process of being conscious, intersubjectively aware personal agents. Purpose in the social person is not 'given', nor is it imposed by society, but it is sourced in being a person with social relations, 'doing' not merely 'behaving'. There is not much room for doubt that in his dash for science Spencer made man into what Cairnes described as a 'conscious automoton'. And here we come back to Bosanquet's diagnosis of Spencer's error as his commitment to 'atomic individualism'. It seems to me that it is not so much Spencer's conceptualization of social life or for that matter individual life that is the difficulty, contrary to Bosanquet's verdict. Spencer's understanding covers all the 'moving parts' which a 'thick' understanding of social life requires. What is lacking is a concept of the power of unprogrammed authorship on the part of social individuals in social and personal life. The culprit is indeed Spencer's denial of freedom of the will, not a defective because otherwise stunted grasp of the 'physiology' of social interaction or mutual dependency. The denial was a structural element in Spencer's theoretical edifice, and irrefragable. This is *the* difficulty with Spencer, and, once accepted as such, it should not come as a surprise that, on society and sociology, Spencer can be a richer source of insight than the misplaced gibe of 'atomic individualist' may lead us to suppose. Spencer's insistence on a circumscribed role for government (though one it should perform more effectively than it does) was of course about advocacy and not reliant on an impoverished ontology, though he took it to have sound naturalistic foundations. The denial of freedom of the will was integral to his psychology, but that psychology was not simplistic in its causality: within the parameters set by 'conditions', including social conditions, and the operation of adaptation and the inheritance of its results, it was compatible with and indeed offered an explanation of change in social and personal life. It could even accommodate intellectual conflict in a society, although Spencer was prone to account for the production of novel or 'dissident' ideas (including perhaps his own theory) as the output of the psychology of exceptionally well-adapted persons, and for the spread of those ideas as ahead of or in breach of underlying naturalistic tendencies. The conception of sociality did not reduce to 'atomic individualism', a point reinforced through our reconsideration of Durkheim's interpretation of Spencer from which it emerged that in no relevant sense did Spencer assume that the individual was 'prior to society'. There seem to be no established grounds for counting Spencer as committed to an ontology in which the 'individual' is the atomic source of 'knowledge, conscience and moral obligation' (Vincent, 1995: p. 128). However, and in this he was not isolated, he did not satisfactorily conceptualize what made social life and personal life open-textured, rather than elaborately mechanistic.

One of Spencer's generally acknowledged and notable achievements, perhaps an enduring strength, is that he pioneered the idea of sociology as a science of society against the many voices denying that possibility in the nineteenth century, and did so convinced it had to be in dialogue with the other sciences concerned with human life. He was prolific in signposting where important topics for empirical research could be found. Was the price paid for linking sociology to psychology and biology as indicated unavoidable, or has more recent work in the highly diverse field encompassed by 'biosociology', coupled with contemporary sociology's own (relatively limited) engagement with it, found a richer conception of the life of mutual relations to which it is attempting to connect?

This is of course not the place for a history of 'biosociology', or 'socio-biology', nor even for more than a few comments on recent work, with which I want to try to make a connection. Some bearings, however, are provided by Laland and Brown (2002. For a brief review of earlier 'neo-evolutionary' sociology see Peel, 1969). There are currently several specialities within a general framework committed to applying biologically grounded approaches to the traditional areas of interest of sociology: human behavioural ecology, evolutionary psychology, memetics, and gene-culture co-evolution Each of these approaches is now in the process of developing Darwin-based selectionist explanations of social activity, more or less *terra incognita* to mainstream sociology. Although each of the approaches is distinctive, they share the premise that, because of its success in its original field, 'borrowing Darwinian concepts and methods, suitably adjusted to the structural peculiarities of human culture, is the quickest and easiest path to a reasonable theory of human culture'(Laland and Brown, 2002: p. 275). Spencer, then, it cannot be over-emphasized, does *not* provide the source of the model in question, although as already discussed the *Principles of Sociology* and the Principles of Ethics in particular did make some use of the 'struggle for existence' element of Darwin's thought (on the presence of the idea in the *Psychology*, see Leslie, 2000, 2006). My concern here is the more oblique one of seeing if *current* thinking in biology-based frameworks about social life, whether advanced from within sociology or not, give collateral support to a Spencerian insistence on interdisciplinarity in the study of sociality, as opposed to any specific matter of content.

The approaches in question usually accept as a premise that their conceptualizations and explanations must acknowledge that people live acting and believing they make choices, and assume responsibility for their actions and make their own history, since other starting points are likely to misinterpret human sociality (see Runciman, 1998a: p. 179). The need is also admitted for caution over 'simplification' through the reduction of aspects of social life to quasi-biological events, such as references to 'the evolved design of the psychologies...of political actors' (Curry, 2003: p. 112). As Midgley has observed 'not all simplification is scientific... Science progresses just as often by making distinctions as it does by abandoning them' (2000: p. 70). The main contributions now discussed next may be taken as fulfilling these conditions.

One of the lines of approach, memetics, has developed around Richard Dawkins's idea of 'memes' – units of culture, such as tunes, catch-phrases, fashions and techniques, taken as analogous to genes – which could replicate and mutate in social life (Dawkins, 1976). However, an important variant, and the focus for now, has come from *within sociology itself* through the work of Runciman (1997), who marries a case for 'selectionism' as a paradigm of explanation in social science itself, with the identification of associated changes over time in types and sub-types of society, a quintessentially Spencerian concern as it happens. A selectionist perspective in this context attempts to use a form of Darwinian 'natural selection' (that not all 'variations' produced are 'selected' to survive, see Chapter 2) to explain change in social life. While as it happens certain criticisms advanced against Runciman can be deflected, a less ambitious though still authentically selectionist perspective can be derived from the discussion which is particularly instructive for my present purpose.

Runciman's contribution postulates 'unit practices' as basic to reciprocal social life (1997: p. 173):

> the evolution of a society's modes of production, persuasion and coercion is not a process of 'adaptation' by the society as such, and.... the units of selection are not individuals or groups...but the practices defining the roles of which the society consists. Adaptations, accordingly, are adaptations by roles whose defining practices confer continually shifting competitive advantages on their carriers on a continuously changing distribution of economic, ideological and political power.

Within social science only a theory of social selection 'analogous but not reducible to the theory of natural selection can account for the underlying process by which societies of one kind evolve into societies of another, and it is, therefore, only in the terms of that theory that hypotheses about the causes of particular institutional changes in particular societies can be given adequate grounding' (1997: p. 130). For Runciman, no designed or immutable 'fit' exists between historical entities or sets of social relationships and a 'meaning' or purpose attributed to them in wider social life. Current structures and the outcomes of their presence are contingent matters. He emphasizes the mutability of our social practices in their economic, ideological and political situations. The survival of only some variations is explained by the existence of an adaptive advantage, and a possible constituent of the adaptive advantage is that the end-directedness, or teleonomy, of social actors is actively receptive to those variations, seeking them above others.

Runciman thus insists on the distinction between the factors that initiate change in mutant unit practices and what explains the outcomes of their presence: 'The contingent causes of the introduction of mutant practices by particular role-incumbents can never furnish the explanation of the systemic outcome of which the mutation was a necessary condition, any more than can retrospective diagnosis of the cunning of Lloyd George, the emollience of Baldwin, the pragmatism of Attlee, the deviousness of Wilson, or the hubris of Thatcher (if that is what you think they were)' (1997: p. 127, see also p. 53 and p. 187; and Coleman, 1990). Once the spotlight is placed on what circumstances led to the 'selection' (or 'non-selection') of the outcome of role-incumbents' efforts, *determination* by design is undermined in social evolution. The crucial contribution here is the focus on selection.

Now while Runciman does regard the *course* of social evolution as 'inherently unpredictable', and explanation as 'possible only with hindsight', he applies his new framework to the history of British social policy. He argues that England evolved from one to another 'sub-type' of capitalism after the First World War: 'English society as it had been since approximately 1880 evolved during the First World War and its aftermath into an unmistakably different sub-type of the capitalist mode of production, liberal mode of persuasion, and democratic mode of coercion' (1997: p. 56). His case is built up out of: reports of changes in social life; an explanation of the selective factors at work on these 'mutant practices' (the 'sanctity of private property remained intact', 1997: p. 54); descriptions of *experiences* of the period in question; and an evaluation over time of the actual course and effects of social change independent of actors' experiences. The mutant practices represented by non-contributory old-age pensions (1908), health and unemployment insurance (1911) and inter-war legislation, and consummated in the legislation of 1945–1948, 'were at least as far from the ideology of egalitarian socialism as they were from that of Gladstone and Samuel Smiles...symptoms of a different sub-type...of the distribution of power' (1997: p. 54). However, in whatever manner the changes *after* the Second World War are to be explained, described or evaluated, 'they cannot be reported as an evolution out of one into another sub-type, let alone mode, of the distribution of power' (1997: p. 11).

Runciman's emphasis on the triumvirate of 'production', 'persuasion' and 'coercion', has echoes, intentionally or not, of Spencer's systems of 'production', 'distribution' and 'regulation' (these themes of the *Principles of Sociology* were discussed in Chapter 5 as key elements of the orthogenic 'evolution' of societies. As was shown there and in Chapter 9, while Spencer often introduced references to 'indirect' equilibration or the 'survival of the fittest', although seldom to Darwinian 'variations', evolution as orthogenesis remains his fundamental position). Runciman, however, explicitly distances his account from a Spencerian form of unfolding or directionalism (1998a: p. 167, see also 1998b: p. 51). Nevertheless, within a Darwinian selectionist perspective, the processes of innovation and selection, *not* direction, are the key components, and further comments address these features.

According to Benton (2000: p. 216): '[t]he problem which Darwin solved was how to explain the appearance of design without a designer. Runciman seems to have failed to notice that sociologists have a different problem. Societies, unlike species, do have designers'. However, as already shown, Runciman has pre-empted the force of the criticism. Social change can be influenced by the decisions of incumbents of roles, but these, for the purposes of social science, 'are random impacts to be taken as given, however alien this may seem to readers accustomed to historical and biographical narratives.... Human decisions are not, of course random in the sense that genetic mutations are random. But in the explanation of social evolution, they might as well be' (1997: p. 127; see also 2004). What causes something to occur does not explain the outcome of its presence: social history is less 'one thing *after* another' than 'one thing *instead* of another' (Runciman, 1998a: p. 170). New practices have to be selected, they have to win out over competitors and 'fit' with the appropriate and possibly contested modes of production, persuasion and governance. Otherwise the 'genetic fallacy' is committed, and design presumed (1990a: p. 170; on teleology and the fallacy see Radcliffe Richards, 2000). The process involved in selection can nevertheless include influences for a favourable outcome in these environments – humans make rational models of the world and actors in it, thus reducing uncertainty (Chattoe, 2002: p. 822), but a change is established because it 'fits' and is thus selected, *not* because it was 'guided' (Runciman, 1998a: p. 179). The fact that a person, government or culture intends something to happen does not trump the selective process: the cause of a change does not of itself explain its outcome. 'Teleonomy' or 'teleomechanism', where purposive will steers social individuals in actions and innovations, and then in 'planning' their selection, might appear to be incompatible with non-teleological variation and 'natural' as opposed to 'artificial' selection (see Ingold; 1986: pp. 367–76). However, teleonomy does not need a grander Lamarckian or other teleological *underpinning* for its existence, no appeal to an overall design is entailed. In this sense the survival of something 'artificially' selected amounts to its natural selection. The selection is still achieved without a guarantee and against competing pressures for survival. Human design is real enough; it is not incompatible, however, with the application of the selectionist paradigm.

A further criticism is that the focus on 'unit practices' of 'role-incumbents' as the source of 'mutants' or variations is unduly restrictive. For people to make sense of any 'unit practice' it has to mesh in with a wider framework of meaning and significance: ' "society" is not just a complex built up out of individual practices as its "building blocks". Atomistic accounts of society like this serve to obscure the key insights given to us by sociology – insights into the many complex and more or less subtle ways in which society and our place in it shape us' (Benton, 2000: p. 215). Benton believes that Runciman's 'unit practices' cannot be identified independently of wider and interwoven patterns of social life and meaning. Against this, however, it is a familiar fact that we may nevertheless identify as a 'different practice' distance e-learning, for example, from physical residence at university (see also Chattoe, 2006: pp. 380, 390). More fundamentally, Benton's objection may rest on an itself ontologically fallible idealist conception of society and social life, and on a normatively holistic or organic view which is perhaps 'skyhook'[3] in character in its interpretation of the relationships of the social whole to the mutual relationships of 'social individuals'. In other words, in such a conception our individual 'sociality' or 'moral nature' derives from the will of a whole, ordaining a shared meaningfulness of social life, to the unfolding of which it is assumed we are morally or by purposive design bound in allegiance (see too Runciman's criticism of Durkheim's *conscience collective*, 1998a: p. 170). The familiar exercise by language-using social individuals of their own innovative agency may be difficult to reconcile with this conception[4]. Laland and Brown, themselves active contributors to the development of evolutionary perspectives have, in practical rather than philosophical terms, expressed 'little sympathy' with what they conclude to be 'the obscurant holism that afflicts many of the social sciences'. The human brain is, they add, 'a complex and interconnected system of interacting processes. Yet this has proved no barrier to the unstinting march of neuroscience' (2002: p. 273).

However, Runciman's social analogy of genetic mutations (his 'mutant unit practices') may not itself furnish an indispensable ingredient of a selectionist paradigm in empirical social science. Chattoe (2006), for example, has pointed to a selectionist explanation of church survival which uses *agent-based* simulation of church members to test the significance for their survival of strict churches (demanding on members) versus liberal churches. There may be merit for now in merely highlighting the *general* gains for sociology of thinking in a Darwin-based selective perspective, keeping potentially divisive or controversial commitments to the minimum. For Darwin, after all, our ignorance of 'variations' was profound. At present it may make sense for sociology to examine processes of innovation and extinction in its own subject matter without advance and speculative specification of an underlying master locus or instrument of (quasi-genetic) variation (there is a succinct account of difficulties with memes, such as the matter of why people take up some ideas and not others, in Dickens, 2000: pp. 53–8)[5]. Provided 'innovations' exhibit 'heredity' (replicate themselves) and differential fitness, no more is demanded by Darwin's original insights, though the important qualification must be made that unless it is understood that *explanations* for innovations and extinctions are *being sought* in the examination of the processes involved it may descend to the tautology of whatever is, is. Taken cautiously as an 'experimental' methodological precept, there appears to be nothing inherently incoherent in seeing where it leads.

Such an approach would be concerned with irreducible processes of innovation, survival, and oblivion in social life that constitute the raw materials and outcomes of, applied to social life, 'natural selection', in its basic *form* as presented by Darwin. It is beyond doubt that Mill's comprehensive first sense of 'nature' means that 'natural selection' covers *all* species, so that cases such as Darwin's own examples of even man-induced *biological* selection in plants and animals become subsumed by it. If a non-morally freighted conception of selection in respect of social life were to be adopted, within the framework of biological change set by 'natural selection', that framework simply as a framework would thus grow to accommodate social in addition to biological change. It would recapitulate in formal terms the structure of Darwin's own key insight, before the engine of biological change, genes and their indeterminate course of mutation, was discovered. Key questions would be, therefore, how does innovation in social life occur, what sort of conditions lead to novelty establishing itself and becoming 'persistent', and what factors make for extinction? The pursuit of such questions would not be to colonize social science by biology. Indeed, the modest selectionist perspective proposed is neither an *analogy* nor a *metaphorical construct* (see Kerr, 2003) derived from Darwin's core insight, but an unthreatening exploration of its *formal possibilities*, applied *appropriately* to the social life of human beings, that is, in the sense of taking social life as constituted 'through the creative conduct of persons' (Ingold, 1986: p. 212). Benton considers a selectionist perspective of this type a form of redescription, pressing orthodox social science into 'the service of a new terminology: "old wine, new bottles" ' (2000: p. 217), a verdict, however, which hides its potential status as a *more powerful* framework for interpreting evidence. It would nourish searches for new evidence to furnish *non-teleological* explanations of social change, whilst accommodating teleonomy, and it could lead to a unifying framework of understanding (see also Runciman, 1997: p. 130).[6]

Runciman's own earlier *Relative Deprivation and Social Justice* (1972) partly exemplifies the value of the perspective. It helps explain *how* new micro features of social life arise, undetermined by 'society'. Attitudes, political affiliations and patterns of voting may alter and engender demands for change as a *sense* of deprivation grows in size, intensity or frequency in a population, owing to a redrawn perception of one's position, independent of *actual* deprivations. New information and education or a perceived rise in the prosperity of hitherto 'invisible' others from which one feels excluded, as in the dislocation of wartime, may heighten the magnitude, degree and frequency of a sense of deprivation, while moral or religious teaching may have the converse effect (Runciman, 1972: pp. 27–9).[7]

In this manner one might also re-consider Goffman's *Stigma*. That book explores the experience in interaction of people with attributes regarded as stigmatizing, but counter-productively sidelines the question of *how* an attribute *comes to be* stigmatizing (such as smoking tobacco) or *ceases to be* so seen (such as unmarried cohabitation). A selectionist outlook finds these questions central. For Goffman (1968: p. 45): 'The natural history of a category of persons with a stigma must be clearly distinguished from the natural history of the stigma itself – the history of the origins, spread and decline of the capacity of an attribute to serve as a stigma in a particular society, for example, divorce in American upper middle class society'. However, the 'natural history' of the stigma *is* the product of inputs to and outcomes of interactions, and the appearance or disappearance of an attribute's ability to stigmatize in a given context is the product of selection in the course of everyday interaction over time. Goffman focuses on the persons with an attribute, presumed to be stigmatizing, but not on whether 'normals' among themselves *agree* that the attribute is undesirable. The selectionist perspective yields a powerful corrective: it is as the outcome of the interaction itself, between divorcees and non-divorcees for instance, that changes occur over time in the identification of an attribute as stigmatizing or not. The changes reflect micro-level selection at work, with the actual process of change constituting, to re-deploy Goffman's own phrase, 'one of the primal scenes of sociology' (Goffman, 1968: p. 24), in which the stigmatized may become victors or vanquished.

The actual process of an already-adopted aim of social reform becoming fact, reducing social divisions say, is manifestly and ineluctably two-sided: the product of *both* aspirations cultivated within their interaction by social individuals *and* the balance of the selectional factors working in favour of and against the replication of whatever it is that survives socially. 'Ridicule', wrote Spencer (1854a: p. 46), 'has always been a revolutionary agent. Institutions that have lost their roots in men's respect and faith are doomed; and the day of their dissolution is not far off '. Societies undergo a process of casting off practices, or 'exuviation' (1854a: p. 50). Indeed, the survival element of a selectionist approach became an important supplement in the later Parts of Spencer's *Principles of Sociology* and *Principles of Ethics* to the staples of orthogenesis, ontogenesis and adaptation. Thus for

Spencer old religious and new scientific beliefs were locked in a struggle for survival which science would win: the 'spreading recognition of natural causation ... insensibly weakens' the mythological beliefs 'most at variance with advancing knowledge' (Spencer, 1896b: p. 165).

The case of the decline of the poor law in the years before the First World War might also be illuminated through a selectionist perspective. Chattoe has remarked that 'welfare services must meet the goals of their funding bodies as well as customers (though in varying degrees) if they are to survive. They ... have ... to deliver an output for which there is a demand' (2006: p. 381). Decline is not explained by a historicist Whig reference to a path of 'progress', which would commit the genetic fallacy of taking the alleged causes or motivations behind a novelty as explaining its consequences. We need, rather, to look at *how* the poor law lost political influence, including the impact of the persuasive power associated with growing professional specialization in the fields of public health and medical care, and of criticisms of its stance of 'deterrence' towards users. Account must also be taken of support mustered by its own responses to such developments: workhouses were relaunched by government as 'Poor Law Institutions' in 1913, in a hope 'to save the Poor Law' (Crowther, 1981: p. 87). There is some evidence too of the poor law as popular among its users: 'Some Edwardian workhouse infirmaries even operated a "pay beds" system to meet a rising demand for poor law medical care among more affluent classes' (Harris, 2002: p. 436). In the event, poor law unions and guardians enjoyed a protracted existence until as late as 1930, when they were abolished through a reorganization of local government and its finances (not an 'underlying process' 'unfolding' towards the 'welfare state' of the 1940s).

This schematic discussion can have offered only a foretaste of the potential merits of a selectionist perspective. If Runciman (1972) in a nascent selectivist way shows how 'mutant' social practices may arise,[8] the consideration of *Stigma* and the poor law shows the richness of insight sacrificed when a selectionist orientation is missing in accounts of social change: 'one thing' has indeed occurred *instead* of, rather than *after*, in 'just so' style, 'another thing'. Alongside of this kind of interest in selectionist thought coming from inside the discipline of sociology there is of course also salient work from biologically based sciences, particularly in the field of 'gene-culture coevolution'. Gene-culture coevolution accepts that 'the cultural knowledge an individual adopts may sometimes, although certainly not always, depend on his or her genetic constitution', and it accepts also that 'selection acting on the genetic system is commonly generated or modified by the spread of cultural information' (Laland and Brown, 2002: p. 243). For coevolutionary theorists such as Feldman and Cavalli-Sforza the leash 'that ties culture to genes tugs both ways' (Laland and Brown, 2002: p. 243). In this perspective, culture and social relations are approached as phenomena of ontogeny and human teleonomy, enabled by but not necessarily determined by a genetic envelope. Culture is seen as influencing natural selection pressure, hastening or slowing rates of genetic change, and generating new selection processes, such as group selection – involving social conformity as a tendency which engenders selection of a cultural variation (see Boyd and Richerson, 1985, 2005). Moreover, cultural expressions which might be described as 'adaptive' behaviour might not necessarily indicate the presence of characteristics with an evolutionary history of selection, but could be seen instead as indicating willed, or unwilled, intersubjective creativity. Indeed, the view of Cavalli-Sforza and Feldman (1981) is that cultural expressions and social relations represent phenotypic plasticity with an epigenetic capacity to change and be changed consciously beyond any genetic control. 'Dual-level models', observe Laland and Brown 'could be constructed even if there was no resemblance at all between the two levels' (2002: p. 276). Moreover, genetic evolution does not *have* to be slow, nor cultural evolution fast.

Laland and Brown suggest that such modern evolutionary approaches 'accept that cultural change can occur without accompanying genetic change and that individuals from genetically distinct populations acquire the cultural traits of each other without difficulty' (2002: p. 310). It may be that sociological critics of evolutionary approaches have been tardy in picking up this trend. Gene-culture coevolutionists in particular believe 'that cultural phenomena cannot be fully understood without recourse to the intrinsic processes of cultural change, which are at least partly independent of the processes of biological evolution' (Laland and Brown, 2002: p. 312).[9]

A selectionist perspective, nurtured within sociology itself but also in tune with the gene-culture coevolutionist approach, could probably advance sociological understanding through its concern with the *processes* of innovation and extinction in social life, rather than, of course its *direction*. Of Spencer, Turner declared that ignorance of what he said hurts the progress of social science (1985: p. 7). In considering both Darwin-based and neo-Darwinian models of selectionism this is true ironically: insistent Spencerian whispers mostly serve only to tarnish their potential to illuminate social life. Making explicit the differences between Spencer and Darwin over the mechanism and direction of 'evolution' serves the important purpose of clarifying the potential of selectionism if more widely taken up within sociology. In a selectionist paradigm, novelty and oblivion become key topics: there is though as yet no compelling reason to presume there is one master kind of locus, quasi-genetic or not, in social change.

While the prospect arises of enriching the study of social change within a selectionist perspective, other concerns within social and political theory, such as relations between institutions at particular historical moments, might remain untouched – old wine, old bottles (see Chattoe, 2002). Further reflection upon the empirical application of selectionism in sociology may advance an acceptance within sociology as well as beyond that, since sociologists are especially knowledgeable about social life, the refinement of selectionist perspectives and their application to social life ideally should not remain by default almost exclusively consigned to the biological sciences, and that the incontestable *naturalness* of lived social life indicates, as Laland and Brown conclude, that 'the findings of biology and social science will need to be compatible' if either is 'to rate as satisfactory' (2002: p. 316).

Spencer's denial of the freedom of the will, meaning that his theoretical position could not adequately capture the creativity of man was, after all, not essential for the sciences of man to flourish. The idea of human purpose for Spencer possessed the status of a quasi-biological unwilled freedom. But if this denial can be put on one side, the significance of Spencer for today, beyond his huge importance in intellectual history, can be better grasped. As a matter of principle Spencer refused to ring-fence sociology from psychology and biology. In consequence, while the detail of the ideas just discussed owe very little indeed to Spencer, he as a sociologist uniquely opened the doors to them and would have been positively disposed towards their interdisciplinary spirit in trying to do justice to understanding social life. Spencer's conception of sociology as a scientific activity, with his emphasis on 'preparation' in biology and psychology was, it will now be clear, at odds with the traditions of idealist social thought, committed to man as 'special', requiring both historical interpretation and moral tutelage, and being an inherently difficult subject about which to make meaningful generalizations (den Otter, 1996). In sociology and allied areas of study, idealist social thought became well-rooted. Thus in 1912, the pioneer social work educator E. J. Urwick declared that 'scientific' sociology must remain a very partial aid to the understanding of our social life', it is and must be 'subordinate to the philosophy of that life which passes boldly beyond the domain of any science' (1912: p. vi). In Boucher's later assessment, exponents of idealist thought, 'in demonstrating the relevance of philosophy to ordinary life, exercised a considerable influence in providing a frame of reference for social policy, public administration and education reform well into the twentieth century' (1997: p. xi). It can indeed be argued that this influence was particularly marked in social policy, notably in the writings of Richard Titmuss (Harris, 1989, 1992: pp. 135–7; Offer, 2006a, b). The influence on social work from idealist thought extended to Canada: Moffatt and Irving (2002) point up how John Watson and George Blewett, both previously students of idealism under Edward Caird at Oxford, aligned social work in an idealist direction, particularly at the University of Toronto. This influence was reinforced with the arrival of Urwick from London in 1924. Durkheim's sociological work, it may be suggested, also embodied cognate overarching moral concerns about social life. Yet, for all this, it is, I suggest, Spencer's kind of outlook that strikes us as being more in tune with modern values and attitudes to knowledge, and most likely to yield tangible benefits through substantive research.

The other big and neglected part of Spencer's legacy derives at least in part from Whately's lead, the conception of economic and social life as forming a catallaxy, although for Spencer still an imperfectly realized one. If life in general was 'the continuous adjustment of internal relations to external relations' (1894, i: p. 80) the catallaxy provided an obvious theatre for that adjustment among human beings. Spencer differs from some modern rational action theorists (such as Coleman, 1990) in stressing an elemental and, through social evolution, an increasingly 'thick' social normativity in individual actions, as noted by Zafirovski. Zafirovski adds that 'Spencer, Hayek and other individualists assuming "common ends", "abstract principles", and "shared conventions" underlying individual behaviour' come to a point of convergence which meets with 'Durkheim, Parsons and other holists emphasizing the role of "normative consensus" ' (2000: p. 560), doing so in a manner which shows that the traditional sociological dichotomy between individualism and holism is specious (see also Gray, 1996, as discussed in Chapter 5). Although of course occurring within what are themselves sociologically significant parameters involving, not least, asymmetrical power, the phenomena associated with voluntary co-operation and free-market exchange, as contrasted with coercive direction and regulated and rationed distribution, remain familiar features of much social life. Spencer's sociology points up the need for the catallaxy's dynamics, use of resources, consequences, and frameworks of regulation to be part of the contemporary sociological gaze (Spencer's associated critiques of governmental bureaucracy, beyond that necessarily involved with the administration of 'justice', not least in *The Man versus The State*, remain bracing today). Spencer was explicit and in the process presciently modern, after all, in insisting that in this conception of what counts as a society: 'the members of the body-politic are not to be regarded as separated by intervals of dead space, but as diffused through a space occupied by life of a lower order. In our conception of a social organism, we must include all that lower organic existence on which human existence, and therefore social existence, depend (1860a: p. 275). Beyond doubt, a joint focus on catallaxy and selectionism today in sociological thought would provide Spencer's own ambitions with an apt memorial. Nevertheless, its protean nature is one of the fascinating qualities of sociology, and it would be unwise to think that with any such development sociologists will or indeed should thereby narrow the characteristic diversity of the questions they pursue.

Notes

1 Early Spencer: Influences and Ideas

1. Francis appears to imply some model of the authentic emotionally fulfilled life from which Spencer fell short. Duncan's *Life and Letters* volume (originally published in 1908) had not been 'arranged' in the sense of constrained by Spencer as Francis suggests (2007: p. 19).
2. Published in London in 1860, and New York in 1876. Anecdotal evidence suggests it made the study of geometry and Euclid notably more palatable and comprehensible to young minds than competing texts.
3. Mozley much later published four volumes of reminiscences, two entitled *Reminiscences Chiefly of Oriel College and the Oxford Movement* (1882), and *Reminiscences Chiefly of Towns, Villages and Schools* (1885). A Church of England clergyman and writer of leaders for *The Times*, Mozley irritated Spencer in 1882 both by questioning his father's faith and for implying that his 'System of Synthetic Philosophy' owed unacknowledged debts to George Spencer. Spencer's responses to Mozley are dealt with in the *Autobiography*, particularly in Vol. 1, pp. 549–56. There is no evidence of anything approaching plagiarism (see Lamar, 1953). Both sets of *Reminiscences* contain material on George Spencer. Mozley was also taught mathematics by Thomas Spencer in 1827 (see Mozley, 1885, vol. 2: pp. 174–85).
4. J. E. Bicheno's chief publication (*An Inquiry into the Poor Laws, Chiefly with a View to Examine them as a Scheme of National Benevolence and to Elucidate their Political Economy* of 1824 – a revision of an earlier version of 1817) has some similarity with Spencer's early writing. For Bicheno, 'political science' shows that 'the social polity is the result of wise and immutable laws bearing the stamp of omniscience; that these laws may be assisted, but cannot be contravened; and that they are to be discovered by the study of mankind, under all climes' (1824: p. 75). In species of animals we see that the 'constant struggle for subsistence' (1824: p. 101) improves 'faculties', and this principle applies throughout mankind: 'man, being an animal endowed by the Creator with a larger capacity and a more improveable nature than any other, is benefited by this struggle for subsistence in a far greater degree than the rest; his moral powers being also developed, and the spring of civilization and refinement set in motion' (1824: p. 114). Bicheno also served on the Royal Commission on the poor in Ireland which Whately chaired.
5. On Whately see also Akenson (1981), McKerrow (1981) and Rashid (1977). Whately had held the Drummond Chair in political economy at Oxford until his move to Ireland in 1831 as Church of Ireland Archbishop of Dublin. A leading Oriel Noetic or 'reasoner' he contributed prolifically to Christian political economics. Whately did much to develop the study of economics in Ireland.
6. 'Library catalogues', Lyon notes, 'indicate that a number of them were reprinted between ten and 28 times, resulting in between 10,000 and 28,000 copies. Few other polemicists could match such a prodigious impact' (1999: p. 157). Anna Spencer on occasion also wrote, in her case on local history matters (1844).

7. Vidler (1961: p. 90) points to other clergymen in Thomas Spencer's position on the corn law.

8. References to Lamarck and Lamarckianism in this study concern Spencer's own interpretation of Lamarck's claims. For recent reassessments of Lamarck's science see Corsi (1988b) and Burkhardt (1995).

9. On phrenology in general see Van Wyhe (2004). Combe's phrenology and Spencer is discussed in Chapter 4.

10. Francis couples his own misleading analysis with the unnecessary comment that his analysis of Spencer's early political thought, as at odds with David Weinstein's in fact mostly conventional reading (1998), is not an analysis 'of a kind that an American such as Weinstein would feel comfortable with' (2007: p. 398).

11. As portrayed in *Crotchet Castle*, Chapter 2.

12. The quotation included is from John Morley's *Life of Richard Cobden* (1881: p. 142).

13. Persons of course belong to and comprise communities and societies; so it is difficult to read Spencer here as committed to the kind of contrast which Francis has suggested in his study: 'The young Spencer was certain that the community – not the individual – possessed moral standing' (2007: p. 263). Francis omits Spencer's last sentence from his own quotation from Spencer.

14. Spencer noted his inability to decide whether legislative restrictions on traffic in shares was desirable (1904, i: p. 290).

15. As translated by Marian Evans.

16. 'At what time was formed the resolution to set forth my views on political ethics, is uncertain; but during those early months of 1846, I commenced a course of reading in furtherance of my project' (1904, i: p. 304).

17. In the process he encountered Isambard Kingdom Brunel who was apparently angered by the implied challenge to his estimate of costs for the line. In the *Autobiography* Spencer catalogued what to his mind were some of Brunel's professional misjudgements and a failure to give credit to one of his engineering colleagues, Hughes, who, for his work on bridge foundations in deep water which had led to the award of the Telford medal, had made an invaluable contribution to permitting as a possibility Brunel's celebrated Saltash Bridge over the River Tamar: for having done 'much work which had to be undone, wasted many millions of national capital, and entailed great losses upon multitudes of citizens, Mr. Brunel was knighted and is commemorated by a statue on the Thames Embankment' (1904, i: p. 328).

18. Not the same James Wilson associated with *The Pilot*. On the *Economist* see Ruth Dudley Edwards, *The Pursuit of Reason: The Economist 1843–1893*, 1995.

19. The question of Spencer's intellectual indebtedness to Hodgskin was raised by Elie Halévy (1903). It is clear that Spencer visited Hodgskin at home and consulted his collection of books, but nothing more substantial emerged in A. E. Taylor's investigation (1955). Francis quotes from and discusses a letter from Spencer to Hodgskin of April, 1855, which suggests that Hodgskin may have helped confirm Spencer in his drift away from accepting the rigid categories of the 'faculty' psychology of the phrenologists (2007: p. 175).

20. On Comte and Spencer's choice of the expression see Eisen (1967: p. 229).

21. Milne-Edwards was already well-established in French biological circles as a result of his research into comparative physiology. So far as I can ascertain no English translation of his work was published before 1856. Spencer also recalled that it was 'a little book just published' (in Duncan, 1911: p. 542). It is thus probable

the book Lewes had brought with him was the one issued in 1851 in Paris by the publisher Masson, *Introduction à la zoologie générale, ou, Considérations sur les tendances de la nature dans la constitution du regne animal.*

22. The widespread confusion afflicting the date of origination of 'survival of the fittest' is discussed in Paul (1988).

23. Nor is the opportunity spurned for a libertarian jibe at public expressions *versus* actual developments in France: 'Whatever it maybe in theory, it is clear that in practice the French idea of liberty is – the right of every man to be master of the rest' (1852b: p. 343). On the phrenological psychology underpinning the essay see Denton (1921).

24. Von Baer (1828/1837). On the influence of Von Baer see Ospovat (1976).

25. Notably Francis (2007). A discussion of Eliot's responses in her fiction to Spencer's ideas as well as of their personal connections is available in Paxton (1991).

26. Although Spencer revised his individual essays when they were later collected together for publication in book form, the references here to evolution all date from the original *Westminster Review* version.

2   Middle Spencer: Towards a Tapestry of the World

1. Thompson himself was using words taken from the *Life of Goethe* by Lewes, whom he describes as Spencer's 'closest friend'.

2. When this essay was later republished Spencer added a note at this point explaining that the sentence was 'written before the publication of the *Origin of Species*. I leave it standing because it shows the stage of thought then arrived at'.

3. In 1893, Sir William Flower invited Spencer to join the committee to arrange a memorial to Owen. Although he did on further reflection agree to join the committee, his first reaction was to refuse, to which effect he replied in blunt terms to Flower: 'large though Owen's claims may be in the way of achievement, he lacked a trait which I think essential – he was not sincere. He did not say out candidly what he believed, but tried to please both parties, the scientific world and the religious world. This is not my impression only, but that, I believe, of many' (in Duncan, 1911: p. 325).

4. The reference to 'sociology' at 1857b, 102, is one of his earliest, and the acceptance of 'direct metamorphosis' in social life was novel for Spencer and seldom discussed later, though the point does reappear in the first volume of the *Sociology* (1893: pp. 471–2). One may presume that he came to see that giving prominence to the idea might be perceived as lending support to 'artificial' remodellings of society, undermining the *echt* Spencer postulate that societies were growths, not manufactures.

5. Colonel J. Jacob was the editor of the *Record Book of the Scinde Irregular Horse*, London, 1856. Pelly edited *The Views and Opinions of Brigadier-General John Jacob*, London, Smith Elder, 1858.

6. Some years after publication, Spencer recalled, 'the Rev. Canon Lyttelton applied to me for permission to republish it in a pamphlet along with a sermon of his own on the same subject – a permission which I cheerfully gave. That an ecclesiastic should take a step which coupled his name with mine, curiously exemplified the spread of liberality in religious opinion' (1904, ii: p. 30).

7. François Guizot, 1787–1874, was a French historian and politician, committed to liberty, toleration and the Crown, and steering a course between popular government and absolutism. He was well-connected in England, and briefly prime

minister of France from 1847 to 1848. The book to which Spencer refers was published in 1822, and translated into English in 1852. Spencer's essay concludes with a fanfare for the 'latest developed legislative bodies', which recognize that laws, and representation, must average the interests of various classes: thus they allow 'to each class as much as consists with the claims of the rest' (1860a: p. 303).

8. Hilton discusses Maconochie on the 'mark' system of prison reform and moral regeneration in the context of the politics of atonement, noting that the post-millenialist evangelical Thomas Chalmers congratulated Maconochie, and that Whately's scheme of prison reform had much in common with that of Maconochie (1988: p. 217). Maconochie published *Crime and Punishment* in 1846 and directed the new prison at Winson Green in Birmingham from 1849, but encountered political opposition, bringing his career to an end. On Maconochie's work and ideas see John Gascoigne (2002: pp. 139–45).

9. On Spencer on education see Low-Beer, 1969.

10. Raby remarks (2001: p. 91) that the 'broad evolutionary flow of Spencer's arguments, and their application to social issues, seeped into Wallace's thinking'.

11. Progress is though an incidental concern of the *Origin*. The penultimate paragraph concludes; 'as natural selection works solely by and for the good of each being, all corporeal and mental endowments will tend to progress towards perfection' (Darwin, 1968: p. 459. See Dickens, 2000: p. 12 for a brief account of Darwin's own reflections on the direction of change).

12. William Flower, the Museum's Conservator, later knighted, was helped in his own career by Huxley. In 1844, Flower had been sent to the school in Worksop run by Heldenmaier, known to both Spencer and his father. Baden Powell was Flower's wife's brother-in-law.

13. In *Transactions of the Linnaean Society*, Vol. 25, and Spencer (1894: pp. 536–66).

14. Mill objected to the word 'necessarily', and saw Bentham as entertaining the deduction of 'the effect of action on happiness from the laws of human nature and the universal conditions of human life'. Mill regards the consilience of the results of deductions *and* generalizations from specific experiences, 'each corroborating and verifying the other', as requisite 'to give any general proposition the kind and degree of evidence which constitutes scientific proof' (1961: p. 257).

15. 'That division of Biology which concerns itself with the origin of species', Spencer insists, 'I hold to be the supreme division, to which all others are subsidiary. For on the verdict of biology on this matter, must wholly depend our conception of human nature, past, present, and future; our theory of the mind; and our theory of society (1864: p. 131).

16. A major problem in assessing Spencer's debt to Comte is that he had indeed not studied him carefully, as a consequence, Spencer on a few occasions found differences where concord was more evident (see Eisen, 1967 and Greene, 1959). A recent study of Comte (Gane, 2006) offers no evidence of hitherto unsuspected elements in Comte of influence on Spencer which would confirm Taylor's belief that Comte was the 'primary model' (2007: p. 43) for Spencer's 'System', tending rather to confirm in particular the independence of Spencer's sociology (2006: pp. 31–2). Relations between Comte and Spencer are briefly discussed in Mary Pickering's intellectual biography of Comte (2009: pp. 484–86).

17. He reported the Club's inauguration to his father on 7 November: 'In pursuance of a long-suspended intention, a few of the most advanced men of science have united to form a small club to dine together occasionally. It consists of Huxley, Tyndall, Hooker, Lubbock, Frankland, Busk, Hirst, and myself. Two more will

possibly be admitted. But the number will be limited to 10. Our first dinner was on last Thursday; and the first Thursday of every month will be the day for subsequent meetings' (1904, ii: p. 115). William Spottiswoode was added shortly after, but no tenth person was ever agreed upon.

18. His period of holiday had encompassed a stay with Masson and his family in the Vale of Yarrow, near Selkirk, a visit to Glenelg for fishing and rambling, three weeks with the Smiths at Ardtornish 'to have another of those interludes in my life which have formed its chief enjoyment' (1904, ii: p. 159), a week in Scarborough after a journey south east, a fruitless search for information on ancestors in Stourbridge, and to end with 'one of my pleasant sojourns' (1904, ii: p. 162) with the Potters at Standish.

19. Spencer also visited Ireland, and grumbled presumably to Youmans: 'I spent three days in Dublin, which has things in it worth looking at. But I found the living bad – slovenly and dirty . . . . Belfast I found worse than Dublin – the most stinking place I was ever in, indoors and out; and I was glad to get away as quickly as possible' (in Duncan, 1911: p. 146).

20. Huxley, Tyndall and Spencer formed a committee to select books for the series (see Howsam, 2000).

21. In a Postscript, Spencer deals with the case of the state-run Post Office, the success of which he sees as equally possible without being run by the state, which as a matter of history came close to being the case. Indeed, much of its success is down to the efficiency of the privately owned agencies which transport the mail. While he does not contend there would be an advantage in replacing public administration in this case, he does suggest that, 'but for State-repression, we should have obtained a postal organization like our present one generations ago!' (1871a: p. 442).

22. Cazelles, having abandoned a career in medicine for the translation of 'philosophical' works by Bentham, Mill and Bain as well as Spencer, was at this time also commencing a career in political administration in southern France. Spencer described him as 'my first and chief French translator' (1904, ii: p. 312).

23. In 1872, Spencer also had his portrait completed by J. B. Burgess, whom he had selected following Mr. Appleton's request for one.

3   Later Spencer: Crafting the *Principles of Sociology*, and Losing Hold

1. Another quite different sign of recognition at this time came with the Minister of Japan to the United States, Mr. Arinori Mori, asking for his opinion about the reorganization of Japanese institutions (Duncan, 1911: p. 161).

2. With the death of Octavius Smith in 1871, not long before, he had already lost an 'admired and valued friend', leaving 'a gap impossible to be filled up' (1904, ii: pp. 229, 230).

3. The data were themselves eventually systematically published in volumes with the generic title, *Descriptive Sociology*.

4. In a note he disclaims teleology associated with his account in *Social Statics*.

5. However, Spencer's points about 'evolution' should not be taken as definitive in relation to his own general practice.

6. Though Spencer expressed reservations about 'cause' in this context. See his letter to A. W. Benn, in Duncan (1911: p. 402).

7. Though later in the same essay (1873a: p. 307) Spencer names the author as John Fletcher Moulton, a Cambridge mathematician, and later a barrister and judge.

8. The controversy was protracted – Spencer fanned the flames by issuing his response to Moulton as a pamphlet early in 1874 – and it 'raged in the correspondence columns of the journal *Nature* from March to June, 1874' (Harman, 2001: p. 188).

9. It showed original tonal variety and distinction in its use of instruments, which in turn yielded 'more marked kinds of effects, each having its distinctive character, and all of them together constituting a more heterogeneous whole' (1904, ii: p. 299).

10. This is the date Spencer gives (1904, ii: p. 299). But an incomplete version appeared in the previous December (Spencer actually gives December, 1873, but this cannot be correct). The missing material in 1876 was from 'Domestic Institutions' (see Carneiro and Perrin, 2002: p. 246).

11. On the same day, Lord Derby (Edward Henry Stanley), who had resigned the previous year as Tory Foreign Secretary, and joined Gladstone's Liberal government in 1882, wrote that he was 'glad to have the opportunity ... of expressing personally to Mr. Spencer his sense of the intellectual obligation under which he lies to a writer whose thoughts he has for many years endeavoured to understand and follow. It is neither his wish nor his right to pay compliments; but he may be allowed to acknowledge a debt' (in Duncan, 1911: p. 199). A year later Spencer met with Lord Derby with hopes that he would found a chair in sociology at the new college at Liverpool, but since he had settled on a chair in Natural History, Spencer's hopes were, he reported to Youmans, 'balked' (in Duncan, 1911: p. 211).

12. The Barnetts' legacy includes the Whitechapel Art Gallery and Toynbee Hall, and Barnett House in Oxford bears Samuel Barnett's name.

13. Other tasks at this time included lobbying to get copyright enforced and pirated editions prevented in America, furnishing the writer Grant Allen with materials for an article, giving advice to Richard Hodgson who wished to answer T. H. Green's criticisms of Spencer which had appeared in the *Contemporary Review*, and writing as well against Green himself (1881a).

14. One report records that since the establishment of the Section, 'nearly the whole of the works of "our great philosopher" have been considered and subjected to an exhaustive and searching exposition and criticism, in which most of those students in the town and neighbourhood actively interested in the spread of the doctrine of evolution have at times taken part; the proceedings whereof have been published from time to time in the Midland Naturalist' (Hughes, 1890: p. 20). W. R. Hughes was a key figure in the Birmingham Society and a friend of Spencer's. His daughter Edith Hughes was invited to stay with Spencer in St. Leonard's in 1894.

15. On the Liberty and Property Defence League, its members and Spencer's support see Mason (1974), Soldon (1974), and Taylor (1992).

16. Brooke gives no citation for this quotation from Spencer, and as far as I can ascertain it does not appear in either *The Man versus The State* or 'Ecclesiastical Institutions', the obvious publications matching the date of 1884 provided by Brooke.

17. The suppressed book did, though, resurface without permission, as *The Insuppressible Book*, published in Boston by Cassino (Duncan, 1911: p. 266).

18. Naden, Hughes recorded, had expressed her intention 'to act as Honorary Secretary to the proposed Society, and suggested that the preliminary meetings might be held in her drawing room; but for her untimely death [in 1889] there is no

doubt that she would have, with her usual energy and devotion to the cause of evolution, succeeded in carrying into effect the object suggested' (1890: p. 46).

19. Six months after Naden's death Spencer wrote to Robert Lewins, who was collaborating with Hughes on the *Memoir*: 'Very generally receptivity and originality are not associated, but in her they appear to have been equally great. I can tell you of no woman save George Eliot in whom there has been this union of high philosophical capacity with extensive acquisition...' (in Duncan, 1911: p. 296).

20. Herbert lived at Old House in the New Forest. Here he occasionally entertained and went riding with Beatrice Potter whom he had met through Spencer – marked political differences did not prevent warmth, but a projected joint novel, *Looking Forward*, came to nothing.

21. Spencer by now had become well-acquainted with the Canadian-born science writer and general author Grant Allen. Spencer sent Allen an early version of the 'From Freedom' essay. In a letter to him Spencer wrote: 'I hear that you have turned socialist. I hoped, when I heard of it from Miss Potter, that there might be some mistake; but a verification reached me a day or two ago under the form of a statement that you have been lecturing on the subject.

     If you have, I suppose it is useless to say anything; for my experience is that when definite views have once been taken, the probability of change is very small. Nevertheless, I send something in the shape of an antidote. It is to be an introduction to a forthcoming volume of essays. Of course, you will not let it pass out of your hands' (quoted in Allen, 1904: p. 626).

22. In June 1891, there had come a surprise yielding up pure joy. A grand piano had arrived, a gift from Carnegie. In thanking him he theorized about the distribution of wealth: 'I have all along sympathized in your view respecting the uses of wealth, but it never occurred to me that I should benefit by the carrying of your view into practice.... what an immensity of satisfaction of a high kind is obtained by its distribution during life, as compared with the pleasure of one who heaps up and bequeaths. You are much to be envied...' (in Duncan, 1911: p. 305).

23. A year further on, though, and Spencer was sounding much less sanguine, confiding to Lord Wemyss (prominent in the Liberty and Property Defence League and other Individualist associations) his disillusionment with the 'dull, bovine unintelligence' of the 'stupid English public', who behave as if railway companies and manufacturers 'have a right to make noises of any degree of loudness, with any degree of frequency, at whatever times they please'. They do not, they will not, make a fuss and demand their right not to submit to an 'enormous evil' of 'daily aggressions' (in Duncan, 1911: p. 314).

24. See Spencer (1897: pp. 125–8) for a published sample.

25. As others have shown, Spencer's ideas themselves were available in Japanese from the 1870s, and widely discussed, along with Mill's *On Liberty* (Nagai, 1954; Howland, 2000).

26. Sidney Webb had now been married to Beatrice Potter since 1892.

27. An attempt, however, by Spencer to show that he had been misunderstood by the Italian writer and socialist, Enrico Ferri, was neatly turned back on him by Ferri: 'No socialist has ever dreamt to include among the supporters of Socialism the greatest living philosopher.... But it is necessary to distinguish between the personal opinions of H. Spencer and the logical outcome of the positive theory of universal evolution, which he has developed better than any other writer, without however obtaining an official patent against the unrestricted expansion

which is daily given to that theory by the work of other thinkers' (in Duncan, 1911: p. 368).

28. Tönnies Papers, Schleswig-Holsteinische Landesbibliothek, Kiel. It appears to have been written on receipt of a copy of Tönnies's article on Spencer on sociology of 1889.

29. Another earlier attempt to secure a portrait, this time by G. F. Watts, was stillborn (Spencer's lack of admiration for Watts was reciprocated by the artist: to W. S. Blunt, Watts described Spencer as 'wholly selfish').

30. The portrait is now held by the National Galleries of Scotland.

31. 'The pedantic may sneer at the trivialities of this book and the unsympathetic may scoff at our weakness, but we cannot let the personal reputation of the man we learned to know and admire and reverence go down to posterity tarnished with the suspicion of meanness, pettiness and vulgarity that most of the stories that are told about him suggest' ('Two', 1910: pp. 8–9).

32. Spencer's *Autobiography* records that in 1881 he had read Black's *A Daughter of Heth* and *White Wings* while staying on the west coast of Scotland and where the novels were set (1904, ii: p. 360).

33. Dr. B. Vetter, Spencer's main German translator, had died early in 1893, but Spencer was fortunate to have the Leipzig zoologist Professor Victor Carus, who had already translated Darwin, take his place.

34. West Sussex Record Office, Chichester, Blunt Mss, Box 55.

35. Spencer's funeral was described, accompanied by photographs, in Rhys, 1904.

36. Shyamaji Krishnavarma testified briefly to 'the great debt owed by the philosophical students of his native country to Herbert Spencer's works and influence' (Rhys, 1904: p. 174). Krishnavarma had been educated at Balliol College, and had responded with enthusiasm to Spencer's work. He was championing the cause of Indian Independence in England and shortly to begin publication of the monthly *The Indian Sociologist* to further that aim.

37. On 9 December, Francis Galton wrote to *The Times*: 'While conversing with him I had frequent occasion to admire the easy precision with which he dealt in generalizations; there was neither vagueness nor change in the sense in which he used them. I concluded from this that observations from which those generalizations were deduced were habitually present to his mind in large number, consciously or unconsciously, at the moment of speaking'. Spencer's trustworthiness in generalization was thus 'much enhanced'.

38. 'Herbert Spencer dead', *New York Times*, 9 December 1903.

4 Evolution and Mind

1. It will be helpful at this point to expand upon this kind of guide to Spencer by recording that the 1892 edition of *Social Statics* is indeed as he described it an abridged and revised version, abridged and revised in a general sense to be compatible with the theory on evolution, the full illustration of which was by then nearly completed, and in a detailed sense to incorporate changes of analysis in such respects as his views on the status of women. It should be noted too that the first edition of the *Principles of Psychology* pre-dated *First Principles*, and that the first edition of *First Principles* was recast and extended in the second edition, with further changes up to the sixth and final edition of 1900. I have tried to indicate throughout this book where significant variations in Spencer's ideas between the

editions of all of his publications may be noted, a matter on which rather more commentators on Spencer have been negligent than one might have expected.

2. The word 'evolution' was *not* 'added in' at the later date when Spencer revised the article for inclusion in his *Essays*.

3. On Chambers see Secord, 2000.

4. In 1831, Whately's interest in phrenology led to a 'personal acquaintance' with Combe, and Combe made a phrenological analysis of a cast of Whately's head (Gibbon, 1878, i: pp. 264–76, p. 264).

5. Sources variously identify 1827 and 1828 as the date of first publication of *The Constitution of Man*. Combe himself gave 9 June 1828 in the sixth edition of 1845. Spencer makes no mention of Combe, but the broad contents of *The Constitution of Man* are highly likely to have been familiar to him. Young notes that there is 'no evidence that Spencer read it' (1970: p. 158).

6. While grappling with Hamilton's Scottish metaphysics, Spencer was approached for a testimonial by Alexander Campbell Fraser in 1856, then a candidate to succeed to Hamilton's Edinburgh chair (in which ambition he was successful). Spencer had not then read anything by Fraser. In the *Autobiography* he recorded, 'I thought I might be able to read as much as was requisite, and I did so; but the result was a break-down, and an undoing of what good had been done during some previous months' (1904, i: p. 483).

7. It may be added that C.U.M. Smith has drawn a comparison between Spencer and Martin Heidegger (1983: pp. 9–11).

8. Malcolm Guthrie, in three philosophically astute books (1879, 1882 and 1884), found the logic of the cosmic philosophy unpersuasive. In 1884, he considered that when carefully examined it proved to be 'constructed of terms which had no fixed and definite meaning, which were in fact merely symbols of symbolic conceptions, conceptions themselves symbolic because they were not understood – and the moment we begin to put them to use as having definite values they landed us forthwith in alternative contradictions!' (1884: p. vii). What at first sight seemed grand and alluring 'will not stand the ordinary handling of scientific language and logical statement as between man and man' (1884: p. ix). Spencer regarded Guthrie's criticisms as 'formidable if measured by bulk' (1904, ii: p. 358).

9. Tait, in *Nature*, July 17.

10. Sir Peter Medawar (1969) provides a succinct discussion of some of the problems in Spencer on 'evolution' and 'force' from the point of view of modern science.

11. The eulogy is contained in Duncan (1911: pp. 478–81). On Spencer's cremation see the previous chapter.

12. As it happens I do not think Haines makes the case out convincingly against Peel and Freeman. Neither author seems to me to interpret Spencer as confused over the process and causes of change.

13. It should be noted, though, that the passage quoted earlier from Spencer's essay 'The Americans' (1883) might well appear to lend *some* limited support to Haines's position.

14. On this important point of contrast between the logic of the positions of Darwin and Spencer see Alland (1974), responding to Carneiro (1973).

15. It may be desirable, to avoid any risk of confusion, to indicate that the making of this point should *not* be taken as an endorsement of a judgement such as that offered by Andreski, eccentric even at the time, that Spencer's theory of social evolution is 'one of the most securely based generalisations of sociology' (1964: p. 73).

5 Mind and Society

1. On Mivart see Gruber (1961), Richards (1987: pp. 353–63), and Rylance (2000: pp. 235–9). Mivart's religious beliefs and interest in metaphysics led him to publish articles which criticized Darwin and Spencer over what he regarded as the special status of man as a knowing and moral being. *On the Genesis of Species* of 1871 is his best-known book. Nature could not have 'accidentally' produced man. It was Mivart whom Samuel Butler noted had written: 'With regard to the conception as now put forward by Mr. Darwin, I cannot truly characterize it but by an epithet which I employ only with much reluctance. I weigh my words and have present to my mind the many distinguished naturalists who have accepted the notion, and yet I cannot hesitate to call it a *"puerile hypothesis"* ' (in Butler, 1911: p. 371, first edition 1879).
2. Cairnes held chairs in Political Economy at Dublin, Galway and University College London. Cairnes's criticisms of Spencer were very quickly made available in America in the *Popular Science Monthly*, for March, 1875. In 'From the Editor's Table' (pp. 616–20), written presumably by Spencer's supporter and firefighter, Youmans, Cairnes's comments were confronted by a litany of points made by Spencer not noted by Cairnes. Yet Youmans, if it was he, left matters more blurred than clarified.
3. To Cairnes the problem Spencer presented was his inadequate idea of 'human nature'. Much later the philosopher Peter Winch noted that what we can ascribe 'to human nature does not determine what we can and cannot make sense of; rather what we can and what we cannot make sense of determines what we can ascribe to human nature. It is indeed for precisely this reason that the concept of human nature is not the concept of something fixed and given; i.e. the reason for this is a philosophical, not a sociological one' (1971: p. 10).
4. For a brief summary of Spalding's work see Richards (1987: pp. 387–8). Bain's *The Emotions and The Will* was published in 1859.
5. It is not, therefore, unreasonable to see Spencer both as 'the founder of modern neurology' (Riese, 1959: p. 199, quoted in Young, 1970: p. 198) and as a highly significant influence on new physiological thought, given David Ferrier's own expressions holding Jackson's advances in high regard (see Young, 1970: pp. 197–200 and pp. 235–7).
6. Indeed Perrin suggests that Durkheim is 'too often' ascribed the status of 'a faithful expositor of Spencer's views' (1995: p. 341; see also Perrin, 1976).
7. See also Seidman (1983: p. 284).
8. In contrast with the one-way traffic control of the *conscience commune* present in the societies displaying mechanical solidarity.
9. On the range of distinctions which Durkheim's use of 'individual' and 'social' tended to conflate see Lukes (1971: p. 329).
10. It should be noted that Spencer later introduced the concept of a 'pro-altruistic sentiment of justice' which comes into play 'before there is any social organization' (1910, ii: pp. 29–30). This is discussed later in Chapter 9.
11. Taylor misleadingly represents Spencer as meaning by 'super-organic' merely 'aggregates of individuals' (2007: p. 95).
12. See also p. 50 for a further reference to 'survival of the fittest'.
13. It may be noted that Spencer is critical of J. F. McLennan's *Primitive Marriage* of 1865, which he interprets as overstating the arguments for early exogamous practices.

14. Spencer also discusses Sir John Lubbock's *Origin of Civilization* on property, but suggests it is possible that ownership of property (such as weapons) predated rather than followed that of women.

15. This passage, which inaugurates 'Ceremonial Institutions', with its highlighting of a world of mundane yet universal communication, had sufficient resonance for Erving Goffman to prompt him to place it at the very start of his essays in 'microstudies of the public order', *Relations in Public*, published in 1971.

16. This topic also figures in 'Addenda' at the conclusion of the whole section, in which Spencer includes a riposte to E. B. Tylor (Spencer refers to Tylor's *Primitive Culture* and *Researches in to the Early History of Mankind*). Spencer had interpreted mutilations as acts of propitiation leaving signs of allegiance and subordination that in due course came to be seen as decorative. Tylor regarded Spencer's method in anthropological research as the speculative deduction of customs from unproven 'laws of nature', and preferred to interpret mutilations as, when not purely decorative, a means of keeping records. Spencer in turn simply questions the breadth of evidence on which Tylor's 'inductive' claim is made.

17. These matters are discussed further in Chapter 7 since they bear closely on Spencer's discussion of the characteristics of his well-known contrast between 'militant' and 'industrial' types of society.

18. In January, 1886, Sidgwick was reading 'Political Institutions' and thought 'much more highly of it now that I come back to it after reading other, especially German books. He is, as always, over-confident in generalisation, but it is a more vigorous and useful essay towards the construction of scientific sociology; I do not know anything as good' (in Carneiro and Perrin, 2000: p. 251).

19. Spencer illustrates the division of labour with references to the growth in the diversity of tasks during his lifetime in the Midland Railway workshops of his home town, Derby.

20. This observation prompted in Spencer a significant wider reflection on social evolution as a process whereby what has come to be seen as 'constructed', 'contrived' or 'symbolic' was once the unconsciously real: 'Erroneous interpretations of social phenomena are often caused by carrying back modern ideas into ancient times, and supposing that motives which might then have prompted us to do certain things were the motives which prompted uncivilized or semi-civilized men to do them. One example occurs in the usual belief that the symbols which everywhere meet us in the accounts of men's usages, were consciously chosen – that symbols originated as symbols. But in all cases they were the rudiments of things that were once in actual use' (1896b: p. 440).

6   The Social Organism

1. Spencer does not discuss the interesting case of John of Salisbury's *Policraticus* in the twelfth century (see Nederman, 1987, John of Salisbury, 1990).

2. Spencer notes, though, that for some lower animals such sensitiveness can exist in all parts, and further that the members of a society vary in 'feeling': 'The classes engaged in laborious occupations are less susceptible, intellectually and emotionally, than the rest; and especially less so than the classes of highest mental culture' (1860a: p. 276).

3. Spencer quotes approvingly Liebeg's remark in *Familiar Letters on Chemistry* that 'Silver and gold have to perform in the organism of the state, the same function as the blood-corpuscles in the human organism' (in 1860a: p. 293).

4. A good parliament 'is one in which the parties answering to these respective interests are so balanced, that their united legislation allows to each class as much as consists with the claims of the rest' (1860a: p. 303).

5. Spencer concludes by admitting that he has not discussed what he calls the 'different types of social organization', or 'social metamorphoses'. If by this he means as seems probable a reference to the distinction between 'militant' and 'industrial' 'types of society' and change from one to the other, these issues were pursued subsequently in *First Principles* and the *Principles of Sociology*.

6. In the 1870s, Huxley moved to circumvent such difficulties of description through introducing the concepts of zooids and metamerism.

7. As noted in Chapter 2.

8. In his retrospective essay, 'The Filiation of Ideas', written in 1899, Spencer judged that in this rejoinder to Huxley he emphasized more than before 'the truth that from the beginning war has been the cause of the development of centralized governmental structures, which become coercive in proportion as war is the dominant social activity; while growth of that decentralized co-operation characterizing sustaining structures, becomes more marked as war ceases to be chronic; a corollary being that social types are essentially distinguished by the proportion between the militant structures and the industrial structures, and undergo metamorphoses according to the growth or decline of either order of activity' (in Duncan, 1911: p. 568). This aspect is considered further in the next Chapter.

9. Spencer also refers to these interests as 'altruism'. Together, 'egoistic' and 'altruistic' feelings are powers which 'amply suffice to originate and carry on all the activities which constitute healthy national life' (1871a: p. 437). Spencer points to altruistic institutions in the fields of medicine, and in education, founded to teach rich and poor, and now already encouraging science.

10. Whately described economics as 'catallactics' but Spencer, as far as I can ascertain, uses neither 'catallaxy' nor 'catallactics', though he is referring to what 'catallaxy' denotes. On Whately and economics see Rashid, 1977. On Whately, Mises and Hayek, and the distinction between 'sociologics' and 'catallactics' see Zafirovski, 2003.

11. As Chapter 7 discusses, this situation can at best pertain to a small degree in a society where 'militant' social forms predominate.

12. On this reading, it should be noted that Walter Simon was at least partly unfair to Spencer when he alleged and reflected upon a tendency in Spencer to write 'indifferently of "society" and "a society". Now' Simon continued, 'we may grant, for the sake of argument, that human society as a whole, or mankind, is an organism, and that various parts of it, also confusingly called societies, may likewise be organisms. But Spencer, who scorned the study of history, tacitly equated the highly unnatural units called states with the natural organisms or species called societies which carried on, at its highest level, the universal struggle for existence' (1960: p. 162).

13. It should be noted too that Spencer also regarded structures and functions, and men's physical make-up, as themselves subject to adaptation to 'external' factors as well.

14. According to Ingold, the British anthropologist Radcliffe-Brown stressed this aspect of organismic thought: 'The analogy is not between organism and society as things, but between organic life and social life considered as movements' (1986: p. 154).

15. See especially 'Concluding Reflections' below.

16. Spencer was indeed searching for 'a universal grammar for sociology' (Peel, 1971: p. 191).
17. Burrow noted in this kind of context that individuals are seen by Spencer as sources of 'facts from which facts about social institutions will be derivative' (1966: p. 200).
18. For Spencer, the 'class-bias' 'warps working-men's judgments of social relations – makes it difficult for working-men to see that our existing industrial system is a product of existing human nature, and can be improved only as fast as human nature improves' (1873b: p. 254: Spencer's reference here to 'social relations' as a concept deserves to be noted).
19. There is a connection here to Roland Wilson's *Province of the State*. Although Wilson shared substantial political ground with Spencer he was critical of the social organism conception since individuals often belonged to more than one society, and shared interests across societies could trump the ties of geographical propinquity (1911: pp. 223–4).
20. Bosanquet later went on to add, largely ignoring the way Spencer had argued for what he understood by the 'social organism', that 'human society corresponds in many of its features rather to a local variety of a species than to an individual organism'. He notes, though, that Spencer 'does not really mean that a human society has no more intrinsic bond between its members than the local group of an animal species'. To indicate its 'true nature', Bosanquet observes, he gives us 'a good word' – but a word only – the word 'super-organic'. Bosanquet spends no time examining Spencer on 'social self-consciousness' or co-operation, instead announcing peremptorily that the word brings us to the limit of what 'biological sociology is able to suggest with regard to the unity of a human commonwealth, and points us to something beyond' (1920: p. 24).
21. Charles Loch too, Secretary of the Charity Organisation Society, largely shared this hostility.
22. Hetherington wrote of Jones that he considered Spencer could not capture the fact that 'the relation of parts to the whole in a social, which is a spiritual, unity has an intensity and concreteness unattainable by any merely physical organism...man is all through an ethical being, aware of a good, and set upon its realization' (1924: p. 28). Jones also 'kicked out' in a lecture at Herbert Spencer (Hetherington, 1924: p. 105).
23. In Taylor's view, Wordsworth Donisthorpe, in general sympathy with Spencer's views, 'completely misunderstood the nature of the analogy which Spencer drew' in his study, *Individualism: A System of Politics*, of 1889 (Taylor, 1992: p. 151).
24. Wiltshire further comments that the added attempt by Spencer to point to inner and outer contrasts in the tasks for government in the social organism is deficient in clarity – what, after all, of import and export relations? As expressed by Spencer, this may be so, but Spencer could have in addition pointed to the need to protect the security of the organism in such transactions.
25. Certainly this was not a view that gripped Spencer, since *The Study of Sociology* and all three volumes of the *Principles of Sociology* at this point remained in the future.

7   Militant and Industrial Social Types

1. The first volume of the *Sociology* first appeared in December, 1876 (although the relevant instalments had been issued to subscribers during 1875 and 1876).

2. In England, the Local Government Board's increasingly centralized regulation of the poor law practices of local guardians illustrates according to Spencer this type of change in process (1893: p. 571).

3. In comparing the two types from a more structural point of view, Spencer again finds that the industrial type of society, 'with its decentralized structures, is the highest, because it is the one which most subserves that happiness of the units which is to be achieved by social organization, as distinguished from that happiness of the aggregate which is to be achieved by individual organization with its centralized structures' (1893: p. 588).

4. The identical passage occurs in the first edition of 1876 at pp. 595–6, except for the first 'inversion of' being rendered as 'inverting'.

5. With reference in particular to modern times, Spencer declares the situation to be less that 'a social life passed in peaceful occupations is positively moralizing, as that a social life passed in war is positively demoralizing' (1891c: p. 640).

6. It is tempting to speculate at this point that the Whately of the *Introductory Lectures* was alive in Spencer's psyche: 'War, which, if Christianity were heartily and generally embraced, would be wholly unknown, has been, even as it is, much mitigated by that humanizing influence. Now War is, in the present day, generally regarded, though to a far less degree than it really is, as a great destroyer of wealth. But the direct demoralizing effect of War is probably still greater than its impoverishing effect. The same may be said of Slavery' (Whately, 1832: Lecture 8).

7. While Spencer did not accept in full the views of Maine on patriarchy as the earliest form of family, he admitted that Maine prompted him to become aware of a lacuna: 'reflection made it clear that intrinsically as well as extrinsically, the traits of its family-life form an important group in the traits presented by each society; and that a great omission had been made in ignoring them' (1904, ii: p. 289; see also Duncan, 1911: pp. 188–9).

8. A kind of fulfilment which but partially has a parallel with beneficence as present in the conduct of wider social life.

9. Rules of behaviour, Spencer thus insists, are 'natural products of social life which have gradually evolved' (1891c: p. 211), not conventions at some time deliberately made. In time the untruthfulness which has been associated with militancy declines, confronted by a spreading resentment at dishonest obeisance. The discipline that has been involved in militancy nevertheless has served as the formative process 'by which men are adapted to a higher social life', educating 'the anti-social nature into a form fitted for social life' (1891c: p. 221).

10. It was Spencer's analysis of the growth of militancy in social life at this time that probably prompted the idealist-influenced Ernest Barker's remark that the 'social organism will, as it were, constantly insist on coming to *life*, and being a living substance, and Spencer has to resort to far-fetched devices to kill it again, in order to assert a mechanical conception of the state as a compound of physical units' (1915: p. 13).

11. As argued earlier in this study, logically considered, both Spencer's 'guidance' and the nature of its impact must be products determined by the mechanisms of psychological and social evolution, principally the inheritance of acquired characteristics, acting in accord with the theory of *First Principles*.

12. Here, it may be noted, Spencer does not introduce any discussion of 'early' societies displaying voluntary co-operation and peaceful coexistence, in other words conforming to the industrial type, advanced by him, as noted earlier, in the *Principles of Sociology*.

13. Blunt Papers, West Sussex Record Office, Chichester.
14. Indeed, limiting the application of what can be described as 'evolved' to what is the 'perfect', is simply not, and did not need to be, Spencer's practice.
15. That Spencer himself sometimes failed to grasp that 'historical generalizations and ideal types are different things' is emphasized by Peel (1971: p. 192).
16. E. F. Paul correctly describes Spencer as regarding militancy and industrialism as at least in modern times 'commingled' in societies (1983: p. 539. Other aspects of Paul's article were commented on in Taylor, 1989, to which in turn Paul, 1989, replied).
17. On which see Spencer (1883) and Werth (2009).
18. To Spencer: 'The social man has not reached that harmonization of constitution with conditions forming the limit of evolution, so long as there remains space for the growth of faculties which, by their exercise, bring positive benefit to others and satisfaction to self. If the presence of fellow-men, while putting limits to each man's sphere of activity, opens certain other spheres of activity in which feelings while achieving their gratifications, do not diminish but add to the gratifications of others, then such spheres will inevitably be occupied' (1910, i: p. 147).
19. Not least of course in relation to his overarching framework of a Lamarckian mechanism as the engine of directional evolutionary change in social life.
20. Adopting Popper's term 'historicism' (as presented in his *The Poverty of Historicism*), Paul suggests that Spencer may be considered an 'historicist' (1983). Yet his highly individualized version of 'organicism' (discussed in Chapter 6) and the rejection here that his use of 'militant' and 'industrial' stood for separate and deterministic stages in the direction of social evolution weakens that case. On the other hand the physical, psychical and social adaptation to which individuals are subject, and their simultaneous 'output' into social life, all seem deterministic in nature, and thus 'historicist' in the spirit of Popper.
21. Spencer's explicit identification here of 'militant industrialism' clearly undermines Harris's criticism that he did not even make the 'cursory glance' towards actual European and American history of which she accused him.

8   Understanding Music

1. Principally Darwin (1871), Gurney (1876), Newman (1905), and Wallaschek (1891, 1893).
2. In the anonymous 'Some memories of Herbert Spencer' of 1904, written by 'One of a family whose friend he was', Spencer's participation in domestic music-making is recalled as a source of pleasure for all concerned. This short article refers to a family home in Yarrow, which suggests the author was a member of David Masson's family.
3. 'A week or so was passed at Andarroch, a farmhouse a few miles to the north of Dalry, and a short distance from the banks of the river. Spending leisure time, now in rambling over the moors, now in trying with one or other lure to tempt some salmon which were lying below the falls of the Ken, I spent the mornings in writing part of the essay on the "Origin and Function of Music" ' (1904, i: p. 507).
4. Pleasurable or painful 'feelings' mean that Carlo barks, puss purrs, lions roar and canaries chirp (1857c: p. 403).
5. Newman (1905) noted that Spencer's replies to Gurney's reservations were seldom convincing.
6. Wallaschek's article was very largely incorporated into Chapter 9 of Wallaschek (1893).

7. In Spencer's replies to Wallaschek (1891d) and Newman (1902: pp. 140–42) (Newman had earlier published some criticisms of Spencer in his *Aspects of Wagner*) Spencer made no attempt to protect his position beyond insisting that he was concerned with the *origins* of music, not the nature of developed music.

8. The first edition of Scholes's *Listener's History of Music* was published in 1923.

9. On this point see Ryle (1949: Ch. 4, and 1954: pp. 56–72 and 1971, ii: pp. 272–86).

10. See also Adorno, on Schoenberg (1967), Hatch and Watson (1974), and Schutz (1971: pp. 159–78).

11. Mellers applied formal analysis to Beatle songs, at a stroke violating the usual assumptions made by analysts about the reach of their operations. Indeed Mellers was clearly alert to this and to other sources of antipathy to his project: 'Some people seem to find it inherently risible that pop music should be discussed in technical terms at all; when the senior critic of The Times wrote the first musically literate piece about the Beatles it was greeted with hoots of mirth both from the Beatles themselves and from their hostile critics. This is curious, for there is no valid way of talking about the experiential 'effects' of music except by starting from an account of what actually happens in musical technique, the terminology for which has been evolved by professional musicians over some centuries' (1973: p. 15).

12. A passage retained in subsequent editions, and taken up from 1857a: p. 31. In the sixth edition of 1900 it appears on p. 329.

13. In the 1900 edition this passage is at pp. 298–9.

14. Arthur Schopenhauer had identified music, because of its ability to transcend the mundane, as the supreme form of art in his *The World as Will and Idea*.

15. A topic also raised earlier here, in Chapter 5. As sacerdotalism declines, ecclesiastical institutions will come to deal with 'matters concerning individual and social welfare', and a 'chief function of one who stands in the place of a minister, will be not so much that of emphasizing precepts already accepted, as that of developing men's judgments and sentiments in relation to those more difficult questions of conduct arising from the ever-increasing complexity of social life' (1896b: pp. 157–8).

16. See earlier, Chapter 3.

17. Further references to Parry's book are at pp. 42–3 and p. 177.

18. Two works chosen as especially satisfying by Spencer are Beethoven's Septet and Haydn's 'Seven Last Words'.

19. In fact the nature of opera and the logic of opera criticism are complex matters. The writings on opera of Wagner are key texts: for discussion see J. Stein's *Richard Wagner and the Synthesis of the Arts* (1973) and B. Magee's *Aspects of Wagner* (1972: Ch. 1). Wagner's thinking was influenced by Schopenhauer's philosophy of art (see Gardiner, 1963). On the topics more generally R. J. Yanal (1981). It is just worth noting in addition that even if Spencer's target was Meyerbeer's music alone, evidence on its theatricality drawn from a piano reduction of the full score is likely to be unreliable: orchestration as well as notes can be theatrical. As it happens, Spencer's experience of music in later life seems largely to have been confined to piano reductions: 'ill-health has prevented me from hearing an opera or concert for the last twenty years' (1902: p. 180).

20. This book, not perhaps the first such to have drawn on Spencer, is of great significance because of the degree to which it did this and because of its popularity, testified to by it reaching a 10th edition in 1931.

21. From this perspective, Parry commented: 'If a man's ideas are worth expressing, and are capable of being expressed completely within the limits of his resources, his productions may be in a certain sense completely mature at almost any epoch in the progress of artistic development. If Palestrina had introduced discords more freely and treated them with less reserve, and had aimed generally at a stronger type of expression, the balance of his work would have been destroyed, he would have gone beyond the limits which were then inevitable for completely artistic work' (1931: p. 175).

22. How far music historiography in America followed a similar path I am unsure, but there are approving references to Spencer in Lucas, 1908, which was published in New York.

23. The questionable impact of evolutionary ideas on the treatment of melody in music histories in general has been explored by Solie (1982).

24. This point, though should not be taken as a denial in principle of the applicability of *explanatory* perspectives first developed within biology to the sociological understanding of social life.

9   Sociology, Ethics and Well-Being

1. Later in the volume, Spencer responded quite adroitly to criticisms advanced by Henry Sidgwick in his *Methods of Ethics* against the usefulness of his conception of 'absolute' ethics (1910, i: pp. 271–9).

2. Turner's discussion of Spencer excludes discussion of the *Ethics*, apparently because Turner believes, mistakenly I suggest, that it is not sociological in intent, but a study in *laissez-faire* 'moral philosophy' (1985: p. 13).

3. Spencer places the rearing of offspring under the umbrella of altruism.

4. It should be noted that now, writing in the 1890s, Spencer makes reference here and at other points to a Darwinian struggle for existence as an explanation for what survives, though there is no apparent commitment to Darwin's 'variations'. After about 1890, references in this sense to the 'survival of the fittest' become more common than hitherto in both the *Ethics* and the relevant Parts of the *Sociology*. Spencer persists, however, in maintaining also his trust in the inheritance of acquired characteristics as a mechanism producing organic change, particularly in respect of adjustment by men to 'higher' social life.

5. In modern days exemplified, notes Spencer, in Paley's writings. For Spencer, Paley, 'in his official character, derived right and wrong from divine commands, and in his unofficial character derived them from observation of consequences' (1910, i: p. 320).

6. On the philosophical difficulties of Spencer's position here, principally that it confuses the maximizing of 'being' with the maximizing of 'well-being' (which is qualitative in nature) see Sidgwick (1876). Similarly, in 1892, the philosopher and Cornell University President, J. G. Schurman noted a confusion in Spencer between 'living' and 'living well' (1892: pp. 82–3). It is probable that Sidgwick, writing as he was ahead of the appearance of any division of the *Ethics*, had already detected this difficulty in the *Psychology*.

7. In pro-ethical militant societies the low status of women is accompanied by unchastity; it should not be assumed, though, that all peaceful societies value chastity highly.

8. 'May we not reasonably infer that the state reached by these small uncultured tribes may be reached by the great cultured nations, when the life of internal enmity shall be unqualified by the life of external enmity?' (1910, i: p. 472).

9. Spencer also considers marriage and parenthood, making out a case for birth control and a case against parents yielding their responsibility for the individual mental culture of their children to public authority and the public purse.

10. However, Spencer notes that before offspring reach the stage of self-sustentation, they must, to survive, receive benefits which are inversely proportionate to merits.

11. Spencer thus exclaimed indignantly that 'every act of parliament which takes money from the individual for public purposes and gives him public benefits is tending to assimilate militancy with socialism'. At stake was the endangering of a true idea of justice: 'For while no energy is spared in so reforming our judicial administration that everyone may obtain and enjoy all he has earned, great energy is shown in providing for him and others benefits which they have not earned' (1910, ii: p. 44).

12. This 'positive' element is of key importance in understanding Spencer's idea of justice, and often glossed over. For an exception, see Smith (1981: p. 400).

13. The freedom to use limbs and move from place to place is also an ethical desideratum, and progressively being acknowledged. Similarly, Spencer notes that rights to, for instance, unpolluted air are increasingly recognized in practice.

14. See also Bannister (1970) and Steiner (1982). Both F. B. Jevons (1892) and Sidgwick (1892), criticized Spencer's proposals to award compensation.

15. On the right of making gifts to others than offspring Spencer muses that the evidence of the Charity Organisation Society on 'the results of careless squandering of pence' might lead to the inference that benefit would ensue 'if almsgiving were forbidden', but cedes that the belief in this right of gift is so strong that 'no one dreams of denying it for reasons of apparent expediency' (1910, ii: p. 119).

16. Providing a check against a 'tyranny of the majority' was Mill's primary concern in 1859 in his *On Liberty*.

17. Ready access to the administration of 'justice' was a theme in Spencer running back to *The Proper Sphere of Government*, and such access was to serve not only against interferences with the equal freedom principle arising from government, but from fellow citizens. I would suggest that Michael Freeden misrepresents Spencer's position in stating that 'Spencer was perturbed by legal constraints far more than by the straightforward coercive acts of individuals' (1996: p. 285). For Spencer on the constraints to liberty presented by social conditions see Chapter 5 above on trade unions and wages. The scope for negative beneficence to soften the dictates of 'justice' is of course discussed in this Chapter. While only thinly developed it does seem to me that Spencer recognizes that coercion into agreeing to a contract by 'the conditions of social life' (Vincent, 1990: p. 149) is not compatible with the equal freedom principle.

18. Since all citizens benefit, the costs of the state should be borne by all, according in some way to their means. Indirect taxation Spencer opposes since it serves only to camouflage the real cost of government, disguising the need for economy in the performance of necessary functions and reducing resistance to the assumption of unnecessary functions. Experience shows that 'representation without taxation entails robbery' (1910, ii: p. 200).

19. With his concern with 'beneficence' as contrasted with 'justice' Spencer was writing in a tradition familiar to Adam Smith in his *Theory of Moral Sentiments*, as noted by J. E. Bicheno (1824: p. 150). Bicheno himself distinguished 'beneficence' from 'benevolence': benevolence 'may signify either the *principle*, or that intuitive instinct or impulse which excites in us sympathy towards the distressed, and a desire to relieve and communicate happiness; or, it may signify the *exercise* of the

principle in the actual communication of happiness. This, in order to distinguish it from the former, has been frequently called *beneficence*' (1824: p. 78). Bicheno championed beneficence over poor law provision.

20. The authors of books 'which contain neither facts nor thoughts of any value, do not simply entail loss to the community in paper and print thrown away, but help to smother things of true worth … Negative beneficence commands silence' (1910, ii: p. 325).

21. A topic explored in Offer (2006a,b, 2009).

22. There are in fact occasional cognate passages elsewhere, most notably in *The Man versus The State*. Apocalyptic perhaps, but they arise in connection with what Spencer regarded as the juxtaposition of an artificially created niche of a 'bad' environment and the consequential (but temporary) vicious operation of his Lamarckian mechanism of adaptation, the inheritance of acquired characteristics; in time a squeeze is predictable on those too selfish to work to support themselves and their families, which will force adaptation to the normal social state, and during which process the 'penalty' of suffering will be exacted (1910, ii: p. 394). This is *echt* Spencer, it may be noted, not in need of re-description as 'social Darwinism'.

23. 'It only remains for the author to avow his obligation to the teaching of Mr. Herbert Spencer,' wrote Mackay in the Preface to his *The English Poor* (1889).

24. Aspects of the theoretical and practical significance of a focus on beneficence in research associated with social policy and the idea of a 'welfare state' are discussed in Bulmer (1985, 1986, 1987), and also Offer (1999a).

25. Such passages reignited Sidgwick's concern expressed in 1876 that Spencer was apt to mix up description with prescription. Writing in 1899 after the whole System of Synthetic Philosophy was complete, Sidgwick now challenged a tendency for sociological description to partake confusedly of ethical reflection: 'The sociologist who brings his optimism into his sociological reasonings must, I think, find the tendency almost irresistible to give a one-sided prominence to those facts in the past history of society which make for a favourable view of its future progress and to ignore those facts which make for the opposite conclusion. It is only in this way that I can account for Mr. Spencer's belief, regarded by him as a strictly scientific inference from a survey of sociological facts, that the evolution of society will produce "pleasure unalloyed by pain anywhere" ' (1899: p. 20).

26. Francis (2007), it seems to me, compromises his anti-individualist reinterpretation of Spencer by excising rather arbitrarily discussion of Spencer's account of equal freedom and 'justice'.

27. David Miller, 1976 and Tim Gray, 1981, have offered contrasted expositions of Spencer's idea of justice in respect of the weight attached to considerations of the element of desert in outcomes compared to the element of entitlement to opportunities. See also Weinstein (1998: pp. 57–61).

28. The main direction of Sidgwick's essay of 1876 was to a similar end. With Spencer as target, Schurman commented: 'whoever denies the power of free choice dissipates the common notion of desert, and undermines the foundation of Justice as ordinarily understood (1892: p. 84).

29. Commentary on Spencer's concern with 'animal ethics' has sometimes followed Calderwood's drift, and viewed the idea as an eccentricity. Yet, though without reference to Spencer, a concern of Alasdair MacIntyre's recent philosophical work has lent support to some version of the ethical continuum to which Spencer was committed. MacIntyre now regards it as an error to suppose 'an ethics

independent of biology to be possible'. He cites two reasons: 'The first is that no account of the goods, rules and virtues that are definitive of our moral life can be adequate that does not explain – or at least point us towards an explanation – how that form of life is possible for beings who are biologically constituted as we are, by providing us with an account of our development towards and into that form of life. That development has as its starting point our initial animal condition. Secondly, a failure to understand that condition and the light thrown upon it by a comparison between humans and members of other intelligent animal species will obscure crucial features of that development' (1999: p. x).

Concluding Reflections

1. 'New Liberalism' involved David Lloyd George, Winston Churchill and Herbert Samuel, among others (see Wasserstein, 1992).
2. Beatrice Webb's membership of the Commission engendered the dissenting Minority Reports, with the contrasting but in key structural respects idealist principle that *the state* must assume responsibility for a national minimum of civilized life (see McBriar, 1987; Offer, 2004, 2009). There were separate Majority and Minority Reports on England and Wales, Scotland, and Ireland.
3. See Radcliffe Richards (2000: p. 18), and Runciman (1997: p. 128; 1998b: p. 54). 'Skyhook' comes from Daniel Dennet and refers to things that descend from above to pull up what allegedly cannot lift itself, 'cranes', by contrast, are on the ground and can lift things from the ground to a 'higher' level. Darwinism renders needless explanation in terms of 'skyhooks'. See also Cohen (1973). It is worth adding that Spencer's conception of a society as a 'superorganism' was as the co-operative resultant of 'incorporated human nature' (1873b: p. 60) and 'social relations' (1873b: p. 254), not as a new kind of thing.
4. Spencer of course rejected the conception of society under consideration here, and thus did not have this particular problem about the powers of agency of social individuals. For a discussion of Hayck's argument that societies should be seen not as organizations but as 'open', or as 'catallaxies', see Miller (1989: pp. 62–3).
5. Memes as a cultural replicator are considered evolutionary because they exhibit variation, heredity and differential fitness. They also have longevity, fecundity and relative copy fidelity. Dennett has sketched a meme's-eye view of the world: 'A scholar is just a library's way of making another library' (Dennett, quoted in Laland and Brown, 2002: p. 205). As yet empirical work on memes is thin, and there are questions over exactly what memes replicate – ideas, information, behaviour, neural structures, or artefacts? 'Postulating memes for this and that risks a circulation of meaning, if memes are not only "what we think" but also the explanation of what we think' (Laland and Brown, 2002: p. 236).
6. Marx regarded himself as attempting a selectionist approach, interpreting social individuals as agents in a struggle with historical constraints in a manner comparable with the theory of natural selection (see Warren, 1987). Marx, though, may shed little light on how a modest selectionist perspective relates to social matters today, the question now addressed. The 'precedent' of Marx has difficulties over orthogenesis and directionalism derived from Marx's Hegelian roots.
7. Transnational migration or 'returning home' may also stimulate new comparisons of 'selves' and feelings of deprivation, among people on the move and those hosting them (Ramji, 2006). In a selectionist framework, though, the explanation of the *survival* of a change in social life, brought about by a sense of deprivation,

must derive from independent evidence about social life in the receiving social environment the change is situated in, not merely point back to its origins.

8. One might also consider the novelty, if that is what it is, of privileged individual selves finding ways of navigating the management of risk by taking personal responsibility to assure private security, assuming sufficient and appropriate resources (Beck, 1996; Elliot, 2002). On this reading, some agents are adopting strategies to confront special risks associated with novelty, survival and oblivion, while others perforce remain outside the security gates.

9. Indeed, in relation to the production of variations, Dickens reports a radical potential development, pointing to Jablonska and Lamb (1995) as indicating that 'some contemporary biologists do indeed go even further and suggest that characters acquired during an organism's lifetime can be inherited by future generations' (2000: p. 114). This is to break with the established Weismann principle rigidly separating the germ plasm from the somatic cells of the body. However, any prospect of a possible revival of Lamarck's fortunes is both somewhat distant and beyond this book's scope.

Bibliography

Adams, W. E. (1903) *Memoirs of a Social Atom*, London, Hutchinson.

Adorno, T. (1967) *Prisms*, London, Neville Spearman.

Akenson, D. H. (1981) *A Protestant in Purgatory*, Connecticut, Archon.

Alland, A. (1974) 'Why not Spencer?', *Journal of Anthropological Research*, Vol. 30, reprinted in Offer (ed.) (2000), Vol. 2, pp. 460–470.

Allcock, J. B. (1982) 'Emile Durkheim's encounter with pragmatism', *Journal of the History of Sociology*, reprinted in Hamilton (ed.) (1990), Vol. 1, pp. 214–233.

Allen, G. (1904) 'Personal reminiscences of Herbert Spencer' *Forum*, 35 (April), pp. 610–628.

Allen, W. D. (1962) *Philosophies of Music History*, New York, Dover (first published in 1939).

Alpert, H. (1937) 'France's first university course in sociology', *American Sociological Review*, Vol. 2, reprinted in Hamilton (ed.) (1990), Vol. 1, pp. 15–22.

Andreski, S. (1964) *Elements of Comparative Sociology*, London, Weidenfeld and Nicolson.

Anon (1904) 'Some memories of Herbert Spencer' (probably a Masson family member), *The Bookman*, January, pp. 173–177.

Austin, W. (1953) 'The idea of evolution in the music of the 20th century', *Musical Quarterly*, Vol. 39, pp. 26–36.

Bain, A. (1855) *The Senses and the Intellect*, London, Parker.

Bain, A. (1859) *The Emotions and the Will*, London, Parker.

Balfour, A. J. (1892) *A Fragment on Progress*, Edinburgh, David Douglas, reprinted in Offer (ed.) (2000), Vol. 1, pp. 44–59.

Bannister, R. C. (1970) ' "The survival of the fittest is our doctrine": history or histrionics?', *Journal of the History of Ideas*, Vol. 31, reprinted in Offer (ed.) (2000), Vol. 2, pp. 165–185.

Barker, E. (1915) *Political Thought in England from Herbert Spencer to the Present Day*, London, Williams and Norgate.

Barnes, H. E. (1921) 'Some typical contributions of English sociology to political theory', *American Journal of Sociology*, Vol. 27, reprinted in Offer (ed.) (2000), Vol. 3, pp. 20–47.

Barnett, H. O. (1921) *Canon Barnett: His Life, Work and Friends*, London, Murray.

Barton, R. (1990) ' "An influential set of chaps": the X-Club and Royal Society politics 1864–85', *British Journal for the History of Science*, Vol. 23, Part 1, No. 76, pp. 53–81.

Barton, R. (1998) ' "Huxley, Lubbock, and half a dozen others": professionals and gentlemen in the formation of the X Club, 1851–1864', *Isis*, Vol. 89, No. 3, pp. 410–444.

Beck, N. (2004) 'The diffusion of Spencerism and its political interpretations in France and Italy', in *Herbert Spencer: the Intellectual Legacy*, edited by G. Jones and R. A. Peel, London, Galton Institute, pp. 37–60.

Beck, U. (1996) 'Risk Society and the provident state', in S. Lash, B. Szerszynski and B. Wynne (eds) (1996) *Risk, Environment and Modernity: Towards a New Ecology*, London, Sage.

Bell, D. and Sylvest, C. (2006) 'International society and Victorian political thought: Herbert Spencer, T. H. Green and Henry Sidgwick', *Modern Intellectual History*, Vol. 3, No. 2, pp. 207–238.

Bennett, A. (1971) *The Journals*, Harmondsworth, Penguin.

Benton, T. (2000) 'Social causes and natural relations', in H. Rose and S. Rose (eds) (2000), pp. 206–224.

Bicheno, J. E. (1824) *An Inquiry into the Poor Laws, Chiefly with a View to Examine them as a Scheme of National Benevolence, and to Elucidate their Political Economy*, 2nd edition, London, Hunter.

Bixby, J. T. (1882) 'Herbert Spencer's *Data of Ethics*', *Modern Review*, Vol. 3, reprinted in Offer (ed.) (2000), Vol. 3, pp. 292–310.

Black, R. D. C. (1990) 'Jevons, Marshall, and the utilitarian tradition', *Scottish Journal of Political Economy*, Vol. 37, No. 1, pp. 5–17.

Black, R. D. C. (2002) 'The political economy of Thomas Edward Cliffe Leslie (1826–82): a re-assessment', *European Journal of the History of Economic Thought*, Vol. 9, No. 1, pp. 17–41.

Blackley, W. L. (1878) 'National insurance: a cheap practical and popular means of abolishing poor rates', *Nineteenth Century*, November, pp. 834–857.

Blunt, W. S. (1932) *My Diaries: Being a Personal Narrative of Events, 1888–1914*, 2 Vols, London: Secker.

Bosanquet, B. (1889) Review of T. Mackay, *The English Poor*, in *Charity Organisation Review*, Vol. 5, September, pp. 460–466.

Bosanquet, B. (1895) 'Socialism and natural selection', in D. Boucher (1997) (ed.) *The British Idealists*, Cambridge: Cambridge University Press.

Bosanquet, B. (1920) *The Philosophical Theory of the State*, London, Macmillan (first published 1899).

Boucher, D. (ed.) (1997) *The British Idealists*, Cambridge, Cambridge University Press.

Boyd, R. and Richerson, J. (1985) *Culture and the Evolutionary Process*, Chicago, Chicago University Press.

Boyd, R. and Richerson, J. (2005) *Not by Genes Alone: How Culture Transformed Human Evolution*, Chicago, Chicago University Press.

Boylan, T. A. and Foley, T. P. (1983) 'John Elliot Cairnes, John Stuart Mill, and Ireland', *Hermathena*, 135, pp. 120–137.

Boylan, T. A. and Foley, T. P. (1992) *Political Economy and Colonial Ireland*, London, Routledge.

Bradley, F. H. (1876) *Ethical Studies*, London, King.

Bray, C. (1841) *The Philosophy of Necessity, or, The Law of Consequence: As Applicable to Mental, Moral and Social Science*, 2 Vols, London: Longman, Orme, Brown, Green and Longmans.

Brinton, C. (1962) 'Spencer', in his *English Political Thought in the 19th Century*, New York, reprinted in Offer (ed.) (2000) Vol. 3, pp. 187–196.

Brooke, J. H. (1991) *Science and Religion: Some Historical Perspectives*, Cambridge, Cambridge University Press.

Brown, K. D. (ed.) (1974) *Essays in Anti-Labour History*, London, Macmillan.

Buck, P. C. (1969) *The Scope of Music*, Freeport, Books for Libraries (first published in 1924).

Buckle, H. T. (1857) *The History of Civilization in England*, London.

Bulmer, M. (1985) 'The rejuvenation of community studies', *The Sociological Review*, Vol. 33, No. 3, pp. 430–448.

Bulmer, M. (1986) *Neighbours: The Work of Philip Abrams*, Cambridge: Cambridge University Press.

Bulmer, M. (1987) *The Social Basis of Community Care*, London: Allen and Unwin.

Burkhardt, R. W. (1995) *The Spirit of System: Lamarck and Evolutionary Biology*, Cambridge, MA: Harvard University Press.

Burrow, J. W. (1966) *Evolution and Society: A Study in Victorian Social Theory*, Cambridge, Cambridge University Press.

Butler, S. (1911) *Evolution, Old and New; Or the Theories of Buffon, Dr. Erasmus Darwin, and Lamarck, as Compared with that of Charles Darwin*, London, Fifield, first published in 1879.

Bynder, H. (1969) 'Emile Durkheim and the sociology of the family', reprinted in Hamilton (ed.) (1990) Vol. 4, pp. 294–306.

Cahnman, W. J. (ed.) (1973) *Ferdinand Tönnies: A New Evaluation*. Leiden, Brill.

Cairnes, J. E. (1875a) 'Mr. Spencer on social evolution', *Fortnightly Review*, Vol. 17, reprinted in Offer (ed.) (2000) Vol. 3, pp. 125–145.

Cairnes, J. E. (1876b) 'Mr. Spencer on the study of sociology', *Fortnightly Review*, Vol, 17, reprinted in Offer (ed.) (2000) Vol. 3, pp. 146–160.

Calderwood, H. (1892) 'Animal ethics as described by Herbert Spencer', *Philosophical Review*, Vol. 1, No. 3, reprinted in Offer (ed.) (2000) Vol. 3, pp. 352–359.

Carneiro, R. L. (1972) 'The devolution of evolution', *Social Biology*, Vol. 19, reprinted in Offer (ed.) (2000) Vol. 2, pp. 426–440.

Carneiro, R. L. (1973) 'Structure, function and equilibrium in the evolutionism of Herbert Spencer', *Journal of Anthropological Research*, Vol. 29, reprinted in Offer (ed.) (2000) Vol. 2, pp. 441–459.

Carneiro, R. L. (1981) 'Herbert Spencer as an anthropologist', *Journal of Libertarian Studies*, Vol. 5, reprinted in Offer (ed.) (2000) Vol. 2, pp. 563–624.

Carneiro, R. L. and Perrin, R. G. (2002) 'Herbert Spencer's *Principles of Sociology*: A centennial retrospective and appraisal', *Annals of Science*, Vol. 59, pp. 221–261.

Carpenter, W. B. (1842) *Principles of Human Physiology: With Their Chief Applications to Pathology, Hygiene and Forensic Medicine*, London, Churchill.

Carroll, J. (2003) 'Introduction' to *On the Origin of Species by Means of Natural Selection* by Charles Darwin, edited by J. Carroll, Ontario, Broadview.

Cattell, J. McK. (1891) 'On the origin of music', *Mind*, Vol. 16, pp. 386–388.

Cavalli-Sforza, L. and Feldman, M. (1981) *Cultural Transmission and Evolution: A Quantitative Approach*, Princeton, NJ, Princeton University Press.

Chalmers, T. (1808) *Inquiry into the Extent and Stability of Natural Resources*, Edinburgh, printed for Oliphant and Brown.

Chambers, R. (but initially anonymous) (1844) *Vestiges, of the Natural History of Creation*, London, Churchill.

Chattoe, E. (2002) 'Developing the selectionist paradigm in sociology', *Sociology*, Vol. 36, No. 4, pp. 817–833.

Chattoe, E. (2006) 'Using simulation to develop testable functionalist explanations: a case study of church survival', *British Journal of Sociology*, Vol. 57, No. 3, pp. 379–397.

Clark, T. N. (1968) 'Emile Durkheim and the institutionalization of sociology', *European Journal of Sociology*, Vol. 9, reprinted in Hamilton (ed.) (1990) Vol. 1, pp. 104–136.

Clodd, E. (1900) *Grant Allen: A Memoir*, London, Grant Richards.

Cohen, L. J. (1973) 'Is the progress of science evolutionary?', *British Journal of the Philosophy of Science*, Vol. 24, pp. 41–61.

Coleman, J. S. (1990) *Foundations of Social Theory*, Cambridge, MA, Belknap Press.
Coleridge, S. T. (1848) *Hints Towards the More Comprehensive Formulation of a Theory of Life*, London, Churchill.
Collier, E. C. F. (ed.) (1944) *A Victorian Diarist: Extracts from the Journals of Mary, Lady Monkswell, 1873–1895*, London, John Murray.
Collier, J. (1904) 'Reminiscence of Herbert Spencer', in Royce, J. (1904), *Herbert Spencer: An Estimate and a Review*.
Collins, F. H. (1889) *An Epitome of the Synthetic Philosophy*, London, Williams and Norgate.
Collins, R. (1994) *Four Sociological Traditions*, New York, Oxford University Press.
Combe, G. (1828) *The Constitution of Man and its Relations to External Objects*, Edinburgh, Anderson, and London, Longman.
Combe, G. (1846) *Moral Philosophy; or The Duties of Man Considered in his Individual, Domestic and Social Capacities*, Edinburgh, Maclachlan Stewart, and London, Longman.
Cooley, C. H. (1920) 'Reflections upon the sociology of Herbert Spencer', *American Journal of Sociology*, Vol. 26, reprinted in Offer (ed.) (2000) Vol. 3, pp. 7–19.
Copleston, F. (1949) 'Herbert Spencer – progress and freedom', *Ideas and Beliefs of the Victorians*, London, Sylvan Press, reprinted in Offer (ed.) (2000) Vol. 1, pp. 105–110.
Corning, P. A. (1982) 'Durkheim and Spencer', *British Journal of Sociology*, Vol. 33, reprinted in Offer (ed.) (2000) Vol. 2, pp. 307–329.
Corsi, P. (1988a) *Science and Religion: Baden Powell and the Anglican Debate, 1800–1860*, Cambridge, Cambridge University Press.
Corsi, P. (1988b) *The Age of Lamarck: Evolutionary Theories in France, 1790–1830*, Berkeley, LA: University of California Press.
Crook, D. P. (1984) *Benjamin Kidd: Portrait of a Social Darwinist*, Cambridge, Cambridge University Press.
Cross, J. W. (ed.) (1885) *George Eliot's Life as Related in her Letters and Journals*, Edinburgh and London, Blackwood.
Crowther, M. A. (1981) *The Workhouse System, 1834–1929*, London, Methuen.
Curry, O. (2003) 'Get real: evolution as metaphor and mechanism', *British Journal of Politics and International Relations*, Vol. 5, No. 1, pp. 112–117.
Darwin, C. (1859) *On the Origin of Species*, London, Murray.
Darwin, C. (1871) *The Descent of Man, and Selection in Relation to Sex*, London, John Murray.
Darwin, C. (1968) *The Origin of Species*, edited by Burrow, J. W., Harmondsworth, Penguin.
Dawkins, R. (1976) *The Selfish Gene*, Oxford, Oxford University Press.
De Laveleye, E. (1885) 'The state versus the man: a criticism of Mr. Herbert Spencer', *Contemporary Review*, Vol. 47, reprinted in Offer (ed.) (2000) Vol. 4, pp. 122–144.
den Otter, S. (1996) *British Idealism and Social Explanation: A Study in Late Victorian Thought*, Oxford and New York, Clarendon Press.
den Otter, S. (1997) ' "Thinking in communities": late nineteenth-century liberals, idealists and the retrieval of community', *Parliamentary History*, Vol. 16, pp. 67–84.
Denton, G. B. (1921) 'Early psychological theories of Herbert Spencer', *American Journal of Psychology*, Vol. 32, reprinted in Offer (ed.) (2000) Vol. 3, pp. 228–237.
Desmond, A. (1997) *Huxley: From Devil's Disciple to Evolution's High Priest*, London and New York, Penguin.
Desmond, A. and Moore, J. (1991) *Darwin*, London and New York, Penguin.
Dewey, J. (1904) 'The philosophical work of Herbert Spencer', *Philosophical Review*, Vol. 13, reprinted in Offer (ed.) (2000) Vol. 1, pp. 31–43.

Dibble, J. (1992) *C. Hubert H. Parry: His Life and Music*, Oxford, Oxford University Press.

Dickens, P. (2000) *Social Darwinism*, Buckingham, Open University Press.

Dingwall, R. and King, M. (1995) 'Herbert Spencer and the professions: occupational ecology reconsidered', *Sociological Theory*, Vol. 13, reprinted in Offer (ed.) (2000) Vol. 2, pp. 644–659.

Donisthorpe, W. (1889) *Individualism: A System of Politics*, London, Liberty and Property Defence League.

Drummond, H. (1894) *The Lowell Lectures on the Ascent of Man*, London, Hodder and Stoughton.

Dudley Edwards, R. (1995) *The Pursuit of Reason: The Economist 1843–1893*, Boston, Mass, Harvard Business School Press.

Dugdale, B. E. D. (1939) *Arthur James Balfour*, London, Hutchinson.

Durkheim, E. (1933) (first published in 1893) *The Division of Labour in Society*, London, Macmillan.

Duncan, D. (1911) *The Life and Letters of Herbert Spencer*, London, Williams and Norgate.

Eisen, S. (1967) 'Frederic Harrison and Herbert Spencer: embattled unbelievers', *Victorian Studies*, September, reprinted in Offer (ed.) (2000) Vol. 1, pp. 144–165.

Elliott, A. (2002) 'Beck's sociology of risk', *Sociology*, Vol. 36, No. 2, pp. 293–315.

Elliott, P. (2003) 'Erasmus Darwin, Herbert Spencer, and the origins of the evolutionary worldview in British provincial scientific culture 1770–1850', *Isis*, Vol. 94, pp. 1–29.

Elliott, P. (2004) ' "Improvement, always and everywhere": William George Spencer (1790–1866) and mathematic, geographical and scientific education in nineteenth-century England', *History of Education*, Vol. 33, No. 4, pp. 391–417.

Elton, W. (ed.) (1954) *Aesthetics and Language*, Oxford, Basil Blackwell.

Elwick, J. (2003) 'Herbert Spencer and the disunity of the social organism', *History of Science*, Vol. 41, pp. 35–72.

Finch, J. and Mason, C. (1993) *Negotiating Family Responsibilities*, London, Routledge.

Fiske, J. (1894) *Life and Letters of Edward Livingston Youmans*, London, Chapman and Hall.

Flew, A. G. N. (1967) *Evolutionary Ethics*, London, Macmillan.

Francis, M. (2007) *Herbert Spencer and the Invention of Modern Life*, Ithaca and London, Cornell University Press; Stocksfield: Acumen.

Freeden, M. (1976) 'Biological and evolutionary roots of the new liberalism in England', *Political Theory*, Vol. 4, No. 4, pp. 471–490.

Freeden, M. (1978) *The New Liberalism: An Ideology of Social Reform*, Oxford, Clarendon Press.

Freeden, M. (1996) *Ideologies and Political Theory: a Conceptual Approach*, Oxford, Oxford University Press.

Freeden, M. (2000) 'Short notice' of David Weinstein, *Equal Freedom and Utility*, *English Historical Review*, Vol. 115, No. 463, pp. 1006–1007.

Freeman, D. (1974) 'The evolutionary theories of Charles Darwin and Herbert Spencer', *Current Anthropology*, Vol. 15, No. 3, pp. 211–237, reprinted in Offer (ed.) (2000), Vol. 2, pp. 5–69.

Froude, J. A. (1849) *The Nemesis of Faith*, London, Chapman.

Fuller, S. (2006) *The New Sociological Imagination*, London, Thousand Oaks, New Delhi, Sage.

Gane, M. (2006) *Auguste Comte*, Abingdon and New York, Routledge.

Gardiner, P. (1963) *Schopenhauer*, Harmondsworth, Penguin.

Gascoigne, J. (2002) *The Enlightenment and the Origins of European Australia*, Cambridge, Cambridge University Press.

Gaus, G. (2001) 'Bosanquet's communitarian defense of economic individualism: a lesson in the complexities of political theory', in A. Simhony and D. Weinstein (eds), *The New Liberalism*, pp. 137–158.

Gay, H. (1998) 'No "heathen's corner" here: the failed attempt to memorialize Herbert Spencer in Westminster Abbey', *British Journal of the History of Science*, Vol. 31, pp. 41–54.

Gay, H. (1999) 'Explaining the universe: Herbert Spencer's attempt to synthesize political and evolutionary ideas', *Endeavour*, Vol. 23, No. 2, pp. 56–59.

George, H. (1879) *Progress and Poverty: An Inquiry into the Cause of Industrial Depression, and of Increase of Want with Increase of Wealth – The Remedy*, San Francisco (also London, Kegan Paul, 1882).

George, H. (1892) *Herbert Spencer: A Perplexed Philosopher; Being an Examination of Mr. Herbert Spencer's Various Utterances on the Land Question*, New York, Webster.

Gibbon, C. (1878) *The Life of George Combe*, 2 Vols, London, Macmillan.

Giddens, A. (1971) 'The "individual" in the writings of Emile Durkheim', *European Journal of Sociology*, Vol. 12, reprinted in Hamilton (ed.) (1990) Vol. 2, pp. 300–317.

Goffman, E. (1968) *Stigma: Notes on the Management of Spoiled Identity*, Harmondsworth, Penguin.

Gondermann, T. (2007) 'Progression and regression: Herbert Spencer's explanations of social inequality', *History of the Human Sciences*, Vol. 20, No. 3, pp. 21–40.

Graves, C. L. (1926) *Hubert Parry: His Life and Works*, 2 Vols, London, Macmillan.

Gray, J. N. (1982) 'Spencer on the ethics of liberty and the limits of state interference', *History of Political Thought*, Vol. 3, reprinted in Offer (ed.) (2000) Vol. 4, pp. 234–249.

Gray, J. N. (1995) *Liberalism*, Milton Keynes, Open University Press.

Gray, T. (1981) 'Herbert Spencer's theory of justice – desert or entitlement?', *History of Economic Thought*, Vol. 2, reprinted in Offer (ed.) (2000), Vol. 3, pp. 381–403.

Gray, T. (1996) *The Political Philosophy of Herbert Spencer: Individualism and Organicism*, Aldershot and Brookfield, Vermont, Avebury.

Green, T. H. (1883) *Prolegomena to Ethics*, Oxford, Oxford University Press.

Greene, J. C. (1959) 'Biology and social theory in the nineteenth century: Auguste Comte and Herbert Spencer', in M. Clagett (ed.) *Critical Problems in the History of Science*, Madison, reprinted in Offer (ed.) (2000) Vol. 2, pp. 203–226.

Greenleaf, W. H. (1983) *The British Political Tradition, Vol. 2: The Ideological Heritage*, London, Routledge.

Grew, E. M. (1928) 'Herbert Spencer and music', *Musical Quarterly*, Vol. 14, No. 1, pp. 127–142.

Ground, W. D. (1883) *An Examination of the Structural Principles of Mr. Herbert Spencer's Philosophy*, Oxford, Parker.

Grove, Sir William (1846) *The Correlation of Physical Forces*, London, Longman, Green.

Gruber, J. W. (1961) *A Conscience in Conflict: The Life of St. George Jackson Mivart*, New York, Columbia University Press.

Gurney, E. (1876) 'On some disputed points in music', *Fortnightly Review*, Vol. 26, July, pp. 106–130.

Guthrie, M. (1879) *On Mr. Spencer's Formula of Evolution as an Exhaustive Statement of the Changes of the Universe, Followed by a Résumé of Criticisms of Spencer's First Principles*, London, Trübner.

Guthrie, M. (1882) *On Mr. Spencer's Unification of Knowledge*, London, Trübner.

Guthrie, M. (1884) *On Mr. Spencer's Data of Ethics*, London, Modern Press.

Haines, V. A. (1988) 'Is Spencer's theory an evolutionary theory?', *American Journal of Sociology*, Vol. 93, reprinted in Offer (ed.) (2000) Vol. 2, pp. 471–493.

Haines, V. A. (1991) 'Spencer, Darwin and the question of reciprocal influence', *Journal of the History of Biology*, Vol. 24, reprinted in Offer (ed.) (2000) Vol. 2, pp. 70–89.

Halévy, E. (1903) *Thomas Hodgskin (1787–1869)*, Paris, Société Nouvelle de librairie et l'édition.

Halliday, R. J. (1971) 'Social Darwinism: a definition', *Victorian Studies*, Vol. 15, No. 4, reprinted in Offer (ed.) (2000) Vol. 2, pp. 133–148.

Halsey, A. H. (2004) *A History of Sociology in Britain*, Oxford and New York, Oxford University Press.

Hamilton, P. (ed,) (1990) *Emile Durkheim: Critical Assessments*, 4 Vols, London and New York, Routledge.

Harman, P. M. (2001) *The Natural Philosophy of James Clerk Maxwell*, Cambridge, Cambridge University Press.

Harris, J. (1989) 'The Webbs, the Charity Organisation Society and the Ratan Tata Foundation: social policy from the perspective of 1912', in M. Bulmer, J. Lewis and D. Piachaud (eds), *The Goals of Social Policy*, London, Unwin Hyman, pp. 27–63.

Harris, J. (1992) 'Political thought and the welfare state 1870–1940: an intellectual framework for British social policy', *Past and Present*, Vol. 135, pp. 116–141.

Harris, J. (1993) *Private Lives, Public Spirit: A Social History of Britain, 1870–1914*, Oxford, Oxford University Press.

Harris, J. (2002) 'From poor law to welfare state? A European perspective', in *The Political Economy of British Historical Experience, 1689–1914*, D. Winch and P. K. O'Brien (eds), pp. 409–438, Oxford, Oxford University Press.

Harris, J. (2004) 'Spencer, Herbert', in *Oxford Dictionary of National Biography*, Oxford, Oxford University Press.

Harrison, F. (1905) 'Herbert Spencer', *Herbert Spencer Lecture*, Oxford, Oxford University Press.

Hatch, D. J. and Watson, D. R. (1974) 'On hearing the blues', *Acta Sociologica*, Vol. 17, pp. 162–178.

Hawkins, M. (1997) *Social Darwinism in European and American Thought, 1860–1945*, Cambridge, Cambridge University Press.

Hennell, S. (1860) *Thoughts in Aid of Faith, Gathered Chiefly from Recent Works in Theology and Philosophy*, London, Manwaring.

Heraud, B. J. (1970) *Sociology and Social Work*, Oxford, Pergamon.

Herbert, A. (1884) *A Politician in Trouble About His Soul*, London, Chapman and Hall.

Herbert, A. (1885) *The Right and Wrong of Compulsion by the State*, London, Williams and Norgate.

Herbert, A. (1893) 'A cabinet minister's vade-mecum', *Nineteenth Century*, October, pp. 504–522.

Herbert, A. (1894) 'The ethics of dynamite', *Contemporary Review*, May reprinted in Mack (ed.), 1978, pp. 191–226.

Herbert, A. (1908) *The Voluntaryist Creed: Being the Herbert Spencer Lecture Delivered at Oxford, June 7, 1906, and A Plea for Voluntaryism*, London, Oxford University Press.

Hill, R. (1928) 'Herbert Spencer and music', *Musical Opinion*, February, pp. 496–497.

Hilton, B. (1988) *The Age of Atonement*, Oxford, Clarendon Press.

Hirst, P. Q. (1976) *Social Evolution and Sociological Categories*, London, Allen and Unwin.

Hiskes, R. P. (1983) 'Spencer and the liberal idea of community', *The Review of Politics*, Vol. 45, pp. 595–609, reprinted in Offer (ed.) (2000) Vol. 3, pp. 44–55.

Hobhouse, L. T. (1911) *Social Evolution and Political Theory*, New York, Columbia University Press.

Hobson, J. A. (1904) 'Herbert Spencer', *South Place Magazine*, Vol. 9, No. 4, reprinted in Offer (ed.) (2000) Vol. 1, pp. 12–18.

Hodgson, G. M. (2006) *Economics in the Shadows of Darwin and Marx*, Cheltenham, Edward Elgar.

Hodgson, S. H. (1872) 'The future of metaphysic', *Contemporary Review*, November, pp. 819–838.

Hofstadter, R. (1944) *Social Darwinism in American Thought*, New York, Braziller (revised edition 1955).

Holyoake, G. J. (1875) *The History of Cooperation in England*, 2 Vols, London.

Holyoake, G. J. (1905) *Bygones Worth Remembering*, 2 Vols, London, Fisher Unwin.

Howland, D. (2000) 'Society reified: Herbert Spencer and political theory in early Meiji Japan', *Comparative Studies in Society and History*, pp. 67–86.

Howsam, L. (2000) 'An experiment with science for the nineteenth-century book trade'. *British Journal for the History of Science*, Vol. 33, pp. 187–207.

Hudson, W. H. (1897) *An Introduction to the Philosophy of Herbert Spencer: with a Biographical Sketch*, London, Chapman and Hall.

Hudson, W. H. (1904) 'Herbert Spencer: a character study', *Fortnightly Review*, Vol. 75 (new series), reprinted in Offer (ed.) (2000) Vol. 1, pp. 5–11.

Hughes, K. (1998) *George Eliot: The Last Victorian*, London, Fourth Estate.

Hughes, W. R. (1890) *Constance Naden: A Memoir*, Birmingham, Bickers.

Hunt, L. (1853) *The Religion of the Heart: A Manual of Faith and Duty*, London, Chapman.

Hutchinson Harris, S. (1943) *Auberon Herbert: Crusader for Liberty*, London, Williams and Norgate.

Hutton, R. H. (1869) 'A questionable parentage for morals', *Macmillan's Magazine*.

Huxley, T. H. (1871) 'Administrative nihilism', in *Fortnightly Review*, Vol. 10, reprinted in Offer (ed.) (2000) Vol. 4, pp. 56–74.

Ingold, T. (1986) *Evolution and Social Life*, Cambridge, Cambridge University Press.

Jablonska, E. and Lamb, M. (1995) *Epigenetic Inheritance and Evolution*, Oxford, Oxford University Press.

Jacob, J. (1856) *Record Book of the Scinde Irregular Horse*, London.

Jacoby, E. G. (ed.) (1974) *Ferdinand Tönnies: On Social Ideas and Ideologies*, New York, Harper and Row.

Jacyna, L. S. (1980) 'Science and social order in the thought of A. J. Balfour', *Isis*, Vol. 71, pp. 11–34.

Jacyna, L. S. (1983) 'Immanence or transcendence: theories of life and organization in Britain, 1790–1835', *Isis*, Vol. 74, pp. 310–329.

James, W. (1911) 'Herbert Spencer's Autobiography', in *Memories and Studies*, New York, Longmans, Green (first published in the *Atlantic Monthly* for July, 1904), reprinted in Offer (ed.) (2000) Vol. 1, pp. 19–30.

Jensen, J. V. (1970) 'The X Club: fraternity of Victorian scientists,' *The British Journal for the History of Science*, Vol. 5, No. 1, pp. 63–72.

Jevons, F. B. (1892) 'A review of Spencer's *Justice*', *Economic Review*, Vol. 2, reprinted in Offer (ed.) (2000) Vol. 2, pp. 287–291.

Jevons, W. S. (1874) *The Principles of Science: A Treatise on Logic and Scientific Method*, London, Macmillan.

John of Salisbury (1990) *Policraticus*, edited by C. Nederman, Cambridge, Cambridge University Press.

Jones, R. A. (1974) 'Durkheim's response to Spencer: an essay toward historicism in the historiography of sociology', *Sociological Quarterly*, Vol. 15, reprinted in Offer (ed.) (2000) Vol. 2, pp. 267–286.

Jones, R. A. (1975) 'Durkheim in context: a reply to Perrin', *Sociological Quarterly*, Vol. 16, reprinted in Offer (ed.) (2000) Vol. 2, pp. 296–306.

Jones, T. R. (1845/1852), *The Natural History of Animals*, 2 Vols, London, Van Voorst.

Kennedy, M. (1964) *The Works of Ralph Vaughan Williams*, London, Oxford University Press.

Kerr, P. (2002) 'Saved from extinction: evolutionary theorising, politics and the state', *British Journal of Politics and International Relations*, Vol. 4, No. 2, pp. 330–358.

Kerr, P. (2003) 'Keeping it real! Evolution in political science: a reply to Kerr and Curry', *British Journal of Politics and International Relations*, Vol. 5, No. 1, pp. 118–128.

Kidd, B. (1894) *Social Evolution*, London and New York, Macmillan.

Kidd, B. (1902) *Principles of Western Civilisation*, London and New York, Macmillan.

Kidd, B. (1908) *Individualism and After, the Herbert Spencer Lecture Delivered in the Sheldonian Theatre on the 29th May 1908*. Oxford, Clarendon Press.

Kidd, B. (1918) *The Science of Power*, London, Methuen.

Kingsley, C. (1877) *Charles Kingsley: his Letters and Memories of his Life* (edited by his wife), 2 Vols, London, King.

Kirkman, T. P. (1876) *Philosophy Without Assumptions*, London, Longmans, Green.

Laland, K. N. and Brown, G. R. (2002) *Sense and Nonsense: Evolutionary Perspectives in Human Behaviour*, Oxford, Oxford University Press.

Lamar, L. B. (1953) 'Herbert Spencer and his father', *Studies in English*, Vol. 32, reprinted in Offer (ed.) (2000) Vol. 1, pp. 182–189.

Lamont-Brown, R. (2005) *Carnegie: The Richest Man in the World*, Stroud, Sutton.

Laugel, A. (1864) 'Les etudes philosophiques en Angleterre', *Revue des deux mondes*, Vol. XLIX.

Lecky, W. E. H. (1908) 'Carlyle's message to his age', in his *Historical and Political Essays*, 1908, London, Longman's Green.

Lee, D. and Newby, H. (1983) *The Problem of Sociology*, London, Hutchinson.

Leinster-Mackay, D. (1981) 'John Hullah, John Curwen and Sarah Glover: a classic case of "whiggery" in the history of music education', *British Journal of Educational Studies*, Vol. 29, No. 2, pp. 164–167.

Leonard, T. (2009) 'Origins of the myth of Social Darwinism: the Ambiguous Legacy of Richard Hofstadter's *Social Darwinism in American Thought*', *Journal of Economic Behavior and Organization*, Vol. 71, No. 1, pp. 37–51.

Leslie, T. E. C. (1879) 'Political economy and sociology', in his *Essays in Political and Moral Philosophy*, Dubliln, Hodges, Foster and Figgis, and London, Longmans, Green.

Leslie, J. C. (2000) 'Herbert Spencer and selectionism in psychology', in Offer (ed.) (2000) Vol. 3, pp. 267–278.

Leslie, J. C. (2006) 'Herbert Spencer's contributions to behavior analysis: a retrospective review of *Principles of Psychology*', *Journal of the Experimental Analysis of Behaviour*, Vol. 86, No. 1, pp. 123–129.

Letwin, S. (1965) *The Pursuit of Certainty*, London, Cambridge University Press.

Lewes, G. H. *Biographical History of Philosophy*, 4 Vols, London: Knight.

Lewis, J. (1995) *The Voluntary Sector, the State and Social Work in Britain*, Aldershot, Edward Elgar.

Linton, W. J. (1895) *Memories*, London, Lawrence and Bullen.

Lissa, Z. (1967) 'Musicology and the universal history of music', *Actes du 11 Congrès d'Histoire, des Sciences*, Ossolineum, Warsaw, Vol. 2.

Low-Beer, A. (ed.) (1969) *Herbert Spencer*, London and Toronto, Collier Macmillan.

Lubbock, Sir J. (1882) *Origin of Civilization*, 4th edition, London.

Lucas, C. (1908) *The Story of Musical Form*, London, Scott, and New York, Scribner's.

Lukes, S. (1969) 'Durkheim's "Individualism and the Intellectuals"', *Political Studies*, Vol. 17, reprinted in Hamilton (ed.) (1990) Vol. 4, pp. 166–183.

Lukes, S. (1971) 'Prolegomena to the interpretation of Durkheim', *European Journal of Sociology*, reprinted in Hamilton (ed.) (1990) Vol. 2, pp. 318–342.

Lyon, E. G. (1999) *Politicians in the Pulpit: Christian Radicalism in Britain from the Fall of the Bastille to the Disintegration of Chartism*, Aldershot, Ashgate.

Lyell, C. (1830/1837), *Principles of Geology: Being an Attempt to Explain the Former Changes of the Earth's Surface by Reference to Causes Now in Operation*, 3 Vols, 5th edition, London, John Murray.

Lynn Linton, E. (1894) 'Professor Henry Drummond's discovery', *Fortnightly Review*, September, pp. 448–457.

McBriar, A. M. (1987) *An Edwardian Mixed Doubles: The Bosanquets versus The Webbs*, Oxford, Clarendon Press.

McClelland, K. (1994) 'The British intelligentsia', *Twentieth Century British History*, Vol. 5, No. 3, pp, 391–397.

McGowran, K. (2004) 'Bevington, Louisa Sarah', in *Oxford Dictionary of National Biography*, Oxford University Press.

McKerrow, R. E. (1981) 'Archbishop Whately, human nature and Christian assistance', *Church History*, Vol. 50, pp. 166–181.

MacIntyre, A. (1999) *Dependent Rational Animals: Why Human Beings Need the Virtues*, London, Duckworth.

McLennan, J. F. (1865) *Primitive Marriage*, Edinburgh, Black.

Mack, E. (ed.) (1978) *The Right and Wrong of Compulsion by the State and Other Essays by Auberon Herbert*, Indianapolis, Liberty Fund.

Mackay, T. (1889) *The English Poor*, London, John Murray.

Mackay, T. (ed.) (1891) *A Plea for Liberty*, London, John Murray.

MacLeod, R. (1970) 'The X-Club: a social network of science in late-Victorian England', *Notes and Records of the Royal Society of London*, Vol. 24, No. 2, pp. 305–322.

Maconochie, A. (1846) *Crime and Punishment: The Mark System, Framed to mix Persuasion with Punishment, and make their Effect Improving, yet their Operation Severe*, London, Hatchard.

Magee, B. (1972) *Aspects of Wagner*, London, Panther.

Magee, B. (1997) *Confessions of a Philosopher*, London, Phoenix.

Maine, Sir H. (1861) *Ancient Law: Its Connection with the Early History of Society, and its Relation to Modern Ideas*, London, Murray.

Maine, Sir H. (1871) *Village Communities in the East and West: Six Lectures Delivered at Oxford*, London, Murray.

Maine, Sir H. (1875) *Early History of Institutions*, London, Murray.

Maine, Sir H. (1883) *Dissertations on Early Law and Custom*, London, Murray.

Mallock, W. H. (1898) *Aristocracy and Evolution*, London, Black.

Malthus, T. R. (1798) *An Essay on the Principle of Population*, reprinted in A. Flew (ed.) (1970) *Malthus: An Essay on the Principle of Population*, Harmondsworth, Penguin.

Mandler, P. (1990) 'Tories and paupers: Christian political economics and the making of the new poor law', *Historical Journal*, Vol. 33, pp. 81–105.

Mandler, P. (2002) 'Book review forum', *Victorian Studies*, Summer, pp. 654–662.

Mansel, H. (1858) *Limits of Religious Thought: Examined in Eight Lectures Preached before the University of Oxford in the year 1858 on the Foundation of . . . John Bampton*, Oxford: John Murray.

Mansel, H. (1866) *The Philosophy of the Conditioned: Comprising Some Remarks on Sir William Hamilton's Philosophy, and on Mr. J. S. Mill's Examination of That Philosophy*, London, Strahan.

Marshall, A. (1925) *Memorials of Alfred Marshall*, edited by A. C. Pigou, London, Macmillan.

Martineau, J. (1866) *Essays, Philosophical and Theological*, London, Trübner.

Martineau, J. (1872) 'The place of mind in nature, and intuition of man', *Contemporary Review*, June.

Marx, K. (1934) *The Eighteenth Brumaire of Louis Napoleon*, Moscow, Progress (first published in 1852).

Mason, J. W. (1974) 'Thomas Mackay: the anti-socialist philosophy of the Charity Organisation Society', in Brown (ed.), *Essays in Anti-Labour History*, Ch. 12.

Meadowcroft, J. (1995) *Conceptualizing the State: Innovation and Dispute in British Political Thought 1880–1914*, Oxford, Clarendon Press.

Medawar, Sir P. (1969) 'Herbert Spencer and the law of general evolution' in *The Art of the Soluble* (Harmondsworth: Penguin), reprinted in Offer (ed.), 2000, Vol. 1, pp. 111–125.

Mellers, W. (1973) *Twilight of the Gods*, London, Faber and Faber.

Merton, R. K. (1968) *Social Theory and Social Structure*, New York, Free Press.

Midgley, M. (1985) 'The religion of evolution', in J. Durant (ed.), *Darwinism and Divinity*, Oxford, Blackwell, pp. 154–180.

Midgley, M. (2000) 'Why memes?' in H. Rose and S. Rose (eds), *Alas, Poor Darwin*, (2000), pp. 67–84.

Mill, J. S. (1859) *On Liberty*, reprinted in *Essential Works of John Stuart Mill*, edited by M. Lerner, New York, Toronto, London, Bantam (1961), pp. 255 360.

Mill, J. S. (1961) *Utilitarianism*, reprinted in M. Lerner (ed.) *Essential Works of John Stuart Mill*, New York, Toronto, London, Bantam (1961) pp. 189–252.

Mill, J. S. *On Nature*, reprinted in M. Lerner (ed.) *Essential Works of John Stuart Mill*, New York, Toronto, London, Bantam (1961) pp. 367–401.

Miller, D. (1976) *Social Justice*, Oxford, Oxford University Press.

Miller, D. (1989) *Market, State and Community*, Oxford, Clarendon Press.

Miller, W. L. (1982) 'Herbert Spencer's drift to conservatism', *History of Political Thought*, Vol. 3, reprinted in Offer (ed.) (2000), Vol. 4, pp. 172–184.

Milne-Edwards, H. (1851) *Introduction à la zoologie générale, ou, Considérations sur les tendances de la nature dans la constitution du regne animal*, Paris, Masson.

Mineka, F. E. and Lindley, D. N. (eds) (1972) *The Later Letters of John Stuart Mill*, *(Vols. 14–17 of The Collected Works of John Stuart Mill)*, Toronto and Buffalo, Toronto University Press, and London, Routledge and Kegan Paul.

Mivart, St. G. J. (1871) *On the Genesis of Species*, New York, Appleton.

Mivart, St. G. J. (1873) 'Herbert Spencer', *Quarterly Review*, reprinted in Offer (ed.) (2000), Vol. 3, pp. 201–227.

Moffatt, K and Irving, I. (2002) ' "Living for the brethren": Idealism, social work's lost enlightenment strain', *British Journal of Social Work*, Vol. 32, pp. 415–427.

Moore, G. E. (1901) *Principia Ethica*, London, Cambridge University Press.

Morley, J. (1881) *The Life of Richard Cobden*, 2 Vols, London: Chapman and Hall.

Morley, J. (1917) *Recollections*, 2 Vols, New York: Macmillan.

Mozley, T. (1882) *Reminiscences Chiefly of Oriel College and the Oxford Movement*, 2 Vols, London, Longmans.

Mozley, T. (1885) *Reminiscences Chiefly of Towns, Villages and Schools*, 2 Vols, London, Longmans, Green.

Muirhead, J. H. (1939) *The Man versus the State as a Present Issue*, London, Allen and Unwin.

Müller, M. (1873) 'Lecture delivered at the Royal Institution', *Fraser's Magazine*, May.

Nagai, M. (1954) 'Herbert Spencer in early Meiji Japan', *Far Eastern Quarterly*, Vol. 14, pp. 55–65.

Nederman, C. (1987),'The physiological significance of the organic metaphor in John of Salisbury's *Policraticus*', *History of Political Thought*, Vol. 8, pp. 211–223.

Neill, E. (2003), 'Evolutionary theory and British idealism: the case of David George Ritchie', *History of European Ideas*, Vol. 29, pp. 313–338.

Newman, E. (1905) *Musical Studies*, London, Lane.

Newman, F. (1849) *The Soul, her Sorrows and her Aspirations: an Essay towards the Natural History of the Soul, as the True Basis of Theology*, London, Chapman.

Newman, F. (1850) *Phases of Faith*, London, Chapman.

Nisbet, R. A. (1969) *Social Change and History: Aspects of the Western Theory of Development*, New York, Oxford University Press.

Nozick, R. (1974) *Anarchy, State, and Utopia*, Oxford: Basil Blackwell.

Offer, J. (1983) 'Dissonance over harmony: A Spencer oddity', Sociology, Vol. 17, No. 2, reprinted in Offer (ed.) (2000), Vol. 2, pp. 494–498.

Offer, J. (ed.) (1994) *Herbert Spencer: Political Writings*, Cambridge, Cambridge University Press.

Offer, J. (1999a) 'Idealist thought, social policy and the rediscovery of informal care', *British Journal of Sociology*, Vol. 50, No. 3, pp. 467–488.

Offer, J. (1999b) *Social Workers, the Community and Social Interaction*, London, Jessica Kingsley.

Offer, J. (ed.) (2000) *Herbert Spencer: Critical Assessments*, 4 Vols, London and New York, Routledge.

Offer, J. (2004) 'Dead theorists and older people: Spencer, idealist social thought and divergent prescriptions for care', *Sociology*, Vol. 38, No. 5, pp. 891–908.

Offer, J. (2006a) *An Intellectual History of British Social Policy*, Bristol, The Policy Press.

Offer, J. (2006b) ' "Virtue", "citizen character" and "social environment": social theory and agency in social policy since 1830', *Journal of Social Policy*, Vol. 35, No. 2, pp. 283–302.

Offer, J. (2009) 'The poor law commission of 1905–1909: a view from a century on', in K. Rummery, I. Greener and C. Holden (ed.) *Social Policy Review*, Vol. 21, Bristol, The Policy Press, pp. 109–129.

Oldroyd, D. R. (1980) *Darwinian Impacts*, Milton Keynes, Open University Press.

Ospovat, D. (1976) 'The influence of Karl Ernst Von Baer's embryology, 1828–1859', *Journal of the History of Biology*, Vol. 9, pp. 1–28.

Paley, W. (1785) *Natural Theology*, in *The Works of William Paley*, Edinburgh, Brown and Nelson, 1830.

Parker, G. (1990) *With Due Care and Attention*, London, Family Policy Studies Centre.

Parry, C. H. H. (1896/1931) *The Evolution of the Art of Music*, London, Kegan Paul, Trench, Trubner.

Paul, D. B. (1988) 'The selection of the "survival of the fittest" ', *Journal of the History of Biology*, Vol. 21, No. 3, pp. 411–424.

Paul, E. F. (1983) 'Herbert Spencer: the historicist as a failed prophet', *Journal of the History of Ideas*, Vol. 64, reprinted in Offer (ed.) (2000), Vol. 2, pp. 528–555.

Paul, E. F. (1989) 'Herbert Spencer: second thoughts, a response to Michael Taylor', *Political Studies*, Vol. 37, reprinted in Offer (ed.) (2000), Vol. 2, pp. 556–562.

Paul. J. (1982) 'The socialism of Herbert Spencer', *History of Political Thought*, Vol. 3, reprinted in Offer (ed.) (2000) Vol. 4, pp. 185–199.

Paxton, N. L. (1991) *George Eliot and Herbert Spencer: Feminism, Evolutionism and the Reconstruction of Gender*, Princeton, NJ, Princeton University Press.

Peel, J. D. Y. (1969) 'Spencer and the neo-evolutionists', *Sociology*, Vol. 3, reprinted in Offer (ed.) (2000), Vol. 2, pp. 625–644.

Peel, J. D. Y. (1971) *Herbert Spencer: the Evolution of a Sociologist*, London, Heineman.

Peel, J. D. Y. (2004) 'Spencer in history: the second century', in G. Jones and R. A. Peel (eds) *Herbert Spencer: the Intellectual Legacy*, London, Galton Institute, pp. 126–149.

Pelly, L. (ed.) (1858) *The Views and Opinions of Brigadier–General John Jacob*, London, Smith Elder.

Perrin, R. (1976) 'Herbert Spencer's four theories of social evolution', *American Journal of Sociology*, Vol. 81, reprinted in Offer (ed.) (2000), Vol. 2. pp. 508–527.

Perrin, R. (1993) *Herbert Spencer: A Primary and Secondary Bibliography*, New York and London, Garland.

Perrin, R. (1995) Emile Durkheim's *Division of Labour* and the shadow of Herbert Spencer, *Sociological Quarterly*, Vol. 36, reprinted in Offer (ed.) (2000), Vol. 2. pp. 339–360.

Pickering, M. (2009) *Auguste Comte: An Intellectual Biography*, Vol. 3, New York, Cambridge University Press.

Pinker, R. (1971) *Social Theory and Social Policy*, London, Heineman.

Pinker, R. (1974) 'Social policy and social justice', *Journal of Social Policy*, Vol. 3, pp. 1–19.

Popper, Sir K. (1961) *The Poverty of Historicism*, London, Routledge and Kegan Paul.

Potter, B. (1891) *The Cooperative Movement in Great Britain*, London, Allen and Unwin.

Powell, B. (1860) 'On the study of the evidences of Christianity', in *Essays and Reviews*, London, Parker.

Pringle Pattison, A. (1904) 'Life and philosophy of Herbert Spencer', *Quarterly Review*, July, pp. 240–267.

Raby, P. (2001) *Alfred Russel Wallace: A Life*, London, Chatto and Windus.

Radcliffe Richards, J. (2000) *Human Nature after Darwin*, London, Routledge.

Ramji, H. (2006) 'British Indians "returning home"', *Sociology*, Vol. 40, No. 4, pp. 645–662.

Rashid, S. (1977) 'Richard Whately and Christian political economy at Oxford and Dublin', *Journal of the History of Ideas*, Vol. 38, pp. 145–155.

Rhys, E. (1904) 'The funeral of Herbert Spencer', *The World Today*, Vol. 6, pp. 171–174.

Richards, R. J. (1987) *Darwin and the Emergence of Evolutionary Theories of Mind and Behaviour*, Chicago and London, University of Chicago.

Riese, W. (1959) *A History of Neurology*, New York, MD.

Ritchie, D. G. (1885) 'Mr. Herbert Spencer's political philosophy', *Time*, Vol. 2, reprinted in Offer (ed.) (2000) Vol. 4, pp. 103–121.

Robertson, J. M. (1901) 'Herbert Spencer', in his *Modern Humanists*, London and New York, reprinted in Offer (ed.) (2000) Vol. 3, pp. 48–83.

Roche, M. (1973) *Phenomenology, Language and the Social Sciences*, London and Boston, Routledge and Kegan Paul.

Rogers, J. A. (1972) 'Darwinism and social Darwinism', *Journal of the History of Ideas*, Vol. 33, reprinted in Offer (ed.) (2000) Vol. 2, pp. 149–164.

Rose, H. and Rose, S. (eds) (2000) *Alas, Poor Darwin*, London, Cape.

Royce, J. (1904) *Herbert Spencer: An Estimate and a Review*, New York, Fox Duffield.

Rumney, J. (1934) *Herbert Spencer's Sociology*, London, Williams and Norgate.

Runciman, W. G. (1972) *Relative Deprivation and Social Justice*, Harmondsworth, Penguin.

Runciman, W. G. (1997) *A Treatise on Social Theory*, Vol. 3, Cambridge, Cambridge University Press.

Runciman, W. G. (1998a) 'The selectionist paradigm and its implications for sociology', *Sociology*, Vol. 32, No. 1, pp. 163–188.

Runciman, W. G. (1998b) *The Social Animal*, London, Harper Collins.

Runciman, W. G. (2004) 'The diffusion of Christianity in the Third Century AD as a case-study in the theory of cultural selection', *European Journal of Sociology*, Vol. 45, No. 1, pp. 3–21.

Rylance, R. (2000) *Victorian Psychology and British Culture 1850–1880*, Oxford, Oxford University Press.

Ryle, G. (1949) *The Concept of Mind*, London, Hutchinson.

Ryle, G. (1954) 'Feelings', in Elton (ed.), 1954, and Ryle's *Collected Papers*, Vol. 2, London, Hutchinson (1971), pp. 272–286.

Scholes, P. A. (1954) *The Listener's History of Music*, 3 Vols, (1st edition, 1923), London, Oxford University Press.

Schneider, M. (1957) 'Primitive music', in E. Wellesz (ed.) *The New Oxford History of Music*, Vol. 1, London, Oxford University Press.

Schopenhauer, A. (1883) *The World as Will and Idea*, 3 Vols, translated by R. B. Haldane and J. Kemp, London: Routledge and Kegan Paul.

Schurman, J. G. (1892) 'Review of *Justice*', *Philosophical Review*, Vol. 1, pp. 79–88.

Schutz, A. (1971) 'Making music together', in his *Collected Papers*, Vol. 2, pp. 159–178, The Hague, Martinus Nijhoff.

Seal, H. S. (1893) *On the Nature of State Interference*, London, Williams and Norgate.

Secord, J. A. (2000) *Victorian Sensation: The Extraordinary Publication, Reception and Secret Authorship of 'Vestiges of the Natural History of Creation'*, Chicago, Chicago University Press.

Seidman, S. (1983) 'Modernity and the problem of meaning: the Durkheimian tradition', *Sociological Analysis*, Vol. 46, reprinted in Hamilton (1990), Vol. 1, pp. 277–304.

Seth, J. (1889) 'The evolution of morality', *Mind*, Vol. 14, reprinted in Offer (ed.) (2000), Vol. 3, pp. 333–351.

Shapin, S. (2007) 'Man with a plan: Herbert Spencer's theory of everything', *New Yorker*, August 13.

Sidgwick, H. (1873) 'Review of Spencer's *Principles of Psychology*', *The Academy*, April, pp. 131–134.

Sidgwick, H. (1876) 'The theory of evolution in its application to practice' *Mind*, Vol. 1, pp. 52–67.

Sidgwick, H. (1877) *The Methods of Ethics* (2nd edition), London, Macmillan.

Sidgwick, H. (1892) 'Critical notices [Spencer's *Justice*]', in *Mind*, Vol. 1 (NS), reprinted in Offer (ed.) (2000), Vol. 3. pp. 370–380.

Sidgwick, H. (1899) 'The relation of ethics to sociology', *International Journal of Ethics*, Vol. 10, pp. 1–21.

Simhony, A. and Weinstein, D. (eds) (2001) *The New Liberalism*, Cambridge, Cambridge University Press.

Simon, W. M. (1960) 'Herbert Spencer and the "social organism"', *Journal of the History of Ideas*, Vol. 21, reprinted in Offer (ed.) (2000), Vol. 3, pp. 161–166.

Skilton, J. (1889) *Evolution of Society*, Brooklyn, New York, Brooklyn Ethical Association.

Smith, A. (1759/2002) *The Theory of Moral Sentiments*, K. Haakonsson (ed.), Cambridge, Cambridge University Press.

Smith, A. (1776/1999) *The Wealth of Nations*, 2 Vols, A. Skinner (ed.), London, Penguin.

Smith, C. U. M. (1982) 'Evolution and the problem of mind, Part 1 – Herbert Spencer', *Journal of the History of Biology*, Vol. 15, reprinted in Offer (ed.) (2000), Vol. 3, pp. 238–266.

Smith, C. U. M. (1983) 'Herbert Spencer's epigenetic epistemology', *Studies in History and Philosophy of Science*, Vol. 14, No. 1, pp. 1–22.

Smith, G. H. (1981) 'Herbert Spencer's theory of causation', *Journal of Libertarian Studies*, Vol. 5, reprinted in Offer (ed.) (2000), Vol. 2, pp. 384–425.

Soldon, N. (1974) '*Laissez-faire* as dogma: the Liberty and Property Defence League, 1882–1914', in Brown (ed.) (1974), *Essays in Anti-Labour History*, Ch. 9.

Solie, R. D. (1982) 'Melody and the historiography of music', *Journal of the History of Ideas*, Vol. 43, No. 2, pp. 297–308.

Spalding, D. (1873) 'Review: Spencer, *The Principles of Psychology*', *Nature*, Vol. 7, pp. 298–300.

Spencer, A. (1844) *Some Account of Hinton Charterhouse and Hinton Abbey*. A paper given at The Temperance Festival in the grounds of Hinton Abbey, 8 July 1844), London, Gilpin, and Bath, Gibbs.

Spencer, H. (1836) 'Poor laws – reply to "TWS"', *Bath and West of England Magazine*, March, reprinted in Offer (ed.) (1994).

Spencer, H. (1843) *The Proper Sphere of Government: a Reprint of a Series of Letters Originally Published in 'The Nonconformist'*, London, Brittain, reprinted in Offer (ed.) (1994).

Spencer, H. (1851) *Social Statics: or the Conditions Essential to Human Happiness Specified, and the First of Them Developed*, London, Chapman.

Spencer, H. (1852a) 'The development hypothesis', *Essays*, 1, pp. 1–7, first published in *The Leader*, March 20.

Spencer, H. (1852b) 'A theory of population', *Westminster Review*, April.

Spencer, H. (1852c) 'The philosophy of style', *Essays*, 2, pp. 333–369, first published in the *Westminster Review*, October.

Spencer, H. (1853) 'Over-legislation', *Essays*, 3, pp. 229–282, first published in the *Westminster Review*, July.

Spencer, H. (1854a) 'Manners and Fashion', *Essays*, 3, pp. 1–51, first published in the *Westminster Review*, April.

Spencer, H. (1854b) 'The genesis of science, *Essays*, 2, pp. 1–73, first published in the *British Quarterly Review*, July.

Spencer, H. (1854c) 'Railway morals and railway policy', *Essays*, 3, pp. 52–112, first published in the *Edinburgh Review*, October.

Spencer, H. (1855) *Principles of Psychology*, London, Longmans, Brown, Green and Longmans.

Spencer, H. (1857a) 'Progress: its law and cause', *Essays*, 1, pp. 8–62, first published in the *Westminster Review*, April.

Spencer, H. (1857b) 'Transcendental physiology', *Essays*, 1, pp. 63–107, first published as 'The ultimate laws of physiology' in the *National Review*, October.

Spencer, H. (1857c) 'The origin and function of music', *Essays*, 2, pp. 400–451 (the *Postscript* of 1891 is at pp. 425–451), first published in *Fraser's Magazine*, October.

Spencer, H. (1857d) 'Representative government – What is it good for?', *Essays*, 3, pp. 283–325, first published in the *Westminster Review*, October.

Spencer. H. (1858a) 'State-tamperings with money and banks', *Essays*, 3, pp. 326–357, first published in the *Westminster Review*, January.

Spencer, H. (1858b) 'The nebular hypothesis', *Essays*, 1, pp. 108–181, first published in the *Westminster Review*, July.

Spencer, H. (1859) 'The morals of trade', *Essays*, 3, pp. 113–151, first published in the *Westminster Review*, April.

Spencer, H. (1860a) 'The social organism', *Essays*, 1, pp. 265–307, first published in the *Westminster Review*, January.

Spencer, H. (1860b) 'Parliamentary reform: the dangers and the safeguards', *Essays*, 3, pp. 358–386, first published in the *Westminster Review*, April.

Spencer, H. (1860c) 'Prison-ethics', *Essays*, 3, pp. 152–191, first published in the *British Quarterly Review*, July.

Spencer, H. (1861) *Education*, London, Williams and Norgate.

Spencer, H. (1862) *First Principles*, London, Williams and Norgate.

Spencer, H. (1864) 'The classification of the sciences', and 'Reasons for dissenting from the philosophy of M. Comte', *Essays*, 2, pp. 74–117 and pp. 118–114, first published as a brochure.

Spencer, H. (1865) 'Mill *versus* Hamilton – The test of truth'. *Essays*, 2, pp. 188–217, first published in the *Fortnightly Review*, July.

Spencer, H. (1867) *First Principle* (2nd edition), London, Williams and Norgate.

Spencer, H. (1870) *First Principles* (3rd edition), London, Williams and Norgate.

Spencer, H. (1871a) 'Specialized administration', *Essays*, 3, pp. 401–444, first published in the *Fortnightly Review*, December.

Spencer, H. (1871b) 'Morals and moral sentiments', *Essays*, 1, pp. 331–350, first published in the *Fortnightly Review*, April.

Spencer, H. (1872) 'Mr. Martineau on evolution', *Essays*, 1, pp. 371–388, first published in the *Contemporary Review*, June.

Spencer, H. (1873a) 'Replies to criticisms', *Essays*, 2, pp. 218–320, first published in the *Fortnightly Review*, November and December.

Spencer, H. (1873b) *The Study of Sociology*, London, King.

Spencer, H. (1876a) 'The comparative psychology of man', *Essays*, 1, pp. 351–370, first published in *Mind*, January.

Spencer, H. (1876b) *The Principles of Sociology*, Vol. 1, (1st edition), London, Williams and Norgate.

Spencer, H. (1881a) 'Prof. Green's explanations, *Essays*, 2, pp. 321–332, first published in the *Contemporary Review*, February.

Spencer, H. (1881b) *The Principles of Psychology*, 2 Vols (3rd edition), London, Williams and Norgate.

Spencer, H. (1883) 'The Americans', *Essays*, 3, pp. 471–492, first published in the *Contemporary Review*, January.

Spencer, H. (1884) *The Man versus The State*, London, Williams and Norgate, reprinted in Offer (ed.) (1994).

Spencer, H. (1886) 'The factors of organic evolution', *Essays*, 1, pp. 389–466, first published in the *Nineteenth Century*, May.

Spencer, H. (1888) 'The ethics of Kant', *Essays*, 3, pp. 192–216, first published in the *Fortnightly Review*, July.

Spencer, H. (1890) 'Absolute political ethics', *Essays*, 3, pp. 217–228, first published in the *Nineteenth Century*, January.

Spencer, H. (1891a) 'From freedom to bondage', *Essays*, 3, pp. 445–470, first published in T. Mackay (ed.), *A Plea for Liberty*.

Spencer, H. (1891b) 'Letter on the Society for the Prevention of Cruelty to Children,' *Pall Mall Gazette*, 28 May, p. 3.

Spencer, H. (1891c) *The Principles of Sociology*, Vol. 2 (2nd edition), New York, Appleton.

Spencer, H. (1891d) 'On the origin of music', *Mind*, Vol. xvi (OS), pp. 535–537.

Spencer, H. (1892) *Social Statics, Abridged and Revised*, London, Williams and Norgate.

Spencer, H. (1893) *The Principles of Sociology*, Vol. 1 (3rd edition), London, Williams and Norgate.

Spencer, H. (1894) *The Principles of Biology*, 2 Vols, London, Williams and Norgate.

Spencer, H. (1896a) 'The relations of biology, psychology and sociology', *Essays*, 2, pp. 467–479, first published in *Appleton's Popular Science Monthly*, December.

Spencer, H. (1896b) *The Principles of Sociology*, Vol. 3, London, Williams and Norgate.

Spencer, H. (1897) *Various Fragments*, London, Williams and Norgate.

Spencer, H. (1899) 'The filiation of ideas', in Duncan (ed.), *The Life and Letters of Herbert Spencer*, 1911, pp. 533–576.

Spencer, H. (1900) *First Principles* (6th edition), London, Williams and Norgate.

Spencer, H. (1901) *Essays: Scientific, Political and Speculative*, 3 Vols, London, Williams and Norgate.

Spencer, H. (1902) *Facts and Comments*, London, Williams and Norgate.

Spencer, H. (1904) *An Autobiography*, 2 Vols, London, Williams and Norgate.

Spencer, H. (1910) *The Principles of Ethics*, 2 Vols, New York and London, Appleton.

Spencer, T. (1836) *The Successful Application of the New Poor Law to the Parish of Hinton Charterhouse*, London, Ridgway.

Stanford, C. V. and Forsythe, C. (1916) *A History of Music*, London, Macmillan.

Stapleton, J. (1999) 'Historiographical review: Political thought, elites and the state in modern Britain', *Historical Journal*, Vol. 42, No. 1, pp. 251–268.

Stark, W. (1961) 'Herbert Spencer's three sociologies', *American Sociological Review*, Vol. 26, reprinted in Offer (ed.) (2000), Vol. 3, pp. 115–124.

Steeman, T. M. (1963) 'Durkheim's professional ethics', *Journal for the Scientific Study of Religion*, Vol. 2, reprinted in Hamilton (1990), Vol. 1, pp. 55–77.

Stein, J. (1973) *Richard Wagner and the Synthesis of the Arts*, Westport, Greenwood.

Steiner, H. (1982) 'Land, liberty and the early Herbert Spencer', *History of Political Thought*, Vol. 3, reprinted in Offer (ed.) (2000), Vol. 4, pp. 200–217.

Stumph, C. F. (1885) 'Musikpsychologie in England', *Vierteljahrsschrift für Musikwissenschaft*, Vol. 1, pp. 261–349.

Strauss, D. F. (1846) *The Life of Jesus, Critically Examined*, translated by Marian Evans, London (Strauss's study was originally published in Tubingen 10 years earlier).

Taylor, A. J. (1955) 'The originality of Herbert Spencer: a footnote to "Herbert Spencer and his father"', *Studies in English*, Vol. 34, reprinted in Offer (ed.) (2000), Vol. 1, pp. 190–195.

Taylor, M. (1989) 'The errors of an evolutionist: a reply to Ellen Frankel Paul', *Political Studies*, Vol. 37, reprinted in Offer (ed.) 2000, Vol. 2, pp. 548–555.

Taylor, M. W. (1992) *Men Versus The State: Herbert Spencer and Late Victorian Individualism*, Oxford, Oxford University Press.

Taylor, M. W. (2007) *The Philosophy of Herbert Spencer*, London and New York, Continuum.

Thompson, D. W. (1913) 'On Aristotle as a biologist, with a proaemion on Herbert Spencer', in *Herbert Spencer Lecture*, Oxford, Oxford University Press.

Titmuss, R. M. (1970) *The Gift Relationship*, London: Allen and Unwin.

Tönnies, F. (1887) *Gemeinschaft und Gesellschaft*, Leipzig, Fue's Verlag (R. Riesland).

Tönnies, F. (1889) 'Herbert Spencers sociologisches Werk', *Philosophische Monatshefte*, Vol. 25, pp. 40–85 (reprinted in Tönnies's *Soziologische Studien und Kritiken*, Jena (1925), Vol. 1, pp. 75–104.

Tönnies, F. (1892) 'Werke zur Philosophie der Geschichte und des socialen Lebens', three articles, *Philosophische Monatshefte*, Vol. 28, pp. 37–66, 444–461, 592–602, reprinted in the third volume of *Soziologische Studien und Kritiken*, Jena (1929), pp. 132–196.

Tönnies, F. (1898) 'Herbert Spencer, The Principles of Sociology, Vol. 3', *Archiv für Systematische Philosophie*, Vol. 4, pp. 498–501.

Tönnies, F. (1974) 'Herbert Spencer (1820–1903)', in E. G. Jacoby (ed.) *Ferdinand Tönnies*, 1974, pp. 95–118, first published in 1904 in *Deutsche Rundschau*, pp. 368–382.

Tönnies, F. (2001) *Community and Civil Society*, Jose Harris (ed.), Cambridge, Cambridge University Press (a new translation of *Gemeinschaft und Gesellschaft*).

Troughton, W. (1938) 'Herbert Spencer's last years: some personal recollections', *Rationalist Annual*, pp. 59–65, reprinted in Offer (ed.) (2000) Vol. 1, pp. 186–202.

Turner, J. (1985) *Herbert Spencer: A Renewed Appreciation*, Beverly Hills, Sage.

'Two' (1910) *Home Life with Herbert Spencer* (new edition), Bristol, Arrowsmith.

Tylor, C. (2006) (Edward Caird's) 'Spencer', *Collingwood and British Idealism Studies*, Vol. 12, No. 1, pp. 5–38.

Tylor, E. B. (1865) *Researches into the Early History of Mankind*, London, John Murray.

Tylor, E. B. (1871) *Primitive Culture*, 2 Vols, London, John Murray.

Urwick, E. J. (1912) *A Philosophy of Social Progress*, London, Methuen.

Van Wyhe, J. (2004) *Phrenology and the Origins of Victorian Scientific Naturalism*, Aldershot and Burlington VT, Ashgate.

Vaughan Williams, R. (1963) *National Music*, Oxford University Press, London.

Vidler, A. (1961) *The Church in an Age of Revolution*, Harmondsworth, Penguin.

Vincent, A. (1984) 'The Poor Law report of 1909 and the social theory of the Charity Organisation Society', *Victorian Studies*, Vol. 27, pp. 343–363.

Vincent, A. (1990) 'Classical liberalism and its crisis of identity', *History of Political Thought*, Vol. 11, pp. 143–161.

Vincent, A. (2005) 'The ontology of individualism', *Theoria*, Vol. 85, pp. 127–149.

Von Baer, K. E. (1828, 1837), *Ueber Entwicklungsgeschichte der Thiere*, 2 Vols, Konigsberg, Gebrüder Bornträger.

Wachsmann, K. (1973) 'Spencer to Hood: a changing view of non-European music', *Proceedings of the Royal Anthropological Institute of Great Britain and Ireland*.

Wallaschek, R. (1891) 'On the origin of music', *Mind*, Vol. 16, pp. 375–386.

Wallaschek, R. (1893) *Primitive Music*, reprinted in New York, Da Capo, 1970.

Ward, L. F. (1894) 'The political ethics of Herbert Spencer', *Annals of the American Academy of Political Science*, Vol. 4, reprinted in Offer (ed.) (2000), Vol. 4, pp. 75–102.

Ward, L. F. (1897) *Dynamic Sociology: or Applied Social Science as Based upon the Less Complex Sciences*, Vol. 1, New York, Appleton.

Warren, M. (1987) 'The Marx-Darwin question: implications for the critical aspects of Marx's social theory', *International Sociology*, Vol. 7, No. 3, pp. 251–269.

Wasserstein, B. (1992) *Herbert Samuel: A Political Life*, Oxford, Oxford University Press.

Waterman, A. M. C. (1991) *Revolution, Economics and Religion: Christian Political Economy 1798–1833*, Cambridge, Cambridge University Press.

Webb, B. (1926) *My Apprenticeship*, London, Longmans.

Webb, B. (1948) *Our Partnership*, London, Longmans, Green.
Webb, S. and Webb, B. (1894) *History of Trade-Unionism*, London, Longmans, Green.
Webb, S. and Webb, B. (1910) *English Poor Law Policy*, London, Longmans, Green.
Weinstein, D. (1998) *Equal Freedom and Utility: Herbert Spencer's Liberal Utilitarianism*, Cambridge, Cambridge University Press.
Weikart, R. (2004) *From Darwin to Hitler: Evolutionary Ethics, Eugenics and Racism in Germany*, New York and Basingstoke, Palgrave Macmillan.
Wells, H. G. (1914) *An Englishman Looks at the World*, London, Cassell.
Werth, B. (2009) *Banquet at Demonico's*, New York, Random House.
Westrup, J. (1955) *An Introduction to Musical History*, London, Hutchinson.
Whately, R. (1832) *Introductory Lectures on Political Economy*, London, Fellowes.
Whately, R. (1861) 'On the origin of civilisation', Lecture 2 in *Miscellaneous Lectures and Reviews*, London, Parker and Bourn.
White, J. (1979) 'Andrew Carnegie and Herbert Spencer: a special relationship', *American Studies*, Vol. 13, pp. 57–71.
Wilson, Sir R. (1911) *The Province of the State*, London, King.
Wiltshire, D. (1978) *The Social and Political Thought of Herbert Spencer*, Oxford, Oxford University Press.
Winch, P. (1971) 'Human nature', in *The Proper Study* (Royal Institute of Philosophy Lectures, 1969/70), London and Basingstoke, Macmillan.
Wright, D. F. (1975) 'Musical meaning and its social determinants,' *Sociology*, Vol. 9, pp. 410–435.
Yanal, R. J. (1981) 'Words and music', *Journal of Philosophy*, Vol. 76, No. 4, pp. 187–202.
Young, P. M. (1980) *George Grove*, London and Basingstoke, Macmillan.
Young, R. M. (1967) 'The development of Herbert Spencer's concept of evolution', *Actes du 11 Congrès International d'Histoire des Sciences*, Vol. 2, Warsaw, Ossolineum, reprinted in Offer (ed.) (2000), Vol. 2, pp. 378–383.
Young, R. M. (1970) *Mind, Brain and Adaptation in the Nineteenth Century*, London, Oxford University Press.
Zafirovski, M. Z. (2000) 'Spencer is dead, long live Spencer: individualism, holism, and the problem of norms', *British Journal of Sociology*, Vol. 51, No. 3, pp. 553–579.
Zafirovski, M. (2003) *Market and Society: Two Theoretical Frameworks*, Westport CT, Praeger.

Index

Harris, Jose, 1, 218, 244, 248
Harrison, Frederic, 104, 110, 153–4
Hartley, David, 167
Hartog, Marcus, 126
Hawkins, Mike, 19
Hayek, F.A., 182, 313, 327, 339, 347
Hegel, G.W.F. and Hegelianism, 58, 102,
    131–3, 218, 299, 310, 348
Herbert, Auberon, 6, 8, 16, 121–3
heredity, 63, 81, 126, 298, 307, 342, 347
Herkomer, Hubert, 129
heterogeneity, 62–3, 117, 137, 233, 257,
    263
    see also homogeneity
Hilton, Boyd, 2, 32–3, 36, 304, 305,
    331
Hirst, Thomas Archer, 87
historicism, 342
history, 91, 97–8, 162–4, 224
Hobbes, Thomas, 193, 199
Hobhouse, L.T., 18, 300–1, 310
Hobson, J.A., 14, 18, 151, 215–16
Hodgskin, Thomas, 6, 329
Hodgson, Shadworth H., 101
Hofstadter, Richard, 19
Holmes, Oliver Wendell, 112
Holyoake, G.J., 194
Home Rule for Ireland, 123–4
homogeneity, 62–3, 117, 137, 233, 263
    see also heterogeneity
Hooker, Joseph Dalton, 8, 21, 80–2, 86,
    119
Hudson, William Henry, 18, 132, 141
Hume, David, 145, 171
Hunt, Alfred, 60
Hunt, Leigh, 51
Husserl, Edmund, 146
Hutton, R.H., 173
Huxley, Thomas Henry, 6, 8, 52–4, 64,
    77, 86, 118, 127, 170, 308–9
    on *First Principles*, 75
    on organic analogy, 203–4
    on Spencer's theory of evolution,
        125–6, 170

idealism, 5, 6, 16, 24, 102, 129,
    131–2, 146, 216–19, 299–301,
    321, 326
ideal types, 244
individualism, 85, 125, 178–80

individuation, 143, 177, 198
industrial social relations, 5, 108, 179,
    226–7, 229–30, 341
    and evolution, 244
    and family, 234–7
influence and admirers, 2–3, 6, 8–9, 12,
    14–15, 20, 119–20, 133–5, 171–2
Ingold, Tim, 2, 181, 211, 313, 316
inheritance of acquired characteristics, 9,
    74, 77, 79, 126, 156, 170, 303, 306,
    313, 344
    and social evolution, 162
    see also Lamarck, Jean-Baptiste
institutions
    'Ceremonial Institutions', 187–8,
        236
    'Domestic Institutions', 185–6
    'Ecclesiastical Institutions', 116,
        190–1, 265
    'Industrial Institutions', 192–3, 237
    'Political Institutions', 188–9, 236–7
    'Professional Institutions', 191–2, 210
    see also Spencer, Herbert, *Principles of
        Sociology*
integration, 198, 226
    and differentiation, 90

Jackson, G.B.W., 39–40
Jackson, Hughlings, 124, 172
James, William, 6, 27, 151–3, 269
Japan, 125, 334
Jevons, F.B., 345
Jevons, W.S., 8, 103
Jones, Henry, 217–18
Jones, T. Rymer, 35
justice, 5, 15, 72, 281, 287–91, 297, 301,
    345
    and altruism, 176, 287
    and class, 70
    and prisoners, 71–2
    see also equal freedom

Kant, I., 45, 101–2, 114, 171
Kidd, Benjamin, 6, 18, 215, 307
Kingsley, Charles, 55, 305
Knowles, James, 91, 96
Krishnavarma, Shyamaji, 335
Kropotkin, Prince Peter (Pyotr)
    Alexeyevich, 288

and progress, 188
and tribal society, 183, 283
see also natural selection
Swift, Jonathan, 58
Sylvester, J.J., 112
sympathy, 11, 50, 99, 165, 175, 180, 241, 246, 249
and animals, 175
and justice, 250
and music, 265

Tait, Peter, 152
Taylor, Michael, 1, 50, 157–8, 183, 196
Thompson, Henry, 129
Thompson, Wentworth D'Arcy, 9, 62
Titmuss, Richard, M., 301, 326
Tönnies, Ferdinand, 6, 128, 216–18, 251–2, 269
trade unions, 193–4, 298
transcendental physiology, 63–5, 201–2, 208–12, 310
tribal society
domestic organisation of, 183, 185–6
industrial social relations of, 227, 231, 233
intelligence and sentiment in, 173, 183
and music, 255, 257–8, 261
pro-ethics of, 285
and supernatural beliefs, 184
and use-inheritance, 83
Whately, on, 74
Troughton, Walter, 128, 129, 132, 254
Turner, Jonathan, H., 2, 160, 247–8
Tylor, E.B., 8, 105, 338
Tyndall, John, 8, 21, 59, 76, 86, 105, 127, 145

Urwick, E.J., 326
use-inheritance, 77, 83
and variations, 81
see also inheritance of acquired characteristics
utilitarianism, 10, 83–4, 278
see also Bentham, Jeremy

Vincent, A.W., 299, 310, 317
Von Baer, K.E., 52–3, 62, 143, 156, 330

Wagner, Richard, 105, 266–9, 343
Wallace, Alfred Russel, 72, 77, 134
Wallaschek, Richard, 254, 260
war, 197, 223–5, 251, 339, 341
Ward, Lester Frank, 127, 251, 297–9
Watts, G.F., 335
Webb, Beatrice, 6, 8, 10, 132–3, 153, 194, 299, 307
see also Potter, Beatrice
Webb, Sidney, 10, 194, 299
Weber, Max, 244
Weinstein, David, 10, 161, 245, 329, 346
Weismann, August, 126, 307, 348
welfare, 17, 21, 25, 70, 176, 178, 189, 207, 217, 281, 283
welfare state, 324, 346
see also caring and beneficence
Wells, H.G., 135
Westminster Review, 51–2
Whately, Richard, 7–8, 33, 74, 93, 181, 223, 304, 313, 326, 328, 339, 341
Whately, Thomas, 36
Whewell, William, 170
Wilson, James, 48–9, 67
see also Economist
Wilson, Roland, 10, 340
Wiltshire, David, 4, 159, 194, 220–1, 244, 340
Wolff, Caspar, Friedrich, 62
women, 90, 173, 183, 186, 231, 234, 290, 295, 338, 344
see also suffrage; tribal society

X Club, 86–8, 123

Youmans, Edward Livingston, 6, 9, 13, 15, 68, 76, 107, 112–13, 118
Young, Robert, M., 159

Zafirovski, M., 181, 327
Zoist, 45

CPSIA information can be obtained at www.ICGtesting.com
Printed in the USA
LVOW070925101112

306743LV00008B/70/P